# ILLUSTRATED GUIDE TO IRELAND

Published by
The Reader's Digest
Association Limited

LONDON · NEW YORK · SYDNEY
MONTREAL · CAPE TOWN

# ILLUSTRATED GUIDE TO
# IRELAND

The publishers wish to express their gratitude to the following people for their contributions to the book:

CONSULTANTS
Bord Fáilte, Dublin
Dr Peter Harbison
Irish Tourist Board, London
Northern Ireland Tourist Board

MAJOR CONTRIBUTORS
John Booth  John Dodd  Anne Flaherty
Ronan Foster  Anne Gatti  Norman Gelb
William Geldard  Derek Hall  Penny Hart
Ian Hill  Robert Kiener  Jennifer Mackenzie
John Man  Anthony Mason  Vic Mayhew
Colin Reid  Gerry Thornley  David Ward

PHOTOGRAPHERS
Christopher Hill  Barry Hitchcox  Neil Holmes
Tom Kelly  Susan Lund  John Vigurs
Jon Wyand  Peter Zoeller

ARTISTS
Richard Bonson  Tony Lodge  Gill Tomblin

**Project Editor**  Sandy Shepherd
**Art Editor**  Bridget Morley

ILLUSTRATED GUIDE TO IRELAND
was edited and designed by The Reader's Digest
Association Limited, London

First Edition Copyright © 1992
The Reader's Digest Association Limited, Berkeley
Square House, Berkeley Square, London W1X 6AB
Copyright © 1992
Reader's Digest Association Far East Limited
Philippines Copyright 1992
Reader's Digest Association Far East Limited

Printed in Milan
ISBN 0 276 42033 0

# CONTENTS

# INTRODUCTION

'Céad Míle Fáilte', 'a hundred thousand welcomes', is the slogan proclaimed all over Ireland – and it is one the Irish live up to. Strangers are eager to pass the time of day with you, whether on remote country roads, in busy streets, or in the pubs over 'a pint of plain'. But it is also easy to get away from it all. Ireland is still largely a pastoral country, where a cow is more frequently met along a country lane than a car, and you may not see another soul out on the heather-cloaked slopes of the Mourne Mountains, or Macgillycuddy's Reeks. There is much to draw walking enthusiasts, from the dramatic coasts of north Antrim, where extraordinary basalt columns form the Giant's Causeway, to the sweet wooded valleys of Killarney and the whispered chatter of its sparkling streams.

Ireland has no lack of water – its many lake systems lie in shining fragments like shattered mirrors, and a string of shards draped from north to south forms the River Shannon, Ireland's longest river. The waters are thick with salmon and trout, and anglers are rarely disappointed. The drowsy canals and waterways are ideal for cruising and for birdwatching among the reed fringes. The rivers were the routes used by the earliest settlers of Ireland, who found them safer and easier to traverse than the dense woods and soggy peatbogs through which they wandered.

The first settlers, and those that followed, left their marks all over Ireland, in tombs older than the pyramids, ring-forts, creeper-clad crumbling castles, and the ruins of innumerable monasteries, such as Glendalough and Clonmacnoise, centres of learning famed throughout Europe. The monasteries also bequeathed Ireland a wealth of treasures, from illuminated manuscripts to exquisitely decorated reliquaries, which now fill Ireland's museums.

The more recent legacy of the Anglo-Irish gentry is visible in the big houses scattered around the countryside – places like Florence Court and Castle Coole, in Fermanagh, and Castletown in Kildare. Many have also left splendid gardens – from the regimented order of Powerscourt to the subtropical profusion of Ilnacullin on Garinish Island, washed by the warm Gulf Stream, and the exotica of Mount Stewart, which flourish in the mild climate of the north-east coast.

The towns and cities of Ireland are as varied in their character as is the countryside: 'dear, dirty Dublin', city of writers, pubs and Georgian elegance; Belfast, solidly but elegantly Victorian; the neatly ordered Plantation towns of Ulster; the medieval mazes of Galway and Waterford. And in marked contrast to them all are the scattered villages in the remote west, the last bastions of the Irish language and a traditional way of life. There, beliefs in the 'little people' are strongest and Ireland's rich body of myths is kept alive. Ireland should be savoured slowly, like the golden whiskey it produces. It will leave you with a mellow aftertaste and a warm glow.

*Boats at Dunmore East harbour, Co Waterford (right). Following pages: the Glanmore valley, Co Cork (left); cottages at Dunmore East (top centre); a decorated front at Fethard-on-Sea, Co Wexford (centre); Castletown Bearhaven, Co Cork, at dawn (bottom centre); fishermen on Lough Eske, Co Donegal (right).*

## Finding Your Way Around Ireland

Ireland has been divided in this book into eight main regions, each with a detailed, large-scale map. If, for example, you plan a holiday in Donegal, first refer to the map on the right. Donegal falls within the North-West region, and the figure 244 indicates that the region begins on that page.

The regional maps show the number of touring areas the regions have been divided into, giving the number of the first page on which each area appears. The touring centre for each area is marked with a large orange dot. Smaller dots of the same colour show selected towns of interest within easy reach. The border crossing points given between the Republic and Northern Ireland are approved by Customs. It is advisable to stick to these.

Each touring area has its own map indicating places of interest which are described in the text for that area. Place names in the main text are given in English and Irish. The English names used are those approved by the Irish Ordnance Survey. Additional information on walks, cruises, events and sports are given for each touring area, with a contact number for the local tourist office.

The North-West
page 244

Northern Ireland
page 274

The Drumlin Belt
page 68

Connaught Counties
page 198

The Central Lowlands
page 12

The Lower Shannon
page 128

The Leinster Ridge
page 162

The South-West
page 86

DONEGAL · LONDONDERRY · ANTRIM · Belfast · TYRONE · FERMANAGH · ARMAGH · DOWN · MONAGHAN · SLIGO · LEITRIM · CAVAN · LOUTH · MAYO · ROSCOMMON · LONGFORD · MEATH · WESTMEATH · DUBLIN · Dublin · GALWAY · OFFALY · KILDARE · LAOIS · WICKLOW · CLARE · Limerick · CARLOW · LIMERICK · TIPPERARY · KILKENNY · WEXFORD · WATERFORD · KERRY · CORK · Cork

## KEY TO ZONE MAP SYMBOLS

| | | | |
|---|---|---|---|
| ◎ | Touring centre | / | Beach |
| • | Town or village | 🏠 | House or castle |
| ═ | Motorway | 🏰 | Ruined castle |
| ▬ | Major road (class 'A' or 'N') | ✿ | Garden |
| ▬ | Secondary road (class 'B' or 'R') | ☀ | Viewpoint |
| ─ | Minor road | ✝ | Church or cathedral |
| ----- | Footpath | ✚ | Abbey, monastery etc. |
| ∿ | River, lough | ⊤ | Ancient monument |
| ⊢⊢⊢ | Canal | 🏛 | Museum |
| – – – | National boundary | ♉ | Country or forest park |
| ☆ | Frontier crossing (approved) | ⚑ | Lighthouse |
| ℤ | Information centre | ∘ | Other interest |
| ⊕ | Airport or airfield | 🏃 | Racecourse |
| ▲ | Hill or mountain peak | ♪ | Golf course: 18 hole |
| | | ♪ | less than 18 holes |

## The regions, counties and touring areas of this magical island

**THE CENTRAL LOWLANDS**
**Co. Dublin**
Dublin City 16
Dun Laoghaire 22
Howth 24
Lucan 26
**Co. Kildare**
Athy 28
Kildare 30
Naas 32
**Co. Laois**
Abbeyleix 36
Mountrath 38
Port Laoise 40
**Co. Longford**
Ballymahon 42
Longford 44
**Co. Meath**
Kells 46
Navan 48
Slane 50
Trim 53
**Co. Offaly**
Birr 58
Clara 60
Tullamore 62
**Co. Westmeath**
Athlone 64
Mullingar 66

**THE DRUMLIN BELT**
**Co. Cavan**
Bailieborough 72
Belturbet 74
Cavan 76
**Co. Louth**
Drogheda 78
Dundalk 80
**Co. Monaghan**
Castleblayney 82
Monaghan 84

**THE SOUTH-WEST**
**Co. Cork**
Bantry 90
Clonakilty 92
Cork City 94
Around Cork City 96
Fermoy 100
Macroom 102
Mallow 104
Skibbereen 106
Youghal 108
**Co. Kerry**
Cahersiveen 112
Dingle 114
Kenmare 118
Killarney 120
Listowel 122
Tralee 124

**THE LOWER SHANNON**
**Co. Clare**
Ennis 132
Kilkee 134
Killaloe 136
Lisdoonvarna 139
**Co. Limerick**
Kilmallock 144
Limerick City 146
Around Limerick City 148
Rathkeale 150
**Co. Tipperary**
Caher 152
Nenagh 154
Thurles 156
Tipperary 158

**THE LEINSTER RIDGE**
**Co. Carlow**
Carlow 166
Muine Bheag 168
**Co. Kilkenny**
Kilkenny 172
Thomastown 174
**Co. Waterford**
Dungarvan 176
Waterford 179
**Co. Wexford**
Enniscorthy 182
Gorey 184
New Ross 186
Wexford 188
**Co. Wicklow**
Baltinglass 190
Blessington 192
Bray 194
Wicklow 196

**CONNAUGHT COUNTIES**
**Co. Galway**
Ballinasloe 202
Carrowroe 204
Clifden 208
Galway City 211
Loughrea 214
Oughterard 216
Tuam 218
**Co. Mayo**
Ballina 222
Ballinrobe 224
Belmullet 226
Castlebar 228
Charlestown 230
Louisburgh 232
Westport 234
**Co. Roscommon**
Boyle 238
Castlerea 240
Roscommon 242

**THE NORTH-WEST**
**Co. Donegal**
Ardara 248
Buncrana 250
Donegal 252
Dunglow 254
Letterkenny 256
Rathmelton 258
**Co. Leitrim**
Carrick-on-Shannon 260
Drumshanbo 262
Manorhamilton 264
**Co. Sligo**
Ballymote 266
Sligo 268

**NORTHERN IRELAND**
**Co. Antrim**
Ballycastle 278
Ballymena 280
Belfast City 282
Greater Belfast 286
Bushmills 288
Cushendall 292
Larne 294
Lisburn 296
**Co. Armagh**
Armagh 300
Portadown 302
**Co. Down**
Ballynahinch 306
Banbridge 308
Downpatrick 310
Newcastle 314
Newry 316
Newtownards 318
**Co. Fermanagh**
Belleek 320
Enniskillen 322
Lisnaskea 324
**Co. Londonderry**
Coleraine 326
Londonderry 328
Maghera 330
**Co. Tyrone**
Cookstown 332
Omagh 334
Strabane 336

Opening times of buildings and gardens are included, but visitors are advised to check for themselves before visiting an area. Further information can be obtained from the local tourist offices listed. Advice on recreational amenities in Ireland, in addition to that given separately for each region, will be found on pp 341-343.

# THE CENTRAL LOWLANDS

AYERS of history spread across these softly moulded lands, from their great Stone Age burial sites to the legendary Hill of Tara, seat of ancient Celtic power; from the fortifications and great houses that marked out Anglo-Norman control to Dublin, the political, artistic and cultural centre of Ireland.

With about one-third of Ireland's population living around Dublin, the eyes of the country are focused on the capital. It is a compact and manageable city nestling between Dublin Bay and the surrounding hills, its two halves united by a series of bridges over the River Liffey. Predominantly Georgian, the city has a comfortable air, the elegant ease of a well-worn suit. The great treasures of Ireland have been collected here, in the National Museum, Trinity College Library and the National Gallery. Jonathan Swift, Oliver Goldsmith, Gerard Manley Hopkins and W.B. Yeats lived and worked in Dublin; the careers of J.M. Synge and Sean O'Casey were nurtured at the Abbey Theatre, focus of the Irish Literary Revival; Oscar Wilde, George Bernard Shaw, James Joyce and Samuel Beckett spent their formative years here. And Dublin was probably the birthplace of the Duke of Wellington, although this is disputed by some.

Dublin was founded around AD 840 by Vikings who built on a swampy settlement inhabited since about the 2nd century. It remained in Danish hands until 1014, when the great Irish king, Brian Boru finally broke Viking power at the Battle of Clontarf, now a Dublin suburb. But subsequent Irish control of the city lasted only 150 years, until 1170, when Dermot MacMurrough, the hapless King of Leinster, invited the Norman Earl of Pembroke – known as Strongbow – to help him oust the High King of Ireland. The country would never be the same again. For the next 750 years Dublin was the stronghold of English rule. Until Tudor times, this rule was mainly limited to an area around Dublin known as the Pale, a moving border marked today by the embattled ruins of military outposts and fortified manor houses. What

MORRISSEY'S BAR *A grocery and pub are combined in this atmospheric bar in Abbeyleix.*

WHERE CELT AND CHRISTIAN MEET *The churchyard at Tara contains an ancient pillar carved with the image of a pagan god and a Bronze Age standing stone.*

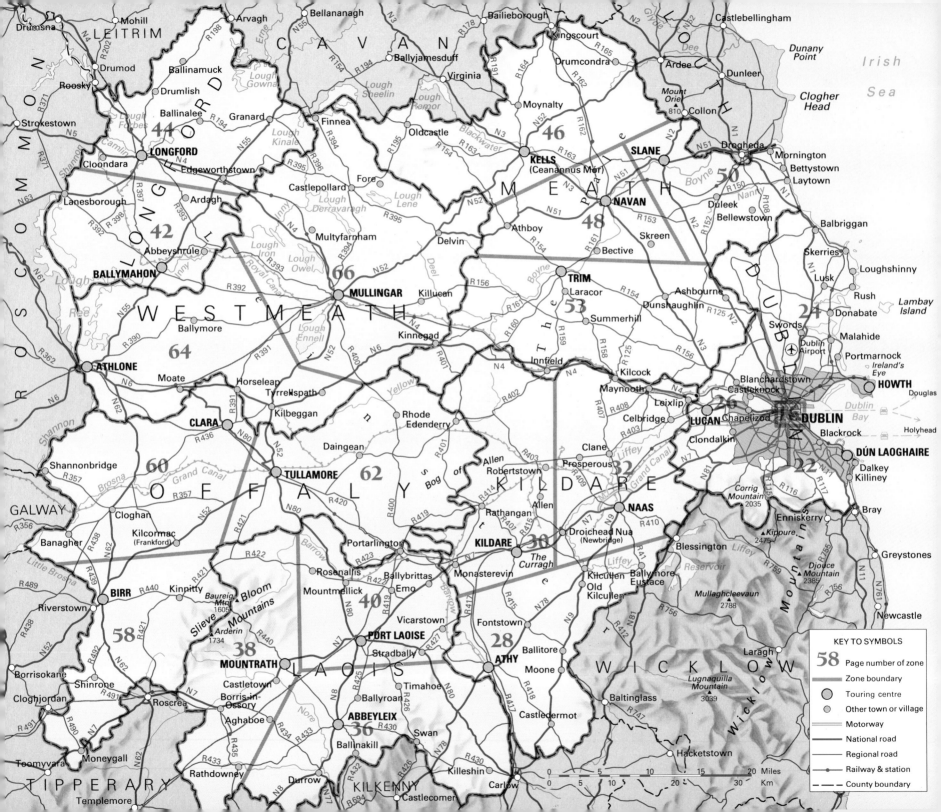

## INDEX OF TOURING AREAS

went on outside these limits was shrugged at as being 'beyond the Pale'.

To the south of Dublin lies the wild and rugged scenery of the Wicklow Mountains, but fanning out to the west and north are the limestone plains of the midlands. Unlike the industrial British Midlands, the Irish midlands are predominantly rural. There are six counties in this region besides County Dublin – Meath, Westmeath, Longford, Offaly, Laois and Kildare – and beyond the dormitory towns surrounding the capital these counties are sparsely populated.

The region contains some rich grassland, in County Meath and around the Curragh in County Kildare, where some of the world's most valuable racehorses are raised. The racecourse there dates back to pre-Christian times. But large tracts of land in this region are given over to bog – notably the Bog of Allen – where gentle domes of damp peat have been built up by century upon century of decaying moss. Elsewhere, the plains are broken up by outcrops of hills laid down in earlier geological eras, such as the Slieve Bloom Mountains on the border between counties Laois and Offaly, with their wooded glens and rolling moorland. Longford and Westmeath are known for their multitudinous loughs and streams, the beloved haunt of anglers.

Throughout the region there is evidence of prehistoric habitation – ring-forts, crannogs (lake dwellings), standing stones and burial sites. If the sheer quantity of archaeological evidence is anything to go by, the richly fertile valley of the River Boyne, flowing through Meath, was particularly favoured in prehistoric times. Excavations at Navan have revealed traces of human activity in the Stone Age, but it is the Stone Age burial sites of 3000 BC that have given the Boyne valley its place in archaeological textbooks. The most famous of these is Newgrange, with its long gallery aligned to catch the light of the rising sun on the day of the winter solstice.

It was also in Meath, at the Hill of Tara, that the High Kings of Ireland had their seat. This was the heartland of Celtic Ireland and a sacred centre of pre-Christian cults. Some of the great early Christian settlements were built in this region, including Ardagh in Longford, founded by St Patrick, and Kells in Meath, a great centre of learning and the source of one of the world's finest illuminated manuscripts, the *Book of Kells*.

Later, the ruling Anglo-Irish families built great houses, whose comfortable grandeur is still to be seen in several stately homes open to the public, such as Newbridge House in County Dublin, and Castletown House in Kildare.

But the region has other attractions besides its historical sites. On the east coast there are some fine beaches and resorts, particularly at Skerries, Rush, Laytown and Bettystown. Ireland's most famous racecourses, the Curragh and Punchestown in Kildare, and Fairyhouse in Meath, lie within striking distance of Dublin, while at Laytown, once every summer, horses race across the beach at low tide in one of Ireland's quainter race meetings. There are numerous golf courses, including the championship Portmarnock Golf Club and the Royal Dublin; inland rivers and lakes for anglers wishing to catch coarse or game fish; and excellent facilities for sailors and windsurfers at Dublin, Dun Laoghaire, Howth, Malahide and Skerries. For plant lovers there is a fine arboretum at Birr Castle, in Offaly, the Botanic Gardens in Dublin, and the Japanese Gardens in Kildare. Or if you simply want to see Ireland at 3mph, hire a canal cruiser or narrowboat and travel up the 18th-century canals. The Grand Canal, the Royal Canal (under restoration) and the navigable River Barrow connect Dublin with the River Shannon and with Waterford in the south.

EARLY MORNING IN DUBLIN *The rising sun on the Grand Canal in Ireland's capital city silhouettes the barges and St Mary's Church.*

SWEET MOLLY MALONE *On Dublin's Grafton Street a statue commemorates the heroine of the traditional ballad, who sold cockles and mussels from her wheelbarrow.*

# In Dublin's Fair City

*Dubh Linn, meaning 'dark pool', is today called Baile Átha Cliath, 'the town of the hurdle ford', crossing the River Liffey that cuts Dublin in two. The well of St Patrick may recall a visit by the nation's apostle in 448. Four centuries later it was settled by Norwegian Vikings, and after them came the Danes. The Norse command of Dublin was not broken until 1014, when they were defeated by the great Irish king, Brian Boru. The Anglo-Norman warrior Strongbow stormed the town in 1170, establishing English power in Ireland, and from then on Dublin was the focus of political, religious and cultural upheavals.*

*Today it is a gracious city with two faces, on either side of the Liffey. The north side of the Liffey has the wide boulevard of O'Connell Street, one of the grandest streets in Europe; the Custom House, a masterpiece of 18th-century architecture; Moore Street market, which rings with raucous Dublin cries; and unpretentious pubs frequented by real Dublin characters. Dublin's south side is the cultural and fashionable part of the city with its elegant Georgian buildings, two cathedrals and a castle, and Ireland's treasure houses, the National Gallery, National Museum and Trinity Library.*

## Christchurch Cathedral

The square, parapeted tower of the splendidly restored Cathedral of the Holy Trinity, the cathedral's official name, towers above buildings on the south bank of the Liffey. Founded in 1038 by the Norse king Sitric Silkenbeard, its crypt, crossings and transepts date from the 12th century, and are fine examples of early Gothic architecture. It was here that the pretender, Lambert Simnel, was crowned Edward VI of England in 1487. In the magnificent nave is a tomb said to be that of Strongbow, the Anglo-Norman Richard de Clare, who died in 1176. And in a metal box is preserved the heart of St Lawrence O'Toole, Archbishop of Dublin at the time of Strongbow's invasion in 1170.

Blocked-off underground passageways from the crypt are said to have led at one time to nearby Dublin Castle. Preserved in a glass case down there are the bodies of a cat and a mouse, about 120 years old, both caught in full flight as their chase led them through the pipes of the organ, where they both got stuck, the mouse only a few inches ahead of the cat's paws.

## Dublin Castle

Only the Norman Record Tower survives as a reminder that this castle was once part of Dublin's defensive system, built between 1204 and 1268. The rest of the building dates from later periods, but contains much to admire. On one side of the Castle Yard are the State Apartments, reached by a grand staircase of Connemara marble. They include the vast St Patrick's Hall, with a painted ceiling and a frieze bearing the arms of the Knights of St Patrick. It is here that Irish presidents are inaugurated. The castle's Throne Room, where English kings and queens received their subjects, has a massive throne believed to have been presented by William of Orange and last used by George V in 1911. The oval Wedgwood Room is decorated in the blue-and-white style of Wedgwood china, and contains a Waterford glass chandelier, Chinese-style Chippendale chairs and an Adam marble fireplace.

The Record Tower served as the centre of British administration in Ireland from the 18th century until 1922.

**Opening times** *Mon-Fri 10am-5pm; Sat, Sun and Bank Holidays 2-5pm. Tel: (01) 777129.*

### The Garden of Remembrance

Close to Parnell Square, a little north of O'Connell Street, is a peaceful retreat of manicured lawns and a lake in the form of a cross. It is dedicated to all who died in the cause of Irish freedom. On this spot the Irish Volunteer movement was formed in 1913, and it was here three years later that the Volunteers were held overnight after their week-long Rising, before being transferred to prison. A bronze sculpture at one end of the lake represents the legend of the Children of Lir, who were changed into swans and condemned to tread the waters of Lough Derravaragh, in County Westmeath, for 300 years.

The Garden of Remembrance was opened in 1966, on the 50th anniversary of the Easter Rising.

### Grafton Street

Pedestrians and street buskers have the place to themselves in Dublin's most fashionable walkway with its gaudy shop signs, department stores, restaurants and cafés. At one end of Grafton Street is St Stephen's Green Park, an area known to Dubliners simply as 'the Green'. Laid out in its present form in 1880 by Sir Arthur Guinness, it is surrounded by some of the city's most attractive Georgian houses. The green is one of Dublin's best-loved parks and squares, with lawns, flowerbeds, fountains and ponds, a Victorian bandstand and numerous bronze statues.

At the end of the tiny Johnson Court alley off Grafton Street is a striking example of tasteful renewal, in Powerscourt House. It was built in 1771 as a town house for Viscount Powerscourt, and has been meticulously renovated and brought back to life as a shopping centre. The fine courtyard has been given a glass roof and over its three storeys are spread art galleries, shops, craft workshops, restaurants and cafés.

A VIEW FROM THE BRIDGE *One of Dublin's loveliest views is from O'Connell Bridge, with the slender Halfpenny Bridge spanning the Liffey downstream.*

INSTANT ENTERTAINMENT *Street buskers draw audiences of all ages in lively Grafton Street.*

### National Gallery of Ireland

Francis Fowke, architect of London's Victoria and Albert Museum, designed this elegant building, built between 1859 and 1864. Its greystone façade fronted by a columned porch was added later. Inside, the impressive collection of works is arranged around a spiral staircase that ascends to the skylighted roof. The collection includes more than 2400 paintings and some 300 pieces of sculpture. Apart from a range of Irish works, including paintings by Jack B. Yeats (1871-1957), considered to be Ireland's greatest painter, there are works representing just about every European school. The Italian masters represented include Titian, Canaletto and Veronese, while the French works include Degas' *Ballet Girls*, and the Spanish room has paintings by El Greco and Goya.

**Opening times** *Mon-Sat 10am-6pm, Thur 10am-9pm, Sun 2-5pm. Tel: (01) 615133.*

## National Museum of Ireland

Irish antiquities are imaginatively displayed here, creating a vibrant image of Ireland's past. The museum's ground floor houses relics of both native and Viking occupation of the country. Pride of place goes to the fabulous collection of artefacts from the Wood Quay site in Dublin, where the Vikings established a harbour some 800 years ago. Wood Quay was the subject of much controversy in the 1970s and 1980s, when developers and conservationists clashed over whether a proposed office block should go ahead there or whether it should be fully excavated by archaeologists and then a museum built on the site to house the finds. The compromise, though it barely satisfied the conservationists, was for a stay to be put on the development to allow some excavation to be carried out. The items that were recovered, including swords, combs, brooches, cloak pins, weighing scales and tools, are now on show in the museum. In the upper rooms are fine collections of glass, lace and musical instruments including 17th and 18th-century Irish harps. The museum's Treasury House numbers among its hoard the 8th-century silver Ardagh Chalice and the Tara Brooch.

The Natural History Museum, housed in Merrion Street, contains a huge collection of animals from Ireland's past and present, including an Irish elk and a basking shark.
**National Museum of Ireland** *Tues-Sat 10am-5pm, Sun 2-5pm. Tel: (01) 618811.*
**Natural History Museum** *Opening times and telephone number as above.*

## O'Connell Street

A statue of Daniel O'Connell, 'The Liberator', stands at the southern end of the street named after him, overlooking O'Connell Bridge, the city's main north-south link. Around the plinth fly bronze angels of victory, their wings pierced with bullet holes from the Easter Rising of 1916. Behind the victor in the struggle for Catholic emancipation runs a central, tree-lined pavement with more statues and, at its northern end, the massive bronze of Charles Stewart Parnell who led the Home Rule movement in the 19th century.

The central walk between the two statues gives the best views of Dublin's most famous street, and without doubt its most impressive building is the General Post Office of 1814-18. Above its gleaming white portico of fluted columns are figures of Hibernia, Mercury and Fidelity, and in the main hall is a

THE CUSTOM HOUSE *Dublin's finest public building, with the figure of Hope surmounting the dome, dates from 1791.*

DYING HERO *A bronze statue of the hero Cuchulainn stands in the General Post Office.*

superb bronze statue of the dying Cuchulainn, hero and leader of the Red Branch Knights in Irish mythology. During the 1916 Rising, the GPO was the headquarters of the rebel Irish Volunteers. It was relentlessly shelled and shot at by the British, and the great Ionic columns of the portico still show the scars.

A short walk from O'Connell Street, along Henry Street, leads to the Moore Street market where modern-day 'Molly Malones' sell cockles and mussels, as well as fruit and vegetables.

## Phoenix Park

Few cities in the world have a park of such magnitude. Phoenix Park covers 1752 acres and is surrounded by a wall 7 miles long. Within them are gardens, lakes, woods and playing grounds for just about every sport from cricket to polo, not to mention the motor-cycle race meetings held on its roads.

The park, whose name comes from the Irish *fionn uisce*, or 'clear water', in reference to a freshwater spring in the Furry Glen, was once part of the grounds of Kilmainham priory nearby. It was opened as a deer park in 1662 by the Duke of Ormonde (its present herd of 300 or so deer is descended from the original stock), and was laid out in 1747 by Lord Chesterfield.

Phoenix Park is entered by the main gate at its south-eastern corner. To the left of the gate is a 190ft tall obelisk honouring the Duke of Wellington, who was born in Dublin. It is said that he played down his Irish ancestry, and when reminded that he was a Dubliner replied: 'Just because you were born in a stable, it doesn't mean you're a horse!' The park is also the home of the world's third oldest zoo, established in 1831.
**Opening times** *6.30am-11pm, all year.*

STREETS BROAD AND NARROW *Moore Street is Dublin's venue for barrow vendors.*

## Rotunda Hospital

Built in 1750, this was Europe's first purpose-built maternity hospital, founded by Dr Bartholomew Mosse (1712-59). The Doric portion of the complex facing O'Connell Street was intended to serve as assembly rooms to generate financial support for the hospital, but has since been converted to a cinema.

TRANSPORT OF DELIGHT *Horse-drawn coaches are still a familiar sight in Dublin's streets.*

HALFPENNY BRIDGE *The bridge reflected in the Liffey's waters was once a toll bridge.*

DUBLIN DOORWAYS *Georgian Dublin boasts many fine doorways with gleaming brass knockers and filigree fanlights.*

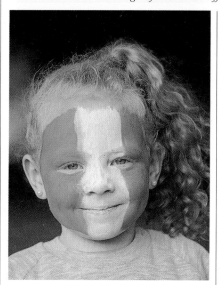

PATRIOTIC FACE *A young Dubliner wears Ireland's colours for St Patrick's Day.*

### A VIKING ADVENTURE

The Vikings came to Ireland in 795, and in 841 settled on the banks of the Liffey, probably upriver of what is now Wood Quay. By the 10th century, Dublin had become the largest Viking town in Ireland, and was probably a slave port from where slaves captured from the monasteries were exported to Scandinavia. Excavations on Wood Quay have produced a wealth of Viking artefacts which are on display in the National Museum. In High Street, on Dublin's south side, a Viking street has been re-created on the site of their settlement. Called 'Irish Life Viking Adventure', it presents everyday life in the town of 1000 years ago, with video displays and a tour led by a 'Viking' through the street with its realistic sights, sounds and smells.

In the adjacent St Audoen Heritage Foundation is the dramatic 'Flame on the Hill' presentation, a large-screen, ten-projector show that tells the story of Ireland before the coming of the Vikings.

Topped by a three-storey tower and copper cupola, the building takes its name from the 80ft diameter hall designed in 1764 by John Ensor and modified in 1786 by James Gandon, one of Ireland's foremost 18th-century architects. Above the main entrance hall is the chapel, with exquisite baroque plasterwork by Barthélemy Cramillion.

### St Mary's Abbey

Off Capel Street is what was once the largest and most important Cistercian monastery in Ireland. Founded by the Benedictine order in 1139, it was transferred to the Cistercian order 12 years later. In the 17th century much of the original monastery was dismantled and the stone used to build the Grattan Bridge, which crosses the Liffey at Capel Street. Now only the chapter house remains. It measures 45ft by 24ft and its vaulted roof has groins and moulded crossribs.

The chapter house is where, in 1534, the Lord Deputy and 10th Earl of Kildare, Silken Thomas Fitzgerald (so called because of his love of fine clothes), declared his defiance of Henry VIII and his reordering of the Church. Fitzgerald also pronounced himself an enemy of the king because he believed him to have had his father killed. There followed a brief period of rebellion, which ended with Fitzgerald's capture and execution in 1537. **Chapter House** *Mid-June to mid-Sept, Tues-Sun 12-6pm. Tel: (01) 721490.*

TAVERN IN THE TOWN *Dubliners enjoy a 'pint of plain' in one of the city's many bars.*

## St Patrick's Cathedral

This majestic cathedral, at 300ft long, is Ireland's largest church. It was founded in 1190 on a site where, it is said, St Patrick baptised converts to Christianity in the 5th century. There has been a church on this site ever since. The present one was first built around 1225 but has been enlarged and restored several times. Jonathan Swift, author of *Gulliver's Travels*, was Dean here from 1713 to 1745, and the pulpit he preached from is still to be seen, although it is no longer in use. Swift's tomb is in the south aisle, and over the door of the robing room is his epitaph: 'He lies where furious indignation can no longer rend his heart.'

One of the more curious sights here is the door of the medieval Chapter House, with a hole in the middle of it. It was cut by the Earl of Kildare in 1492 so that he might reach through and shake the hand of the Earl of Ormonde who had taken refuge there, thus ending a bitter feud between the two ruling families in Ireland at the time.

THE BOYLE MONUMENT *Among the monuments in St Patrick's Cathedral is one erected in the 17th century to the Boyle family, Earls of Cork.*

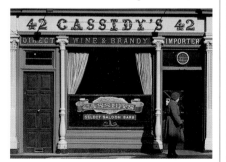

LASTING ATTRACTION *Many Dublin pubs have eye-catching façades, unspoilt by modernisers. Inside, too, they are mellow with old wood and brass, which must foster conviviality for it is good talk as much as velvet pints that draws today's regulars – just as it drew James Joyce's Dubliners to Mulligan's.*

## Trinity College

Founded by Elizabeth I in 1592, Trinity is the sole college of Dublin University. Its 300ft façade, with graceful columns and pilasters, dates from the mid-18th century. The college looks out onto trim lawns and College Green, flanked by statues of two of the college's most famous graduates, the orator Edmund Burke (1729-97) and playwright Oliver Goldsmith (1728-74). Other graduates who went on to win distinction include Jonathan Swift, Samuel Beckett, Oscar Wilde and Bram Stoker, creator of the novel *Dracula*. Trinity College is unusual in that it allowed women students to enter as early as 1903, although it was many years later before Catholics were allowed to attend, with special dispensation from the Church in Rome.

The Front Gate leads to the cobbled Parliament Square, dominated by the campanile of 1853, and beyond the square is the Trinity Library. Its reading room, the Long Room, stretches 210ft, is 41ft wide and soars 40ft to a superb barrel-vaulted ceiling. It houses some 200,000 of the college's collection of more than 2 million volumes, and its treasures are many, including the 7th-century *Book of Durrow* and the 8th-century *Book of Dimma*. But the most priceless manuscript it has is the *Book of Kells*, a Latin text of the Four Gospels with illuminated pages, which dates from about AD 800. Two of the book's four volumes are usually on display.

**Trinity College** *Mon-Fri 9.30am-4.30pm, Sat 9.30am-12.30pm.*

**Trinity Library** *Mid-Oct to mid-June, Mon-Fri 9.30am-10pm, Sat 9.30am-1pm; mid-June to mid-Oct, Mon-Fri 9.30am-5pm, Sat 9.30am-1pm. Closed last two weeks in July. Tel: (01) 772941.*

HALL OF LEARNING *The Long Room of the Old Library in Trinity College, completed in 1732, houses many exquisitely illuminated manuscripts.*

---

**OTHER PLACES TO SEE**

**Abbey Theatre** National theatre of Ireland, specialising in works of Irish playwrights.

**Civic Museum** Devoted to history of the city and county. Open Tues-Sat 10am-6pm, Sun 11am-2pm. Tel: (01) 794260.

**Custom House** Imposing 18th-century building designed by James Gandon, with 375ft façade, arched windows, arcades and copper dome 120ft high, topped by 16ft figure of Hope.

**The Four Courts** The High Court and Supreme Court of Ireland, built 1786-1802, designed by James Gandon.

**Guinness Brewery** Europe's largest stout-producing brewery, with visitor centre explaining how Guinness Stout is made. Open Mon-Fri 10am-3pm. Tel: (01) 536700.

**Hugh Lane Municipal Gallery of Modern Art** Irish and European 19th and 20th-century paintings and sculpture, with fine collection of French Impressionists.

Open Tues-Fri 9.30am-6pm, Sat 9.30am-5pm, Sun 11am-5pm. Tel: (01) 741903.

**Leinster House** Georgian mansion designed 1745 by Richard Cassel, now seat of The Dáil, the Irish Parliament.

**Mansion House** Built in 1715, official residence of Dublin's Lord Mayor. Round Room open to public every day. Mansion House open by appointment. Tel: (01) 762852.

**National Library** Large collection of books and

manuscripts of national importance, as well as records, newspapers and documents covering several centuries. Open Mon and Tues 10am-5.15pm, Wed and Thur 10am-9pm, Fri and Sat 10am-1pm. Tel: (01) 618811.

**National Wax Museum** About 200 wax dummies including politicians, pop stars, even the 12 Apostles and Christ at the Last Supper. Open Mon-Sat 10am-5.30pm, Sun 12-5.30pm. Tel: (01) 726340.

**St Michan's Church** Founded in 1095. The church vaults contain bodies 'mummified' by the absorbent limestone. Open Mar-Oct, Mon-Fri 10am-5.30pm, Sat 10am-12.45pm. Guided tours by special arrangement, Nov-Mar. Tel: (01) 724154.

**WALKS**

**City Centre Walks** Tel: (01) 532407.

**Literary, Medieval and Georgian walks** Feb-Dec. Tel: (01) 6794291.

**EVENTS**

**Dublin International Organ Festival** Late June.

**Dublin Theatre Festival** Late Sept-early Oct.

**Dublin Traditional Music Festival** Mid-June.

**Kerrygold Dublin Horse Show** Aug.

**Spring Season of International Opera** End Apr-early May.

**INFORMATION**

Dublin Tourism. Tel: (01) 747733.

# The Dubliners' Playground

*A handful of miles south of Dublin's city centre lies a region of outstanding natural beauty. The Dublin Mountains rise in purple majesty and embrace a landscape of wide bays and little villages with lovely coastal views and an almost Mediterranean atmosphere. At Dun Laoghaire a vast harbour shelters colourful yachts that bob and sway in the wake of the ferries plying to and from the English mainland.*

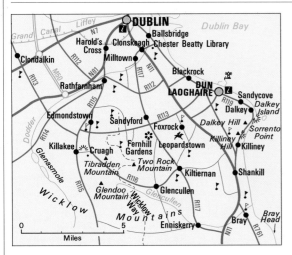

**OTHER PLACES TO SEE**

**Blackrock** Fashionable coastal village near Dun Laoghaire, with two Martello towers.

**Chester Beatty Library** Ballsbridge. Museum of Oriental and Middle Eastern books, including the world's largest collection of Korans. Open Tues-Fri 10am-5pm, Sat 2-5pm. Tel: (01) 2692386.

**Clonskeagh** Village containing Roebuck Lodge, home of Maude Gonne MacBride (1865-1953), nationalist and friend of poet W.B. Yeats.

**Fernhill Gardens** At Sandyford, 40 acre site of woodlands, garden and park with fine collection of trees and shrubs. Open Mar-Nov, Tues-Sat 11am-5pm, Sun 2-6pm. Tel: (01) 956000.

**Grand Canal** One of Dublin's two canals, with attractive walks between Portobello Bridge and Mount Street Bridge.

**Killiney** Village 2½m S of Dalkey with coastal and mountain views from Sorrento Point and Killiney Hill.

**WALKS**

**Cruagh and Tibradden** S of Rathfarnham, forest walks, nature trails and picnic spots.

**EVENTS**

**Bloomsday** Sandycove, June 16.

**Circuit of Ireland Car Rally** Dun Laoghaire, mid-Apr.

**Dun Laoghaire Arts Week** Early to mid-Sept.

**Dun Laoghaire Summer Festival** End June-early July.

**Greyhound racing** Harold's Cross, Tues, Thur, Fri. Tel: (01) 971081. Shelbourne Park, Dublin, Mon, Wed, Sat. Tel: (01) 683502.

**Horse racing** Leopardstown, all year.

**King of Dalkey Festival** Mid-July.

**Yachting races** Dun Laoghaire, May-Sept.

**SPORT**

**Angling** Game fishing: River Dodder. Sea fishing: Dun Laoghaire to Bray.

**Bathing** Killiney Beach and White Rock.

**Golf** Carrickmines Golf Club, 18-hole course. Tel: (01) 955972.
Dun Laoghaire Golf Club, 18-hole course. Tel: (01) 2801055.
Elm Park Golf Club, 18-hole course. Tel: (01) 2693438/2693014.
Killiney Golf Club, 9-hole course. Tel: (01) 2851983.
Milltown Golf Club, 18-hole course. Tel: (01) 977060.
Old Conna Golf Club, 18-hole course. Tel: (01) 2826055.
Woodbrook Golf Club, 18-hole course. Tel: (01) 2824799.

**Yachting** Dun Laoghaire.

**INFORMATION**

Dublin Tourism. Tel: (01) 747733.
Dun Laoghaire Tourist Office. Tel: (01) 2806984.

## Dalkey/Deilginis

There is an air of the past in this seaside village that was once a medieval walled settlement known as the Town of Seven Castles. Only two of the castles remain, in the tiny main street. One, the 16th-century Archbold's Tower, has three storeys rising to its battlemented parapets. The other has been reconstructed and is now the Town Hall. Directions to the keyholder can be found on a sign on the tower, or enquire locally.

The village's two harbours, Coliemore and Bullock, are home to a small fishing fleet. Up on Dalkey Hill is Torca Cottage, home to George Bernard Shaw from 1866 to 1874. The cottage is privately owned and is not open to visitors.

The Vico Road, which leads south to the next village, Killiney, climbs up the hillside and has superb views across the sea. Offshore is a group of rocky islands, the largest of which is Dalkey Island, on which are a Martello tower and a ruined medieval Benedictine church, St Begnet's Oratory. Dalkey Island can be reached by boat trips that run from Coliemore in the summer.

Every year Dalkey celebrates a ritual crowning of the 'King of Dalkey'. The ceremony dates from 1797, when it began as a naval prank, but the joke turned sour when, in the following year, the year of the Irish rebellion, the occasion took on a political significance and the ceremony was banned. It began to be celebrated again in the 1950s and is now an annual event.

## Dublin Mountains

South of Dublin's city limits are the so-called Dublin Mountains, part of the Wicklow mountain range. With their forest walks, gentle, undemanding strolls, craggy treks and scenic drives they have for generations been the playground of Dubliners.

An excellent drive starts at Enniskerry, just inside the County Wicklow border, and wends northwards to the city suburbs of Rathfarnham. Take the road up the Glencullen valley to the village of the same name, and then follow the road with Two Rock and Tilbradden mountains to the north-east of the road and Glendoo Mountain to the southwest. Along the way, numerous routes lead off into the quiet hills and valleys.

Farther west is the lovely Glenasmole valley, where the River Dodder rushes through fields and wooded hillsides, and at Killakee there are sweeping views of Dublin.

## Dun Laoghaire

Visitors from Britain by ferry get their first glimpse of Ireland at Dun Laoghaire, and it does not disappoint with its rows of brightly painted houses laid out in terraces beyond the slender, arching arms of the harbour piers. The harbour was built by the celebrated Scottish engineer John Rennie between 1817 and 1852, and each of the granite piers is more than a mile long. The East Pier, with a lighthouse at the far end, makes a pleasant stroll, especially in the evening when its granite glows golden in the setting sun. The town is Ireland's largest yachting centre, and is the headquarters of the Royal Irish, the National, and Royal St George yacht clubs.

In Haigh Terrace the former Mariners Church of 1837 now houses the National Maritime Museum of Ireland. Among the wide display of nautical exhibits are the Baily Optic, a light that once shone from the Baily lighthouse at Howth, on the north side of Dublin Bay. A model of Isambard Brunel's steamship *Great Eastern* is a reminder that a Wicklow man, Captain Robert Halpin, commanded the ship when it laid the first transatlantic telegraph cable in July 1866.

**National Maritime Museum** *May-Sept, daily exc Mon 2.30-5.30pm. Weekends only, Oct and Nov. Check first. Tours by arrangement. Tel: (01) 2800969.*

## Sandycove/Cuas an Gaineamh

A short way down the coast from Dun Laoghaire is a promontory that shelters the tiny village of Sandycove. It was put on the literary map by the author James Joyce (1882-1941), who mentioned it in the opening pages of his novel *Ulysses*: 'They halted, looking towards the blunt cape of Bray Head that lay on the water like the snout of a sleeping whale.' In 1904 Joyce stayed for a week in the village's Martello tower, some 40ft high with 8ft thick granite walls, and one of several built along the west coast in the early 19th century to guard against a possible invasion by Napoleon. It is now a museum known as Joyce Tower, and contains some of the author's personal possessions, including his guitar, cane and cigar case, as well as letters, documents and first editions. Devotees of Joyce make a pilgrimage to the museum on Bloomsday, June 16, the day on which all the events in *Ulysses* took place.

**Joyce Tower** *Apr-Oct 10am-5.30pm, Sun 2.30-6pm. Nov-Mar, by appointment. Tel: (01) 2808571/2809265.*

## DUBLIN'S PRODIGAL SON

Of all the great writers born in Dublin, none has been more controversial than James Joyce, both in the content of his novels and in his love-hate relationship with the city that he called 'dear dirty Dublin'.

Born in suburban Dublin in 1882 and educated at University College, he left Dublin in 1904 after failing to find a publisher for his first book, *Dubliners*, and lived from then on in Rome, Trieste, Paris and Zurich – self-exiled and often in poverty. His bitterness against his homeland emerged in *Gas from a Burner*, privately published in 1912, in which he wrote:

*'This lovely land that always sent
Her writers and artists to banishment.'*

In 1922 Joyce published in Paris his most famous novel, *Ulysses*, considered by some to be a turning point in modern fiction, but to many a work of pornography. In it he describes June 16, 1904, a day in the life of Dublin and its citizens, and in particular of Leopold Bloom and his promiscuous wife, Molly.

Yet Joyce's heart was always in Dublin, and he once said that after his death 'Dublin' would be found inscribed on his heart. He died in Zurich in 1941.

BRACING TROT *The owner of a horse-drawn gig, or jaunting car, goes for a trot along the Dublin coast.*

DUN LAOGHAIRE *The name, pronounced Dunleary, means 'Leary's fort'. Over the centuries this pretty harbour has become Dublin's main ferry port.*

23

# Dublin's Rocky Coast

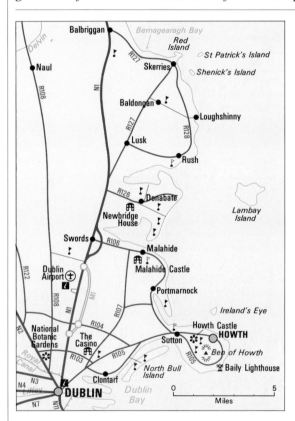

*North of Dublin a coast road gives spectacular seascape views, including rocky offshore islands such as the long strip of North Bull Island in Dublin Bay, the tiny, distant Ireland's Eye and the once-volcanic Lambay Island. Each town and village along the way has its own treasure to offer, from the lovely gardens of Howth to the ancient grandeur of Malahide Castle, home of a national portrait collection.*

**OTHER PLACES TO SEE**
**Donabate** Site of Newbridge House, Georgian mansion built for Archbishop of Dublin. Superbly decorated, with dairy and forge, also museum of curiosities, aviary and doll museum. Open Mon-Fri 10am-6pm, Sun 2-6pm. Tel: (01) 436534/5.

**National Botanic Gardens** Founded in 1795; has some 20,000 varieties of plants, shrubs and trees, and a 400ft long tropical glasshouse. Open Mar-Oct, Mon-Sat 10am-6pm, Sun 11am-6pm; Oct-Mar, Mon-Sat 10am-4.30pm, Sun 11am-4.30pm. Tel: (01) 374388.

**WALKS**
**Bernagearagh Bay** 2m NW of Skerries, picnic site.
**Skerries** Along coast on either side of bustling holiday town.

**EVENTS**
**All-Ireland Football Finals** Croke Park, Dublin, Sept.
**All-Ireland Hurling Finals** Croke Park, Dublin, Sept.
**Howth Jazz Festival** Mid-Apr.

**SPORT**
**Angling** Game fishing: River Delvin. Sea fishing: Balbriggan, Howth, Loughshinny, Rush, Skerries.
**Boating** Balbriggan, Howth.
**Golf** Beaverstown Golf Club, 18-hole course. Tel: (01) 426439.
Clontarf Golf Club, 18-hole course. Tel: (01) 311305.
Corballis Golf Club, 18-hole course. Tel: (01) 436346.
Donabate Golf Club, 18-hole course. Tel: (01) 436059.
Howth Golf Club, 18-hole course. Tel: (01) 323055.
The Island Golf Club, 18-hole course. Tel: (01) 450248.
Portmarnock Golf Club, 27-hole course. Tel: 323082.
Royal Dublin Golf Club, 18-hole course. Tel: (01) 336346.
Skerries Golf Club, 18-hole course. Tel: (01) 491204.
**Sailing** Malahide.
**Windsurfing** Portmarnock.

**INFORMATION**
Dublin Tourism.
Tel: (01) 747733.

## The Casino

There are no longer any gaming tables in this splendid building, started in 1762 for the 1st Earl of Charlemont as an out-of-town house, but it remains one of the world's finest Georgian houses. It was built to the design of Sir William Chambers (architect of Somerset House in London), in the form of a Greek cross and took 15 years to finish. It is surrounded by 12 Tuscan columns, four at the corners and two in each of the four porticoes, with stone lions guarding the approaches. The balustraded flat roof is decorated with urns, which are in fact chimneys leading from ornate fireplaces. Inside, the Casino has elaborate plaster ceilings.
**Opening times** *Early June to mid-Sept, daily 10am-6.30pm. Tel: (01) 331618/613111.*

## Howth/Binn Éadair

At the northern end of a long, gently curving road that hugs Dublin Bay is the Howth peninsula. A winding road from the pretty little village leads up to Ben of Howth, a hill 560ft high topped by an ancient stone cairn. From every point there are tremendous views – past seagulls riding the strong up-draughts of wind against the cliffs to North Bull Island and northwards to the islands of Ireland's Eye and Lambay, with the distant Mourne Mountains visible on a clear day. The novelist H.G. Wells called it 'the most beauti-ful view in the world'. The view is also spectacular at night, when the ferries can be seen entering and leaving Dun Laoghaire Harbour across the bay to the south, and the street lights glitter on the coast road, earning it the title 'the string of pearls'.

Howth was once an island, its narrow link with the mainland now submerged in the sea. It is said to have been inhabited since 3250 BC. Today, Howth is one of Ireland's five major fishery harbours, crammed with trawlers. At weekends the piers throng with families in search of a walk in the fresh air and some freshly landed fish. Its lighthouse dates from 1814, and stands on the site of a light erected in 1670. An optic from the old lighthouse is in the National Maritime Museum at Dun Laoghaire.

West of the harbour is Howth Castle, home of the St Lawrence family since 1177. The oldest parts of the castle are more than 700 years old, though it was much rebuilt in the 18th century. The castle is not open to the public, but its gardens are. Spread over 30 acres, these include some 2000 varieties of rhododendrons. The gardens also contain a half-mile long, 30ft high beech-hedge walk, planted in 1710, at the entrance to which stands an elm planted in 1585. It is Ireland's oldest introduced tree.
**Howth Castle Gardens** *All year, 8am to sunset. Tel: (01) 322624.*

Malahide Castle *The 14th to 18th-century castle has an impressive interior and art collection.*

the bustle and clamour of the seafront are many places to explore. At Red Island, now part of the mainland, there are indentations in the rocks said to be the footprints of St Patrick, who locals claim began his mission to Ireland there in the 5th century. On St Patrick's Island, reached by boat from Skerries, are the remains of a church where a national Synod was held in 1148. At low tide it is possible to walk to Shenick Island, with its Martello tower.

A cliff walk to the south of Skerries leads to the pretty fishing village of Loughshinny.

## Swords/Sord

Now a dormitory town for Dublin, this ancient village was the site of a monastery founded in the 6th century by St Columba. The monastery has long since vanished, but there are still some ancient relics in this now thoroughly modern community. At the northern end of the town is the pentagonal Swords Castle, built about 1200 by the Archbishop of Dublin as a fortified house.

In the grounds of the Protestant church are two towers. The Round Tower, 82ft high, dates from the 11th century, and close by a square tower is all that remains of a 15th-century church.

DUBLIN BAY *The silvery waters of the bay mirror brooding hills at Howth Head.*

## Lusk/Lusca

A few miles inland the tiny village of Lusk boasts a small collection of antiquities, including a 10th-century Round Tower that is 84ft high. It stands on the site of a 6th-century monastery, which was dissolved four centuries later, crushed by successive Viking and Irish assaults. The ground level has risen substantially over the centuries, and the doorway is now not far above ground. Enquire in the village about obtaining the key to the tower.

There is also a 16th-century tower on the site, and a mid-19th-century church with medieval tombstones inside it.

## Malahide/Mullach Íde

South-west of this seaside resort is the stately, greystone Malahide Castle, home of the Talbot family from 1185 until 1973, when the last Lord Talbot de Malahide died. Its core is 14th century, though the turrets and battlements are later additions. Inside are rooms furnished with period furniture, including the striking Great Hall with a Minstrels' Gallery, which dates from 1475 when the Lord of Malahide was made Admiral of Malahide and the Adjoining Seas. Also impressive is the Oak Room, a dark room with ornate 16th and 17th-century carved panelling and ogee-arched windows. The rooms are hung with portraits from the National Gallery of Ireland, including works by Joshua Reynolds and Nathaniel Hone.

The Talbot Botanic Gardens, spread over 20 acres, were created by Lord Talbot between 1948 and 1973 and contain several thousand species of plants, particularly from Australasia.

**Malahide Castle** *Mon-Fri 10am-5pm. Apr-Oct, Sat 11am-6pm, Sun 2-6pm; Nov-Mar, Sat and Sun 2-5pm. Tel: (01) 452655/452337*
**Gardens** *All year round. Tel: (01) 450940.*

## Skerries/Na Sceirí

A sandy beach and bracing climate have made Skerries the biggest and most popular resort on the coast north of Dublin. But away from

SERENE SCENE *Beneath a seagull-speckled sky, colourful cottages line Skerries' quiet harbour.*

# Along The Liffey Valley

*Only a few miles west of Dublin city centre the Liffey valley becomes heavily cloaked with woods as it probes its way inland towards the heart of the central lowlands. Thrusting up to the south of the river are the Dublin Mountains, the start of the Leinster range that runs down almost as far as the south coast. To the north the level valley floor leads to the edge of the rich grasslands of County Meath.*

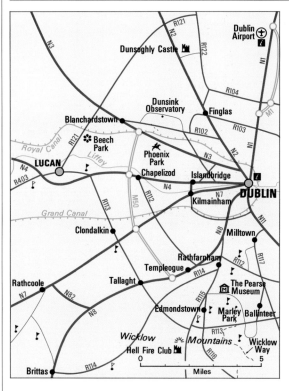

**Dunsoghly Castle** 15th-century castle on hillock surrounded by marsh. Four-storey tower with square corner towers, and still with original roof beams. Good views from parapet.

**Finglas** Site of monastery marked by 9th-century High Cross.

## WALKS
**Dublin Mountain foothills** Many well-signposted walks.
**Wicklow Way** 82m walk from Marley Park to Clonegall, County Carlow.

## SPORT
**Angling** Game fishing: River Liffey, best from around Lucan and Islandbridge.
**Golf** Beech Park Golf Club, 18-hole course. Tel: (01) 580522/580100.
Castle Golf Club, 18-hole course. Tel: (01) 904207.
Edmondstown Golf Club, 18-hole course. Tel: (01) 932461.
Grange Golf Club, 18-hole course. Tel: (01) 932832.
Hermitage Golf Club, 18-hole course. Tel: (01) 265396.
Lucan Golf Club, 9-hole course. Tel: (01) 280246.
Marley Park Golf Club, 9-hole course. Tel: (01) 934059.
Newlands Golf Club, 18-hole course. Tel: (01) 592903.
Stackstown Golf Club, 18-hole course. Tel: (01) 942338/941993.

## INFORMATION
Dublin Tourism.
Tel: (01) 747733.

## OTHER PLACES TO SEE
**Beech Park** At Clonsilla, 7m W of Dublin, walled garden of Regency house with rare cottage-garden plants. Open first Sun of the month, Mar-Nov 2-6pm. Tel: (01) 212216.
**Clondalkin** Site of friary founded in 6th century by St Mochua, with 84ft Round Tower still complete with conical cap, and two granite High Crosses standing in cemetery opposite.
**Dunsink Observatory** Observatory of Trinity College, from 1782-1921, and one of the oldest observatories in the world. Its South Telescope, dating from 1863, has a 12in refractor. Open Sept-Mar, 1st and 3rd Sat 8-10pm.

## Hell Fire Club
A short drive into the Dublin Mountains from the city's suburbs of Rathfarnham and Templeogue leads to Montpelier Hill, the wooded site of a hunting lodge where, according to legend, the Devil appeared to a group of men playing cards. Their midnight game came to an abrupt end when one of the players noticed that under the cloak of an unknown member of the company there extended not a boot but a cloven hoof. The story may have influenced the rakish young Dubliners who founded the Hell Fire Club in the 18th century, which indulged in gambling and other outlandish activities. Though whether they enjoyed these under the patronage of the Devil is not recorded.

The hunting lodge in which the club met is believed to have been built in 1720 for William Conolly, MP and later Speaker of the Irish Parliament. The revellers once set fire to the building while they remained drinking inside, to see what Hell would be like. Now ruined, the symbol of decadence and diabolism is surrounded by woodlands which draw visitors to their many marked forest walks and picnic sites. From the hill there are broad views of the western parts of Dublin city.

## Islandbridge/Droichead na hInse
On the south side of the River Liffey, close to Phoenix Park, are the War Memorial Gardens dedicated to the 49,400 Irish soldiers who died during the First World War. Sir Edward Lutyens, architect of London's Cenotaph in Whitehall, designed the gardens in 1931, with pathways, fountains, rose gardens and pagodas. In the middle of a lawn is the War Stone. South of the stone stands a great cross, modelled on an ancient Celtic High Cross. Four stone pavilions house illuminated volumes, which contain the names of all those killed in the war, and a wooden cross brought from near the battlefields of Guillemont and Gichy, in France, where many Irish soldiers died.

Trees and shrubs give a gentle edge to the gardens' solemn air, and have been carefully selected to provide a tranquil and beautiful backdrop at all times of the year.
**War Memorial Gardens** 8.30am-twilight.

## Kilmainham/Cill Mhaighneann
On the western outskirts of Dublin is Ireland's most infamous building, the jail that has become a shrine of Irish independence. Between 1796 and 1924 the jail housed many

RUSHING WATERS *The River Liffey cascades noisily over a weir at Lucan.*

political prisoners, the last being Eamon De Valera, later to become Taoiseach (Prime Minister), then President of Ireland, who was released from the jail on July 16, 1924. Here also the ringleaders of the 1916 Easter Rising, including Patrick Pearse and James Connolly, were shot by firing squad in the stone-breaking yard.

The jail is now a museum, restored to its grim original condition, with dark passages, tiny cells with massive iron doors, punishment cells and execution room. The execution yard, surrounded by a high granite wall, contains the Irish flag and two timber crosses, and a plaque bears the names of the executed nationalist leaders.

Nearby is the Royal Hospital, a restored hospice, built in 1680 for pensioner soldiers by the Duke of Ormonde, and modelled on Les Invalides in Paris. The first such hospice in the British Empire, it is now the National Centre for Culture and the Arts, and houses the Irish Museum of Modern Art. It is a two-storey structure built around a quadrangle, with a tower rising from the centre of one face. Its Great Hall has huge roof beams and

DARK MEMORIES *Kilmainham Jail, now a museum, is symbolic of Ireland's fight for independence.*

A KING'S FAVOUR *Kilmainham's Royal Hospital was built under a charter granted by Charles II.*

white pine panelling and is hung with some fine portraits. Nearby is the chapel, a baroque building recently restored.

**Irish Museum of Modern Art** *Tues-Sun 11am-6pm. Tel: (01) 718666.*

**Kilmainham Jail Museum** *June-Sept, daily 11am-6pm; Oct-May, Wed and Sun 2-6pm. Tel: (01) 535984.*

## Lucan/*Leamhcán*

The bridge over the River Liffey in the village of Lucan is a pleasant place to linger a while and watch the patient anglers fishing from the river bank. Lucan is one of the best spots on the Liffey to catch a decent salmon. There are also walks on its banks, past a tumbling weir where roach, perch and eel can be caught.

Patrick Sarsfield (d.1693), 1st Earl of Lucan, is the village's most famous son, and hero of the 1691 Siege of Limerick.

## Marley Park

At Ballinteer is Marley Park, with a craft centre, a golf course and a miniature steam railway. Marley Park marks the start of the Wicklow Way, a long-distance walk of 82 miles that leads to the village of Clonegall in County Carlow. Seasoned walkers may cover 18-20 miles a day, and complete the walk in four days, but many ramblers do the walk in 10-12 days.

**Opening times** *10am-sunset. Check for closing times. Tel: (01) 934059.*

## The Pearse Museum

Near the suburb of Rathfarnham, in St Enda's Park, is the 18th-century home of the poet Patrick Pearse. He founded St Enda's school here, a bilingual institution which aimed to revive Irish as a language. It also served as an arsenal. Pearse was one of the leaders of the Easter Rising of 1916, and kept the arms for the rebellion hidden in the house. The house has been restored and displays the Pearse family memorabilia. The history of the Easter Rising is presented in a video documentary.

**Opening times** *Dec and Jan 10am-3.30pm; Nov and Feb 10am-4.30pm; Mar, Apr, Sept and Oct 10am-5.30pm, May-Aug 10am-6pm. Tel: (01) 934208.*

### THE EASTER RISING

On Easter Monday, April 24, 1916, the simmering resentment of English rule in Ireland erupted into a violent, bloody rebellion. Led by Patrick Pearse (right) and James Connolly, some 2000 members of the Irish Volunteers and the Irish Citizens Army seized 14 key buildings in Dublin, including the General Post Office in O'Connell Street, which became the rebels' headquarters. Here Pearse defiantly read out a proclamation calling on all Irish men and women to fight for their freedom. For six days bitter street fighting took place between the rebels and 20,000 British troops. The end was inevitable, and when the rebels finally surrendered 64 had died along with 134 police and soldiers and more than 220 civilians.

The devastation they had caused turned public opinion against the rebel leaders, but they achieved martyrdom when 15 of the rebels, including Pearse and Connolly, were shot by firing squad in Kilmainham Jail.

# The Basin of the Barrow

*Behind the dark green hedgerows that line a warren of small roads, a concentration of Bronze Age settlements, disused monasteries, old churches and Celtic High Crosses tells the tale of south Kildare's ancient history. Early invaders pushed their way up the basin of the River Barrow into Kildare, the Celtic kings of Leinster made their seat here, and later still the Normans left their mark.*

WHITE'S CASTLE *The remarkably well-preserved castle was built in 1507 to defend the Crom-a-boo Bridge, which straddles the fast-flowing River Barrow.*

## Athy/Baile Átha Í

Narrow, busy streets crowded with little shops make this the very essence of the Irish country market town. The 'town of the ford of Í', named after a Munster chieftain who was killed here in the 2nd century, developed in the 13th century when the Anglo-Normans fortified it to control an important crossing over the River Barrow. The bustling town is still dominated by the well-preserved 16th-century White's Castle, a rectangular turreted tower that sits imposingly by the bridge over the Barrow, in the heart of the town. The tower is now a private home. The bridge is named 'Crom-a-boo', after 'Cromadh Bhu', the battle cry of the Earls of Desmond, one of whom was governor here in 1420.

Just 3 miles north-east of Athy is one of the largest Norman mottes in the country, Ardscull motte. The 35ft high mound with its surrounding ditch is believed to have been created in the 12th century. Close by is the battle site where Edward Bruce, brother of Robert, and his Scottish supporters defeated a strong English army in 1316.

## Castledermot/Díseart Diarmada

A step through a gateway at the southern end of this straggling town takes visitors back 800 years in an instant, into the stillness of a 13th-century Franciscan friary, which was plundered by Robert Bruce in 1317. Later, in 1541, the friary was suppressed. Only the walls of the church remain, attached to a square building known as the Abbey Castle, which possibly dates from the 15th century and was where the monks lived. The ruins are set back from the main road by only two or three feet, which makes it all the more remarkable that they have survived for so long. The solid stonework is well preserved, seeming as secure and strong as the day it was first assembled. It is a thought-provoking place, worth spending a few moments in, pondering on the life of its original inhabitants. The key is available from the caretaker's house next door.

A short walk from the friary is a churchyard just off the main road, which goes back even farther in time, to the 12th century and even to the 9th. It lies on the site of a

ROMANESQUE DOORWAY *Incised arches and mellow stonework make the doorway at Castledermot a fine example of the Irish Romanesque style.*

monastery founded around 800 by the father of St Diarmuid, after which Castledermot takes its name. The monastery was raided by the Vikings in the 9th century, but continued its existence at least until the 12th century.

All that is left today is a splendidly reconstructed Romanesque doorway, which came from a church that has since vanished, a 10th-century Round Tower, 65ft high with a granite base, and two magnificent High Crosses, probably 9th century. Richly carved with depictions of the Crucifixion, Adam and

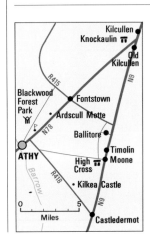

**OTHER PLACES TO SEE**
**Ballitore** 2m N of Timolin. Charming village founded by Quakers in 1700s. Meeting House now a museum. Open 10am-6pm daily.
**Blackwood Forest Park** 4m NE of Athy on road to Kildare. Attractive forest walks.
**Kilkea Castle** 6m SE of Athy. Stronghold of FitzGeralds, rulers of Kildare, now a hotel. Scenic paths through the nearby forest park lead walkers to picnic site, ring-fort and wishing well.
**Timolin** 6m N of Castledermot. 12th-century effigy of local knight lies in churchyard. Pewter mill and craft centre. Open daily.

**EVENTS**
**Athy Festival** End July.

**SPORT**
**Angling** Coarse fishing: River Barrow. Game fishing: River Barrow.
**Golf** Athy Golf Club, 9-hole course. Tel: (0507) 31729.

**INFORMATION**
County Kildare Tourist Office.
Tel: (0404) 69117/69118.
Midlands-East Tourism.
Tel: (044) 48650.

ST DOMINIC'S CHURCH *Overlooking the River Barrow at Athy, this Dominican church was built in 1963-5 to a revolutionary design. It has five sides and a double-curved roof.*

Eve, Daniel in the Lions' Den, the Sacrifice of Isaac, and the Miracle of the Loaves and Fishes, these High Crosses are among the best preserved of the granite crosses in the Barrow valley. The North Cross shows David with his harp, one of the few images from this time of an Irish harp.

Also in the churchyard are the foundations of a medieval church and early Christian and medieval grave slabs.

### Knockaulin/Dún Ailinne

Once the seat of the kings of Leinster, the hilltop fort on Knockaulin is a significant landmark in Kildare. The circular wall that surrounds the fort is some 1350ft across and about 15ft high, and, unusually, a defensive ditch runs around the inside. The site was settled from the Stone Age and abandoned by the kings in the first few centuries AD. But recent excavations, which have unearthed the foundations of wooden buildings, suggest that the fort may have been lived in until around AD 400.

### Moone

A short drive off the road through the tiny village of Moone takes visitors to a slender, granite, 9th-century High Cross reaching 17ft high. The cross, and the crumbling walls of a 13th-century church, stand on the site of a monastery allegedly founded by St Columba in the 6th century. The cross is intricately carved with 51 panels, including animals and Biblical scenes, among which are Daniel and the Lions, the Sacrifice of Isaac, Adam and Eve, the Crucifixion, the Apostles, the Miracle of the Loaves and Fishes and the Flight into Egypt.

### Old Kilcullen

Overlooking the basin of the River Barrow and with fine views of the plain that stretches to Dublin are the vestiges of a monastery founded in the 5th century by St Patrick, the patron saint of Ireland, credited with bringing Christianity to the island. Like many Irish monasteries it was raided and burnt several times by the Vikings who forayed from their secure base in what is now Dublin, and their stronghold in Leixlip, to the north. All that remains is the shaft of a granite High Cross like those at Moone and Castledermot, with few of the carved figures now identifiable, the shaft and base of another cross, and a crumbling Round Tower damaged in the fighting during the 1798 rebellion against British rule.

*Castledermot's 9th-century High Cross, 10ft 3in high, has the typical Celtic form of a cross over a circle and is decorated with spiral designs in the style known as La Tène.*

A reminder of the penetrating and lasting influence of Christianity on Ireland crops up at almost every turn, in the form of High Crosses. These were preceded by standing stones that monks carved with simple motifs in the 7th century. By the 9th and 10th centuries whole crosses were carved out of blocks of stone, usually sandstone, although in the Barrow valley in Kildare granite was used. High Crosses are characterised by tall stone shafts topped by a circle that surrounds the arms of the cross. They were decorated on every face with panels depicting scenes from the Old and New Testaments, such as Adam and Eve on either side of an apple-laden tree, with the Crucifixion in the central position.

*The carvings on the north face of Old Kilcullen Cross may possibly depict a bishop with his crozier, axe and bell, a saint destroying a pagan idol and, on the base, David and the Lion.*

*The 9th-century Moone Cross stands 17ft high, carved with charming figures. On the north base is The Temptation of St Anthony, and below mythical serpents fight with lions.*

Interlaced patterns with motifs taken from metalwork were carved around these panels, and some of the decoration includes ornamental studs and angle mouldings which suggest that the designs were first cast on sheets of metal and then translated into stone.

One of the finest High Crosses is Muiredach's Cross at Monasterboice in Louth. It is carved out of a single sandstone block 17ft 8in high, and has an inscription on its base asking for a prayer for Muiredach, who had the cross made.

It has been suggested that the crosses marked the graves of important people, but it is more likely that they were an illustrated Bible, used as a means of instruction.

# Birthplace of Thoroughbreds

*Deep-green pasturelands and quiet hedge-lined roads dotted with dozens of stud farms make up the heart of Ireland's famous bloodstock and racing industries. The early mornings frequently see steaming strings of sleek thoroughbred racehorses in full career across the great open spaces of The Curragh, their warm nostrils rhythmically puffing out little clouds of breath. But this part of Kildare is also a place of ancient towns and villages, ruined monasteries and Round Towers, and small communities clustering beside the canals.*

### The Curragh/An Currach

The 5000 or so acres of softly rolling grasslands that constitute The Curragh seem slightly out of place among the otherwise heavily planted and hilly landscape that is typical of most parts of the county of Kildare. The main road cuts right through The Curragh and gives a good view of the racecourse of the same name, where many major events in the racing calendar are staged. Every small roadway for miles around seems to be lined with studs owned by horse enthusiasts ranging from local families to international oil billionaires. It is hardly possible to cross The Curragh without seeing at least one group of sinewy, lean racehorses being put through their paces on the wide open grassy spaces.

A favourite place for leisurely walks and weekend picnics, The Curragh is also home to the largest army base in the country and the army's main training and manoeuvres camp. The camp is an open one and a roadway runs right through it, but taking pictures is not allowed.

### The Japanese Gardens

Ornamental Japanese Gardens, tracing human life in 20 stages from birth to old age and eternity, strike a delightfully incongruous note in the middle of lush grasslands outside the town of Kildare. The Japanese gardener Eida, and his son Minora, were employed by Lord Wavertree, landowner and horse-breeder, to lay them out between 1906-10.

JAPANESE GARDENS *A stone lantern and a wooden bridge mark one of the 'paths of life' in the garden.*

The journey leads the pilgrim soul from a cavern in a rock, through the stages which include the Cave of Birth, the dark Tunnel of Ignorance, up the steps of the Hill of Learning, topped with a lofty pine tree, to the Parting of the Ways. One of these leads across stepping stones to the Island of Joy and Wonder and then the Engagement and Marriage bridges. These cross to the Hill of Ambition where past disappointments, successes and failures, in the form of difficult crossings and dead-ends, can be looked back upon. From there the Well of Wisdom is reached, where 'the couple' may wish for enlightenment before passing over the Red Bridge of Life to the Garden of Peace and Contentment beyond.

A specially chartered ship was used to bring materials from Japan, including stone lanterns, a tea house and a miniature village carved out of rock from Mount Fuji.

Symbolic meanings apart, the gardens have a fine collection of unusual shrubs and trees and some particularly striking mature bonsai trees.

**Opening times** *Easter-Oct, daily. Tel: (045) 21251.*

### Kildare/Cill Dara

Solid and settled, Kildare is secure in the affluence it has won by horse-breeding and racing. The town's Irish name, Cill Dara, means 'the church (or monastery) of the oak tree'. The monastery in question was founded in AD 490 by St Brigid, and today St Brigid's Church of Ireland cathedral, on what is believed to be the same site as the monastery, is the dominant feature of the town. Its precise age is uncertain, though some say the odd-looking Round Tower, with its entrance doorway located 12ft up the wall for extra security and accessible then as now only by ladder, was built in the 10th century. The main parts of the cathedral were started in 1223, though several reconstructions have been undertaken over the years since.

Kildare is an excellent base for exploring the surrounding countryside, including the Bog of Allen, the largest bogland area in Ireland, which stretches from the western edge of the county to touch the Shannon to the west.

### The National Stud

Established in 1902 by Colonel William Hall-Walker, later Lord Wavertree, who also set up the Japanese Gardens next door, the stud is today owned and run by the Irish Government, and provides expert advice and breeding services to bloodstock interests all over the country. It also carries out veterinary research into thoroughbred breeding.

The basis of the stud's operations is a stable of stallions housed in 'lantern' boxes, so called because they have skylights, in keeping with Hall-Walker's belief that the moon and stars affected the fortunes of racehorses as well as people. He would study the astrological chart of each foal born in the stud, and if it was favourable he would keep the foal; if not, it would be sold. Hall-Walker's methods were surprisingly successful.

Guided tours of the stud take in the stallion boxes, the foaling unit and a museum which tells the story of the evolution of the horse from ancient times to the present day. One of the more bizarre exhibits is the skeleton of Arkle (1957-70), one of the greatest steeplechasers ever, which had to be put down after cracking a bone in its foreleg.

The stud grounds were designed in part by the same hands that laid out the Japanese Gardens. They contain an ornamental lake with mineral-rich drinking water for horses, credited with helping to produce good bone

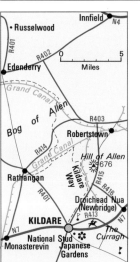

### OTHER PLACES TO SEE

**Hill of Allen** 15 minute climb to summit for panoramic views.
**Monasterevin** Canal town with its own drawbridge; home of the poet Gerard Manley Hopkins (1844-89). Moore Abbey, home of famous tenor John McCormack (1884-1945), has forest area and picnic site in grounds.
**Rathangan** An excellent base for coarse fishing.
**Russelwood** Picnic sites and forest walks.

### WALKS

**The Kildare Way** A walk from Kildare town to Edenderry through the Bog of Allen and along the banks of the canals.

### EVENTS

**Kildare Derby Festival** End June.
**Monasterevin Festival** First week in July.
**Racing Classics at The Curragh** June-Sept.

### SPORT

**Angling** Coarse fishing: Monasterevin, Grand Canal.
**Boating** Grand Canal and Royal Canal.
**Golf** The Curragh Golf Club, 18-hole course. Tel: (045) 41238/41714.
Cill Dara Golf Club, 9-hole course. Tel: (045) 21433.

### INFORMATION

County Kildare Tourist Office. Tel: (0404) 69117/69118.
Midlands-East Tourism. Tel: (044) 48650.

ARKLE *The most famous steeplechaser is preserved for posterity in the National Stud Museum.*

THE CURRAGH *Racehorses canter over the springy turf on their morning exercises.*

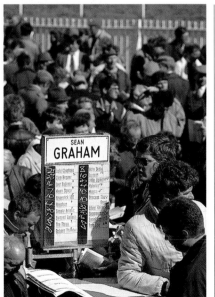

RACE DAY *Crowds jostle the bookies' boards.*

BETWEEN RACES *Dressed up for The Budweiser 1987, racegoers throng the terraces.*

formation. There is also a Zen Garden of Meditation where large rocks and sand have been arranged to symbolise simplicity, constancy and timelessness. And as if this were not sufficient to keep the horses content, soft music is played to the mares over a sound system in their stalls.

The lake has several islands with a collection of rare and unusual plants, such as giant parsnips that, with their seed heads, reach 20ft high. These, and the bamboo plantings, are home to a wide range of bird life, including kingfishers, yellow wagtails and coots.

*Tours daily. Tel: (045) 21251.*

### Robertstown/Baile Riobaird

Robertstown is one of the most charming of the little towns centred on the Grand Canal, which runs from the centre of Dublin city all the way to the River Shannon. With the Royal Canal, which cuts through Kildare near its northern border with County Meath, they were once important thoroughfares. The Grand Canal carried some 100,000 passengers a year up to the mid-1800s, and was used by freight barges up to the 1960s. Now the waterways have no commercial purpose, but they still provide recreation: both are used by coarse fishermen, and Robertstown is a base for canal cruises.

# The Plain of the River Liffey

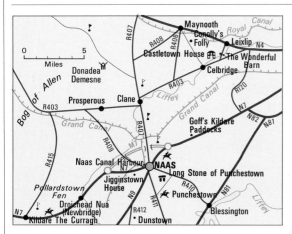

*Many early nobles chose these heavily wooded lands for their strongholds, leaving this part of Kildare with some of the finest manorial houses and castles to be found anywhere in Ireland. Charming old-style towns and villages dot the rolling plain of the River Liffey, whose waters teem with wild salmon and trout.*

### Castletown House

At the end of a long tree-lined avenue leading off Celbridge's main street is Castletown House, one of Ireland's most imposing mansions and largest private houses. Built in 1722 for William Conolly, a Member of Parliament for Donegal and later Speaker of the Irish Parliament, it is acknowledged as the finest example of its type in the country. It is a solid greystone building modelled on a 16th-century Italian town palace, with a wide flight of steps leading to a simple doorway framed by pilasters, rectangular columns set into the wall, and flanked by two curving colonnades which link the house to a wing on either side. One wing houses the kitchens, the other the stables. A trimmed yew hedge and regularly spaced, conical yew trees face the mansion, emphasising its elegant neatness.

Much of the internal design, with its graceful stucco work framing paintings, and the 80ft long Pompeian Gallery, was the work of Lady Louisa Lennox, who married into the Conolly family in 1758 at the age of 15. On two levels, connected by a sweeping stone staircase, are a magnificent hall with a black-

CONOLLY'S FOLLY *A series of lofty stone arches is topped by a soaring obelisk which rises into the sky, at the end a glorious 2 mile long vista from Castletown House.*

such as the semi-aquatic snail.
**Prosperous** Small 1780's village with cotton mill near Grand Canal; walks along the canal towpath and coarse fishing.

### EVENTS
**Celbridge Horse Trials and Flower Festival** Aug.
**Celbridge Summer Festival** End July, early Aug.

### SPORT
**Angling** Coarse fishing: Grand Canal, at Prosperous. Game fishing: River Liffey.
**Golf** Bodenstown Golf Club, 18-hole course. Tel: (045) 97096.
Clongowes Golf Club, 9-hole course. Tel: (045) 68202.
Knockanally Golf Club, 18-hole course. Tel: (045) 69322.
Naas Golf Club, 9-hole course. Tel: (045) 97509.

### INFORMATION
County Kildare Tourist Office. Tel: (0404) 69117/ 69118.
Midlands-East Tourism. Tel: (044) 48650.

### OTHER PLACES TO SEE
**Donadea Demesne** 10m N of Naas. Forest park with walks and castle ruins.
**Dunstown** Picnic site, forest walks.
**Goff's Kildare Paddocks** 3m NE of Naas. Yearly auctions here sell more than half of Ireland's thoroughbred horses for tens of millions of pounds to buyers who come here from around the world.
**Naas Canal Harbour** Once-busy terminus with Grand Canal. Good towpath walks.
**Pollardstown Fen** Largest area of marshy ground in Ireland and area of international ecological interest. Noted for its unusual bird and plant species, such as Savi's warbler and Pugsley's marsh orchid, and molluscs

and-white chequered floor, several drawing rooms with period furniture, a dining room, a study, a print room, and a raft of bedrooms.

From the back of the house an obelisk can be seen in the distance, mounted on a series of stone arches. This 140ft high structure, known as Conolly's Folly, was designed by Richard Cassel and built at the behest of Conolly's widow as a means of creating work for local men after the severe winter of 1739 which led to famine. The folly, 2 miles away over the fields from the house, can be reached by driving out of Celbridge for about a mile towards Maynooth, and taking the first turning right.
**Opening times** *Guided tours all year. Tel: (01) 6288252. Gift shop. Coffee shop, afternoons and weekends.*
**Restaurant** *pm. Tel: (01) 6288502.*

### Celbridge/Cill Droichid

No small country town wanting to be recognised for its charm and character could ask for a better setting than that of Celbridge. The River Liffey flows strongly through the village, and its gentle burble lends an air of peaceful, watery stillness.

Like Maynooth, Celbridge was planned to complement the nearby manor house, in this case Castletown House. Its main street runs right up to the entrance of the great estate, and from there a long avenue leads to the sweeping gravel forecourt of the house.

The Gothic Revival Celbridge Abbey, in the town, was the home of Esther Vanhomrigh, Jonathan Swift's 'Vanessa' (1690-1723). She was regularly visited by the Dean, and at the river's edge is a seat which is said to have been their favourite retreat. The abbey is now occupied by a religious order and visits are by arrangement only.

In the town, on the river bank, is the old workhouse, a striking neo-Gothic structure with diamond-paned windows, built in 1841. It has been partly restored and is now used as a factory.

**Celbridge Abbey** *Tel: (01) 6271849.*

### Leixlip/Léim an Bhradáin

The little village on the wooded banks of the Liffey has its origins in a settlement established by the Vikings a little over a thousand years ago. The name Leixlip derives from the old Norse for 'salmon leap' – and indeed the River Liffey, as it flows through Leixlip, frequently yields the first salmon of each year's new fishing season.

The glorious days of Leixlip's more

### SWIFT'S VANESSA

Early 18th-century Celbridge was home to Esther Vanhomrigh, a woman who has been immortalised as 'Vanessa' in the writings of Jonathan Swift, Dean of St Patrick's Cathedral in Dublin and author of *Gulliver's Travels*. Swift met her in London in 1708 and over the years their relationship developed, but it is a romantic conundrum that Swift scholars have still not managed to sort out. History suggests that he was her lover and may have given her a child.

Esther followed Swift to Ireland and settled in her father's house at Celbridge. But involved as he was with 'Stella' Johnson Swift could not make Esther happy. A year before she died, in 1723, Esther broke off with him and even cut him out of her will.

Celbridge still pays tribute to 'Vanessa', and many of the small roads there bear names like Vanessa Grove and Vanessa Lawn in memory of her.

recent past were centred largely in and around Leixlip Castle, a 13th-century building whose two battlemented towers, one round, the other square, rise above the tree tops. It was from here that King John set out to hunt moose, red deer and wolves along the river banks and through the great oak forests of County Kildare, accompanied by knights and barons from England. The castle was occupied over the centuries by, among others, the Honourable William Conolly, nephew of the Speaker of the Irish Parliament. Now the headquarters of the Irish Georgian Society, it is not open to the public.

A mile south-west of Leixlip is a conical stone building with a staircase spiralling up it on the outside. This is 'The Wonderful Barn', built as a famine-relief project in 1743 for Lady Conolly of Castletown House. It has five storeys, each of which has a vaulted ceiling and a hole in the floor through which sacks could be hauled. It is now on a private farm and is not open to the public.

### Maynooth/Maigh Nuad

With the orderly layout typical of a manorial village, the university town of Maynooth proclaims its noble origins to all who enter it. Just outside the entrance to St Patrick's College, on the right, stands the ruin of the medieval Maynooth Castle, begun by Gerald FitzMaurice, the Baron of Offaly, in 1203, and occupied for generations by his Fitz-Gerald successors, the rulers of Kildare. Many parts of the huge structure, especially the keep, the great hall and the gate-tower, are preserved. Visitors can get the key from the caretaker's house directly across the road.

St Patrick's College was founded in 1521, but closed in the Protestant Reformation. It opened again in 1795 when the penal laws suppressing Catholics were relaxed. One of the finest Catholic seminaries, it now has full university status, and lay and clerical students study here side by side.

The college's fine Gothic Revival square is a haven of tranquillity that seems a million miles removed from the bustle of the streets outside. Its chapel was designed by J.J. McCarthy, the 'Irish Pugin', and was built from 1874 to the 1890s. An ecclesiastical museum houses a fine collection of unusual artefacts, including vestments made by Marie Antoinette, and others given by Elizabeth, the wife of the Emperor of Austria. Phone for an appointment to visit.

**Ecclesiastical museum** *Tel: (01) 6285222.*

ST PATRICK'S COLLEGE *This Catholic seminary is an elegant example of the Gothic Revival style.*

### Naas/An Nás

The 'Castle of the Kings', as its Irish name translates, was at one time a centre of the kings of Leinster who are said to have governed from a castle on the large North Motte in the town. Naas became a fortified town under the Anglo-Normans in the early 14th century and was later put to the torch by Edward Bruce. But gradually it gained prominence again and is now the county town of Kildare, a bustling place full of shops, with a healthy commercial life and a smattering of interesting buildings and ruins. A signposted walking tour of the town takes in the remains of a 13th-century castle in the grounds of St David's Protestant church.

The town's commercial success is fuelled, like so much of Kildare's business life, by one aspect or another of the racehorse business. There are regular meetings at two local racecourses, Naas and Punchestown. In part of the grounds of Punchestown is a 23ft granite standing stone, the Long Stone of Punchestown, discovered in the 1930s to have a Bronze Age burial site at its base.

Just a mile to the south-west of Naas is the unfinished Jigginstown House, which was to have been a palace for King Charles I. The building work stopped in 1641 and now only the cellars and ground-floor rooms remain, but they have been vandalised, leaving a dangerous ruin.

# HORSE COUNTRY

*Where horse breeding, trading, racing and gambling are a national pastime*

Along with gambling, Guinness and religion, horses and horse racing are one of the major preoccupations of the Irish. The horse – known as 'capall' in Gaelic – has been part of Irish folklore since ancient times. Horses were first introduced into Ireland by Stone Age farmers, around 2000 BC. About 1500 years later, Celtic invaders brought chariots drawn by fiery horses which mixed with the native ponies. And in the 16th century it is thought that Spanish Arab stallions, which escaped from shipwrecks off the Galway coast, mated with the indigenous Connemara ponies, producing a faster breed.

THE IRISH HORSE There are now some 55,000 horses in Ireland, of which 15,000 are racehorses. Apart from these there are draught horses, used for generations to plough Irish fields, to cart barrels of beer and to help families move house. Crossed with thoroughbreds, draught mares produced the Irish Sport Horse used worldwide for show-jumping and eventing. But the most special of the non-thoroughbreds are Connemara ponies. These docile, hardy creatures breed in Connemara itself, where they feed on sea grasses. Feeding on richer grasses elsewhere, they tend to grow too big to be registered as Connemara ponies.

Irish thoroughbreds have a lordliness, beauty and power which sets them apart from others. Some say that their strength is drawn from the limestone that lies under most of Ireland, which makes the soil and therefore the grass rich in minerals and calcium and gives the horses strong bones. But whatever the reason, their power and grace are renowned, and have been for centuries. In the 18th and 19th centuries the quartermasters of many European armies, including those of France and Russia, came to horse fairs in Ireland to buy horses for their elite cavalry regiments. Napoleon's horse Marengo is said to have come from Ireland.

HORSE FAIRS Horse fairs, or sales, still attract buyers from around the world. The main bloodstock sales are held in Kill, County Kildare, and the principal national hunt sales are the Tattersalls Sales in Fairyhouse, in County Meath. But for interested observers, possibly the best of all are the traditional non-thoroughbred sales, of which the oldest and most famous is in Ballinasloe, County Galway, held in October, where as many as 4000 animals may change hands in a day.

Buying and selling here often follows an ancient ritual. After hovering discreetly around a horse, a potential buyer declares an offer, spits on his hand and slaps it against the seller's open palm. The offer is bound to be refused, and the seller's price – with another spit and slap – draws a gasp of disbelief from the buyer, who starts to walk away. An enthusiastic crowd gathers to give advice.

This is the moment for a 'tangler' to appear and act the broker between the parties. Bit by bit, with dramatic gesturing, the prices narrow. Finally, perhaps with a coin tossed to settle the last few pounds, a deal is struck, and hands are shaken. The ritual requires that, before they go their separate ways, the seller slips some 'luck money' to the buyer – usually around 5 per cent of the agreed price. It is an old custom that says the horse means more to both of them than the money it can earn.

HORSE RACING The actual racing of horses is as old as the nation itself. The legendary Red Branch Knights raced among themselves, as did the Fianna warriors in the 3rd century AD. Early racecourses were the private greens of kings or chiefs, although sport was not confined solely to the aristocracy. At fairs or public assemblies, racing was a common feature, with the most famous of these fairs held at The Curragh, in County Kildare. Beaches at low tide were also used occasionally as racecourses.

In the 17th century the sport nearly died off, first after Cromwell banned Sunday racing, and later in the tumultuous times following the Battle of the Boyne in 1690. It was during this time that steeplechasing started, although it was not given its name until 1752, when Mr O'Callaghan raced Mr Blake from Buttevant to Doneraile, keeping the spire of Doneraile's St Leger Church in

RIGOROUS DIET *The hardy Connemara ponies survive on short sea grasses.*

JUMPING TO WIN *The great showjumper Rockbarton, an army horse, carries Captain Gerry Mullins to glory.*

DAILY TIPPLE *Arkle, the champion racehorse of the 1960s, was reputed to be fed daily with a bottle of Guinness.*

SIGNED, SEALED AND DELIVERED *A buyer concludes a deal at the Ballinasloe horse fair.*

RIDING PARTNERS *The jockey Pat Taaffe rode the steeplechaser Arkle to 27 victories out of 35 starts in the 1960s. Three of these victories won him the Cheltenham Gold Cup.*

LAYTOWN RACES *The annual 2 mile race at Laytown is the only official race meeting to be held on a beach in Europe.*

sight. In 1731, when hundreds of race meetings were being held around Ireland, Dickson's newspaper, *The Dublin Intelligence,* noted: 'Horse racing is become a great diversion in the country.' In 1790 the Turf Club was formed to supervise racing, 40 years after the Jockey Club had been set up in England.

It was only a matter of time before great horses and great races emerged. The Irish Grand National was first run in 1837 or 1839 and the Irish Derby was first run in 1866 at The Curragh. In 1880 the Irishman Henry Eyre Linde won the English Grand National with the mare Empress, and some 20 years later, 'Boss' Croker's Orby became the first Irish-trained horse to win the Epsom Derby.

In 1945 the Irish National Stud was formed to improve the quality of bloodstock in Ireland by providing high-class stallions at a reasonable fee. Its founder believed in astrology and had skylights fitted to the stables so that the moon and stars could exert their influence fully on the horses. The Stud's museum boasts among other things the skeleton of the peerless Arkle, who won the Cheltenham Gold Cup three times in a row in the 1960s.

The highlight of the equestrian year is the Dublin Horse Show in August, which attracts spectators and contestants from around the world. With the recent revival of Sunday racing, there are now roughly 280 meetings in Ireland each year, including the Irish Derby held on the last Sunday in June or the first Sunday in July, and the Irish Grand National held at Fairyhouse on Easter Monday. The Irish, with their love of horses and of gambling, find these meetings irresistible – they bet just over IR£90 million a year on the horses.

One race that is uniquely Irish is held on the beaches of Laytown, usually in July or August – depending on the tide. The Laytown races have been run on the sands at this sleepy little resort since 1876. Although hardly Ireland's answer to the elegance of Royal Ascot or the sophistication of Longchamps, Laytown does have a quirky charm. As soon as the tide goes out, a tractor marks out the course and workers hurry to put up a strip of fencing leading to the finishing post. All the races are 'about 6 furlongs' or 'about 2 miles'. Unlike other races, however, they are run with uncharacteristic punctuality – in a race to get through before the tide comes in.

# A Quiet Land with a Lively Past

*Empty roads, scattered villages with stone dwellings, disused coal mines and the isolated ruins of great monasteries – these are the human marks on this lonely landscape of bogland and, to the east, limestone hills. Once a lively centre of religious and cultural life, south-east Laois is now a quiet farming region.*

### Abbeyleix/Mainistir Laoise

The elegant town, centred around a wide and spacious main street, is the result of a piece of 18th-century town planning by the first Viscount de Vesci. Landowners of that period often adapted, improved or replaced towns in this way and Abbeyleix is a particularly good example of this remodelling. The original town encircled a Cistercian monastery, founded in 1183, which has long since disappeared, although its memory lives on in the name of Abbeyleix.

Abbeyleix House, the family seat where the de Vescis still live, was designed by James Wyatt in 1773 and given a new façade in the 19th century. It has extensive gardens, but neither the house nor the garden are open to the public.

One uniquely Irish establishment in the area is Morrissey's public house and grocery store. Turn left on entering for provisions; right for a glass of porter in the dark, timbered bar.

### Ballyadams/Baile Adam

The 'house of Adam' was in fact a castle, built on the site of a Norman castle by a member of the O'Moore family in the 15th century. Enough is left of the building to give an idea of its impressive scale – it has five storeys connected by a spiral stone staircase, and two towers, the highest of which is 75ft. Unusually, the iron-studded oak doorway has survived.

The bloodthirsty history of Ballyadams includes many battles. It was taken in 1548 by the Earl of Desmond's army who turfed out the O'Moores when they burnt the town and monastery of Athy. The O'Moores never regained possession and the castle was taken over in 1551 by Welshman John Bowen, known as 'Shane-a-feeka' or John of the Pike, whose cruelty was renowned even in those harsh times. When Bowen was threatened by Castlehaven, a royalist general who called on him to surrender, Bowen told him: 'I will cover that part, or any other, your lordship

Cecil Day-Lewis (1904-72), poet and detective novelist, was born in Ballintubbert, a tiny village in Laois where his father was the Church of Ireland vicar.

Educated in England, Day-Lewis was a contemporary of the poets W.H. Auden and Stephen Spender. In the 1930s he was a member of the Macspaunday Beast, a literary group comprising satirical poet Louis MacNeice, Spender, Auden and Day-Lewis himself; the group was given its name – a blend of the members' surnames – by another contemporary poet and satirist, Roy Campbell.

Day-Lewis married in 1928 and fathered two children, then finding himself short of money he took to writing detective novels under the pseudonym Nicholas Blake. He was an active member of the Communist Party for three years, but during this time his writing suffered and he decided to go and live in the pastoral tranquillity of Musbury, in Devon, where he could make himself 'a better poet'.

In Musbury he commanded the Home Guard platoon during the war. He also had a tumultuous affair with the wife of a local farmer, which later inspired his autobiographical book *The Private Wound*, published in 1968, the year he became English Poet Laureate. In 1951 he

*The distinguished Irish poet C. Day-Lewis (centre), relaxes with his peers, W.H. Auden (left) and Stephen Spender, in Venice in 1949.*

remarried, and in the same year became Oxford professor of poetry.

Day-Lewis recollected his father's rectory at Ballintubbert, in *The House Where I Was Born*:

*'Elegant house, how well you speak*
*For the one who fathered me there,*
*With your sanguine face, your woody*
*                                        provincial charm*
*And that Anglo-Irish air*
*Of living beyond one's means to keep up*
*An era beyond repair.'*

The actor John Hurt now lives in the house.

---

chooses to shoot at, by hanging both my daughters in chairs.'

Because of the unsafe condition of Ballyadams, visitors are advised to view it only from the road.

### Ballinakill/Baile na Coille

The broad main street and large central square reflect Ballinakill's standing in the 17th century when it was an important centre. A monument in the square is dedicated to local men who died in the 1798 Rebellion. The Protestant and Catholic churches standing side by side today, reflect more tolerance. The Protestant church, St Peter's, was built in 1821 and has a delicately decorated gilt ceiling and a number of fine stained-glass windows. Glebe House, built for the vicar in 1810, is a handsome country house set in 50 acres. It is now a guesthouse.

On the edge of the village are the Italianate gardens that were created in 1906 by the famous landscape designer Lutyens,

for Colonel Poe, owner of Heywood House, which was demolished in 1950. The gardens, built at a cost of £250,000, are a rarity in Ireland. They fell into neglect but were restored recently by volunteers and members of the Salesian Order, a missionary and educational Catholic order who are members of the Society of St Francis de Sales, and who have a school nearby.

A folly in the garden grounds uses decorative masonry taken from the ruined abbey of Aghaboe, near Durrow. The gardens have a circular walled rose garden at the centre, some leafy walks and a number of lakes with good coarse fishing. The gardens are open by appointment only.
**Heywood Gardens** *Tel: (0502) 33334.*

### Durrow/Darú

Castellated walls in the centre of the village mark Castle Durrow, built in 1716 and the first great Palladian house in this part of Ireland. The house is now a convent but

---

founded by St Fiach, Bishop of Leinster at the time of St Patrick.

**SPORT**
**Angling** Coarse fishing: Heywood, and Mass Lough. Game fishing: Rivers Nore and Erkina. Contact Southern Regional Fisheries Board, Clonmel, County Tipperary. Tel: (052) 23624.
**Golf** Abbeyleix Golf Course, 9-hole course. Tel: (0502) 31450.

**INFORMATION**
Port Laoise Tourist Information Office. Tel: (0502) 21178.
Midlands-East Tourism. Tel: (044) 48650.

**OTHER PLACES TO SEE**
**Ballyroan** Interesting motte and bailey to be explored.
**Cullahill** Ivy-covered, melancholy, 15th-century ruined castle, once principal stronghold of the MacGillapatricks, ruling chieftains of the Upper Ossory region.
**Sleaty Church** Two impressive granite crosses and remains of medieval church lie on site of monastery

visitors may go through the gates to view it from outside.

Durrow itself was built as a planned estate village in the late 18th and early 19th centuries, although there has been a settlement here since medieval times. Its charter for a fair was granted in 1245. For political reasons Durrow was transferred by the Duke of Ormonde to County Kilkenny in the 17th century, and it took an Act of Parliament to restore it to Laois in the 19th century. The village is on the pretty River Erkina, which has excellent trout fishing.

## Killeshin/Cill Uisen

In the 6th century St Comghán founded a monastery here, which became not only a place of prayer but also a noted centre of culture and learning. The monastery was razed in the 11th century and the present ruins date from the 12th century. The most notable remnant is a carved doorway, one of the finest examples of Irish-Romanesque architecture. On the abaci, the stonework above the beautifully carved heads, is an

St Comghán's Monastery *Each receding arch of this well-preserved Romanesque doorway has capitals adorned with human faces.*

Timahoe Tower *The 12th-century Round Tower rises 96ft over gentle wooded countryside.*

inscription which has been interpreted as reading 'Prayer for Diarmit, King of Leinster'. The carvings, in four recessed arches in the doorway, are said to contain 12 faces, but it is not easy to find them all. Nearby is the holy well of St Diarmuid which dates at least from the 6th century.

Unfortunately, no trace remains today of a 105ft high Round Tower, reputed to be one of the tallest in Ireland, which stood next to the monastery. This was demolished by an 18th-century landowner who said he was afraid it might fall and injure his cattle. The ruins are along a narrow lane just above a church built in 1823. From the hills above Killeshin, some say, as many as ten counties can be seen.

### The Pass of the Plumes

It was a sad day for the English but a great victory for the Irish when in 1599 troops of

the Earl of Essex were defeated in a battle with the men of Owen O'Moore near Ballyknockan and Ballyroan.

Essex and his men had been dispatched by Queen Elizabeth to quell the unrest in Ireland. After bloody combat, the English soldiers fled the battlefield, leaving it strewn with their plumed helmets – hence the name, The Pass of the Plumes.

The name is as romantic as the battle was gruesome, but today the pass looks deeply peaceful with roads winding through soft green fields and low, wooded hills.

### Timahoe/Tigh Mochua

One of the best-preserved Round Towers in Ireland rises 96ft above the village of Timahoe, or 'Mochua's house', and is surrounded by trees inhabited by a large and vociferous colony of rooks. There are about 70 Round Towers still standing in Ireland,

and there has been some disagreement about their purpose. But it is now generally accepted that they functioned as bell towers, used to call the monks to prayer from their work in the fields, as lookouts and as places of retreat.

Entrances to the towers are almost always several feet above ground – 16ft in the case of Timahoe – and the monks reached them using a rope or wooden ladder which they could have pulled up after themselves. At Timahoe the entrance has elaborate carvings around the arch which show bearded heads.

Round Towers date from AD 900 to the 13th century and Timahoe's probably dates from the 12th century. One theory is that it may be older, perhaps dating from the 7th century when St Mochua, the patron saint of Laois who died in 657, founded a monastery at Timahoe.

37

# The Land of the Cow

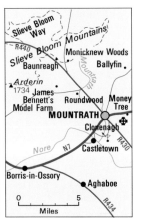

*They say a piper played in west Laois, causing the rocks and trees to jig up and down and form the Slieve Bloom Mountains. But that is the stuff of legend. What is certain is that the red-sandstone mountains were for centuries a refuge for people and have allowed a rich variety of wildlife to flourish. The sandstone is widely used in buildings and walls in the area, giving it a distinctive character. The flat spread of pastureland in the south is dotted with historic monasteries whose monks once referred to it as 'the land of the cow'.*

### Aghaboe/Achadh Bhó

Sleek cattle graze contentedly in the grounds of the abbey in the 'land of the cow', as its Irish name translates, much as they must have done when the monks lived and worked here in the 6th century. The abbey's substantial remains are visible from the road and are easily accessible.

The first church on the site was founded by St Canice in the 6th century and became an important religious centre. St Virgil is said to have left here to become Bishop of Salzburg, Austria, from 755 to 784, just one of a number of Irish missionaries of the period who were to have great influence in Europe. This debt is acknowledged even today, and to honour St Virgil's activity, the church, which probably stands on the site of the ancient monastery, was restored in 1984.

The ruins are principally those of a late 14th-century Dominican abbey, and include much of the church with some fine stonework around the arched windows. A tower from the abbey ruins has been incorporated into the Protestant church just behind the site and decorative stonework was removed to adorn a folly at Heywood House, Ballinakill, in 1773.

### Ballyfin/An Baile Fionn

One of Ireland's most sumptuous houses, Ballyfin was built in 1826 by the 9th baronet Sir Charles Coote to replace a former, plainer dwelling. Most of the architectural and design work was done by Richard Morrison, a pupil of James Gandon.

The sober exterior of the house gives no clue to its magnificent interiors, where glossy inlaid parquetry floors mirror the vaulted ceilings with their remarkable plasterwork. The drawing room, or Gold Room, is richly embellished in the style of Louis XV. Marble

BALLYFIN *Gold-leafed plasterwork adds splendour to Louis XV furnishings in the Gold Room.*

columns surround the domed central hall, or rotunda, the lilac-coloured ceiling of which is decorated with ornate plasterwork motifs.

Ballyfin was created in an age when the cost of materials and craftsmanship were obviously not principal considerations for the designers. Sir Edward Lutyens was hired to landscape the gardens, which feature a large lake facing the house. The graceful conservatory at the side, dating from 1850, is attributed to Richard Turner, the designer of the Palm House at Kew Gardens, London. Today the house is owned by the Patrician Brothers.

Near Ballyfin is Roundwood, an elegant country house built in 1740 for the Quaker Anthony Sharp. At one time there were so many Quaker tenants on the estate that it was known as Friendstown after the Quakers' name for themselves. The house was bought by the Irish Georgian Society in 1970 and is now run as a country house hotel.
**Ballyfin House** Tel: (0502) 55245. *Visits by arrangement only.*
**Roundwood House** Tel: (0502) 32120.

---

**OTHER PLACES TO SEE**
**Baunreagh** 5½m NW of Mountrath, forest walks and picnic sites.
**Borris-in-Ossory** Village with splendid Catholic church.
**James Bennett's Model Farm** 6m NW of Mountrath. Environmental demonstration cattle and sheep farm. Tours by appointment. Tel: (0502) 35097.
**Monicknew Woods** 5m NW of Mountrath; woodland walks, waymarked nature trails and picnic sites.

**SPORT**
**Angling** Game fishing:

Mountrath Angling Club, the Rivers Mountrath and Nore.
**Golf** Mountrath Golf Club, 9-hole course. Tel: (0502) 32558.
Rathdowney Golf Club, 9-hole course. Tel: (0505) 46170.
**Orienteering** Slieve Bloom Mountains. Maps and course details obtainable from Michael Dooley, Kinnitty. Tel: (0509) 37036.

**INFORMATION**
Port Laoise Tourist Information Office. Tel: (0502) 21178.
Midlands-East Tourism. Tel: (044) 48650.

### Castletown/Baile an Chaisleáin

The castle from which the village gets its name was the object of an act of Irish self-destruction. Built by the Normans in the 13th century, it was taken by the Irish ruling family of Fitzpatrick who burned it to the ground in 1600 to prevent it from falling into English hands. The remnants of its thick walls are a testament to the formidable castle-building skills of the Normans. Today Castletown is a peaceful Georgian village set around a large green with the sparkling River Nore flowing by.

### Clonenagh

A few mounds in a field are all that remain of one of Ireland's greatest monasteries, which stood here from the 7th to the 16th centuries. Founded by St Fintan, the monastery was at one time a famous seat of learning, and had 4000 foreign students.

The monastery's famous *Book of Clonenagh*, a record of literature and laws, was last seen in the 17th century but has since vanished.

### Mountrath/Maighean Rátha

Now a small market town, Mountrath gives little impression of its past as a leading industrial centre with a thriving ironworks, cotton mill and tannery.

The iron industry was established in the early 17th century by Sir Charles Coote, whose family built Ballyfin, and flourished for a century and a half. It resulted in the devastation of the surrounding forests, whose timber fuelled the industry, but turned Mountrath into a prosperous outpost, in a wild, often turbulent region.

---

### THE MONEY TREE

Once a great monastery founded by St Fintan in the 7th century stood on a site between Mountrath and Port Laoise. Nothing remains of it now except a few low mounds in a field. But a story is told locally of a farmer who refused to allow pilgrims visiting the monastery to enter his land to drink water from the stream. Miraculously, a well appeared in the heart of a tree in the land opposite the monastery.

Although there is no evidence of the well, a tree certainly grows on the site. It is known as the Money Tree, because travellers press coins into it in thanks for the miracle, and perhaps in anticipation of others to come. The tree stands beside the road, completely unmarked or signposted, and is unremarkable until it is approached, when closer examination reveals it to be studded with thousands of coins. The tree still flourishes with its treasures embedded in its bark.

---

Sir Charles settled the town with English families, but a chronic labour shortage forced him to get special permission to take on 500 Irish workers – provided they lived within a musket-shot sound of the works.

Today the town is mainly agricultural and is an excellent centre for exploring the Slieve Bloom Mountains. It has a pretty picnic area in the town centre in the shadow of St Fintan's, the Catholic church whose spire can be seen for miles around. It is an elaborate example of Gothic Revival architecture. The River Mountrath nearby has good fishing.

---

### THE IRISH HARE

A relative of the blue hare found in Scotland and Scandinavia, the Irish hare (*Lepus timidus hibernicus*) is smaller than its cousins, with shorter ears, a buff to yellow coat and a white belly and under tail. It is found in all regions of Ireland in lowlands and in the mountains, yet unsettled argument surrounds the hare: the question is whether its fur turns white all over in winter, or whether it remains the same shade all the year round. Diplomatic naturalists say that some individual hares may turn partially white in winter.

---

SLIEVE BLOOM MOUNTAINS *Lush pastureland, studded with farms, slopes up to the mountains.*

### Slieve Bloom Mountains

Rising steeply from the surrounding plain is the 600sq mile range of Slieve Bloom. Although not high by mountain standards – the tallest point, Arderin, is only 1734ft – the range seems higher because it swells above a flat landscape. The hills are said to have been named after Bladhma, an ancient hero who once took refuge there. After him, other Irishmen who lost their lands after the Cromwellian wars took to the remote glens, where they lived as outlaws.

The area is a delight for walkers, with miles of tracks and paths in the numerous glens, 24 of them signposted. One of them, the 20 mile circular Slieve Bloom Way, covers a variety of terrain from high, often desolate places in the hills, to meandering streams in the foothills.

Large areas have been turned over to forestry, mostly coniferous sitka spruce and lodgepole pine, but the mountains still support numerous wild flowers and the rare mountain pansy, *Viola cornuta*. They are also home to the rare pine marten, Irish hares, fallow deer and mountain goats. An abundant bird life of 85 recorded species includes the hen harrier.

Walkers are advised to take a good map and warm, weatherproof clothing. The mountains are benevolent when it's fine, but they can be very bleak if the weather changes.

# Domain of the Fort Protector

*North-east Laois is a land of undulating terrain and shining waters, where the sudden height of the Slieve Bloom Mountains to the west contrasts dramatically with the lower-lying plain. In the middle of this rich agricultural country sits Port Laoise, once Fort Protector, a military post surrounded by wild country and hostile clans, but now a dignified county town populated by a welcoming people.*

BALLYBRITTAS *The tiny cottage is a museum of traditional life.*

### Ballybrittas/Baile Briotáis

Although its name means 'town of the fortified place', the most interesting building in Ballybrittas is a rebuilt traditional thatched cottage behind The Old Pound. The town's name may suggest that an Irishman's home is his castle, but the two-room cottage surrounded by pretty gardens with an aviary, seems very small.

The dim living room houses an old settle bed which slept four at night and became a seat by day. The room also contains some fine cooking and butter-making equipment. A large brass bedstead and a 200-year-old cradle fill most of the tiny bedroom.

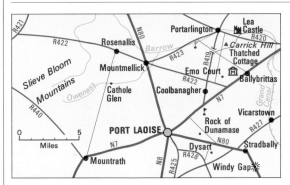

you can see six counties as well as the Barrow valley.

### EVENTS
**Port Laoise Jazz Festival** First week in June.
**Stradbally Flower Festival and Steam Rally** Early Aug.
**Vicarstown Easter Festival** Festival and boat rally.

### SPORT
**Angling** Coarse fishing: Vicarstown, on the Barrow canal.
Trout fishing: River Barrow.
**Golf** Heath Golf Club, 18-hole course. Tel: (0502) 46533.
Portarlington Golf Club, 9-hole course. Tel: (0502) 23115.

### INFORMATION
Port Laoise Tourist Information Office. Tel: (0502) 21178.
Midlands-East Tourism. Tel: (044) 48650.

### OTHER PLACES TO SEE
**Carrick Hill** 1m S of Portarlington, picnic site and forest walks.
**Dysart** 4m E of Port Laoise, forest walks and viewing points.
**Lea Castle** Ruins of a once-great Norman castle, used as a mint by confederates before it was taken by Cromwell in 1650. Its square walls and round, corner towers can still be seen.
**Rosenallis** Ireland's oldest Quaker cemetery. Burial-place of William Edmundston, 17th-century founder of Quaker movement.
**Vicarstown** Pretty village on a quiet stretch of canal.
**Windy Gap** A beauty spot from where local people say

COOLBANAGHER CHURCH *Gandon's spare and elegant spire soars into the sky.*

### Coolbanagher

The most impressive building in this little village is its 1786 Protestant church, designed by James Gandon (1743-1823), one of Ireland's foremost architects. The starkly neo-classical church contains a finely carved 15th-century font and the imposing Portarlington mausoleum, also by Gandon.

## Emo Court/Ioma

A fine Georgian mansion, put up in 1796 for the Earl of Portarlington, stands in a commanding position overlooking the estate. It was built by James Gandon, best known for the Custom House and the Four Courts in Dublin.

The gardens have been created in two parts. The Clucker, so called because it was once the site of the women's quarters of an ancient abbey, is filled with azaleas, rhododendrons and Japanese maples. The Grapery, which has since proved more suitable for growing hops than grape vines, has an abundance of trees and flowering shrubs.

**Opening times** *House: Mon pm by arrangement. Gardens: daily. Tel: (0502) 26110.*

## Mountmellick/Móinteach Mílic

The surrounding land is still 'soft bogland', the meaning of the Irish name, just as it was in the 17th century when the Quakers settled here and remained to bring prosperity to the town. Mountmellick lies on a bend of the River Owenass, almost ringed by it, at the north-eastern end of the Slieve Bloom Mountains. Nearby is Cathole Glen with its cascades and trout pools.

The Quakers industrialised the town, establishing iron and woollen industries in the early 18th century and, later, a cotton industry. The town has a legacy of 18th-century houses and work-buildings left by the prosperous merchants of the period.

Mountmellick was famous in the 18th century for its lace, which is still made by the sisters of the Presentation Convent next to St Joseph's Roman Catholic church. A stone cross stands there, in memory of 'eleven brave men' of Mountmellick, hanged after the defeat of the 1798 Irish uprising against English landowners.

## Portarlington/Cúil an tSúdaire

The River Barrow divides this town and places it in two counties – Laois and Offaly. The 1696 Protestant church of St Paul's is of most historical interest. The town was founded in 1666 by Sir Henry Bennett, later Lord Arlington, of the same family that had Emo Court built. He was granted much of the land that had been confiscated from the rebellious Irish and brought English settlers to live here.

General Rouvigney, Earl of Galloway, added a Huguenot colony to the settlement in the late 17th century. The Huguenots built the Protestant church (which was rebuilt in 1851), where the services were given in French until 1861. They also brought prosperity and established Portarlington as a centre for silver and banking. Unfortunately, nothing is left of the houses they built that faced inwards, looking onto small orchards, but some of the gardens remain. There are still some good examples of Georgian architecture, in former merchants' houses, and French surnames such as Le Blanc and Champs are still found.

The small museum has a collection of exhibits, from 4000-year-old axe heads to memorabilia of this century. The keys are with the barber across the road, who will happily share his local knowledge.

**Portarlington Museum** *Sun, or by appointment.*

## Port Laoise

A great fort, the Fort Protector, was built here in 1547 to guard the English settlers from the Irish and as a garrison which served to oust the warlike local O'Moore clan. In the reign of Mary Tudor (1553-8) the O'Moores were dispossessed and sent to County Kerry, and replaced by the English. The town was renamed Maryborough and the county Queen's County until 1920. Little remains of the original fortification. Today Port Laoise is the county town and an ideal place from which to explore the area.

## Rock of Dunamase/Dun Masg

A dramatic 150ft rock outcrop crowned by the ruined walls of Masg Castle (or Dun Masg) soars above the low Laois countryside. Before the arrival of St Patrick in AD 432, the rock and surrounding land were the property of the O'Moore clan chieftain Laois Ceannmor, who gave his name to the area. One of the most ancient sites in Ireland, it was shown by the Greek geographer Ptolemy in his map of AD 140.

The rock, veteran of many battles, was an important fortification throughout much of Ireland's history. It was plundered by the Vikings in the 9th century, became a Norman stronghold in the 13th, was rebuilt by the O'Moores in the 15th and was finally destroyed by Cromwellian guns from the east in the 17th century.

It is a short walk up the hill to the stronghold, which is easily reached from the rear. The castle's remains are considerable, partly due to the thickness of its walls.

ROCK OF DUNAMASE *Ancient castle ruins ring the high crag known even to the Greeks.*

## Stradbally/An Sráidbhaile

Every year in August, the town becomes a rainbow of colour with its flower festival. At the same time it clangs and hisses to the sound of the steam rally organised by the Irish Steam Preservation Society. Both events attract thousands of visitors from Ireland and abroad. There is also a steam museum with permanent exhibits such as an 80mph Belfast fire engine and a former Dublin tram.

The town is largely 18th century and was developed by the Cosby family, some of whom live in 17th-century Stradbally Hall, which is not open to the public.

On the east side are the remains of Ougheval Abbey, St Colman's 6th-century monastery, thought to be the place where *The Book of Leinster*, a remarkable historical collection, was collated by monks. It is now preserved in Trinity College, Dublin.

**Stradbally Steam Museum** *By appointment. Tel: (0502) 25136.*

# Poet's Country

*A network of pretty back lanes weaves through rich pastures, leading from small communities hidden away on the gently sloping shores of Lough Ree to villages known by their association with the poet and dramatist Oliver Goldsmith. This is the threshold of the gentle spread of land that has become known as 'Poet's Country', where visitors can pay their respects at Goldsmith's birthplace and the country house that was once mistaken for an inn by the playwright.*

### Abbeyshrule/Mainistir Shruthla

The village of Abbeyshrule is charmingly situated at the point where the weed-choked Royal Canal crosses the River Inny. It is popular with fishermen, since its many stone bridges provide easy access to the Inny's pike, trout, bream and roach.

On the east bank of the Inny, in an unkempt cemetery, stand the forlorn vestiges of the Cistercian abbey that gave the village its name. O'Farrell founded it and it was colonised by the abbey at Mellifont in County Louth, in about 1150. The abbey was badly damaged by fire in 1476 and repaired, but now only the choir and part of the nave of the church survive. When Queen Elizabeth I suppressed the monasteries, she presented this abbey and all its lands to Robert Dillon, Earl of Roscommon.

The village has a small but thriving airfield from which visitors can take short flights over the surrounding countryside.

### Ardagh/Ardach

Victorian houses grouped neatly around a limestone clock tower, a small green and a village pump in the centre of Ardagh, stand in testimony to the village's 'improving' landlords, the Fetherstones, who acquired the local estates in the 18th century. Lady Frances Fetherstone, who built the houses for her tenants in the 1860s, was inspired by the order of Swiss town planning, a legacy that still survives for the village has several times won the national 'Tidy Towns' competition.

The Fetherstone family home, Ardagh House, was once mistaken for an inn by the young poet Oliver Goldsmith, an incident which inspired his still-popular play and masterpiece *She Stoops to Conquer*, written in 1773. The neoclassical house, at the end of a tree-lined avenue, is now a domestic science college for girls.

Behind the village's dilapidated Protestant church are the remains of one of Ireland's

**OTHER PLACES TO SEE**
**Forgney** 2½m SE of Ballymahon. Church with window of Goldsmith's 'Sweet Auburn'.
**Lough Ree** Second-largest midland lake, with wildfowl such as tufted duck.
**Royal Canal** Walks along towpath from Ballymahon.

**EVENTS**
**Abbeyshrule Fly-In** Early Aug.
**Goldsmith Week** Forgney, Whitsun. Contact tel: (044) 57590.
**Goldsmith Weekend** Abbeyshrule, early June.
**Lakeland Vintage Club Annual Rally** Abbeyshrule, last weekend in May.

**SPORT**
**Angling** Coarse fishing: Lough Ree, River Inny. Trout fishing: River Inny.

**INFORMATION**
Midlands-East Tourism. Tel: (044) 48650.

## GOLDSMITH'S GOLDEN WORDS

'Sweet Auburn, loveliest village of the plain,' was how Oliver Goldsmith began his poem *The Deserted Village*. Now Auburn exists in name only, yet its associations still draw thousands of Goldsmith's fans each year to Longford and Westmeath.

Goldsmith was born in 1728 at Pallas, near Ballymahon in County Longford. Most of his boyhood was spent near Auburn in the parsonage at Lissoy, County Westmeath. Lissoy parsonage is now just a ruin, with only a plaque to mark its significance.

Goldsmith was described by his first teacher as 'impenetrably stupid', and an attack of smallpox left him with an unprepossessing appearance – 'small, lumpish, with a lively, sad, ugly face, much pitted by the smallpox'. He lived in London for a time, where he was known as a buffoon, and he died in 1774, terribly in debt. But he gained lasting recognition as a writer, with his classic novel *The Vicar of Wakefield*, as a poet, and as a dramatist, with the play *She Stoops to Conquer*.

Although much of Goldsmith's working life was spent in London, it was to Ireland that he looked for inspiration. In *The Deserted Village* Goldsmith fondly recalled 'The never-failing brook; the busy mill, The decent church that topt the neighbouring hill'. The busy mill, which worked until the mid-19th century, can be seen at the entrance to the Three Jolly Pigeons pub, on the Ballymahon road out of Athlone. The millstone itself is said to be built into the pub.

oldest churches, traditionally known as St Mel's Cathedral. They include a 20ft by 30ft stone rectangle dating from the 8th or 9th centuries, and restored 6ft walls. Massive, rough foundation stones carry huge slabs that were individually shaped to fit the church's foundations.

St Patrick brought the Christian faith to Ardagh in the mid-5th century and left behind his nephew Mel as first Bishop of Ardagh. St Mel's original wooden building has long since vanished, but Ardagh church was the seat of the diocese until it was destroyed in the 16th century. The seat of the bishopric moved to Longford when St Mel's Cathedral was built there in the 19th century.

### Ballymahon/Baile Uí Mhatháin

A broad street is the focus for four main roads that meet across the River Inny in this picturesque town. A riverside park built at the foot of long-abandoned barracks provides a good picnic spot beside the river. Farther downstream, towards Red Bridge, the coarse fishing is excellent.

Ballymahon has many associations with the famous poet Oliver Goldsmith. It is said that the area around the town had a strong influence on him and was an inspiration for many of his works.

### Barley Harbour

On the shores of the silent expanse of Lough Ree, tucked down small, winding roads, the harbour is a mooring place for cruisers and other boats going through Lough Ree on their way up and down the Shannon. It is one of the most beautiful spots in the country, although that is not the reason for its fame. A few hundred yards back from the harbour is the workshop and home of Michael Casey, a sculptor with a unique craft – he works with bog wood that is semi-petrified after being preserved in peat for several thousand years.

Casey has worked with wood since he was 14 years old, starting out first as a carpenter. After travelling in North America, he returned home and began building gypsy caravans for tourists. But, unfulfilled, he turned to bog wood, devoting himself exclusively to his craft from 1970. Now an engaging, white-haired man in his 60s, Casey has built up an international reputation.

Bog wood has been used in country areas for centuries to make tools and door frames, but Casey is the first to use it for aesthetic purposes. First he allows the wood to dry out for almost two years. He then carves it, smooths it with sandpaper, and finishes it with beeswax to produce works as hard and smooth as ivory and stone, and with a texture and colour all their own. He works with pine, yew and oak, all of them hardened and blackened by peat, and allows the shape and grain of the wood to suggest the final form – perhaps a mother and child, a snake, or a dancer.

## Inchcleraun

On this island in Lough Ree, six churches make up the extensive remains of a monastery founded in the early 6th century by St Diarmuid. These include the Belfry Church, set on the highest point on the island, an unusual Romanesque church with a square tower at the west end and stairs with two doors in the north wall. There is also a church, probably dedicated to the Blessed Virgin and known as the Woman's Church. Teampull Mór, 13th century and called the Big Church, is rectangular with two lancet east windows. The earliest church is probably St Diarmuid's.

The legendary Queen Maeve is said to have been killed on the island by a sling stone fired from the shores of the lough while she was bathing.

Inchcleraun can be reached by boat from Coosan Point, Athlone, or Lanesborough.

## Newtown Cashel/Baile Nua an Chaisil

This little village has a folk museum housed in a traditional whitewashed cottage, with an open hearth fire and a collection of agricultural and domestic artefacts. Teas are served there in the summer.
**Folk museum** May-Oct, daily 2-6pm. Tel: (043) 45698.

SAINT'S ISLAND *The ruins of a 14th-century Augustinian monastery gave this peninsula, once an island in Lough Ree, its name.*

SINUOUS SCULPTURE *Michael Casey's graceful carving is made from wood preserved for thousands of years beneath the bog.*

ARTIST AT WORK *In his workshop, Casey carefully carves a piece of bog wood, before sanding and buffing it to a silky finish.*

# The Ancient Land of Annaly

*From the reedy shores of Lough Gowna to the broad flood plain of the Shannon, across red-brown bogs, meadows and woodland, lie areas of great natural beauty as yet little explored. The boggy north of the county offers poor land to farmers, but to visitors it presents surprising variety, from the county town itself to pretty villages on the Shannon, excellent fishing and absorbing historical remains.*

### Ballinamuck/Beal Atha na Muc

Sitting astride a hill overlooking a valley is the small village whose size gives no notion of its past importance. Its time for death and glory came in 1798, when a small French invasion force supported by Irish insurgents was routed here by the British, an event which is marked by a memorial in the centre of the village; it depicts an Irish pikeman and cannon and displays a map of the campaign.

Another monument stands above Ballinamuck, on Shanmullagh Hill, site of the battle itself, and 3 miles north, in an old cemetery at Tubberpatrick, are memorials to General Blake, an Irish officer in the French army, who was captured and hanged, and to the heroic Gunner Magee and his cousins. These doughty defenders, when they ran out of ammunition, ingeniously improvised a supply of grapeshot by breaking up camp cooking equipment. They fought to the last, dying in the battle.

The town's role in this battle was recently replayed when a television series was made in 1981 based on Thomas Flanagan's historical novel *The Year of the French.*

Ballinamuck's hotel, The Pikeman, is a popular base for fishermen drawn by the ten small loughs strung along the county border to the west and north.

### Carrigglas Manor

Ireland's first Victorian country house stands on a 650 acre estate, proclaiming a grand past. The site was the Jacobean seat of the Bishops of Ardagh, and has been the home of the Lefroy family since the late 18th century, when their Huguenot ancestors came over from France. The house was rebuilt completely in 1837, with fashionable Tudor-Gothic turrets.

Today, Jeffry and Tessa Lefroy give a lively guided tour that takes in ancestral portraits, Victorian costumes and 18th-century furniture, including the dining table, which has been laid with part of a 19th-century Spode dessert service.

Each item sparks an anecdote. One Lefroy was said to have been romantically involved with Jane Austen, becoming the model for Darcy in *Pride and Prejudice.* Another, Hugh Lefroy, was an eccentric who grew potatoes on the roof and pruned the apple trees by night so as to cause least distress to them. He also insisted on meals being served at unpredictable intervals, so that guests might find breakfast being served at supper time. His wife, a rich Polish countess, spent all her money in a vain attempt to convert the local Catholics to Protestantism.

Strangely, the house itself is less interesting architecturally than the stable block, which has grand entrance arches and fine stonework. The stables were built in the late 18th century and designed by James Gandon, who created Dublin's magnificent Custom House. Now they are partially converted into self-contained holiday accommodation. An

CARRIGGLAS MANOR *Period furniture still graces this Victorian ancestral home.*

informal woodland garden contains flowers in their natural wild setting and includes rare plants such as pink cow parsley.
**Opening times** *June-Sept, pm, except Wed and Thur. Tel: (043) 45165.*

### Corn Hill

Rising above meadows, brown peat fields and woodland, along the road from Drumlish to

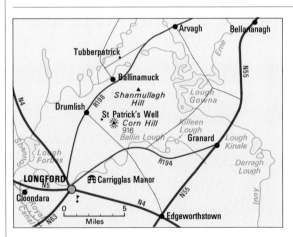

ash. Breeding and overwintering ground for wildfowl, including wigeons, golden-eyes and wild swans.

**EVENTS**
**Granard Harp Festival**
Granard, mid-Aug.
**Longford Summer Festival**
Third week in July.

**SPORT**
**Angling** Coarse fishing: Ballinamuck, Ballin Lough, Granard, Killeen Lough, Loughs Gowna, Derragh and Kinale, and River Erne. Trout fishing: Loughs Gowna and Derragh, and River Erne. For more information contact Granard Angling Club. Tel: (043) 86529.
**Golf** Longford Golf Club, 18-hole course. Tel: (043) 46310.

**INFORMATION**
Midlands-East Tourism. Tel: (044) 48650.

**OTHER PLACES TO SEE**
**Cloondara** The end of the Royal Canal, at Richmond Harbour; charming mooring spot with meadow on one side and line of pastel-coloured houses along the other.

**Lough Forbes** Large lake on Shannon system whose shores are home to woodland birds and wintering wildfowl, particularly white-fronted geese.
**Lough Gowna** Shallow lake fringed with willow, alder and

## THE BATTLE OF BALLINAMUCK

An Irish rebellion against harsh British rule erupted in May 1798. Three months later it had almost been crushed, when France was persuaded to send troops to support the rebels. A combined Franco-Irish force landed in Mayo on the west coast in August 1798, and moved across the country, winning two battles on the way and collecting a few more Irish to the cause.

The little army, now 2300-strong, was aiming to link with other patriots in Granard. But they never made it. On Shanmullagh Hill, above the village of Ballinamuck, they faced a vastly superior British force of 12,000 in an unequal battle with a predictable outcome. The Irish and French were sent scattering downhill, leaving 500 bodies on the battlefield – except for a gunner named Magee, and his two cousins. They held out to the last, even when the wheel of Magee's gun was smashed and he ran out of ammunition. It is said that they made grapeshot by breaking up the camp cooking equipment, and while Magee's cousins supported the gun, he fired a final round. It was a heroic, futile act. The recoil of the gun broke the backs of the two men, and Magee was then killed by British cavalry. The Irish general, Blake, was captured and hanged, and many others fleeing the battle were taken prisoner and executed.

Edgeworthstown, is the 916ft Corn Hill, the county's highest point. Visitors must walk the last half mile up a paved road, but will be rewarded with a fine view of the surrounding area, dotted with half-a-dozen loughs and a scattering of white-walled bungalows. The name is a corruption of 'cairn' hill.

In the lee of the hill, set back in rough pasture, stands St Patrick's Well, with a modern statue of the saint watching over a well with coins thrown in as offerings. A large rose bush behind the well is draped with strips of cloth, tied on as thanks for cures effected by prayers offered to St Patrick.

## Edgeworthstown/Meathas Troim

The 19th-century novelist Maria Edgeworth (1767-1849) lived here, and it was after her family that the town of Mostrim, or Meathas Troim, was recently renamed. Maria, daughter of the educationalist, scientist and author Richard Lovell Edgeworth, was the second of 24 children. While helping her father to run the estate, she drew inspiration from the local community for her satirical novels and established a fashion for 'regional' works, of which the first and best-known was *Castle Rackrent*. She was admired by Jane Austen, and Sir Walter Scott wrote that in his own historical novels he hoped 'in some distant degree to emulate the admirable Irish portraits drawn by Miss Edgeworth'.

Still sprightly at the age of 80, she achieved a different sort of fame, in her work to relieve the effects of the Famine. She was particularly loved in the United States. Boston sent her 150 barrels of flour and rice and it is said that she was so well known that one relief parcel reached her addressed only to 'Miss Maria, Ireland'. She died aged 82, worn out by her efforts, and was buried in St John's Church in the town.

Her home, set in a bend at the Dublin end of the town, is now a nursing home, a graceful, porticoed white house with a portrait of Maria in the entrance hall.

## Granard/Gránard

Framed by a backdrop of fields, distant hills and glinting loughs is Ireland's highest Norman motte, constructed in 1199, at 534ft a projection that causes the main street of this busy market town to veer sharply to the south. The motte is now almost hidden by a Victorian church when seen from the town, but there is easy access to it behind the church. It is no longer topped by a bailey, but

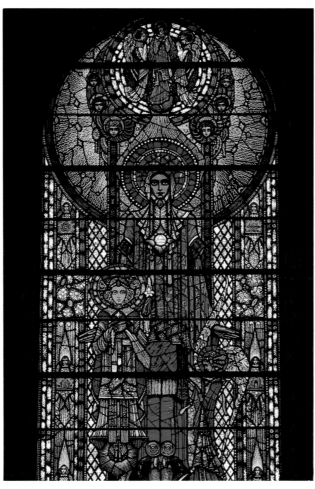

ST MEL'S CATHEDRAL *Reds, golds and blues radiate from Harry Clarke's vivid interpretation of Christ in glory.*

THE NAVE IN ST MEL'S *Classical colonnades bear the lofty vaulted roof.*

ST PATRICK'S WELL *A modern statue of the saint presides over the well on Corn Hill, in which coins are tossed as offerings.*

is crowned by a 1932 statue of St Patrick.

Granard is a good centre for fishermen – local loughs and the Inny offer pike, perch, roach and tench – and for nature lovers. Two rare plants, bedstraw and stonecrop, have been found on the motte itself, and other rarities – creeping willow, hedge mustard and wild pansy – are known to grow in the surrounding countryside.

## Longford/An Longfort

A castle built by the O'Farrell princes of Annaly, as Longford was before 1547, gave this busy county town its name. There is

nothing left of it, and of the 1641 castle built by the Earl of Longford only a few overgrown stone walls remain. The town's wide streets and handsome 18th and 19th-century buildings are dominated by the 200ft tower of St Mel's Cathedral. Like a huge pepperpot, it is an incongruous addition to the Italian Renaissance style of the cathedral. This is because work on the church, started in 1840, was stopped by the Famine, and it was not completed until 1893. The spacious forecourt has an imposing portico of pillars topped by a triangular frieze. Inside, colonnades support the vaulted roof, and two stained-glass windows combine with an unusual rose-tinted roof to colour the monochromatic stone.

Behind the cathedral is a small Diocesan Museum with an intriguing collection of old tools, penal crosses, elk antlers, Bronze Age spear heads and stones. Pride of place goes to 10th-century St Mel's Crozier, found in the original St Mel's Cathedral in Ardagh. Another museum, in the post office, contains an array of old tools, weapons and memorabilia of the Republican struggle in the 1920s.
**Diocesan Museum** *June-Sept: Mon and Wed 11am-1pm, Sat 12-2pm, Sun 4-6pm. Tel: (043) 46465.*

# The Fount of Early Christianity

*The ancient town of Kells, one of Ireland's first Christian settlements and the source of many early Christian treasures, is cradled within an arc of spectacular hills. These rise in the west to Meath's highest points, some of which form the Slieve na Calliagh, or Hill of the Witches, topped by several tombs. From this summit and others nearby there are superb views of the chains of loughs to the east.*

### Drumcondra/Droim Conrach

Every year, this normally placid village buzzes and bristles with the reels and rods of fishermen from around the world. They come to take part in Drumcondra's annual angling festival which is held on the surrounding loughs where the waters are so thick with fish that in 1989 three men caught 500lb between them in a day. Even at less competitive times of the year Drumcondra (also sometimes spelled Drumconrath) attracts those anglers who like to fish in peace the small secluded loughs that dot the wooded countryside.

Most loughs have car parks and slipways for boats, and some have wooden platforms for fishermen. Forests with nature trails and picnic areas on the lake shores make this an attractive area even for non-anglers.

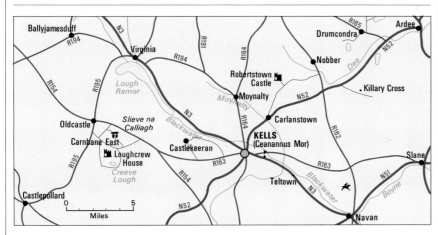

### OTHER PLACES TO SEE
**Castlekeeran** 4m W of Kells. Ruins of 9th-century church and monastery called Diseart Chiaráin, the 'Hermitage of Ciarán', with three High Crosses and an ogham stone.
**Killary Cross** 11m NE of Kells. Shaft of a 10th-century High Cross with carved Biblical illustrations.
**Robertstown Castle** 7½m NE of Kells. A three-storey, 17th-century castle with gabled roof and two towers. Key obtainable from the house 200yds behind the castle.
**Teltown** 4m SE of Kells. Said to be a pagan graveyard and the site of an ancient palace probably built by King Tuathal (1st or 2nd century AD), where assemblies and games took place every Aug.

### EVENTS
**Drumconrath Tara Mines Angling Festival** Summer.

**Moynalty Steam Threshing Festival** Second Sun in Aug.

### SPORT
**Angling** Coarse fishing: Drumcondra and surrounding loughs, and near Kells.
**Golf** Headfort Golf Club, 18-hole course. Tel: (046) 40146.

### INFORMATION
Midlands-East Tourism. Tel: (044) 48650.

### Kells/Ceanannus

One of the great centres of Celtic Christianity, where the Book of Kells may have been written and illustrated, this busy little crossroads today offers numerous reminders of its glorious past. Kells is also known as Ceanannus Mór.

In AD 563, St Colmcille, also known as St Columba, founded a monastery on the Hebridean island of Iona. When the Vikings raided it in 802, some of its monks sought refuge at Kells, where they founded a new Columban monastery in 804. It probably survived until around 1200. The circular shape of this monastery is followed today in the street pattern of the modern town.

The monks continued to be hounded by Vikings, who plundered the settlement four times, and nothing is left of the several churches the monks built. However, a house and Round Tower can still be seen. The Round Tower, 90ft high, was built before 1076, and stands in the churchyard. It has a door that was once 15ft above the ground, reached by a ladder which the monks could have drawn up after them when threatened by Viking raids. Once the tower would have contained about five floors, connected by an internal staircase. Now these floors are gone and the tower is as empty as a chimney.

The house, now called St Colmcille's House, was perhaps a monastic library. (The key is available from Lower Church View, 100yds down the road.) Today, its vaulted interior has only an attic storey of three tiny rooms beneath the steeply pitched stone roof, where vellum – the calfskin that the monks used to write on – may have been stored. Perhaps it was in this house that the monks completed the writing and decoration of the Book of Kells. This richly illuminated copy of the Gospels is now kept in Trinity College, Dublin, although impeccable reproductions can be seen in Kells town hall and in the Protestant church.

Three ornately carved stone crosses from the 9th century stand in the churchyard, and a fourth at the crossroads below it. These High Crosses are similar to many others elsewhere in Ireland, some of which probably marked sites for open-air religious devotions. One of these Kells crosses, at the foot of the Round Tower, is more than 9ft tall and, unusually, has a Latin inscription. The 8ft high cross in Market Square, the busy centre of Kells, probably marked the edge of St Colmcille's monastery. It is decorated with 30 panels of carved illustrations, including Adam and Eve, the Sacrifice of Isaac, Daniel in the Lions' Den, the Crucifixion, and the Resurrection. The cross was badly damaged in the religious wars, but was repaired and put up again in 1688. Its base is interestingly grooved where, it is said, English soldiers sharpened their swords.

### Loughcrew House

A well-preserved square of walls at the foot of the Slieve na Calliagh, the 'Hill of the Witches', is all that is left of the kitchen garden of a now-vanished mansion, Loughcrew House, birthplace of the martyred Archbishop of Armagh, Oliver Plunkett (1625-81). The garden had a dual purpose: apart from providing food it also concealed the mound that today lies exposed and which is the roof of a superb 'souterrain'. This was an underground chamber designed as a short-term refuge from marauders, probably dating from the time of the Viking raids between the 8th and 11th centuries.

The souterrain can be visited, with permission from the owner who lives in the big house nearby. A muddy crawl along a pitch-black passage leads to two spacious chambers, some 10ft high and 20ft across, whose conical stone roofs are in almost perfect condition. Empty and eerie, their silence is broken only by the sound of an occasional drip from the damp stones.

Below the walled garden, beside a beautiful avenue of yew trees, stands a high mound which is a Norman motte of the 12th century. Once ringed by a stone wall and topped by a keep, it is now an abrupt grassy knoll 20ft high with a tree sprouting from its flat crown.

To the south-east, in Creeve Lough itself, is another fortification. This is a small, tree-covered, artificial island known as a crannog, built of stone laid on the lake bed. The crannog stands in 30ft of water and would once have been reached by boat, but today it is not accessible.

The walled garden, the yew avenue and the surrounding land once formed part of the great estate of the Plunkett family. Among their members was St Oliver Plunkett, martyred in 1681 and canonised in 1975. A ruined church near the motte is dedicated to him, his shinbone is displayed in a shrine in Oldcastle's Catholic church, and his skull rests in a shrine in St Peter's Church, Drogheda, in County Louth.

VIEW OF CAIRN T *The mound of this passage-grave rises above the springy turf on the Slieve na Calliagh, or 'Hill of the Witches'.*

CAIRN T *Huge boulders prop up the roof of this Stone Age tomb, which is richly decorated with an intricate array of circles, spirals, chevrons, stylised suns and diamond shapes, carved with skilful precision into the stone.*

### Slieve na Calliagh

Prehistoric sites almost 5000 years old lie on these three peaks, also known as the 'Hill of the Witches'. They are reached by foot from a car park, on a steep walk that leads up over grass to a 911ft summit – Meath's highest point. Of the 30 tombs known, only two are in good condition. Entries to both are locked, but the keys are available from the keeper's house at the bottom of the access road. Visitors should take a torch to make their way safely round the tombs.

Embedded in the mound of stones of the eastern tomb, known as Carnbane East, is a huge stone called the 'Hag's Seat', shaped like an altar or a broad chair. Its origins and purpose are still a mystery.

A masterpiece of early Irish art, this illuminated manuscript is thought to have been started in a monastery on Iona, in Scotland, or in Kells itself around AD 804, where it was completed. The book is a richly coloured, minutely decorated version of the Gospels, written on vellum. For a while the book lay in Kells church. It was stolen from there in 1007 and found 2½ months later in a bog, without its jewel-encrusted cover. The book was returned to Kells, but in the 17th century it was given to Trinity College, Dublin, where it remains today.

# The Heart of Celtic Ireland

*According to the legends, here is where the story of Ireland began. Hidden among the low hills is a wealth of prehistoric, Celtic and early Christian sites, chief among them the Hill of Tara, the heart of Celtic Ireland. Once the seat of the High Kings, this Iron Age hill-fort is now a collection of grassy hillocks and ridges. Even so, nearly 1000 years after the kings abandoned it, Tara's past lives on, attracting pilgrims from all parts of the world.*

### Bective Abbey

The collection of ruins that was Bective Abbey has a beautiful setting, in open fields stretching down to the River Boyne. The abbey was once the focus of a gruesome dispute. In 1186, 40 years after the abbey was founded, Hugh de Lacy, Henry II's governor of Ireland, was murdered. He was beheaded by a furious workman in Durrow, County Offaly, who was outraged that he would demolish Durrow Abbey to build a castle. His headless trunk was buried at Bective and his head at St Thomas's Abbey, Dublin. A decree proclaimed that certain lands would become the property of the abbey that held Hugh's body – but which half constituted the true body? In 1205 an episcopal court decided in favour of the head, and St Thomas's.

The abbey was founded as a Cistercian monastery by Murchad, King of Meath, but most of the ruins are those of a 15th-century reconstruction. After the Dissolution in 1536 the abbey became a fortified manor house, the battlemented tower dating from then. The site is entered through a wicket gate, and visitors can wander over trim lawns, through the old chapter house, church, cloisters, tower and monks' living quarters.

ANCIENT BRIDGE *Near Bective Abbey ruins, the arches of a stone bridge span the River Boyne.*

### Hill of Tara

In ancient legend this was the palace of the High Kings of Ireland, and it is crowned with the remains of forts. It has a passage-grave where Bronze Age burials have been found, including one of a young man wearing a necklace of amber and faience. The hill rises 300ft above undulating, tree-studded pastures, giving glorious views all around.

### Hill of Ward

Towering above the Meath countryside is a hilltop crowned with the ramparts of a large Iron Age fort. This was the Palace of Tlachtga, a local sorceress, and was one of the principal meeting points for Meath's pagans, who assembled for the great Celtic festival of Samhain, held on November 1 every three years to mark the beginning of winter. Some sources even say that human sacrifices were carried out here on Samhain Eve. The fort is now just a vague pattern of mounds heavily trampled by cattle, but it has a fine all-round view of the surrounding land.

DUNMOE CASTLE *The crumbling turrets of the 15th-century Dunmoe Castle, former home of the Darcy family, tower above the River Boyne. Cromwell is said to have fired on it from the opposite bank in 1649, but it was not destroyed until 150 years later.*

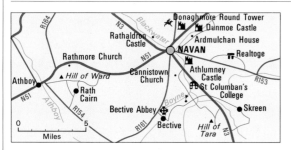

### OTHER PLACES TO SEE

**Athboy** (early closing Wed) Once a walled stronghold of the Pale, now a quiet agricultural town in wooded country on the banks of the River Athboy (also called the Tremblestown).

**Athlumney Castle** Ruins of 15th-century tower house with 17th-century Tudor addition, on east bank of River Boyne 1½m S of Navan. Key obtained from convent on other side of road.

**Cannistown Church** Early 13th-century church with 15th-century additions, S of Athlumney Castle. Interesting chancel arch and grotesque stone masks.

**Donaghmore Round Tower** 2m NE of Navan, next to a 15th-century church with a fine Crucifixion above the doorway. Said to be on site of first monastery built by St Patrick.

**Rathaldron Castle** 15th-century quadrangular tower with an adjoining castellated mansion built in the 19th century.

**Realtoge** 5m SE of Navan. Massive Celtic ring-fort about 120ft wide surrounded by earth banks, with underground passage, and traces of hut foundations.

### EVENTS

**Market Day** Fri, in Navan.
**Rath Cairn Gaelic Festival** First week in July.
**Senior Cup Golf Final** Royal Tara Golf Club, end July.

### SPORT

**Angling** Game fishing: Rivers Blackwater and Boyne.
**Golf** Royal Tara Golf Club, 18-hole course. Tel: (046) 25244.
**Horse racing** Navan, various meets.

### INFORMATION

Midlands-East Tourism.
Tel: (044) 48650.

BOYNE VALLEY *Cattle graze in the rich, lush grassland with Dunmoe Castle in the distance.*

### Navan/An Uaimgh

From Navan, the county town of Meath, a splendid walk leads alongside the River Boyne for 4 miles towards Slane. Known as The Ramparts, it begins where the Blackwater meets the Boyne, on a path signposted 'Boyne Way'. The path heads east over a small 18th-century humpbacked bridge, which spans one of 20 locks on the Boyne Canal. Built between 1759 and 1800 to bypass the Boyne's rapids between Navan and Drogheda, the canal never paid its way, and was abandoned in 1923.

The path leads along a steep bank, from newly planted woodland to old woods and pastures and the towering, romantic ruin of Dunmoe Castle, built in the 15th century but burned down in the 1798 Rebellion. Opposite Dunmoe lies the estate of Ardmulchan House, a private home.

On the road above the path, several access points allow cars down to the river. At Ardmulchan, a track signposted 'Scenic Views' leads to a bluff overlooking the full width of the valley.

### Rath Cairn

Tucked away down tiny lanes lies a thriving 'Gaeltacht', or Gaelic-speaking community, where English is rarely heard. Rath Cairn – pronounced 'Racharran' (soft 'ch') in Gaelic – was founded in 1935 when 27 families from the impoverished west coast accepted the chance of a new life with land, equipment and houses provided by the government. The experiment worked, and now Rath Cairn is the largest Irish-speaking community in the central and eastern counties, and runs language courses for people from all over the country.

The enthusiasm for Irish can best be seen at the village's two festivals for performers of unaccompanied storytelling. One is a competition, the other a series of lectures and performances in memory of a much-admired singer, Dudley Kane (Dharach Chathain in Irish). There is also a spring drama festival for Irish acting groups.

### Rathmore Church

This 15th-century church, standing prettily in isolated ruins in a green field, was built by the Plunkett family of Dunsany. Inside it are the tombs of the Plunketts, and its delicate tracery is still intact. The church was abandoned in the 17th century, but its rough and tussocky graveyard is still in use.

### St Columban's College, Dalgan Park

A 500 acre nature reserve with 30,000 hardwood trees and a fine view of the Hill of Tara surrounds this imposing greystone building, completed in 1940 to train missionaries for work in the Far East.

The college and the missionary group who run it, the Columban Fathers, are named after St Columbanus – Colman in Irish – who, between 590 and his death in 615, devoted his life to working among the poor. It has a fine barrel-vaulted chapel with Irish decorations, in a style known as Hiberno-Romanesque. Visitors can also view rooms which display art and objects from the five main regions in which Columbans have been active since their foundation in 1916: Burma, China, Korea, Japan and the Philippines.
**College museum** *Daily, 9am-9pm.*

### Skreen

On the sharp summit of the hill of Skreen, 2½ miles east of Tara, perch the remains of a 14th-century church and its tall tower, probably from the 15th century. Ruined in Elizabethan times, it is now secured from further collapse. The key is kept in the little pub that is one of the half-dozen houses on the top of the hill. The ascent of the church tower is not for the faint-hearted – a tight spiral of uneven stone steps leads to a flat roof that has no guard rail. But the brave are rewarded with a dramatic, if unnerving, view that includes the Hill of Tara in silhouette.

Skreen was not the hill's first name. In the 3rd century, after the death of High King Cormac, there was a rebellion against his son, Cairbre. He defeated his foes in a bloody battle at the base of this hill but was himself killed. His distraught wife keened over the body for so long that the place became known as Cnoc Ghuil, 'The Hill of Weeping'.

It was renamed in 875, when the relics of St Columba were brought from Iona to a monastery he had founded at Skreen three centuries earlier. The word 'skreen', or 'skryne' in the preferred local spelling, is the equivalent of the English word 'shrine'.

# A Stone Age Cemetery

*Five-thousand years ago settlers first came here, attracted by the swift-flowing Boyne river, which gave them access to the interior and the rolling green hills that surveyed the surrounding land. Now their tale is told by the stones, mounds and tombs they left behind, such as Newgrange, one of the most important and spectacular prehistoric monuments in Europe, part of an enormous Stone Age cemetery whose enigmatic decorations and sheer size continue to fascinate visitors.*

### Bettystown/Baile an Bhiataigh

Every year, the glorious 2 mile stretch of hard sands between Bettystown and Laytown is dramatically transformed by the drum of hooves and the hum of the crowd when the annual race meeting is held here, in June, July or August, depending on the tides. Nowhere else in Europe is an official race meeting held on a beach. Behind the sands north of Bettystown are the rolling dunes known as the 'Burrows', where there is a popular golf course.

The villages of Bettystown and Laytown, or An Inse, straggle between the mouths of the Nanny and Boyne rivers. At Mornington, beacons at the northern end of the sands mark the mouth of the Boyne and warn approaching mariners of the river bar. Two of these beacons are the 60ft Maiden Tower, built in the 16th century, and the nearby, smaller, Lady's Finger. There is a popular local story that says a girl threw herself from the top of Maiden Tower in great distress believing that her lover had been lost at sea. When she fell, her arm broke in such a way that one finger was left sticking up. This, they say, is how the towers got their names. In fact, Maiden Tower is probably named after Elizabeth I. From the top of Maiden Tower there is a good view of the town of Drogheda and the tidal reaches of the Boyne. The tower is open all year round.

### Duleek/Damhliag

Ireland's oldest stone church, St Cianán's, built in the 5th century when Christianity first came to the land, gave this village its Irish name, which means 'stone church'. The

BETTYSTOWN TOWERS *The Maiden Tower, on the left, and Lady's Finger, stand sentinel at the mouth of the River Boyne, life-saving beacons to seafarers.*

church has disappeared, and the ruins that now stand on the site may be those of a 12th-century monastery, St Mary's Abbey. The abbey's graveyard contains the ornately carved North Cross, smaller than the 9th-century High Crosses in Kells, and a reminder of the village's early Christian origins. The cross is decorated with the Crucifixion, Celtic interlacing and weather-worn figures.

Among the ruins are those of a 15th-century church with a tower that has a groove in one face, where its stones were cut to fit against the long-vanished Round Tower of St Mary's. The church contains the tomb of Lord John Bellew, a Catholic who died in 1691 at the Battle of Aughrim, where the Protestant armies sealed their victory after the Battle of the Boyne. He is recorded as being shot in the stomach – proof that he died facing the enemy. The last skirmish in the Battle of the Boyne was fought near Duleek, and King William is said to have spent the night after the battle here.

### Fourknocks/Fornocht

The Stone Age passage-tomb of Fourknocks can be seen as a grassy knoll over the rim of a hill from the narrow lane that runs below it. Its Irish name means 'bleak place'. The site is kept locked, but the key is obtainable from the house nearby. Inside the tomb, a 17ft long passageway leads to a chamber 21ft across, far larger than the chamber at Newgrange. It has a few rough zigzag and circular decorations, one of which could represent a human form.

### Newgrange

The most impressive Stone Age tomb in Europe stands on a hill above the Boyne's fertile valley, part of a huge prehistoric cemetery known as Brugh na Bóinne. It is older than Stonehenge, and even older than the Egyptian pyramids. A pear-shaped mound, Newgrange reaches 36ft high and about 300ft across, and is surrounded at its base by large stones engraved with geometric patterns. The entrance to the tomb is marked by an ornately carved, 10 ton stone. The semicircular courtyard, faced with granite, has been reshaped to accommodate the flow of people.

A mile away from Newgrange lie the dramatic passage-tombs of Dowth to the north-east and Knowth to the north-west. With two burial chambers set back to back, and with 17 satellite graves, Knowth is more complex than Newgrange, although Dowth is larger. Knowth is under excavation, and Dowth is not open to the public.

**Newgrange** *Open 10am daily, exc Mon and Sun from Nov–Mar. Closing varies. Tel: (041) 24488.*

### Oldbridge

The little bridge that crosses the Boyne to Oldbridge on the south bank gives this hamlet its name, but it reveals nothing of the momentous battle that was contested on the hills above it. The Battle of the Boyne, fought in 1690, was the decisive confrontation in which the Protestant forces supporting William of Orange routed the army of the exiled English Catholic king, James II.

A flight of 75 uneven steps leads up from a small car park to a viewing-point across part of the battlefield. A map displayed there indicates the course of the battle, and signposts mark the spots of its various stages: such as the ford at Rossnaree, where William detached part of his army, and Grove Island, where General Schomberg rushed the ford below Oldbridge.

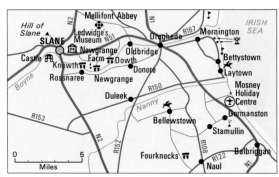

**OTHER PLACES TO SEE**
**Ledwidge's Museum** The cottage home of poet and member of the Irish Volunteers, Francis (Frank) Ledwidge (1891-1917), and now a museum. Opening times vary. Tel: (041) 24285/24244.
**Mosney Holiday Centre** 300 acres of beach, dunes and woods, with camp site. Late May-late Aug. Tel: (041) 29200.

**Newgrange Farm** Tours Apr 1-Aug 31, Mon-Sat 10am-6pm, Sun 2-6pm. Tel: (041) 24119.
**Stamullin** Ruins of church with 14th-century cadaver grave.

**EVENTS**
**Bellewstown Races** Early July.
**Laytown Races** July/Aug.

**SPORT**
**Angling** Sea fishing: Bettystown and Laytown.
**Golf** Laytown and Bettystown Golf Club, 18-hole course. Tel: (041) 27170.
**Swimming** Mornington.

**INFORMATION**
Midlands-East Tourism. Tel: (044) 48650.

FOURKNOCKS PASSAGE-TOMB *The grassy knoll (above) marks this huge tomb high on the hills above Ardcath. Inside, a passage (top) leads to the vast, eerie, inner chamber with carved stones.*

## Slane/Baile Shláine

Looking north across the Boyne, Slane is a pretty sight. The main road sweeps down beside a ruined church to a long, narrow bridge, and beyond that, on a hillside, rises the well-planned 18th-century village. The octagonal focal point where the roads meet at its centre is distinguished by four dignified Georgian houses built diagonally opposite each other.

This stretch of the Boyne, a playground for picnickers, walkers and canoeists, is dominated by Slane Castle, a mile upriver. A late 18th-century creation for the Marquis of Conyngham, the castle had several architects, mainly because they were antagonised by the marquis's temper. He also hired Capability Brown to plan the gardens, which he did – at a safe distance – from England.

The present owner, the Earl of Mount Charles, has turned the castle into a restaurant and nightclub, but visitors may see the ground floor, which includes a superb Gothic Revival circular ballroom, and a library built in the early 19th century. Lady Elizabeth Conyngham, the first Marchioness, was the last mistress of George IV, and the house contains several gifts that he sent her, including a spectacular portrait of himself, which now hangs in splendour in the round ballroom.

Above the village is the Hill of Slane, where the first Easter fire was lit by St Patrick in 433 to symbolise the arrival of Christianity in Ireland. This act defied an order by Laoghaire, the High King of Tara, but when St Patrick explained himself, Laoghaire was impressed by his message and gave him permission to preach the gospel.

The hill was also the site of a 6th-century monastery and church. These buildings and those that succeeded them were ravaged in turn by Vikings, Normans and Cromwell's troops. Today's ruins are those of a 16th-century priestly college and a church, which were abandoned in 1723. The church tower has a narrow spiral stairway that leads to a flat roof with panoramic views of Meath.

At the foot of the hill, on the village side of the bridge, an 18th-century mill houses a Folk and Transport Museum. It contains vintage and classic cars and motoring memorabilia, as well as traditional interiors, and has a tea room.

**Slane Castle** *Tours: Mar-Oct, Sun, or by prior arrangement. Tel: (041) 24207. Restaurant: All year, Wed-Sun pm.*
**Old Mill Folk and Transport Museum** *June-Aug, daily; Sept-May, Sun. Tel: (041) 51827.*

## THE BATTLE OF THE BOYNE

Driven from the throne in the Glorious Revolution of 1688, England's Catholic king, James II, fled to France, while his Dutch Protestant son-in-law, William of Orange, and his daughter Mary, took the English throne. In 1689 James landed in Ireland backed by French troops, hoping to oust the Protestant settlers brought in under Cromwell 50 or so years earlier and to restore Ireland to its native Catholics. He was also seeking to raise an army to help him regain the English throne.

James failed to take the Protestant towns of Londonderry and Enniskillen, and in 1690 William and his army landed to confront him. On Sunday, June 29, James crossed the Boyne with his 30,000 men, and set up camp on the hills on the southern side of the river, in a field below Donore church.

William's army, 36,000 strong, established itself in the hills to the north, around Mellifont Abbey. His aim was to seize the bridge over the River Nanny at Duleek and so cut off James's retreat to the

*Protestant King Billy leads his soldiers against the Catholic forces of James II.*

south. The Williamite soldiers were to wear sprigs of green leaves to distinguish themselves from the Jacobite soldiers who were adorned with pieces of paper, which resembled the White Cockade of France. These badges were essential since there was no recognisable uniform on either side.

On July 1, William sent 10,000 men to cross the Boyne at Rossnaree, near Slane. James countered with massive forces, thinking that the main attack was being made on his left. William then sent other forces across the Boyne at Oldbridge, when the tide was low. They marched ten abreast across the river, waist deep in the water, to drums and fifes playing *Lillebullero*.

The day became one of sally and counter-sally, with James's men gradually retreating towards Duleek. The action vanished over the hill during the course of the afternoon. James's troops fought a rearguard action to defend the Duleek bridge, covering his escape. James fled back to France a few days later, his cause lost. William lost 500 men, James lost 1500.

# HILL OF TARA

## The seat of the High Kings of Ireland

A heritage of fact, hearsay and legend has woven the name of Tara into the heart of Irish history – and nowhere more memorably than in Thomas Moore's poem:

*The harp that once through Tara's halls*
*The soul of music shed,*
*Now hangs as mute on Tara's walls*
*As if that soul were fled.*

For centuries the hill was the seat of Celtic kings, and at its height, under King Cormac MacAirt in the 3rd century, Tara was one of the wonders of Europe, an Irish Camelot. Nothing remains of the wooden structures that once made up the hilltop's forts and houses. But the outline of the ditch and earthen rampart that enclosed the site – about 300yds across – can still be seen.

'THE PLACE WITH A WIDE VIEW' It is easy to see why Tara was chosen as a seat of royal power – the hill rises 300ft above the surrounding countryside, commanding an all-round view over the undulating, tree-studded pastures of Meath; in fact, Tara's Gaelic name 'Teamhair' derives from a word meaning 'the place with a wide view'.

There was another reason why the Celts chose this hill as the seat of their kings. It had formerly been a Stone Age burial site, the remains of which now form a steep knoll, and therefore had sacred importance.

Some time after the Celtic invasions of around 500 BC, Tara became associated with supreme royal authority. Whoever ruled Tara termed himself High King, claiming supremacy over all Ireland's other kings. But giving the claim reality was quite another thing, and no king of Tara ever ruled all Ireland.

To prove his claim was valid, according to myth, the High King stood upon a magic Stone of Destiny, the Lia Fáil, which roared approval if the choice of king was apt. A stone known as the Lia Fáil, which stands in Cormac's House today, was placed there to commemorate the deaths of 37 men in the 1798 Rebellion, but its origins are unknown. Probably in the years before the Christian era, the Celtic kings built a number of circular 'raths', or enclosures. Two lie inside

ANCIENT SIGNS *From the air, the rings of Cormac's House, on the right, and the Royal Seat, are clearly visible within the Royal Enclosure, as is the Mound of the Hostages, in the foreground.*

REPEAL MEETING *In 1843 nearly 1 million people, with banners and symbols of Ireland, gathered on the Hill of Tara to hear the Irish patriot Daniel O'Connell speak against union with Britain.*

the huge Royal Enclosure. Another is named after Cormac's daughter, Gráinne, whose flight from Tara with her lover Diarmuid forms an Irish Romeo-and-Juliet legend. Gráinne was betrothed to Finn MacCool, a hero, but ageing. To avoid marrying him, she eloped with Diarmuid. The couple wandered around Ireland for years before Diarmuid was killed, by a boar.

FEASTS FIT FOR KINGS At one end of the hilltop are two parallel lines, said to be the foundations of what is now called the Hall of Banquets. This area – more than 250yds long and 30yds wide – is believed to have been a single immense hall, the site of a feast held every three years. The grandest of these feasts are associated with Cormac, who reigned as High King from 218 to 254; they are said to have been phenomenal events, at which 1000 people celebrated for a week.

Princes, poets, athletes and priests ate goose, mallard, venison, oxen and boar, and the higher their rank, the better they ate. The royal family and nobles gorged on ribs of beef; the druids and soothsayers ate the shins; the historians fed on the haunches, the musicians on shoulder of pork; and the jesters ate shoulder fat. It took 'thrice fifty steaming cooks' to prepare the meals, and 300 men to serve them.

TARA'S DECLINE Tara's loss of importance is associated with the arrival of Christianity. One of the enclosures, the Fort of the Synods, is named after the meetings of Christian and pagan leaders on Tara's hill. The first confrontation was supposedly between High King Laoghaire and St Patrick in the 5th century, after the saint had challenged the king's authority by lighting a fire on the nearby Hill of Slane. Summoned by the king to explain his action, St Patrick so impressed him that he was allowed to go free and preach Christianity. The king, however, said he was too old to change. A late 19th-century statue of St Patrick commemorates his visit.

The last feast was held in 560, and Tara was abandoned sometime afterwards. The wooden buildings rotted and the walls and ditches weathered down to their present haunting shapes. But history became legend, and the name of Tara became a talisman for those eager to conjure Irish nationalism from the misty past.

# Norman Stronghold of the East

*Villages and castles that date from Norman times to the 19th century shelter snugly, sometimes completely hidden, among the low hills. To the north is the charming town of Trim, Norman guardian of the upper River Boyne and Dublin. It is a fascinating combination of ancient and modern, the broken walls of its old towers and castle scattered among grassy fields that stretch right into the centre of the town. To the south the Royal Canal cuts through the lowlands, with the towpath alongside it leading to the emerald heart of Ireland.*

## Ashbourne/Cill Dhéaghláin

A monument like a ship's prow, set into a Y-junction, honours two nationalists from Ashbourne who were killed by British soldiers a mile north of here in the only action outside Dublin during the 1916 Easter Rising. The monument carries a plaque inscribed with a line from a poem by the men's leader, Thomas Ashe, who was also the village schoolmaster: 'Let me carry your cross for Ireland, Lord.' The statue, sculpted in 1959 by Peter Grant, shows a man bearing a cross. It is a dual image – on one side the figure takes the form of Christ, on the other, that of a bare-torsoed nationalist. More figures may be added in the next few years.

The Fairyhouse racecourse, south-west of Ashbourne, holds a race meeting on Easter Monday and Tuesday every year, with the Irish Grand National among the races.

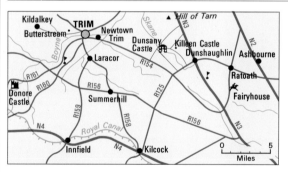

### OTHER PLACES TO SEE
**Donore Castle** 9m SW of Trim. A handsome 15th-century, three-storey turreted castle, roughly 20ft long, 16ft wide and 40ft high, which conforms to the measurements of what were known as £10 castles. These were built after Henry VI promised £10 to every subject that built such a castle before 1439 in Dublin, Kildare, Louth and Meath. The key can be obtained from the house across the road.

**Dunshaughlin** A 10th or 11th-century church with a carved lintel depicting the Crucifixion; a figure on Christ's right brandishes a spear, while that on the left offers a cup of vinegar at the end of a pole.
**Laracor** The village of which the satirist and poet Jonathan Swift was rector from 1699 to 1713.

### WALKS
Town walks and coach tours around Trim start from the town's High Street. Tel: (046) 36633.

### EVENTS
**Irish Grand National** Fairyhouse, Easter Mon and Tues.
**Trim Pony Races** This event includes a Nun Run, in which nuns from around the world race on ponies. Late June. For exact dates contact Sean Dempsey, Trim Pony Race Committee. Tel: (046) 31813/25097.
**Trim Vintage and Veteran Car Rally** Mid-July.

### SPORT
**Angling** Coarse fishing: Royal Canal at Innfield. Contact Trim-Athboy Angling Association.
**Golf** Blackbush Golf Club, 18-hole course. Tel: (01) 250021.
Trim Golf Club, 18-hole course. Tel: (046) 31463.

### INFORMATION
Midlands-East Tourism. Tel: (044) 48650.

## Dunsany Castle

On the southern slopes of the Hill of Tara is one of the oldest continuously inhabited houses in Ireland. A Norman stone fortress, it was built in 1180 to guard the road between Trim and Dublin, where it crosses the River Skane, against the 'savage Irish'. Only the four towers remain of the original castle, which was altered much over the centuries, but it is still a solid and imposing battlemented structure, with neo-Gothic windows. Its owners since the 15th century have been the lords of Dunsany, heads of the Plunkett family who also once owned two other local estates, Killeen and Rathmore.

The castle is still a family home, but is open to the public on 90 days each year. It is a rambling, friendly house, full of treasures and knick-knacks gathered over the centuries. Weapons, posthorns, shields, shooting trophies and Meissen porcelain decorate walls and shelves with an endearing informality. Among the oddities is one of the many manuscripts of the 18th Lord Dunsany (1878-1957), a writer of short stories, poems and plays. The manuscript is written in a book 3ft high with quills from his own specially reared geese. Other intriguing items include 'heart jars', in which the embalmed hearts of knights killed in the Crusades were returned home. The hearts are no longer inside the jars.

A library stretches the length of one of the towers, and on the walls of the large staircase are works of art that include paintings by Opie, Cuyp, Van Dyck, and Jack Butler Yeats.

Just inside the gates of the castle is the crumbling 15th-century church of St Nicholas, open to the sky, its nave overgrown with grass. From the top of the tower on its west side it is possible to see Killeen Castle, once part of the estate of the Plunketts of Dunsany and whose church is thought to have been the model for this one.

The church font, carved around 1445 with elaborate images of the Crucifixion and several apostles, is one of the finest in Ireland. It may have been commissioned by Sir Christopher Plunkett and his wife, Anna Fitzgerald, whose effigies lie on the altar tomb.

Facing the north-east entrance to the castle is part of a carved stone cross thought to date from around 1600. The images on it depict the apostles. Its base may have held holy water, with which travellers could bless themselves.

**Opening times** *May to mid-Aug, Mon-Sat 9am-1pm. Guided tours at 9am, 10am and noon. Tel: (046) 31845.*

DUNSANY CASTLE *Standing in splendid parkland, the sun reflected in its Gothic windows and setting its mellow brickwork aglow, this impressive castle still has four of its original towers.*

### Innfield/An Bóthar Buí

By the bridge in Innfield is a slip road that leads to the Royal Canal, which in turn leads to the heart of Meath. Completed in 1817, the canal runs 100 miles inland, from Dublin to Cloondara, just west of Longford. It was closed in 1957 but is now being restored, and the stretch from Dublin to Mullingar, 20 miles west of Innfield, is in working order. From a small parking area trails a towpath along which walkers can head west for Mullingar. Even a few minutes' stroll between two of the many bridges, through quiet pastures and past hedgerows thick with birds and butterflies, is a pleasure. Mallards, moorhens and the occasional stately heron thrive on the canal, and there is excellent coarse fishing – for tench, bream and perch – to be enjoyed along the canal, which is free.

Innfield – called Enfield when the Midland Great Western Railway Company misspelled the name of the station, and still the local and postal name for the town – also provides a slipway where small boats can be launched onto the canal.

### Summerhill/Cnoc an Línsigh

The attractive village green running down the middle of the main street of Summerhill once formed a gracious approach to a Georgian mansion and a castle. The estate was originally owned by the Lynch family, who built the castle around 1600. Forty years later, they were evicted by Cromwell. In the early 18th century Lynch's Castle was finally abandoned when its then owner, Hercules Rowley, built the mansion, Summerhill House, on the hill-top. The mansion was burnt down in the 1922 civil war. Ambrosio O'Higgins (1730-1801), Viceroy of Peru and father of Bernardo O'Higgins (1778-1842), liberator of Chile, is said to have grown up on the estate.

A public-spirited landlord, Rowley created the village of Summerhill, at the beginning of the avenue of trees that led up to his mansion. The village still exists much in its original form, but the avenue now leads, incongruously, to a bungalow. Lynch's Castle, ruined and unsafe, stands to the left of the avenue on private ground. Visitors should enquire at the bungalow.

### Trim/Baile Átha Troim

Once destined to be the capital of Ireland, Trim is now a small market town. But it is dominated by its medieval ruins and has been designated a 'Heritage Town'. It straddles the

YELLOW STEEPLE *The 14th-century bell tower, standing above fields strewn with medieval ruins, turns a golden colour at sunset.*

TRIM TOMB *Sir Lucas Dillon and his wife lie for ever in stone, divided by the sword of purity.*

Boyne, and takes its name from the Irish for 'ford of the elder tree'. Signs of its past importance are still visible in a mile-long sweep of open land that contains Ireland's largest Anglo-Norman castle and many other ruins, all accessible by car or an easy walk along the banks of the Boyne.

In 1172 Meath's first Norman baron, Hugh de Lacy, founded the castle that was to be the keystone of Norman rule in eastern Ireland. The castle was built on the south bank of the Boyne, towards the edge of the Pale, the perimeter of the English-controlled area. There it guarded the north-west approach to Dublin against invaders.

Damaged by Cromwell's troops in 1649, the castle is now a safe and well-preserved ruin in a sea of grass, on a 3 acre site. At its centre is a 75ft high square keep, built around 1200. A great wall, punctuated by watch-towers, sweeps round the ruins in a gentle curve to the river. Dublin Gate, in the south wall, is the only complete tower and barbican in the country. The wall along the river is now a grassy bank that forms part of a pitch-and-putt course.

Across the river are the ruins of a 13th-century Augustinian abbey, St Mary's, which lies in meadowland grazed by cattle from a nearby farm. A fortified manor house, Talbot's Castle, was built on the site of the abbey; confusingly, it is also known as St Mary's Abbey. Talbot Castle became the diocesan school in the 18th century, and it was there that Arthur Wellesley, later Duke of Wellington, received his early education.

At the top of the slope behind St Mary's looms the gaunt 125ft ruin of a 14th-century bell tower, the Yellow Steeple, so called because of the colour of its stone which at sunset glows a wonderful mellow yellow. It was partially blown up during the Cromwellian siege in 1649 and it now has a rather odd jagged appearance. It was once part of the Augustinian monastery of St Mary. The approach to the tower is along a narrow unmarked lane, but the tower itself is fenced off. Near the tower is Sheep Gate, a small arch that once formed part of the old town wall.

Trim Castle and the Yellow Steeple are at the western end of an open expanse of meadow that runs down either side of the Boyne for a mile. At the eastern end of the meadow, about half a mile towards Newtown Trim, on the northern side of the river, are more ruins. The first are those of the medieval cathedral of St Peter and St Paul, and the remains of a medieval parish church. These well-preserved but broken walls, surrounding neatly gravelled floors, lie in Newtown cemetery, which is still in use and beautifully tended.

The parish church contains a tomb that is the centre of a curious tradition. An Elizabethan tombstone displays the images of Sir Lucas Dillon, who died in 1593, and of his wife, Lady Jane, separated by a sword, a medieval symbol of purity. In the runnels of the bas relief, where rainwater gathers, are dozens of pins, placed there as part of a ritual that supposedly cures warts. Rub a pin on your wart – so local people say – then place the pin in the water, and as the pin rusts, so the wart vanishes.

Immediately to the south of the cathedral is the ruined abbey of the Canons Regular of St Victor, a religious order, built around 1200 by Simon de Rochfort. Only crumbling walls remain of the Victorine abbey, but they are noted for their echo, which can be heard from the road on the other side of the river, particularly at a gate known locally as Echo Gate.

Downstream from the abbey the river is spanned by St Peter's, one of Ireland's oldest stone bridges, thought to date from the 15th century. It is still used by pedestrians and traffic. On its south side the road leads to the ruins of a priory and a medieval hospital.

From this distance, Trim appears as a town of verticals: the castle, the Yellow Steeple, two church spires, and a pillar bearing a statue of Arthur Wellesley, who was the MP for Trim from 1790 to 1795 and was later given the title Duke of Wellington.

*A Tuscan temple, wide flagstones and a water-lily pond, enclosed by box hedges and clipped bay, form a tranquil Roman garden.*

Tucked behind high hedges a quarter of a mile along the road from Trim to Kildalkey lies one of Ireland's finest gardens, the inspired creation of one man, an archaeologist named Jim Reynolds. Butterstream's 2½ acres consist, in fact, of a series of small gardens that run beside the little stream after which the place is named, and were inspired by Vita Sackville-West's garden in Sissinghurst, Kent. Each garden is individual, with its own colours and flowering times, and hidden from the others by hedges. Yet all form part of an overall design linked by paths of grass, slate and gravel.

Plants such as polyanthus and hosta form a 'wild garden'. The rose garden has the finest collection of wild roses in Ireland. A

*The series of different gardens are separated by neatly cut hedges and narrow paths, some with statues or sundials.*

'white' garden with white leaves and blooms is hedged by box, with formal paths surrounding an 18th-century sundial and a Victorian Gothic seat. The Classical garden contains a miniature Tuscan temple created from the owner's archaeological finds. In autumn the foliage garden is a blaze of reds, oranges and yellows.

Butterstream was created over 20 years, a labour of love that involved a constant struggle to find the best plants to suit the damp clay soil and chilly winds. Reynolds uses hardly any machinery, except for a lawn mower and, for thorn hedges, a hedge trimmer. Beech and box, he insists, need sensitive treatment with hand clippers. Access to the gardens is by arrangement with the owner. Tel: (046) 36017.

# THE STONE AGE LANDSCAPE

## The tombs, dolmens and standing stones that dot the Irish countryside

All over Ireland huge rounded forms and massive stones sculpted by the weather of centuries shape the countryside. These are Stone Age tombs, sacred sites and observatories – clear evidence that more than 5000 years ago Ireland was inhabited by a group of people skilled in architecture and astronomy. The most spectacular of these structures is Newgrange in the Boyne valley, older than the pyramids of Egypt, and among the finest of all Europe's Stone Age monuments.

THE PALACE OF THE BOYNE Newgrange, which dates from around 3000 BC, is one of 40 passage-tombs found in the Boyne valley, at a veritable city of the dead called Brúgh na Boínne, 'the palace of the Boyne'. The passage-tombs are so called because the burial chamber is built at the end of a long passage dug into a man-made mound. The passages were lined with huge stones, and covered with a mound of earth, turf sods or stones.

Newgrange received its name in medieval times when the land on which it stands became one of the outlying farms, or 'new granges', of Mellifont Abbey. It was discovered in 1699 by the Welsh antiquary Edward Llwyd.

The grassy mound under which the tomb lies reaches about 300ft across, and is partially ringed with glistening white granite, on a low hill. A great circle of 97 slabs 8-10ft long shores up the outside base of the mound. Beneath the mound is the passage, which is 62ft long, and three chambers, lined with massive standing stones, intricately carved with spirals and zigzags. The huge slabs form a roof that curves inwards to a height of 20ft, and were so perfectly fitted that the roof is still as secure and dry as when the tomb was built. A ring of enormous pillar stones once surrounded the mound; of the original 35, only 12 are left.

This wonder of Stone Age architecture contains a structure that puzzled archaeo-

GATEWAY TO THE UNDERWORLD *The Kildooney More dolmen towers above the high moors of northern Donegal. Its capstone is nearly 14ft long.*

logists for almost 100 years. Above the entrance to the passage that leads to the central chamber is a stone box with a slit some 8in across. In 1969 the site's chief archaeologist, Michael O'Kelly, decided to test his theory that the box had some astronomical significance. At 8.58am on December 21, the shortest day of the year, he recorded, 'the first pencil of direct sunlight shone through the roof-box and right along the passage to reach across the tomb'. For 15 minutes the beam of light passed through the slit in the roof-box and along the passage to

the central chamber, bathing it in a golden glow. So Newgrange was shown to be not just a grave, but also an observatory designed to monitor the turning point of winter.

Ancient Irish folklore says the tomb is the burial place for the High Kings of Tara, but in fact the graves predate Tara by 3000 years. Early Celtic myths call Newgrange the abode of Aengus, the great god of love. However, it is most likely to have been a mausoleum for the select few – a dynasty of kings, perhaps – and may have been looked after by priests.

COURT-TOMBS AND WEDGE-TOMBS Older even than the passage-graves are the court-tombs, which date from around 3500-2500 BC and are found only north of a line that runs from Dundalk Bay, off County Louth, to Galway Bay. Their name comes from the semicircular open space lined with standing stones in front of the tombs. Ceremonies were probably performed in these courtyards before the bodies were cremated and buried. The tombs themselves consist of a long chamber divided into burial compartments, where the ashes of the dead were interred together with pottery

GUARDIAN STONE *The massive entrance stone in front of the tomb at Newgrange is carved with a pattern of spirals and concentric semicircles. The meaning of these symbols is not known.*

SOLAR OBSERVATORY *Sunlight pierces the gloom of Newgrange, whose passage and inner chambers are aligned with the rays of the rising sun of December 21, the winter solstice.*

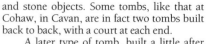

CREEVYKEEL COURT-TOMB *A plan of this tomb in County Sligo shows that it consists of a large open court, behind which is a burial chamber divided into two.*

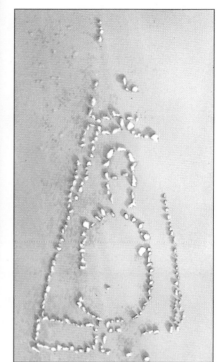

and stone objects. Some tombs, like that at Cohaw, in Cavan, are in fact two tombs built back to back, with a court at each end.

A later type of tomb, built a little after 2000 BC, is the wedge-tomb, which is wider at one end than another. Many of these tombs, once buried under a mound of earth and stones, now lie exposed, looking like nothing more than a jagged heap of rocks. Among them is Labbacallee, in County Cork.

GIANTS' TABLES AND HENGES The most abundant and most obvious Stone Age tombs are the dolmens – groups of three or more huge standing stones topped by one, sometimes two, enormous flat slabs that can each weigh up to 100 tons. The word 'dolmen' means 'stone table' in Breton. Most were built around 2000 BC along Ireland's eastern coast. Long after the people that raised them had gone, the Celts wove them into their legends – Diarmuid and Gráinne, the Irish Romeo and Juliet, allegedly slept on the capstones when they eloped; locals today describe them as giants' graves.

The construction of the dolmens was an extraordinary feat of engineering: the capstones were apparently dragged up a mound of earth built around the standing stones, and then hauled into position. The surrounding mounds have since disappeared. Of more than 1400 in Ireland, among the most impressive are those at Proleek in Louth, and Browneshill and Haroldstown in Carlow.

Stone circles, or henges, also dot the countryside. They can be found together with tombs, but are often solitary – strange stone groups in open fields. Most are from the Bronze Age, from around 1750 BC. They are thought to have been sacred sites, and probably also had some astronomical purpose.

Ireland's tombs and standing stones may be very old but they still have an active part in its culture. Apart from their role as features in the landscape, they are also the inspiration of rich folk tales and legends. Many have been left untouched for centuries because the local people believed they were the home of the fairies and should not be disturbed.

A ROYAL GRAVE *Inside the tomb at Newgrange, 60 standing stones 5-8ft high line the passage and three chambers. The tomb was probably a burial place for kings, whose ashes were placed in large stone bowls in the chambers.*

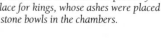

# The Very Navel of Ireland

*In the southern reaches of Offaly, at the country's centre, the fields are luxuriant and green, and the farmland has a prosperous feel to it. The towns, such as Birr, have a genteel air, a legacy of their Georgian past. To the east the countryside is dominated by the beautiful Slieve Bloom Mountains, clear-cut in the crisp, pure country air.*

### Birr/Biorra

Ancient writers called this town 'The Navel of Ireland', or 'Umbilicus Hiberniae', since it is virtually at the geographical centre of the country. This point was once marked by the ancient Seefin stone that stood on the road south to Roscrea, but is now displayed in John's Mall in the town.

Birr was founded in the 6th century at the junction of two rivers, the Little Brosna and the Camcor, by St Brendan of Birr, but its neat and well-planned Georgian layout, which makes it one of Ireland's most attractive towns, is due to the Parsons family. Englishmen from Norfolk, they were granted 1000 acres of the land in 1620, and built the town around their castle.

The castle's builder, Lawrence Parsons, had a reputation as a martinet, laying down severe penalties for seemingly trivial 'crimes'. Townsfolk could be banished for lighting fires except in stone chimneys, and women caught serving beer might be 'sett in the stocks by the constable for three whole markett dayes'. To his credit, however, he helped the locals by establishing a glass factory, and started a weekly market, which boosted Birr's commercial prosperity.

Birr's spacious and elegant tree-lined streets, solid architecture and imposing squares can still be seen. In the centre of the town is Emmet's Square, edged with some of the best of Birr's buildings, which owe their existence to the 2nd Earl of Rosse, a member of the Parsons family. Among them is Dooley's Hotel, an old coaching inn, built in 1747. It was set on fire in 1809 by members of the Galway Hunt who were celebrating there and let their enthusiasm run away with them – an act which earned them their nickname of the 'Galway Blazers'. The tall column in the middle of the square once carried a statue of the Duke of Cumberland, known as 'Butcher' Cumberland, whose English forces defeated the Highlanders at Culloden in Scotland on April 16, 1746, thus ending the Jacobite uprising of 1745. The statue, which may have been put there as a warning to Irish Catholics, became unsafe and was taken down in 1925.

DRIVING TRIALS *A driver and groom race a gig through water at the competition held at Birr Castle.*

West of Emmet's Square, in John's Mall, are some fine Georgian houses with delicate fanlights and heavily panelled doors. A monument to the astronomer William Parsons, the 3rd Earl of Rosse, stands in John's Place. A curiosity of the town is 'Crotty's Church', in Castle Street, which marks the only schism in the Irish Catholic Church. In trouble with the law after a minor offence, Father Crotty and the local parish priest argued about his return to the parish. Crotty defied him and returned to Birr as an independent priest and led the Birr Reformation, conducting his services in English instead of Latin, rejecting 'servility to popish domination' and denouncing the doctrine of purgatory by which people paid to save their souls, as 'an invention of clerical avarice, a pious fraud to draw money from the pockets of people'. By 1832 he was excommunicated and was hounded out of Ireland by the law and religious opposition and eventually died in an asylum in Belgium.

From Oxmantown Bridge, over the River Camcor, a tree-shaded riverside walk gives fine views of the town and leads to the 1817 St Brendan's Church, with its glorious stained-glass windows, and the Convent of Mercy, designed by Pugin. There is also good fishing for brown trout in the river.

### Birr Castle and Demesne

Sir Lawrence Parsons, whose family was later ennobled as the Earls of Rosse, built this massive castle in the 1620s on the site of the Offaly stronghold of the O'Carrolls, the local clan described as 'a hospitable, fierce, yellow-haired race'. The Earls of Rosse live there to this day. A fire badly damaged the castle in 1823 and soon afterwards it was rebuilt, largely in Gothic Revival style.

Birr Castle's superb ornamental gardens, spread over 100 acres, are planted with flowering magnolias, cherry and crab-apple trees, hornbeam alleys and 34ft high box hedges, claimed to be the tallest in the world. The remains of the 3rd Earl of Rosse's giant telescope, built in the mid-19th century, can be seen in the grounds. The castle is not open to the public, though the grounds can be visited all the year.
**Birr Castle Gardens** *9am-6pm. Tel: (0509) 20056.*

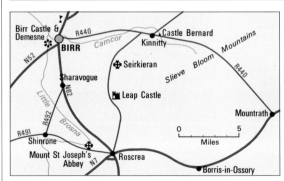

**OTHER PLACES TO SEE**
**Leap Castle** Ivy-clad ruin that guards the valley between the provinces of Munster and Leinster and was once the main fortress of the O'Carrolls. Nearby are ring-forts.

**Seirkieran** 2m N of Leap Castle. Traces of a monastery founded in the 5th century by St Ciaran the Elder, as well as the base of a High Cross, and many sculpted stone fragments.

**EVENTS**
**Birr Vintage Week** Aug.
**Horse Driving Trials** Aug/Sept. Tel: (045) 83618.

**SPORT**
**Orienteering** Outdoor Pursuit Centre, Birr.

**INFORMATION**
Midlands-East Tourism. Tel: (044) 48650.

BIRR CASTLE AND GARDENS *A long drive sweeps up to the stately home of the Earls of Rosse, past colourful and rare flowering shrubs.*

## *Kinnitty/Cionn Eitigh*

Set against the green backdrop of the serene Slieve Bloom Mountains is the tiny village of Kinnitty, laid out in the late 18th century. Inside its Church of Ireland church is an early Christian grave slab. At nearby Castle Bernard, built in Tudor Revival style in the early 19th century, the shaft of a 9th-century (or even earlier) High Cross from the monastery of St Finan Cam has been set up.

## *Mount St Joseph's Abbey*

Mount St Joseph's, Roscrea, is the home of present-day Cistercian monks who carry on their way of life just as their predecessors did centuries ago. The abbey was founded in 1878, and its 40 monks lead strict, austere lives. They run a dairy farm, a guesthouse and a boys' boarding school that has the

ST CIARAN'S BUSH *A hawthorn named after the saint divides the road from Birr to Kinnitty.*

distinction of producing more members of the Irish Parliament than any other.

Visitors are welcome to stay in the guesthouse for a few days of peace and contemplation, or to take part in the simple services of prayer that are held in the abbey. No questions are asked of visitors, but the monks are always ready to discuss problems or their own way of life. Tel: (0505) 21711.

---

### PEERING INTO SPACE

What was once the largest telescope in the world is now a blind eye, but still pointed at the heavens, in the grounds of Birr Castle. The giant 72in reflecting telescope was constructed in 1845 by William Parsons (1800-67), the 3rd Earl of Rosse, and for 75 years remained the largest ever built. It enabled the earl to see more than 10 million light years into space – much farther than any previous astronomer – and revealed the spiral structure of nebulae, bodies of rarified gas and dust in interstellar spaces of galaxies, of which he made meticulous and detailed drawings.

William's son Lawrence, the 4th earl (1840-1908), became the first man to measure the heat of the Moon. And another son, Sir Charles Parsons (1854-1931), built the compound steam turbine that drove battleships such as the *Dreadnought*.

*The 3rd Earl of Rosse and family with his 72in telescope.*

# Meadows and Monasteries

*First settled almost 9000 years ago, west Offaly is rich in prehistoric treasures. The people who left them probably came up the River Shannon, the longest river in Ireland, which bounds the western edge of Offaly and cuts a giant swathe through a green patchwork of meadowland on either side. Beside it are the evocative remains of one of the largest monasteries founded in Ireland, with an equally poetic name – Clonmacnoise, 'the meadow of the son of Nos'.*

### Banagher/Beannchar

The pace of life in this charming, quiet town on the River Shannon seems dictated by the slow flow of the river. Banagher consists of a long street of tidy late-Georgian houses running right up to the river, where a sweeping bridge links Offaly with Galway. The bridge is fortified on the west side by a Martello tower, a small circular fort built against possible invasion by the French in the Napoleonic Wars. The most appealing of Banagher's buildings is Crank House, with its bowfronted doorway, curving fanlights and pediment. It is now the local tourist office.

The novelist Charlotte Brontë (1816-55) and her husband, the curate Arthur Ben Nicholls, honeymooned here in 1854, in Cuba Court. The house now lies in decaying ruins. Another literary figure to stay here was Anthony Trollope (1815-82). In 1841 he was appointed Post Office Surveyor at Banagher, where he developed a taste for hunting, bought a hunter, and began to write the novels that made him famous.

### Blackwater/An Abhainn Dubh

At Blackwater the Irish Peat Board, Bord na Móna, has provided an excellent and safe way of getting a close look at the boglands of Offaly, in the form of The New Bog Road, the second largest railway system in Ireland. Travelling between Blackwater and Clonmacnoise on part of the Bord's 800 miles of rail track, visitors can listen to a running commentary provided by a tour guide. Small lakes, pools and little springs break up the hummocks of sphagnum moss speckled with bright red cranberry and bog rosemary, the County Offaly flower. Dragonflies hover and dart over cotton grass, sedge and heather, home to golden plovers and snipes, among other birds.
**Bord na Móna** *Tel: (0905) 74114.*

### Clara/Clòirtheach

This pretty little village surrounded by boglands was originally a Quaker settlement, and is now a thriving commercial centre. Its Protestant church was built about 1770.

Clara Bog, a mile to the south on the road to Rahan, is run as a nature reserve by the Irish Wildlife Service. The bog, which formed about 10,000 years ago, is a layer of moss peat, which reaches a depth of over 20ft. It is rich in insect-eating plants such as sundews, pitcher plants and bladderworts, and many species of moss. It teems with wildlife such as Irish hares, foxes and lizards, as well as thousands of spiders, butterflies, moths, dragonflies and frogs, all a rich source of food to the birds that live here, among them grouse, snipe, merlins, kestrels and skylarks.

Walkers should wear wellingtons or sturdy footwear, bring protective clothing, and keep to the two gravel tracks that lead to the bog, avoiding its pools and marshy areas.

### Clonmacnoise/Cluain Mic Nois

If there is anywhere in Ireland suited to contemplation and pondering the meaning of life, it is surely here, at this ancient monastic site beside the Shannon. A monastery was founded here in AD 545 by St Ciaran on a fertile meadow, or *cluain*, surrounded by bog. It could be reached only by river or along the esker ridge known as the Pilgrims' Road. The monastery flourished for 600 years as a centre of learning and religious instruction, as well as providing much of Ireland's finest Celtic art and illuminated manuscripts. The earliest-known manuscript in the Irish language, *Lebor na hUidre* ('The Book of the Dun Cow', so called after a cow that belonged to St

some 9000 years old have been found at nearby Boora Bog.
**Garry Castle** 1m S of Banagher, a tower house and 18th-century farmhouse with a sheela-na-gig, a female figure, 32ft high on the wall.
**Kilcormac** Formerly called Frankfurt or Frankford, contains a ruined Carmelite priory, which in the 14th century produced an illuminated missal now in Trinity Library, Dublin.

### EVENTS
**Feast of St Ciaran**
Clonmacnoise, Sept 9.

### SPORT
**Angling** Trout fishing: River Shannon, beside Banagher, and River Brosna.
**Boating** River Shannon.

### INFORMATION
Midlands-East Tourism.
Tel: (044) 48650.

### OTHER PLACES TO SEE
**Boher** The 12th-century shrine of St Manchan, a bronze and yew box containing the saint's relics.
**Cloghan Castle** 3½m SW of Banagher, a 15th-century tower house with 19th-century additions.
**Clonony Castle** Ruined 16th-century tower house used in the 17th century by a German, Mathew de Renzi, as a base for an unsuccessful attempt to colonise this part of Offaly.
**Gallen Priory** ½m S of Ferbane, site of a 5th-century priory, with collection of 8th to 11th-century grave slabs preserved in the modern priory. Stone Age weapons

St Manchan's Shrine *Long figures and a cross, worked in bronze, adorn the saint's reliquary.*

ANGEL'S VIEW *Clonmacnoise monastery, its well-preserved ruins and layout seen from the air, was once one of the greatest ecclesiastical centres of Europe.*

Ciaran), was written here in about the 11th century, and today forms part of the design of an Irish £1 note. Clonmacnoise was also the burial place of the kings of Connaught and of Tara. The last High King of Ireland, Rory O'Conor, was buried here in 1198.

The monastery survived numerous attacks from warring clans, Vikings and Normans, until 1552, when it was destroyed by the English. The ruins are the most extensive of their kind in Ireland, consisting of a cathedral, eight churches, two Round Towers, three High Crosses, 200 grave slabs and a 13th-century castle. The Nuns' Church, a 12th-century Irish-Romanesque building, was a simple church with only a nave and chancel. The chancel arch is beautifully carved with geometrical patterns, in three orders. The church was built in 1167 by Dervorgilla, the wife of a Breifne chieftain, whose abduction by Dermot MacMurrough, King of Leinster, ultimately resulted in the Anglo-Norman invasion of Ireland.

The grave slabs, which date from the 8th to the 12th century, are the largest and most significant collection in Ireland, and are inscribed with crosses and memorial prayers in Irish. They are now in the Visitor Centre, protected from souvenir hunters.

Among the most fascinating of the remains is the 1000-year-old Cross of the Scriptures, depicting episodes from the life of Christ. It was put up in the 9th or 10th century and bears an inscription which reads: 'A prayer for Colman who made this cross for King Flann.'

The Crozier of Clonmacnoise, a gold handle inlaid with interlaced patterns in silver and decorated with animals, which protected the wooden staff of a saint, is one of the best preserved in Ireland, and is now in the National Museum of Ireland in Dublin.

From the graveyard the road leads to Clonfinlough church and a huge recumbent, or fallen, stone 9ft 9in by 8ft 3in, engraved with Bronze Age motifs.

Just west of the site near the car park is the so-called Bishop's Castle, built in 1220 by the Normans who had attacked and plundered Clonmacnoise and the surrounding

CROSS OF THE SCRIPTURES *Apart from the usual Biblical scenes depicted on High Crosses, this one shows King Dermot helping St Ciaran erect the first corner post of Clonmacnoise monastery, in the bottom panel on the shaft.*

countryside. It was destroyed in the 17th century to render it useless as a stronghold and now only its courtyard can be seen, as well as a small square tower that leans towards the moat.

## Shannonbridge/Droichead na Sionainne

This comfortable townscape of one and two-storey houses and shops is dominated by a massive peat-fired power station, from which files of colossal pylons stride out across the boglands.

Only slightly less imposing are the huge artillery fortifications, built in Napoleonic times to guard the bridge over the river, from which Shannonbridge gets its name. The river here is one of the best angling spots on the Shannon, known for the large size of its bream and rudd.

THE LIFE OF ST CIARAN

St Ciaran, the founder of Clonmacnoise, was born in the western province of Connaught in AD 512, the son of a journeyman cartwright and chariot-builder. He was educated at the monastic school of Clonard in Meath, which was founded in about 530 by St Finian, and soon became renowned for his religious way of life and good works.

Ciaran established his first monastery on Hare Island, in Lough Ree, County Westmeath, but after a few years resigned as abbot and set off downriver for the isolation of Clonmacnoise. He died in 545, aged 33, only seven months after the first huts were built there. Despite his short life, St Ciaran's influence spread across Ireland into Britain, and eventually extended across Europe as far as Bavaria.

# Treasures of the Bog

*Eastern Offaly is a modest place whose main feature – a cloak of 'brown gold', or bog turf – discreetly envelops the whole landscape. Formed over the past 8000 years, with a layer of peat over 30ft deep in many places, it teems with fascinating plant and animal life. This is also Fir Cell country, of the 'man of the church', so-called because it was once thick with monasteries, the remains of which rise in jagged heaps above the flat landscape.*

### Charleville Castle

The finest Gothic Revival building in Ireland stands surrounded by a forest of broad-leaved trees. The turreted and ivy-clad mansion was built in 1800-12 by the Irish architect Francis Johnston, for Charles William Bury, a wealthy landowner who became Lord Tullamoore, and eventually Earl of Charleville. His intention was 'to exhibit specimens of Gothic architecture, as collected from cathedrals and chapel-tombs, and to show how they may be applied to chimneypieces, ceilings, windows, balustrades, etc. In 1798 he bought 'tuppenny' etchings of Gothic and neo-Gothic buildings and used them to model his castle on. For example, the fan-vaulted ceiling in the ballroom is from Strawberry Hill, a Gothic Revival mansion built in the mid-18th century in Twickenham, Middlesex, and the fireplace in the dining room is a replica of the west door of Magdalen College Chapel in Oxford. The castle has 55 rooms, including a superb gallery that runs the whole width of the building.

The earl and his wife, Lady Charleville, scandalised the literary world of their time when in 1796 they translated into English a lampooning poem on Joan of Arc, *La Pucelle*, by the French satirist Voltaire.

> *Her bubbies round as bowl, and firm as rock*
> *In russet beauty swell'd above her smock.*
> *With vigorous address she trod the land,*
> *And with a delicate, tho' nervous hand,*
> *Now carried burdens, and now pour'd out wine*
> *And serv'd the rustic Squire or sleek Divine.*

Visitors are welcome to look around Charleville, by arrangement. Tel: (0506) 21279.

### Daingean/An Daingean

Unlikely as it may seem today, this little town, formerly the seat of the O'Conors, chiefs of Offaly, was once Offaly's county town. Offaly was one of the first counties to be 'planted' – colonised with English settlers – in the 1550s, during the reign of Mary Tudor. In honour of her husband, Philip II of Spain, Offaly was called King's County, and Daingean was named Philipstown. But despite its colonisation, Daingean's remote situation in the middle of vast boglands did little to help it to flourish as a commercial centre, and in the 1830s it lost its status as the county town to Tullamore.

The name Daingean is Irish for 'castle' – the French word *'donjon'* is similar – and derives from a 16th-century fortress that once stood there, but of which nothing is left now. The town's classical Georgian courthouse was designed in 1810 by James Gandon, architect of many buildings, including the King's Inns, the Four Courts and the Custom House in Dublin.

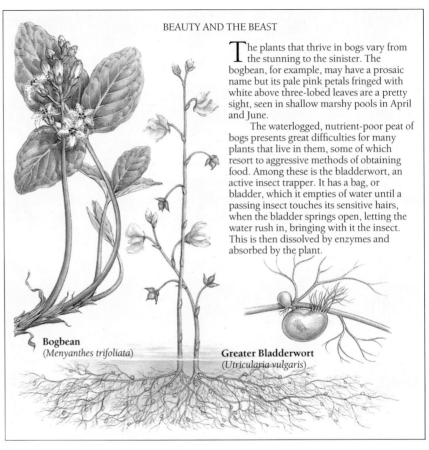

BEAUTY AND THE BEAST

The plants that thrive in bogs vary from the stunning to the sinister. The bogbean, for example, may have a prosaic name but its pale pink petals fringed with white above three-lobed leaves are a pretty sight, seen in shallow marshy pools in April and June.

The waterlogged, nutrient-poor peat of bogs presents great difficulties for many plants that live in them, some of which resort to aggressive methods of obtaining food. Among these is the bladderwort, an active insect trapper. It has a bag, or bladder, which it empties of water until a passing insect touches its sensitive hairs, when the bladder springs open, letting the water rush in, bringing with it the insect. This is then dissolved by enzymes and absorbed by the plant.

**Bogbean** (*Menyanthes trifoliata*)

**Greater Bladderwort** (*Utricularia vulgaris*)

### Durrow Abbey

Little is left of this once-great abbey, founded in 553 by St Columba, or Colmcille. The Venerable Bede called it 'a noble monastery known as Dearmach, the Field of Oaks, because of the oak forest in which it stands'. Though it was plundered and burnt several times during the Dark Ages, its 9th or 10th-century High Cross survives, as do a number of early tombstones and a well. The cross is carved with scenes from the Bible, now weathered and indistinct, including the Sacrifice of Isaac, the Crucifixion, and soldiers guarding the tomb of Christ. Durrow is the source of the 7th-century illuminated manuscript, the *Book of Durrow*, now in the Library of Trinity College, Dublin.

In 1186 the Anglo-Norman lord of Meath, Hugh de Lacy, was killed here by a workman. De Lacy was overseeing the final

**OTHER PLACES TO SEE**

**Blackwood Forest** 4m SW of Tullamore, secluded forest ideal for walking and picnicking.

**Croghan Hill** The top of an extinct volcano 769ft high and the site of Bronze Age burials, with views over Offaly and the surrounding counties.

**Geashill** Village on a plain that was once a granary of Gaelic tribes; said to have oldest Anglo-Norman motte in Ireland.

**Rhode** 4m E of Croghan Hill, tiny village with little church and various enterprises dealing with peat and peat products.

**SPORT**

**Angling** Coarse fishing: Grand Canal. Trout fishing: River Boyne at Edenderry.

**Boating** Grand Canal.

**Golf** Edenderry Golf Club, 9-hole course.
Tel: (0405) 31072.
Tullamore Golf Club, 18-hole course. Tel: (0506) 21439.

**INFORMATION**

Midlands-East Tourism.
Tel: (044) 48650.

GOTHIC CONFECTION *Romantic Charleville Castle is well placed in this lyrical landscape.*

demolition of Durrow Abbey, on the site of which he planned to build a castle, and the workman, outraged at such profanity, struck his head off with an axe.

### Edenderry/Eadan Dóire

This spacious Georgian town, with a long, straggling main street lined with neat houses and shops, marks the westward limits of the Pale, the region centred on Dublin that was under direct English rule, and which gave us the expression 'beyond the pale'. Still to be seen dotted around the area are the crumbling walls of border castles, such as Blundell's Castle, on a hilltop just off the main street.

Edenderry was largely built by Lord Downshire, who inherited it late in the 18th century. It was formerly an important trading centre on the Grand Canal that linked Dublin to the Shannon, and is today a busy market town. The canal is popular among anglers.

The town is also the gateway to the Bog of Allen, the largest area of bog in Ireland, which stretches in every direction as far as the eye can see. It is the centre of the thriving peat industry, and the source of much of the region's prosperity.

### Tullamore/Tulach Mhór

This is the only town in Ireland that owes a major part of its development to a peacetime explosion. In 1785 a hot-air balloon flying over the town fell to the ground and exploded in the centre of the town, destroying 100 houses (but sparing the pub). The present town centre owes much to the rebuilding and restoring scheme that followed. Among the fine buildings that were saved is a bow-fronted house dating from 1750 and the old market house built in the late 1780s.

Tulach Mhór means 'Great Assembly Hill', but also became Tullamoore after the Moore family who owned it in the 18th century. The Grand Canal from Dublin reached the town in 1798, greatly increasing its prosperity, and Tullamore became a centre for brewing, flour-milling and distilling. The seductive Irish Mist liqueur is made in the town – visitors can see it being made at the Irish Mist Liqueur Company, Bury Quay, where the liqueur can also be sampled free.

Tullamore has been the county town of Offaly since 1833, and has more than its fair share of interesting buildings. One of the finest is St Catherine's, a Gothic Revival church of 1818 designed by Francis Johnston, the architect of Charleville Castle.

Among the treasures in the Library of Trinity College, Dublin, is an exquisitely illuminated manuscript of the Gospels known as the *Book of Durrow*. It is said to have been written at Durrow Abbey in about AD 675, although some scholars say it may have been created in Iona or Northumbria. It is one of the earliest manuscripts to cover a whole page with ornament, called a 'carpet' page. The manuscript disappeared in the 16th century, when the monastery was dissolved, but was found a century later and given to Trinity College. Its survival in the intervening period is a miracle, because during that time it belonged to a local farmer who used to pour water onto it to cure his cattle.

# The Capital of the Midlands

*The historic town of Athlone, spanning the River Shannon, has for centuries been the vital link between east and west Ireland. To the east of this magnetic centre is a countryside pervaded by a sense of timelessness, where aromatic hedge-lined lanes lead to almost-hidden villages. To the north is country made famous by writer Oliver Goldsmith, and to the west Lough Ree, whose secluded shores offer many a quiet bit of fishing and stretches for messing about in boats.*

### Athlone/Baile Átha Luain

Guardian of the main Shannon crossing since the 12th century, and the link between east and west Ireland, this historic town is now a compact commercial centre and the capital of the midlands. Its focal point is the castle, a squat 13th-century Anglo-Norman building which was severely damaged in 1690-1, when the Irish withstood the advance of William of Orange's Protestant forces. The Williamites bombarded the castle massively, and after a siege that lasted a week the Irish surrendered.

The remains of the castle keep now contain a folk museum with a wide-ranging collection of objects: early Christian grave slabs, the locks of the town's ancient gates, devices for filling cartridges, gear for rope-making, old razors, even the gramophone that belonged to one of the most glorious tenors of this century, John McCormack (1884-1945). The house where he was born, in the Bawn off Mardyke Street, is marked with a bronze plaque, and there is a bronze bust of the singer in Dean's Grange cemetery in Dublin, where he was buried.

Opposite the castle is the 1937 Catholic church of St Peter and St Paul, whose two spires and Italianate dome can be seen from most parts of the town. It has a neo-

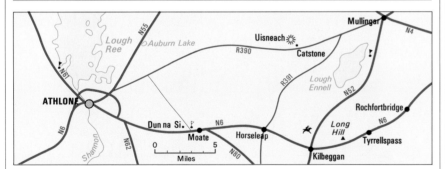

CHURCH OF ST PETER AND ST PAUL *Twin spires are reflected in the Shannon's waters.*

Renaissance interior and vivid modern stained-glass windows, most of which were designed by the studios of Harry Clarke, one of Ireland's most successful stained-glass designers.

Downriver, the Shannon's grassy banks support thousands of water birds, including swans and wigeon.
**Castle Folk Museum** *Mar-Nov, 10am-7pm or by appointment. Tel: (0902) 94630.*

### Kilbeggan/Cill Bheagáin

St Becan founded a monastic settlement here in the 7th century, but the village is now known for its distillery. Built in 1757, Locke's distillery operated until it was abandoned in 1954. Recently revived as a showpiece of the whiskey-distilling process, it is one of the world's oldest licensed distilleries, producing a small quantity of Irish triple-distilled whiskey. The process is visible through glass

## OTHER PLACES TO SEE

**Horseleap** Near border with Offaly, village with restored drawbridge over which Hugh de Lacy is said to have leaped, when fleeing angry villagers.
**Lough Ree** A broad, reedy lake speckled with islands. The grassy shoreline gives easy access to the water, and the woodland offers interesting walks.

## EVENTS

**Kilbeggan Horse Races** Three times yearly: late May, late June and mid-Aug.
**Lough Ree Yacht Club Annual Regatta** Athlone, early Aug.
**Shannon Boat Rally** Athlone, end July.

## SPORT

**Angling** Coarse fishing:

Auburn Lake, Lough Ree and the River Shannon. Trout fishing: Lough Ree.
**Boating** Lough Ree Yacht Club. Tel: (0902) 75976.
**Golf** Moate Golf Club, 9-hole course. Tel: (0902) 81271.
**Waterskiing** Lough Ree.

## INFORMATION

Athlone Tourist Information Office. Tel: (0902) 94630.

screens from walkways where the soft splashing of a water wheel can be heard filtering through the cavernous 18th-century interior. The distillery is powered by an 1878 steam engine to supplement the water wheel. Visitors can see the huge vats, or mashtons, in which the grain mash is stirred by rotating arms and levers, and the cooperage where wooden barrels are checked and repaired. There is also a restaurant and craft shop, and an antique shop that doubles as a museum of local artefacts.

**Distillery** *Mon-Sat 10am-6pm; Sun 2-6pm. Tel. (0506) 32115/32154/32183.*

## Long Hill

Jutting out from the surrounding landscape is a tree-crowned ridge 370ft high which is an esker – a deposit of sand and gravel left when an Ice Age glacier melted away, dumping its stony contents as a mile-long rib of blue-grey stones. Eskers provided Ireland's first inhabitants with important high roads between the boggy lowlands.

Long Hill is an ecological rarity because its ancient woodland crown of hazel, hawthorn and ash is still intact. Access is not easy, so finding a way up requires agility.

## Moate/An Móta

This cattle-market town was founded by Quakers at the end of the 17th century and named after the motte that rears up behind the main street. Its oldest building is a 16th-century castle, now a private home. Next to the castle is a Quaker cemetery. Folk festivals and musical evenings are held regularly in the town's bars.

A mile from Moate is a thriving cultural heritage centre, Dún na Sí – 'the Fort of Fairies'. The 5 acre site doubles as the headquarters of a travelling folklore group that performs song, dance and mime internationally, and as a school for students of Irish music, language and folk traditions. There is also a mock-up of an early Christian village, complete with thatched round houses, domestic tableaux and a display of agricultural tools. The centre also houses a genealogical research unit for Westmeath, where people whose ancestors came from the area can trace their family tree from the computerised records of the county's parishes.

**Moate Historical Society Museum** *June-Aug, 2-5pm. Tel: (0902) 81209.*

**Dún na Sí Arts and Cultural Centre** *Tel: (0902) 81260/81183.*

TYRRELLSPASS *The semicircular green with its neat cottages gives the village a quiet elegance.*

VILLAGE SCENE *Farmers share a joke by a traditional cottage bright with pots of geraniums.*

## Tyrrellspass/Bealach an Tirialaigh

A strategic pass through the bogs to the north of the village was the scene of a massacre in 1597, when Captain Richard Tyrrell and a small Irish force ambushed a large Elizabethan army and annihilated it. The Anglo-Norman Tyrrells settled here in about 1180. Their 15th-century castle, whose squat tower once guarded the western edge of the settlement, is now a private home.

## Uisneach

In pre-Christian times, on Beltane, the first day of May and of summer, clans would gather on this hilltop site to dispense justice, exchange goods, share entertainment and compete in sports. Now, all that remains of the hill-fort is a few scattered stones and grassy undulations in a thistly meadow.

The site is signposted, and from the highest point of Uisneach (620ft), pronounced 'Ushna', the astounding view stretches south to the Wicklow Mountains, 90 miles away.

Down the main road another signpost points over a stile to the Catstone, so called because it resembles a cat looming over a mouse. It is thought to have been deposited by a glacier. Once known as 'The Stone of the Divisions', tradition claims that it was where the borders of Ireland's five ancient kingdoms were established – Meath was the fifth, then considered to be a province.

### WESTMEATH'S CARUSO

Born in 1884 in the midland town of Athlone, from humble origins, John McCormack made his opera debut in Italy when he was only 22. The following year he arrived in triumph at Covent Garden, performing the role of Turiddu in *Cavalleria Rusticana*. His beautiful tenor voice was soon recognised internationally, and in 1909 he was asked to sing at the Manhattan Opera, performing Alfredo in *La Traviata*. Soon, with his extrovert personality and extraordinary voice, he built a following of millions and made a fortune. He became America's foremost tenor after the death of the great Caruso, and performed with other opera greats, such as Tetrazzini and Melba, as well as popular performers like Bing Crosby. He finally returned home to Ireland to indulge his passion for horse racing.

McCormack received the greatest of his many honours in 1928 when he was made a Papal Count for his services to the Roman Catholic Church and to Catholic charities. The accolade was all the rarer for being made hereditary. And just four years later, John McCormack performed to his biggest audience ever, when over a million people gathered in Dublin's Phoenix Park for the Eucharistic Congress. He died in 1945.

# Lakes Shrouded in Legend

*Steep hillsides rise to glorious hilltop views and fall sharply to boggy flats, home of bog cotton and geese. This is cattle-raising country, and the rich pastureland is studded with romantic ruins, sturdy castles and loughs shrouded in legend. Lough Derravaragh is said to have been the haunt of the Children of Lir, who were changed into swans by a jealous stepmother, and spent 300 years on the lough's dark waters before being turned back into people by a holy man.*

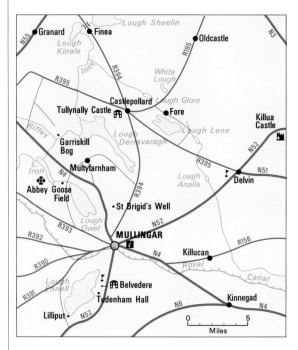

house, now used as a study centre.
**Lough Derravaragh** Lake associated with the legend of the Children of Lir.
**Lough Lene** Good bathing, fishing and walks.
**St Brigid's Well** Ancient spring, traditionally associated with St Brigid. A path of stones representing the Stations of the Cross leads to a small stone beehive chapel.

## EVENTS
**Mullingar Agricultural Show** Cullion, end July.
**Mullingar Festival** Mid-July.
**Pike-fishing Competition** Lough Owel, June.
**Royal Canal Boat Rallies** End May-Aug. Tel: (01) 387230.
**Trout-fishing Competitions,** Lough Owel, Apr, Aug and Sept.

## SPORT
**Angling** Coarse fishing: Loughs Analla, Derravaragh, Iron and Owel, River Inny, Royal Canal. Trout fishing: Loughs Derravaragh, Ennell, Glore, Lene, Owel, Sheelin and White.
**Golf** Clonyn Golf Club, 18-hole course. Tel: (044) 64171.
Belvedere Golf Club, 18-hole course. Tel: (044) 48366.

## INFORMATION
Midlands-East Tourism.
Tel: (044) 48650.

## OTHER PLACES TO SEE
**Delvin** Subject of *Valley of the Squinting Windows*, 1918, by Brinsley MacNamara. Villagers, outraged by seeing themselves thinly disguised, burnt the book in the village square.
**Killua Castle** Ruins of late 18th-century house, once the seat of the Chapman family. Thomas Robert Chapman sired a number of illegitimate children, among them T.E.

Lawrence (1888-1935) who was renowned as Lawrence of Arabia.
**Killucan** Pretty village near Royal Canal with locks, bridges and canal-side walks. 18th-century wayside crosses.
**Lilliput** Park once owned by Boyd Rochforts, admirers of Swift, and named after the tiny people in his *Gulliver's Travels*. Boating, picnic spots, fishing, sports area, adventure playground and historic

## Belvedere
Commanding a magnificent view from a hilltop above Lough Ennell is a beautifully proportioned 18th-century house. It was built in 1740 for Robert Rochfort, Lord Belfield, later first Earl of Belvedere. Its interiors have rococo plasterwork ceilings which are among the finest of their kind in Ireland. Belvedere's immaculate gardens fall away to formal terraces overlooking the lough. There is a Gothic folly known as The Jealous Wall, built by Rochfort to hide the sight of his wealthier brother's residence at nearby Tudenham Hall, and a walled garden with a fine collection of roses and hydrangeas. The estate also has a 2 mile walk through woods of oak, beech and ash.
**Opening times** *Apr-Sept. Tel: (044) 40861.*

## Finea/Fiodh an Átha
The bridge at Finea (pronounced Finnay), was made famous in 1646 when Myles 'The Slasher' O'Reilly and a group of 100 men held off a Cromwellian force of combined Scottish and Irish troops numbering 1000. After a battle that lasted all day, O'Reilly was attacked by a gigantic Scotsman who thrust the point of his sword through O'Reilly's cheek. Closing his jaw on the blade O'Reilly held it as if in a vice, and slew the Scotsman, cutting him through his steel helmet down to his chin with one blow. A cross on Main Street commemorates his heroism.

Finea is a pretty village leading down to an old stone bridge flanked by two slip roads to the River Inny. At each side, boats are for hire. The boats on the right can be rowed upriver to Lough Sheelin, while those on the left can be taken downriver as far as Lough Kinale.

IRELAND'S HORATIO *'Slasher' O'Reilly defended Finea bridge against Cromwell's troops.*

## Fore/Baile Fhobhair
In a valley between two ranges of hills lie ancient Christian ruins adjoining the 'town of the spring', named after St Fechin's Spring which bubbles up beside the ancient church. Around 630 St Fechin founded a monastery there, which had grown into a large community of 300 monks by the time he died of the 'yellow plague' in about 665. Between 771 and 1169 Fore was burnt 12 times. St Fechin's Church, a roofless nave and chancel with walls almost 3ft thick, was built in two periods – the nave perhaps in the 11th century, and the chancel in the early 13th century. Local opinion, however, believes that the church goes back to the time of St Fechin, and legend claims that the huge lintel above its west doorway, which shows a Greek cross within a circle, was magically placed there by St Fechin himself on the strength of his prayers, a feat known as one of the 'seven wonders of Fore'.

In the 13th century the de Lacys, Norman landlords, built a Benedictine priory in the valley nearby. Some of the buildings that remain are from the 15th century and have been restored throughout this century, making Fore Abbey the largest group of Benedictine remains in Ireland. Its 13th-century church still has some decoration and graceful arcaded cloisters. Attached to the church are the broken walls of two towers, where the monks once lived.

On the hillside above the old church of St Fechin is a diminutive chapel, the Anchorite's Church, an extension of a cell once occupied by a hermit, or anchorite. The 8ft by 12ft cell in the chapel's tower was used by hermits until the 17th century. The last hermit in Ireland lived there until 1616, a man called Patrick Beglan who is commemorated on a stone tablet in the cell. The chapel is kept locked, and the key can be obtained from the Seven Wonders pub which stands nearby.

## Garriskill Bog
It takes 15 years for all traces of a footprint to be eradicated from a raised bog such as Garriskill, one of half a dozen almost undisturbed and protected raised bogs in Ireland.

The bog, half a mile across, is bounded by a railway and the Rivers Inny and Riffey. A walk crosses the railway to the borders of the bog and leads to a quiet wilderness with a raw beauty. Above the surface dance hosts of white bob-tailed stems of bog cotton, whose mineral-rich roots are a prime source of food for the white-fronted geese, or 'bog geese', that winter here. But this world is potentially treacherous. Garriskill, like all bogs, is a combination of semi-decayed plants and water where sumps of viscous, mossy water can form, in which a struggling person can sink. (To escape, do not try to stand upright. Sink down into the mud and swim.) For this reason, visitors are advised not to walk on the bog alone.

## Mullingar/An Muileann gCearr

The Royal Canal loops round Mullingar, Westmeath's busy county town, almost encircling it. The towpath makes an attractive walk round the largely 19th-century town, where an important cattle and sheep market is held on Tuesdays. Mullingar is dominated by the 140ft high twin towers of its 1939 Catholic cathedral, which contains post-war mosaics by the Russian-born artist Boris Anrep (1883-1969). They show Mary being presented to the Temple, and St Patrick lighting the Easter fire on the Hill of Slane in Meath, in AD 433. The cathedral has an ecclesiastical museum, whose prize possessions are the 17th-century vestments of St Oliver Plunkett, Bishop of Armagh, hanged for treason in 1681 and canonised in 1975, a collection of penal crosses, made by Catholics to preserve their faith during their persecution in the 17th and 18th centuries, and models of the cathedral, one of which is made with matches – 68,750 in all. Museum visits are by arrangement only.
**Church museum** *Tel: (044) 48338.*

## Multyfarnham/Muilte Farannáin

At the edge of the small village stands a 700-year-old Franciscan friary whose grounds include quarters for eight priests and brothers, an extensive garden and an agricultural college. The friary was suppressed by Henry VIII in 1540, but undaunted, the friars preserved a presence there – 'a nest of scorpions', as Queen Elizabeth I described them, until they were finally scattered by Cromwell's men in 1651.

The abbey was restored in 1973 and its new stained-glass windows show the burning of the abbey in 1601, a priest holding a secret mass, and the legend of the Children of Lir, who were turned into swans living nearby on Lough Derravaragh. The tabernacle is a millstone with a huge copper ear of wheat, a symbol of the bread of life, soaring through it.

TULLYNALLY CASTLE *The Victorian castle stands in beautiful gardens overlooking a lough.*

ROYAL CANAL *Calm waters and daisy-dotted banks make this a paradise for rowers and ramblers.*

The painted crucifix is copied from one in San Damiano, near Assisi, the church in which St Francis heard a heavenly voice instructing him: 'Go and repair my church.'

## Tullynally Castle

The greystone, castellated Victorian castle, home of the Earls of Longford, lies a mile outside the pretty village of Castlepollard. Its landscaped gardens contain fine rhododendrons, many splendid trees, and a lake.

Spectacular views of Lough Derravaragh can be seen from the castle's grotto.

The 17th-century castle, remodelled in 1803 by the Irish architect Francis Johnston (1760-1829), was enlarged in 1840. The main hall, with its 25ft high ceiling and built-in organ, is often used for concerts, and the library, with some 8000 volumes, is one of Ireland's greatest private collections.
**Opening times** *Mid-July to mid-Aug. Tel: (044) 61159/61425. Grounds open all year.*

# THE DRUMLIN BELT

SMALL rounded hills crop up in their thousands all over the region – sometimes standing alone, sometimes joined together in a hummocky jumble, and sometimes sticking up as islands in the many lakes that speckle the landscape. They are the drumlins – teardrop-shaped humps up to half a mile long and 100ft high. All are aligned with their tears pointing in the same direction. Drumlins were shaped from rock rubble and clay by the great ice sheet that once covered most of Ireland – and were exposed when the ice retreated 10,000 years ago. Today they provide pasture for cattle with the occasional field of crops on their gentler slopes. They also dictate the winding pattern of the country roads that wander endlessly round them.

The counties of Louth, Monaghan and Cavan occupy the central part of the 'Drumlin Belt'. This is border country, lying along the southern boundary of Northern Ireland. But it is a border that has been redrawn during the 20th century. Counties Cavan and Monaghan, together with Donegal, are part of the province of Ulster, now separated from the other six Ulster counties of Northern Ireland. Historically, the terrain of these counties, more thickly forested and boggy in the past than today, has always placed them on the margins.

To the east, Louth has a long, sandy coastline interrupted only by the rocky promontories of Clogher Head and Dunany Point. Dundalk, the county town, is set in a bay bordered by saltmarshes, home to a bird sanctuary and gathering place for thousands of oystercatchers, godwits and other waders. To the north, the beautiful Cooley peninsula juts into the Irish Sea, its mountains providing spectacular views over Carlingford Lough to the Mourne Mountains across the border. It was here that Cuchulainn, the great hero of ancient Ulster, battled with the warriors of Queen Maeve of Connaught for the Brown Bull of Cooley, as recounted in the legendary *Táin bó Cuailgne*. The fertile Plain of Murtheimne to the west

SAINTLY ARCHBISHOP *St Joseph's, Carrickmacross, has eight glorious modern windows.*

MUCKNO LAKE *The 900 acres of island-freckled lake in County Monaghan are a paradise for anglers, ramblers and boatmen.*

of Dundalk is where Cuchulainn was said to have been born and raised, and where, exhausted by battle, he died strapped to a stone pillar (still to be seen at Knockbridge near Dundalk), in accordance with his wish to die standing up, facing his enemies.

To the west, the landscape becomes progressively more rugged. Sporadic woodland and gorse-covered scrub invade the unproductive slopes, while water meanders between the hills, often trapped in the folds to form tiny lakes or areas of damp, heather-cloaked bog.

Farther west again, the Cavan landscape breaks up into numerous streams. Two great rivers have their sources here. The Erne begins its tortuous journey to the sea near Shercock and continues through the maze of islands in Lough Oughter, while the Shannon, the longest river in Ireland, rises under Cuilcagh mountain. With its abundance of water, this county is a cherished centre for coarse fishing and hosts many fishing competitions throughout the year.

The rivers provided waterways that allowed successive groups of people to penetrate the interior and settle on the pockets of fertile ground, while the inaccessibility of the surrounding landscape made their settlements comparatively easy to defend. Stone Age tombs, cairns and dolmens – notably the impressive Proleek dolmen at Ballymascanlan, in Louth – show that the whole of this region has been inhabited since prehistoric times.

Early Christians, spreading out from St Patrick's base in Armagh just to the north, also found sanctuary in the knolls and glens of the drumlin landscape and there are numerous testimonies to the unfolding story of the Irish Church in these counties. Monasterboice in Louth has one of the loveliest High Crosses in Ireland, beautifully carved with Biblical themes. Mellifont, also in Louth, was the first Cistercian monastery in Ireland, playing a leading role in the 12th-century reform of the Church.

The coastal plains were overrun by the Normans, who exercised their authority from a series of forts, including the massive Carlingford Castle overlooking Carlingford Lough. But the chieftains remained in control of the remoter regions, comparatively undisturbed by the Normans or the English. However, here, as elsewhere in Ireland, the 17th century proved a turning point.

In the 1590s the Irish clans, such as the O'Reillys and McGoverns of County Cavan and the MacMahons of County Monaghan threw in their lot with Hugh O'Neill and Red Hugh O'Donnell in their rebellion against encroaching Tudor power, which ended with the defeat of the Irish at the Battle of Kinsale in 1601. The region put up fearsome resistance during the ensuing turmoil, notably under Owen Roe O'Neill in the 1640s. But it suffered severely for its stand. In 1649, Drogheda in Louth became the first town to taste the ruthlessness of Cromwell's campaign in Ireland. Many of its people were massacred and others deported. Subsequently, these counties were heavily 'planted' with landowners loyal to the English Crown.

The landscape, much of it turned to the development of the linen, woollen and tanning industries, began to take on the more orderly look associated with plantation, punctuated by market and garrison towns, such as Cootehill in County Cavan and Carrickmacross in County Monaghan, with their Planter's Gothic churches and solid Georgian homes. The woodlands of beech, chestnut, sycamore and lime – all introduced trees – date from this time, originally imported to adorn the estates attached to the houses of the new ruling class.

The site of Cuilcagh House, near the old garrison town of Virginia in Cavan, marks the home of Thomas Sheridan, grandfather of the playwright, Richard Brinsley Sheridan, and a friend of the writer Jonathan Swift. Swift is believed to have written much of his *Gulliver's Travels* here. But the writer most readily associated with this region is the 20th-century poet Patrick Kavanagh, who was born and raised around Inishkeen in County Monaghan.

TIMELESS PURSUITS *Exquisite lace is still made by hand in Carrickmacross by a few women, whereas sheep markets thrive as they have done for centuries in Carlingford.*

# Cavan's Rolling Hills

*Low hills interlaced with rivers, streams, marshes and loughs make up the gentle watery landscape of east Cavan. These hills, or drumlins, carved by glaciers about 50,000 years ago, provided early settlers with ideal sites for defence, and the area is thick with ring-forts and ancient stone tombs, unmarked and undisturbed. Centuries later, English and Scottish settlers also left their mark here, in the layout and architecture of the 'plantation' towns they founded.*

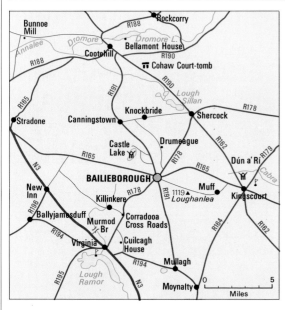

## OTHER PLACES TO SEE

**Bunnoe Mill** Only working water mill in County Cavan, dating from 1830. It works from Sept to Mar.

**Cohaw Court-tomb** 3m SE of Cootehill. Double tomb, 85ft long, with a semicircular court at each end. It is a fine example of a 5000-year-old megalithic tomb.

**Cootehill** Typical early 17th-century planter's town laid out in an orderly way, with a large number of churches testifying to an extraordinary tolerance of religious sects.

**Knockbride** Ivy-covered ruins of a pre-Reformation church, once used by Catholics in the morning and Protestant settlers in the evening.

**Mullagh** Holy well of St Killian (c. AD 640-689), assassinated in Würzburg, Germany, by the wife of the local duke, who had been converted by the saint; she feared that her husband would leave her to follow the saint. St Killian is said to have been born at Mullagh.

**Shercock** Playwright Richard Brinsley Sheridan (1751-1816) lived here. Nearby Lough Sillan has excellent coarse fishing.

## WALKS

**Ancient Celtic Road** Now a farm track that runs between Virginia and Bailieborough.

**Cootehill Walk** Roughly 5½m; takes in 2 ring-forts.

**Virginia-Murmod Walk** Roughly 10m.

## EVENTS

**Bailieborough Angling Festival** Late Apr.

**Bailieborough Community Festival** Late June.

**Ballyjamesduff Music Festival** Late July.

**Cootehill Arts Festival** Mid-Oct.

**Cootehill Fishing Championship** Late Sept.

**Ed Reavy Festival Week** Cootehill, early Aug.

**Queen of Ramor Festival** Lough Ramor, early to mid-July.

**Virginia Agricultural Show** Early Sept.

## SPORT

**Angling** Coarse fishing: Loughs Ramor and Sillan.

**Golf** Kingscourt, 9-hole course. Tel: (042) 67189. Virginia Park, 9-hole course. Tel: (042) 65766.

## INFORMATION

Cavan Town Tourist Office. Tel: (049) 31942.
North West Tourism. Tel: (071) 61201.

## Bailieborough/Coill an Chollaigh

During the plantation of Ulster with English and Scottish Protestants in the early 17th century, the Scottish Bailie family was granted land in this area and founded Bailieborough. Like many other plantation towns it has a wide main street dominated by a Protestant church at one end, in the high-spired style known as Planter's Gothic, and a market house at the other, symbols of the two most important moving forces of plantation society. Opposite the Protestant church is the Catholic cathedral of 1942, which contains paintings of the Stations of the Cross by George Collie (1904-75).

In 1629 the Bailies built a castle beside the lake to the north-west of the town. Nothing remains of the castle, but the banks of Castle Lake, as it is known, are now a secluded, wooded picnic spot with tranquil views of the water.

The ancestors of the novelist Henry James were tenant farmers on the Bailieborough estate, at the foot of Loughanlea mountain, before they left for the New World. In 1837, Henry's father caused something of a stir locally when he arrived with his Negro servant Billy Taylor to visit his Cavan cousins. Later he often spoke of the open doors in Bailieborough Main Street, with whiskey on every table.

## Ballyjamesduff/Baile Shéamais Dhuibh

*Oh, the grass it is green around Ballyjamesduff,*
*And the blue sky is over it all;*
*And tones that are tender and tones that are gruff,*
*Are whispering over the sea,*
*'Come back, Paddy Reilly, to Ballyjamesduff,*
*Come home, Paddy Reilly, to me'.*

Percy French's song *Come Back Paddy Reilly* brought fame to this small, but spaciously laid out town built down the slopes of a hill, whose only importance until then came from its cattle market. At the wide crossroads, where tractors outnumber cars on market day, is a small, raised garden with a fountain and plaque dedicated to the memory of 'an Irish troubadour who immortalised this village'. *Come Back Paddy Reilly*, written in 1912, is said to have been inspired by a Ballyjamesduff man who occasionally drove French around the country. Reilly left to work in

### THE THREE-FACED IDOL

About the year 1885 a farmer stumbled across a curious three-faced head on Drumeague, or the Ridge of Maodhóg, in east Cavan. The Corleck Tricephalos, as the head is known, proved to be one of the most important archaeological finds in the county. Associated with the site – which may have been some kind of Celtic 'head shrine' – are a ring-fort and what was probably a Stone Age passage-tomb. The Celts worshipped heads, believing that they were the centre of the human spirit.

The three-faced head is thought to represent Lug, the Celtic creator, Dagda the preserver, and Ogma the destroyer, a trinity similar to the Hindu gods Brahma, Vishnu and Siva. Other head idols were found on the site, including a stone with a ram's head at one end and a bearded man's head at the other. These now form the Drumeague Pantheon Collection in the National Museum in Dublin.

Scotland for 15 years and then did come back to Ballyjamesduff, where he died aged 88. Behind the Percy French memorial is the greystone market house, built in 1813.

### Bellamont House

One of the finest Palladian villas in Ireland stands on high ground overlooking Dromore Lough. It was built in the early 18th century for the local landlord, Thomas Coote, and has remained in the family since. The wide stone steps of this country mansion lead up to a Doric portico decorated with a classical frieze. In the marble-floored hall, alcoves hold busts of members of the Coote family crowned with laurel wreaths, like Roman emperors. The drawing and dining rooms that lead off it are richly decorated with stucco work, and the upper floor, with elaborate pillars, has one of the first central glass cupolas to be built in the British Isles. The house is being carefully restored, with the original paint colours on the walls and the furniture of the period. Although not open to the public it can be seen by private arrangement with the owner. Tel: (049) 52461.

### Cuilcagh House

Dean Swift (1667-1745) regularly stayed for months at a time at Cuilcagh House, the home of his great friend, the clergyman and classical scholar Dr Thomas Sheridan (1687-1738). Swift was far from comfortable in the house, and was given to breaking into poetry on the subject:

*'Let me thy properties explain:*
*A rotten cabin with dropping rain,*
*Chimneys with scorn rejecting smoke,*
*Stools, tables, chairs and bedsteads broke,*
*Here elements have lost their uses,*
*Air ripens not, nor earth produces;*
*In vain we make poor Sheelah toil,*
*Fire will not roast, water will not boil.'*

But despite its discomforts this was where Swift wrote some of his best satires and letters and conceived the idea for *Gulliver's Travels*. He is said to have modelled his Brobding-nagian farmer on a local man known as 'Big Doughty', who amazed the Dean by lifting a Manx pony onto his shoulders to show his strength.

Today, only one part of the original house remains, tucked behind a later façade which can be seen from the road. It is not open to the public, who may see only the outside of the house from the drive.

### Dún an Rí Forest Park

For centuries people have visited the holy wishing well called Tobar na Splinnc, 'the well of the cliff, or 'ledge', set into a rocky terrace above the River Cabra, where it slips over moss-covered boulders into the pool below. Today they are just as likely to be attracted to the well-marked walks and nature trail in this 565 acre forest park. The walks wander through woodland that is teeming with wildlife, including red squirrels and Irish hares.

At the top of the hill above the car park it is possible to see from the Mourne Mountains in the north to Louth in the east. The view also takes in the ruined fortress of Gerald Fleming, standing above the gorge. It was

DÚN AN RÍ FOREST PARK *Vegetation grows in lush profusion by the River Cabra which rushes under the high stone arches of Cromwell's Bridge.*

built in 1607, after Elizabeth I granted land in the district to the Anglo-Norman Fleming family, in the hope that they would put a stop to raids by the locals on the rich neighbouring farmlands of Meath. But the fortress was destroyed by Cromwell only 42 years later. The keystones of this and the O'Reilly castle at Muff were said to have been marked out by an informer, which enabled Cromwell to dismantle the castle's doorway and gain access.

Above Lady's Lake is an ice house, a stone-lined pit in which ice from the lake would be packed in winter to provide a cold store for the local Pratt family. Nearby is Sarah's Bridge, built in 1801 in memory of a member of the family. According to local legend, Sarah had been meeting the same swain on the bridge for 30 years, when one evening he suddenly proposed marriage. Sarah was so surprised that she fell off the bridge and drowned.

### Kingscourt/Dún an Rí

Built with the stones of Cabrach, a village that stood in what is now the Dún an Rí Forest

ST MARY'S CHURCH *Glowing windows depict Evie Hone's interpretation of the Ascension.*

Park, Kingscourt was started in 1760 by local landowner Mervyn Pratt. The town is now home to some of the most distinguished modern art in Ireland: the stained-glass windows in St Mary's Catholic church are by Evie Hone (1894-1955). She was a renowned member of the Irish school of stained glass that flourished in the first half of this century, and was influenced by French abstract artists. The windows, finished in 1948, depict the Apparition of the Virgin Mary at Fatima, the Annunciation, Crucifixion and Ascension.

### Virginia/Achadh an Iúir

This spacious plantation town, set on the wooded north shore of the dog-leg shaped Lough Ramor, exudes a relaxed charm. Its wide, curving main street sweeps round from the tall Protestant church at the head of the town to an old stone mill and a bridge over the river at the eastern end. On one side of a leafy, central triangle stands the old court-house, still with its original, polished wooden benches in the courtroom. A long, straight drive leads off Main Street to the tranquil shores of the lake and grassed picnic areas.

# The Ancient Kingdom of Glan

*North-west Cavan is the ancient Kingdom of Glan, whose rulers were the Magaurans, or McGoverns, still the most common family name in the area. Abandoned farmhouses and crumbling dry-stone walls, the legacy of mass emigration to the United States, are scattered throughout this lonely, windswept and mountainous country where unkempt hedges of gorse, hawthorn and blackthorn straggle across fields dappled by the ever-changing light.*

## Ballyconnell/Béal Átha Conaill

Conall Cearnach, a Celtic chieftain and warrior of Ulster, defended a ford here against invaders from Connaught, and it is from him that this neat village is said to have taken its name. Ballyconnell became famous in early Christian times for its monastery of Tomregon, a centre of healing and learning, which reached its peak in the 7th century.

Tomregon's most notable surgeon was St Bricin, whose name is preserved in the local townland, or district, of Slieve Bricken. The carved Tomregon Stone, which leans against the side wall of Ballyconnell's handsome 17th-century Protestant church, may well be a memorial to St Bricin's skill as a surgeon. This triangular stone, about 3ft high, has a primitive head at its apex and legs down the sides, and a skull held in the left hand. The stone was taken from a medieval church about 2½ miles south-east, where it probably served as the arch stone of a door or window, and is thought to show an operation carried out by St Bricin on a local chieftain.

Ballyconnell is at the centre of an ambitious plan to achieve an old dream – to unite the Rivers Erne and Shannon and so create a very large and important waterway system, the Ballinamore-Ballyconnell Canal. The Woodford river, which runs through the village, would be a crucial link, joining Garadice Lough in Leitrim to the Erne. The Ballinamore-Ballyconnell Canal is due for completion in 1994-5.

TOMREGON STONE *The 7th-century surgeon, St Bricin, may be portrayed here, performing an operation on a chieftain's head. Another suggestion is that the carving is a pagan image of the Earth Mother, her right hand holding a young creature and the left a skull to demonstrate her power as life-giver and destroyer.*

## Belturbet/Béal Tairbirt

Built on rising ground beside the River Erne, and at the centre of a fractured landscape of lakes, Belturbet's original strategic importance was as a point of defence against invaders. Nowadays the invaders of this small but busy town are anglers and boating enthusiasts. Motor-cruisers bob at their moorings on one side of Belturbet bridge, and on the other side trout fishermen try their luck with rod and line.

Belturbet is a 'plantation', or resettlement town. It was founded by the Butlers, the English Earls of Lanesborough, who were granted 384 acres in 1610 as part of a scheme to populate the area with English and Scottish settlers who would bring commerce to the region. The layout of Belturbet is typical of a plantation town, with an imposing town hall at the head of the main street, and behind it, on the crest of the hill, a 17th-century Protestant church. Built from sandstone, with a square tower and tall spire, it is characteristic of the style known as 'Planter's Gothic'. Its austerity contrasts with the Italianate Catholic church next to it, whose domed bell tower dominates the skyline.

Below the town are walks along the river banks, one of which, on the opposite bank, leads along a spit of land to Turbet Island, where there is a Norman motte and bailey. The flat-topped mound gives views across the River Erne to the town.

## Blacklion

A thatched, 18th-century posthouse on the coach and mail route between Sligo and Enniskillen gave this one-street village its name. Now all that remains of the old inn are stables behind the present Blacklion bar. Blacklion is the starting point of a 16 mile walk known as the Cavan Way, from Blacklion to Dowra.

About 3½ miles south of Blacklion, west of the Moneygashel Post Office, is a 19th-century sweathouse, an early version of a sauna, and one of a number in west Cavan. It is a stone construction covered with turf and reaches just over 6ft high. The sweathouse was last used in 1923.

The name Moneygashel means 'thicket of the round cashels' – near the post office are the remains of three cashels, or stone forts, thought to be more than 1000 years old.

Across a field 2 miles west of Blacklion, in a tranquil spot overlooking the beautiful Lough Macnean Upper, are the crumbling walls of the oldest church in the district, the 12th-century Killinagh Church. Stone tablets there bear the names of American families whose ancestors came from Blacklion.

Nearer the lake is St Brigid's Stone, a 5ft wide boulder with depressions in its surface, which was probably an ancient communal mill for grinding corn.

IRISH SAUNA *The sweathouse was a type of sauna used in the 19th century. A turf fire was lit and left to burn for about six hours until the stones were hot. Then the fire would be raked out and fresh rushes spread on the floor to provide steam. Two people could crawl through the entrance into the sweathouse, the door was closed behind them, and they were left to perspire. Sometimes the process was followed by a dip in a nearby stream.*

## OTHER PLACES TO SEE

**Bawnboy** Hamlet with access to glens and mountains.
**Corleggy Craft Shop and Goat Farm** Belturbet. Tel: (049) 22219.
**Doobally Church** Rebuilt in the 1920s and again in the 1980s; contains a famine-pot, from which gruel was served during the 1840s Famine.
**Drumlane Abbey** Medieval church, with fine stonework around the doorway. An interesting Round Tower with carvings stands nearby.
**Gubaveeny** Two sweathouses.

## WALKS AND RIVER TRIPS

**Cavan Way** A 16 mile hike from Blacklion to Dowra.
**Heritage River Trips** Along the River Erne or on Lough Oughter. Contact Donal Carlin. Tel: (049) 22637.

## EVENTS

**Ballyconnell Festival** Mid-Aug.
**Festival of the Erne** Belturbet, early Aug.
**Market Day** Dowra, Sat.

## SPORT

**Angling** Coarse fishing: Lough Macnean Upper, and Rivers Woodford and Blackwater. Game fishing: Rivers Claddagh and Erne.
**Boating** River Erne.
**Golf** Belturbet Golf Club, 9-hole course. Tel: (049) 22498/22287. Blacklion Golf Club, 9-hole course. Tel: (072) 53024.
**Potholing** Blacklion.

## INFORMATION

Cavan Town Tourist Office. Tel: (049) 31942.
North West Tourism. Tel: (071) 61201.

### Burren

At the top of the limestone hill south of Blacklion, overlooking the marshlands below, are the 200 forested acres of Burren, or 'stony place'. Five-thousand years ago farmers settled here and left a rich concentration of wedge-tombs, court-tombs, passage-graves and dolmens. Among them are a rocking stone estimated to weigh 6 tons, and the Druid's Altar – a dolmen, or portal grave, with a massive capstone. There is also a tomb that is said to be the grave of a giant who collapsed and died after attempting two jumps across the nearby Giant's Leap.

The Burren Forest can be reached only on foot, by one of two routes: along the Cavan Way from Blacklion, or by a path off the minor road that runs south from Blacklion to Dowra.

### Swanlinbar/An Muileann Iarainn

In its heyday in the 18th and 19th centuries, Swanlinbar was a spa resort that glittered with gentry from the surrounding districts, who gathered here in summer to sample its waters. As sea bathing became more popular in the middle of the last century, inland resorts such as Swanlinbar declined – but it has retained something of its spa charm. It is attractively sited on the River Claddagh at the foot of the eastern slopes of the Cuilcagh Mountains, with a main street north of the river and clusters of whitewashed cottages to the south.

Efforts are today being made to revive the reputation of Swanlinbar water. In 1987 one well was restored, on the road that leads south-east from the village and just beyond the sharp northwards bend, where it is reached through a cut in a roadside hedge. Covered by a stone canopy, the circular pool of blue-tinged water quivers with the slight bubbles that rise to the surface. Enthusiasts travel from around Ireland to collect supplies. But the taste of the water is an acquired one: its high sulphur content gives it a strong smell of bad eggs.

Swanlinbar produced iron from the 17th to the 19th century from ore found in the Cuilcagh Mountains, hence the town's Irish name, which means Iron Mill. But the smelting was fuelled by charcoal, and once the wood from the surrounding forests was exhausted, the industry collapsed. The mill's founders, Messrs Swann, Linn and Barr, became immortalised in the English name of the town.

REMOTE UPLANDS *Grassy fields slope gently under an open sky on the road from Ballyconnell to Dowra.*

### THE SHANNON POT

Ireland's longest river, the Shannon, starts its 250 mile journey to the Atlantic in a hole called the Lug-na-Sionna, or Shannon Pot, in a boggy field on the west side of the Cuilcagh Mountains. Rivulets gush from the slopes into a dark circular pool 50ft wide, overhung by lichen-covered trees. The river is named after Sionna, granddaughter of the great sea god Lir. Legend says she was seized with the desire for knowledge, the possession of man alone, and went to Connla's well, a mythical place, to catch the Salmon of Knowledge. The salmon received its wisdom by eating the nuts from the sacred hazel trees of science, poetry and knowledge, which grew round the well, so whoever ate the salmon would become all-knowing. As Sionna bent down to trap the fish, it leaped and lashed its tail in rage. The well overflowed and Sionna was swept into it and down into the earth through the Lug-na-Sionna, or Shannon Pot.

The infant Shannon soon becomes a fair-sized stream. Within 3 miles of its source it is joined by the Owenmore, which drains the Cuilcagh Mountains, and by the time it reaches Dowra, about 5 miles away, a wide stone bridge is needed to cross it.

# Lakeland Labyrinth

*Cavan people are fond of saying that there is a lake in the county for every day of the year, and they are not far wrong. The centre of Cavan is a vast fragmented jigsaw puzzle of hills, islands, lakes and waterways fringed with trees. Now a pleasure ground for boating enthusiasts and anglers, the waterways were once 'highways' along which the early Celtic settlers penetrated what was then a densely forested region. Traces of their fortifications and burial sites are scattered everywhere.*

### Ballyhaise/Béal Átha hÉis

A pretty, arched bridge crosses the River Annalee into the quiet village of Ballyhaise, whose parish church can boast that its walls were once those of a cathedral. In 1942 the neo-Gothic Catholic cathedral of Cavan was dismantled to make way for a grander, more modern replacement. The stones were transported to Ballyhaise, which had no church at that time, and were used to build a simpler place of worship.

Overlooking the village, from a terraced hillside, is the striking redbrick-and-sandstone Ballyhaise House. Built in 1705, it was reconstructed in 1733 by one of Ireland's leading architects, Richard Cassel, who was born in Germany but anglicised his name to Castle when he settled in Dublin. At the back of the house, a very early example of a curved bay window forms one wall of a fine oval saloon, the first oval room in Ireland, with curved doors and chimneypiece, and which still has its original plaster decoration. The house is remarkable too for the steel shutters guarding the ground-floor windows. They are fitted with musket holes through which the inhabitants could aim their muskets at would-be attackers. Since 1906 Ballyhaise House has been used as a state-sponsored agricultural college, the oldest of its kind in Ireland. Visitors may see the hall and main rooms on request.
**Ballyhaise House** *Tel: (049) 38300/38257.*

### Cavan/An Cabhán

Resting in a hollow – the meaning of its Irish name – Cavan grew up with a castle at its head and an abbey at its heart. The castle stood on the hill that rises behind Main Street, known as Gallows Hill after its use for public executions in the 18th century. Built in the 13th century, the castle was the seat of the O'Reillys, the enterprising ruling clan of the old kingdom of East Breifne. The O'Reillys were renowned for their talent for commerce, and even had their own mint. Only traces of the castle remain now, on Fair Green.

Below the castle, near the river, Giolla Íosa Rúadh O'Reilly founded a friary for the Franciscans around 1300. It continued to exist until 1608, despite having burned down in 1451 through the carelessness of an inebriated friar. The friary, the castle and the whole town were burned in 1576 as a result of the jealousy of an O'Reilly woman.

Being near the Ulster border, Cavan has frequently been a battleground and suffered extensive damage over the centuries. Most of its buildings therefore date from the 19th century and later. Two of the most prominent are churches, whose spires dominate the end of Farnham Street. The shorter one, at 140ft, tops the Protestant church of 1810. Opposite is the 200ft spire of the Cathedral of St Patrick and St Felim, seat of the Catholic bishops of Kilmore. Completed in 1942, the cathedral has an airy interior based on the shape of a Roman basilica, with an attractive high altar of green and pink Irish marble. The Stations of the Cross and the mural behind the altar were painted by the Irish artist George Collie (1904-75).

Visitors in search of their Cavan roots will find help in an unlikely place – a former prison at the top of the hill behind Farnham bus station. Here local authority workers are painstakingly compiling lists of births, marriages and deaths from handwritten parish records.

On the Dublin Road just outside Cavan, classic Irish glassware is made at the Cavan Crystal glassworks. Visitors can watch craftsmen blowing and skilfully shaping the molten crystal, using tools and techniques that have barely changed since the 18th century. Most of the crystal made here is exported.
**Cavan Crystal** *Viewing: June-end Oct, daily except weekends. Shop: All year, daily. Tel: (049) 31800.*

**Killashandra** 11m from Cavan, on Lough Oughter. Good fishing and pleasant walks.

**EVENTS**
**Cavan Lakes and Vales Festival** Mid-July.
**Cavan Open Fishing Competition** Mid-Aug: Lough Oughter.
**Killashandra Festival of Irish Music** Early June.

**SPORT**
**Angling** Coarse fishing: Butlers Bridge, Loughs Gowna and Sheelin, Killykeen Park. Trout fishing: Lough Sheelin.
**Golf** County Cavan Golf Club, 18-hole course. Tel: (049) 31283.

**INFORMATION**
Cavan Town Tourist Office. Tel: (049) 31942.
North West Tourism. Tel: (071) 61201.

**OTHER PLACES TO SEE**
**Corr House** 4m from Cavan. The Pighouse Collection, articles from the past. Visits by arrangement. Tel: (049) 37248.

BALLYHAISE BRIDGE *Stone arches loop over the River Annalee on the approach to the village.*

## Cloughoughter Castle

Rising from an island in Lough Oughter is a massive, circular stone tower, 59ft high. The lower storey, with walls 6½ft thick, was built in the 13th century on an existing crannog, or artificial island, which had natural rock as a foundation.

During the 17th-century struggles between the Irish and the Ulster settlers, William Bedell, Protestant Bishop of Kilmore, was imprisoned in the tower by the O'Reillys of Cavan. Soon after, Cromwell landed in Ireland and attacked the stronghold, which surrendered, the last confederate fortress to succumb to the Protestants. The tower can be reached by boat from Inishconnell.

FINN MacCOOL'S FINGERS *Ancient boulders are grouped together in a quiet glade.*

## Finn MacCool's Fingers

In a quiet pine glade on Shantemon Hill, five great boulders stand in a row on the emerald grass. Named after the legendary Irish giant-slayer Finn MacCool, or MacCumhaill, the stones are thought to have been erected during the Bronze Age (between 1750 and 500 BC), but their original purpose is unknown. Shantemon Hill is said to have been the inauguration place of the O'Reillys. This site was also the scene of an annual gathering to celebrate the harvest, on Bilberry Sunday, usually the last Sunday in July. It was probably last celebrated in the 1940s.

## Killykeen Forest Park

Coill Chaoin, the Irish name for Killykeen, means 'delightful wood', an apt description of the 600 acre park beside Lough Oughter. Winding trails lead through forests filled with birdsong and along shores graced with herons, kingfishers and great crested grebes. The lough waters are filled with eels, pike, bream, roach and perch, which can be fished. Scattered throughout the park are early for-tifications, among them part of a ring-fort.

LOUGH RAMOR *Still and chill in the early morning, the lough's silky waters take on a warmer gleam as the pale sunlight caresses them.*

## Kilmore/An Chill Mhór

A tree-shaded drive up a hill leads to the Church of Ireland cathedral of St Feithlimidh, a neo-Gothic cathedral built in 1858-60, with an intricately carved Irish-Romanesque vestry door, probably once part of an early church on Trinity Island in Lough Oughter. The graveyard beside the cathedral contains the grave of Bishop Bedell (1571-1642), who translated the English Bible into Irish and was imprisoned in Cloughoughter tower in 1641. Well-preserved remains of a Norman motte and bailey can be seen nearby.

### FINN MacCOOL, LEGENDARY HERO

Standing stones in many parts of Ireland are named after Finn MacCool (or MacCumhaill), a celebrated Irish hero thought to have lived in the 3rd century AD and the subject of a cycle of Irish legends. He became immensely wise after he devoured a Salmon of Knowledge, and when an enemy threw water at him from a magic well, he swallowed it and acquired the powers of a sorcerer. Leader of the Fianna, a band of legendary soldiers, he was a great hunter and fighter. His two hounds were his nephews, and his son Ossian was the child of a woman transformed into a deer. Finn was betrothed to Gráinne who eloped with Diarmuid, taking refuge under dolmens as they fled. He never caught up with them and Diarmuid was killed by a boar. It is not certain how or when Finn died, or where his death took place.

# Just Beyond the Pale

*Ireland's central plains and southern hills are dotted with religious sites, including the country's first Cistercian abbey and its finest High Cross. But the rural calm disguises a turbulent past. Drogheda, once the largest English town in Ireland, stood just outside the frontier of the Pale, the part of Ireland over which the English held control, and was the scene of a horrific massacre by Cromwell's soldiers.*

## Drogheda/Droichead Átha

This close-packed town, with its old buildings clustered in 13th-century streets, retains a medieval feel. Two towns were founded on either side of the River Boyne by the Anglo-Norman Hugh de Lacy. In 1412 they were united by charter to become the largest English town in Ireland at the time.

**OTHER PLACES TO SEE**

**Ardee** Small town with two castles: one, 13th century, is private; the other, Ardee Castle, 15th century, is the courthouse, and once the largest fortified home in Ireland.

**Castlebellingham** Crossroads village with two little triangular greens, thatched craft shop, semi-circle of Victorian houses, and 18th-century castle now occupied by a hotel.

**Clogher Head** Headland with fine view across Dundalk Bay to the Cooley peninsula and Mourne Mountains. Nearby is Clogherhead, fishing village with pier.

**Collon** 2m from Mellifont, and site of 'Mellifont Abbey (Collon)', built in 1930s by Cistercians, with its 1000 acre wildlife sanctuary. Visitors are welcome to walk around the lake.

**Dromiskin** Cemetery on site of 6th-century monastery, with 55ft high 10th-century Round Tower and part of much-worn 10th-century High Cross.

**Smarmore Castle** Medieval castle and recreation centre with swimming pool and 16 acres of woodland. Tours of castle by arrangement. Tel: (041) 53474.

**Termonfeckin** Village with well-restored 15th or 16th-century tower house with fine beehive stone roof. (Key available from house opposite entrance.)

**Townley Hall** 4m W of Drogheda. Georgian mansion, 1794, now a private educational centre; near site of 1690 battle. Extensive grounds with walks, picnic sites and nature trail.

**EVENTS**
**Castlebellingham**
**Agricultural Show** Mid-Aug.
**Clogherhead Prawn Festival** Mid-July.

**SPORT**
**Angling** Game fishing: Rivers Boyne and Dee, and Killineer Reservoir. Sea fishing: Clogher Head.
**Bathing** Clogherhead.
**Golf** Ardee Golf Club, 18-hole course. Tel: (041) 53227.
County Louth Golf Club, 18-hole course. Tel: (041) 22327.

**INFORMATION**
Dundalk Tourist Information Office. Tel: (042) 35484.

Overlooking Drogheda, and providing excellent views over the town, is the Millmount, a hill that surges up on the south side of the River Boyne, topped by an early 18th-century Martello tower. The mound itself, probably of Celtic origin, was built up by the Normans into a huge motte. The Millmount Museum, once an army barracks, now displays gloriously painted banners of the old trade guilds and long-obsolete machines and tools used in weaving, brewing, distilling, coopering and metal-casting. A prize exhibit is a coracle, a traditional circular fishing vessel, in use locally until 1948. Its willow frame is covered by the leather hide of a prize bull.

Old buildings that reflect Drogheda's long and sometimes stormy past are scattered through the town. The most prominent, the 1224 Magdalene Tower, is a landmark in the northern part of town, with a two-storey tower rising from a Gothic arch. It was the belfry tower of a once-extensive Dominican friary. The 13th-century St Lawrence Gate, with two imposing round towers flanking a portcullis entry, formed an advance fortification outside the town walls and is one of the finest of its kind in Ireland. Both are unsafe and closed to the public.

St Peter's Roman Catholic church, an imposing Gothic Revival building reached by a double flight of steps, houses a shrine containing the embalmed head of St Oliver Plunkett, Archbishop of Armagh, who was disembowelled, beheaded and burnt in London in 1681.

The cemetery of the Protestant St Peter's Church includes an interesting 'cadaver' gravestone which represents the occupants as skeletons, once a common way to remind the living of their final end.

**Millmount Museum** *May-Sept, Tues-Sun 2-6pm; Oct-Apr, Wed, Sat, Sun 3-5pm. Tel: (041) 33484.*

## Kildemock Church

According to legend, the wall of this ruined 14th-century church 'jumped' inward to place the grave of an excommunicated person outside its hallowed bounds. The wall, some 16ft high and weighing many tons, now stands about 3ft inside the end of the 'Jumping Church'. Certainly the wall looks as if it has leaped forward – it stands clear of its apparent foundations and its stonework slopes into the ground at a dangerous angle. But a plaque in the church suggests a more

JUMPING CHURCH *The wall is said to have 'jumped' forward to avoid a grave.*

pedestrian explanation – that the wall was blown inward in the great storm of 1716.

## Louth/Lú

In a field outside this tiny village stands the delightful little building known as St Mochta's House, which, according to legend, sprang up in a single night to protect the sleeping saint. In fact, St Mochta died in 534, and the house probably dates from the 12th century. The house is permanently open and consists of two rooms, one above the other, linked by a minute spiral staircase, with ceilings of stone slabs carefully set in a fan-shape to create vaults. The upper vault supports a fine, heavy stone roof. Nearby stand the remains of a 14th or 15th-century church. Like St Mochta's House, they are the remnants of a religious community founded by St Mochta in the 6th century.

Outside the village on the Castlebellingham road are the remains of St Oliver's Church, named after St Oliver Plunkett, who defied British anti-Catholic legislation to preach there, until his arrest in 1678.

## Mellifont Abbey

A few low stone walls and ruined buildings, cupped in a hollow of protective hills, are all that is left of Ireland's first Cistercian abbey. It was founded in 1142 by St Malachy, Bishop of Armagh, after a stay in the French Cistercian monastery at Clairvaux. St Bernard, Clairvaux's abbot, later sent over an architect to design Mellifont Abbey, which was finally completed in 1225, and other Cistercian monasteries – 35 in all – soon followed. Mellifont survived for over four centuries, until it was suppressed in 1539.

The main sections that remain are an imposing doorway and a finely carved, octagonal washing area, or lavabo, built with

BRIGHT FIELDS *A vivid yellow field of oilseed rape in flower is spread below a church spire, a presiding presence that is never far away in the Irish countryside.*

Romanesque arches. Other fragmentary remains reveal traces of the church, chapter house, refectory, kitchen and dormitories.
**Opening times** *Mid-June to mid-Sept, 10am-6pm.*

## Monasterboice/Mainistir Bhuithe

This former monastery is one of Ireland's best-known and oldest religious sites, with the ruins of two churches, a Round Tower, a pre-Gothic sundial, a decorated grave slab and three High Crosses all packed into a cemetery. Founded in the 6th century by St Buite, or Boyce, the monastery became a great seat of learning, wealthy enough to acquire a good library and support fine artists.

The 95ft Round Tower dates from the 10th or 11th century, when monks needed quickly accessible places of refuge from marauding Vikings and Irish warlords. Once the inhabitants had locked themselves in and hauled up the access ladder, the smooth, round surface offered no niches or footholds to attackers. It was, however, vulnerable to fire, perhaps delivered by flaming arrows. Once its interior was ablaze, it would have acted like a factory chimney. Possibly that was the way monastic life at Monasterboice

THE CROSS OF MUIREDACH *Biblical images over 1000 years old are still sharp in detail.*

ended. A sign directs visitors to the holder of the key.

Pride of place among the site's remains is held by the High Crosses, towering stone sculptures carved with beautifully intricate decorations and panels illustrating Biblical themes, intended as reminders of the Christian message in a largely illiterate society.

The best of the three is the South Cross, known as the Cross of Muiredach, a massive 17ft 8in monolith which is remarkably well preserved despite more than 1000 years of weathering. Among its dozens of facets and panels, the more easily identifiable scenes include Cain slaying Abel, the Adoration of the Magi, Adam and Eve, and David and Goliath. The whole west face of the cross depicts the Ascent of Christ to the Cross.

Nearby is the more slender West Cross, or Tall Cross, almost 4ft taller than Muiredach's, making it the tallest High Cross in Ireland. Unlike Muiredach's Cross, the West Cross was made in separate sections and its panels have suffered more severe erosion. At some time in its recent history, people seem to have removed parts of the shaft. Of the third cross, only the top section remains, with several unfinished panels.

### THE MASSACRE OF DROGHEDA

In 1649, Drogheda was the scene of a massacre that had a searing effect on Irish history. By that year, Cromwell had won the civil war against Charles I in England. But in Ireland the conflict still raged and Cromwell sailed there to complete his conquest.

The garrison at Drogheda stood against him, under its Catholic commander, the one-legged English royalist Sir Arthur Aston. After breaching the walls, Cromwell's troops drove the defenders back into Millmount Fort and forced them to surrender. Cromwell then ordered the garrison to be killed. Sir Arthur Aston was battered to death with his own wooden leg. 'I think that we put to the sword altogether about 2000 men,' Cromwell wrote self-righteously, in the firm belief that he was doing God's will. 'It is right that God alone should have all the glory.'

Drogheda became the Catholic symbol of Protestant perfidy. And even though English officers were among the garrison's defenders, the massacre is remembered as an atrocity against the Irish.

# Cuchulainn Country

*In Ireland's smallest county lies the spectacular Cooley peninsula, a wild, mountainous region jutting into the Irish Sea. Forested slopes plunge down to Carlingford Lough to the north-east, while to the south, gentler hills and plains lead to Dundalk Bay and the county town. Also known as Cuchulainn Country, this is the setting for the 'Táin bó Cuailgne', an ancient saga which features the hero Cuchulainn in battle against the invading armies of Queen Maeve.*

## Carlingford/Cairlinn

Slieve Foye, highest peak of Carlingford Mountain, provides a 1935ft backdrop of scenic grandeur to the charming medieval town of Carlingford. King John's Castle, a massive D-shaped fortress completed in the early 13th century, and now a ruin, towers above the harbour and commands the entrance to Carlingford Lough. The castle is safe enough to be walked around.

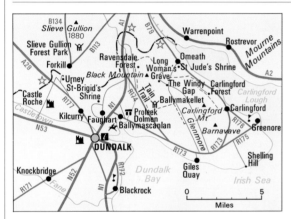

**OTHER PLACES TO SEE**
**Blackrock** Village stretched out along coastal road, with fine sandy beach; seaside resort of Dundalk.
**Giles Quay** Pretty village with line of white houses built along quayside; long, clean sandy beach nearby.
**Greenore** Privately owned port, once terminus of rail links with Newry and Dundalk. Built by Welsh company, and has air of Welsh mining village.
**Omeath** St Jude's shrine lies ½m S, surrounded by trim garden containing modern statues created to represent Stations of the Cross.
**Urney** Quiet little graveyard, overlooked by peaks of Slieve Gullion; burial place of Peadar Ó Doirnín, 18th-century Irish poet persecuted for writing and teaching in Irish.

**WALKS**
**Ballymakellet Forest Park** Walks, picnic sites, views.
**Carlingford Forest** On side of Carlingford Mountain; superb view overlooking Carlingford Lough.
**Ravensdale Forest** On western slopes of Black Mountain; contains nature trail, walks and picnic spots.

**EVENTS**
**Annual Great Leprechaun Hunt** Carlingford, end Apr/early May.
**Carlingford Medieval Weekend** June.
**Carlingford Oyster Festival** Mid-Aug.
**Cooley Vintage Festival** Cooley peninsula, early Aug.
**Cuchulainn Games** Dundalk, May.
**Dundalk International Maytime Festival** End May to early June.
**Omeath Gala Week** Late Aug.

**SPORT**
**Angling** Game fishing: Rivers Ballymacscanlan, Castletown and Fane. Sea fishing: Carlingford Lough, Greenore.
**Bathing** Giles Quay, Shelling Hill.
**Golf** Dundalk Golf Club, 18-hole course. Tel: (042) 21379.
Greenore Golf Club, 18-hole course. Tel: (042) 73212.
**Sailing** Carlingford Sailing Club. Weekends only. Tel: (042) 73238.

**INFORMATION**
Dundalk Tourist Information Office. Tel: (042) 35484.

The town itself is a huddle of old streets, houses and ancient buildings which grew up in the shadow of the castle. In the Middle Ages, it was a place of substance, partly because of its oyster fishing. But Carlingford's early wealth was undermined by the development of Newry in the 17th century, and the town remained frozen in time for the next 300 years, little touched by the wars that ravaged other towns.

Among its old buildings are the town hall, or Tholsel, an arched town gate just wide enough to allow a car through, a fortified 15th-century townhouse called The Mint, decorated with finely carved Celtic heads and knots, and Taafe's Castle, a 16th-century fortified house. None of these buildings is open to the public.

The town is the recommended point to start the 19 mile Táin Trail, which heads north-west through thick forest and returns from the south-west along the ancient Golyn Path between the peaks of Slieve Foye and Barnavave.

## Castle Roche

The most romantic ruin in Louth, Castle Roche is built on a pinnacle of rock, which commands spectacular views of the countryside. It has a large D-shaped curtain of castellated walls and a fine twin-towered gatehouse, around uneven, grassed-over floors. It was built in the 13th century to defend the frontier of the Pale, a British-controlled area centred on Dublin. A window in the west wall is known as the 'murder window' because Rohesia de Verdun, the original Norman owner, was said to have had the castle's builder thrown through it. The castle is in a field next to the road and is approached across a stile and up a grassy incline.

## Dundalk/Dún Dealgan

The busy port and county town of Dundalk guards a gap in the hills, where it was once an outpost of the Pale. To the west stands the fort after which the town takes its Irish name, Dún Dealgan, 'the fort of thorns'. It is an imposing Norman motte, now overgrown with beeches, capped by an 18th-century folly, and can be climbed. Tradition claims it was once a Celtic site and home of the legendary hero Cuchulainn.

In the town centre is a neoclassical courthouse with a Doric portico, built between 1813 and 1818 to the exact proportions of the Temple of Theseus in Athens.

The Protestant church of St Nicholas, known as the Green Church because its copper roof has turned a bright moss green with verdigris, is a fine greystone building, built originally in the 15th century. It was remodelled extensively in the 18th and 19th centuries. Agnes Galt, sister of the poet Robert Burns, is buried here.

### THE CATTLE RAID OF COOLEY

'*Some things in it are devilish lies, and some poetical figments; some seem possible and others not; some are for the enjoyment of idiots.*'

This was a 12th-century scribe's description of the *Táin bó Cuailgne*, a fantastic tale possibly set around the 1st century AD, which has become Ireland's national epic. It tells of Queen Maeve's envy of her husband Ailill's White-Horned Bull, Fuinbennach, which spurred her to win the Brown Bull of Cooley from Ulster. (One version claims that Ailill's White Bull had originally belonged to Maeve but had refused to be a woman's property and joined the king's herd.) Unable to buy the Brown Bull, Maeve and Ailill declared war on the Kingdom of Ulster and tried to take the bull by force.

For much of the tale, all the men of Ulster except Cuchulainn, the hero known as the Hound of Ulster, lie sick or under a spell of sleep cast by a sea witch, leaving the hero to fend off the invading armies alone. Fighting raged across the Cooley peninsula while the bull stayed hidden in Dubchoire, the Black Cauldron, a secluded hollow in Glenmore. Cuchulainn picked off 100 men with his sling, and in revenge Queen Maeve's troops tore up the earth at what is now known as 'The Windy Gap'.

Finally, Cuchulainn was mortally wounded, and the invading armies captured the bull. But, ironically, 'The Táin' finishes with a battle between the Brown Bull of Cooley and Ailill's bull, Fuinbennach. The Brown Bull won the fight, but was fatally wounded and charged back to Cooley with the mangled remains of Fuinbennach hanging from its horns.

LOUGH VIEW *Wind-blown heather and kelp-strewn rocks edge Carlingford Lough (above).*
HOLY HEIGHTS *St Brigid's Shrine high up on a hill draws pilgrims and travellers alike (below).*

WINDOW ON A CASTLE *The impressive ruins of Castle Roche rear up from a rocky outcrop.*

## Proleek Dolmen

Standing like a giant mushroom on three uprights is a 5000-year-old tomb with a huge capstone, known as 'The Giant's Load'. Local legend claims that the capstone, which weighs some 46 tons, was placed there by a giant. In fact it was probably hauled into position up an earth ramp that was then removed. Visitors who can throw three pebbles that then remain on top of the capstone will be granted a wish, it is said.

The Proleek Dolmen is signposted along a path around the back of the Ballymacscanlan House Hotel.

Nearby is an unkempt gallery-grave made of rocks that seem to outline a great bed, said to be the grave of a Scottish giant who came to challenge the Irish hero Finn MacCool, and lost the fight.

Back on the road lies a single line of terraced houses that form the village of Ballymacscanlan. It is one of the smallest villages in Ireland, with only six houses.

## St Brigid's Shrine, Faughart

On a hill that looks north to the brooding mountains of Armagh and south to the plains by Dundalk Bay is the shrine of St Brigid, said

A GIANT'S LOAD *The huge capstone of Proleek Dolmen is said to have been laid by a giant.*

to have been born nearby in 453. It is an extensive site, as befits a saint so beloved that she is known as 'The Mary of the Gael'.

The area was landscaped in 1933. Now stones line a prayer route beside a stream, where St Brigid is said to have performed miracles, and steps lead up to the white-and-gold shrine. On the path which leads up to the shrine, plaques mark the Stations of the Cross, at St Brigid's Well, St Brigid's Pillar and St Brigid's Stone. Steps also lead down to a grassy clearing and a grotto, which contains a statue of St Brigid being visited by Mary.

The shrine is at a road junction. In a field over the road from the junction are 'healing' stones, each indented with a shape corresponding to the part of the human or animal body to be cured – a head stone, a hoof stone, an eye stone. A supposed relic of St Brigid – an inch-wide fragment of skull – is kept in the church at Kilcurry a few miles away.

Edward Bruce, brother of Robert Bruce of Scotland, is buried in the local churchyard at Faughart, the site of an early Christian monastery whose patron saint was St Brigid. He was defeated and died here in 1318 after coming to Ireland with an army of Scots. Two years before his death Bruce crowned himself King of Ireland within sight of Faughart. Nearby is a stone on which, so legend says, Edward was decapitated.

## The Windy Gap

Four small steep roads, all with dramatic views over uplands scarred by rocky outcrops and gorse patches, come together to make a level pass entirely hemmed in by crags and hills. According to the *Táin bó Cuailgne* – the Cattle Raid of Cooley – it was here that the armies of Queen Maeve tore up the earth.

In rain and mist it seems a sinister spot, and for this reason, perhaps, local legend has spun a tale around a jumble of rocks nearby known as the Long Woman's Grave, marked with a plaque.

The story tells of a local man, Lorcan O'Hanlon, who courted a Spanish princess whom he had rescued from Moorish pirates. He promised her that in his homeland he owned all that could be seen in any direction from this hill. One version says that he had been tricked out of his inheritance. In any event, on their arrival all he could show her was The Windy Gap with its restricted view. When she saw the narrow limits of his realm, she died of shock and was buried on the spot.

# A Little Lake District

*Grand stretches of island-speckled water give south Monaghan a little lake district of its own. Rising from them are uplands scattered with traces of early settlers, whose monuments are mostly still unexplored because local people believed that fairies lived in them. Links with the past are stronger in this region – Irish was still spoken here long after it faded from use in north Monaghan.*

### Ballybay/Béal Átha Beithe

Set on a rising curve above Lough Major, the main street of Ballybay is distinguished by its fine 18th and 19th-century buildings, built when Ballybay was a successful linen town. Arched 'entries', or passageways, which lead from the street, give intriguing glimpses of the houses and yards behind the shopfronts, where poor families used to live. On Lower Main Street is a handsome, 1848, two-storey market house constructed of blackstone.

The original settlement of Ballybay, which probably consisted of only a few mud cabins, was near a ford on the birch-lined banks of the river, hence its Irish name, 'the mouth of the ford of the birches'. In the 1750s, a canny Presbyterian called Hugh Jackson decided to build a new town near the old ford because the area was particularly suitable for growing flax, the raw material for producing linen. By the end of the 18th century, Ballybay was the third-largest linen market in the county after the towns of Monaghan and Clones.

Nowadays the talk is more likely to be of fishing than flax because of the town's central position among south Monaghan's rivers and lakes. Anglers have only to take a few steps from Lower Main Street to reach Lough Major, the headwaters of the Dromore river that links the chain of loughs to Cootehill in County Cavan.

Just west of Ballybay, at Derryvally, are two, almost identical, handsome barn-type Presbyterian churches, the result of a serious rift in the congregation. In the early 19th century, some members of the flock believed the minister of First Ballybay Presbyterian Church to be a 'landlords' man' and they broke away to build their own church nearby,

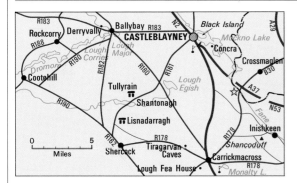

### OTHER PLACES TO SEE
**Lisnadarragh** 1m N of Shercock, wedge-tomb dating from around 2000 BC.
**Tiragarvan** 2½m W of Carrickmacross. Interesting limestone caves.
**Tullyrain** Just N of Shantonagh, triple ring-fort dated 8th-10th century.

### WALKS
**Black Island** Muckno Lake, forest walks and nature trails.
**Concra** SE of Castleblayney, forest walks and nature trails.

### EVENTS
**Ballybay International Fishing Competition** Mid-Sept.
**Castleblayney Angling Competition** Mid-Apr.
**Castleblayney Festival** Early Aug.

### SPORT
**Angling** Coarse fishing: River Dromore, Loughs Corries, Egish, Major, Monalty, Muckno and other lakes near Carrickmacross.
**Golf** Castleblayney Golf Club, 9-hole course. Tel: (042) 40197.
Nuremore Golf Club, 18-hole course. Tel: (042) 61438.

### INFORMATION
Monaghan Tourist Office. Tel: (047) 81122.

MONAGHAN LACE

*Carrickmacross lace with typical swan motif is compared with Clones lace, which is crocheted.*

Monaghan is graced with two centres of lacemaking, Carrickmacross and Clones. Carrickmacross lace, the oldest of the Irish lace industries, was introduced in the early 19th century by Mrs Gray Porter, a rector's wife who learned lacemaking on honeymoon in Italy. On her return home she taught her skills, until overproduction led to a decline in the industry. After the 1840s Famine, lacemaking was revived when Belgian Guipure lace was brought to the town and the technique of tracing designs on a cambric base was introduced.

In 1898 the craft of fine lacemaking was revived once more in Carrickmacross, by the Sisters of St Louis convent who now support a lacemaker's cooperative of local women. Their fine work, some pieces of which are now collector's items, incorporates traditional emblems such as shamrock, harps, swans and flowers. The lace is distinguished by its fine loops, and coloured work has recently been introduced. The lacemaking is labour-intensive work – one small handkerchief takes about 30 hours to make.

Clones lacemaking started in 1847 when the wife of the rector of Clones invited a lacemaking teacher to show women from impoverished families how to earn some income. Soon 1500 women were working, to a style based on snippets of old ecclesiastical lace, and by 1910 Clones was Ireland's main centre for crochet lace. Modern work still features a distinctive small raised knot, the Clones 'dot'.

the Derryvally Presbyterian Church. When the minister of the original church died in 1831, a dispute over his successor led to yet another split, and a third church – the Second Ballybay Presbyterian Church – was built, in Ballybay, in 1834. The congregations were united once more in 1972.

## Carrickmacross/Carraig Mhachaire Rois

The chief agricultural centre for the south of the county is often called 'the rock on the wooded plain', and is a busy town with traditions of robust trading and exquisitely fine lace.

At one end of Carrickmacross's broad main street is the 200-year-old St Finbarr's Church, with its octagonal spire, and at the other the austere William Caldbeck courthouse of 1844. In between, the street is lined with handsome Georgian buildings and pretty shopfronts. The old 1861 market house, at the top of the main street near the square, is a U-shaped building with an iron-pillared arcade. It now houses council services and a collection of local lace.

The graceful spire of the Gothic Revival St Joseph's, built between 1861 and 1897, signals one of the finest Catholic parish churches in the county. It contains eight windows from the 1920s by Harry Clarke, a leading member of the Irish school of stained glass. The tenth of the Stations of the Cross includes the face of Stalin, regarded at the time as the antichrist.

Outside the town, to the south-west, is Lough Fea House, a sinister-looking Victorian mansion built in the Tudor-Gothic style, overlooking a lake and surrounded by woods. It has a vast baronial hall with a hammerbeam roof and a large, handsome library. Its chapel has two pulpits and a gallery. Admission is by request to the Agent on Main Street.

## Castleblayney/Baile na Lorgan

On the western shores of Muckno Lake is the market town that takes its name from Sir Edward Blayney, who received a grant of land from James I in 1611 and started to build the town. Almost two centuries later, the 11th Lord Blayney, who was responsible for much of the town's development, raised a regiment in the Napoleonic Wars, which was known as 'Blayney's Bloodhounds'. He had the 1622 Church of Ireland church rebuilt in 1808 and had a Catholic church erected. South of the

ST JOSEPH'S CHURCH *St Ceara, a local saint who had a convent nearby, is portrayed vividly in scarlet and yellow in this striking window created by Harry Clarke in 1926.*

town are five red-brick almshouses built for the poor under the will of his son, the last Lord Blayney, who died in 1874.

An imposing 1856 courthouse stands in the centre of the triangular marketplace, built on top of the lower storey of the old market house. Off the marketplace, two gatehouses indicate the entrance to Hope Castle, a 17th-century mansion close to where Castle Blayney once stood. The castle itself cannot be visited, but from it there are panoramic views of the lough.

Castleblayney is also a recreational centre. The nearby Lough Muckno Leisure Park and Youth Hostel, on the 900 acres of island-dotted Muckno Lake, provides for water sports such as boating, water-skiing, fishing and swimming. There are forest walks and nature trails at Black Island, which can be reached by crossing a timber footbridge, or at Concra to the south-east.

## Inishkeen/Inis Caoin

The harshness and glories of life amid the hills around Inishkeen have been celebrated by poet Patrick Kavanagh (1905-67) and have ensured that the village is now better known for the poet than for its founding saint, St Daig, who died in AD 586.

Signposts by the road point to places mentioned in Kavanagh's work, such as Shancoduff, a hill with views of the surrounding counties, and the scene of his 'black hills'.

*'My black hills have never seen the sun rising, Eternally they look north toward Armagh.'*

Kavanagh spent his formative years working on the family farm, off the Carrickmacross road. The farmhouse, a plain 1791 building, is signposted, but the public cannot go inside. Kavanagh's grave lies in the family plot at the local church.

Close to the Fane river, which runs through the village, is the 42ft lower half of a Round Tower with a doorway 14ft above the ground accessible only by ladder, and the remains of the 6th-century monastery founded by St Daig. An old stone church on the site houses a small museum containing local artefacts and railway memorabilia.

On the road to Carrickmacross is a striking, round modern church whose unusual shape and curved roof were inspired by a cockleshell, symbol of a pilgrim, a theme that is continued inside.

**Church museum** *By arrangement. Tel: (042) 78102.*

# The Place of Little Hills

*True to the meaning of its Irish name, Monaghan is a place of 'little hills', egg-shaped mounds of boulder clay formed by glaciers some 10,000 years ago. From a distance this landscape looks like a great green ocean swell. A closer view shows the countryside to be on an intimate scale: the farms are small, the villages and market towns compact, the woods little. Ragged hedges crisscross the smooth hill slopes, and a maze of lanes and ancient paths leads to peaceful fishing lakes.*

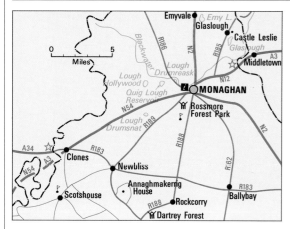

CLONES TOMBSTONE *Gruesome symbols remind passers-by of death.*

## Clones/Cluain Eois

Its Irish name means 'the meadow on the height' and Clones sits on a hill, which gives a slope to the town's Diamond – the Ulster 'square' that characterises plantation towns of the 1600s.

St Tighearnach, or Tierney, c. 470-548, first gave prominence to Clones by establishing a monastery there. The monastery was destroyed by Vikings in 836, but undaunted the monks continued their work. The roofless 12th-century church is in a quiet yard off Abbey Street, and among the graves are curious round stones, crudely carved in the 18th and 19th century with symbols of mortality: the skull and crossbones, an hourglass and the bell and coffin. More of these stones appear in St Tighearnach's graveyard, a short distance away, along with an early Round Tower and a 12th-century stone sarcophagus with a roof-shaped lid.

The sculpted High Cross that stands in the Diamond consists of parts of two separate 9th or 10th-century crosses mounted on top of one another. The capstone probably dates from the 18th century. The carving is weathered but some of the Biblical scenes can be identified, among them the Fall of Adam and Eve, and the Adoration of the Magi. South-west of the Diamond is an earthwork once used by invading Normans, and now surrounded by undergrowth.

Among Clones's 19th-century buildings, reflecting its wealth and status, are the Church of Ireland church, at the high point of the Diamond, which was built in 1822, a huge 1847 market house, which now houses the County Library, and a sternly plain courthouse from the mid-1840s.

## Glaslough/Glasloch

The neat, charming village clustered beside the wall of the 1000 acre Castle Leslie estate stands out from the surrounding fields and woods like an outcrop of grey stone. The 'green lake', the meaning of Glaslough, is at the centre of the estate, overlooked by the brooding Scottish Baronial castle of 1878. Also known as Glaslough House, it is a vast mansion of grey stone and red Scottish sandstone. Descendants of the Scottish scholar and bishop, John Leslie (1571-1671) have lived there since he acquired the property in 1665. Leslie was known as the 'fighting bishop' for his energetic part in resisting the Catholic uprising of 1641. A vigorous man, he married, at the age of 70, a bride of 18, and fathered ten children.

The bishop built a little Church of Ireland church by the lake, to which stained glass was added in Victorian times. The church still stands and is open for services on Sunday. From it, a broad drive curves round to the castle. In its Edwardian heyday, the castle's grounds were formally laid out, but now they consist mainly of rough grass and fine, mature trees.

**Glaslough House and Garden** *May be seen by appointment.* Tel: (047) 88100.

## Monaghan/Muineachán

From the severe Presbyterian church to the orderly town layout, the stamp of the industrious Scots who built up Monaghan's prosperity is evident. Even today, the local accent carries an echo of Scotland that sounds through the Irish brogue.

But Monaghan contains reminders of an even longer history, in the crannog that rises from the lake in the grounds of the St Louis convent. This fortified, man-made island was

---

**OTHER PLACES TO SEE**
**Dartrey Forest** Woodland walks, Georgian stables and a 1774 monument.
**Rossmore Forest Park** Forest and lakeside walks.

**EVENTS**
**Clones Agricultural Show** First week in July.

**Monaghan Band Festival** End June.
**Monaghan County Arts Festival** End Sept/early Oct.
**Monaghan Jazz Festival** Mid-Sept.

**SPORT**
**Angling** Coarse fishing: Loughs Drumreask, Drumsnat and Hollywood, River Blackwater and Quig Lough Reservoir. Trout fishing: Emy Lough and Glaslough.
**Golf** Clones Golf Club, 9-hole course. Tel: (049) 56017.
Rossmore Park Golf Club, 18-hole course. Tel: (047) 81316.
**Horse riding** Glaslough.

**INFORMATION**
Monaghan Tourist Office. Tel: (047) 81122.

GLASLOUGH PUB *Bulging with curiosities, this snug, wood-panelled parlour is full of character. The ancient pots crowded into the fireplace, and other objects, give it a pleasant flavour of the past.*

MONAGHAN CATHEDRAL *A supremely elegant spire complements this splendid Gothic Revival building.*

where the ruling MacMahon clan made their base in the 14th century.

The centre of Monaghan is made up of three wide interconnected squares. Two of these are graced with solid, authoritative 19th-century civic buildings, but linked by bustling, narrow streets of 18th-century character. The Diamond was originally the market place, at the foot of the walls of a long-vanished castle, and contains the elegant, classical, 1792 Market House, with its delicately carved decorations and rounded corners typical of many of the town's buildings. The Market House now houses the Tourism Office. The Diamond is dominated by the Rossmore Memorial, a Victorian drinking fountain whose eight grey marble columns support an elaborate canopy of sandstone. The 17th-century market cross was moved to Old Cross Square to make way for it.

The Diamond lost its central role when Church Square was built, where the 1829 courthouse, with its Doric columns, contrasts with the lighter elegance of the Regency Gothic of St Patrick's Church. A massive obelisk commemorating a local notable, Col. Thomas Dawson, who fell in the Crimean War, completes the square's civic character.

Old Cross Square, reached from the Diamond by Dublin Street, recalls an earlier, less solemn age. This area of town used to be known as the Shambles, the centre of the butchery trade. The curious market cross in the square – moved here from the Diamond – is in fact a sundial. Unfortunately the polygonal block on top of the column was put back upside down, so that the cups hollowed into three of its faces to show the hour at different seasons of the year are now useless.

Old Cross Square also contains the Presbyterian church, built in 1901 above the original one of 1827, now serving as a church hall underneath. It is fronted by some fine iron railings.

St Macartan's Cathedral surveys the town from the hill above. Built between 1861 and 1892 to designs by J.J. McCarthy (1817-82), the 'Irish Pugin', it is considered one of his best works.

After the cathedral, the proudest possession of Monaghan is its museum which won a Council of Europe Museum prize in 1980. It is housed in a fine town house just above the market house. The processional Cross of Clogher, dating from about 1400 and embossed with figures and ornaments, is one of the most important and beautiful objects on display here.

Monaghan was the birthplace of Charles Gavan Duffy (1816-1903), Prime Minister of Victoria, Australia.

**Monaghan County Museum** *Tues-Sat, 11am-5pm. Tel: (047) 82928.*

---

### GREGG'S SHORTHAND

Born in 1867 in Shantonagh, Monaghan, John Robert Gregg was the son of the local stationmaster. At the age of ten he taught himself shorthand, and finding the system unsatisfactory began to compile his own version based on the sounds of words and written in a more cursive style than Isaac Pitman's.

Later, Gregg went to work in Liverpool, where he developed the system into one of the best-known types of shorthand in the world. When he was 21 he published it in a pamphlet entitled *Light-Line Phonography*. In 1893 he took the system to America, where it became known as Gregg Shorthand. It is now taught in most of the schools that teach shorthand in the United States. It is also published in many other languages, including Hebrew, Japanese, Thai and Polish.

---

### Newbliss/Cúil Darach

A linen village built in the mid-18th century by Robert Kerr, Newbliss suffered hard times when the industry collapsed, but it has since revived due to a flourishing activity in the arts. Only 3 miles away, overlooking a lushly wooded lake, is the Victorian Annaghmakerrig House, former home of theatre director Sir Tyrone Guthrie (1900-71) and now an artists' retreat. He left the property to the state so that artists from Ireland and abroad could gather in the peace of the 400 acre estate to complete work in progress, whether a book, a painting, a piece of sculpture or a musical composition. Members of the public can enjoy the inspiring surroundings, with its picnic sites and forest walks.

### Rockcorry/Buíochar

Named after the Corr family, Rockcorry is a former flax-growing village, and the place where John Robert Gregg (1867-1948), inventor of Gregg Shorthand, grew up.

Before the Corr family took over the surrounding land, the place was known as Gribby, from the Irish for yellow clay. It was this stiff local clay beneath a shallow covering of loam that attracted the flax-growers.

Opposite the church is a terrace of greystone and red-brick almshouses, built in 1846 by Joseph Griffiths, 'gentleman of Cootehill', for widows of 'respectable character'. They are still inhabited.

CRAFT SHOP *Items made locally are popular.*

# THE SOUTH-WEST

THE touchstone against which all other beauty spots in Ireland are popularly measured is Killarney in County Kerry. This is a charmed landscape of lakes and wooded vales, rolling sandstone hills and rich, green pastures where herds of black-and-white cows graze, producing much of Ireland's famous butter and cream. To the east lies Cork, the second-largest city in the republic, with broad, gracious streets and 19th-century limestone bridges.

But it is the west of this region, with its rugged mountains and wave-lashed coves, that has drawn flocks of visitors since the mid-18th century. Here the grandeur of the scenery is softened by memorable detail – a red deer glimpsed among the oaks, furze and bell-heather clinging to the headlands. The Gulf Stream brings a touch of Caribbean warmth to the climate, fostering an exceptional range of wild flowers, including fragile, white Kerry lilies, and the strawberry tree, a Mediterranean shrub which in Kerry grows to tree-size.

Fine scenic roads, including the famous Ring of Kerry, trace the coastline of mountainous fingers jutting out into the Atlantic. Off one of these peninsulas is Puffin Island, pockmarked with the burrows of thousands of puffins. And the rocky pinnacles of Little Skellig island form one of the world's largest gannetries, hosting some 20,000 nesting pairs. Shearwaters, skuas and petrels, too, settle on the coast in the intervals between their Atlantic migrations.

This part of Ireland has long been the point of access to and from the Continent and, in more recent centuries, the New World. The waterfront at Cobh, the port of Cork, with its multicoloured façades of shops and houses, has a poignant beauty, for this was the last sight of Ireland for many emigrants on their way to new lives in America and Australia.

The Anglo-Normans recognised the strategic threat implied by south-west Ireland's ease of access from the Continent and built fortresses and tower houses across the region – and not without reason.

MACGILLICUDDY'S REEKS *Ireland's highest mountains dominate the Kerry landscape.*

A MERCURIAL COAST *The silvery stillness of the Cork coast is shattered at times by fierce Atlantic gales.*

Some 4000 Spaniards came to help Gaelic chieftains Hugh O'Neill and Red Hugh O'Donnell in 1601 when they made their last stand against English rule. It was, however, fewer than expected, and the Irish clans were defeated at the Battle of Kinsale. Almost two centuries later, in 1798, a French fleet organised by Wolfe Tone arrived in Bantry Bay to back the rebellion of the United Irishmen, only to be beaten back by a spell of the fearsome weather that the Atlantic regularly throws at this coast.

Some of Ireland's great poets have been inspired by the region. Among them Aodhagán Ó Rathaille, who is buried at Muckross Friary, near Killarney. The area has inspired English writers too. The ruined castle at Kilcolman, County Cork, was once owned by the Elizabethan poet Edmund Spenser, who is thought to have written the first three books of his masterpiece *The Faerie Queene* there.

Christianity is believed to have reached the south-west region before St Patrick landed in the north-east, and nowhere in Ireland is the self-imposed, contemplative isolation of the early monks more movingly revealed than on the rocky island of Great Skellig. There a cluster of simple, beehive cells has survived for more than 1000 years, perched some 600ft above the ocean.

The remoteness of the far west has meant that the Irish language has survived there, particularly on the Dingle and Iveragh peninsulas. The region is known as a Gaeltacht, an Irish-speaking area, and is an active centre of Irish culture. Among its quaint charms is the Rose of Tralee International Festival, in which the 'Rose' is selected from girls of Irish descent who come to the festival from all over the world. And in August, Killorglin holds the Puck Fair, in which a goat is paraded around the town. On the more serious side, Cork city is known for its lively arts festivals; it has a choral and folk-dance festival in May, and jazz and film festivals in October.

For sports lovers, the region boasts several tournament golf courses, and Tralee, Killarney, Listowel and Mallow all have well-known racecourses. Indeed racing history was made at the north Cork town of Buttevant. In 1752, riders raced from Buttevant Church to Doneraile some 5 miles away, guided by the steeple of Doneraile Church, in the first ever 'steeplechase'. Southern Cork is one of the yachting centres of Ireland, with schools, clubs and charter facilities along the coast; there are boats for sea anglers and excellent game fishing in the lakes and rivers inland. And there are several stately homes for the public to escape into on rainy days.

THE GOAT KING AND THE ROSE *At the annual Puck Fair in Killorglin, a goat is crowned King of the Town in an exuberant celebration that has all the atmosphere of an ancient Celtic feast (left). And in Tralee, one of Ireland's biggest festivals takes place each September, in which beautiful girls of Irish descent from all over the world hope to be chosen the Rose of Tralee (below).*

*Atlantic Ocean*

Brand Mount ▲ 3197

Smerwick Harbour

Ballyferriter

Dunquin  Ventry  R559 Connor DING

Great Blasket Island

Slea Head

Blasket Sound

Ding

CAHERSIVEEN

Valencia Island

Bray Head

Portmagee

N70

Waterville

Great Skellig  Little Skellig

St Finan's Bay

Ballinskelligs Bay

Scarriff Island

Dursey Island

Dursey Head

Kilkee
Kilrush
N67
N68
Loop
Head
Askeaton
LIMERICK
N69
N20
R503
Thurles
N8
N62
Cappamore
R505
R691
Ballybunnion
Mouth of the
Shannon
Ballylongford
Tarbert
R552
R551
R553
N69
Patrickswell
Adare
Rathkeale
R512
R513
N24
R497
R616
R505
Cashel
N74
R692
R689
R660
Ballyduff
Causeway
R551
Kerry
Head
R557
R556
N69
LISTOWEL
**122**
Abbeyfeale
Athea
R523
Ardagh
Newcastle
N21
Croom
R511
R516
R515
N20
Tipperary
R662
R515
Kilmallock
Galty Mountains
Caher
N24
R665
Clonmel
R668
N8
Fethard
R516
TIPPERARY
Ballyheige
Banna
Ardfert
Magharee
Islands
Rough
Point
Tralee
Bay
Fenit
**124**
TRALEE
Stack's Mts
Glanaruddery Mts
N21
Mullaghareirk Mountains
Drumcollliher
R579
Rathluirc
(Charleville)
R517
R513
Ballyhoura Mountains
Mitchelstown
Knockmealdown Mountains
Monavullagh
Mountains
WATERFORD
Castlegregory
R559
N22
N21
Castleisland
R578
R576
Liscarroll
Buttevant
R522
N73
Kildorrery
R668
R669
R671
R672
Camp
Slieve Mish Mts
R561
Maine
N23
R577
R578
Newmarket
R580
Doneraile
Glanworth
Castletownroche
Anascaul
Inch
Castlemaine
Harbour
Farranfore
**104**
Banteer
Kanturk
Killavullen
**100**
FERMOY
Blackwater
Lismore
N72
Killorglin
R563
Rathmore
R582
R577
MALLOW
Ballyhooly
N72
Tallow
R627
Dungarvan
Glenbeigh
N70
R562
Laune
**120**
KILLARNEY
Blackwater
Nagles
Mountains
R628
N25
of Kerry
Lough
Caragh
Lough
Leane
N22
Millstreet
Boggeragh Mountains
R619
N20
R614
N8
R626
**K   E   R   R   Y**
Macgillycuddy's Reeks
Derrynasaggart
Mountains
**C    O    R    K**
R634
**108**
YOUGHAL
**112**
**118**
KENMARE
R568
R569
Kilgarvan
Ballyvourney
**102**
MACROOM
R618
Coachford
Blarney
Killeagh
Midleton
Castlemartyr
Cloyne
Ardmore
Head
Sneem
Ring of Kerry
R571
Ballingeary
R584
Inchigeelagh
Farran
N22
**96**
CORK
Lee
Cork
Airport
Ringaskiddy
Great
Island
Cobh
Youghal
Bay
Ballycotton
Bay
Ballycotton
herdaniel
Lauragh
Glengarriff
R584
R585
R581
Cappeen
R586
Beanablath
Innishannon
R611
Crosshaven
Kenmare River
Caha
Mountains
Dunmanway
**92**
Kilbrittain
Ballinspittle
Swansea
Le Havre
Roscoff
Eyeries
Adrigole
Whiddy
Island
BANTRY
R586
R586
R588
Ballinascarty
Bandon
Kinsale
Castletown
Bearhaven
Bear
Island
Bantry
Bay
**90**
Drimoleague
R599
R600
Timoleague
Kinsale
Harbour
Old Head of
Kinsale
Ballydehob
**106**
Leap
Courtmacsherry
CLONAKILTY
Sheep's
Head
Dunmanus Bay
R591
R592
Skull
SKIBBEREEN
Glandore
Carbery
Clonakilty
Bay
Seven
Heads
Three Castle
Head
Goleen
Lough
Hyne
Castletownshend
Galley
Head
Crookhaven
Mizen
Head
Brow
Head
Clear
Island
Baltimore
Sherkin
Island
Fastnet
Rock

KEY TO SYMBOLS

**90** Page number of zone
Zone boundary
Touring centre
Other town or village
National road
Regional road
Railway & station
County boundary

0    5    10    15    20    25    30    35    40    45    50 Miles
0   5   10      20      30      40      50      60      70      80 Km

# Flower of the Gulf Stream

*Between rocky promontories jutting into the Atlantic lies Bantry Bay, one of the world's largest and most beautiful natural harbours. The Caha Mountains form the spine of the rugged Beara peninsula to the north. Farther south the Mizen peninsula pokes into the Atlantic like a gnarled finger. The scenery ranges from rock-strewn desolation to wooded glens and luxuriant gardens warmed by the Gulf Stream.*

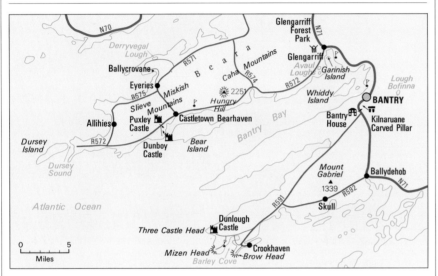

BANTRY HOUSE *The dining room, with period furniture, sparkles with family silver and porcelain.*

**OTHER PLACES TO SEE**
**Ballycrovane** Site of Ireland's tallest ogham pillar, an inscribed standing stone 17½ft high.
**Barley Cove** On S coast of Mizen peninsula. Magnificent beaches.
**Brow Head** SE of Barley Cove; Martello tower built in 19th century against invasion by the French, and radio mast built by Guglielmo Marconi to communicate with Atlantic shipping; spectacular views from headland.
**Dursey Island** The only cable car in Ireland crosses over Dursey Sound to reach this island.
**Kilnaruane Carved Pillar** Just S of Bantry; 9th-century carving, showing the ship of the church.

**EVENTS**
**Bantry Mussel Festival** May.
**Crookhaven Regatta** Aug.
**Skull Festival** Early July.

**SPORT**
**Angling** Coarse fishing: Lough Bofinna. Game fishing: Derryvegal Lough, Lower and Upper Avaul Lough, Lough Bofinna, and Skull reservoir. Sea fishing: Bantry Bay and Beara peninsula. Deep-sea fishing: Castletown Bearhaven.
**Golf** Bantry Park Golf Club, 9-hole course. Tel: (027) 50579.
Barley Cove Hotel, 9-hole course. Tel: (028) 35234.

Berehaven Golf Club, 9-hole course. Tel: (027) 70164/70469.
Glengarriff Golf Club, 9-hole course. Tel: (027) 63150.
**Hang-gliding and para-gliding** Mike Tanner, Bantry. Tel: (027) 51567.
**Horse riding** West Cork Horse Trekking Co, Bantry. Tel: (027) 50221/51412.
**Sailing** Bantry, Castletown Bearhaven, Glengarriff, Skull.
**Skin diving** Matt O'Connor, Bantry. Tel: (027) 50221.
**Water-skiing** Matt O'Connor, Bantry. Tel: (027) 50221.

**INFORMATION**
Skibbereen Tourist Office. Tel: (028) 21766.

## Bantry/Beanntraí

Fishing port, market town, tourist centre and gateway to Ireland's mountainous south-west, Bantry sits comfortably in the shelter of wooded hills at the head of Bantry Bay, bathed in the warm waters of the Gulf Stream. It was twice unsuccessfully attacked by French fleets, first in 1689 in support of the exiled James II, and again in 1796, when General Hoche's ships were dispersed by storms lasting six days. On board one of them was the Irish revolutionary leader Wolfe Tone, after whom Bantry's main square is named. He said later: 'We were close enough to toss a biscuit ashore.'

On the town's southern fringe is Bantry House, an elegant Georgian mansion built around 1750 of mellow red brick and set in superbly laid-out gardens. Originally the seat of the Earls of Bantry, it is still owned and occupied by descendants of the family. What adds to its charm is its lived-in atmosphere: no areas are roped off, though the family keeps a few private rooms for themselves. Among the objets d'art on display inside the house are Gobelin tapestries, mosaics from Pompeii, fine family portraits, and Chippendale and Sheraton furniture. In the yard of the house is a recently opened Armada centre.

Bantry is ideally placed for most holiday activities, and is a convenient base for touring the local peninsulas. With its lush country-side, wide beaches, and remote lakes and rivers, it is perfect for activities from walking to skin diving, and from horse riding to golf. For the more adventurous, it also has a hang-gliding and para-gliding school.

Whiddy Island, which guards the sea-ward access to Bantry, has many remains of 19th-century fortifications. It is an off-loading terminal for oil tankers, but the storage tanks are discreetly sunk into the landscape.
**Bantry House** *Daily, 9am-6pm, and later in summertime. Tel: (027) 50047.*

## Castletown Bearhaven/Baile Chaisleáin Bhéarra

The Beara peninsula's main town, popularly known as Castletownbere, is sheltered on the north by the Slieve Miskish Mountains and protected to the south by Bear Island. It stands beside a natural haven, which until 1937 was the fortified anchorage of the British Atlantic fleet. Today the town makes its living mainly from fishing (including deep-sea angling), and holds a lively fish auction several evenings a week.

One mile south-south-west of the town are the ruins of Dunboy Castle, set in water-fringed woodland. It was the last castle to hold out against the English after the Battle of

Kinsale in 1601, but in the following year it was captured after a siege and its Spanish-Irish garrison was massacred.

Between the castle and the town is the dilapidated shell of Puxley Castle, once the home of the Puxley family, who made their fortune from the copper mines at nearby Allihies. Daphne du Maurier based her novel *Hungry Hill* on their family history. Hungry Hill itself, rising to 2251ft, is the highest point of the Caha Mountains, with stupendous views and a 770ft waterfall.

### Glengarriff/An Gleann Garbh

Despite its Irish name, 'Rugged Glen', Glengarriff is an oasis of subtropical colours and lush woodland at the head of an islet-dotted inlet at the top of Bantry Bay. The Gulf Stream allows palm trees and subtropical flowers to flourish in the sheltered parts of the valley, and the climate often feels like the Mediterranean. There are also sturdy northern woodlands of oak and holly, which hug the shoreline and provide the nucleus of the Glengarriff Forest Park, with its walks and nature trails. Glengarriff's 9-hole golf course is among the prettiest courses in the world.

Lying offshore is Garinish Island, easily reached by boat from Glengarriff. In the early

FIERY SKIES *Streaks of red and gold fill the evening sky above Bantry Bay, while boats rock gently below the huge silhouette of Hungry Hill.*

ITALIAN GARDENS *On Garinish Island a temple leads the eye to the water and mountains beyond.*

19th century it was chosen as a defence point against Napoleonic invasion and a Martello tower was built there. It is still intact, surrounded by superb Italian gardens.

The island was bought early this century by Scottish MP Annan Bryce, whose wife had fallen in love with it. In the 1920s they turned the island's 37 acres into a Garden of Eden with the help of Harold Peto, architect and garden designer. Exotic species were planted, such as New Zealand privet, sacred bamboo, scented mahonias and rhododendrons, as well as magnolias, camellias and rare conifers. They now grow around stone balustrades and Grecian pillars. Garinish was bequeathed to the Irish people in 1953.

It was here that George Bernard Shaw is said to have written his play *St Joan*.

### Mizen Head/Carn Uí Néid

This is Ireland's Land's End. Its 700ft cliffs are a marvellous vantage point overlooking spectacular coastal scenery. On wild days, tremendous Atlantic waves assault the cliffs. When it is calm, seals bask on the rocks and gannets wheel over the sea before diving into the placid waters.

### Skull/An Scoil

This popular yachting harbour (also spelled Schull) shelters between rolling green hills at the foot of 1339ft Mount Gabriel. The village, whose Irish name means 'school', after the monastic school founded here in the 10th century, is little more than a single main street of brightly coloured terraced houses, shops and bars.

The two enormous golfball-like white domes visible on top of the mountain are part of an international aircraft-tracking system. Skull has the only planetarium in the Irish Republic. Its founding was inspired by a German scientist, Joseph Menke, who donated its £130,000 projector.

### Three Castle Head/Dun Locha

The imposing ruins of Dunlough Castle stand on a western promontory of the Mizen peninsula. On one side of it 300ft cliffs plummet down to the sea, while on the other a pretty lake gives it a quite different character. The castle was one of a number built here by the warring O'Mahoney clan from 1200 to 1500. It was once formed by three buildings joined together, hence its English name.

# Buskers and a Moving Statue

*From Kinsale Harbour in the east round to Galley Head in the west, the Cork shoreline twists and darts in and out of creeks, bays and coves. Inland is a tranquil pastureland of soft green hills where fat milking cows graze. Once it was thickly forested and haunted by wolves, but the last of these was killed in the early 18th century.*

## Ballinascarty/Béal na Scairte

This was the family village of the car maker Henry Ford. Like thousands of others, the Fords left Ireland for America in 1847, fleeing from the potato famine. They travelled by cart to Cork, and sailed from there to Quebec. Henry was born in Michigan, in 1863. It is said that a fall from a horse encouraged him to invent a less temperamental form of transport. Around 1930 Henry Ford's son came here and took the hearthstone from the family home to America, and now only a playing field, hostel and bookshop are reminders of the village's Ford ancestors.

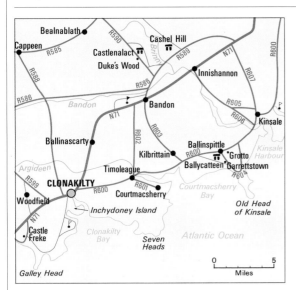

**Cork** Clonakilty, July.
**Clonakilty Agricultural Show** Early June.
**Clonakilty Busking Festival** Last weekend Aug.
**Clonakilty Festival of Music** End July.
**Timoleague Harvest Festival** End Aug.

### SPORT
**Angling** Game fishing: Rivers Argideen, Bandon and Brinny, and lakes of the locality. Sea fishing: Clonakilty Bay, Courtmacsherry and Timoleague. Deep-sea fishing: Courtmacsherry Sea Angling Centre. Tel: (023) 46427.
**Bathing** Clonakilty Bay, Courtmacsherry, Garrettstown, Inchydoney, Kilbrittain.
**Boating** Courtmacsherry Sea Angling Centre. Tel: (023) 46427.
**Golf** Bandon Golf Club, 18-hole course. Tel: (023) 41111.
Dunmore Golf Club, 9-hole course. Tel: (023) 33352.
**Pony trekking** Ardnavana House Hotel, Ballinascarty. Tel: (023) 39135.

### INFORMATION
Skibbereen Tourist Office. Tel: (028) 21766.

### OTHER PLACES TO SEE
**Courtmacsherry** Near Clonakilty. Family holiday resort on Seven Heads peninsula, with its seven jutting headlands. Good beaches, excellent for swimming, fishing and birdwatching.
**Kilbrittain** Near Timoleague. Village in wooded countryside, offering good fishing, forest walks and views of the restored Kilbrittain Castle.
**Old Head of Kinsale** Promontory off which the passenger liner *Lusitania* was sunk by a German submarine in 1915.

### WALKS
**Castle Freke** On coast, 6m from Clonakilty.
**Duke's Wood** 4m N of Bandon.

### EVENTS
**Annual Festival of West**

## Ballinspittle/Béal Átha an Spidéil

In the summer of 1985 fame came to Ballinspittle when two local women vowed that a plaster statue of the Virgin in a grotto outside the village had swayed and waved its hands. Soon thousands of pilgrims flocked to Ballinspittle – and hundreds claimed to have seen the Virgin move. The crowds became so large that areas had to be roped off as viewing and praying enclosures. Visitors still come to the grotto, but no further movements of the statue have been reported.

Near Ballinspittle is the ring-fort of Ballycatteen. It is made up of three concentric rings, is 400ft in diameter and is said to date from about AD 600. Excavations at the site have uncovered fragments of imported pottery – proof of Ireland's early trading links with the outside world.

MOVING VISION *Pilgrims flock to Ballinspittle's statue of the Virgin, which is said to 'move'.*

## Bandon/Droichead na Bandan

The walled town of Bandon lies surrounded by prosperous farming country, on the banks of the beautiful River Bandon. (In fact, the town's Irish name means 'Bandon bridge'.) Like Clonakilty, it was founded on land seized from local clans for English settlers, by Richard Boyle, 1st Earl of Cork. The land was expropriated in 1608. In those troubled times Catholics and Nonconformists were not allowed inside the town wall, parts of which

BUSKERS' HOLIDAY *Every summer the lilting music of buskers trips down Clonakilty's streets.*

still stand today. The old town stocks and whipping post are preserved inside Kilbrogan Church, which was built in 1610 and is the oldest surviving post-Reformation Church of Ireland church.

Modern Bandon has a large cattle market and is a popular fishing centre. To the north are some fine standing stones at Castlenalact, and a large oval hilltop fort on Cashel Hill.

## Clonakilty/Cloich na Coillte

At the top of a winding inlet is this lively market town, laid out in 1614 by the 1st Earl of Cork. The tall-spired Catholic church dominates the square. The handsome Presbyterian church, built in 1861, was converted into a post office after its once-prosperous congregation, mainly farmers and land stewards, had gradually died out.

In the street outside the courthouse is the 19th-century pump known as the Wheel of Fortune, which formed part of a water scheme for the area promoted by the Earl of Shannon, a descendant of Richard Boyle.

Clonakilty became notorious during the devastating 1847 Famine, when hundreds of starving farm labourers and their families struggled to the town in the hope of finding food. Many either died there in the workhouse or carried on to Cobh, where they boarded ships sailing to America.

Today Clonakilty has a far more cheerful reputation and hosts an international busking festival, when the town resounds to music and frolics and becomes one joyous 'gettogether' or 'hooley'. It also has several bars where traditional music is played.

INCHYDONEY ISLAND *Miles of soft sand swirl in a beautiful curve around the promontory, which used to become an island when the tides rolled in higher than they do nowadays.*

Clonakilty Bay has fine sandy beaches, excellent for swimming and fishing.

### Inchydoney Island/Oileán Inse Duine

At the head of Clonakilty Bay is a peninsula known as Inchydoney Island, and so called because up to 1845 it was cut off from the mainland at high tide. The tide no longer rises high enough to isolate Inchydoney, and two causeways now link the 'island' to the mainland, giving easy access to its sandy beaches.

Inchydoney has seen violent times in the past. In 1642, during an Irish rising, two companies of Scottish soldiers were cut to pieces on the streets of Clonakilty. Reinforcements of English troops tried to force the rebels onto Inchydoney, but when the tide came in more than 600 were drowned in the marshy land around the island.

### Timoleague/Tigh Molaige

The extensive remains of a Franciscan friary, once one of the most important religious houses in Ireland, dominate the village of Timoleague, beside the mud flats of the River Argideen. Its Irish name means 'house of Molaga', from the saint who founded the first monastery on the site in the 6th century. The ruins are of the abbey built in the 14th century by an Irish prince, Donal Glas MacCarthy. Today it is one of the better-preserved of the 62 Franciscan friaries built in Ireland before the Reformation, with the kitchen, library, dining hall and infirmary still distinguishable.

In 1642 the abbey was sacked by English Parliamentary forces, and during Cromwell's campaigns of suppression it became a local burial place. The Franciscans remained in the area until around 1700, but the abbey was no longer a place of worship. A good deal of the church survives, including the chancel, nave and south transept, and the graceful 67½ft tower. Near the transept window is a squint – an opening which allowed lepers to observe the service.

### Woodfield

This village was the birthplace of Michael Collins (1890-1922), soldier, statesman and one of Ireland's greatest heroes. A memorial has recently been built outside the place where he was born, and another stands in the centre of the village. Opposite is the pub where he is said to have had his last drink on the day he was shot in an ambush in a narrow lane at Béalnablath, a few miles to the north.

---

#### MONKEY BUSINESS

On April 7, 1943, an American Flying Fortress on its way from North Africa to England strayed off course, ran out of fuel and crash-landed on marshland between Clonakilty and Inchydoney. The crew of ten, a passenger and a pet monkey, Tojo, all survived and were at once besieged by an excited crowd.

Clonakilty took on a carnival atmosphere as the local defence force accompanied the lucky survivors to O'Donovan's Hotel in the town. Eventually a temporary runway was laid and the plane took off for England, leaving Tojo behind.

When he died, he was buried in the hotel yard with full military honours; a plaque inside the building commemorates the crash-landing.

# The City of Spires

Ireland's second largest city grew from a 7th-century monastery founded by St Finbarr on the marshland of the River Lee (its Irish name, Corcaigh, means 'marshy place'). Shipping has always been important here, and today Cork is a prosperous harbour city. The River Lee flows through the middle of Cork, splitting into two channels which pass around either side of the main business and shopping centre. The result is a profusion of quays and bridges. Cork is a city of spires, bow windows, Georgian houses, bustling markets and bars; a city of hidden alleys, pedestrian walkways and modern shops.

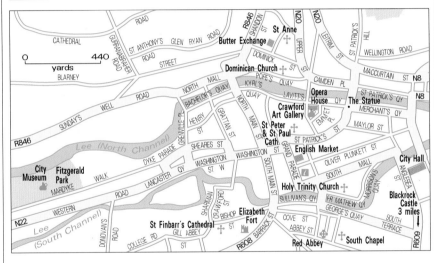

HARBOUR CITY *The spires of Cork's churches and its City Hall crowd the banks of the harbour.*

## OTHER PLACES TO SEE

**Blackrock Castle** 19th-century castle whose handsome battlements overlook the River Lee 3m downriver from Cork. Originally built in 1582 as a harbour fortification by Lord Mountjoy, Queen Elizabeth I's Viceroy of Ireland, destroyed by fire and rebuilt in 1829. Has seen many famous visitors including Queen Victoria. Now a restaurant. Tel: (021) 357414.

**Dominican Church** Built in 1839 on land beside the River Lee with fine neoclassical interior.

**English Market** Off St Patrick's Street, 18th-century covered market in use today as a flea market.

**Holy Trinity Church** Designed by Pain brothers, and begun in 1834 by Father Mathew.

## WALKS

**Tourist Trail** From Grand Parade to Coal Quay market, Paul Street (artisan area), Fitzgerald Park and Cork City Museum, Butter Exchange, St Anne's Church, Crawford Art Gallery and Cathedral of St Peter and St Paul.

## EVENTS

**Cork International Choral and Folk Dance Festival** Apr/May.

**Cork International Film Festival** Oct.

**Cork Jazz Festival** Oct.

## SPORT

**Angling** The Lough.

**Golf** Cork Golf Club, 18-hole course. Tel: (021) 353263.

## INFORMATION

Cork Tourist Information Office. Tel: (021) 273251.

## Butter Exchange

The disused 18th-century Butter Exchange is not far from St Anne's Church, Shandon. Here deals were struck for the export of Cork and Kerry salted butter to countries all over the world, and the foundations for Cork's prosperity as a commercial centre were first laid. The Exchange opened in 1770, and by the end of the 19th century was exporting 500,000 casks of butter a year, valued at £1½ million. It closed in 1924. Part of the Butter Exchange now houses the Shandon Craft Centre which sells local crafts including Shandon Crystal, from Monday to Saturday.

## Cork City Museum

Set in the pretty grounds of Fitzgerald Park, off Mardyke Walk, is the Cork City Museum. Its exhibits include a fascinating display of Cork's history, the dart that the city's mayor annually threw into the water to mark the limits of his jurisdiction, and a working model of an early flour mill, with an unusual horizontal water wheel.

**Opening times** *Mon-Fri, 11am-5pm; Sun, 3-5pm.* Tel: (021) 270679.

BLACKROCK CASTLE *The 19th-century castle guards the river approach to Cork City.*

## Crawford Art Gallery

The city's main art gallery, beside the opera house in Emmet Place, has a striking façade of red brick dressed with limestone. It was built in 1724 as the customs house, when the street alongside was the King's Dock, where ships unloaded their cargoes. In 1832, when Cork's shipping operations moved downstream a couple of miles, the customs house became an art gallery. Exhibits include sculptures by John Hogan (1800-58) and works by more modern Irish artists.
**Opening times** *Mon-Sat, 9.15am-5.30pm.*

## Elizabeth Fort

Just off Barrack Street is a fortification built about 1600 on the orders of Queen Elizabeth to guard against the threat of a Spanish invasion. Part of the fort is accessible to the public all year round, and gives fine views of Cork from its high walls.

## Red Abbey

A square tower, in Red Abbey Street, is all that survives of the 14th-century Augustinian priory that once stood in marshland outside the eastern walls of the city. Despite its name it is not red, but grey limestone.

During the siege of Cork by the English army in 1690, the Duke of Marlborough watched from the tower as his heavy guns in the abbey gardens below battered down the city walls. The tower is the oldest surviving piece of architecture in the city. It is open to visitors at all times.

## St Finbarr's Cathedral

The three graceful Gothic spires of Cork's imposing and highly ornamented Church of Ireland cathedral are visible from all over the city. It stands very near the south channel of the River Lee, the site where, in about AD 600, Cork's patron saint, the scholarly, fair-haired St Finbarr, built a monastic school that attracted scholars from all over Europe.

The present building is the third cathedral on the site. The medieval cathedral was badly damaged in the siege of Cork by the English in 1690, replaced in 1735, to be replaced again by the present building. Designed in the French Gothic style, it was completed in 1870.

Inside are some rich carvings and fine mosaics. Also displayed is a cannon ball that was fired during the siege of 1690 and afterwards found in the tower. A brass memorial commemorates Elizabeth Aldworth, the

CELESTIAL VISION *The apse ceiling of St Finbarr's Cathedral depicts Christ in glory surrounded by angels. Below the paintings, stained-glass windows illustrate the events of Christ's life. The roof and arches are supported by slim pillars made from Irish marble.*

only woman who was ever made a Freemason. As a young girl, in 1712, she hid and listened in on the proceedings of her father and other Masons, at her home in Doneraile. But she was discovered, and to ensure that she kept their secrets she had to be enrolled in their masonic lodge.

## South Chapel

The Roman Catholic church, built in 1766, is hidden in a back street, reflecting the low profile adopted by Catholics as the penal laws that forbade them from practising Catholicism were just being relaxed. The old stone exterior gives way to a simple interior which includes an altar sculpted from Carrara marble by the Irish sculptor John Hogan.

## The Statue

At one end of St Patrick's Street is a statue commemorating Father Mathew, an apostle of temperance and helper of the poor, particularly during the famine years of 1845-7. It is known by Cork people as 'The Statue' and was created by John Foley (1818-74), who also made the Group of Asia and the figure of Prince Albert for the Albert Memorial in London's Hyde Park.

# A Kiss for Eloquence

*Just outside the city of Cork you are in the heart of some of Ireland's most fertile land with thickly wooded valleys where rivers meander lazily. The countryside is dotted with ancient castles, such as Blarney and its famous stone, and busy seafaring towns such as Cobh and Kinsale. Along the coast remote sandy beaches offer quiet swims and walks.*

## Blarney/An Bhlarna

The village of Blarney was planned in the late 18th century as a linen and wool-processing centre, using water-powered machinery. Today it is chiefly a craft and tourist centre, where visitors can buy Irish glass, pottery, knitwear and linen. The Blarney Woollen Mills, which were built around 1750 and once employed many people in the area, have been converted into a hotel and craft centre.

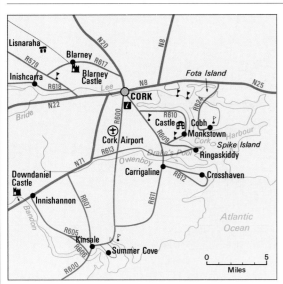

**OTHER PLACES TO SEE**
**Drake's Pool** Near Crosshaven. In 1587 Sir Francis Drake hid his ships in this reach of the River Owenboy while being chased by Spanish men-of-war. Although they combed the inlets, they missed this little haven – and Sir Francis lived to fight the Armada the following year.
**Innishannon** Village on River Bandon, which is tidal up to this point. Beside it are ruins of 15th-century Downdaniel Castle. Good centre for forest walks.
**Lisnaraha** 4m NW of Blarney. Fine medieval ringfort and standing stones.
**Monkstown Castle** Overlooking Cork Harbour. The builder of this Elizabethan house stipulated that everyone working on it should buy food from her. As a result, by the time the house was completed she was only one groat out of pocket.
**Spike Island** In estuary S of Cobh. Once a detention centre where 19th-century Irish political prisoners were held before being transported to Australia; there is still a prison on the island.

**EVENTS**
**Cobh International Folk Dance Festival** July.
**Cobh Regatta** Aug.
**Kinsale Gourmet Festival** Oct.
**Kinsale Regatta** Aug. (Yacht and dinghy racing also at various other times.)

**SPORT**
**Angling** Coarse fishing: Inishcarra reservoir. Game fishing: Inishcarra reservoir, Rivers Bandon, Bride and Lee. Sea and deep-sea fishing: Cobh, Crosshaven, Kinsale.
**Canoeing** Inishcarra reservoir.
**Golf** Cobh Golf Club, 9-hole course. Tel: (021) 812399. Harbour Point Golf Club, 18-hole course. Tel: (021) 353094. Kinsale Golf Club, 9-hole course. Tel: (021) 772197. Monkstown Golf Club, 18-hole course. Tel: (021) 841225.
**Sailing** Inishcarra reservoir.
**Water-skiing** Inishcarra reservoir.

**INFORMATION**
Cork Tourist Information Office. Tel: (021) 273251.

**Blarney Woollen Mills** *Daily, 9am-6pm. Tel: (021) 385280.*

## Blarney Castle

This 15th-century castle is the mecca of first-time visitors to Ireland, who hope to win the gift of eloquence by kissing the Blarney Stone. The magnificent keep, with walls 85ft high and 12ft thick at the base, was built in 1446 by Cormac MacCarthy, and withstood many sieges during the 16th and 17th centuries. The castle was finally captured in 1690 by King William III's army, and was largely demolished.

The Blarney Stone is a block of rough limestone measuring 4ft by 1ft, set 83ft high in the battlements. To kiss it, you have to lie on your back and lean out over a sheer drop, with a pair of strong arms gripping your shins. It is scrubbed with disinfectant four times a day to prevent any risk of transmitting disease. Father Prout, the 19th-century humorist and poet, wrote of it

> *. . . a stone that whoever kisses*
> *O he never misses*
> *To grow eloquent.*

Blarney Castle House, on the estate, is a 19th-century Scottish Baronial mansion with a renovated interior and splendid gardens.
**Blarney Castle** *Mon-Sat, 9am-sundown; Sun, 9.30am-5.30pm.*
**House and Gardens** *June-Sept, Mon-Sat, 12.30-5.30pm. Tel: (021) 385252.*

## Cobh/An Cobh

Steep, narrow streets climb the hill above Cobh's fine natural harbour, giving wide views across the bay. Its name, pronounced 'cove', is simply the Irish for 'haven'. In the 19th century it was named Queenstown after Queen Victoria, who first stepped on Irish soil there in 1849. It remained a British naval base until 1937. Now a popular holiday resort and yachting centre, it was the headquarters of the Royal Cork Yacht Club, founded in 1720 and the oldest such club in the world. The Yacht Club building survives.

Cobh was once the main departure point for emigrants to America and was a stopping place for transatlantic liners. The *Sirius* sailed from Cobh in 1838 to make the first-ever Atlantic steamer crossing. The doomed *Titanic* called there in 1912. And it was from Cobh that naval ships set out in search of survivors from the *Lusitania*, torpedoed by a German submarine in 1915. A monument to the *Lusitania*'s 1198 dead stands in Casement Square, and many of them are buried in the Old Church cemetery. A visitor centre features Cobh's role in the emigration, and its naval history.

Towering over Cobh is the magnificent Gothic-style St Colman's Protestant cathedral, which was built in 1868. It is faced with blue granite, its floor is laid with mosaics and it is supported inside by pillars made from local marble topped with intricately carved capitals. The cathedral is floodlit at night,

### LEGENDARY ELOQUENCE

The legend connecting Blarney with the gift of eloquence is said to date from the time of Queen Elizabeth I. The smooth-talking Lord of Blarney, Cormac MacDermot MacCarthy, was asked by George Carew, the Queen's Deputy in Ireland, to give up the tradition whereby Irish clans elected their chiefs, and to transfer his allegiance to the English Crown. MacCarthy kept on sidetracking Carew with promises, until the Queen exploded: 'Blarney! Blarney! What he says he never means. It's the usual Blarney!'

The public ritual of kissing the Blarney Stone seems to date from the 18th-century development of the Blarney Castle Estate by the Jefferyes family. Some say the stone is part of the Stone of Scone, the ancient crowning seat of Scotland's kings, now in Westminster Abbey.

COBH HARBOUR *Pretty shopfronts and St Colman's Cathedral look down on the harbour.*

PLASTER CONFECTION *The drawing room of Fota House has an exquisite ceiling decorated with panels of cupids and gilded plasterwork reflected in long Italian mirrors.*

STAR PROTECTOR *The 40ft high star-shaped walls of Charles Fort protected the entrance to Kinsale harbour in the 17th century.*

when it makes a dramatic sight. Its carillon of 42 bells is claimed to be the largest in Ireland.

### Cork/Corcaigh See pages 94-95.

### Foaty Island

Surrounded by mud flats where wildfowl thrive, Foaty island (also called Fota island) includes a 70 acre wildlife park owned by the Royal Zoological Society of Ireland. The park contains cheetahs, and, wandering virtually unhindered, giraffes, zebras, wallabies and a large collection of other animals. There is also an arboretum, established in 1820, in which many unusual and beautiful specimen trees and shrubs from around the world flourish.

Also on the island is Fota House, originally a modest 18th-century hunting lodge that was remodelled and enlarged in Regency style in 1820. It is not open to the public.
**Arboretum** *Easter-Oct, Mon-Sat, 10am-5.15pm; Sun, 11am-5.15pm. Tel: (021) 276871.*
**Wildlife Park** *End Mar to early Sept, Mon-Sat, 10am-6pm; Sun, 11am-6pm. Sept and Oct, weekends only, 11am-6pm. Tel: (021) 812678.*

### Inishcarra/Inis Cara

West of Cork City, at the point where the River Bride joins the Lee, a section of the valley has been transformed into a huge reservoir as part of a hydroelectric scheme. This has been done so beautifully that the reservoir enhances the lovely Lee valley. Inishcarra is now a recreational centre for water sports.

### Kinsale/Cionn tSáile

An ancient seaside town, Kinsale is full of style and character. It is also a winner of the National Tidy Towns Competition. In the 17th and 18th centuries it was an important English naval base, and it still has a distinct Georgian flavour. With its yacht-filled harbour, brightly painted cottages, bow-windowed houses and displays of flowers in pots, tubs and hanging baskets, it marks the beginning of scenic west Cork, and well deserves its booming tourist industry. Only 18 miles from Cork, it is ideally placed as a deep-sea angling and yachting centre.

In 1601 Kinsale was the scene of a battle in which English troops defeated a mixed Irish-Spanish force. It was followed by the 'Flight of the Earls', when many of the Irish aristocracy surrendered their lands and fled to mainland Europe. In 1690, after his defeat at the Battle of the Boyne, James II escaped from Kinsale to exile in France. Not long after, in 1703, the 90 ton *Cinque Ports* sailed from the port with Alexander Selkirk on board. Selkirk's survival, after being marooned on the Pacific island of Juan Fernandez, gave Daniel Defoe the idea for his novel *Robinson Crusoe*.

The town's Dutch-gabled 18th-century courthouse is now the Kinsale Regional Museum. Among its fascinating exhibits is a toll-board giving the sums levied on food and other goods passing through the town gates. It includes the waiver: 'No fee is to be taken out of a smaller quantity of potatoes than three weights brought to town on women's or children's backs.'

Other notable buildings include the 13th-century St Multose Church with its massive west tower. The north transept and font are probably original and both are noteworthy. The 16th-century Desmond Castle, a tower house used in Napoleonic times to house French prisoners of war, is also worth a visit.

Two miles outside the town, at Summer Cove, are the 40ft walls of Charles Fort, dating from 1677. It is one of Europe's best-preserved star forts, so called from their star-shaped ground plan. The barracks inside were occupied by British troops until 1922.
**Charles Fort** *May-Oct, 11am-4pm. Tel: (021) 772044.*

# GAELIC GAMES

*The skilful, thrilling Irish sports of hurling, Gaelic football and road bowls*

Only general elections command as much attention and animated debate in Ireland as sports. And of the sports played, the Gaelic games – hurling and Gaelic football – and road bowls are deeply entwined in Ireland's social and political culture.

THE GAME 'MEN CALL HORLINGS' Hurling dates from pre-Christian times and was played by teams of warriors for days on end. In 1367 the Kilkenny Parliament tried to ban the game 'men call horlings with great sticks upon the ground', saying that it led to a neglect of military service. At about the same time, Archbishop Colton of Armagh threatened to excommunicate Catholics who played the game, blaming it as the cause of 'mortal sins, beatings and . . . homicides'.

Hurling is a fast game played with an ash stick or 'hurley', from $30\frac{1}{4}$in to 37in long, with a striking end curved broadly, rather like a hockey stick. This is used to hit, or carry, a leather ball known as the 'sliotar', which is smaller than a cricket ball and weighs between $3\frac{1}{2}$ and $4\frac{1}{2}$oz. The sliotar can be driven along the ground or struck over the players' heads, although most activity takes place in between.

The game is played by two teams of 15 who score by striking the sliotar into the opponents' goal. Players are not allowed to carry the sliotar in their hands for more than four steps, though they may balance or carry it on the hurley. There is no offside, so players can propel the ball for great distances. A referee, two linesmen and four umpires monitor the game.

Hurling is played mainly in the provinces of Munster and Leinster, and County Galway, in the Irish Republic, and County Antrim in Northern Ireland. Its 'capital' is Cork, which frequently holds the All-Ireland crown. A county 'derby' at Cork's stadium, Páirc Ui Chaomh, can attract crowds of up to 50,000.

GAELIC FOOTBALL The first record of Gaelic football is in the Statutes of Galway (1527), which allowed football but banned hurling. Today it is played in every county, although it does not have much support among Protestants. Kerry, another Munster county, leads in the games.

Like hurling, the game is played by two teams of 15, but with a round ball slightly smaller than a soccer ball, on a pitch between 140 and 160yds long and between 84 and 100yds wide. At either end of the pitch are goalposts like rugby posts but with a net. A goal is scored by kicking the ball into the net, and counts for three points. Sending the ball over the crossbar and between the posts counts as one point.

Gaelic football requires great strength and skill, with high jumping, solo runs, catching and long kicks. The players may catch the ball and pass it with either foot or fist, but may not throw it. The ball may be carried for only four steps without being bounced, or played from foot to hand any number of times before it is released, but cannot be bounced from the ground more than once unless it is touched by the foot between each bounce. As in hurling, the game is supervised by a referee, two linesmen and four umpires, and there is no offside.

In the early 19th century both hurling and Gaelic football were either discreetly discouraged or openly prohibited by priests and landlords, perhaps because of fear of violence and drunkenness, but mainly out of suspicion of nationalism. They were often right. In 1884 the Gaelic Athletics Association (GAA) was formed, originally to 'combat the influence of other games and customs which threatened to destroy the surviving cultural inheritance of Gael'. But despite attempts to prevent the games, today about 300,000 men play them in Ireland, with strong support among Irish communities in the United States, Canada and Australia.

Capacity crowds of up to 65,000 gather in September at Croke Park, Dublin, for the All-Ireland finals, the culmination of inter-county knock-out championships for hurling and football. Hill 16, where the Dublin fans congregate, is a sea of blue flags, banners and clothing. Elsewhere, pockets of green and gold mark supporters of Meath and of Kerry, or 'The Kingdom', as it is known. And anyone

FOOTBALL FINALS *The green and gold colours of Meath fly at the All-Ireland football finals (left). At the Leinster football final (above), Dublin's Clarke and Kennedy tackle Meath's O'Rourke.*

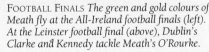

can participate. Jack Lynch, Prime Minister of the Irish Republic between 1966 and 1979, won six successive All-Ireland titles during this period: five for hurling and one for Gaelic football, all for Cork.

ROAD BOWLS Another predominantly Irish game is road bowling. This is played on Sunday afternoons, mainly in August, on the winding country roads of Armagh and Cork.

Spectators gather on the roadside in clusters, with men moving among them taking money for bets until their hands, full of notes, look as though they are holding small cabbages. A man tears handfuls of grass from

HURLING FINALS *Galway's Kilkenny reaches for the sliotar from Corrigan, playing for Offaly (above), at the 1990 semi-finals held in Dublin's Croke Park (top).*

the verge, tossing them in two piles on the road surface. The first player comes up to these grass 'butts', then walks back some 30 paces. The player's 'handler' stands with his legs apart at the next corner of the road. Holding an iron ball, or 'bullet', which can weigh 16, 21 or 28oz, the player runs up, bounding into the air at the butt and releases the bowl underarm as he lands. The aim is to make the bowl fly a few feet from the ground, land at about 40yds, bounce between the handler's legs, spin off the kerb and turn the

corner. The course is about 3 miles long and the winner plays the course in the fewest shots. A good thrower can curl and spin the ball in the manner of a bowler at cricket, taking corner after corner, and the spectators have to be as agile as the players. If the bowl leaves the road the player is penalised.

A similar game, played with a 16½oz wood-and-iron ball, takes place in north Friesland, in the Netherlands. And in 15th-century Amsterdam, a game called 'kloot-schiesse' was banned for damaging the town walls – as road bowls was banned in Londonderry in 1714. It is thought that soldiers of the Dutch-born William III may have brought the game with them to Ireland.

# The Golden Vale

*This area of green fields, gentle hills, wooded valleys and meandering streams and rivers is known as the Golden Vale. It is the perfect playground for those who enjoy walking, riding, fishing, canoeing or golf in idyllic countryside. It also has fine old towns, ancient castles, historic country houses, mature gardens and prehistoric tombs, evidence of the region's importance in earlier centuries.*

### Annes Grove

For any nature lover, the botanical gardens beside the River Awbeg are a joy. On this large 18th-century estate, the wild and the formal, the exotic and the native, the rare and the common are grown together with spectacular effect.

Among the principal features are a walled garden, woodland walks and rare trees and shrubs. Many of the specimens grow to an unusually large size because of the mild climate. In spring, a magnificent collection of azaleas and rhododendrons, many raised from seeds collected in Tibet and Nepal, creates a blaze of glorious colour. Beside the Awbeg is a water garden with swamp cypresses and tufted bamboos, and naturalised astilbes and primulas cover the valley floor. The house in the gardens is not open to the public.
**Gardens** *Easter-Oct, Mon-Fri, 1-6pm, weekends, 10am-5pm. Tel: (022) 26145.*

ANNES GROVE GARDENS *Fiery berberis and marsh plants thrive at the edge of the River Awbeg.*

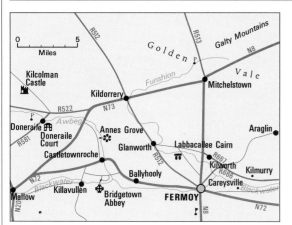

### WALKS
Ballyhooly, Doneraile Forest Park, Fermoy, Killavullen, Kilworth.

### EVENTS
**Gracious Homes and Gardens Festival** Open week, on various days, early May. Tel: (021) 273251.

### SPORT
**Angling** Coarse fishing: River Blackwater. Game fishing: Rivers Blackwater and Funshion, and Careysville and Kilmurry Fisheries.
**Boating** Fermoy Rowing Club. Tel: (025) 31328.
**Golf** Doneraile Golf Club, 9-hole course. Tel: (022) 24137.
Fermoy Golf Club, 18-hole course. Tel: (025) 31472.
Mitchelstown Golf Club, 9-hole course. Tel: (025) 24072.

### INFORMATION
Mallow Tourist Information Point. Tel: (022) 42222.
Cork Tourist Information Office. Tel: (021) 273251.

### OTHER PLACES TO SEE
**Araglin** Village NE of Fermoy, in extreme NE corner of Cork. Wide views of Cork, Tipperary and Waterford.
**Ballyhooly** Village on River Blackwater, with picturesque bridge and ancient castle of Roche family, restored in 19th century. Good base for forest walks.
**Kildorrery** Well-preserved 19th-century village; Bowen's Court, now demolished, was home of novelist Elizabeth Bowen (1899-1973), buried in graveyard there. Members of the Gate family, of Cow and Gate company, also buried at Kildorrery.
**Killavullen** Blackwater village with two castles. One of them is Ballymacmoy House, ancestral home of Hennessy family of brandy fame. The caves by the lake have ancient rock carvings.

### Castletownroche/Baile Chaisleáin an Róistigh

This village by the River Awbeg takes its name from the stronghold built there by the Roche family. In 1650, when Cromwell's armies were subduing the country, Lord Roche, a suspected royalist, fled from the castle, leaving his wife to command the defence of the fortress. Lady Roche was taken prisoner and was later hanged at Cork. The present-day Castle Widenham incorporates a tower of the Roche castle.

The village's Church of Ireland church stands on a rise above the river. Below the churchyard, on the way down the hill into the village, is the 'Old Rustic Bridge by the Mill', the subject of a song by the 19th-century ballad composer Thomas P. Keenan, who is buried at Castletownroche:

*I'm thinking tonight of the old rustic bridge*
*That bends o'er the murmuring stream.*
*'Twas there, Maggie dear, with our hearts*
*full of cheer,*
*We strayed 'neath the moon's gentle gleam.*

The bones of extinct Ice Age animals, such as giant reindeer and Irish elk, have been found in caves below the village, where the River Awbeg flows through a limestone gorge. The remains are now in the National Museum, Dublin. Nearby, below an old railway viaduct, are the ivy-covered ruins of Bridgetown Abbey, an Augustinian priory founded in the early 13th century and suppressed during the Reformation. Its church has pretty lancet windows, as does the refectory, and some overgrown walls remain.

### Doneraile Court

A herd of native Irish red deer browse in Doneraile's 400 acres of superbly landscaped park, which is now a wildlife sanctuary. Doneraile Court, a fine building in Queen Anne style dating from 1725, was once the home of the powerful St Leger family, who made their fortune during the land confiscations of the late 16th and 17th centuries. William St Leger, who first owned the house, was an ancestor of the Viscount Doneraile. The tomb of the 1st Viscount Doneraile, who died in 1727, lies in the church. It was to this church that two men rode in 1757, from Buttevant, using the steeple to guide them in the first recorded 'steeplechase'.

The only recorded initiation of a woman into the rites of Freemasonry took place at Doneraile Court. In 1712 Elizabeth (later Lady Aldworth), daughter of the 1st Viscount Doneraile, hid in the library to spy on a Masonic meeting. When the outraged masons discovered her, they decided that the only way to ensure her silence was to enrol her in their Lodge. The house is being restored for future opening to the public.

### Fermoy/Mainistir Fhear Maí

This prosperous market town straddles a tree-lined stretch of the River Blackwater on the main Cork-Dublin road. But crumbling barrack ruins mark Fermoy as a former British garrison. It owes its origins to a farsighted Scots merchant, John Anderson, who bought the land in 1791, laid out the town, provided the site for a barracks, and started a mail-coach service between Cork and Dublin. By about 1800 Fermoy was a wealthy military centre with a busy social life. Anderson was also remarkable for his religious tolerance. He believed that 'Irish Papists are as well entitled as Protestants to live all the days of their lives'.

The British Army is long gone, but reminders of the wealth the military and the mail-coach brought to the town still stand in its centrepiece, the handsome market house on the south side of Pearse Square. The high-arched entry to the stable yard of the Grand Hotel, on Ashe Quay, is a reminder of its days as a coaching inn. It was built in the early 1800s. Fermoy also has several charming 19th-century shopfronts.

Fermoy is an excellent centre for angling and touring the Blackwater valley.

### Glanworth/Gleannúir

The River Funshion flows through Glanworth where it is spanned by a low stone bridge dating from 1446, the oldest in the county. It has 12 arches and is 150yds long. Above it are the massive ruins of an ancient castle of the Roches and an old woollen mill.

In prehistoric times Glanworth was the principal settlement of this richly fertile area – a fact reflected in the number of local antiquities. Most notable is Labbacallee Cairn, on Labbacallee Hill 2 miles south-east of the village. It is 3500 years old and is one of the biggest and best-preserved wedge-tombs (so called because of their shape) in Ireland. Its Irish name means 'Hag's Bed'. When the cairn was first excavated, in 1934, a headless female skeleton was found in the inner chamber. The skull was in the outer chamber with some male skeletons. Archaeologists have made similar finds in tombs of about the same age in Brittany.

In the river east of the tomb is a large rock, which, according to legend, was thrown by the Hag at her absconding husband, pinning him to the riverbed. This legend may hint at an ancient matriarchal society – as perhaps do the male skeletons in the tomb.

GLANWORTH BRIDGE *The 12-arched stone bridge spans the River Funshion in the shadow of the ruins of the Roche family castle.*

### Kilcolman Castle/Cill Cholmáin

A single small tower is all that remains of the castle where, during the late 16th century, the poet Edmund Spenser lived. In 1580 he had gone to Ireland as secretary to the Lord Deputy, who was in charge of crushing the rebellious Irish population. As a reward for his part in subjugating the province of Munster, Spenser was granted Kilcolman, where he wrote most of *The Faerie Queene*, his masterpiece. In 1598 the castle was attacked by a mob and burnt. Though Spenser and his wife escaped, their infant son lost his life.

### Mitchelstown/Baile Mhistéala

This thriving town, with a lively market on Thursdays, lies at the foot of the Galty Mountains. It was planned in the early 19th century, and has fine broad streets and two splendid squares. The town was largely the creation of the Earls of Kingston, whose Gothic Revival castle was burnt down by Republican troops in 1922. Its site is now occupied by a large creamery, the town's principal industry, but the castle gardens are worth visiting.

GLANWORTH LABBACALLEE *Light filters between the huge stones set around an open pit in one of Ireland's best-preserved wedge-tombs, where once a decapitated female skeleton was found.*

# A Remote Beauty Spot

*West of Cork city is rocky, wild countryside alternating with farmland, thick forests, rivers and lakes. In the more remote areas, scattered communities glean a living by raising sheep. This is also a Gaeltacht – an area where Irish is the everyday language, where villages keep alive Irish cultural traditions, and where first-time travellers may lose their way because all the signposts are in Irish.*

### Ballingeary/Béal Átha an Ghaorthaidh

People go to Ballingeary's Irish college to learn the native language, with nothing to distract them but glorious countryside. At the head of a nearby lake is an old stone 'clapper' footbridge made of long slabs of stone laid on uprights rising from the water of the River Lee. The village is a good base for exploring the Derrynasaggart Mountains.

CLAPPER BRIDGE *An old crossing of huge flat stones still spans the River Lee at Ballingeary.*

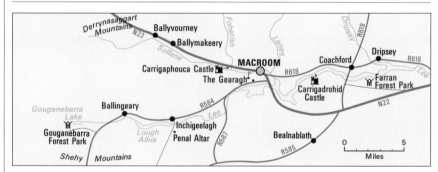

### Ballyvourney/Baile Bhuirne

Like the twin village of Ballymakeery down the road, Ballyvourney lies in an area of beautiful forest and mountain scenery. But visitors are also attracted to Ballyvourney by the shrine of St Gobnat, a 6th-century saint who founded a convent here. She practised beekeeping and cured the ailments of both her nuns and the local villagers, and is said to have kept the plague away from Ballyvourney. She is still the object of widespread devotion and is commemorated in a statue, which portrays her as a beekeeper, outside the graveyard. The remains of the convent lie in and around the village. They include St Gobnat's house and church, her grave and a holy well. Pilgrims visit them in turn, beginning at the circular stone hut where St Gobnat lived.

### Carrigadrohid Castle/Caisleán Carraig an Droichid

Between Coachford and Macroom an ancient bridge spans one of the loveliest reaches of the River Lee, and on a rock in the river stand the ruins of Carrigadrohid, once a stronghold of the MacCarthy clan. The name translates as 'the rock of the bridge'.

A plaque on the wall records a grim event that took place here in 1650. The Bishop of Ross, Bishop MacEgan, had been captured by Cromwell's troops but was promised his freedom if he persuaded the garrison in the castle to surrender. Instead, he urged them to fight to the end, telling them 'Hold out to the last for religion and country'. He was hanged from a nearby tree by the reins of his horse, while the garrison, who held out, watched helplessly from the battlements.

### The Gearagh/An Gaoire

Two miles south of Macroom, on the River Lee, is The Gearagh, a rare relic of the Ice Age. Its Irish name means 'the wooded river', and it is indeed a swamp, a 3 mile long maze of little reed-fringed, wooded islands and interlacing streams. It is a haven for wildlife and a rich diversity of plants.

### Gouganebarra Lake

This mountain lake is one of Ireland's most famous beauty spots, much visited in spite of its remoteness. It is set in a dramatic glacial valley and is the source of the River Lee.

The valley's Irish name means 'St Finbarr's Cleft', after the patron saint of Cork. It was on a tiny island in the middle of the lake,

LAKESIDE SOLACE *A tiny stone chapel overlooks the calm waters of Gouganebarra Lake.*

**OTHER PLACES TO SEE**
**Carrigaphouca Castle** 3m W of Macroom. A 15th-century castle, built on a rocky mound, which gets its name from the *púca* or goblin (the English 'puck').
**Dripsey** Woollen mills originally run by water power. Mill shop sells products made there.
**Farran Forest Park** Picnic sites and nature trails, small lake and wildlife enclosure with deer, ducks and geese.

**Penal Altar** 1m S of Inchigeelagh. Plaque inscribed: 'Altar of Penal Times. Mass was said here 1640-1800.'

**EVENTS**
**Pilgrimage** Gouganebarra, Sept 29.
**Pilgrimages** St Gobnat's shrine, Feb 11 and at Whitsuntide.

**SPORT**
**Angling** Coarse fishing: Rivers Dripsey and Lee,

Lower River Sullane and Lough Allua. Trout fishing: Rivers Dripsey, Foherish and Laney, Middle River Lee, River Sullane and Gouganebarra Lake.
**Golf** Macroom Golf Club, 9-hole course. Tel: (026) 41072.
**Waterskiing** Farran Forest Park. Tel: (026) 41771.

**INFORMATION**
Cork Tourist Information Office. Tel: (021) 273251.

EMERALD PATCHWORK *Geometrical green fields hemmed by bushy trees stretch as far as the eye can see from Gouganebarra.*

under mountain crags and surrounded by pine forests, that the saint set up a hermitage in the 6th or 7th century, before moving downriver to build his monastery at Cork City. He is also said to have drowned a monster here. Today nothing is left of the original hermitage. The ruins on the island – reached by a modern causeway – were built by Carmelite Father Denis Mahony in the 18th century. There is also a relatively modern Romanesque-style chapel.

Beyond the island stretches the 1000 acre Gouganebarra Forest Park, the first such park to be set up in Ireland. Among the conifers and birch trees are rowans and arbutus, the strawberry tree.

### Inchigeelagh/Inse Geimhleach
This small village, a popular resort for artists, spreads along the banks of Lough Allua, where the River Lee widens into a lake. The white water lilies growing in the lake make a delightful picture against the looming backdrop of the Shehy Mountains, which rise to almost 1800ft.

### Macroom/Maigh Chromtha
An ancient market town, whose Irish name means 'sloping field', Macroom stands on the banks of the River Sullane just above the point where it joins the Lee. The market square is dominated by the impressive entrance to Macroom Castle. This entrance, which has recently been renovated, is virtually all that remains of the 15th-century stronghold that was formerly the seat of the MacCarthys of Muskerry.

In 1654 Oliver Cromwell granted the town and castle to Admiral Sir William Penn, father of the William Penn (1644-1718) who founded Pennsylvania. It was while looking after his father's Irish estates that the young Penn became a confirmed Quaker. Near the entrance to the castle is a good local museum, which is open only during the summer.

# Where the Horse is King

The north-west corner of County Cork, bordering on Limerick and Kerry, is a region of standing stones, hills and country estates, of studs and riding stables set in picturesque parkland. Across it flow the upper reaches of the River Blackwater, with the slopes of the Boggeragh Mountains rising to the south. It is an underpopulated area with remote villages, some dwarfed by the ruins of ancient castles.

### Boggeragh Mountains/An Bhograch

Ring-forts, stone circles, standing stones and other prehistoric remains are scattered throughout the Boggeragh Mountains. They stretch south of the Blackwater valley between Millstreet and Mallow, a region of high moorland cut by marshy valleys. Of the 93 stone circles discovered in Cork and Kerry, about 16 are in the Boggeraghs – it is an archaeologist's treasurehouse.

The most notable of the circle remains stand at Knocknakilla, south of Millstreet, where five stones rear up on open moorland on the north flank of Musherabeg. From the site there are superb panoramic views over the surrounding hills and valleys. There is another fine circle west of Knocknakilla, at Glantane East.

Of the 30,000 ring-forts so far discovered in Ireland, 196 are in Millstreet parish alone. One of the best is at Donoure, near Kilcorney. Its great ring, measuring 50yds across, has a high bank and deep ditch, and underground workings.

KNOCKNAKILLA STONE CIRCLE *Five stones speak of ancient rituals on the windswept moor.*

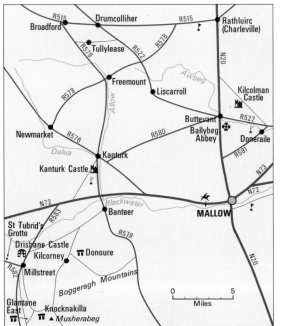

**OTHER PLACES TO SEE**
**St Tubrid's Grotto** 1m W of Millstreet, holy well beside a grotto sacred to St Tubrid. **Tullylease** 12m N of Kanturk. Site of monastery established by St Berchert in 8th century. Inscription on beautifully carved cross-slab, once probably marking Berchert's grave, asks for a prayer for him.

### EVENTS
**Buttevant Busking Festival** End Aug.
**Cahirmee Horse Fair** Buttevant, mid-July.
**Mallow Folk Festival** End July.
**Millstreet International Horse Show** Early Aug.

### SPORT
**Angling** Coarse fishing: River Blackwater. Game fishing: Rivers Allow, Awbeg, Dalua and Blackwater.
**Golf** Charleville Golf Club, 18-hole course. Tel: (011) 81257.
Kanturk Golf Club, 9-hole course. Tel: (029) 50534.
Mallow Golf Club, 18-hole course. Tel: (022) 21145.

### INFORMATION
Cork Tourist Information Office. Tel: (021) 273251.

### Buttevant/Cill na Mallach

Once a year, on July 12, this busy market town becomes one of Ireland's horse-trading centres. Its streets are given over to the ancient Cahirmee Horse Fair, when thousands of pounds and many mounts change hands. In 1752 a keen amateur rider, Edward Blake, challenged a neighbour to race him from Buttevant Church to St Leger Church in Doneraile, 4 miles away. By keeping the Doneraile steeple in sight, both riders could steer cross-country to the finishing point by the most direct route. Thus the term 'steeple-chasing' entered the language.

The ruins of Ballybeg Abbey, a 13th-century Augustinian priory, are a mile south of the town. The west wall of the church has two fine windows, and the central and west towers still stand. But the most interesting part of the priory is the dovecote, said to be the best-preserved in Ireland from this time. Nearby, the River Awbeg is a favourite with trout fishermen.

### Kanturk/Ceann Toirc

'Boar's Head', the Irish name of this attractive and historical town, rests on the northern slopes of the Blackwater valley. It stands at the meeting point of two small rivers, the Dalua and the Allow, which are spanned by three arched bridges, the oldest of which was built in 1745. The poet Edmund Spenser, who lived at Kilcolman Castle not far away, mentions both rivers in his masterpiece *The Faerie Queene*. The local clan, the Mac-Carthys, had a fortified house here in the 17th century, but never lived in it. The house is now just a shell.

Kanturk was developed in the 18th century by the Earls of Egmont, who had been granted the land after the Irish rebellion in 1641. At its centre is the market square with its handsome early 19th-century Clock House.

### Liscarroll/Lios Cearúill

The extensive remains of a massive castle dominate the village of Liscarroll. It is believed to have been built by the Barry family in the 13th century, to set the seal on their dominance of the region. The vast central quadrangle is surrounded by curtain walls 30ft high, with a great circular tower at each corner. Restoration has been carried out over many years, but the castle is currently closed to the public.

### Mallow/Mala

In the 18th and 19th centuries, visitors flocked to Mallow to enjoy the waters of its spa, which bubbles out of the limestone rock at a constant 22°C. This led to its nickname

BUTTEVANT HORSE FAIR *Sleek Irish horses wait patiently while buyers and sellers haggle over prices.*

### BUILDER IN A RAGE

Kanturk Castle, a mile south of Kanturk village, is a fine example of Jacobean architecture. It was begun in about 1601 by a local clan chief, MacDonagh MacCarthy, but never completed. It is said to be the biggest house ever undertaken by an Irish chieftain. It is built around a central quadrangle and is defended by four-storey towers. While it was still being built, its obvious strength so aroused the suspicions of the English government that in 1615 they ordered further building to be stopped, saying that the castle was 'much too large for a subject'. It was to have been roofed with blue glass tiles, but MacCarthy was so furious when the work was stopped that in a rage he smashed them all, leaving his castle without roof, beams or floors.

BLACKWATER VALLEY DRIVE *Ireland's finest river scenery can be enjoyed along this route.*

MALLOW MASTERPIECE *Lively paintwork gives this traditional cottage a Mediterranean air.*

'The Irish Bath'. Today it is a centre for processing sugar beet, and for touring, fishing and hunting in the Blackwater valley.

The town has an Elizabethan castle surrounded by a public park that contains a herd of white fallow deer, descendants of a pair given by Queen Elizabeth 400 years ago to her god-daughter Elizabeth Norrey, then living at the castle. It was her father, Sir Thomas Norrey, who replaced Mallow's medieval castle with the present handsome fortified house. The stables have been converted into a mansion, which is still lived in.

During the 19th century the novelist Anthony Trollope lived for a time in Mallow while working for the Post Office.

One building from its fashionable heyday is Spa House, charmingly restored and privately owned. Inside, behind an ornamental balustrade, spa water bubbles into a basin in the front living room, providing the owner with natural central heating.

An 1850 neo-Tudor Clock House stands on the site of an older building which was a meeting place in late-Georgian times of a group of wild young bucks celebrated in the traditional song *The Rakes of Mallow*:

*Beaving, belling, dancing, drinking,*
*Breaking windows, damming, sinking,*
*Ever raking, never thinking,*
*Live the Rakes of Mallow.*

Mallow's rakes were notorious enough for the Cork-Mallow stagecoach to take its name after them.

### Millstreet/Sráid an Mhuilinn

Overshadowed by the Boggeragh Mountains, Millstreet is an ideal centre for hill walking and exploring the area's antiquities. It has Ireland's largest showjumping ring outside Dublin, and thousands of visitors flock here each summer to watch the international stars.

Just outside the village, in parkland beside a convent, is Drishane Castle, a well-preserved tower house with panoramic views, built in 1450 by Dermot MacCarthy.

# The Yachtsmen's Coast

*The coastline from Ross Carbery to Baltimore twists round creeks, sandy bays; harbours and headlands, luring the traveller to fresh discoveries. Behind the beaches are small lakes and quiet picnic spots, which give way farther inland to rolling hills, crisscrossed by lanes, or 'boreens', some little more than farm tracks with grass sprouting in the middle, nicknamed 'dual cabbageways'.*

### Baltimore/Dún na Séad

The harbourside village is a favourite port of call for fishermen and yachtsmen, because of its sheltered position behind Sherkin Island. In McCarthy's, one of its quayside pubs, a wall chart testifies to the marine mayhem that took place over the centuries in nearby Roaringwater Bay. Around 1600, a defeat was inflicted on the local warlords when 'several ships of the O'Driscoll fleet sank in an affray with a fleet from Waterford', within sight of the 15th-century O'Driscoll stronghold towering above the village. In 1620 a Spanish galleon was sunk offshore. A much stranger misfortune befell in 1631 when Baltimore was raided by Algerian pirates, who carried off 200 inhabitants into slavery. Many of them were English settlers.

BALTIMORE BEACON *The huge white cone thrusts into the sky, an important marker for boats.*

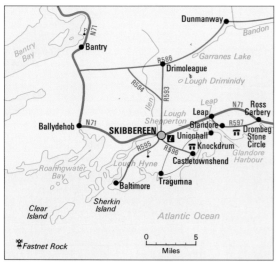

**OTHER PLACES TO SEE**
**Knockdrum** 1m from Castletownshend, ring-fort with underground passage.
**Ross Carbery** Foundations of St Fachtnan's 6th-century monastery. Good point for the signposted detour to the scenic coastal drive to Skibbereen via Glandore, Unionhall, Castletownshend and Tragumna.

**Sherkin Island** Secluded island with beautiful beaches, a ruined 15th-century Franciscan friary, and a castle. Boat from Baltimore.

**EVENTS**
**Castletownshend Autumn Festival** End Oct.
**Castletownshend Festival of Music** End July/early Aug.
**Dunmanway Agricultural Show** End July.
**Maid of Isle Festival** Skibbereen, end July/early Aug.
**Skibbereen Cattle Market** Tues and Wed.
**Skibbereen Harness and Trotting Grand Prix** Mid-Aug.

**SPORT**
**Angling** Coarse fishing: Loughs Driminidy, Garranes and Shepperton. Game fishing: Rivers Bandon and Ilen, and surrounding lakes. Sea fishing: Baltimore, Castletownshend, Glandore, Ross Carbery.
**Bathing** Glandore, Ross Carbery, Tragumna.
**Boating** Skibbereen.
**Golf** Skibbereen Golf Club, 9-hole course. Tel: (028) 21227.
**Pony trekking** Ross Carbery and Skibbereen.
**Sailing and boat hire** Baltimore Sailing Centre and at Ross Carbery.
**Tennis** Dunmanway and Skibbereen.

**INFORMATION**
Skibbereen Tourist Office. Tel: (028) 21766.

Today Baltimore is quieter and makes its livelihood from fishing and tourism. It has a boat-building yard and sailing schools, and is the starting point for ferries to Sherkin and Clear Islands.

### Castletownshend/Baile an Chaisleáin

In this beautiful old village, on a winding creek, the aristocratic cousins Somerville and Ross, Edith Somerville and Violet Martin, from Ross, County Galway, wrote their classic tales of Irish life in Edwardian times, *Some Experiences of an Irish R.M.* (Resident Magistrate). Wandering down the village's steep main street, past pretty cottages to its picturesque harbour, visitors half expect to bump into one of the characters of their stories, such as Major Yeates or Slipper, coming out of a pub. The two authors wrote at Drishane House, one of the 'big houses' at the upper end of the village. They are buried at nearby St Barrahane's Church, where Edith Somerville was organist.

The village was originally called Castletown, but took its present name from the Townshends, a local family whose descendants still live in the castle, now a thriving guesthouse.

### Clear Island/Oileán Cléire

Gulls, cormorants, puffins, kittiwakes and other seabirds, can all be seen from the bird observatory on this high, rocky island reached by boat from Baltimore. It is also the birthplace of the 6th-century St Ciaran, whose church and holy well are signposted. Irish is still the spoken language of its dwindling population of fishermen and farmers, who number fewer than 100.

### Dunmanway/Dún Mánmhaí

Sir William Cox, Lord Chancellor of England under William III, founded the town, introducing a colony of linen weavers to take advantage of the flax which was widely grown in County Cork. The linen industry has long gone, and Dunmanway now rests quietly among wooded hills in land intersected by slow-moving rivers which provide excellent fishing.

### Glandore/Cuan Dor

The tree-shaded little village and its twin, Unionhall, or Bréantrá, eye each other from opposite sides of Glandore harbour, two of the loveliest villages on the coast. Dean Swift, who lived in Unionhall in 1723, was so delighted with the local scenery that he praised it in a Latin poem – *Carberiae Rupes*, which translated means 'Rocks of Carbery'.

The Drombeg Stone Circle, 2 miles east of Glandore, is one of the finest recumbent stone circles in west Cork. Nearby are the remains of an ancient cooking place, or *fulacht fiadh*, probably used for cooking meat eaten at feasts. It is a stone trough, which was filled with water from a spring alongside and heated with stones made red hot in a fire. The water could be brought to the boil in about 30 minutes.

### Leap/An Léim

Tucked into the innermost corner of Glandore harbour, where the River Leap flows through a deep gorge, is the tiny village of Leap whose name, pronounced 'lep', refers to O'Donovan's Leap. Legend has it that a member of the O'Donovan clan, fleeing from the forces of law, urged his horse to a mighty jump across the gorge. As the pursuing posse halted and watched in wonder, not daring to attempt the leap themselves, O'Donovan landed safely on the far side and fled to freedom, hence the local saying: 'Beyond the leap, beyond the law.'

### Lough Hyne

The gloriously forested hills between Skibbereen and Baltimore surround Lough Hyne (or Ine), a landlocked salt lake with a remarkable ecosystem. It has a maximum depth of 160ft, and is linked to the ocean by a narrow channel through which the tide races over rapids for four hours, then reverses slowly for eight and a half hours, leaving many rare and exotic fish trapped in the lake, among them such subtropical visitors as the triggerfish and red-mouth goby. There are billboards posted around the lake with pictures of the fish that can be seen and information about the different species, so that visitors can identify them.

### Skibbereen/An Sciobairín

The 'little boat harbour' is a thriving market town, regarded as the capital of the area known as The Carberies. Standing on the River Ilen, at a point where the river widens into a creek, it was founded after Algerian pirates sacked the neighbouring port of Baltimore in 1631. In the 17th century it produced two 'battling bishops': one was killed in 1602 fighting the forces of Queen Elizabeth, and the other was hanged on Cromwell's orders in 1650.

## YACHTSMEN'S STORMY GOAL

A few miles out to sea, beyond the offshore Sherkin and Clear Islands, is an outline like a giant swan sitting on the horizon. It is the Fastnet Rock, Carraig Aonair, with its lighthouse flashing a navigational warning to shipping every five seconds. Fastnet is the western turning-point in the celebrated Fastnet Yacht Race, held every two years, in which yachtsmen from all over the world take part. The race, run since 1925, starts from Cowes in the Isle of Wight.

The lighthouse dates from 1906, after an earlier tower had yielded to the Atlantic storms, and was constructed not in Ireland but in Cornwall. Each block of Cornish granite was dovetailed into the next, and assembled and tested in Cornwall to be certain of an exact fit. Then the lighthouse was taken apart, transported to Fastnet, and reassembled on the rock.

*The Fastnet Lighthouse is the western turning-point in the twice-yearly Fastnet Yacht Race.*

DROMBEG STONE CIRCLE *More than 2000 years old, this stone circle surrounds a pit where cremated bones were placed.*

# An Ancient Walled Port

*A gentle charm pervades east Cork, particularly inland where walkers and fishermen can explore the rich, undulating farmland and river valleys. Its towns, such as the ancient walled port of Youghal, once the home of Sir Walter Raleigh, echo with turbulent history, and in recent years it has become something of a gastronomic centre.*

KILLEAGH PUB *Old-world charm oozes from this ivy-draped thatched cottage.*

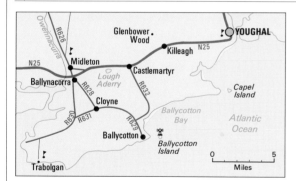

**EVENTS**
**Midleton All-Ireland Ploughing Championships** Oct. Tel: (0507) 25125.
**Youghal Potato Festival** Late June–early July.

**SPORT**
**Angling** Sea fishing: Ballynacorra, near Midleton, Ballycotton, Youghal. Deep-sea fishing: Contact Sea Angling Centre, Youghal.
**Golf** East Cork Golf Club, 18-hole course. Tel: (021) 631687.
Trabolgan Golf Club, 18-hole course. Tel: (021) 661551.
Youghal Golf Club, 18-hole course. Tel: (024) 92787.

**INFORMATION**
Cork City Tourist Information Office. Tel: (021) 273251.
Youghal Tourist Office. Tel: (024) 92390.

**OTHER PLACES TO SEE**
**Castlemartyr** The keep and walls of a 15th-century castle now form part of a Carmelite priory. Visits by arrangement only. Tel: (021) 667113. Lough Aderry, a short way west, has picnic sites.
**Killeagh** Behind the thatched pub is the entrance to Glenbower Wood, with an ornamental lake, nature trail, and delightful forest walks.
**Trabolgan** 10m S of Midleton. All-weather holiday centre of 140 acres of coastal wood and meadowland, with a heated swimming pool with water-slide and views over the Atlantic.

BALLYCOTTON HARBOUR *Fishing boats prepare to leave the harbour for deeper waters.*

## Ballycotton/Baile Choitín

The charming village stands high above a neat little harbour, from which fishermen have gone out for centuries to the rich fishing grounds of Ballycotton Bay. The harbour is packed with trawlers and pleasure craft, and anglers can enjoy themselves with rod and line from the end of the quay, or hire boats for sea-fishing trips. Beyond the village are spectacular clifftop walks, 200ft above the sea.

On Ballycotton Island, just outside the harbour, is a lighthouse which is painted black. At the beginning of this century a lighthouse was begun on neighbouring Capel Island, but halfway through its construction the ship owners who commissioned it decided to switch to Ballycotton Island instead. Since local fishermen tended to confuse the unfinished stump on Capel Island with the completed Ballycotton Island lighthouse, it was painted black so that it could be distinguished more easily.

## Cloyne/Cluain

A Round Tower between 800 and 900 years old rises 100ft high above this ancient village, and commands superb views across the countryside. Its original conical top has been replaced by battlements. The key to the tower can be obtained from the cathedral house.

Cloyne was founded by St Colman in the 6th century. The nearby St Colman's Cathedral, built in 1250, was disappointingly restored in the 19th century. Among its monuments is the magnificent alabaster tomb of the philosopher George Berkeley (1685-1753), Bishop of Cloyne from 1734 to 1752. During his time at Cloyne he wrote on the benefits of drinking tar water, founded a workhouse and taught improved methods of farming. On the opposite side of the road is another Round Tower, whose original conical top has been replaced by battlements.

Cloyne is a centre for producing contemporary pottery. Not only do local shops

THOUGHTFUL REPOSE *An alabaster effigy of the philosopher George Berkeley covers his tomb in St Colman's Cathedral.*

stock a good selection of modern pieces, but a number of potters encourage people to buy by selling their wares at the roadside direct from their studios.

WHISKEY GALORE *Gallons of the golden liquid ferment in this gleaming copper pot still.*

### Midleton/Mainistir na Corann

If the wind is blowing in the right direction, you can tell when you are approaching Midleton by the aromatic vapours wafting from its distillery, one of the most modern in Europe. At the head of the Owennacurra estuary, Midleton is a thriving market town with a distillery that produces vodka and gin as well as whiskey. It has a working water wheel, 23ft in diameter, which claims to be the largest in Ireland, and a beam engine dating from 1825. Its magnificent centrepiece is the world's largest pot still – a vast, gleaming copper flask, with a capacity of 33,333 gallons of wash, a fermented liquid which is then distilled. The distillery has a heritage centre, which tells the story of Irish whiskey and shows the processes of its manufacture.

Midleton's wide streets were laid out in the 18th century, and among the buildings of that time are the market house, built in 1789, which is topped by a clock tower and weathercock. The dignified Church of Ireland church dates from the 1820s.
**Distillery and Heritage Centre** *Tel: (021) 631821.*

### Youghal/Eochaill

Once a strongly fortified harbour town, Youghal (pronounced 'yawl') is now a popular seaside resort with wide sandy beaches. Its Irish name means 'yew wood', from the forests that once covered the hinterland.

Youghal is strategically placed at the mouth of the River Blackwater. It may have been occupied briefly by Norse pirate-traders in the 9th century, and after them the Anglo-Normans in the 13th century. It was first properly fortified by Edward I in 1275. Because of the wealth of architecture these medieval settlers left behind, Youghal has been classified as a 'Theme Town'.

The town's most famous landmark is the unusual Georgian clock tower that spans the main street. It was built in 1777 from mellow red sandstone. Four storeys high, it connects two buildings which together formed the prison. Steps leading from the clock tower climb the steep hill to the top of the town, where the walls and turrets of the medieval defences can still be seen. Among the best-preserved town walls in Ireland, they probably date from the 15th century, and were refortified during the Civil War in 1642.

Nearby is St Mary's, the Church of Ireland parish church, a large 13th-century building and one of the few medieval Irish churches still in regular use. It has an unusual feature – holes in the chancel walls, behind which are pottery jars, placed there to improve the acoustics. Among its monuments is the imposing 1619 tomb of Sir Richard Boyle, 1st Earl of Cork, and his wife.

In Viking times it is said that the forerunner of Youghal lighthouse was maintained by nuns from the nearby St Anne's Convent. There was an underground passage from the convent to the beacon. Every night 12 nuns took it in turn to keep alight the beacon that guided the longships into the harbour.

Sir Walter Raleigh, who brought both the potato and tobacco to Europe, was Youghal's mayor in 1588-9. He lived at Myrtle Grove, an Elizabethan mansion, and is said to have grown Ireland's first potatoes on his extensive estates. Apparently when Raleigh first sampled a potato plant he ate the berry, and finding it inedible told his gardener to dig the plant out. The gardener dug it up and discovered the tuber, which he then cooked and ate with pleasure. Thereafter the potato became Ireland's traditional staple food.

A local story tells how one day Sir Walter was sitting under a tree in his Myrtle Grove

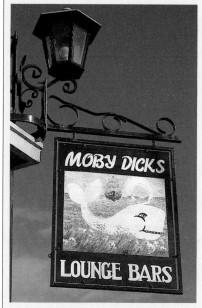

*The white whale Moby Dick grins cheekily from a local pub sign.*

In 1956 Youghal achieved Celluloid prominence as the location for the film *Moby Dick*, directed by John Houston, with Gregory Peck playing the one-legged Captain Ahab obsessed with finding the white whale. After a wide search for a suitable location, the producers chose Youghal, because it was unspoiled and perfectly matched the New England whaling port of Herman Melville's classic novel. Scores of townsfolk were used as extras, and for weeks Youghal's stone houses were transformed with a 'skin' of New England-style clapboard. Photographs and memorabilia can be seen in the Moby Dick seafront bar.

garden quietly smoking a pipe. A maid-servant, seeing the clouds of smoke billowing round his head, thought he was on fire and threw a bucket of water over him. She was roundly cursed by Raleigh, who had been enjoying his first smoke in Europe.
**Myrtle Grove** *Tues, Thur and Sat. Tel: (024) 92274.*

# FORTRESS IRELAND

## A history of invasion and fortification

At almost every turn in the Irish countryside there are remnants of ancient forts, some now reduced to mounds overgrown with grass, others the crumbling fragments of once-massive strongholds. The story they tell is of a harsh and often dangerous existence endured over thousands of years.

Life in ancient Ireland was characterised by an almost constant series of disputes and skirmishes between neighbouring kingdoms. At various times in its history the island was divided into as many as 80 kingdoms, each ruled by a king, or 'Ri', elected by the clan. Status was determined by the amount of land a king controlled and by the number of cattle the clan possessed. Consequently, territorial invasions and cattle raids were common.

THE FIRST FORTS As early as 600 BC the first rudimentary 'forts' were being built, either on natural islands in lakes or else on artificial islands called 'crannogs'. These were constructed by piling up stones on the lake bed and then covering them with brushwood and a layer of soil. One or two houses of wattle and mud or, later, timber and thatch, were built to house people and animals, and a crude palisade was often constructed around the houses as a final deterrent. The islands were reached by boat, and any approaching enemy could easily be repelled.

Crannogs survived as a means of defence for more than 2000 years. But their usefulness came to an abrupt end with the invention of the cannon, which made them easy to attack from the mainland. All that is left of the hundreds of crannogs that once speckled Irish lakes is a mosaic of grass-covered islands. Lough Gara, in County Sligo, was discovered during a drainage programme to have more than 200 crannogs, thought to have been inhabited until about AD 1000. The lake has been filled again, but the tree-covered crannogs are still visible.

On the mainland, farmsteads were surrounded by a ring of earthen or stone walls up to 200ft in diameter. These 'ring-forts' were often sited on hilltops to make approach more difficult for an enemy, although many were modest affairs, intended more to fend

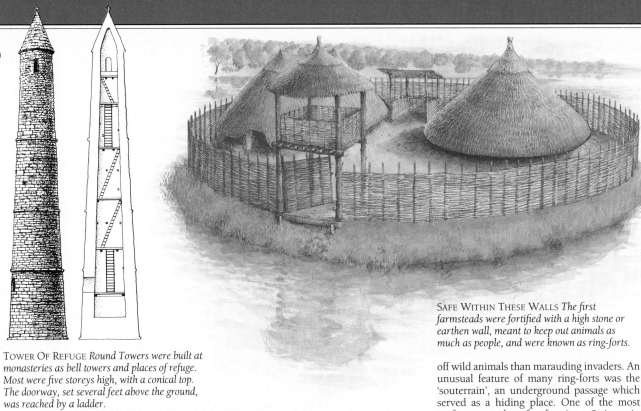

TOWER OF REFUGE *Round Towers were built at monasteries as bell towers and places of refuge. Most were five storeys high, with a conical top. The doorway, set several feet above the ground, was reached by a ladder.*

SAFE WITHIN THESE WALLS *The first farmsteads were fortified with a high stone or earthen wall, meant to keep out animals as much as people, and were known as ring-forts.*

ISLAND RETREAT *Early settlers constructed crannogs, or islands, with one or two houses for people and livestock, surrounded by a fence.*

off wild animals than marauding invaders. An unusual feature of many ring-forts was the 'souterrain', an underground passage which served as a hiding place. One of the most perfect examples of a fort is at Staigue, in County Kerry. Ring-forts were in use from about 200 BC right up to the 17th century.

Other types of fort included hill-forts, like the one on the Hill of Tara, which were much larger than ring-forts and often included burial mounds from earlier times, which implied that they had some religious significance. The forts were surrounded by a large stone wall, and often had a ditch on the inside of the wall rather than outside it.

There were promontory forts, too, so called because they were built on promontories, which were naturally defended on three sides by the sea and on the fourth by banks and ditches. Dunbeg fort on the Dingle peninsula is a good example.

DEFENDING THE MONASTERIES In 795 the sporadic skirmishes of the Celtic kings were overshadowed by a much darker threat – the Vikings. These fierce, heavily armed warriors first raided coastal settlements and then struck deeper into the country. More sophisticated defences were called for, particularly

DUNLUCE CASTLE *This guardian of a rocky headland on the north Antrim coast was occupied and rebuilt several times from the late 13th century when Anglo-Normans controlled the area.*

at the monasteries, the focus of Viking raids. Whereas monasteries had previously been built of wood or wattle, they were now made from stone. Added to them was the Round Tower, which doubled as a bell tower and lookout post in times of peace and a place of refuge during raids. These towers, built in the 10th to 12th centuries, were up to about 100ft high with thick walls that tapered, and contained about five storeys linked by an internal staircase. Entrance to these towers was by a ladder to a doorway set several feet above ground level, so once the ladder was hauled up, the towers were nearly impenetrable. They were, however, vulnerable to fire, perhaps from a flaming arrow through one of the windows set high above the ground, and those monks who were not smoked out also risked being starved out by a long siege. Round Towers can be seen in many of the monastic sites scattered around Ireland – at Kells, Clonmacnoise and Monasterboice, for example.

The Vikings were finally routed at Clontarf in 1014, and the Irish kings were left once more to fight among themselves. During one of these feuds, Dervorgilla, the wife of the King of Breifne, was abducted. In the battles that followed, her abductor, Dermot Mac-Murrough, lost his lands, and invited the Anglo-Normans to come to his aid. In 1169 the Norman invasion of Ireland began.

MOTTES AND CASTLES To protect themselves during their forays into the countryside, when defences needed to be established quickly, the Normans built a stop-gap fort – the motte. This was a large mound of earth with the top levelled to provide a flat base for a timber tower, which served as a lookout. Frequently a 'bailey' was added at the foot of the motte. This was a sort of 'corral', enclosed by a bank of earth and a ditch, or by wooden palisades, and it housed livestock at night.

But these structures were not enough to maintain the Normans' position as conquerors of the land, and to establish themselves more securely they constructed substantial castles, one of the most impressive of which is Carrickfergus in County Antrim, built by John de Courcy around 1180. These strongholds had massive keeps protected by a curtain of thick walls with rounded towers at the corners, and were easily defended.

The wars continued, with the Irish chiefs battling to oust the Normans and regain their land. Outside the walled towns, homes remained fortified, many of them built as square towers surrounded by a 'bawn' or high wall with turrets at the corners. In the 16th and 17th centuries, as the last chiefdoms disintegrated, these towers started to be built with comfort in mind as much as defence, marking the easing of the fortress mentality.

# The Ring of Kerry

*The awesome mountain and coastal scenery of the Iveragh Peninsula lies on the route known as the 'Ring of Kerry'. This circuit starts in Killarney, wanders through villages, and dips and rises in a roller-coaster run, hugging the mountainside high above a twisting shoreline before dropping to luxuriant woodland and sandy coves. The wild hinterland of the peninsula is jewelled with glassy lakes.*

### Cahersiveen/Cathair Saidhbhín

At the head of Valencia Harbour is the capital of the Iveragh peninsula (also known as Cahirciveen), dominated by two enormous buildings. One, in the main street, is the massive O'Connell Memorial Church, built to mark the 1875 centenary of the birth of Daniel O'Connell, 'The Liberator', who fought for Catholic emancipation. The other building, beside the river bridge, is the towering ruin of a police barracks, burned to a shell in 1922. The barracks was designed for the north-west frontier of India, but due to a bureaucratic mix-up over the plans it was built in Cahersiveen instead.

The bridge across the river gives splendid views of Valencia Harbour and the remains of a 15th-century castle, of which the O'Connells were once guardians, or senechals. After the Cromwellian wars in the mid-17th century, the leading O'Connell was banished to County Clare.

Some 12 miles north-east of Cahersiveen is Lough Caragh, a 4 mile long lake set amid the wooded foothills of the poetically named Macgillycuddy's Reeks, frequently shortened to 'the Reeks', another word for 'mountains'. This wall of red sandstone peaks, which rears up above the plains of Kerry, takes its name from an old Irish family, the MacGillycuddys.

### Derrynane/Doire Fhionain

The Irish name means 'St Fionan's wood' after the 6th-century monastery founded there by St Fionan. There is no trace of the monastery. Centuries later, Derrynane harbour became a thriving centre for trading with Spain and France. There are stories of attempts by 18th-century customs men to impede the export business run by the O'Connells and others from Derrynane and the little harbours along the Kenmare River. Some of the 'exports' included young people going in search of education and employment in Europe, which, as Catholics, were denied them in Ireland.

Wide, sandy beaches and dunes stretch from the harbour for miles and the rocks yield particularly delicious mussels. It is an atmospheric place, especially at sunset when, as the twilight lingers over the flat sea and wet sands, it is easy to believe, as the Gaels did, that sunrise and sunset were points of transition where one could slip from the real world into the faerie one. A legend says that Bull Rock, the nearest of two great rocks in the mouth of the estuary, is the entrance to the Kingdom of Donn, God of the Dead, and that when the sun shines through a hole in the middle of the rock, it becomes the golden gate to the next world.

Just outside Derrynane are several ruined wedge-tombs, relics of the Beaker folk who arrived here 4000 years ago to prospect for copper. There is also a Stone Age grave, or

---

### CRUISES
**Skelligs Cruise** 2½ hour cruise around the rocky island group, the Skelligs. Contact Des Lavelle, Valencia Island.

### SPORT
**Angling** Coarse fishing: Lakes Coomasaharn, Coomnacronia and Coomaglaslaw. Game fishing: Glenbeigh, Waterville. Sea fishing: Caherdaniel, Cahersiveen, Derrynane, Portmagee, Reenard Point, Valencia Harbour, Waterville.
**Bathing** Caherdaniel, Cahersiveen, Derrynane, Glenbeigh, Waterville.
**Golf** Dooks Golf Club, 18-hole course. Tel: (066) 68205.
Waterville Golf Club, 18-hole course. Tel: (066) 74102.
**Windsurfing** Caherdaniel.

### INFORMATION
Cork Kerry Tourism.
Tel: (064) 31633.

### OTHER PLACES TO SEE
**Caherdaniel** Pretty village near Derrynane Bay. Just outside it is a stone fort (caher) and the ruins of a much older fort. Copper ore was mined in the nearby mountains 4000 years ago.
**Glenbeigh** Small holiday and fishing resort on the northern lap of the Ring of Kerry, with a 4m stretch of golden sand with views across the bay to the Dingle mountains.
**Lough Caragh** The road past this lake travels through some of Kerry's best mountain scenery.

---

### IRELAND'S LIBERATOR

Daniel O'Connell (1775-1847), lawyer, politician and statesman, was born just east of Cahersiveen at Carhan House, now in ruins. He came from an old Gaelic family of traders and smugglers and their home was a major centre of Gaelic culture. Daniel's grandmother had 22 children and was a great wit. Her daughter, Eilin Dubh (Dark Eileen), composed a magnificent lament for her husband who was shot dead because he would not, under laws discriminating against Catholics, give up his fine horse.

The young O'Connell went to a local school, then to France, and later studied law in London, becoming a barrister of great distinction. Throughout his life he fought for civic freedom for Irish Catholics, and achieved Catholic emancipation in 1829. He then became Ireland's first Catholic MP and was hailed as its 'Liberator'.

He lived in the magnificent mansion of Derrynane House, south of Waterville, where he was adopted by a rich uncle, Muiris 'Hunting Cap' O'Connell (so called because of his habitual headgear). In 1802, when Daniel married his distant cousin, Mary, one of ten children of a Tralee physician, his uncle furiously opposed the marriage because Mary brought no dowry. However, the marriage proved to be an unusually happy one and the uncle relented. In 1825, on his uncle's death, Daniel inherited Derrynane, where he lived and worked for the rest of his political life.

*The portrait of the Catholic champion and his porcelain figure are in Derrynane House.*

dolmen, beyond the pub, which may date from 5000 years ago.

Derrynane House is set in mature woodland that forms part of a 320 acre National Park. The house was the home of Daniel O'Connell, and is now a national monument, filled with period furnishings and a collection of his personal possessions. It probably stands on the site of St Fionan's monastery.

**Derrynane House** *Oct-Apr, Tues-Sun 1-5pm; May-Sept, Mon-Sat 9am-6pm, Sun 11am-7pm. Tel: (066) 75113.*

### Portmagee/An Caladh

Smuggling, shipwrecking and fishing were once the chief interests of this village on the Portmagee Channel, named after the local smuggler, Theobald Magee. He was an officer in King James' army at the Battle of the Boyne in 1690 before setting up home and a smuggling business in Portmagee.

The village has a fine natural harbour and modern pier to serve the fishing trawlers. A road behind the village leads steeply to Ballinskelligs via the Coomanaspig Pass (1000ft), one of the highest places in Ireland accessible by car.

### Great and Little Skellig

Eight miles off the Kerry coast lies a group of three rocky islands. Great Skellig, or Sceilg Mhichil, the largest of them, has a 500ft climb up a 1000-year-old stone stairway, a test of stamina that brings adventurous visitors to one of the most magnificent monastic sites in Europe, dating from around AD 800. Surprisingly well-preserved stone beehive huts, in which the monks lived centuries ago, cling to the cliff edges, along with oratories, cemeteries, stone crosses, holy wells and the Church of St Michael.

Nearby Little Skellig, An Sceilg Bheag, is a sea-bird sanctuary, home to more than 20,000 pairs of gannets, as well as hundreds of kittiwakes, guillemots, petrels, shearwaters and fulmars. They are best seen in June, July and August. Puffin Island, farther north, is also a bird sanctuary.

### Staigue Fort

Near Caherdaniel is probably the finest example of a cashel, or stone fort, anywhere in Ireland. Set on a hill within a valley it is perfectly located for defence, and has survived for about 2500 years. Despite the fort's age its 13ft thick, tightly fitting dry-stone walls are superbly preserved.

### Valencia Island/Dairbhre

A popular holiday resort, Valencia Island is reached by a modern bridge that spans the 120yd wide channel from Portmagee. On the west side of the island is a dark grotto with sacred figures appearing out of the gloom, set high in the cavernous entrance to an old slate quarry hundreds of feet above the sea. The cliff-top road to the quarry gives stunning views of the Dingle peninsula and the Great Blasket Island. Knight's Town, by the harbour, has a heritage and natural history centre that tells the fascinating story of the laying of the first transatlantic telegraph cable from Valencia in 1866.

**Heritage Centre** *May-Sept.*

### Waterville/An Coireán

Charlie Chaplin spent many holidays at this seaside resort in the sixties and seventies, and happy snaps of Chaplin and his family line the walls of the 'Chaplin Lounge' in the seafront hotel – The Butler Arms – where he stayed. Among the other celebrities to frequent Waterville were Walt Disney and George Bernard Shaw. Its beautiful beach is a great attraction and there are several good fishing lakes nearby.

BALLINSKELLIGS BAY *Hog's Head, on the left, and Bolus Head dominate the wide-sweeping bay.*

ANCIENT FORT *Staigue Fort, built around 1000 BC, is one of the best-preserved 'cashels' in Ireland.*

# Ireland's Most Westerly Point

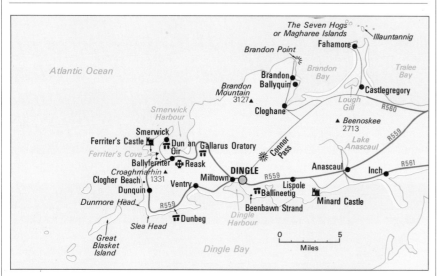

*The Dingle peninsula thrusts out into the Atlantic to claim Ireland's most westerly point. Here, majestic hills soar green and purple over vast bowls of unspoiled valleys, glittering mountain streams tumble down to lakes, summer hedgerows blaze with fuchsias, and soft, golden beaches stretch for miles. The peninsula is a Gaeltacht, an area where the Irish language is preserved. The region also has some 2000 sites of prehistoric and early Christian remains.*

### Anascaul/Abhainn an Scáil

At the west end of this attractive, one-street village, tucked between the sea and mountain peaks, is the South Pole Tavern. It commemorates Tom Crean, born here in 1877, who was a member of Scott's Antarctic Expedition and discovered the bodies of the team who died of exposure on their ill-fated return journey.

North of the village, in a wild, boulder-strewn gorge, is a glittering expanse of water – the beautiful Lake Anascaul. Here, according to legend in the 1st century AD, a giant tried to seize a young girl named Scál, but the brave and fierce warrior, and noted womaniser, Cuchulainn, came to her rescue. The giant and the warrior fought for the maiden, hurling boulders at each other until Cuchulainn was wounded and fell. He survived, but Scál, thinking him dead, drowned herself in the lake, which was then named after her.

South-west of Anascaul village is Minard Castle, once a stronghold of the Knights of Kerry, built in the early 16th century, when it was the largest fortress on the peninsula. Cromwellian troops destroyed it in 1650, after a long siege, and all that remains are three vast, crumbling walls, towering on rising ground beside a storm beach.

MINARD CASTLE *The blackened shell of what was once the largest fortress on the peninsula overlooks the sandstone boulders tossed up on a stretch of storm beach on Dingle Bay. On the green rise behind it are the remains of an ancient stone fort, or cashel.*

## OTHER PLACES TO SEE

**Dunquin** Village where *Ryan's Daughter* was filmed. Only schoolhouse remains from village built for film set.
**Inch** Haunt of 18th-century shipwreckers, and site of Iron Age beach-dwellers. Splendid 4m beach. Location for film *The Playboy of the Western World*, and scenes of *Ryan's Daughter*.
**Lispole** Ballineetig standing stone, largest on peninsula, 13ft high and 5ft wide.
**Milltown** A gallan, or standing stone, 10ft tall by 5ft wide, stands in garden of guesthouse. Two others in adjacent field known as the 'Gates of Glory'. Possibly erected to celebrate legendary Fianna victory in prehistoric Battle of Ventry.
**Smerwick** Norse settlement in 9th and 10th centuries. Smerwick means 'butter harbour' in Norse – butter was exported from here to a settlement at Limerick.

## WALKS

**Dingle Way** Just over 31m from Tralee to Dingle, along lanes and mountain tracks. The path is in three sections, each manageable in a day.

## EVENTS

**Dingle Cultural Festival** Mid-July.
**Dingle Races** Aug.
**Dingle Regatta** Aug.

## SPORT

**Angling** Coarse and trout fishing: Lough Gill. Sea fishing: Ballyquin, Castlegregory, Dingle Harbour Mouth, Dunquin, Ferriter's Cove, Inch and Ventry.
**Bathing** Ballyferriter, Castlegregory, Smerwick Harbour, Ventry.
**Golf** Ceann Sibeal Golf Club, 18-hole course. Tel: (066) 56255.

## INFORMATION

Killarney Tourist Office. Tel: (064) 31633.

GREAT BLASKET ISLAND *This island is said to have emerged when Atlantis sank under the sea.*

## Ballyferriter/Baile An Fheirtéaraigh

The pretty, crescent-shaped village curls at the foot of 1331ft Croaghmarhin mountain in the heart of an Irish-speaking enclave. An excellent heritage centre in the main street tells the history and geology of the area through displays of prehistoric and early Christian artefacts.

Another centre farther down the street has an exhibition of the wild animals and plants of the Dingle peninsula.

To the north-west of the village are the remains of 15th-century Ferriter's Castle, birthplace of the soldier-poet Piaras Ferriter, the last Irish chief to hold out against Cromwell's army. The crumbling ruins once formed part of an Iron Age defence. Not far away, bordering Smerwick Harbour, is a similar Iron-Age promontory fort called Dún an Oír (Fort of Gold). It was here, in 1580, that 600 Irish and Spanish soldiers were massacred after surrendering to the English. Just outside the village is the superb and recently excavated monastic site of Reask, which gives a clear idea of the layout of an early Christian monastery. Dating from the 5th or 6th centuries, when the site was enclosed by a dry-stone wall, the ruins include the lower sections of beehive huts, an oblong oratory, cross-inscribed pillars and slabs, and a corn-drying kiln.

**Ballyferriter Heritage and Natural History Centres** *June-end Sept. Tel: (064) 56100.*

## Blasket Islands

Two miles beyond Dunmore Head, the westernmost tip of the peninsula, monstrous humps of rock with dizzying cliff faces rise from the sea among a multitude of lesser rocks and reefs. These are the Blasket islands, scene of many shipwrecks over the centuries and once the home of a close-knit fishing and farming community. Since 1953, they have been uninhabited. The largest island, Great Blasket, is 4 miles long, 1 mile wide and nearly 1000ft high at its peak.

## Castlegregory/Caisleán Ghriaire

At the neck of a sandy peninsula dividing the bays of Tralee and Brandon, is a seaside resort whose lovely beaches are tucked beneath 2713ft Beenoskee mountain and surrounded by glorious hill scenery. To the west lies Lough Gill, filled with trout and the winter home of that lovely migrant from Arctic Siberia, Bewick's swan.

At the tip of the peninsula, at Fahamore, a colourful harbour is packed with fishing trawlers and currachs, traditional canoe-like

REASK STONE *The cross-pillar, inscribed with a Maltese cross at its head, marks the site of an early monastery at Reask. Such pillars were precursors of the Celtic High Cross.*

HIGH RELIEF *From the dizzying heights of Connor Pass a breathtaking view stretches over a wild, boulder-strewn and lake-dotted landscape to the 3127ft peak of Brandon Mountain.*

fishing boats made of tar-impregnated canvas stretched over a wooden rib cage. A group of small islands, known as the Seven Hogs, or Magharee Islands, lies off the peninsula. On the largest, Illauntannig, are the ruins of a 7th-century monastery, founded by St Seanach, consisting of two oratories, three beehive huts and an enclosing wall. Boat trips to these islands can be arranged at Fahamore.

## Connor Pass

This is the highest mountain pass in Ireland, linking the north and south shores of the peninsula across the magnificent Brandon range with Ireland's second highest peak, Brandon Mountain (3127ft). Travelling north from Dingle town, the narrow road winds up the sides of the great green bowl for 4½ miles to a height of 1500ft, with wonderful coastal views. It then corkscrews down to Brandon Bay past great cliffs, a dazzling waterfall and lakes on boulder-cluttered hillsides.

Travelling westward from the bottom of the pass, the road leads through verdant countryside to Cloghane, a pretty, flower-decked, waterside village, and on to Brandon harbour and a sweep of red sands at Ballyquin. At Brandon Point, a few miles farther along, there are more stupendous coastal views from the cliff top.

## Dingle/An Daingean

A thriving, colourful fishing port and tourist centre, the town is a jumble of attractive streets tumbling down a hillside and jerking to a halt at the handsome pier. In the 14th and 15th centuries Dingle was Kerry's leading port and later became a centre for smuggling, at one point even minting its own coins.

In the 19th century a uniquely successful attempt was made to woo the Kerry Catholics from their faith when a Protestant curate began preaching in Irish, establishing schools and building houses on the peninsula as inducements for converts. There is no longer a thriving Protestant community.

## Gallarus Oratory

The most complete example of early Christian architecture to be found anywhere in Ireland is Gallarus Oratory, on a signposted site a mile inland from Smerwick Harbour. It has been dated to between 800 and 1200 and is a remarkable stone structure, shaped like an upturned boat and measuring 10ft by 15ft inside. It has a small window in the east wall and a narrow 5ft 6in high door in the west side. Although it was built of unmortared stone, it is still waterproof after many centuries of existence. Such oratories were common on monastic sites, but in most cases the roofs have fallen in.

## FUNGIE, THE DINGLE DOLPHIN

In 1984 a dolphin was sighted at Beenbawn Strand off the Kerry coast by two snorkellers. Friendly from the start, he amused the divers with his seductive antics and the huge perpetual smile spread across his face. Now thousands of people every year take boat trips from the quay to watch Fungie, as he was named by local fishermen, play. As soon as the dolphin hears the boat engines throbbing he starts his tricks – leaping out of the water, falling onto his back with a mighty splash, throwing fish into the air and catching them in his mouth. He clearly enjoys the company of humans and will often follow the boats home in an effort to try to get people to stay with him.

Dolphins are highly intelligent creatures and Fungie is no exception. Once, a disabled person was lowered into the water to meet him. The dolphin reacted with unusual tenderness, restraining his natural exuberance.

### Ventry/Ceann Trá

The white and pastel-coloured cottages of Ventry sit at the head of a deep bay at the southern end of the peninsula overlooking a superb, crescent-shaped beach with safe bathing and good fishing. The harbour was the scene of a 3rd-century legendary battle, when the hero Finn MacCool eloped with both the wife and daughter of the King of France. The bereft king sought vengeance and, aided by the King of Spain, arrived with a fleet of ships. In the ensuing battle the King of Spain was killed, while the King of France went mad.

Four miles west, down a signposted path in a field, are the extensive ruins of Dunbeg fort, one of the most interesting Iron Age promontory forts in Kerry. Perched on a 60ft cliff, with a sheer drop to the waves below, it has four defensive earth banks and, inside these, a stone wall which seals off the promontory. At the roofed entrance, which has two guard rooms, there is a souterrain, or underground escape passage.

Half a mile down the road towards Slea Head, in a field on the inland side, is an equally fascinating collection of prehistoric beehive dwellings inside a fortification whose walls are 10ft thick. These simple circular huts are known in Irish as clocháns.

ATLANTIC ROLLERS *Clogher Beach, pounded by Atlantic waves, looks out on the Blasket islands.*

DINGLE HARBOUR *Bright fishing boats bob in the waters of this natural harbour.*

GALLARUS ORATORY *This early chapel is the most complete of its kind in Ireland.*

117

# Warm Verdant Shores

*The broad and beautiful Kenmare River, an inlet of the sea, thrusts like a spearhead deep into the Kerry coast. Warm Gulf Stream waters lap these shores, above which sub-tropical palm trees, yuccas, bamboos, rhododendrons and fuchsias mingle with oak, willow, arbutus and blazing yellow gorse. Rock-strewn mountains tower on either side of this deep cleft, making it an area of outstanding natural beauty.*

## Caha Mountains/An Cheacha

Like a great, bony spine the Caha Mountains run down the centre of the Beara peninsula, dividing Cork from Kerry. Here and there in this boulder-strewn wilderness glaciers of an age long gone scooped out a corrie lake which now, with its ever-changing hues, reflects each day's weather patterns. Lower down, towards the seashore, smaller lakes shimmer in the verdant tranquillity of the forested foothills. It is a region where climbers, hill walkers and, above all, anglers are in their element – there are 40 lakes where brown trout slip through the waters.

The road climbs from Killaha, where a hoard of copper axes, a halberd and a dagger, dating from the early Copper Age (2000-1800 BC), was found on a site on the left, close to the road. The road eventually turns south through the village of Lauragh and rises into the Caha Mountains up to the 1081ft Healy Pass, where the views on the dizzying descent to Bantry Bay are spectacular.

## Derreen/Doirín

The magnificent woodland gardens on the outskirts of the village of Lauragh have a luxuriant display which includes wild rhododendrons, camellias, tree ferns, bamboos and many fine shrubs and specimen

SHEPHERDS' DAY *Sheep markets are a frequent sight in the pretty town of Kenmare.*

trees. The gardens, begun in the mid-19th century, form part of the estate of Derreen House, once home of the Marquess of Lansdowne, a descendant of Kenmare's founder, Sir William Petty.

Most of the land around here was acquired by Petty after the Cromwellian wars. As Cromwell's surveyor-general, he made some excellent maps and bought up confiscated land all over Ireland, much of it in Kerry. The house is not open to the public.
**Gardens** *Apr-Sept, daily 11am-6pm. Tel: (064) 83103.*

## Inchiquin Lough/Loch Inse Uí Chuinn

The still waters of Inchiquin lie amid quiet woods and pastureland set against a backdrop of the rugged Coomnadiha Mountain (2116ft). A wild and glorious place to explore, it is of exceptional botanical interest. In early summer the large-flowered butterwort, *Pinguicula grandiflora*, blooms here in all its glory. Irish spurge, saxifrages and arbutus also flourish, and across the lake is Uragh Wood, a protected area of primeval sessile oaks, remnants of the forest that once covered much of Ireland. Along a tarred road at the edge of the lake is a superb view of a waterfall, tumbling from another lake above. Inchiquin teems with salmon and trout.

## Kenmare/Neidín

The old name of Kenmare, Ceann Mara, means 'Head of the Sea', and once there used to be a town on the south side of the Kenmare River. The present one sits at the head of the river, providing a perfect link between two scenic routes – the Ring of Kerry and the Ring of Beara.

A colourful market town with attractive limestone houses, Kenmare is an excellent example of town planning. It was founded in 1670 by Sir William Petty (1623-87), Cromwell's surveyor-general, and an ancestor of the first Marquess of Lansdowne who in 1775 designed the town like a giant 'X', with two wide main streets.

A fine Catholic church with interesting roof timbers lies beyond the market house that faces the park. A Poor Clare convent next door, founded in 1861, was where the nun Mary Frances Cusack wrote an acclaimed *History of Kerry*, and was instrumental in launching a successful appeal for the starving locals in the famine of 1879. The convent is now famous for its needlepoint school.

Among the town's numerous antiquities is the finest example of a stone circle in the Kerry-Cork area. The circle, on the banks of the River Finnihy, is 3000 years old and consists of 15 stones with a 'burial boulder' lying in the middle. Nearby is Cromwell's Bridge, a stone bridge built without mortar. Its name has nothing to do with The Pretender, but derives instead from the Irish *crombheal*, meaning 'moustache', referring to its shape.

---

### KENMARE LACE

An exhibition of ancient and modern Kenmare lace is on display in Kenmare's Main Street, opposite the Lansdowne Arms Hotel. Such was the reputation of this exquisite needlepoint that Queen Victoria was presented with a Kenmare lace collar in 1881. In 1886 a lace bedcover was sold to the wife of an American millionaire for £300, an astronomical figure for a bedspread then.

The lacemaking was originally introduced into the town by nuns in a local convent, St Clare's, as a means of giving employment to women and girls during the famine years. After decades of prosperity it slumped to virtual extinction, but has recently been revived.

---

**OTHER PLACES TO SEE**
**Cnoc an Cappeen** 2m E of Kenmare. 'The mountain with a hat' – an enormous stone mushroom twice the height of a man, a geological oddity left on the landscape by the last Ice Age.
**Kilgarvan Motor Museum** Display of classic cars.

**EVENTS**
**Kenmare Cibeal (Arts Festival)** June.
**Kenmare Regatta** Aug.
**Kenmare Walking Festival** Easter weekend and first weekend in June.
**Sneem Regatta** Aug.

**SPORT**
**Angling** Game fishing: Inchiquin Lough and Rivers Blackwater, Roughty and Sneem. Sea fishing: Kenmare River.
**Boating** Kenmare River.
**Golf** Kenmare Golf Club, 9-hole course. Tel: (064) 41291.
Parknasilla Golf Club, 9-hole course. Tel: (064) 45122.

**INFORMATION**
Killarney Tourist Office. Tel: (064) 31633.

WHITE WATER SPECTACULAR *South of Sneem, boulders whip the river to a creamy foam as it thunders on its way to the sea.*

## Sneem/An tSnaidhm

A charming village, lined with gaily painted cottages, Sneem stands on the estuary of the River Sneem which flows into the Kenmare River. In front of the bridge over the river stands a pretty 18th-century Protestant church with a salmon weather vane, a reminder that this is great fishing country. A museum on the west side has an intriguing display of antique agricultural and domestic implements and furniture.

The village marks a junction point for scenic tours, such as the main 'Ring of Kerry' road that leads east by woodland and coast to Kenmare. Another route, to the north-east, leads directly to Moll's Gap, across wild and rugged country with majestic mountain views including Ireland's highest mountain, Carrauntoohill (3414ft), in Macgillycuddy's Reeks. The rugged cliffs of the Black Valley, near Moll's Gap, are home to hooded crows and the rare chough.

### WHOOPER SWAN

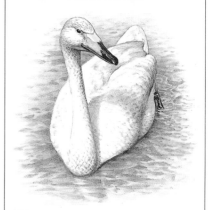

Every winter the lovely Black Valley is visited by a group of whooper swans, handsome birds that enjoy the salt water of the coast as much as the fresh water of lakes. Their name comes from their whooping, bugle-like call, which carries well over long distances and is easily recognisable. Whooper swans, which have shiny black legs and a bright yellow-and-black bill, breed in several parts of the Arctic and north-western Europe – in Lapland, Iceland and occasionally in Scotland – making large nests with a soft, downy lining and laying three to five eggs.

## Parknasilla/Páirc na Saileach

The benign effects of the Gulf Stream are seen at their best in this delightfully sheltered and idyllic resort on the southern Ring of Kerry, where subtropical plants flourish by manicured lawns at the edge of the sea. Over the past 100 years, Parknasilla has drawn many celebrities to its shoreside hotel, the Great Southern, among them Prince Rainier and Princess Grace of Monaco. George Bernard Shaw, a frequent visitor, wrote much of his great play *St Joan* there.

# The Killarney Lakeland

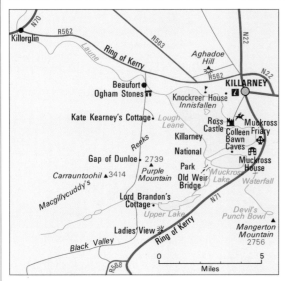

*With its spectacular scenery, unusually mild climate and rapid changes in light and weather, this is a bewitching place of intense beauty. Ireland's highest mountains, Macgillycuddy's Reeks, raise a jagged edge to the sky while at their feet rest three still lakes, studded with little islands, set among forests and lush glens thick with grand trees, wild fuchsias and scented orchids. The stillness can be almost eerie.*

**OTHER PLACES TO SEE**

**Aghadoe Hill** 2m W of Killarney. Outstanding panoramic view across gleaming lakes towards mountains. Also ruins of Round Tower, castle and 12th-century church with beautiful Irish-Romanesque doorway and ogham stone on the south wall.

**Knockreer House** In part of National Park, best reached through Deenagh Lodge gate. Built 1958 and formerly home of Grosvenor family. Now contains displays of plants and animals of area. Also houses Park Information Office, open in July and Aug. Tel: (064) 31947.

**Muckross Friary** Renovated remains of Franciscan friary, with remarkable cloisters enclosing ancient giant yew said to date from abbey's foundation in the 15th century. Graveyard contains remains of the last King of Desmond, as well as remains of various O'Sullivan, MacGillycuddy and O'Donoghue chieftains.

**Muckross Lake** Sometimes known as Middle Lake; fringed with thick woods inhabited by wild red deer. In the 18th century a popular pastime among the noble families living nearby was to hunt deer down from the hillsides and into the water, where the chase would continue in boats.

**WALKS**

**Killarney National Park** Nature trails are marked throughout the park, many close to Muckross House but others leading farther afield. Lucky visitors may see wild goats and otters. Picnic sites provided.

**Killarney Tourist Trail** A marked route through the town leads past the main points of interest. Takes about 2 hours walked at a leisurely pace.

**EVENTS**

**Easter Folk Festival** Killarney.

**Killarney Races** May, June and July.

**Killarney Regatta** July.

**Puck Fair** Killorglin, Aug.

**Rally of the Lakes** (motor-rally) Dec.

**St Patrick's Week Festival** Killarney, Mar.

**SPORT**

**Angling** Game fishing: Killarney Lakes, Kilbrean Lake, River Laune.

**Canoeing** Killarney Lakes, Lough Guitane.

**Golf** Killarney Golf Club, 18-hole course. Tel: (064) 31034.

**Windsurfing** Lough Leane.

**INFORMATION**

Killarney National Park Office. Tel: (064) 31665 or 31947 in July and Aug.

Killarney Tourist Office. Tel: (064) 31633.

### Kate Kearney's Cottage

Kate, a local beauty reputedly free with her charms, ran a shebeen (an illegal drinking-house) here in the mid-19th century, selling poteen to travellers passing through the Gap of Dunloe. She was constantly hounded by the law, but the final blow came when blight attacked the potato crop, the mainstay of her business. One night she vanished, leaving her poteen-making equipment behind.

Today, Kate Kearney's Cottage is a pub, café and souvenir shop, as well as the starting point for pony trap, or ponyback, trips through the Gap of Dunloe. Visitors cross a rugged 6 mile mountain pass between Macgillycuddy's Reeks and Purple Mountain, then by boat down river and across a lake to Ross Castle and back again, taking in the most glorious of all Killarney's scenery.

### Killarney/Cill Airne

In 1750 the local magnate, Lord Kenmare, decided to capitalise on nature's bounty and started to develop tourism in the area. Today it is a multi-million-pound business, and Killarney town bulges with hotels, bars, restaurants and shops.

Among the town's historical attractions is the 1855 St Mary's Catholic cathedral, designed by Augustus Pugin (1812-52) in the Early English style. It is a magnificent lime-stone structure with a massive square tower capped by a soaring spire. Opposite the Franciscan friary, built in 1860 with superb stained-glass windows, is a monument by Seamus Murphy to Kerry's four best-known Gaelic poets. There is a Transport Museum with a fine collection of vintage cars.

From the town centre, jaunting cars can be hired. These charming little two-wheel carts, drawn by horses and driven by men known as jarveys who act as guides, are the ideal way to view the sights and scenery of Killarney.

**Killarney Transport Museum** *Apr-Oct 10am-6pm. Tel: (064) 32638.*

### Killarney National Park

Some 25,000 acres of luxuriant woodland and three major lakes lie within this National Park, which is a nature-lover's delight. On the encircling mountain slopes can sometimes be seen Ireland's only herd of red deer, said to have established itself here in the Ice Age. In the woodland areas roam wild goats and Japanese sika deer, while other wildlife in the park includes otters, badgers, foxes, hares and hawks. There are attractive picnic sites throughout the park.

The Old Weir Bridge links Killarney's Upper Lake with Lough Leane and Muckross Lake at a place called the Meeting of the

MONASTIC SECLUSION *MacCarthy Mór, last King of Desmond, founded Muckross Friary in 1448.*

Waters. Here boats 'shoot the rapids' on the all-day tour of the Gap of Dunloe and the lakes. On the northern shore of Muckross Lake are the Colleen Bawn Caves, hollowed out of limestone by the lake waters. Special to the area is the pink-berried arbutus, or strawberry tree, which grows in profusion.

Ladies' View, on the Killarney-Kenmare road, gives the best views of the Killarney valley, taking in the Gap of Dunloe, Black Valley, the lakes and Ross Castle. It derives its name from the delight expressed by Queen Victoria's ladies-in-waiting on their first visit to the spot over 100 years ago.

Just outside the western fringe of the park, close to the village of Beaufort, stands a group of eight ogham stones, enclosed behind an iron railing and easily visible from the road. They are magnificently preserved, with their writing – the most ancient in Ireland, dating from the early Christian era – splendidly clear. Ogham stones usually bear the name of a person and his father or ancestor, but their original purpose is not known.

Along the Kenmare road, the waters from the Devil's Punch Bowl, high on Mangerton Mountain, plunge 60ft over sandstone crags to form one of Ireland's prettiest waterfalls. Tradition has it that if a childless woman drinks the icy waters of the Devil's Punch Bowl, her wish to bear children will be answered.

The centrepiece of Killarney National Park is the magnificent Muckross House with its splendid gardens sweeping down to the shores of Muckross Lake. They include a beautiful water garden, an unusual rock garden made out of the natural limestone and, in summer, stunning displays of rhododendrons and azaleas. The 65-room mansion, now The Kerry Folklife Centre, was built in 1843 in Tudor style. The museum houses craftsmen who can be seen working at their various trades – blacksmiths, weavers, potters and others. There is a craft shop, an exhibition of Kerry's music and poetry, and another of ancient farm machinery.
**Muckross House** *Mar-June and Sept-Feb 9am-6pm; July-Aug 9am-7pm. Tel: (064) 31440.*

## Killorglin/Cill Orglan

At the gateway to the beautiful Iveragh peninsula, beyond Killarney and on the renowned Ring of Kerry, slopes the town of Killorglin, built on a steep hill overlooking

HIGH AND MIGHTY *The rugged Mangerton Mountain rises to 2756ft above Lough Leane.*

the wide and wandering Laune, a clear river noted for its salmon and trout fishing. A busy, friendly, market town, it is famous for its Puck Fair – a horse and cattle fair held each August, when a wild goat from the mountains is caught, 'crowned' and enthroned in the centre of the town as a signal for nonstop merrymaking.

## Lough Leane/Loch Léin

The largest of Killarney's three lakes, this is also called Lower Lake. With Muckross and Upper Lakes, it lies in a mountain-ringed valley of outstanding beauty, dotted with islands. Apart from jaunting-car trips, no visit to Killarney is complete without an excursion on the lakes. Starting from Lord Brandon's Cottage at the western end of Upper Lake, and finishing at the landing stage of Ross Castle on Lough Leane, the waterborne traveller is treated to view after view of exhilarating beauty. Ross Castle, which dates from the 15th century, was the stronghold of the local chieftains, the O'Donoghues. It was the last castle to surrender to the Roundheads during the Cromwellian wars. A 15th-century tower house still remains and also a dwelling house dating from the 17th century.

A story goes that when the O'Donoghues owned all the land, the chief of the clan made his exit from this world by diving into the water from the castle, so entering the 'Land of Eternal Youth' – which, as every Irishman knows, lies beneath Killarney! He is said to be seen each May Day emerging from the water at sunrise.

Lying serene in the blue waters is the enchanting, uninhabited Innisfallen island, once the site of a 7th-century monastery founded by St Finan Lobhar ('the Leper'). Now there are only the ruins of a 12th-century Augustinian priory, and some fine Romanesque decoration in the little 11th to 12th-century church. The great Irish king, Brian Boru is said to have been educated at the monastery, in the late 10th century.

### THE KILLARNEY STRAWBERRY TREE

*My love's an arbutus*
*By the borders of Lene*
*So slender and shapely*
*In her girdle of green.*

The 1890 song alludes to the beauty of the strawberry tree, *Arbutus unedo*, which has glossy, dark green leaves, clusters of waxy, chaste-white flowers and cinnamon-red bark, and thrives in the very mild climate of Kerry. It flowers profusely from September to December and is then hung with masses of round, red fruits, which take a year to ripen. They are edible, but the Latin species name *unedo*, which means 'I eat one', suggests that one may be enough!

# A Smuggler's Coast

*Coves and sea caves that once sheltered smugglers, long strands of soft, golden sand with soaring dunes, lofty cliffs and rocky inlets make the north Kerry coastline an exciting one. The region's violent history is no less compelling – from the first landings by Stone Age beach-dwellers (7000-4000 BC) to Viking and Anglo-Norman invasions, shipwrecks and clan wars.*

### Ballybunnion/Baile an Bhuinneánaigh

This popular resort has many attractions: long beaches, excellent fishing, hot seaweed baths, and a coast riddled with caves. Dividing the main beach is a promontory on which stands the wall of the 16th-century Ballybunnion Castle, once a Fitzmaurice stronghold. The wall, 30ft high and 6ft thick, is pierced by two large holes and five window slits, and has become Ballybunnion's badge.

At the south end of the beach are fine caves, which can be reached at low tide. Above the main beach, a superb clifftop walk leads around the headlands to Nun's Beach. Halfway round, plunging down inside the cliff, is a 12ft wide 'blow hole'. It is fenced off for safety, but from it the sea can be heard crashing on the rocks 100ft below. Called Nine Daughters' Hole, its name derives from the legend of the 13th-century O'Connor chief who had nine daughters. He was justifiably proud of them until, one day, he

discovered that all nine were planning to elope with Norsemen, his hated enemies. In fury he hurled his daughters down the hole to their death on the rocks below.

Just outside the town, a large stone by the roadside marks the site of a Marconi Wireless Station from which 'wireless telephonic communication was made for the first time from east to west in March 1919 to Louisberg, Cape Breton, Nova Scotia'.

### Ballyduff/An Baile Dubh

South of the farming village a lane leads to Rattoo where, in a cul-de-sac beside the ruins of an ancient monastery, stands probably Ireland's most beautifully preserved Round Tower and the only complete one in Kerry. Reaching a height of 92ft and with a circumference of 48ft at its base, it probably dates from the 10th or early 11th century.

At the opposite end of the village stands the handsome new Rattoo Heritage Museum and Interpretive Centre. It contains local

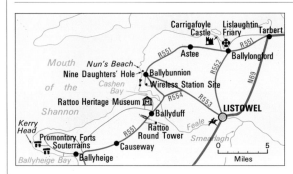

## SPORT

**Angling** Coarse fishing: River Feale. Game fishing: Rivers Feale and Smearlagh. Salmon hatchery at Cashen Bay, S of Ballybunnion. Sea fishing: Ballyheige.
**Bathing** Seaweed baths, Ballybunnion. Tel: (068) 27469. Sea bathing: Ballyheige and Beale.
**Golf** Ballybunnion Golf Club, two 18-hole courses. Tel (068) 27146.

## INFORMATION

Listowel Tourist Office. Tel: (068) 22590.
Tralee Tourist Office. Tel: (068) 21288.

## OTHER PLACES TO SEE

**Causeway** Several ring-forts on road between Ballyduff and Ballyheige. Causeway's name comes from stepping stones being laid there for people to cross the bogland.

## EVENTS

**Listowel Harvest Festival** Sept.
**Listowel Races** Oct.

The father of Jesse James, one of America's most notorious outlaws, was born in the neat little village of Astee, between Ballybunnion and Ballylongford. He emigrated to Missouri, where Jesse was born on September 5, 1847. The American Civil War, in which Jesse's family joined the Southern cause, brought ruin to their home. In revenge, young Jesse joined a guerrilla force where he quickly made a name for himself as a marksman. Soon he was leading his own gang, robbing trains and banks. It was members of that same gang, the Ford brothers, who eventually shot him dead and collected a $10,000 reward. The life of Jesse James has been the subject of many books and Hollywood films, and in Astee a pub bears his name.

archaeological discoveries, including Stone and Bronze Age tools and weapons. Graphic panels illustrate north Kerry's fascinating history and folklore.
**Rattoo Heritage Museum** *May-Sept, Mon-Sat 10am-6pm, Sun 2-6pm; Oct-Apr, Mon, Fri 10.30am-5.30pm, Sun 2-5.30pm. Tel: (066) 31000.*

### Ballyheige/Baile Uí Thaidhg

Long, sandy beaches lapped by the Gulf Stream, splendid views of the Dingle peninsula, and the claim that it has the driest and brightest weather in Kerry, make Ballyheige a favourite among seaside resorts. The shell of a neo-Gothic castle built by the Crosbie family in 1812 dominates the town. It looks for all the world like a substantial castle in a Hollywood film, but, like a Hollywood film set, close inspection reveals only a castellated front wall with nothing behind it.

In 1730 the Danish bullion ship *Golden Lyon* ran aground here, in one of the most notorious crimes of the 18th century. Sir Thomas Crosbie engaged two men to lure the ship onto the shore with a lantern hung from a horse's neck, whose tossing made it look like the light of another craft. The men took the *Golden Lyon*'s captain and crew – and its cargo of silver bullion worth £15,000 – to the Crosbie castle 'for safe keeping'. Apparently as a result of the night's exertions, Sir Thomas thereupon died. There were rumours of poisoning, however, and the Danish captain remained Lady Margaret's 'guest' for some months, as it was considered too dangerous to transfer the bullion to Dublin.

On June 4, 1731, a group of men – apparently promised a reward by the Crosbie family and the gentry of Tralee – staged a mock attack on the castle. The 12 bullion chests were loaded onto farm carts – but this was just a ruse. The chests were empty, and the silver was being hidden in caves beneath the castle. However, the *Golden Lyon*'s captain recognised one of the attackers as a nephew of Lady Margaret, and guessed that the robbery was a mock one. As a result, nine men were thrown in prison by Sir Edward Denny, Governor of Tralee. But by then the silver had been spirited away.

### Ballylongford/Béal Átha Longfoirt

To the north of this little farmland village stand the imposing Gothic ruins of Lislaughtin Friary, built in 1478 by John O'Connor Kerry.

This once-magnificent friary stands in verdant countryside, ivy-clad and roofless, its tower and cloisters gone and bushes growing out of its centre. But the remaining walls are well preserved. Its east window is divided into four pointed lights by stone mullions. There is a beautifully carved sedilia, a three-seated bench for the priest and his assistants on the south side of the altar, and three handsome windows.

The friary had a violent history, including an incident in 1580 when three aged monks were beaten to death by English soldiers.

### Carrigafoyle Castle

West of Ballylongford is the stronghold that was once the seat of the O'Connors of Kerry, originally built in 1490 by the chieftain Conor O'Connor. The castle measures 60ft by 30ft, with walls 8ft thick and a little over 80ft high – but only three walls remain. At the riverside entrance, a wide spiral staircase of more than 100 steps leads to the tower battlements with magnificent views across the Shannon estuary.

Once considered impregnable, Carrigafoyle Castle was attacked by Queen Elizabeth's forces on Palm Sunday, 1580. The castle held out against this bombardment until, reportedly, a maidservant who had fallen in love with an English officer betrayed the castle's defenders by holding a lighted candle in a window at the weakest part of the structure. Concentrated fire then made the breach in the wall that can be seen today.

### Kerry Head/Ceann Chiarraí

High above the wave-lashed cliffs of Kerry Head, at the most westerly point of the headland, stand two 2000-year-old promontory forts, stone-built defences strung across the neck of sea-girt promontories to reduce the area of attack. Today only crumbling semicircles of stone wall a few feet high survive, with sheer 60ft cliffs behind them and acres of wild, wind-blown bogland in front. To reach them, follow the southern coast road until it becomes a track through a farmyard and across bogland.

A few miles along the same road from Ballyheige, close to the sea, is a number of

TRANQUIL BAY *Peace reigns on the sands of Ballyheige Bay, once the scene of an infamous shipwreck.*

BREACHED WALLS *Carrigafoyle Castle bears scars made by Elizabeth I's cannons in 1580.*

souterrains – underground chambers – with a group of corbelled beehive houses.

### Listowel/Lios Tuathail

A lively inland town, Listowel has the ruin of a 15th-century castle – little of which remains apart from two ivy-clad towers – and a striking central square. It is dominated by two early 19th-century Gothic-style churches: the Catholic St Mary's facing the Protestant St John's. Listowel is also the home of Maurice Walsh (1879-1964), author of *The Quiet Man*, which was turned into an Oscar-winning film.

The town was once the terminus of the world's first monorail system, the Lartigue Railway, devised by a Spanish engineer of that name, which ran between Listowel and Ballybunnion from 1888 to 1924. Engines, carriages and wagons were divided into two sections, hanging on either side of a central rail. It inspired the ballad *The Song of Lartigue*.

> *The old train's held together with rope,*
> *And the tackling they say won't endure, Sir,*
> *Sure they balance the people with soap,*
> *And sometimes with bags of manure,*
>  *Sir . . .*

### THE KERRY BLUE TERRIER

Loved by generations of Kerrymen, the lively Kerry Blue Terrier was said to have descended from the long-haired blue dogs that swam ashore from the Spanish Armada warships, wrecked on the Kerry coast. The truth is that these dogs are a native Irish breed and have similar traits to those of the Irish Terrier and other Irish dogs. Robert Madgett, of Ballymacadam, near Castleisland, is credited with originating and promoting the breed in the 18th century.

In the early 1800s a breed of silver-blue terriers was used by farmers for hunting, fighting, ratting, guarding hearth and herd and even churning butter. They are thought to have some wolfhound in their makeup because when the Irish peasants were forbidden by their overlords to own pure hunting dogs, they arranged clandestine mating of their terriers with the lordly wolfhound. The hybrid was today's Kerry Blue. These dogs have a dandy stylishness about them with their bushy beards and moustaches and well-clipped coats. They are very intelligent and vivacious. However, they are often quite fierce and make good hunting and guard dogs. Their silky, thick and curly coats, which give them their name, vary in colour from dark to pale blue.

# The Vale of Tralee

*The beautiful Vale of Tralee, celebrated in the love song, 'The Rose of Tralee', lies at the heart of fertile farmland bounded by high, rolling moorland and the Slieve Mish and Stack's Mountains. To the west, sandy beaches stretch for miles. Sailing, fishing and watersports abound but the area is also rich in antiquities and historical sites, and has several cave systems for the adventurous.*

LONE SURVIVOR *Standing stark against the purple, mist-shrouded Slieve Mish Mountains is Ireland's only commercially operated windmill, at Blennerville.*

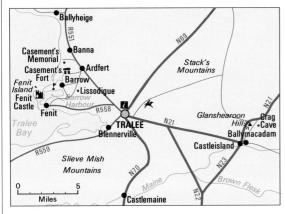

**OTHER PLACES TO SEE**
**Blennerville** Ireland's only remaining windmill that is being operated commercially.

Built in 1780 and recently restored. Apr-Oct. Coffee shop and gift shop. Tel: (066) 21064.

**Lissodigue** 3m NE of Fenit, limestone cave running deep into hill can be explored for more than 700ft.

**EVENTS**
**Rose of Tralee International Festival** Last week in Aug.
**Tralee Market** Thur pm.

**SPORT**
**Angling** Coarse fishing: Rivers Brown, Maine and Flesk. Sea fishing: Banna and Fenit Island.
**Bathing** Fenit Strand.
**Golf** Tralee Golf Club, 18-hole course. Tel: (066) 36379.
**Sailing** Tralee Bay.

**INFORMATION**
Tralee Tourist Office. Tel: (066) 21288.

## Ardfert/Ard Fhearta

This small village was once the ecclesiastical capital of Kerry. Today the reminders of its days of glory are extensive ruins of a cathedral and abbey that owe their foundation to St Brendan the Navigator (AD 483-577). Young St Brendan was educated at the missionary post established here in the 5th century. The monastery he founded became the centre of Anglo-Norman ecclesiastical influence in Kerry, although some of the three surviving buildings have pre-Norman features.

The 13th-century St Brendan's Cathedral is roofless now, its massive walls standing stark against the skyline, the haunt of rooks, but it stubbornly retains an air of its former grandeur. The lovely Irish Romanesque doorway, the arcaded west wall and the soaring, graceful lancet windows that once lit the handsome nave, catch the eye immediately. The graveyard contains ancient tombs and a 5th-century stone carved with the ancient Irish script called ogham. Nearby are the Temple-na-Hoe (Temple of the Virgin), built in the late 12th century, and the 15th-century Temple na-Griffin (Temple of the Griffin), in the north wall of which are two winged dragons with crossed necks, representing evil devouring itself.

## Banna

In a bush-surrounded ancient ring-fort close to Banna's extensive beach, Sir Roger Casement (1864-1916), the Irish patriot and revolutionary leader, was found hiding and was arrested on Good Friday morning in 1916. He had landed on Banna beach from a German submarine, but was ill and hid in the fort while his companions went to Tralee for help. The police, already alerted, found the trio's rubber dinghy and hastily buried pistols, and soon discovered the fugitive. Casement was sent to London to stand trial.

He was found guilty and hanged as the only 'traitor' of the 1914-18 war, despite his plea that he had landed in Ireland in the hope of putting off the rising planned for Easter Sunday. From the dock he said: 'Ireland is treated today, among the nations of the world, as if she were a convicted criminal . . . . if it be treason to fight against an unnatural fate as this, then I am proud to be a rebel and I shall cling to my rebellion with the last drop of my blood.' The fort where he hid, now thickly overgrown, is signposted 'Casement's Fort', and a memorial at the site of his capture stands beside Banna beach.

## Castleisland/Oileán Ciarraí

Now a thriving market town this was once the formidable power base of the Earls of Desmond. Their Kerry headquarters, the supposedly impregnable 'Castell of the Island' (an island formed by diverting the waters of the River Maine into a moat around the 13th-century castle), is today an ivy-covered stump, seen on the right as the town is entered from Killarney. Castleisland is now noted for its distinctive red marble quarried here and used locally. From Glanshearoon Hill, to the north, there is a fine view of the Vale of Tralee.

Close to Castleisland is a recently discovered fossil cave system called Crag Cave. It is a cool, spectacular world where pale forests of stalagmites and stalactites, thousands of years old, throw eerie shadows around vast echoing caverns.

Magical names identify many of the cave's special features – Minas Tirith is the largest chamber – and the great love story of Irish mythology, the Passion of Diarmuid and Gráinne (a saga that is part of the North Kerry folklore), has been woven into the tour-guide story of Crag. From a maze of side passages come the distant gushing sounds of underground streams traversing the depths of one of Ireland's longest cave systems – it is just over 2 miles long.
**Crag Cave tours** *Mid-Mar to Dec. Tel: (066) 41244.*

SUBTERRANEAN MAGIC *Crag Cave is a colourful wonderland of stalactites and stalagmites.*

### Castlemaine/Caisleán na Mainge

The castle from which this attractive little market town derived its name was built in 1215 to guard a crossing over the nearby River Maine. It was destroyed by Cromwellian troops, but Castlemaine was to live on in song and legend as the home of the famous Australian outlaw, 'The Wild Colonial Boy'.

> There was a wild colonial boy,
> Jack Duggan was his name,
> He was born and reared in Ireland
> in a place called Castlemaine.
> He was his father's only son,
> his mother's pride and joy,
> And dearly did his parents love
> the Wild Colonial Boy.

The traditional ballad contains incidents from an earlier one, 'Bold Jack Donahoe', which relates the exploits of an Irish convict in New South Wales, in the late 1820s. The song became so popular that government authorities feared it might encourage rebellion among the Irish population in Australia, and for ten years it was illegal to sing the ballad in pubs.

### Fenit/An Fhianait

St Brendan the Navigator was born at Fenit, and from there he is said to have set sail for America over 1400 years ago. Fenit is now a major port busy with fishing boats and dinghies, and renowned for its oyster beds. From Fenit a scenic route by Barrow through Ardfert and Banna to Ballyheige has lovely views of miles of unpolluted golden beaches. On Fenit Island, north-west of the village, are the crumbling remains of Fenit Castle, built around 1800 to guard the entrance to Barrow Harbour which once had a busy trade with Spain and the Low Countries.

### Tralee/Trá Lí

The Rose of Tralee International Festival, which any woman with even remote Irish connections may enter in the hope of becoming the 'Rose of Tralee', has made the chief town of Kerry famous. The event is accompanied by a week of pageantry, music and merrymaking. 'The Rose' is also the subject of a love song, *The Rose of Tralee*, written in the 1800s by C. Mordaunt Spencer. The song is said to be based on the story of Mary O'Connor and her sweetheart, a young soldier sent to fight abroad in the British Army, who arrived home from the wars hoping to marry her, only to see her coffin being carried to the graveyard – a tragic victim of an early death.

Tralee originally grew up as a fortified settlement around the 13th-century Desmond Castle, the seat of the Desmond earls, which has long since gone. Once composed of streets of thatched cottages, the town and its castle were destroyed in the mid-17th century by Cromwellian troops. But today some majestic 18th-century houses can be seen in Denny and Castle Streets. Just off Castle Street is the impressive 19th-century courthouse with a splendid Ionic portico, designed by Sir Richard Morrison. Two cannon flank it, commemorating Kerrymen killed in the Crimean War of 1854 and in the Indian Mutiny of 1857-8. At Day Place, on the site of a 13th-century friary, is the 1861 Dominican church designed by Edward Pugin, which has some fine stained glass. St John's church, built in 1870 in Castle Street, is reputed to have the tallest spire in Ireland, soaring to 200ft.

The town is also home to the delightful Siamsa Tíre Theatre, a centre for mime, dance and folk theatre. It holds regular concerts of traditional music with flutes, pipes and fiddles and the artistes dress in colourful native costume.

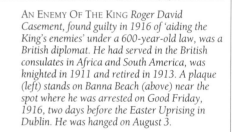

AN ENEMY OF THE KING *Roger David Casement, found guilty in 1916 of 'aiding the King's enemies' under a 600-year-old law, was a British diplomat. He had served in the British consulates in Africa and South America, was knighted in 1911 and retired in 1913. A plaque (left) stands on Banna Beach (above) near the spot where he was arrested on Good Friday, 1916, two days before the Easter Uprising in Dublin. He was hanged on August 3.*

PRIDE OF TRALEE *Proud home owners in Tralee's Denny Street have made the most of their rich 18th-century heritage. Every doorway, no two alike, glows with colourful paintwork and shiny brass.*

# THE LANGUAGE OF POETS

*The story of Irish, a soft and magical tongue*

The Celts arrived in Ireland around the 3rd and 4th centuries BC, having spread westward from central Europe across France and into Britain. Unlike the Continent and Britain, Ireland was never invaded by the Romans and so the Irish version of the Celtic language, 'Goedelic', or Gaelic, was not greatly affected by Latin. Even three centuries of Viking raids and settlements left only a minimal influence on the Gaelic vocabulary. In fact, it was the Irish who planted their own language abroad, when they invaded the Isle of Man and Scotland and set up a kingdom in present-day Argyll in AD 500. The native Picts gradually adopted Irish as their language and eventually it was spoken throughout Scotland – 'Scot' in medieval times meant 'Irish speaker'. When St Patrick landed in Ireland in AD 432, he found a fiercely independent people who valued their poets as highly as their warriors and nurtured an oral tradition that stretched back into the mists of time.

As Christianity spread across Ireland many of the Gaelic poets and their descendants became monks who worked to create and record their literature in Irish. Latin ecclesiastical terms were absorbed into the Irish language. By the 11th century the first manuscripts were being written in Irish, in the distinctive Irish uncial script that remained almost unaltered until the 20th century. Epics such as *Lebor na hUidre* (The Book of the Dun Cow) and *Táin bó Cuailgne* (The Cattle Raid of Cooley) retell the grand deeds of legendary heroes and heroines such as Finn MacCool, Deirdre, Cuchulainn and the bellicose Queen Maeve.

When the first Anglo-Normans settled in Ireland at the end of the 12th century, they clung to their own language – Norman French. But they adopted Irish culture so successfully that the English administration became alarmed, and passed the Statutes of Kilkenny in 1367, which made speaking Irish a treasonable offence. Despite these laws, by the 16th century only a few towns were English-speaking, and these lay within the Pale – the English-controlled enclave around Dublin. A more forceful approach was decided on to change the Irish 'course of government, apparel, manner of holding land, language and habit of life' – by 'planting' Scots and English settlers in Ireland. The Plantation, followed by Cromwell's invasion in 1649 and the anti-Catholic penal laws of the early 18th century, set in motion the decline of the Irish language. Added to this, the terrible potato famine of 1846-8 hit the poorer, Irish-speaking families very badly and resulted in mass emigration to the United States. By the end of the 19th century less than a quarter of the population spoke Irish.

IRISH TODAY In 1922, when the Irish Free State was established, Irish was designated the national language. Today, only a small number of people speak it as their first language – perhaps as few as 30,000. But it is still widely heard. You won't travel far without seeing a signpost in Irish, you'll hear snatches of it on the radio and on television, and you can buy Irish books, magazines and papers and attend church services in Irish.

Roughly 780,000 people – nearly a quarter of Ireland's population – consider themselves Irish-speaking. This includes those who can just get their tongues around the basic greetings as well as those who can follow current affairs programmes on the television channel RTE and Raidió na Gaeltachta.

All government legislation is written and passed in both Irish and English, and in the courts every citizen has the right to be heard in Irish. All children in state-supported schools must learn it and it is a requirement for entry into the National University.

In recent years, Irish language arts have blossomed. Conradh na Gaeilge (The Gaelic League) hosts the 'Oireachtas', an annual festival of Irish music, dancing, poetry, drama and painting. Many Irish amateur drama groups have been formed, and Deilt, a professional theatre company, tours the country regularly. The number of Irish language writers has mushroomed – it includes the late Máirtín Ó Cadhain and poets such as Nuala Ní Dhomhnaill – and many have seen their works translated into other languages.

CITY EMBLEM *The emblem of the Cork City Town Hall includes the Irish phrase 'Erin Gobradh' (Ireland For Ever).*

BRIGHT SIGNS *The post office in the Gaeltacht area of Dunquin (top), and a craft shop nearby (above) are gaily signposted in Irish.*

## PLAIN TALK

Irish speakers will be visibly delighted if you make the effort to greet them in Irish. Here are some essential, and a few not-so-essential, words and expressions. However, pronunciations vary from place to place as there are three main dialects: Munster, Connaught and Ulster.

| | |
|---|---|
| Hello (*to one person*) | **Dia duit** (dee-a gwith) (*God be with you*) |
| Hello (*in return*) | **Dia's Muire duit** (dee-as mwir-a gwith) (*God and Mary be with you*) |
| Hello (*to several people*) | **Dia daoibh** (dee-a gweev) |
| How are you? | **Conas tá tú** (kunas thaw thoo) |
| I'm well | **Táim to maith** (thawim gu moh) |

| | |
|---|---|
| Thank you | **Go raibh maith agat** (gu ru moh aguth) |
| Please | **Le do thoil** (leh duh hell) |
| You're welcome | **Tá fáilte romhat** (thaw foil-cha ro-ath) or just 'fáilte'. |
| Health | **Sláinte** (slawncha) |
| Whiskey | **Uisce beatha** (ishka baha) |
| Good luck, safe journey | **Go n-éirí do bhóthar leat** (gu nire-ee du voher lath) (*may the road rise with you*) |
| Goodbye (*to person leaving*) | **Slán leat** (slawn lath) |
| Goodbye (*to person staying*) | **Slán agat** (slawn aguth) |
| Goodnight | **Oíche mhaith** (ee-ha woh) |

'AT THE FEIS' *Jack Yeats's drawing depicts a storytelling competition, or 'feis', in which the entrants tell their tales in Irish. These events are still held in Ireland every year.*

Iryſhe.    Latten.    Engliſhe,

Coneſ ta tu,      Quomodo habes,    How doe you.
Taim ſo maih,     Bene ſum.          I am well,
ſo ſo maih aſaſ,  Habeo gratias,     I thancke you,
In eoloſo ſealaſ  Poſſis ne ~~~      Cann you ~~ }
ſo lauaſſo, ~~    hibernice loqui,}  speake Fryſhe
Abaſſ laſſen,     Dic latine.        Speake Latten
Dia leſiuſan ]    Deus adiuat ~~ }   God saue the
ſaſoma ~ ~~}      Reginā Angliæ}     Queene off
                                     Englande:

QUEEN ELIZABETH'S IRISH PRIMER *An Irish phrasebook was written by Christopher Nugent, Baron Delvin, to be used by Elizabeth I, and given to her as her personal copy. She also had the first Irish fount cut for her, in 1571, so that books could be printed in Irish.*

## FINDING YOUR WAY IN IRISH

Most place names in Ireland have their roots in the Irish language. Many are linked to the natural world of fords, lakes, rocks and hills. Others belong to the supernatural world of bean sí (banshee) and fairy mounds, or to the religious one of churches and saints. The Irish name is followed by the English meaning, and a sample place name.

| | | |
|---|---|---|
| **Ard** | *height, high* | Ardglass (*the green height*) |
| **Áth** | *ford* | Athdare (*ford of the oak tree*) |
| **Bal, Baile, Bally** | *town, settlement* | Ballybunnion (*town of the sapling*) |
| **Carrick, Carraig** | *rock* | Carrickfergus (*rock of Fergus*) |
| **Cluain** | *meadow* | Clonmel (*meadow of honey*) |
| **Drom, Drum** | *ridge, drumlin* | Dromahair (*ridge of the two air demons*) |
| **Dún** | *fort* | Donegal (*fort of the foreigners*) |
| **Ennis, Inis** | *island, river meadow* | Enniskillen (*Ceithleann's island*) |
| **Glen** | *glen, valley* | Glendalough (*valley of the two lakes*) |
| **Kill, Cill** | *church* | Killarney (*church of the sloes*) |
| **Knock, Cnoc** | *hill* | Knock |
| **Lios, Liss** | *fairy mound, ring-fort* | Lismore (*fort of the gamblers*) |

THE GAELTACHT Small pockets of Irish-speaking rural communities, known collectively as the Gaeltachtaí, have survived along the coasts of Donegal, Mayo, Galway, Kerry, Cork and Waterford, and inland in Cork and Meath. Most of the 83,500 people living in these areas are bilingual, but the language spoken in everyday life will be Irish.

Until recently, roads and other communications have been patchy in the more remote areas, so these people have remained closer to their Gaelic roots than people in the rest of Ireland. They put great store in 'good talkers' – those who have a stack of tales, anecdotes, poems and sayings to while away the long winter evenings. And the 'seanchaí'

(traditional storyteller) is a respected figure. Traditional songs are still sung and 'céilithe', or traditional dances, are a weekly event in many villages.

Life in the Gaeltachtaí has always been hard. The land is too poor to support large families, and many people have been forced to move to English-speaking parts of the

country, or to emigrate. However, because the Gaeltacht areas are vital to the survival of the language, the government provides special grants for those who live there, and encourages their traditional industries. For, as the Irish say, 'Daoine gan teanga, daoine gan croí' – 'a people without a language is a people without a heart'.

# THE LOWER SHANNON

As the mighty River Shannon tumbles down from Lough Derg, the last and largest of its lakes, to its deep estuary on the Atlantic coast, it provides a natural border for the three counties that surround its lower reaches – Limerick, Tipperary and Clare. The lowland parts of Limerick and Tipperary are limestone meadows, well watered by the Shannon and its tributaries and by the River Suir to the east. Here is the so-called Golden Vale, famous for its rich grasslands, where cattle, sheep and racehorses are raised. Beyond them, hedged pasture nudges the perimeters of the higher ground, such as the Galty Mountains in southern Tipperary and the Slieve Aughty Mountains on the borders of Clare and Galway to the north. The uplands quickly revert to open, empty landscapes, where peregrines wheel over heather and gorse moors, concealed lakes and neatly squared-off plantations of deep-green conifers.

A rude shock to this pleasantly modulated landscape comes with the Burren, in northern Clare, a fascinating and awesome stretch of land, exposed by some quirk of geology. Huge pavements of grey limestone dotted with massive boulders stretch as far as the eye can see. Clinging to the soil that has collected in the fissures of the rock are spongy tufts of grass and saxifrage, and a surprisingly unusual range of wild flowers – fragile cranesbill geraniums, rock roses, Mediterranean orchids, Arctic-alpine gentians and mountain avens. The Aillwee Caves reveal the underground aspect of this landscape.

Just to the south of the Burren is another of Ireland's great geological wonders – the towering Cliffs of Moher, which surge almost vertically from the sea to a height of 650ft along 5 miles of coastline. Paths lead across the grassy summits of the cliffs, with views to the Aran Islands and across Galway Bay to the mountains of Connemara. Puffins, guillemots and razorbills, along with ravens and choughs, dive and soar in dizzying aerobatic displays up and down the face of the cliffs.

COTTAGE CHARM *Thatched homes line the pretty main street of Adare.*

POULNABRONE DOLMEN *The Burren's wild beauty is a fitting scene for this dramatic prehistoric tomb.*

SUNSET ON THE SHANNON *Another day ends over crumbling Beagh Castle, which still stands watch on the Shannon estuary.*

The Clare coast also has some softer faces, such as the fine beaches at Lehinch and Milltown Malbay, a Victorian resort which offers sea angling, golf, surfing and boardsailing. The spa town of Lisdoonvarna plays host to a curious and ever-popular festival each September – the International Matchmaking Festival, where the young and not-so-young go in search of a partner in marriage.

Counties Clare, Limerick and Tipperary are all part of the province of Munster. In the past, its centre of power was in Tipperary, at the Rock of Cashel, now a majestic cluster of buildings on the crest of an ancient mound, with a ruined cathedral, soaring Round Tower and the exquisite Romanesque Cormac's Chapel. But even before Celtic chieftains made these lands their home, the area around the lower Shannon appears to have been well populated, for it has numerous prehistoric monuments. Among them, the most notable are the rich cluster of sites around Lough Gur in County Limerick, and the spectacular Poulnabrone Dolmen on the Burren.

The Celts left behind them the legends of their great pre-Christian heroes. The grotesque hag Mal is said to have attempted to follow the Ulster hero Cuchulainn in making a giant leap at Loop (or Leap) Head, only to fall into the sea. Her body was washed up at Mal Bay.

Early Christianity saw the foundation of several abbeys, which grew and developed in medieval times under the protection of the Irish chieftains. But this region is perhaps better known for the monasteries built in the 12th century by the austere and reforming Cistercians, such as Monasterananagh in County Limerick, and Kilcooly and Holycross in Tipperary.

Then the Vikings came, raiding the monasteries and villages all the way up the Shannon. They settled in Limerick – now the largest town on the west coast and traditionally a prosperous trading port – in the early 10th century. This was only the beginning of troubles suffered by the region – and Limerick in particular – at the hands of people from overseas. In 1651, Limerick was besieged for 12 months by Cromwellian troops before finally succumbing, and then faced two further sieges in 1690 and 1691. In this final siege, Patrick Sarsfield heroically ambushed the siege train at Ballyneety. But his efforts were in vain, and the 18th and 19th-century elegance of Limerick today reflects the confidence and success of the wealthy English merchants and landowners who became its masters.

Today, however, Limerick is remembered for a more frivolous reason. It is said that a group of Irish poets, who used to meet in the village of Croom in the 18th century, added to their repertoire of verse a humorous, five-line ditty. This style of verse was avidly adopted by English versifiers, and the 'limerick' became popular across the world.

# Echoes of the Middle Ages

The MacNamaras and the O'Briens once vied for control of central Clare, whose eastern hills rise towards Slieve Bernagh and whose southern reaches stretch to the shore of the ever-broadening Shannon. Now, centuries-old fortresses like Bunratty and Knappogue, spectacularly restored, re-create the past for visitors to their medieval banquets a few miles from the modern technology of Shannon Airport.

### Bunratty/Bun Raite

The village whose name means 'the mouth of the River Raite' is commanded by a castle, once the seat of the O'Briens, Earls of Thomond. The 15th-century castle stands on what was once an island surrounded by marshes, but these have since been drained and turned to farmland. The rectangular keep, with four battlemented corner turrets, 48ft high Great Hall, drawbridge, chapel, bedrooms and kitchen, make it a medieval classic.

Bunratty Castle was meticulously

THE LIVING PAST *The kitchen of the farmhouse in Bunratty Folk Park is complete in every detail.*

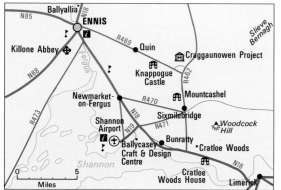

### OTHER PLACES TO SEE

**Ballyallia Riverside Park**
Dinghy sailing, picnic facilities. Overwintering wildfowl can frequently be seen.

**Ballycasey Craft and Design Centre** 3m W of Bunratty. Ancient and modern craft products made for sale in studios in an 18th-century courtyard. Open all year. Restaurant. Tel: (061) 362105.

**Cratloe Woods** Superb protected forest (once entirely oak), said to have provided the oak roof beams for Westminster Hall in London. Car park and walks. Magnificent 50 mile vistas of Shannon and County Limerick to south from Woodcock Hill (capped by telecommunication spheres). Cratloe Woods House (1610), only example of an Irish longhouse still lived in; fine interiors and old farm machinery. Afternoon teas served. Open daily June-Sept, weekdays only May and Oct. Tel: (061) 327028.

**Killone Abbey** 3m S of Ennis, ruined 13th-century convent-abbey with fine Romanesque east window and vaulted crypt, dating to 1225, in beautiful lakeside setting.

**Mountcashel** Also known as Kilmurry Castle. 90ft tower house built before 1470 by the O'Briens in wooded lakeland near Craggaunowen and Knappogue Castles. Restored in 1970s by owner; still lived in. Open daily for refreshments. Tel: (061) 72757.

**Sixmilebridge** Pretty village with attractive Georgian house, Mount Ievers, not open to public.

### EVENTS

**Car Rally** Clare Motor Club, Sept.

**Cois Na hAbhna** Evening stage show of traditional music, song and dance. Ennis, late May. Tel: (061) 71166.

**Ennis Arts Festival** Mid-Sept.

**Fleadh Nua** Week of traditional Irish music, Ennis, May.

### SPORT

**Angling** Trout fishing: River Fergus.

**Golf** Drumoland Castle Golf Club, 18-hole course. Tel: (061) 71144.
Ennis Golf Club, 18-hole course. Tel: (065) 24074.
Shannon Golf Club, 18-hole course. Tel: (061) 61020.

### INFORMATION

Ennis Tourist Office.
Tel: (065) 28366/28308.

restored in 1954, and furnished by its owner, Viscount Gort, who gave it to the nation. It now displays an impressive collection of tapestries, European furniture from the 15th and 16th centuries, furnishings and paintings. The restoration avoids the 'academic chill' that the owner felt pervades so many museums, and brings the castle to life again.

Soon after the opening of the castle in 1960, medieval banquets began to be served, with entertainment by singers and actors, and these are now a regular attraction.

Next to the castle is the Bunratty Folk Park. In the 1960s, a farmhouse rescued from land needed for Shannon Airport was rebuilt here. This was the beginning of what has become a 25 acre living museum of traditional village life. It has 25 houses, a village street complete with a pub, and fully operational workshops such as a blacksmith's forge, a printer's shop and a draper's.

**Bunratty Castle and Folk Park** *Daily, 9.30am-5.30pm; June-Aug, 9.30am-7pm. Tel: (061) 361511. Also, coffee shop and craft shop.*

### Craggaunowen Project

In the grounds of Craggaunowen Castle, set among lakes and hills east of the Fergus estuary, is a reconstruction of daily life in prehistoric and early historic Ireland.

The crannog – an artificial island – in a small lake is a major exhibit. It was built on rocks piled into a shallow part of the lake in the traditional way that was followed for 2500 years. Experiments in planting ancient crops can be seen, and there is a surprisingly efficient 'cooking hole' – a trough into which stones heated in a fire would be thrown to bring 250 gallons of water to the boil in only thirty minutes.

An Iron-Age timber trackway, recovered from a bog in County Longford, has been re-sited here, and a 5th-century ring-fort has been constructed. It is complete with an underground shelter, and a wattle-and-daub kiln in which pottery can be fired.

A conservatory-like building houses the famous leather-hulled 'Brendan' boat, in which explorer and author Tim Severin crossed the North Atlantic in 1976-7, re-enacting the voyages of St Brendan.

The whole historic reconstruction project is the child of John Hunt, an imaginative archaeologist and art historian. It was given birth in the 1960s, when he restored the tall, waterside tower house – originally a Mac-Namara stronghold built in the mid-16th century – and furnished it with medieval religious objects. But his great interest was Irish prehistory, and he wanted to give a feeling of daily life in pre-Christian times. The result is the Craggaunowen Project.

**Opening times** *Mar-Oct, 10am-6pm. Tel: (061) 367178.*

## THE BRENDAN VOYAGE

Brendan the Navigator (c. 484-577) was Abbot of Clonfert in County Galway. He was also reputed to have made a fabulous voyage to America, 500 years before the Vikings got there, but this was long regarded as fanciful legend. Thanks to author and explorer Tim Severin, it is now accepted that the 6th-century Irish missionary and his fellow monks *could* have sailed across the Atlantic.

What Severin did was to build a craft (right) closely following descriptions given in the medieval manuscripts recounting St Brendan's voyage. The hull was formed from oxhide tanned with oak bark and stretched over an ash-wood frame, much as fishermen on Ireland's west coast still make 'currachs', but on a larger scale. The method and materials would give the boat elasticity, of vital importance when ice floes closed in on it. Grease was smeared on the hide to help preserve it in the salt water.

Then, in May 1976, Severin set sail with his companions, via Iceland, Greenland and Nova Scotia, to the USA. It was a difficult journey in which the boat was frequently punctured by sharp ice. The holes were mended by two crewmen – one inside and the other hanging over the side in freezing water – stitching on a leather

patch. The adventure is recounted in Severin's book *The Brendan Voyage* (1979). The boat is now preserved and housed in the grounds of the Craggaunowen Project.

---

### Ennis/Inis

The narrow, one-way streets of Clare's busy county town still have a medieval feel to them. Ennis grew up around a friary founded in the 13th century when wandering Franciscans were befriended by the O'Brien King of Thomond. A famous school flourished in the shadow of the abbey – which still stands, roofless but with its tall tower intact, close to the fast-flowing River Fergus. The cloisters and the church are rich in medieval carvings and the 19th-century tomb in the church incorporates panels from a royal tomb that once stood there, possibly erected in 1470.

A statue of the 19th-century patriot Daniel O'Connell (1775-1847) towers over the High Street on a tall Doric column. In 1828, County Clare elected O'Connell to the British House of Commons, but as a Catholic he was prevented from taking his seat. A year later the Catholic Emancipation Act was passed, and in 1830 he entered Parliament.

The De Valera Museum and Library, housed in a former Presbyterian church across the river, commemorates another Irish patriot, Eamon de Valera (1882-1975). He was elected to the House of Commons by East Clare as early as 1917, and was a leader of the Irish Free State and the Republic as president of the Executive Council and then Taoiseach (Prime Minister) for most of the period 1932-59. He was President from 1959-73.

The area west of the O'Connell monument is laced with bustling markets and old-world lanes. In the Catholic Procathedral, an early Gothic Revival work of the 1830s with a tall, spiky belfry, there is a memorial to Father James Barrett. He is remembered as the childhood guardian of opera singer Harriet Smithson, wife of the French composer Hector Berlioz, who grew up in Ennis.

**Ennis Friary** *May Bank Holiday to mid-Sept, daily 10am-6pm. Tel: (065) 29100.*

### Knappogue Castle/Caisleán Cnapóg

The battlemented keep of Knappogue – built by one of the MacNamaras in 1467 – and its later extensions were rescued from ruin in the 1960s by Mark Edwin Andrews of Houston, Texas, a former assistant secretary of the US Navy, and his architect wife. They transformed a mere shell into an authentic setting for twice-nightly medieval banquets and a pageant of Irish history which tells the story of the women of Ireland – real and mythical queens, saints and sinners – in music, song and dance. The castle is open during the day, when visitors can see the interiors, restored and furnished with items dating from the 15th to 18th centuries.

**Opening times** *May-Oct, 9-30am-5pm. Tel: (061) 71103.*

### Quin/Cuinche

The great landmark of this village is the high-arched ruin of the Franciscan friary, standing in a field, with its cloister almost complete. A stream separates the friary from a second ruin, St Finghin's church. The friary was built in 1402, but the foundation dates from the 13th century. It is a rambling but well-preserved place, with a safe climb to the second-floor dormitory, now grassed over.

KNAPPOGUE *Medieval banquets with singers and actors are held at the castle.*

BY QUIET WATERS *Quin's 15th-century Franciscan friary exudes an air of unruffled tranquillity.*

# Flat Lands by the Shannon

*The Shannon estuary's north shore leads westwards into a flat and treeless peninsula buffeted by the Atlantic's winter gales. On the ocean side, wild, dramatic cliffs alternate with sweeping sandy beaches and fishing villages that have become some of the most popular holiday resorts on Ireland's west coast. Here modern amenities for yachtsmen are being developed alongside more traditional ways of making a living.*

## Carrigaholt/Carraig an Chabhaltaigh

The village is on a well-protected inlet on the Shannon shore, with a sandy beach revealed at low tide. The MacMahon Castle stands on a flat-topped grassy knoll to the west. In a good state of preservation, it has a spiral staircase leading to the top, where there is a wide view of the estuary.

Carrigaholt's Irish name means 'rock of the fleet'. In 1588 the Spanish galleon *La Annunciada* took shelter with six other Armada ships between Carrigaholt and Scattery Island. She was scuttled there, but her crew probably got safely back to Spain on the six other ships.

## Kilkee/Cill Chaoi

A mile-long crescent of sand in Moore Bay, sheltered by a reef from the Atlantic and backed by Victorian guesthouses and hotels, makes Kilkee a popular family resort. The bay's clear water is rich in plant life, and ideal for snorkellers and scuba divers. Special delights are bathing in the low-tide rock pools known as the Pollock Holes and, in stormy weather, watching the Puffing Hole, a blowhole on the south shore that shoots water high into the air. A small Heritage Gallery honours Kilkee's seafaring past, with historic photographs of old-time fishing folk.

Golf links overlook the north of the bay, and to the south there are superb walks along

### OTHER PLACES TO SEE
**Bridge of Ross** 12m SW of Kilkee. Contorted strata eroded by the Atlantic into a natural arch, or bridge. Reached along cliff-top path from parking area.
**Doonbeg** 7m NE of Kilkee. Over 2m of uncrowded sand and dunes sweeping north from village. Armada ship, 736 ton galleon *San Esteban*, was grounded near river mouth, 1588.

**Kilbaha** Scattering of houses around small, stony-beached harbour facing SE on Loop Head peninsula. Scene of the 'Little Ark' episode in 1850s.
**Killimer** Village, and terminal of Shannon car ferry linking County Clare with Tarbert, in County Kerry, avoiding 100m detour via Limerick. Tel: (065) 51324. On hill above is monument to 19th-century heroine Ellen Hanley, the 'Colleen Bawn'.

### EVENTS
**Horse racing** Strand races, Kilkee, usually end Aug.
**Munster Car Rally** Kilkee, usually June.
**Munster Triathlon** Athletics; Kilkee beach, June.

### SPORT
**Angling** Game fishing: Kilkee Reservoir, Knockerry Lough. Sea fishing: Kilrush Creek Marina.
**Golf** Kilkee Golf Club, 9-hole course. Tel: (065) 56048. Kilrush Golf Club, 9-hole course. Tel: (065) 51138.
**Yachting** River Shannon. Charter information from Shannon Maritime Developments Ltd, Kilrush. Tel: (061) 361555 or (065) 52072.

### INFORMATION
Ennis Tourist Office. Tel: (065) 28366/28308.
Shannon Airport Tourist Office. Tel: (067) 61664.

This famous true murder story has been dramatised by Irish playwright Dion Boucicault (1822-90) and made into an opera – called *The Lily of Killarney* – by Julius Benedict (1804-85). The 'Colleen Bawn' (which means 'Shining Girl') was Ellen Hanley (1803-19) from Ballycahane, County Limerick. At 15 she secretly married a local landowner's son, ex-Marine Lieutenant John Scanlan.

In June 1819 the pair were crossing from Kilrush to Glin, in Limerick, with Scanlan's servant-boatman Sullivan and several other passengers, when a storm forced them into Carrigafoyle, on the Kerry shore. The other passengers went on by road next day, and that was the last anyone saw of Ellen until September, when her body was washed up at Money Point.

Scanlan was charged with her murder, his motive presumed to be fear that his peasant bride would embarrass his middle-class family. The trial at Limerick in March 1820 made headlines, the defence being led by no less than Daniel O'Connell, leading champion of Catholic emancipation and later, MP. Although suspicion was cast on the missing Sullivan, Scanlan was convicted and hanged.

In May of the same year, Sullivan was arrested, and made a confession before execution. He had, it seems, been too faithful a servant in dutifully ridding Scanlan of his 'problem'.

*A bronze monument to the 'Shining Girl', Ellen Hanley, is in the churchyard at Killimer.*

the cliffs to Castle Point, 100ft high. Here, mackerel are fished from aprons of rock that swoop down to the sea.

Close by is the Well of St Chaoi, a white-painted wayside shrine set in a circle of raised turf. It bears instructions for curing poor eyesight: '5 Our Fathers, 5 Hail Marys, 5 Glory-Be's, then 9 rounds of the well while reciting the rosary.'
**Heritage Gallery** *July and Aug 11am-5pm. Tel: (065) 56169.*

## Kilrush/Cill Rois

A broad street leads off the bustling market square of Kilrush, down to the head of a creek that connects the town to the wide Shannon about a mile away. Kilrush Heritage Centre provides useful background information for a visit to Scattery Island.

A 250-berth marina project is revita-

lising the area. With a boatyard and a row of fishermen's cottages renovated as shops, the development offers sailing enthusiasts a new west-coast base, with yacht charters and deep-sea angling.
**Heritage Centre** *Early June-end Aug, Mon-Fri 10am-5pm, Sat 10am-4pm. Tel: (065) 51577.*

## Scattery Island/Inis Cathaigh

From Cappagh Pier near Kilrush a boat takes visitors a mile away to uninhabited Scattery Island, a 179 acre microcosm of Irish history. What began in the 6th century as St Senan's retreat grew into a substantial monastic settlement. Remains of several churches dating from the 9th to 15th centuries still stand, as well as one of Ireland's best-preserved Round Towers. It is about 85ft high with a door only 4ft 8in high. The tower is unusual in having the door at ground level.

ROCKY PERCH *Oblivious to the wild seas below, goats graze below the cliffs near Kilkee.*

SAFE HAVEN *Fishing boats shelter in Carrigaholt bay, where ships of the Armada sought refuge.*

SIGHT FOR SORE EYES *Within the diminutive Well of St Chaoi shrine, near Kilkee, are the instructions, appropriately large, for curing poor eyesight.*

## THE 'LITTLE ARK'

The heart-warming story of Father Michael Meehan's triumph over bigotry is remembered at the village of Kilbaha, near Loop Head, nearly 150 years after the events.

Although Catholic emancipation became law in 1829, some local landlords went on trying to eradicate Catholicism in the wake of the 1846 Famine, in particular by denying priests any place to say Mass. Father Meehan knew one place where he was legally outside the landlord's reach: the sea shore between the high and low water marks. In 1852 he paid a carpenter to make a hut on wheels, open with steps at one end. He installed an altar at the other end, and the 'little ark' was trundled down to the beach, where the villagers could hear Mass regularly.

Father Meehan was taken to court for 'obstruction' of the highway, but won his case. Marriages and baptisms followed, and the Catholic faithful were able to continue their worship. The 'ark' itself, made of rough boards, is preserved in the parish church of Moneen.

WHITE SAND AND SEA *Under darkening skies the mile-long arc of White Strand, near Doonbeg, with its grass-knitted sand dunes, is washed by the creamy surf of Atlantic rollers.*

# Home of Hermits and Heroes

*The deep waters of Lough Derg and the Shannon that pours from it frame this part of Clare and make it an anglers' paradise. The lake's winding inlets also create numerous beauty spots and offer a variety of water sports. In this secluded corner steeped in ancient traditions, it seems as if every name on the map is the evocative location of some legend about holy hermits, benign fairies or impetuous heroes.*

### Holy Island/Inis Cealtra

In the middle of Lough Derg is a solitary, uninhabited, 49 acre island whose atmosphere takes visitors back to the golden age of Irish Christianity. St Caimin founded a monastery here in the 7th century. It grew to be a large establishment, the well-preserved remains of which include five churches, a cemetery and a 79ft Round Tower.

Some 80 grave slabs lie in the cemetery, none later than the 12th century. One cross-base is inscribed 'the grave of the ten

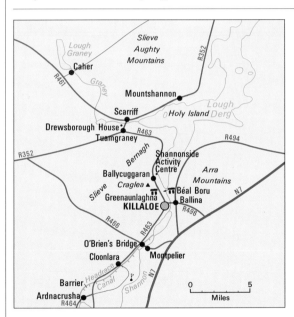

**OTHER PLACES TO SEE**
**Caher** Village clustered on southern shore of Lough Graney, with pretty views of the lake.
**Mountshannon** Neat 18th-century village overlooking Lough Derg. Popular spot for anglers and a favourite centre for walkers and pony trekkers. Good sailing from historic harbour, cruising from new harbour. Motorboat takes visitors across to Holy Island.
**Shannonside Activity Centre** At Ballycuggaran on Lough Derg, 2½m N of Killaloe. Well laid-out recreation centre and moorings, catering for boating, sailing, swimming and water-skiing.
Besides water activities, there is horseriding and walking in the hills. Picnic sites provided. Tel: (061) 376622.

**CRUISES**
**Shannon cruise** On Lough Derg. Derg Line Marina, Killaloe. Tel: (061) 396364. River barges also for hire from Shannon Barge Cruisers and Shannon River Floatels, both in Killaloe.

**EVENTS**
**Midsummer Lakeside Festival** Killaloe, 3rd week June.
**Munster Open Water-ski Championships** O'Brien's Bridge, early June.

**SPORT**
**Angling** Coarse fishing: Lough Derg and O'Brien's Bridge. Game fishing: Lough Derg (especially at Killaloe and Mountshannon).
**Golf** Cloonlara Golf Club, 9-hole course. Tel: (061) 35141.
**Water sports** O'Brien's Bridge Water Ski Club. Tel: (061) 87278. Shannonside Activity Centre, Ballycuggaran. Tel: (061) 37662.

**INFORMATION**
Ennis Tourist Office. Tel: (065) 28366.

ANCIENT STONE *Ogham and runic script adorn a stone in St Flannan's Cathedral, Killaloe.*

men' – perhaps victims of a Viking raid. Nearby, stones form a square hardly larger than a playpen – once a hermit's cell. There are several hollowed-out stones called bullauns, possibly used for mixing herbs, and a 'bargain stone' with a gap below it through which mainlanders and monks shook hands on a sale.

The 10th-century Round Tower is complete except for its conical cap of a roof. According to tradition this tower never had a roof, because an old witch refused to bless the mason's work as she passed by. The furious mason hurled his hammer at her and the witch was turned to stone, but he was unable to finish the roof.

The pilgrimage to Holy Island was famous. A penance of several circuits of the monastery earned sinners absolution, but it was believed that only true penitents could see their reflection in the island's holy well at the end of the round. Those who did not see it in the water had to renew their penance until they did.

The island is reached by motorboat from Mountshannon. Tel: (0619) 21351.

### Killaloe/Cill Dalua

Sheltered by the forested hills of Slieve Bernagh on one side and those of the Arra Mountains in Tipperary on the other, Killaloe lies where the Shannon resumes its course out of the neck of Lough Derg. A narrow, 13-arched stone bridge leads from Killaloe across the river to the town of Ballina in County Tipperary.

WILD AND WONDERFUL *Grey hills rise to shelter the deep waters of Lough Derg, whose quiet ripples run gently to the reed-fringed shores.*

Several sites testify to the local importance of Killaloe, probably since prehistoric times. Kincora is one – the royal palace of the High King Brian Boru (926-1014), founder of the O'Brien clan and one of the greatest kings of Ireland. No traces survive above ground today of Kincora (whose Irish name means 'Head of the Weir'), but it was described in Irish tradition in much the same way as the courts of Argos and Mycenae, in ancient Greece, were described by Homer.

Other sites include Béal Boru ('Boru's Fort'), a wooded mound a mile to the north of Killaloe, surrounded by a ditch. It gives a beautiful view of Lough Derg. Another is the early stronghold of the local kings at Greenaunlaghna (Grianán Lachtna) on the slopes of Craglea, the grey rock above the lough.

At the southern end of Killaloe, close to the Shannon, stands the restored and rather plain 13th-century St Flannan's Cathedral. Inside, a richly carved Romanesque doorway

preserved from an earlier building has been let into the south wall of the nave. The window it now frames filters light over ancient stones.

The slab below the window is said to be the tomb of Murchad (Muircheartach). He died in 1119, and was the last O'Brien to be High King of Ireland. A granite stump in front of the door is, uniquely, inscribed in both the ancient Irish ogham script and runes (the letters used by the Vikings). 'Thorgrim carved this stone', it announces, 'A blessing on Thorgrim'. He was probably a Viking convert to Christianity living around the year 1000.

Two miniature chapels also recall medieval Ireland. One is the 12th-century St Flannan's Oratory – a simple, steep-roofed building with a Romanesque door – in the cathedral grounds. The other was rebuilt close to the modern Catholic church near the bridge: the rudimentary St Lua's (or Dalua's) Oratory. It was rescued from an island in the

Shannon when the great hydroelectric barrier at Ardnacrusha, 7 miles downstream from Killaloe, raised the river level. It is after this chapel that Killaloe takes its Irish name, which means 'Dalua's Church'.

## O'Brien's Bridge/Droichead Úi Bhriain

The ancient 12-arched stone bridge linking O'Brien's Bridge to Montpelier in County Limerick is the last stone bridge to span the Shannon before it reaches the sea. One mile to the north-east, 20th-century progress intrudes: a weir diverts most of the flow into the Headrace Canal that feeds the Shannon hydroelectric scheme downstream.

The village's terraces of old houses now stand on a narrow strip of land between the canal and the river. There is good coarse fishing, and the Shannon is broad enough here for water-skiing – it also has a ramp for ski-jumping competitions.

## Tuamgraney/Tuaim Gréine

In the lake-strewn plain between the Slieve Aughty and Slieve Bernagh Mountains lies the village of Tuamgraney, close to the Scarriff inlet of Lough Derg. The tower of O'Grady's Castle still stands in the village, and traces of a 6th-century monastery are embedded in its former Protestant parish church. Having served for worship since the 10th century, the building is now a heritage centre.

Just to the north of the village runs the River Graney, carrying water down to Lough Derg from Lough Graney, a large and shallow lake ringed with fir trees. The village and lough are linked not only by the river but also by the shared name of a girl called Gile Gréine ('Brightness of the Sun'). A pagan legend says that in a fit of sadness she drowned herself in the lake, and her body was carried down river to be buried under a mound where the village now is. Tuamgraney means 'Tomb of Gréine'.

Drewsborough House, north-west of the village, is the birthplace of the 20th-century novelist Edna O'Brien.

**Heritage Centre** *Daily, 9am-5pm. Tel: (0619) 21351.*

---

### EEVUL OF CRAGLEA

Many tales are told of Eevul, or Aoibheal, the fairy queen of Craglea. According to legend, she lived on the rock projecting from the north slope of Craglea. She was believed to be the supernatural patron of the leading tribe in this part of Ireland. It was also said that she had a magic harp, and whoever heard its music would soon travel to the next world. The rock is still known as Carrickeevul or Aoibheal's Rock.

The legend of Eevul was retold in Gaelic verse by Bryan Merriman (1757-1805). His poem, *Cúirt an Mheadhon Oidhche* (*The Midnight Court*), is bawdy in parts and made Merriman something of an outcast. Among several English versions is one by Percy Ussher (1926):

*Chaste Eevell, hasten to the relief*
*Of the women of Erin in their grief,*
*Wasting their pains in vain endeavour*
*To meet with mates who elude them ever,*
*Till in the ages is such disparity*
*We would not touch them except from*
*charity,*
*With bleary eyes and wry grimaces*
*To scare a maiden from their embraces.*

# Around the Burren's Desolation

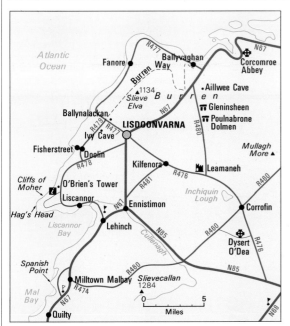

*At the heart of northern Clare is the unique limestone platform of the Burren – a startling landscape that fascinates walkers and naturalists. But there is plenty of evidence, too, of ancient people who lived there when it was still covered by forest. Around it is quite different country, with lakes and rivers to invite anglers and an Atlantic coastline ranging from wide sandy beaches to the towering dark Cliffs of Moher.*

DOG CHEAP *Inflation has not affected the service offered by a Ballyvaghan man and his companions.*

### OTHER PLACES TO SEE

**Ballyvaghan** 19th-century fishing village at northern end of Burren Way. Nearby Corcomroe Abbey is ruin of 13th-century Cistercian monastery.

**Fanore** Popular place for bathing.

**Mullagh More** 6m N of Corrofin. Fine 627ft high rock strata folded and contorted like dough.

**Quilty** Excellent, popular sands, with boats to hire for sea angling.

**Spanish Point** Headland 2m from Milltown Malbay with wide beaches. Its name recalls the events of 1588 when ships from the Spanish Armada were wrecked there.

### CRUISES

**Aran Islands** Ferry crossings daily from Doolin, mid-Mar to Oct (30 min). Tel: (065) 74455/74466.

### WALKS

**The Burren** Guided walking tour (approx 5hrs), May-Dec, Mon-Sat, starts 10am from Ballynalackan Castle, near Lisdoonvarna. Tel: (065) 78066.

### EVENTS

**Horse and pony races** Lisdoonvarna, July and Aug.

**International Angling Festival** Fanore, June.

**International Barbecue Championships** Late Aug and early Sept.

**International Matchmaking Festival** Lisdoonvarna, all Sept.

**Irish and International Softball Championships** Lisdoonvarna, early Sept.

**Lobster Festival** Quilty, July.

**Merriman Summer School** Poetry; various locations in the Burren, late Aug.

**Russell Traditional Weekend of Music** Lisdoonvarna, Aug.

**William Clancy Summer School** Traditional music; Milltown Malbay, mid-July.

### SPORT

**Angling** Coarse and game fishing: Inchiquin lough and many other lakes in Corrofin area. Sea fishing: Lough Donnell, Quilty, Lehinch, Fanore, Doolin and vicinity.

**Golf** Lehinch Golf Club, two 18-hole courses. Tel: (065) 81003.
Spanish Point Golf Club, 9-hole course. Tel: (065) 84198.

### INFORMATION

Ennis Tourist Office. Tel:(065) 28366.

## The Burren/Boirinn

A huge pavement of square limestone slabs, riddled beneath with caves, the Burren is unlike anywhere else in Ireland. The best way to get to know the area is by walking part of the Burren Way. This path stretches 22 miles, from Ballynalackan, near Lisdoonvarna in the south, to Ballyvaghan in the north. Part of it follows the 'green road' – an ancient trackway which runs below 1134ft Slieve Elva, the Burren's highest point.

Bleak though the environment may be, early people clearly took a liking to it. The Burren was well settled in the Stone Age and Bronze Age, long before the Celts arrived in Ireland. It has 70 ancient tombs, one of the most striking of which is the 4500-year-old Poulnabrone Dolmen, with huge, thin slabs like some stone flying-machine ready for takeoff. Excavations revealed that 17 adults and 16 children were buried there.

Just over a mile north is the Gleninsheen wedge-tomb. There, in 1930, a boy out hunting rabbits discovered a fabulous ribbed gold gorget, or collar, dating from about 700 BC. It is a national treasure and is displayed in Dublin's National Museum.

Many of the more than 500 circular earthworks constructed by early herders and farmers that have been counted on the Burren lie on either side of the Burren Way.

That this land was still thought worth fighting for many centuries later is shown by the castles built by the ruling O'Brien family, such as the one at Leamaneh, east of Kilfenora. A mansion was added to the 1480 tower house in about 1640. The house is now just an empty shell, but a good view of the Burren rising to the north can be had from the top of the tower. Legend has it that in 1651, when Cromwell's soldiers brought Conor O'Brien's body back from the battle in which he had been slain, his widow, Maura Rua MacMahon, shouted defiantly at them from a window: 'Take him away! We want no dead men here!'

Just beneath the Burren's grey and pitted limestone surface is dramatic evidence of its geology: the caves gouged out by running water over a period of a million years. The best and safest to visit is the Aillwee Cave, inland from Ballyvaghan, which was discovered only in 1940. Since then, passages have been enlarged, bridges built and lighting and drainage installed, allowing visitors to explore a length of 3400ft under the 'yellow cliff' of Aillwee. The new access building itself has won awards for its architects, Andrzej and Danuta Wejchert.

**Aillwee Cave** *Mid-Mar to early Nov 10am-6pm: July and Aug 10am-7pm. Tel: (065) 77036/77067.*

## Cliffs of Moher/Aillte an Mhothair

Six miles of dark, rough-hewn cliffs plunge into the Atlantic here from heights of up to

668ft. These limestone walls overlaid by thick layers of material have been hammered by the ocean into one of Ireland's most majestic natural features. They can be approached by foot from either Doolin (5 miles away) or Liscannor (3 miles away), or by car as far as the Visitor Centre on top of the cliffs.

A well-constructed footpath leads along the crumbling cliff top, well clear of the edge. On a still, clear summer day the cliffs give little hint of their dangers, but a high wind can whip coin-sized pebbles up from the beach far below, and rainfall can loosen parts of the cliff edge and send sections plummeting into the sea.

The path leads north past O'Brien's Tower, built in 1835 by a colourful character called Sir Cornelius ('Corney') O'Brien, MP and self-publicist. The tower marks the highest point of the cliffs. The view from the tower sweeps from Loop Head and the Kerry mountains in the south around to the Aran Islands and the mountains of Connemara. This is also one of the best places to see the puffins, guillemots, razorbills, kittiwakes, shags, ravens and choughs on the ledges below.

To the south-west the cliff path leads as far as the peninsula of Hag's Head. The length of the cliffs between Fisherstreet and Liscannor can be covered on foot in a day.

**Visitor Centre** *June-Aug 9am-7pm; Sept-May 10am-6pm. Tel: (065) 81565/81171.*

### Corrofin/Cora Finne

This little market village lies in pretty lakeland country near Inchiquin Lough. Its disused Protestant church houses the Clare Heritage Centre, with its well laid-out displays explaining local history, crafts and traditions, the Famine of 1845-8, and the emigration that followed. The exhibits also include something far older: a carved stone 'tau-cross' – an early Christian T-shaped cross nearly 4ft high. Its two arms are carved with faces, perhaps those of the priests of Corrofin and Kilfenora parishes, and it was used to mark the boundaries of the parishes.

The building also houses a genealogical research centre that helps descendants of emigrants from these parts to trace their forebears. It has on file half a million baptismal records, names from gravestones and newspaper announcements, and in one case has traced a family back almost 2000 years.

**Clare Heritage Centre** *Mar-end Oct 10am-6pm; Nov-early Mar, Mon-Fri 9am-5pm. Tel: (065) 27955.*

CLIFFS OF MOHER *The foaming Atlantic waves seem powerless at the foot of the ribbon of cliffs that rise sheer out of the water.*

### Doolin/Dúlainn

A few pubs, scattered farmhouses and dry-stone walls link the village of Doolin with its little port of Fisherstreet, now the terminus for the ferry service to the Aran Islands, which loom 5 miles out to sea. In the distance to the north is the jagged ridge of the Connemara mountains.

The sea angling is good here, but bathing can be dangerous and should only be done when lifeguards are on duty. A major attraction in Doolin's lively pubs is the traditional folk music, which attracts crowds from far afield.

There are many caves in the area between Doolin and Lisdoonvarna. A stalactite in the Ivy Cave, near Ballynalackan Castle, is claimed to be Europe's longest.

### Dysert O'Dea

A stony trail leads around this ancient monastic site, 'O'Dea's Hermitage', and to about 20 signposted sites nearby. They date from prehistoric times to the 19th century. The monastery is said to have been founded by St Tola in the 8th century, but the ruins – a Romanesque church and a Round Tower – date from the 1100s, as does the High Cross, called the White Cross of Tola.

An Archaeology Centre has been established in the restored 15th-century tower house that stands on a rocky outcrop. Its well-designed exhibition and audiovisual display were created by the castle's American owner, John O'Day, a descendant of the original occupant.

**Archaeology Centre** May-Sept 10am-6pm. Tel: (065) 27722.

### Ennistimon/Inis Díomáin

The small market town and fishing centre is set above a waterfall, The Cascades, on the Cullenagh river. The Cascades Walk follows the river bank. Colourful and inventive shopfronts are a feature of the main streets, and the bars draw fans of traditional music from miles around. On a hill above the town is a roofless 18th-century church, and there are fine views down onto the river.

### Kilfenora

The little village tucked into the southern margin of the Burren was once a bishop's see with its own, now ruined, 12th-century cathedral. Three medieval High Crosses, carved with figures and ornament, stand around it. The historical background to these

HEADSTONES *Carved heads form part of the arched doorway of St Tola's Church in Dysert O'Dea.*

BUSINESS MEETING *Farmers discuss prices at the weekly sheep market in Kilfenora's main street.*

local riches is explained in the Burren Display Centre, which also describes the geology of the area.

The models, showcases, charts and audiovisual programmes offer visitors a short cut to understanding the special scientific and historical factors that have gone to make the Burren what it is.

**Burren Display Centre** *June-Aug 9am-7pm; Mar-May, Sept, Oct 10am-4.30pm. Tel: (065) 88030.*

### Lehinch/An Leacht

A popular resort town, Lehinch lies on the sandy Liscannor Bay, with a walled promenade that overlooks a mile-long beach. There is good sea angling here, and boats for deep-sea fishing can be hired at the northern end of the beach.

Lehinch is famous as the 'St Andrews of Ireland', with its two 18-hole golf links: the championship Old Course (which has one of Ireland's best-known holes – the Dell – entirely hidden from the tee by dunes), and the Castle Course.

### Lisdoonvarna/Lios Dúin Bhearna

Mineral-rich waters flow down from the surrounding limestone and peat into this little spa town, renowned for its curative sulphur, magnesium and iron baths. Established in Victorian times as a health resort, Lisdoonvarna ('fort of the gap') is now famous for its matchmaking season, and it holds a special place in Ireland's social history.

Around 1900, wealthy families began using Lisdoonvarna as a meeting place where they could arrange suitable marriages for their children. From late August, with the harvest in, they gathered here for the first of many dances. By the 1970s this sedate tradition had begun to change. City people started coming to the hotels in search of marriage partners, swelling the population to 10,000 on September weekends. The Lisdoonvarna phenomenon resulted in hundreds of marriages. But matchmaking is a seasonal business. A core population of only 800 people remained behind in the winter and, without work, young people left.

Now Lisdoonvarna is developing a year-round economy. The Spa Wells have expanded as a health centre attracting overseas visitors, while new hotels have aided the transformation of Ireland's only active spa.

**Health Centre** *June-Oct 10am-6pm. Tel: (065) 74023.*

# THE BURREN

## A limestone landscape of stark beauty

The Burren is a most un-Irish place – there are no bogs and few pastures, but clean, cracked pavement slabs of limestone, huge boulders and strangely distorted strata. Cromwell's general, Ludlow, dismissed the area as a land 'yielding neither water enough to drown a man, nor a tree to hang him, nor soil enough to bury him'.

This bleak environment is, however, one of Europe's richest botanical areas, with 1100 species of plants out of the 1400 in Ireland as a whole. It is extraordinarily beautiful, with its softly rounded whalebacks of light grey rock dappled by cloud shows and patches of yellow, magenta and blue flowers.

THE GEOGRAPHY Limestone, which formed from the shells of sea creatures at the bottom of shallow seas 300 million years ago, underlies most of Ireland, yet only here, in the Burren (whose Irish name Boireann means 'the rock') were 500sq miles of it scraped clean of topsoil by glaciers, some 15,000 years ago. Water quickly percolates through the limestone to underground streams, leaving the surface dry. Only one river, the Caher, runs overland, running out to sea at Fanore. The few lakes or grassy hollows, which can reach over several acres, are fed from below and can suddenly vanish when the water table sinks. They are called 'turloughs'. Beneath the surface, running waters have turned the rock into a maze of caves, still being mapped by potholers.

THE PLANTLIFE The surface of the Burren is far from a desert. Limestone-loving plants such as foxgloves and rock roses grow there, and the rock's microclimates also nurture plants normally at home much farther north and south. Alpine plants such as mountain avens (**Dryas octopetala**) thrive there, while the warmth stored in the rock through the winter supports Mediterranean plants, such as maidenhair ferns and the bloody cranesbill (**Geranium sanguineum**). Gnarled blackthorn and junipers struggle up from the 'grikes', or joints, in the limestone pavements, where they find protection from the battering Atlantic winds. They grow only a few inches high.

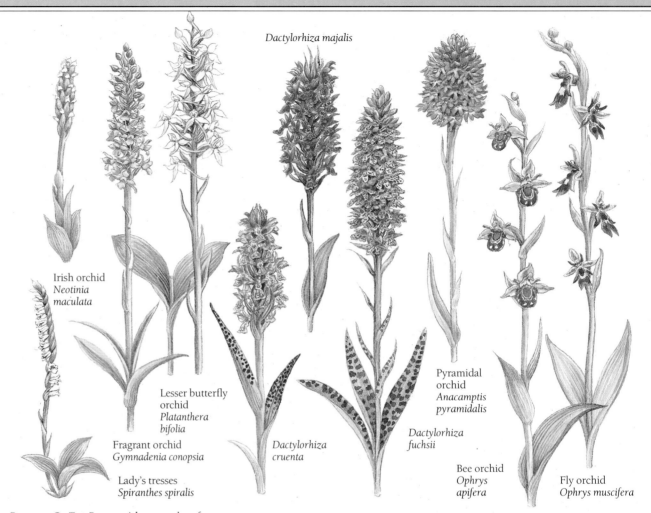

Dactylorhiza majalis

Irish orchid
*Neotinia maculata*

Lesser butterfly orchid
*Platanthera bifolia*

Fragrant orchid
*Gymnadenia conopsia*

Lady's tresses
*Spiranthes spiralis*

*Dactylorhiza cruenta*

*Dactylorhiza fuchsii*

Pyramidal orchid
*Anacamptis pyramidalis*

Bee orchid
*Ophrys apifera*

Fly orchid
*Ophrys muscifera*

BEAUTIES OF THE BURREN *A large number of orchids grow on the Burren, ranging from the white twisted spike of lady's tresses, to the pale pink of the fragrant orchid, to the deep magenta of the pyramidal orchid and the mimic flowers of the bee orchid and the fly orchid.*

The rock's stored heat allows grass to grow all the year round, providing food for the feral goats that live here. The Burren also has a reverse temperature curve, which means its hillsides are warmer in winter than the valleys. Cattle are therefore moved to the uplands to graze in the winter.

ROCK SHELTERS *Hollows and joints in the rock shelter grasses and many types of low-growing plants.*

HIDDEN TREASURES *The Burren's stark moonscape of limestone pavement, littered with boulders and lined with deep cracks, is not as barren as it seems, and hides a treasure trove of plants.*

# A Revolutionary's Village Home

*The majestic Ballyhoura and Galty Mountains make superb walking country and give wide-ranging views over Limerick, Tipperary and Cork. They shelter the broad, rich pastureland known as the Golden Vale, through which the River Maigue meanders on its way to meet the Shannon. On the lower slopes of the Ballyhouras lies the village of Bruree, boyhood home of the Dáil's first President, Eamon de Valera.*

### Bruree/Brú Rí

In 1885, the three-year-old Eamon de Valera was sent by his mother from New York to Bruree to be raised by his grandmother, after his father had died. The village school de Valera attended is now a museum dedicated to him. He became the first President of Dáil Eireann – the unofficial republican parliament – in 1918, and spent his life fighting British rule. He led the anti-Treatyites, who opposed the compromises of the 1921 treaty that created the Irish Free State, and became the President of his country in 1959. De Valera retired at the distinguished age of 91, after serving a second term, and died two years later, in 1975. The De Valera Museum contains relics of his schooldays, including letters, a medal, a pair of glasses, a lock of

BRUREE MILL *A millrace feeds the 27ft diameter wheel of this 19th-century water mill.*

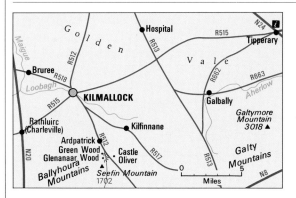

**OTHER PLACES TO SEE**
**Ardpatrick** Steep, half-mile track leads uphill to 13th-century monastery said to have been founded by St Patrick. Remains include 9ft high stub of Round Tower and shell of church. Wide, sweeping views of Limerick.

**Kilfinnane** Hilltop town ideal for exploring Ballyhoura Mountains. Education Centre provides facilities for walking, riding and orienteering.

**WALKS**
**Ballyhoura Trail** 45 mile walk from Ballyhoura to Galty

Mountains; forms part of the O'Sullivan Beara Walk, which runs from Cork to Leitrim.
**Glenroe Loop** Circular walk from Kilfinnane to the Ballyhouras.
Tel: (063) 91300.

**EVENTS**
**Joyce Brothers Summer School** Sept. Tel: (061) 314612.

**SPORT**
**Angling** Game fishing: River Loobagh and rivers around Kilfinnane.
**Horse-riding** Kilfinane Education Centre. Tel: (063) 91300.
**Orienteering** Kilfinane Education Centre. Tel: (063) 91300.

**INFORMATION**
Limerick Tourist Office.
Tel: (061) 317522.

hair, a desk carved with his initials and numerous photographs.

Bruree stretches along a bank above the reedy, rocky River Maigue, spanned there by a six-arched stone bridge. Downstream is a derelict 19th-century water mill. A path continues downstream, and on the opposite bank are a decaying Protestant church and the stump of a Round Tower in the cemetery.

A mile north of the village is the cottage where de Valera lived as a child, a two-up-two-down yellow-painted house surrounded by a trim lawn and furnished just as the family left it. The cottage is kept locked, but instructions for obtaining the key are displayed on a sign.
**De Valera Museum** *Thur and Sun pm. Tel: (063) 91300.*

### Galbally/An Gallbhaile

A village square of surprisingly large proportions stands at the heart of Galbally. It is edged with brightly painted houses, and at one side is a memorial to those who died 'on scaffold, field and from hardships' in the 1921 war of independence.

From almost every point in the village there are superb views of the Galty Mountains, rising almost sheer from the surrounding plain to the 3018ft summit of Galtymore Mountain. Close by runs the River Aherlow, forming the border with Tipperary.

### Green Wood/Coill Glasa

The Green Wood forest covers the slopes of the Ballyhoura Mountains, and from a viewing point in Glenanaar Wood there are fine views of the rolling landscape to the east, dominated by the turrets and chimneys of the red sandstone Castle Oliver, a mid-19th-century mansion. It was built on the site of a house in which was born Marie Gilbert (1818-61), alias Lola Montez, a dancer who dazzled European society in the middle of the 19th century. She finally captured the affections of the mad King Ludwig of Bavaria, who made her Countess of Landsfeld.

From the viewing point, waymarked paths lead through the silent forest of oak, pine, beech and birch, and for the strong in limb the Ballyhoura Trail continues up to the 1702ft peak of Seefin Mountain. Another and even more approach to the peak starts just south of Ardpatrick, where a forest road climbs through fir forests, rank grasses and heather. The view sweeps across north Limerick, taking in foothills and forest, and

SHEER DELIGHT *The Galty Mountains soar above the village of Galbally.*

pastures merging into a blur on the distant horizon. A few hundred yards south, across peaty ground dotted with bog cotton and saxifrage, another viewpoint looks out over Cork.

### Hospital/An tOspidéal

The village takes its name from the Knights Hospitaller of St John of Jerusalem who established an abbey there in the 13th century. The roofless ruin of its church contains three medieval tombs bearing the effigies of chain-mailed knights, one with his lady. The gate into the churchyard is locked, but a sign directs visitors to the caretaker, who will let them in. At the west end of the church is a modern Catholic shrine.

### Kilmallock/Cill Mocheallóg

Once the chief town of the Earls of Desmond, Kilmallock still retains much of its medieval past. It is named after the monastery built here in the 7th century by St Mocheallóg. A large section of its walls, including the mas-

sive Blossom Gate, is still intact. Standing foursquare in the centre of the main street is John's Castle, a 60ft high peel tower where the defenders of the town could make their last effort to hold out if the walls were breached. Close by, a museum illustrates the town's history.

To the north of the main street runs the River Loobagh, and on its banks is the ruined 13th-century Collegiate Church of St Peter and St Paul. Ivy drapes the walls and the roofless Round Tower looks sadly forlorn, but there is still much to impress, including two elaborately carved 17th-century tombs and a richly carved doorway in the south wall.

A footbridge over the Loobagh leads to Kilmallock's 13th-century Dominican priory, a gaunt ruin strangely beautiful in its grassy setting. Its tall, once magnificent tower gapes open at one corner and the gabled stonework is crumbling. However, the chancel has a fine though glassless five-light window and the tracery of a 15th-century window survives in the south transept.

**Kilmallock Museum** *Daily, exc. Sat, pm. Tel: (063) 91300.*

SILENT KNIGHT *The tomb slab of a medieval knight leans against Hospital's ruined church.*

STATELY RUIN *A superb window frames the crumbling tower of Kilmallock Priory.*

145

# A Viking City by the Shannon

*Early in the 9th century, Vikings settled the island between the Rivers Shannon and Abbey. Their crude settlement eventually became today's historic city of Limerick. In the 12th and 13th centuries the Normans left their mark with many fine buildings including the magnificent St Mary's Cathedral and a castle, built by King John in 1210. Later, high stone walls were built that divided the city into Englishtown, within the walls, and Irishtown across the Abbey river. In the 18th century the walls came down, slums were cleared and a Georgian city of charm and elegance – Ireland's fourth largest – arose.*

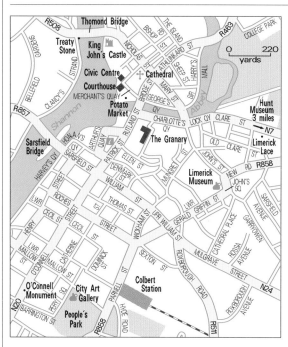

## OTHER PLACES TO SEE

**The Granary** Resplendent four-storey building dating from 1878, now with its stone walls and redbrick-faced windows renovated. It was used as a bonding house during 19th century, holding spirits, wines and tobacco liable for duty. Now converted as a complex containing restaurant, bar, library and company offices.

**Merchant's Quay** Modernised square flanked by porticoed courthouse of 1810, the old Potato Market, the modern Civic Centre, and open to river on the fourth side. Square was first formed when a gap was opened up in the city walls to give merchants access to the Shannon. It gives fine views of the river and of the Thomond and Sarsfield bridges.

**Thomond Bridge** Attractive stone bridge spanning the Shannon in six low, graceful arches, built in mid-19th century on site of King John's 13th-century bridge. The mock medieval tollhouse at castle side of bridge is also Victorian.

### WALKS

**Town tours** June-Sept. Tel: (061) 301587.

### EVENTS

**International Choral Festival** St Mary's Cathedral, end Mar.
**Limerick Show** Mar.
**Limerick Summer Festival** July.
**St Patrick's Week** Mar.
**Son et Lumière** St Mary's Cathedral, June-Sept. Tel: (061) 310293.

### SPORT

**Angling** Coarse fishing: Plassey, and on River Mulkear. Game fishing: Shannon estuary, and River Shannon at Plassey.
**Golf** Castletroy Golf Club, 18-hole course. Tel: (061) 335261.
Limerick Golf Club, 18-hole course. Tel: (061) 44083.

### INFORMATION

Limerick Tourist Office. Tel: (061) 317522.

## Hunt Museum

A pleasant 3 mile riverside walk from the city centre leads to Plassey Technological Park and the University of Limerick, which contains this impressive museum. It is named after John Hunt (1900-76), who established the Craggaunowen Project in County Clare. Well-lit cabinets display a treasure house of objects ranging from Stone Age flints to 18th-century pottery. The exhibits, mostly Irish, include glassware, rare crucifixes, ivory carvings, silverware, and Bronze Age cauldrons, gold waist bands and earrings.
**Opening times** *Apr-Sept, daily 9.30am-5.30pm. Oct, Sat and Sun only, 9.30am-5.30pm.* Tel: (061) 333644.

## King John's Castle

Five irregularly spaced drum towers linked by massive walls are all that remain of the castle that King John built in the early 13th century to keep the peace in Thomond (as the area was then called) between the Norman settlers and the O'Brien clan, kings and later earls of Thomond. Two of the towers are incorporated in the gatehouse, which still has the slots of the portcullis in the stonework of its pointed doorway.

The castle, one of the first to be built without a keep, has had a chequered history. It was captured briefly by the O'Briens and MacNamaras in 1369, and during the Civil War Cromwell's General Ireton forced the Royalist garrison to surrender after bombarding the castle from the foot of Thomond Bridge. It was bombarded again in 1690 and 1691 by the forces of William of Orange, and the marks of the bombardment can still be seen on the walls of the north-western tower.

The courtyard is now an archaeological museum containing relics of the pre-Norman and Norman settlements, revealed when the castle was restored in the 1930s.
**Castle and museum** *Daily, 9.30am-5.30pm. Check opening times in winter months.* Tel: (061) 361511.

## Limerick Museum

On the west side of John's Square, two houses in a simple 18th-century terrace contain an impressive collection of Stone Age pottery vessels, stone axes and arrowheads, and various items from the Bronze and Iron Ages. Other exhibits portray the city's history, and include a 'nail' – a pedestal on which merchants paid their debts, giving rise to the expression 'paying on the nail'.

THE LIBERATOR *The O'Connell monument is overlooked by fine, redbrick Georgian façades.*

ANCIENT ADORNMENT *This Bronze Age dress ornament is displayed in the Hunt Museum.*

POIGNANT PORTRAIT *William Orpen's 'Man of the West' hangs in the City Art Gallery.*

PUBLIC DOMAIN *A Victorian drinking fountain stands amid the trim lawns of People's Park.*

STOUT COMPETITION *Colourful street signs advertise Ireland's favourite beverage.*

Today three ladies keep alive the tradition of handmade lace in Limerick, embroidering veils, stoles, surplices and place mats with the deft skills that once made Limerick city a byword for high-quality lacework. Their workshop, part of the Good Shepherd Convent in Clare Street, is all that remains of an industry that once employed 900 women. When the three ladies retire, the industry will die.

Lacemaking first came to Limerick in 1829, when Charles Walker, an Englishman who had married the daughter of a lace manufacturer, decided to set up a business in Ireland, where labour was cheap. He chose Limerick as the site of his business, and employed English lacemakers to teach their skills to the women of the town. The industry grew, and by the 1850s about 900 people were employed in lacemaking. However, the quality of the work deteriorated until it was revitalised by Mrs Robert Vere O'Brien, who set up a school to teach lacemaking in 1893.

Limerick lace is known as a mixed lace, because it uses two techniques: tambour, so called from the round wooden frame used to stretch the net, which is worked with a needle like a crochet needle; and run work, in which a fine needle is used to darn a pattern onto the net.

*One of the last three Limerick lacemakers weaves an intricate pattern with a sewing needle into the finely meshed, tightly stretched net that distinguishes Limerick lace.*

A newspaper cutting displayed in the museum gives the history of the little-known Limerick Soviet, proclaimed briefly in April 1919 by local trade unionists after Limerick was placed under military rule by the British. Strike committees seized control of the town and even began to print their own money. Martial law was rescinded after two weeks.
**Opening times** *Tues-Sat 10am-5pm. Tel: (061) 47826.*

## O'Connell Monument

Gazing down the street named after him, a bronze statue of Daniel O'Connell (1775-1847) stands on a tall stone plinth amid immaculate flowerbeds. This work by the Irish sculptor John Hogan commemorates the man who became known as 'The Liberator' – the father of Catholic emancipation in 1829.

Close by is People's Park, a delightful little grassy square overlooked by the City Art Gallery, which contains a growing collection of Irish paintings. They include several early works by Jack Yeats (1871-1957).
**City Art Gallery** *Mon-Fri 10am-6pm, Thur 10am-7pm, Sat 10am-1pm.*

## St Mary's Cathedral

Solid and angular, with little of the exterior ornamentation found in many other cathedrals, St Mary's is an imposing building. Its square, turreted tower at the western end rises to about 150ft above the cathedral's most impressive feature – the Romanesque west door, restored in 1895.

The Church of Ireland cathedral stands on the site of the old palace founded around 1170 by Donal Mor O'Brien. Inside, the solid, square pillars of the nave rise to an oak-beamed roof, and there is a beautifully carved choir screen, with two angels. The screen was designed by Conor O'Brien, but he was at sea when it was erected and could not prevent the builder from installing it back to front. The 15th-century choir stools are carved from black oak, decorated with human and animal figures and legendary and imaginary creatures. They are the only examples of their kind preserved in Ireland.

Under the floors of two chapels are buried several of the kings of Thomond. However, one of them – the infamous Murrogh 'The Burner' O'Brien, Earl of Inchiquin – did not stay there for long. A supporter of the English against the Irish rebels in the 1640s, he burnt out the defenders of the Rock of Cashel, in County Tipperary, and put 3000 of them to death. The morning after his interment in the cathedral in 1674 the enraged townsfolk broke into the cathedral, dug up the coffin and hurled his body into the Shannon.

A memorial to the earls of Thomond is set in a Gothic arch in the cathedral's north wall. It includes the black marble lid of Donal Mor O'Brien's coffin. Donal must have been a small man – the coffin is less than 5ft long.

In the north wall of the Chapel of the Holy Spirit is a 'leper's squint' – a slot through which lepers could glimpse the service and receive communion.

## Treaty Stone

A rough-hewn limestone block raised on a pedestal stands across the river from King John's Castle. Traditionally it was on this rock that the Treaty of Limerick was signed in 1691, marking the surrender of the city to William of Orange. Under the terms of the treaty the government promised to respect Catholicism, but the treaty was rejected by the English and Irish Parliaments and its terms were ignored. Thus Limerick became known as 'The City of the Broken Treaty'.

The pedestal is decorated with an image of the castle opposite surmounted by a dome and cross, showing that Limerick was a cathedral city. This symbol is now the civic insignia of the corporation. The Latin inscription is taken from Virgil's description of Troy: 'It was an ancient city, well versed in the arts of war.'

# Monasteries and Music

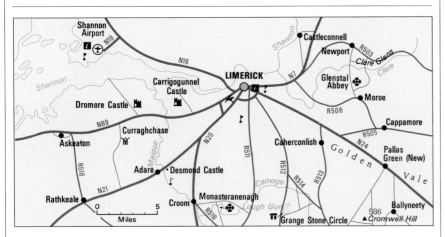

*The picturesque village of Adare, with its three medieval abbeys and annual music festival, is set in the pastoral lowlands that climb gently eastwards from the Shannon's winding course to beautiful, secluded hill country. Beside the county's largest lake, Lough Gur, stands a prehistoric site that was once the home of Stone Age people – an evocative panorama of stone circles, forts and graves.*

## OTHER PLACES TO SEE

**Carrigogunnel** Remains of 15th-century castle, overlooking the Shannon, blasted apart by cannon during 1691 siege of Limerick. Dramatic views across Shannon estuary.

**Castleconnell** Village with short riverside walk to footbridge across the Shannon, only 100yds wide at this point. Salmon rest in the rocky pools here during the spawning season.

**Clare Glens** Waymarked walks on both sides of rocky banks of River Clare, along steep-sided sandstone gorge where the river cascades over waterfalls formed by flat sheets of rock.

**Cromwell Hill** 586ft high mound whose name probably derives from the old Celtic god Crom. It has nothing to do with Cromwell. Scattered with grassy humps of ancient earthworks, with good views of surrounding countryside.

**Croom** Little town surrounded by pretty woods on a bend in River Maigue. Croom Castle, now only grassy mounds and fragments of stone wall, was the Fitzgerald stronghold and gave them their battle cry 'Cromadh Abu' ('Croom For Ever').

**Monasteranenagh** High walls and arches of roofless, ruined, 12th-century Cistercian church.

## EVENTS
**Adare Music Festival** Mid-July.
**Fleadh Cheoil (music festival)** Cappamore, early June.
**Murroe Equine Festival** Early Aug.

## SPORT
**Angling** Coarse fishing: Rivers Maigue and Camoge, River Shannon at Annacotty, Lough Gur and Dromore Lough. Game fishing: Rivers Camoge and Shannon.
**Bathing** River Shannon.
**Boating** River Shannon.
**Golf** Adare Manor Golf Club, 9-hole course. Tel: (061) 86204.
Adare Manor Hotel: 18-hole course being completed 1993. Tel: (061) 396566.

## INFORMATION
Limerick Tourist Office. Tel: (061) 317522.
Shannon Development Tourist Office. Tel: (061) 361555.

## Adare/Áth Dara

Every summer Adare resounds to the music of players, singers and orchestras who come from all over the world to take part in the village's annual music festival. When they are not making music there is much to inspire them in what is often described as Ireland's prettiest village – a broad main street lined with thatched houses, crumbling ruins and a Gothic-style mansion, all set in a bend of the River Maigue.

Adare has an ancient history, with no less than three medieval abbeys and a 13th-century castle. The Trinitarian Priory, founded around 1230, stands in the main street, and although repaired and enlarged in 1852 it still has its original massive central tower. Behind the church is a well-restored medieval columbarium, a stone dovecote which could house 200 doves.

The Trinitarian priory is now the Catholic church, while the Church of Ireland uses the less grand but still imposing Augustinian priory on the edge of the village. Founded in 1315, its tranquil 15th-century cloister still has stone traceried windows and shields bearing the arms of the Kildare and Desmond branches of the Fitzgerald clan.

Few but occasional golfers in search of a lost ball frequent the Franciscan friary, for it stands in the centre of a golf course. Its 72ft central tower is relatively intact, soaring over a roofless nave and transepts, with gable ends gaunt against the skyline. If you wish to visit it, check with the clubhouse first for the best approach path.

The name Desmond occurs frequently in Limerick, and it crops up again in Adare, in the ruined castle that stands by the river bank. It was occupied by the Earls of Desmond during the 16th century, but its actual date of erection is unknown. The best view of the castle is from the 15th-century stone bridge spanning the River Maigue, from where the ivy-clad walls seem to merge with the river bank.

In 1832 the 2nd Earl of Dunraven began building Adare Manor, on the site of an earlier, 17th-century house. As was fashionable at the time, the mansion was built in the Gothic style. Augustus Pugin (1812-52) designed the carved greystone chimneypiece in the Great Hall, as well as the panelled walls and ceilings of the dining room, the carved oak staircases and the minstrels gallery. The manor is now a luxury hotel.

## Curraghchase/An Currach

In this superb 600 acre park, ash, beech, sycamore, elm and hornbeam blend into glorious open forest. A great house once stood here, the home of the 19th-century poet Aubrey de Vere (1814-1902), but was burnt down in 1941 and is now a sad ruin

GREEN PEACE *Mossy boulders shaded by overhanging trees line the banks of Clare Glens.*

with blocked-in windows. Its elegant gardens, lawns and lake survive, however, and are beautifully maintained. Wildlife abounds in the forest and on the lake, with some 80 or more recorded species. A mile-long nature trail leads around the lake. The gardens are open from Easter to mid-September.

### Dromore Castle

The Victorian architect Edward Godwin borrowed from fantasy land when he built Dromore Castle for the 3rd Earl of Limerick. He created a fortress that would have withstood the most determined attack, had such an attack been likely in the 19th century. Tradition has it that Godwin played on the earl's fears of a Fenian uprising (the Fenians were Irish nationalists against Anglo-Irish landowners), in order to give vent to an imagination that produced this fairy-tale place of turrets, towers and battlements.

Dromore is reminiscent of a Bavarian castle, and it is said that Godwin's inspiration came from a castle of the mad King Ludwig of Bavaria. It stands dramatically against a wooded skyline and overlooks a great lake. The castle was partly demolished in the 1940s, and is now roofless.

### Glenstal Abbey

No building could look less like an abbey, for when it was built in the 1830s for the Barrington family, Glenstal was designed as a castle in 12th-century style. It has a great gate and a massive drum tower that resembles the one at Windsor Castle. The Barringtons moved to England in the 1920s, and in 1927 sold the castle and lands to the Benedictine Order. It became an abbey in 1957.

The abbey itself is not open to visitors, but the public are admitted to the beautiful 17th-century walled and terraced gardens, ablaze with rhododendrons in May and June. The church, built in the early 1950s, can also be visited. Its traditional exterior belies the modernistic interior, with a dappled red and green ceiling and four stained-glass windows installed in the 1960s. The church and gardens are open all year round.

### Limerick City/Luimneach

See pp. 146-147.

### Lough Gur/Loch Goir

More than 20 tombs, stone circles, hut foundations, forts and lakeside dwellings have been excavated beside Lough Gur, one of the

STARK RUIN *The cannons of Orange made short work of Carrigogunnel Castle in 1691.*

most complete Stone Age and Bronze Age sites in north-western Europe. A Visitor Centre built in the form of neolithic huts houses a collection of artefacts and models, and there is an audiovisual presentation of the story of Lough Gur.

The most impressive site is the Grange Stone Circle, 50yds across and consisting of some 100 boulders. It probably dates from about 2000 BC and may have been a meeting place for social or religious ceremonies.

When dark clouds roll over the hills and lake they have a haunting beauty that may have inspired a local myth concerning Gerald, Earl of Desmond. He was supposedly under the lake's spell, and every seven years, it is said, he canters over the water on a white horse shod with silver. Only when the horse's shoes are worn away will Gerald be freed from the spell and ride no more.

**Visitor Centre** *May-Sept, daily 10am-6pm. Tel: (061) 85186.*

---

### THERE WAS A YOUNG LADY . . .

The invention of the humorous five-line verse known as the limerick is generally ascribed to Edward Lear, who wrote such poems in his *Book of Nonsense* published in 1846.

*There was an Old Man who supposed
That the street door was partially closed,
But some very large rats
Ate his coats and his hats
While that futile Old Gentleman dozed.*

Lear based his idea on a nursery rhyme that began 'There was an Old Man of Tobago'. But why 'limerick'? It has been suggested that the name derives from an 18th-century soldiers' song, 'Will you come up to Limerick', to which in true army fashion the soldiers added verses of their own.

Another source could have been the group of poets who gathered in and around Croom, and were known as the Maigue Poets, after the river that flows through the town. One of them, Sean O'Tuama, wrote five-line verses with the first, second and fifth lines rhyming, as did the third and fourth lines – the form of the limerick.

In the early 20th century, limericks enjoyed widespread popularity, and limerick competitions were held in magazines. Their popularity continues today, and most describe the nonsensical experiences of a young man or lady of certain towns – but the best ones are usually unprintable!

# Where Flying Boats Landed

*There are many little-explored charms in this corner of Limerick, where flat pastureland, with moody views across the Shannon, gives way to a sweeping semicircle of green hills. At the Shannonside village of Foynes a flying-boat museum recalls the exciting early days of transatlantic flight – a world away from Limerick's ancient castles – while at Drumcolliher a porcelain factory makes 'Dresden' china.*

### Askeaton/Eas Géitine

The River Deel winds through Askeaton where it is spanned by a narrow bridge. The bridge has remained unaltered since it was built by the Earl of Desmond in the 16th century. The town is dominated by a castle standing on a rocky, limestone islet. The castle's origins go back to 1199, and from 1348 until 1580 it was the home of the Earls of Desmond. Its present form dates from the 16th century. Although ruined the tower contains some fine windows and a fireplace on the third floor.

The castle can be explored by obtaining the key from the gatehouse. The climb to the top of the tower is not for the fainthearted, but the views across the river from the top are rewarding.

Downriver, beside the road that bypasses the town, is a ruined 15th-century Franciscan friary – one of the best-preserved ruined monasteries in Ireland. Its cloister, built around a square formed of marble pillars, is 51ft long. In the north-west corner is a carving of St Francis, complete with stigmata, the wounds of Christ. The face of the carving is well worn, for kissing it is said to cure toothache.

### Beagh Castle

A narrow lane opens suddenly onto the Shannon estuary, revealing a short jetty, a line of ruined, ivy-clad cottages and the delapidated keep of the 13th-century castle. It was built by John Fitzjohn Fitzgerald and remained in his family, the Knights of Glin, until it was confiscated by the Crown in 1573. During the Napoleonic Wars a gun battery was built to the west of the castle. It is now, like the castle itself, a crumbling ruin.

### Drumcolliher/Drom Collachair

In this secluded village stand two examples of commercial enterprise, though 70 years separate their foundation. In 1889 the father of Ireland's Cooperative Movement, Henry Plunkett, banded together the local milk-producing farms to establish a creamery, and now the little building houses the Plunkett Heritage Museum, displaying a fully equipped, turn-of-the-century dairy. A beautifully restored steam engine drives the separators, churns and vats used to process the milk.

DANCING GIRL *Deft hands apply the finishing touches to a porcelain figurine at Drumcolliher's Irish Dresden factory. The porcelain clay is mixed to a secret formula, brought over from Dresden in Germany, and each finished product is individually hand painted.*

road plunges down beside Sugar Hill. Dramatic views across low flatlands of Limerick to distant Galty Mountains.

**Newcastle** Village with broad central square containing well-preserved Desmond Banqueting Hall (13th century, rebuilt in 15th), part of castle of Earls of Desmond. Superb wooden vaulting and handsome black fireplace of 1638. Now used as cultural centre.

### EVENTS
**Newcastle West Festival** Mid-July.

### SPORT
**Angling** Game fishing: River Deel, at Rathkeale and Askeaton.
**Golf** Newcastle West Golf Club, 9-hole course. Tel: (069) 62015.

### INFORMATION
Limerick Tourist Office. Tel: (061) 317522.
Shannon Development Tourist Office. Tel: (061) 361555.

### OTHER PLACES TO SEE
**Ashford** Village at foot of steep, craggy mountain on which is a white-painted shrine and its rock altar, called Mass Rock. Masses held there during 18th and early 19th centuries.
**Barnagh Gap** Viewing point where Abbeyfeale-Newcastle

STOUT WELCOME *The word Fáilte, 'Welcome', greets patrons of this colourful pub in Broadford, near Drumcolliher.*

Close by is an even more remarkable enterprise – a porcelain factory with its roots in eastern Germany. In the early 1960s the local quarry closed, facing the village with mass unemployment, so the villagers sought out new business abroad. They found a benefactor in the Saar family, owners of a porcelain factory in Volkstedt, near Halle. They had recently fled to the West and were seeking a new home. They chose Drumcolliher, and established their factory there, calling it Irish Dresden.

Visitors can watch the delicate figurines being produced in nine stages that combine craftsmanship with high technology.

**Irish Dresden factory** *Mon-Fri, 9am-5pm. Tel: (063) 83030.*
**Plunkett Heritage Museum** *Daily, 9am-5pm. Tel: (063) 83113.*

## Foynes/Faing

In the late 1930s, Foynes was as well known to air travellers as Heathrow is today. Flying boats made the first commercial transatlantic crossings and, because Ireland's west coast was the nearest point to America, the placid Shannon between Foynes Island and the shore became their watery runway. The flying-boat museum recalls those pioneering days with models, photographs and dioramas. The original terminal building, radio room and weather-forecasting equipment have been preserved.

**Foynes Museum** *Mar-Oct, daily 10am-6pm, or by arrangement. Tel: (069) 65416.*

## Glenquin Castle

Ireland abounds with fortified tower houses, and Glenquin Castle is one of the best. Rising 70ft and seven storeys high, it is a remarkable mid-15th-century structure, with a spiral staircase linking three high-vaulted rooms, one above the other. Traces of wicker shuttering can be seen on the ceilings of the two private chambers.

## Glin/An Gleann

The road rises from the Shannon estuary to Glin's broad rectangle of terraced houses, shops and pubs, and from almost every point there are sweeping views across the silvery sheen of the river. On the edge of the village lies Glin Castle, the battlemented 18th-century home of the Fitzgeralds, the hereditary Knights of Glin.

The present, 29th, Knight of Glin is Desmond Fitzgerald, a former curator at

CASTLE VISTA *Fine views of Limerick's lowlands stretch from Glenquin Castle's battlements.*

London's Victoria and Albert Museum. Not surprisingly, Glin Castle's grey walls embrace a wonderland of 18th and 19th-century furniture, ceramics and paintings. Set out in rooms leading off from the magnificent hall, with its Corinthian pillars and superb plaster-work ceiling, they reflect the history of Irish artists and craftsmen.

**Castle** *May only. Tel: (068) 34173.*

## Rathkeale/Rath Caola

The town's long main street is flanked by fine Georgian houses with columned porticoes and some ornate fanlights. There is a splendid early 19th-century courthouse, and the remains of a 13th-century abbey and castle. But the town's most intriguing building is Castle Matrix, a 15th-century fortified tower house with outbuildings grouped around a courtyard beside the River Deel.

Abandoned until the 1960s, it was bought by an American, Sean O'Driscoll, who restored it and filled it with antique furniture. In 1970 it was opened as the Irish International Art Centre. Castle Matrix also houses a collection of weaponry from the Middle Ages and earlier, plus axe-heads from the Stone and Iron Ages. No less intriguing than the massive tower, with its overhanging corner

turrets, is its history. Here, it is said, the poet Edmund Spenser met Sir Walter Raleigh, and began to write *The Faerie Queene*.

**Castle Matrix** *Mid-May to mid-Sept, Sat-Tues, pm. Tel: (069) 64284.*

## Shanid Castle/Seanad

Rearing up from a steep hill like a jagged, broken tooth and visible for miles around is the shattered tower of the castle stronghold of the Fitzgeralds, Earls of Desmond. Their war cry, until such cries were banned by Henry VI, was 'Shanid Abu' ('Shanid for ever'). The words continued to be used in the Fitzgerald crest. The castle fell into disuse in the 17th century. It stands in a field a short distance from the road. Its tower, five-sided on the outside but circular within, is some 30ft high with 9ft thick walls and has pastoral views.

## Springfield House

An avenue of lime trees three-quarters of a mile long – said to be the longest in Europe – leads to the seat of the Fitzmaurice family. Rebuilt after a fire in 1923, it has a 15th-century keep as part of its 18th-century courtyard. Though itself not open to the public, Springfield House has spacious grounds that form a deer park which can be visited by arrangement. Tel: (063) 83162.

FLIGHT OF FANCY *Glin Castle's flying staircase is unique in Ireland, and is an outstanding example of 18th-century Irish craftsmanship, with its delicate balustrades and mahogany handrail.*

---

### FOYNES TAKES FLIGHT

The late 1930s were heady times for the village of Foynes. The first Atlantic crossing from here was made in 1937, and a passenger service started in 1939. In those days a PanAm flight to the USA via Newfoundland was a strange combination of ocean-liner luxury and pioneering adventure. Seven-course meals were served aboard the Boeing B314, and there was a honeymoon suite at the rear of the plane.

But the lumbering four-engined machines were able to carry only just enough fuel for the 12-hour crossing between Foynes and St John, Newfoundland. They were often turned back by storms, headwinds or ice on the wings. After one such return, the enterprising barman at Foynes offered the cold, dispirited passengers coffee and cream laced with whiskey. He thus invented 'Irish Coffee'.

War brought an end to commercial passenger flights but a huge surge in military air traffic, conducted in secret to

*A flying-boat model in the Foynes Museum.*

preserve Ireland's neutrality. Foynes became the eastern terminal for transatlantic flying boats, with shuttle connections to England. The war also saw enormous improvements in aircraft design and the construction of many new runways on land. As a result, the flying boat's days were numbered and the last of them left Foynes in October 1945. Its role was taken over by Shannon International Airport across the estuary.

# Ancestral Home of a President

*This prosperous corner of County Tipperary, bordered in the south by the impressive Comeragh Mountains, provides a heady mixture of scenery, history and heritage. Among its tiny villages is the ancestral home of an American president. And on the banks of the River Suir – long a trading route – stands the historic town of Clonmel and the reputed birthplace of an English queen.*

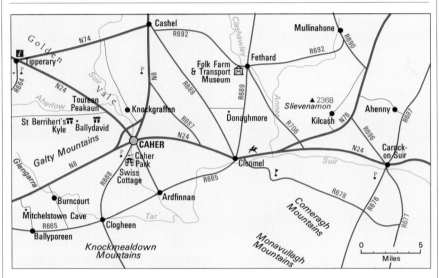

## OTHER PLACES TO SEE

**Ahenny** Small village with cemetery containing two of Ireland's finest High Crosses, from the 8th or 9th century.
**Ardfinnan** Village on banks of River Suir.
**Burncourt** Partly fortified 17th-century castle, destroyed by Cromwell in 1650.'
**Donaghmore** 12th-century Romanesque church with fine windows.
**Fethard Folk Farm and Transport Museum** Includes horse-drawn carriages and hearses and antique bicycles. Open May-Sept, Mon-Sat, 10am-6pm; Sun, 1.30-6pm, or by appointment. Tel: (052) 31516.

**Kilcash** Attractive village in Slievenamon foothills above River Suir, with castle remains and fine early church with Romanesque doorway.
**Knockgraffon** Norman motte with remains of courtyard.
**Mullinahone** Home of novelist and patriot Charles Kickham (1828-82), with memorabilia.
**St Berrihert's Kyle and Toureen Peakaun** Sites of carved stones and, at Toureen Peakaun, remains of 12th-century church.

## WALKS
**Ballydavid** 8m W of Caher. Forest and riverside walks.
**Caher Park** 1½m S of Caher. Forest and riverside walks.

## EVENTS
**Caher Castle Norman Festival** Mid-Aug.
**Clonmel Race Meetings** Mar and June.

## SPORT
**Angling** Game fishing: Rivers Aherlow, Anner, Suir and Tar.
**Golf** Caher Park Golf Club, 9-hole course. Tel: (052) 41474.
Carrick-on-Suir Golf Club, 9-hole course. Tel: (051) 40047.
Clonmel Golf Club, 18-hole course. Tel: (052) 21138.

## INFORMATION
South-East Tourism. Tel: (051) 75823.
Tipperary Town Tourist Office. Tel: (062) 51457.

## Ballyporeen/Béal Átha Póirín
In this little, out-of-the-way village one Michael Reagan was born in 1829. Just 151 years later, his great-grandson Ronald Reagan was elected President of the United States. The village is popular with visiting Americans. The local pub, named The Ronald Reagan, is bedecked inside with pictures of the President and his wife, Nancy, taken when he visited the village in 1984.

## Caher/An Chathair
Set on a rock in the middle of the River Suir is a castle that is every schoolchild's idea of a medieval fortress, and which gives Caher its name (the Irish word *cathair* means 'fortress'). Its high, battlemented walls and towers, massive square keep and barbican gateway are so complete that it looks as if it was built as a film set. In fact, its immaculate condition is due to a major restoration by the Office of Public Works.

Caher Castle was built in the 15th and 16th centuries by the powerful Anglo-Norman Butler family, and remained impregnable until 1599. In that year, the Earl of Essex, made Lord Lieutenant of Ireland by Queen Elizabeth I, battered it with cannon in a three-day siege. Several cannonballs remain embedded in the walls to this day.

The keep is approached through its high-walled outer and middle wards, and then through the gate which has a reconstructed portcullis and hoisting mechanism. The rooms within the keep contain displays of armour and weapons, including broadswords, some 5ft long. The great hall, though it dates only from the 1840s, has a fine hammerbeam ceiling.

Just over a mile south of Caher (also spelled Cahir) is the fairytale Swiss Cottage, with trellised walls and verandahs and dormer windows peeping out from under bonnets of thatch. Inside, the dining room is decorated with Persian wallpaper of 1816, with designs depicting Turks smoking on the banks of the Bosporus. The cottage was built in 1810 for Lord and Lady Caher, and is said to have been designed by John Nash.

Caher is a popular base for hill-walkers, particularly for those climbing the Galty Mountains.
**Caher Castle** May to mid-June, 10am-6pm; mid-June to Sept, 10am-7.30pm; Oct-Apr, daily exc. Mon, 10am-4.30pm. Tel: (052) 41011.
**Swiss Cottage** Mid-June to Sept, Tues-Sun, 10am-6pm. Tel: (052) 41144.

REAGAN'S ROOTS *The pub that bears Reagan's name marks Ballyporeen as his ancestral home.*

CROSS OF AGES *The patterns on the 8th or 9th-century North Cross at Ahenny are weatherworn but still visible.*

## Carrick-on-Suir/Carraig na Siúire

Old quayside buildings line the River Suir and a 15th-century seven-arched bridge spans its fast-flowing water in this little town of narrow, well-kept streets. The soaring town clock of 1784 competes for attention with the tower of St Nicholas Church, completed in 1880 in the Romanesque style, and worth a visit for its stained glass and Kilkenny marble columns.

The town's greatest treasure is the 16th-century Ormonde Castle, a gabled and mullioned manor house built onto a 15th-century castle, and perhaps the finest Elizabethan manor house in Ireland. It was built by Thomas Butler, 10th Earl of Ormonde (1532-1614), who was known as Black Tom for his dark complexion. There is nothing dark about his house, however, and its plasterwork walls and ceilings are truly magnificent. The finest room is the Long Gallery – 100ft long – with panels depicting Edward VI, Elizabeth I and the Royal Coat of Arms, and a massive stone fireplace.

**Ormonde Castle** *Mid-June to mid-Sept, 10am-5.30pm. Guided tours available. Tel: (051) 40787.*

## Clogheen/An Chloichín

The Knockmealdown Mountains rise sheer from the side of the road at Clogheen, forming an impressive setting for the sandstone, brick-trimmed buildings of the village. Inside the gate of the Catholic church stands a Celtic cross erected in 1810 as a memorial to Father Nicholas Sheehy, one of five people hanged at Clonmel in 1776 on a trumped-up murder charge. As a bold champion of oppressed rural people he was feared by the Tipperary establishment. The shaft of the cross, in the mode of early Christian High Crosses, bears religious themes, including the Good Samaritan.

## Clonmel/Cluain Meala

With splendid views of the rugged Comeragh Mountains only a few miles to the south, Clonmel, whose Irish name means 'honey meadow', is one of Ireland's most charming towns. It is Tipperary's county town, with an intimate atmosphere within the remains of its old walls. The town's two gates still stand at either end of the main street. The West Gate is relatively modern, built only in 1831, but the other, Main Guard, dates from 1674 and was built as a courthouse by the Earl of Ormonde. Between the gates the main street has a friendly, good-humoured face, with busy shops and pubs and handsome façades.

Fragments of the 14th-century town walls crop up in parts of the town, the best section being near Old St Mary's Church. In 1650 they stoutly defied a three-week siege by Oliver Cromwell. Even more venerable is the Franciscan Friary, founded in 1269, which contains a tomb with the effigies of a knight and his lady and an inscription to the Butlers, Lords of Caher.

## Fethard/Fiodh Ard

Few places in Ireland have so many antiquities within such a small space as this quiet little town. Its 14th-century walls are still visible here and there, and within them are the 15th-century tower of the Holy Trinity Church, the Augustinian abbey founded in 1306 and rebuilt in 1823, and a fire station, parts of which date from the 16th century.

The little Clashawley stream runs to the east of the town, crossed by a bridge that leads to part of the walls, with a tower still standing and what was once a town gate. On a wall by the gate is a much weathered stone carving known as a sheela-na-gig. It is believed to date from the 14th century, and the frank portrayal of sexual organs suggests that the stone may have played a role in fertility rites or in warding off evil.

## Mitchelstown Cave

Deep below the main road from Caher to Mitchelstown lies a great cave system carved into the limestone by the action of water over the ages. It was discovered in 1833. About half a mile of its length is accessible, a wonderland of huge caverns and rock formations, many with names that describe their weird shapes – the Golden Fleece, Eagle's Wing, Pillars of Hercules, Organ Pipes and Tower of Babel. There is even a feature that has been likened to the face of Christ, called the Turin Shroud.

The most impressive of the caverns, however, is the vast Middle Cave, also known as the House of Lords. It measures 160ft by 90ft and its tapering roof is 60ft high. High in the cavern, on a huge table of rock, is a formation called the Sleeping Warrior, and all around are huge columns with calcite crystals glistening like diamonds in the artificial light. When the lighting was installed in 1972, a banquet for 150 people was held in the cave.

**Opening times** *10am-5.30pm. Tel: (052) 67246.*

RUSTIC RETREAT *The Swiss Cottage at Caher is an example of the cottage orné, 'rustic' surroundings created by the wealthy gentry in the 1800s.*

### THE TIPPERARY FLYER

In France they call him 'Kee-kee', in Spain he is the 'King of the Road', and in 1989 he was named European of the Year. The man with all these nicknames and honours is Sean Kelly, from Carrick-on Suir, the racing cyclist who, in the 1980s, swept all before him on the road circuits of Europe. Winner of the Tour de France in 1988, seven Paris-Nice races, the Tour of Switzerland in 1983 and 1990 and the Tour of Spain in 1988, among many others, he was ranked number one in the world for five consecutive years.

Born into a farming family, Kelly swapped farm tractor for bicycle and rose through the gruelling ranks of international cycling to beat the best in Europe, often on their home ground. For his services to sport, and his unofficial role as an ambassador for Ireland, the President of Ireland presented him with an award. But perhaps his most savoured honour was when his home town named a square after him, a rare distinction for a living person.

*The 'King of the Road', Sean Kelly, pedals to victory in the 1988 Tour de France cycle race, one of his many European victories.*

# Lough Derg's Fertile Plain

*On Tipperary's north-western fringe, the River Shannon broadens into a twisting lake 30 miles long – Lough Derg – that fits into the landscape like a piece in a giant jigsaw puzzle. Lough Derg forms the county border, and along its ragged eastern shore are tiny villages and harbours with spectacular views westwards across to the majestic Slieve Bernagh and Slieve Aughty Mountains.*

### Ballina/Béal an Átha

At the southern end of Lough Derg the River Shannon narrows to cut through a gap between the Slieve Bernagh and Arra Mountains, which, in places, sweep right down to the lake shore. The huddle of houses, shops and pubs on each side of the gap appear to form one town, linked by a 13-arched bridge, but in fact they are two – Ballina on the eastern side and Killaloe on the western, in County Clare.

Ballina is the quieter of the two, though in summer its bright marina is a popular mooring point for the pleasure craft that ply the river, and it has a delightful park for gentle walks by the shore.

### Dromineer/Drom Inbhir

At Dromineer, Lough Derg broadens to its widest point, some 10 miles across, and the village is a haven for watersport enthusiasts. In summer the pier, dominated by a ruined medieval castle, is crowded with sleek cruisers and yachts, while canoes and windsurf boards litter the shore. The village makes full use of its superb location, and offers yachts for hire and sailing and windsurfing courses. The local yacht club, founded in 1837, is the third oldest in the world.

JEWELLED SHRINE *The jewelled face of the shrine of the Stowe Missal is inscribed with 'a prayer for Pilib, king of Ormonde, who covered this shrine, and for Aine his wife'.*

### Lorrha/Lothra

This village in the northern tip of Tipperary is believed to stand on the site of a monastery founded in the 6th century by St Ruadhan, a disciple of St Finian of Clonard and said to be one of the 12 apostles of Ireland. His monastery was destroyed by Vikings in 844. Among many remains on the site are two 9th-century High Crosses, a Norman motte and a ruined Dominican friary founded in 1269. The 13th-century church of the Canons Regular has a Norman doorway decorated with rosettes, bambinos and a female head. Of more recent date is the Catholic church of St Ruadhan and St Patrick, built in 1813. Its stained glass has old Irish spelling and lettering.

Near Lorrha is Lackeen Castle, a 16th-century tower house built for a chief of Ormonde. In the 1730s a jewelled box containing a missal, or prayer book, dating from the 9th century, was found sealed in the castle walls. The Stowe Missal, as it was called, because it became part of the Duke of Buckingham's collection at Stowe House, is now in the Royal Irish Academy, in Dublin.

### Nenagh/An tAonach

The massive round tower of a Norman castle rears up above the roof lines of Nenagh. The castle was built between 1200 and 1220 by

chief sites of interest. May-Sept. Tel: (067) 31610.

**EVENTS**
**Dromineer Gala Day** Aug.
**Dromineer Water Festival** July.
**Lough Derg Annual Regatta** Dromineer, Aug.
**Lough Derg Rally** Aug.
**Nenagh Agricultural Show** Aug.
**Novice Rowing Day** Dromineer, Aug.

**SPORT**
**Angling** Coarse fishing: Lough Derg at Dromineer. Game fishing: Dromineer Bay and River Nenagh.
**Bathing** Dromineer Bay.
**Boating** Dromineer Bay and Ballina.
**Golf** Nenagh Golf Club, 18-hole course. Tel: (067) 31476.
**Windsurfing** Dromineer Bay.

**INFORMATION**
Nenagh Tourist Office. Tel: (067) 31610.
Shannon Airport Tourist Office. Tel: (061) 61664.

**OTHER PLACES TO SEE**
**The Grave of the Leinstermen** Off the Ballina-Portroe road. Burial place of the Leinster men, murdered in about AD 1000 by the soldiers of Brian Boru. The site makes a fine viewing point.

**WALKS**
**Nenagh Town Trail** Takes in

NUMBER PLEASE *A telephone exchange is combined with the imaginatively re-created shop in Nenagh's Heritage Centre.*

Theobald FitzWalter, ancestor of the Butlers of Ormonde and a cousin of Thomas Becket. Its tower is 100ft high and 55ft across, and its walls are 20ft thick.

In the castle's shadow, the town's streets are a mixture of architectural styles, from the overgrown ruins of a 13th-century Franciscan friary to the splendidly classical courthouse of 1843 and the equally elegant, late 19th-century Town Hall with its gas-lamp brackets and acorns and oak leaves carved in the doorway columns.

Close to the courthouse is the Governor's House and the jail block, a grim building where, in 1858, two brothers were publicly hanged for murder on dubious evidence. Their protestations of innocence on the scaffold were accompanied by a raging storm of thunder and lightning. The building now houses the town's Heritage Centre, with a re-created Victorian schoolroom and models of Lough Derg and its villages, but the jail's condemned cells, execution room and scaffold site can still be seen.

Leading away from the town centre is Summerhill, a street of Georgian houses with beautifully proportioned windows, fan-lights – no two alike – and ornate doorways with bootscrapers and mounting blocks. **Heritage Centre** *Mid-Apr to early Nov, Mon-Fri, 10am-5pm; Sat and Sun, 2.30-5pm. Tel: (067) 32633.*

### Portroe/An Port Rua

Dense, green countryside almost envelops this steeply hilled village, with its pretty, cream gritstone church of 1882. A short distance beyond the village, on the Ballina road, is a viewpoint with stirring panoramic views of Lough Derg and the mountains beyond. A forest beside the car park has picnic sites and waymarked nature trails.

### Terryglass/Tír Dhá Ghlas

The neat little lakeside village of Terryglass has, clustered around its quay, a charming collection of quaint cottages, weatherboard houses, a church and a 14th-century castle. The church, the Convent of the Immaculate Conception, was founded by Lucila Larios y Tashara Hickie (1834-80), of nearby Slevoir. It was begun in 1879, and its tower was added 50 years later. Inside the church is a relic of what is claimed to be the True Cross.

The old Court Castle, with the remains of four towers barely distinguishable, stands on high, private ground beside the lake.

ENCHANTED VIEW *Terryglass Quay looks across the sun-tinted waters of Lough Derg.*

CATCHPENNY CASEMENTS *Windows painted on the side of a house in Portroe have a quixotic charm.*

#### A MAN OF MANY PARTS

Nenagh was the birthplace in 1901 of the distinguished scientist J.D. Bernal. A physicist, X-ray crystallographer and pioneer of the study of the crystal structure of substances found in living things, he became professor of physics and later of crystallography at Birkbeck College, London University. But Bernal was a true polymath, interested in a vast range of subjects from molecular biology (of which he was also a pioneer) and the chemical origins of life, to computers, cement and the structure and composition of the Earth's crust.

A lifelong Communist, Bernal was awarded both the US Medal of Freedom (for his scientific work during the Second World War) and the Lenin Peace Prize. He died in London in 1971.

# The Home of Gaelic Sport

*The jagged Devilsbit Mountain in the north and the gentle Slieveardagh Hills to the south embrace eastern Tipperary's landscape of simple, natural charm. This peaceful land, where almost every town and village has an architectural gem, offers several surprises, including a school for policemen and the home of Gaelic sport.*

## Holy Cross Abbey/Mainistir na Croiche

No abbey could have a more tranquil setting, amid green pasturelands with the rock-strewn River Suir lapping its outer walls. Founded in 1180 for Cistercian monks, the great church – with its squat, battlemented tower, groined ceiling and superb decorative stonework – is as impressive now as it was 800 years ago, thanks to a major restoration in 1975.

Holy Cross Abbey is now a national monument. It houses two relics said to be of The True Cross, on which Christ died at Calvary, hence the abbey's name, and is visited by thousands of pilgrims every year. In an adjacent garden are bronze sculptures representing the Stations of the Cross, by the Italian sculptor Enrico Manfrini. Exact replicas were presented to the Pope on his visit to Ireland in 1979.

**Opening times** *Tourist information office, audiovisual centre and coffee shop, open daily. Guided tours available, 10am-5.30pm. Tel: (0504) 43241.*

## Roscrea/Ros Cré

One of Ireland's oldest towns sits astride the Dublin-Limerick road, which cuts through the remains of the 12th-century St Cronan's Abbey. Only the abbey's west façade still stands by the roadside, with a round-arched doorway that contains the moulded figure of a bishop or abbot – probably St Cronan, who founded the monastery around AD 600. The rest of the abbey was demolished early in the 19th century, and a new church was built in the churchyard.

At one side of the church is a weathered, 12th-century High Cross, with carved figures depicting St Cronan and the crucified Christ. On the opposite side of the road is a Round Tower, about 60ft high, and now missing its conical cap. Its door is about 8ft above the ground and has a rounded arch and jambs that tilt inwards.

The massive Gate Tower of Roscrea Castle stands foursquare in the centre of the town, as forbidding now as it must have been when it was built by the Anglo-Normans in the 13th century. The castle has been extensively renovated, the dungeon excavated, and the timber first floor of the Gate Tower replaced. The tower still has its original stone fireplaces and vaulted ceiling. From the top of the tower there are panoramic views towards the distant Slieve Bloom Mountains.

Within the castle walls stands the three-storey, 18th-century Damer House, with an elegant carved stone doorway and a superb red pine staircase. The house is now a heritage centre, providing glimpses of Roscrea's history.

Buildings in a variety of styles make up the rest of the town, including a turreted Temperance Hall that was originally built around 1815 as a prison; the bell tower of a Franciscan friary, dating from around 1470, which is now the gateway to St Cronan's Catholic church; and the Abbey Hall, built in the 1920s in the classical style.

In Rosemary Square stands an ornate fountain constructed in the late 19th century and known locally as the 'fancy fountain', with figures of children around its base. Sadly its jets no longer spray the air. It once adorned Market Square, but to save it from the traffic there it was removed and placed in Rosemary Square.

To the south of Roscrea is the Devilsbit Mountain, where a gap in the hilltop is attributed in local folklore to the Devil who, in a fit of anger, bit out a chunk. Finding the

ITALIANATE EDIFICE *The imposing façade and 120ft bell tower, or campanile, of Thurles Cathedral of the Assumption is modelled on the Cathedral of Pisa in Italy.*

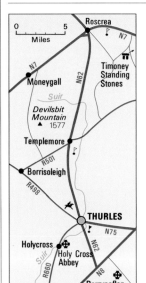

**Derrynaflan** 8m SE of Thurles, site of 6th-century monastery. Its treasures are in the National Museum.

**EVENTS**
**Gaelic Games** Thurles, most Sun.
**Roscrea Festival** Mid-Nov.
**Thurles Races** Apr, May, Sept.

**SPORT**
**Angling** Game fishing: River Suir and tributaries.
**Golf** Roscrea Golf Club, 9-hole course. Tel: (0505) 21130.
Templemore Golf Club, 9-hole course. Tel: (0504) 31720.
Thurles Golf Club, 18-hole course. Tel: (0504) 21983/ 22466.

**INFORMATION**
Nenagh Tourist Office. Tel: (067) 31610.
Shannon Airport Tourist Office. Tel: (067) 61664.

**OTHER PLACES TO SEE**
**Borrisoleigh** Pretty Georgian market town.

DAMER HOUSE *The magnificent hand-carved staircase has an elaborate frieze of foliage.*

taste not to his liking he spat it out, and it landed 22 miles away to the south, where it formed the Rock of Cashel. A short climb to the summit of the Devilsbit is rewarded by wonderful views over the Golden Vale.
**Roscrea Castle and Damer House** *Apr-Sept, 10am-5.30pm; Sun, pm only Tel: (0505) 21850.*

### Templemore/An Teampall Mór

A policeman's lot is a happy one in Templemore, for here young and enthusiastic police cadets receive their training before entering the service of Ireland's police force, the Garda Siochana (Guardians of the Peace). The training centre, which was built as a British military barracks in 1810, has an imposing stone gateway and a square clock tower. The town's military legacy is recalled in the Catholic church. Built in 1790 and reconstructed in 1856, it has mural tablets commemorating Irish soldiers who died in various campaigns overseas from 1868.

A remarkably wide main street, said to have been the widest in Europe when it was built, runs through the town, lined with attractive shops and plain buildings. One handsome building of 1826, built as a market house, still has an onion dome. The town

park has a lake, a nature trail through woodland and a ruined church and castle.

### Thurles/Durlas

The market town of Thurles stands beside the River Suir, dominated by the remains of a 15th-century tower, by the six-arched stone bridge, and Black Castle of the same period, built by the Anglo-Normans to defend the river crossing. The town's focal point is Liberty Square, with a number of ornate shopfronts and a memorial to those who fought for Ireland's independence.

In Liberty Square's Hayes Hotel, the Gaelic Athletic Association was formed in 1884. It promotes native Irish games such as hurling and Gaelic football.

### Timoney Standing Stones

On top of a hill, in a labyrinth of lanes, stand some 300 stones. All about 3ft high and seemingly scattered at random, their origin and significance are a mystery. Many explanations have been put forward – Bronze Age rituals, druidical ceremonies, even medieval follies – but no convincing explanation has stuck. Perhaps they mark the places where warriors fell in some long-forgotten battle.

Archbishop Thomas William Croke is remembered in Tipperary not so much for his undoubtedly successful clerical career but as the man who inspired the Gaelic Athletic Association (GAA). Born in County Cork in 1824, Croke attended the Irish Colleges in Paris and Rome, and after his ordination in 1847 became a professor at Carlow College. He was appointed Bishop of Auckland in New Zealand in 1870, and in 1875 returned to Ireland to become Archbishop of Cashel.

A fervent supporter of anything Irish, including Home Rule, he gave moral and financial support to the GAA, founded in 1884 to popularise native Irish pastimes such as hurling, handball and Gaelic football. Today the GAA is Ireland's biggest sporting association. Croke is remembered for his patronage by a statue in Thurles' Liberty Square. Archbishop Croke retired from public life in 1896, and died in 1902. He is buried in Thurles.

STONE PUZZLE *Folklore or folly — the origin of the lonely Timoney standing stones is unknown.*

# In the Shadow of the Rock

*Tipperary shares with Limerick the rich pasturelands known as the Golden Vale, which stretch southwards as far as the stunningly beautiful Glen of Aherlow and the lowlands of the Galty Mountains. This rich and varied landscape has many intriguing features, such as a peat bog now converted to a nature reserve and the awe-inspiring Rock of Cashel and its soaring 13th-century Cathedral of St Patrick.*

## Cashel/Caiseal

The Rock of Cashel dramatically overshadows Cashel, but the town has its own worthy attractions too – a graceful 18th-century mansion, Cashel Palace, and a main street lined with shopfronts and pubs that have resisted the progress of plastic and glass. Cashel Palace is now a hotel, but it retains many fine architectural features including a panelled hallway and a red pine staircase.

The town has two fine churches, both dedicated to St John the Baptist and one holding the status of cathedral. The Protes-tant cathedral dates from 1749-84. Its imposing gateway, with crossed keys above the arch, leads to a somewhat spartan yet dignified building with a tower and spire. Inside, its chief glories are its stained glass and an organ built by Samuel Green. The Catholic St John's is much grander, built in 1801-55 in the classical style with a colonnaded façade of three semicircular arches and a mosaic representing the Ascension of Christ into Heaven.

Just off the main street is the GPA-Bolton Library, founded in 1744 by Archbishop Bolton, a scholar and the builder of Cashel Palace, who also brought the first public water supply to the town. The library regularly holds exhibitions of silverware, old books, illustrations and maps, and examples of early printing.

The Cashel Folk Village is a re-creation of the town as it was in the 19th century, and has a museum exhibiting items from the 17th century to the present day. There is also the Bothan Scoir, a reconstructed 17th-century peasant dwelling on its original site, with historical artefacts and documents on display inside.

**Bothan Scoir** *Open by appointment. Tel: (062) 61360.*
**Cashel Folk Village** *May-Sept 10am-6pm. Other times by appointment. Tel: (062) 61947.*
**GPA-Bolton Library** *Mon-Sat, 9.30am-5.30pm, Sun 2.30-5.30pm. Tel: (062) 61944.*

## Dundrum/Dún Droma

An enchantingly scenic little village overlooked by rolling hills, Dundrum is the site of the Cappamurra Nature Reserve, centred on some 2000 acres of peat bog that once supplied fuel for local hearths. The peat diggers have gone, and the bog is now a reserve and habitat for hundreds of wildlife species, including butterflies and moths, ferns, mosses, birds, bats, stoats, otters, foxes, red squirrels, badgers and deer. A nature walk through the bog gives the opportunity to see many of its inhabitants. Visits can be arranged between April and October by the Cappamurra Environmental Conservation Committee. Tel: (062) 71127.

## Glen of Aherlow/Gleann Eatharlaí

Peace and tranquillity combine with majestic scenery to make the drive along the winding road through the Glen of Aherlow an exhilarating experience. A deep green patchwork of fields is backed by the magnificent Galty Mountains, and the very names of the scattered low hills – such as Knockaceol (Hill of Music) and Paradise Hill – underline the tranquil atmosphere.

There is a signposted scenic route from Tipperary town towards Bansha which negotiates a series of hairpin bends under a canopy of trees and eventually reveals the glen's full glory. There are also plenty of forest trails for the more energetic.

## Rock of Cashel/Carraig Phadraig

Well before you reach Cashel, the rock that bears its name appears on the skyline, rearing up from the landscape in a series of limestone ridges and topped by the serenely beautiful Cathedral of St Patrick. The cathedral's roofless chancel and nave is 93ft long and its central tower 85ft high. Close by, seeming to be part of the building but detached from it, is

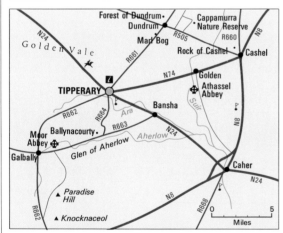

in 1540 during dissolution of monasteries. Nave and chancel remain as mere roofless shell in shadow of tall, slender tower.

**WALKS**
**Cashel Tourist Trail** Apr-Sept. Tel: (062) 61333.
**Forest of Dundrum** Wildlife reserve; includes 2hr Bishop's Wood Walk; picnic sites.
**Marl Bog Forest Walk** Starting from Dundrum village, 2hr walk.

**EVENTS**
**Tipperary Races** Feb, Apr, July and Oct.

**SPORT**
**Angling** Game fishing: Marl Bog Fishery and Rivers Aherlow, Ara and Suir.
**Golf** Tipperary Golf Club 9-hole course. Tel: (062) 51119.

**INFORMATION**
South-East Tourism. Tel: (051) 75823.
Tipperary Town Tourist Office. Tel: (062) 51457.

**OTHER PLACES TO SEE**
**Athassel Abbey** Near Golden, medieval priory founded in the 12th century; abbey church 210ft long, with carved figures.
**Ballynacourty** Forest area with walks and views of the Glen of Aherlow.
**Golden** Has circular tower house built on an island in the River Suir, containing bronze head of Thomas MacDonagh, Tipperary-born patriot executed in the 1916 Rising.
**Moor Abbey** Just inside county border with Limerick are remains of abbey founded in 13th century but destroyed

CASHEL CHEER *Shining paintwork and a bright mural greet customers of a Cashel bar.*

a 12th-century Round Tower, more than 70ft to its pointed roof and still in a fine state of preservation.

The oldest part of this magnificent complex is Cormac's Chapel, with a doorway decorated with chevrons and the heads of dragons and humans. The interior contains a stone sarcophagus, carved with interlacing serpents, which may be the tomb of Cormac McCarthy (d.1138), King of Munster. He is thought to have erected the chapel between 1127 and 1134.

The entrance to the buildings is through the 15th-century Vicars Choral Hall, which once housed the choir members and is the only structure of its kind in Ireland. It now houses a museum, the focal point of which is St Patrick's Cross and Coronation Stone. The former location of the cross outside is now marked by a modern replica. The 7ft tall cross dates from the 12th century, and the robed figure on one face is said to be St Patrick. The pedestal supporting the cross is said to date from the 4th century, and tradition has it that it was the stone upon which the Kings of Munster were crowned.

St Patrick arrived at Cashel during the 5th century and baptised King Aengus and his son at the stone. During the ceremony Patrick carelessly drove his crozier through the king's foot. Asked later why he did not cry out in pain, the king replied that he had thought it was part of the baptismal rite.

**Museum and Rock** *June-Sept, 9am-6pm, although rock closes at 7.30pm. Oct-May, 10am-5pm, with rock closing Nov-Feb at 4.30pm. Tours can be arranged. Tel: (062) 61437.*

## Tipperary/Tiobraid Árann

Though modern developments have largely overtaken Tipperary town, known as 'Arann's well' in Irish, many interesting features remain, including monuments to some of its less law-abiding citizens. The statue of the Maid of Erin commemorates three men known as the Manchester Martyrs, who were executed in England in 1867 for killing a police officer while trying to rescue a Fenian prisoner. The maid is the personification of Ireland. Her statue stands in the middle of the road at the junction of Main Street and O'Brien Street, surrounded by some good examples of traditional shopfronts.

Another statue, outside the Allied Irish Bank, commemorates Charles Kickham (1828-82), a novelist, poet and revolutionary who spent four years in London's Pentonville

VIEW FROM A ROCK *The Round Tower on the Rock of Cashel surveys a patchwork landscape.*

prison in the 1860s. He was born, and died, in the village of Mullinahone, 10 miles northeast of Fethard, and based his novels, such as *Knocknagow*, published in 1879, on rural Irish life. The house where he lived, in Fethard Street, is marked with a plaque, and a Celtic cross stands over his grave in the Catholic churchyard.

There is also a park named after Sean Treacy, leader of the group said to have fired the first shots in the struggle for Irish independence in 1918-22. Nothing, however, commemorates Tipperary's most famous son Red Kelly (c.1820-64), who was deported to Tasmania for various crimes, and was the father of the celebrated Australian outlaw Ned Kelly (1855 80).

Tipperary is probably best known outside Ireland from the First World War marching song 'It's a long way to . . .'. The authors, Harry Williams and Jack Judge, were English and it is likely that they had never been to the town.

UNDER THE HAMMER *Local farmers gather at the cattle auctions in Tipperary town, the heart of the rich pasturelands of the Golden Vale.*

# THE TREASURES OF IRELAND

*Beauty and craftsmanship fused by a nation's masters of metalwork*

The recent discovery of gold in the rocks of Croagh Patrick, St Patrick's holy mountain in Mayo, has created a whirlwind of excitement and controversy among Irish people, and has involved the Church, which, naturally, objects to any excavation of this sacred site. The Church and the shaping of precious metals have been linked since the 7th century. But Irish metalworkers' expertise goes back even farther, to the Bronze Age (1750-c.500 BC), when Ireland's rich mineral deposits began to be exploited.

EARLY MINES AND ARTEFACTS Signs of ancient mining, dating back to about 1700 BC, have been found in Kerry, Tipperary and Cork. The mines on the slopes of Mount Gabriel in west Cork, preserved for centuries under layers of peat, are some of the few surviving prehistoric copper mines in Europe. Bronze Age miners squeezed down its 31 narrow 'drivings', or sloping shafts, one of which

reached 29½ft into the rock face, and used fire and mauls to loosen the rock. This they hauled above ground and crushed to separate the ore from the waste materials.

The first metal artefacts made in Ireland were flat copper axe heads, which were cast in a one-piece open stone mould and then hammered into their final shape. They were hardened by the addition of arsenic. Later, tin was added to the copper to make bronze.

At about the same time the first gold objects were being made, decorated with geometric patterns. Alluvial gold was certainly in good supply in the rivers of County Wicklow and possibly other parts of the country, such as the Sperrin Mountains in County Tyrone. The nuggets panned from these rivers were hammered into thin sheets of gold. They were then shaped into 'sun discs', circles of gold that were probably sewn onto clothes, and 'lunulae', half-moon-shaped collars. Raised designs of concentric

CELTIC PATTERNS *The Turoe stone in County Galway (above), a ritual stone from the 3rd to 2nd century BC, is covered with a curving pattern known as La Tène style. The design was later applied to metal and stylised, as in the spirals on this gilt-bronze plaque (left). An early image of the Crucifixion, it dates from about the 8th century AD. Interlacing and patterns using plant and animal motifs were developed later from La Tène, and can be seen on the arm shrine of St Lachtain (right). It was made in the early 12th century AD, from cast and engraved bronze panels inlaid with silver. Gold foil once covered the panels. The shrine was made to house relics of the saint.*

circles, cones and cable patterns were hammered into them from the back. These delicate, shining ornaments, a sign of wealth and superior social standing, were worn by chieftains and nobles.

From about 1200 BC onwards, goldsmiths started to experiment with twisting sheets of gold, inspired by the twisted jewellery that came to Ireland from the eastern Mediterranean. The bracelets and neck and body rings they produced, known as torcs, are masterpieces. The amount of gold used in some of these torcs is astonishing – one found on the Hill of Tara, County Meath, weighed nearly two pounds.

A new style of decoration, called La Tène, was introduced into Ireland in the 3rd century BC, during the Iron Age. It is named after the site of a 19th-century excavation in Switzerland, where objects were found decorated with curved lines, spirals and stylised plant, animal, bird and human forms. Irish craftsmen first used these designs on bronze objects – scabbards, spear butts and horse bits – and on iron spear heads. The style later spread to other artistic spheres, such as stone carving and manuscript illumination, and influenced Irish craftsmen for hundreds of years to come. It was during the Iron Age, too, that bronze pennanular brooches, hoop-shaped with a small gap and fastened with a free-swivelling pin, came into vogue. The ends of the hoop were often in the shape of various animals' heads.

THE CHRISTIAN INFLUENCE When Christianity was brought to Ireland in the 5th century, metalworkers found a new outlet for their skills in religious objects. The great monasteries, such as Armagh, Kildare and Clonmacnoise, became centres of cultural activity. While scribes were painstakingly copying the gospels and psalms, producing illuminated manuscripts of outstanding artistry, metalworkers were creating highly decorated objects of equal splendour – chalices, bells and shrines among them.

Pieces from the 7th to the 9th centuries are sumptuously decorated with precious metals – gold, silver, gold filigree and engraving. And glorious colours were added to the design by enamelling, coloured glass and semiprecious stones.

Among the most exciting finds from this period are the Tara brooch and the Ardagh

DOMHNACH AIRGID SHRINE *Silver-gilt plaques cast with figures cover the main face of this box, made around AD 800. Its name means 'silver shrine' and it depicts the Crucifixion and saints.*

chalice. The Tara brooch is a solid circle of cast silver-gilt, covered with sheets of gold foil and lavishly decorated with beaded, twisted and plaited wires of gold in the shape of stylised animals, scrolls and tight spirals, and embellished with amber and glass – all this on a circle that is less than 2in in diameter! The silver Ardagh chalice, inspired by Byzantine design, is beautifully made with gold filigree, glass studs and gilt bronze.

The Anglo-Norman invasion of Ireland in 1169, together with the introduction of continental monastic orders and continental styles of art and architecture, led to the decline of native Irish traditions and techniques. They were revived again in Georgian times, when silver teapots and services, coffee and chocolate pots were produced, mostly in Dublin, with a distinctive, unadorned, simple design. These pieces are rare and are collectors' items.

THE CELTIC REVIVAL In the mid-1800s, a number of scholars, among them Dublin antiquary George Petrie, brought early Irish art to the public's attention. Petrie used designs from two shrines and an illuminated gospel on the binding of one of his books, and

so opened the gates for a flood of Celtic-inspired motifs on silver, jewellery, furniture, books, stained glass and ceramics.

At the same time, early Irish art was inspiring craftsmen in England and Scotland, among them Manxman Archibald Knox, who became one of the most influential designers at Liberty & Co. Attracted by the curved lines and interlacings of early Celtic decoration, and by its use of enamelwork and gemstones, Knox designed pewter and silverware decorated with freely flowing Celtic motifs, which became the hallmark of Liberty style at the turn of the century.

Ireland continues to mine – although mostly for silver-bearing lead, and zinc. There is still some gold in the rivers of Wicklow and in the Sperrin Mountains, and even more impressive concentrations of gold-bearing rock in Mayo, Donegal and in several other parts of the country. But no leases have yet been granted to mine these areas.

Meanwhile, a small core of dedicated metalworkers, mainly gold and silversmiths, can still be found delicately hammering, skilfully engraving and lovingly decorating in their workshops, continuing a tradition that started in Ireland nearly 4000 years ago.

ARDAGH CHALICE *In 1868 a boy digging potatoes found this silver chalice, decorated with gilt bronze, gold filigree and glass studs, one of the finest works from the 1st millennium AD.*

DRESS JEWELLERY *Gold lock rings (left), which secured locks of hair, were worn by nobles, as were gold collars such as the Gleninsheen gorget (centre). This was made around 700 BC from a single sheet of gold with discs at each end. The Tara brooch (right), lavishly decorated with gold filigree, amber and coloured glass, was probably worn by a wealthy chief or a Church leader.*

# THE LEINSTER RIDGE

THE granite ridge that forms the lovely Wicklow and Blackstairs Mountains across the south-east corner of Ireland has given this region a distinctive character and history. For centuries it formed a barrier against invaders from the west. As a result, the inhabitants who settled on the fertile land between the mountains and the sea often had more to do with Wales and England, or points still farther east, than with the rest of Ireland. The coastal towns, Wexford, Wicklow and Arklow, and Waterford city, were Viking settlements. Their names reflect their Viking origin – Weissfjord, 'the ford of the goddess Weiss'; Wyking Lo, 'Viking meadow'.

Counties Kilkenny, Carlow, Wexford and Wicklow all form the southern part of the province of Leinster, which also stretched northwards across the midlands. County Waterford has variously been part of Leinster and Munster, settling finally for the latter. When the King of Leinster, Dermot Macmurrough, invited the Anglo-Normans to help him in his struggle against the High King of Ireland, their armies under Strongbow came through Waterford, and quickly established Anglo-Norman supremacy along this strategic coast. But the hinterland remained in the hands of Celtic chiefs – clans such as the O'Tooles and the O'Byrnes – who pestered the Anglo-Normans from their retreats in the Wicklow Mountains.

The dominant family throughout this period was the Butlers, Earls of Ormonde, who based themselves in the massive castle of Kilkenny and ruled from there for 550 years. Their great rivals were the FitzGeralds, Earls of Desmond, from neighbouring Munster, but they found a common enemy in Cromwell. In 1642, the ruling Irish families formed an alliance called the Confederation of Kilkenny to fight against the rule of Protestant England during the 'Great Rebellion' of the 1640s. But they paid dearly for their stand. The result was a new order which saw the replacement of the old Anglo-Norman and Irish families by Protestant landlords 'planted' by the English Crown.

MONASTIC CALM *A horse grazes the sweet pastures in front of Glendalough monastery.*

WILD AND WINDY MOORS *Melting snow glistens on the Wicklow Mountains, once the refuge of bandits.*

163

**INDEX OF TOURING AREAS**

But the south-east did not forswear its traditions of dissidence. It was the focus of the 1798 rebellion of United Irishmen under Father John Murphy, against the British administration, and also produced Charles Stewart Parnell, member of parliament and a key figure in the land reform movement of the late 19th century. He lived at Avondale, County Wicklow, where his home is now a museum.

Today's invaders are the holidaymakers who come from all over Ireland and from across the sea, via Rosslare Harbour, near Wexford. This is the sunniest corner of Ireland. The coast is fringed with long ribbons of silver sand and fine beaches, such as Jack's Hole and Brittas Bay. The hills are a delightful mixture of wooded glens and open, undulating uplands. Roads wind through pretty valleys and bold tracts of bog to the 'Gaps', the old passes to the interior. The wild beauty of Glendalough provides the setting for one of Ireland's most endearing early Christian monuments, the tiny stone-roofed chapel called Kevin's

Kitchen, and its accompanying Round Tower. The contrast between tamed and unfettered nature is beautifully exploited at Powerscourt, where the formal gardens have views across a lake to the weathered pinnacle called the Great Sugar Loaf. Other gardens worth visiting are at Mount Usher.

There are two notable houses open to the public within striking distance of Dublin: Kilruddery House, a rare and elegant survivor from the 17th century; and Russborough House, a splendid Palladian house designed in the mid-18th century by Richard Cassel, which now contains the Beit art collection.

The landscape opens out towards the south in the hinterland to the towns of Wexford and Waterford. County Waterford is in some ways the south-east writ small, with a pretty coastline rising through an undulating landscape of pasture to the Comeragh, Monavullagh and Knockmealdown Mountains. It was settled by a Celtic tribe called the Deisi, and the county is still widely referred to as 'The Decies'. To the north, Kilkenny clips the corner of the limestone country which fills the central regions of Ireland. Visitors to the Dunmore Caves there can follow paths which worm their way through an architecture of fantastical limestone pillars.

The south-eastern coastline, chiselled by the estuaries of the Rivers Slaney, Barrow, Suir and Blackwater, breaks up into beaches and rocky peninsulas, joined by paths that lead over grassy headlands dotted with sea pinks and sea campion. The broad expanses of wetlands round Dungarvan and Tramore are visiting stops for migratory waders and for wintering brent geese. The Slobs, reclaimed land near Wexford town, is a temporary stopover for the largest concentration of migrating Greenland white-fronted geese in the world.

The River Barrow is navigable, and cruisers from the Grand Canal in the midlands can drop down through some fine hill scenery as far south as St Mullin's. The Barrow is also fished for its salmon and trout, while the Blackwater and Slaney are noted salmon rivers. For golfers there is a major seaside links at Rosslare, and a further five agreeable parkland courses making up the so-called South-East Six. Cultural events are offered too: Waterford hosts a celebrated Light Opera Festival; Kilkenny has an arts week in August; and Wexford has an Opera Festival respected for its high-quality productions.

BEACONS OF DANGER *White columns on the clifftops at Great Newton Head warn ships away from the ragged coast.*

165

# Beyond the Walls of the Pale

*Reminders of yesterday's privations exist alongside signs of prosperity in the rolling farmland of northern Carlow. Anglers pit their wits against salmon and perch near great houses surrounded by Famine Walls that were built in the 19th century to provide work and money for starving families. Once-mighty Anglo-Norman castles have now been claimed by nature, and shelter only grazing cattle and sheep.*

### Altamont Gardens

The driveway of Altamont Gardens becomes a river of nodding daffodils in spring. A great sweep of them leads from the Georgian gates to the house and gardens – which offer at least four different kinds of garden experience. First there are formal gardens, with lawns, roses, rare trees, rhododendrons and a tree-shaded nuns' walk that dates back to the 17th century. Next there is the tranquillity of a large, tree-fringed lake which was dug out in the Famine years to give work to local people. Then a magical woodland walk

DUCKETT'S EXTRAVAGANZA *Gothic Revival towers and turrets and ivy tumbling over the walls make Duckett's Grove an enchanted fairy-tale castle.*

ALTAMONT GARDENS *A statue graces the lakeside garden, surrounded by water-loving plants.*

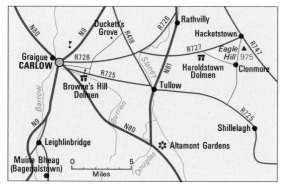

### OTHER PLACES TO SEE
**Duckett's Grove** 2m NE of Carlow, Georgian home of noted Anglo-Irish Duckett family. House later rebuilt as Gothic Revival castle. Scene of celebrated legal case in 1921 between local farmers who bought the land and Bank of Ireland which made them a loan. The dispute centred on how the farmers should divide the land, or pay back the money. The castle burnt down in 1933 and its remains now house a riding school.

**Haroldstown Dolmen** 2m S of Rathvilly. Well-preserved Stone Age burial chamber, with capstones across supporting stones.

### EVENTS
**Carlow Open Golf Week** June.
**Carlow Regatta** June.
**Tullow Horse Show** Aug.

### SPORT
**Angling** Coarse fishing: River Barrow. Game fishing: Rivers Burren, Douglas and Slaney.
**Boating** River Barrow.
**Canoeing** Rivers Barrow and Slaney.
**Golf** Carlow Golf Club, 18-hole course. Tel: (0503) 31695.

### INFORMATION
Kilkenny Tourist Office.
Tel: (056) 21755.

crosses a glen where rare trees and native oaks grow beside huge, moss-covered boulders that were brought down by Ice Age glaciers 10,000 years ago. Add to these a riverside walk beside the swift waters of the Slaney, and Altamont's four faces are revealed.

Altamont's bird life ranges from introduced peacocks to native herons, chiffchaffs and willow warblers. Otters can be seen in the Slaney, and in summer the riverside path is bejewelled with darting peacock butterflies. The house is not open to the public.
**Opening times** *Easter-Oct, Sun only, 2-6pm, or by appointment. Tel: (0503) 57128.*

### Carlow/Ceatharlach

The county capital, Carlow was once an outpost that had to provide its own defence as it was isolated from the Pale around Dublin, which the Anglo-Normans ruled and defended. Carlow developed around a massive Norman keep, built in 1207-13 to guard a strategic crossing of the River Barrow. Today the keep is in ruins, home only to the pigeons that flutter over it.

As befits a frontier town, Carlow's history is turbulent. Lionel, Duke of Clarence, built a wall around it in 1361, but town and castle fell to Art MacMurrough Kavanagh in 1405 and were put to the torch. It was taken again by Rory Óg O'More in 1577. The castle was besieged by Cromwell's forces in 1650, and when it fell the garrison was slaughtered.

But even Cromwell left the castle in better condition than it is now. The main harm was done by a local man, a Dr Middleton, who bought the castle and turned it into a lunatic asylum in 1814. Wanting to enlarge the windows, the intrepid doctor decided to use gunpowder. The explosion blew the castle apart, leaving only the shell of the keep and its corner towers.

Some 16 years earlier, Carlow had been a flashpoint of the 1798 Rebellion against the English. On the morning of May 25, about 4000 poorly armed rebels marched on the town. It seemed deserted as they swarmed through its streets, but they had walked into an ambush. They emerged from Tullow Street into a hail of musket fire. Many ran in panic into nearby houses, but these were set alight. More than 500 were killed in the Battle of Carlow and another 200 were executed later. The remains of 417 rebels were buried across the River Barrow, at Graigue, a site known as the Croppie Grave.

Today's town surrounds the castle walls, and has a number of Georgian houses and

PERIOD STYLE *Nineteenth-century shopfronts make Carlow an attractive county capital.*

some nostalgic 19th-century shopfronts. George Bernard Shaw's aunt lived in Carlow and Shaw donated to the town, among other gifts, the 18th-century building that is now the public library. A plaque to Shaw describes him as a 'self-styled world-betterer'.

Carlow Museum, at the back of the Town Hall, contains some interesting relics of local life, including a Victorian kitchen complete with a 'crane' for swinging pots over the open fire, and a settle bed – a plain wooden bench by day that opened out to become a bed at night. Also on display is the trapdoor

MAY OFFERINGS *Outside Carlow a May bush is decorated with rags in the pagan tradition.*

of the gallows that was used for public executions outside Carlow Jail. The last, in 1820, attracted a crowd of 20,000.

Carlow's courthouse is one of the finest neoclassical buildings in Ireland. It was built in 1830 by Sir Richard Morrison in the Ionic style, with 12 columns supporting the roof.

Squatting like a watchdog next to the lofty Gothic Revival cathedral (1828-33), with its 155ft lantern tower, is the solid St Patrick's College, one of the oldest seminaries in Ireland. It was opened in 1795 to educate priests, following a relaxation of the penal laws that banned Catholic teaching.

Across the roofs of Carlow is the tower of St Mary's, the Church of Ireland parish church. The nave dates from the early 18th century and there is a fine east window. The tower was added in 1834. In the former Scotch Church on Athy Road there is a genealogical centre which advises visitors on ancestral research.

Off the Hacketstown road, in the demesne of Browne's Hill House, stands the grave of a Stone Age chieftain. Browneshill Dolmen, almost 4000 years old, has a massive granite capstone, an estimated 100 tons, the largest in Ireland. Alongside the path leading from the dolmen to the Browne's Hill Road

are examples of so-called Carlow fencing – granite posts, V-shaped at the top, with granite slabs laid across them. This kind of fencing was commonly used in Carlow in the 19th century.

**Carlow Museum** *Tues-Sun 2.30-5.30pm. Tel: (0503) 42666.*
**Carlow Genealogical Centre** *Tel: (0503) 42399.*

### Hacketstown/Baile Haicéid

Rebels on their way back from the Battle of Carlow were ambushed in Hacketstown, and the bloody fighting between rebels and yeomanry continued until 250 rebels lay dead. Today, Hacketstown is a more peaceful place as a centre for walking in the Wicklow Mountains. The 975ft summit of Eagle Hill, a mile south of the town, gives a view that takes in most of County Carlow.

To the south is Clonmore, site of the 13th-century de Lacy castle, now a picturesque ruin. Ivy is rampant over its 7ft thick walls and cattle graze placidly in the bailey where chain-mailed Norman knights once caroused and quarrelled. The castle changed hands several times before it finally fell to Cromwell in 1650. The north-east tower, known as the Six Windows, is well preserved.

Near the castle, the road cuts through a monastery that was founded in the 6th century by St Mogue. The overgrown churchyard contains a large number of early Christian cross-decorated stones. Their number is an indication of the region's importance in the early days of Christianity.

### Rathvilly/Ráth Bhile

Three times in the early 1970s Rathvilly won Ireland's Tidiest Towns Award. This gave local pride a fillip that is still evident in this neat village. In the centre is a monument to Kevin Barry, a local boy who joined the fight for Irish freedom. He was captured, and executed at the age of 18 in Mountjoy Jail, Dublin, in 1920. The deed is remembered in one of the best known of the rebel songs, *The Ballad of Kevin Barry*:

*Early on a Monday morning*
*High upon a gallows tree*
*Kevin Barry gave his young life*
*For the cause of liberty*

In the 5th century, Crimthan, King of Leinster, lived at Rathvilly. He was notorious as a persecutor of Christians until he was converted and baptised by St Patrick.

### Tullow/An Tulach

The town of Tullow is an excellent base for touring the northern part of County Carlow. A statue of Father John Murphy, a leader of the 1798 Rebellion, stands in the market square, near where he was hanged. His vestments are on display at Tullow Museum.

**Tullow Museum** *Tues 10am-4pm, Wed and Fri 2-6pm, Thur 11am-4pm, Sun 2.30-5.30pm. Tel: (0503) 51337.*

MIGHTY MONOLITH *The capstone of Browneshill Dolmen is one of Europe's heaviest.*

---

### THE GRANITE MUSHROOM

Outcrops of granite occur in many parts of Carlow, and local farmers – like those the world over – have put the materials at hand to good use. At Altamont Gardens there are some good examples of the staddle – a device that looks like a granite mushroom.

Before the days of combine harvesters, as late as the 1940s, sheaves of corn would be leaned against each other in the fields to dry in stooks, then later stored in strawricks. A base was made for the ricks using a wheel-like arrangement of staddles, so that rats could not get at the corn – any trying to do so would be unable to climb around the underside of the 'mushroom'.

# A Vision of Versailles

*Some of the roads in the foothills of the Blackstairs Mountains twist and turn so much that, to use the colourful idiom of the local people, 'you'd need to put hinges on a maggot to get round them'. But any amount of twisting and turning is made worth while by the sheer prettiness of southern Carlow, a land steeped in legends of the saints and abounding in charming villages and ruined castles.*

### Borris/An Bhuiríos

The Blackstairs Mountains form a dramatic backdrop to Borris, a Georgian town overlooking the River Barrow. The imposing gatehouse of Borris House, home of the Kavanagh family, is on the main street, but it is not open to the public.

Borris is a good starting point for walking in the Blackstairs. The road south out of the town passes under an impressive viaduct to nowhere. It was built over difficult terrain in the 1860s, when a branch of the railway line was brought down to Borris and Palace East from Muine Bheag (Bagenalstown), but the spur line was abandoned long ago.

At Killoughternane, 5 miles north-east of Borris, a tiny church overlooks the road. It has antae, or projecting walls, an architectural feature that goes back to the temples of ancient Greece. The church was founded by St Fortchern in the late 5th century, although the existing roofless ruins are later.

Hillview Museum, near Corries Cross Roads, 4 miles north of Borris, houses a pleasingly informal jumble of old farming implements and household equipment. There are 100-year-old wind-up gramophones in working order, a collection of ploughs including one which was pulled by a donkey, and an early washing machine in which the tub, as well as the wooden mangle, was turned by hand.

### Huntington Castle

The elegance of Huntington Castle, built at Clonegall in 1625 by Lord Esmond, caught the eye of director Stanley Kubrick, who chose it as the location for his 1975 film *Barry Lyndon*. The castle occupies the site of a monastery, of which little remains except a 600-year-old yew walk, the branches curving over to form a long, cool tunnel. A vine that grows vigorously in the conservatory comes from a cutting that was given to Ann Boleyn (1507-36) by Cardinal Wolsey.

The castle was occupied by Cromwell's men in the 1640s but its dungeon was used as recently as 1921, when the IRA – who occupied the castle briefly – locked up a number of people, including the cook.

For those who like their history spiced with a little mystery, Huntington also offers connections with the Egyptian goddess Isis. The owner of the castle, the Reverend Lawrence Durdin-Robertson, founded the Fellowship of Isis in 1976 along with his wife and his sister. Shrines to the goddess have been set up in the castle's cellars.

**Opening times** *Guided tours only, mid-Mar to Oct, Sun 2.30-5pm. Craft centre. Tel: (054) 77552.*

### Leighlinbridge/Leithghlinn an Droichid

Much of the little town of Leighlinbridge on the River Barrow has the air of an earlier century, with its ruined castle standing guard over the 14th-century bridge, old malt houses rising behind it and walks on the river banks.

The town's original Black Castle, built in 1181, was one of the earliest Norman fortresses in Ireland. It was granted to John de Claville by Hugh de Lacy, the powerful Norman baron who governed Ireland for Henry II. The present castle was built by Sir Edward Bellingham in 1547 and fell to Cromwell's forces in 1650.

The nine-arched bridge across the Barrow, built in 1320 by Maurice Jakis, is said to be the oldest functioning bridge in Ireland. Close by the castle is the site of Ireland's first Carmelite monastery, built in 1272. Half a mile to the south are the remains of Dinn Righ, 'fort of the kings', the ancient palace of the Kings of Leinster. All that remains is a low mound inside a wooded fence.

Size for size, Leighlinbridge has produced as many famous sons as any Irish town. The dashing Captain Myles Keogh, of the Battle of Little Big Horn fame, was born there, as were Cardinal Patrick Moran (1830-1911), Archbishop of Sydney and Australia's first

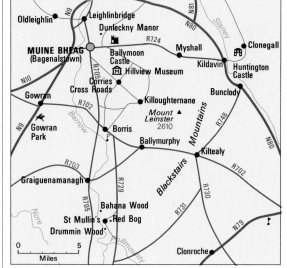

Compelling views from summit; hang-gliding on lower slopes most Suns.

**WALKS**
**Bahana Wood** Near St Mullin's.
**Muine Bheag** Towpaths along canal.
**South Leinster Way** 58m walk from Kildavin to Carrick-on-Suir.
**Wicklow Way** 82m walk from Clonegall to Dublin.

**EVENTS**
**Borris Open Golf Week** 3rd week in July.
**Borris Pattern Day** Mid-Aug.
**Clonegall Village Fair** End July.

**SPORT**
**Angling** Coarse and game fishing: River Barrow.
**Boating** River Barrow.
**Golf** Borris Golf Club, 9-hole course. Tel: (0503) 73143.
**Hang-gliding** Blackstairs Mountains.

**INFORMATION**
Kilkenny Tourist Office. Tel: (056) 21755.

**OTHER PLACES TO SEE**
**Ballymoon Castle** 2m E of Muine Bheag; remains of Anglo-Norman 14th-century castle. Square central enclosure is protected by crumbling towers, 20ft high, 8ft thick walls and a keep.

**Mount Leinster** Highest peak (2610ft) in Blackstairs range, NE of Borris, on Carlow-Wexford border. Nine stones on northern side said to be meeting place of nine kings, or to mark the right of nine families to graze sheep.

ROADSIDE RUIN *The remains of an early Christian church overlook the road at Killoughternane.*

PAGAN PLACE *In the depths of Huntington Castle candles and incense burn in the Temple of Isis, the centre of a cult with a worldwide following.*

cardinal, and Professor John Tyndall (1820-93), a brilliant physicist who in 1867 succeeded Michael Faraday as President of the Royal Institution in London. Among many other achievements, Tyndall explained why the sky looks blue. The ancestors of Canada's Premier Brian Mulroney also hail from there.

## Muine Bheag/Bagenalstown

This quiet little canalside town is a dream that did not quite come true. William Bagenal, of nearby Dunleckny Manor, founded the town in the 18th century, when it was known as Bagenalstown. He planned it to be a hub of commerce, with buildings to vie with the finest of classical times, and made an encouraging start with a number of imposing buildings, including a stately courthouse modelled on the Parthenon in Athens. Bagenal planned to call his town Versailles, after the palace of France's Sun King, Louis XIV. But that idea came to nothing, like the rest of his plans. For Bagenal thought he could bring a coach road through the town, but the decision went against him. Bagenalstown became a backwater, saved only by the arrival of the railway in the mid-19th century. Its neoclassical railway station is almost as impressive as the courthouse.

Today, 20th-century buildings block the view of the courthouse, but it is still possible to catch an occasional glimpse of Bagenal's vision of the town that might have been. The best view is from beside the canal on the road from Leighlinbridge. The panorama includes the spire of St Andrew's Catholic church and the fine tower of the 1841 St Mary's Church

## CHARMS THAT DECEIVE

Wild flowers that once were widespread in Ireland are now becoming rarities as the old boglands are drained and the old permanent pasturelands vanish. But a few places in Carlow have remained undisturbed, among them St Mullin's Red Bog, the Bahana and Drummin woods, and Pollmounty River valley, and in these can be found such plants as the round-leaved sundew, *Drosera rotundifolia*, an insect eater, and the bee orchid, *Ophrys apifera*, an insect deceiver.

The sundew gets its name from the glistening drops of sticky fluid carried on the end of the tiny hairs that cover its leaves. Early naturalists thought this fluid was dew, and midges make the same mistake. When they land to lay their eggs, they are trapped by the stickiness, enfolded in the leaves

*Ophrys apifera*

*Drosera rotundifolia*

and ingested by the plant. Medieval herbalists prized the 'dew' for its supposed magical qualities and used it to burn off warts and to excite lust in cattle.

The bee orchid is designed to deceive bees, but in Ireland this is a case of charm to a degree over and above the demands of necessity. The orchid produces flowers that bear a striking resemblance to bumblebees at rest on its leaves. On the Continent, the deception is carried through to its logical conclusion. Male bees are enticed to land on the flowers and attempt to mate with them. In doing so they pick up pollen which is then passed on to other bee orchids, so bringing about pollination. The ruse is unnecessary in Ireland because the local bee orchids pollinate themselves early in the year, before any bees arrive on the scene.

ANCIENT GREECE REVIVED *Muine Bheag's courthouse was modelled on the Parthenon.*

## HE DIED WITH HIS BOOTS ON

In the 1941 film *They Died With Their Boots On*, starring Errol Flynn, a British officer teaches the US 7th Cavalry a jaunty tune called *Garryowen*. The incident is based on fact, but the officer was Irish rather than English. Captain Myles Keogh, born in 1840 at Orchard House, Leighlinbridge, rode and died with Colonel Custer at the Battle of Little Big Horn against the Sioux, in 1876. But even before that famous massacre, his life had been full of adventure.

When Garibaldi and his Redshirts were uniting Italy in the 1860s, Keogh was among the 700 or so young Irishmen who volunteered to join the pope's army, to protect the Papal States. He was only 20 years old when he was taken prisoner at the Battle of Ancona.

After his release, young Myles looked around for another war, and soon found one across the Atlantic – the American Civil War. He joined the Union side and made a reputation as a daring leader of cavalry on raids deep behind the Southern lines. Keogh emerged unscathed from that war, and at the age of 25 was in charge of a brigade of 3000 men, holding the rank of brevet lieutenant-colonel.

To stay in the US Army after the war, Myles took a drop in rank and it was as Captain Keogh that he joined Custer's newly formed 7th Cavalry. It was said that Keogh was one of the last to die, and that as a mark of respect he was not scalped or otherwise mutilated after the battle. His horse, Comanche, was still alive when the battle was over – the only living thing on the army side.

of Ireland church, added in 1855. The townspeople voted to change the town's name to Muine Bheag (pronounced 'Moon é Beg'), or 'little shrubbery', in the 1950s, but many locals still refer to it as Bagenalstown.

Dunleckny Manor, built in 1835 a mile north-east of Bagenalstown, incorporates the original manor of 1610 and was designed in the Tudor Gothic style with oriel windows. It has been restored to its former glory and is now open to visitors.

**Dunleckny Manor** *Guided tours by appointment. Tel: (0503) 21932.*

### Myshall/Míseal

The village of Myshall, with Mount Leinster and the Blackstairs range towering above it, contains a surprise – a church that is reminiscent of Salisbury Cathedral. It was built by an Englishman, John Duguid of Dover, around the graves of his wife and daughter.

His daughter, Constance, was on holiday when she met a young man from a Carlow family, the Cornwall-Bradys, and fell in love. Tragedy struck when Constance was killed in the 1890s in a hunting accident. Her dying wish was to be buried in the old churchyard at Myshall in the land she loved, near the man she loved. Her father carried out her wish and raised a statue over the grave.

Mrs Duguid died in 1903, and her last wish was to be buried beside her daughter. The distraught Mr Duguid decided to build a memorial church over both graves. He took Salisbury Cathedral as his model, redesigning it as a church. Fine craftsmanship abounds, from the Art Nouveau floor tiles and font to the muted greens, russets and silver of the stained-glass windows.

One of Myshall's famous sons was Peter Fenelon Collier (1849-1909), the founder of *Collier's Magazine*, an illustrated general weekly. He arrived in the United States penniless at the age of 16 and completed his education at a seminary. Starting with a borrowed $35, he was the first man to sell books on the instalment plan. Collier eventually built a publishing empire worth $12 million.

### Old Leighlin/Seanleighlinn

The stubby, crenellated tower of the 13th-century St Lazerian Protestant cathedral stands at Old Leighlin. And nearby is the site of a 7th-century monastery and Lazerian's Well – a place of pilgrimage that after 13 centuries still attracts offerings of medals, crucifixes and rosary beads. The monastery

ROYAL BURIAL GROUND *St Mullin's Church was the burial place of the Kings of South Leinster.*

played a major role in the history of Irish Christianity. It once had 1500 monks, and a synod was held there in 630 to decide the date of Easter that year. St Lazerian, who died in 639, was the pope's delegate to Ireland. The only relics of his monastery are St Lazerian's Cross and Well. The cathedral, refreshingly simple inside, has a Gothic doorway and details from the 13th and 15th centuries. It houses two fonts: a plain one thought to be 11th century, and a 13th-century one with only fluting for decoration.

The Carey family, who run the public house across the road from the cathedral, say theirs is the oldest single-family pub in Ireland – a claim hard to refute, since they have been the publicans since 1542. One of their forebears, Denis Carey, was executed after the 1798 Rebellion, and his gravestone is in the churchyard. On his way to execution, after he had refused under flogging to inform against any of his comrades, he asked his wife what would become of her. 'God and the good neighbours will look after myself and the children,' was her steadfast reply. 'Make no other widows but me.'

### St Mullin's/Tigh Moling

On the east bank of the River Barrow is St Mullin's, a place of history and of legend. A monastery was founded there in the 7th century by St Moling, a prince, poet, artist and artisan, as well as a priest. It is said that he

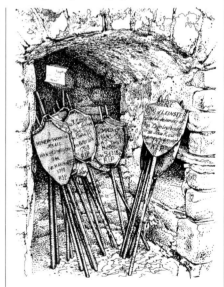

HEROES REMEMBERED *Memorial shields at St Mullin's commemorate some of the men buried there, among them Art MacMurrough.*

dug a mile-long watercourse with his own hands to power his mill – a task that took seven years. He became Bishop of Ferns, died in 697 and was buried at St Mullin's. St Moling's watercourse is still there, but

the original monastery burnt down in 1138. An abbey was built on the site later, in the Middle Ages. A 9th-century High Cross stands outside the remains of the abbey and there are also some domestic medieval buildings, including one that has an unusual diamond-shaped window.

The most notable monument in the packed little churchyard is a penal altar, used in the days when the anti-Catholic penal laws were in force. A Norman motte, once topped by a wooden castle, stands outside the churchyard, and when Mass was being said at the altar some of the congregation would climb the motte to act as lookouts.

A number of South Leinster kings are buried in the churchyard, among them the warrior Art MacMurrough. There is also the grave of Father Daniel Kavanagh, who died in 1813 and is said to have had the gift of healing. People still claim that to cure toothache you should take a pinch of earth from outside the churchyard and exchange it for a pinch of clay from Father Kavanagh's grave. Then say a brief prayer, pop the clay into your mouth and walk down the hill to wash it out with water from St Moling's well – not forgetting to leave an offering.

Every summer on the Sunday before July 25, Mass is held at the penal altar for thousands of people, who visit the graves, draw water from the holy well and take their distresses and ailments to Father Kavanagh and St Moling.

The finely proportioned 19th-century Church of Ireland church at St Mullin's is no longer in use, but there is talk of turning it into a museum. Protestants and Catholics lie side by side in the churchyard, and a story is told in the village of the days when, because there were only a handful of Protestants in the neighbourhood, the local Church of Ireland bishop was thinking of closing down the church. The distraught vicar had a word with the Catholic priest, who had a word with his flock, and on the day of the bishop's visit Catholic families filled the Protestant church, joining in the responses and lustily singing Protestant hymns. The bishop went home delighted and the church remained open.

## THE REMARKABLE MR KAVANAGH

When Arthur MacMurrough Kavanagh (right) was born and held up for his mother to see, she said: 'Thank God the child was born to me and not to anybody else.' For the baby had no arms or legs – only stumps where they should have been. The year was 1831, and a poor family in Borris would have been devastated by the extra hardship of raising a crippled child. But Lady Harriet was one of the Kavanaghs of Borris Hall, the richest landowners in the area, tracing their ancestry back through the ancient Kings of Leinster to 1180 BC.

There was some talk in the village of a peasant's curse, because Arthur's father had turned Protestant. And Lady Harriet rejected her son until his older brothers died and he became the family heir.

Arthur turned out to be the kind of son who took every chance offered. He was given his first pony at the age of four and, strapped to the saddle, controlled the reins by means of a hook tied to his shoulders. He became admired as a fearless horseman when he rode to hounds. He taught himself to fish, to sail, to fell trees, to shoot, even to draw and paint. On a trip to India, he bagged a tiger.

Arthur became head of the family when his brother died in a fire. One of the first things he needed was a wife, and in 1855 he married his cousin, Frances Leathley. They were to have six healthy children. As a prominent landlord, he threw himself into improving the life of his tenants with all the energy of a mid-Victorian reformer. He largely rebuilt the villages of Borris and Ballyragget, brought the railway line down to Borris, built a sawmill and established a local lace industry.

In 1866, he took this energy into national politics, becoming the Conservative Member of Parliament first for County Wexford, then for County Carlow. He lost his seat in 1880 and died nine years later, but the remarkable Mr Kavanagh remains the only totally limbless man ever to sit in the House of Commons.

# Town of Fighting Cats

*'If you ever go to Kilkenny, look for the Hole-in-the-Wall. You'll get 24 eggs for a penny and butter for nothing at all . . .' The old song reflects a land whose pastures and dairies are the source of its wealth. On peaceful meadows of long grass, Friesian cattle graze around ruined Norman castles and abbeys. Yet Kilkenny town was the seat of medieval Irish parliaments and a rival in importance to Dublin.*

## Dunmore Cave

Described in folklore as 'the mouth of a huge wild beast, with ten thousand teeth above his head and as many under his feet', the entrance to this series of limestone caverns is not at all sinister today. Where daylight dims, wild flowers give way to ferns and mosses.

The subdued electric lighting reveals stalactites and stalagmites, lace-like frettings of calcite over the cavern walls and enormous hanging formations like batteries of organ pipes, made over thousands of years by the slow drip of the lime-charged water. One of them, the so-called Market Cross, is 20ft across. There is little to suggest that here, according to legend, Luchtigern – the monster 'Lord of the Mice' – was slaughtered. Nor that the bones of 50 people, mainly women and children, were discovered here in 1973. The bones are presumed to have been the remains of refugees who fled a Viking raid in the early 10th century and who either starved or suffocated, or were killed by the Vikings. A small museum explains the caves' geology and archaeology.

**Guided tours** *Mid-Mar to mid-June, 10am-5pm, exc Mon; mid-June to mid-Sept, 10am-7pm; mid-Sept to mid-Mar, Sat, Sun and public holidays, 10am-5pm. Tel: (056) 67726.*

## Freshford/Achadh Úr

This little Georgian town lies below the softly curved Slieveardagh Hills. Its low, colour-washed houses group around a neat green which has a wheeled water pump and the remains of a cross. In one corner stands a church founded in the 7th century.

St Lachtain, who died in AD 622, built the original church. It was rebuilt in the early 1100s and its richly decorated Irish-Romanesque porch was incorporated into the present church, rebuilt again, in 1730, for Protestant worship. It bears an inscription in ancient Irish asking passers-by to pray for the souls of the builders. The 12th-century reliquary containing the saint's arm and hand is in the National Museum, Dublin.

FRESHFORD GREEN *A wheeled water pump faces Georgian cottages across the village green.*

BENNETTSBRIDGE SPONGEWARE *A sponge dipped in colour is used to decorate a pot.*

## Kells/Ceanannas

The Augustinian priory of Kells – in full, Kells-in-Ossory (or Ceanannas Osraighe), to distinguish it from its more famous namesake in County Meath – was founded by Geoffrey FitzRobert in 1183, shortly after the Anglo-Norman invasion. It was to house the monks he brought to Ireland from Bodmin in Cornwall. For safety, later monks surrounded their 5 acres with a wall that would not have disgraced a castle, and added defensive towers for good measure.

The priory church, domestic buildings, chapels and prior's castle, all built after the 12th century in grey stone, now lie in ruins, approached through a sloping meadow. There are numerous High Crosses, and on the slopes behind is a peaceful little stream.

## Kilkenny/Cill Chainnigh

Before the Normans came in the 12th century, Kilkenny's houses clung to the 6th-century monastery of St Canice and the settlement was the capital of Ossory, a sub-kingdom of Leinster. But the strategic possibilities of the hilltop site were quickly grasped by William Marshal, Earl of Pembroke, who built a castle there in 1192.

At times, Kilkenny vied with Dublin in importance, and numerous Irish parliaments were held there. In 1391 the lordship was bought by James Butler, 3rd Earl of Ormonde, one of a family that figured prominently in Ireland's uneasy history.

The castle was the principal seat of the Ormondes from 1391 to 1935, and during that time evolved from medieval castle to Restoration chateau to Victorian country house. It is this last period that most influences the interior. The long picture gallery with painted beams contains portraits by Kneller, Lely, Van Dyke and the pre-Raphaelites. Kilkenny Castle saw its last struggle in the Civil War of 1922, when it was taken over by Anti-Treatyites (who opposed the treaty with Britain dividing Ireland). But they surrendered peaceably after two days.

The castle's creeper-clad walls rear above the clear waters of the River Nore. Its great drum towers make it look a mixture of a child's toy fort and French chateau. It occupies three sides of a square – the fourth was destroyed in 1659, opening up a splendid view across parkland to distant hills.

St Canice's Anglican cathedral, built in 1280 on the site of the original monastery, incorporates some of the remains. The tall

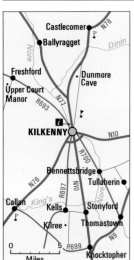

**OTHER PLACES TO SEE**

**Bennettsbridge** Between Kilkenny and Thomastown. 'Sponge' and stoneware potteries. Associated with leatherworkers, silversmiths and glass studio as well.

**Kilree** About 1m S of Kells; chapel with 96ft capless Round Tower. Adjoining field has large carved cross said by some to mark the grave of Niall Caille, a 9th-century king of Ireland.

**Tullaherin** Near Bennettsbridge. Folk museum containing traditional household and farm implements. May-Aug, Sun 3-5pm.

**EVENTS**
**Annual Antique Automobile**
**Auction** Freshford, Upper Court Manor, Sept. Tel: (056) 32174.

**Festival of Kilkenny** Mid-Mar.

**Hurling** Kilkenny, Sun in summer.

**Kilkenny Arts Week** Mid-Aug to late Aug.

**Thomas Moore Weekend** Kilkenny, early Oct.

**SPORT**
**Angling** Game fishing: Rivers Dinin and Nore.

**Golf** Castlecomer Golf Club, 9-hole course. Tel: (056) 41139.
Kilkenny Golf Club, 18-hole course. Tel: (056) 22125.

**INFORMATION**
Kilkenny Tourist Office. Tel: (056) 21755.

tower to one side was used by the monks for refuge. Despite damage by Cromwell's forces, the cathedral remains one of the finest places of worship still in use in Ireland.

It contains black marble monuments to lords, ladies and bishops, and to Edmund Purcell, 16th-century captain of the Ormondes' notorious gallowglasses, or mercenaries. Near this monument is the 12th-century font and St Kieran's chair, built into the cathedral walls and still used in the enthronement of the bishops of Ossory. The bishops' palace and library stand in the churchyard. The library was founded in 1679 and contains 3000 works from the 15th, 16th and 17th centuries, as well as the Red Book of Ossory, a 15th-century manuscript which chronicles the lives of early saints.

Among Kilkenny's other churches is St Mary's Cathedral, 1849, which has a 200ft tower. It contains a statue of the Virgin by

SERENE EFFIGIES *The 8th Earl of Ormonde, Piers Butler, and his wife Margaret lie immortalised in stone in St Canice's Cathedral.*

Giovanni Benzoni (1809-73). An older religious establishment is the Black Abbey, still occupied by Dominicans (the 'Black Friars') 700 years after its foundation, and incorporating the church established by William Marshal in 1225. It has a 13th-century alabaster statue of the Holy Trinity and a pre-Reformation statue – much knocked about – of St Dominic, carved from Irish oak. By the abbey is Black Freren Gate, the only medieval town gate left, named after the Black Friars.

Among Kilkenny's secular buildings, the most important include Rothe House, built by the merchant John Rothe in 1594 (restored 1966). The expansion of his family of 12 children meant he had to build two further houses around cobbled courtyards. The three are now linked and contain the museum and library of Kilkenny Archaeological Society. Opposite is the county courthouse, built in 1794 over a grey, bar-windowed building that in 1220 was Grace's Castle and then later a prison.

Nearby is a Tudor almshouse, a rarity in Ireland. It was built by the lawyer Sir Richard Shee in 1584 and now houses the Tourist Information Centre. Upstairs is the City Scope, a model son et lumière display of Kilkenny in its 17th-century heyday. In the heart of the town, in the Tholsel, once a tollhouse, is the City Hall. The building has

LIGHT IN THE BLACK ABBEY *The Most Holy Trinity and a bright window light up the gloom.*

MERCHANT'S MUSEUM *Rothe House, built as a merchant's home in 1594, is now a museum.*

an octagonal clock and dates from 1761. It contains municipal archives from 1230 and the city's sword, 1609, and mace, 1677.

The Butler Slip is one of the few of Kilkenny's ancient alleys to remain. Close by was the Hole-in-the-Wall Inn, patronised by young bloods who got 'dead drunk for a penny or tipsy for nothing at all'.

**Kilkenny Castle** *Summer, daily 10am-7pm.*
**Rothe House** *Apr-Oct, daily 10am-5pm; Nov-Mar, Sat and Sun 3-5pm.*

# Peace after Past Privations

*' The whole valley swoons in an air so delicately moist that it seems too heavy to move, so that on still wet days even the clouds lie asleep across the distant mountains, and one gets the overpowering sensation of steamy growth, of success over nature, of peace as unbroken as the buzzing of bees.' Seán O'Faoláin's words sum up southern Kilkenny, whose emptiness is echoed in famine cemeteries and roofless manors.*

### Gowran/Gabhrán

The seat of the kings of Ossory is now a village at the junction of the Kilkenny-Borris road, with a racecourse. The village was once strategically important, since it guarded a path through the bogs on the Leinster-Ossory borders, and because of this it was the site of several battles.

In the early 13th century the lands were given to the Anglo-Norman Theobald Fitzwalter, forebear of the Butler Earls of Ormonde. In 1317, when the village had become a town, it was taken by Edward Bruce. A century later it was burnt down in a battle between Irish rebels and Anglo-Normans. Gowran Castle was besieged by Cromwell in 1650, burnt, its entire garrison – all except one of its officers – shot, and the chaplain hanged. No trace of the castle has survived.

The old Gowran collegiate church, which dates from around 1260, has been incorporated into the 19th-century St Mary's Protestant church. These include the tower and a black marble arch which leads into the chancel. In the nave are effigies and tombstones, among them what is perhaps the tomb of the 1st Earl of Ormonde, who died in 1327, and a black marble font.

### Graiguenamanagh/Gráig na Manach

Graiguenamanagh (pronounced Graig-na-manna) means 'dwelling of the monks'. The monks in question were sensible enough to place their abbey in the lee of 1703ft Brandon Hill, in the wooded valley where the Rivers Barrow and Black Water meet. This is the valley whose peace Seán O'Faoláin so evocatively described. The River Barrow is crossed by an 18th-century seven-arched bridge built by George Semple. White water rushes over a weir, and the towpath is merry with wild flowers. Cabin cruisers moor beneath the remains of an Anglo-Norman castle.

There is a long, pebble-dashed building in the centre of the town with an odd little belfry at one end. This is Duiske (Black Water) Abbey, now the Catholic parish church, but once the church of a 13th-century Cistercian monastery, the remains of which have been incorporated into the building. Duiske Abbey, whose buildings encompassed much of the town, began to fall apart in 1536 when it was suppressed. Although the monks continued to occupy it for many years, it gradually fell into ruin. The last tragedy was in 1744, when the tower collapsed into the nave. However, the debris from the tower was smoothed over to create a new floor and the west end was re-roofed to make a place of worship for the Protestant Church of Ireland. In 1812 the church was returned to the Catholic community and the long work of restoration began – to be completed finally in the 1980s.

Its unprepossessing exterior contrasts with a splendid vista once the door is opened. The long nave, with its ancient stone and high clerestory windows, conveys the simplicity and serenity the monks knew. As a link with the past, an effigy of a 13th-century knight found in the ruins was installed by the main entrance. He is unknown – but he makes a suitable guardian. Descend some steps from the south transept – to the original pre-1744 floor level – to see the magnificent Transitional (between Romanesque and Gothic) processional door of about 1220, used by the monks on ceremonial occasions and still there after seven centuries.

### Inistioge/Inis Tíog

Travel to Inistioge by the roundabout way from Graiguenamanagh – or walk along the South Leinster Way – and the whole town can be seen spread out in the valley below: its ten-arched bridge over the River Nore, its churches, its shattered castle, and the 18th and 19th-century houses scrambling up the lanes from the river. High above is Brandon Hill, topped by a cairn.

The town has two centres. The first is a green, tree-lined square surrounded by pastel-coloured cottages. In the square are a

### OTHER PLACES TO SEE

**Jerpoint Glass Studio** Stonyford. Visitors can watch glassware being made by hand. Tel: (056) 24350.

**Kilfane** 2m up the Gowran road, and a little off it; ruined 13th-century church contains Cantwell Fada, rare effigy of knight in 13th-century chain mail, surcoat and rowel spurs.

**Ullard Church** 3m N of Graiguenamanagh, ruins of 12th-century Romanesque church with later staircase and doorway. Two worn carvings above doorway said to be St Fiacre and St Moling, who founded church on site in 7th century. Beside church is 9th-century granite High Cross, with Biblical scenes.

**Woodstock Park** 1m from Inistioge. Arboretum created by Lady Louisa Tighe; has Europe's longest (just over 1m) monkey-puzzle avenue.

### WALKS

**South Leinster Way** Continues Barrow Line south-west from Graiguenamanagh, skirting Brandon Hill and crossing to Carrick-on-Suir, County Tipperary.

### EVENTS

**Horse racing** Gowran Park, all year.

**Open Forest Day** Woodstock Park, late Sept, early Oct.

### SPORT

**Angling** Coarse fishing: River Barrow. Game fishing: River Nore.

**Golf** Mount Juliet Golf Club, 18-hole course. Tel: (056) 24455.

**Riding** Mount Juliet, 2m W of Thomastown.

### INFORMATION

Kilkenny Tourist Office. Tel: (056) 21755.

RURAL IDYLL *The quiet banks of the River Barrow are enjoyed by ponies, as well as anglers.*

THE LADY AND THE BISHOP *A variety of carved figures decorate the pillars of the colonnade running round the cloister at Jerpoint Abbey. Among them are a lady with a pleated skirt, and a bishop.*

ELEGANT EFFIGY *The image of the knight 'Long' Thomas de Cantwell graces Kilfane church.*

SPARE SCULPTURE *A tomb carving at Gowran church has a surprisingly modernist style.*

fountain, put up in 1879 by Lady Louisa Tighe, grand-daughter of the Duke of Wellington, in memory of her husband, and a monument to David Fitzgerald of Brownsford, who died in 1621. The other 'centre' is the river frontage with its lawns running down to the water.

Behind the square are the Catholic church of St Columkille and the Protestant St Mary's, divided from one another by the width of a stony graveyard. St Mary's incorporates part of a 13th-century Augustinian monastery. Its tower served as the mausoleum for the Tighes, the local land-owning family.

Woodstock, the Tighe family estate, stands high above the town and gives a magnificent view of the valley. Its entrance is topped by heraldic beasts, but the long tree-lined drive leads to a roofless, win-dowless house. It once was renowned as among Ireland's finest Georgian dwellings, but in 1922 it was taken over by the notorious British irregular troops, the Black and Tans. After they left it was burnt down by the Republicans.

## Jerpoint Abbey

The dark, biscuit-coloured tower of Jerpoint Abbey, with its battlements, rears above a bend on the road south from Thomastown. The abbey is one of the most awesome religious remains in Ireland, yet, because many of its domestic arrangements are still recognisable, it also gives an intimate picture of monastic life.

The present Cistercian structure dates mainly from about 1180 to 1200, and was probably built on the remains of a Benedictine abbey founded about 1158 by Donal MacGillapatrick, King of Ossory. The oldest parts are the Irish-Romanesque transepts and chancel, where Bishop O'Dulany lies. He died in 1202, and his effigy holds a crozier being gnawed by a serpent. The east window above dates from the 14th century and the magnificent central tower was added in the 15th. Also in the chancel are faded wall paintings, said to be of the heraldic arms of benefactors, while tombs in the transepts bear stylised portraits of saints.

The long run of the nave, where the choristers sang, was completed before 1200. Wooden steps still follow the run of the night stairs down which the choral monks descended to night office. By going up them you reach the roof to look down upon the Dublin-Waterford railway.

The restored cloister piers carry carvings of knights and ladies, bishops, dragons, and even a man with stomachache, echoing the drawings on medieval manuscripts.

The abbey was dissolved in 1540 and its 1880 acres were presented to the earls of Ormonde. A touch of continuity with the past is that local people are still buried in its cemetery.

**Visitor Centre** *Tel: (056) 24623. Off-season, Tel: (056) 21450.*

## Thomastown/Baile Mhic Andáin

Subtropical oleanders grow on the river bank by Thomastown's 18th-century bridge, evidence of the mild climate. Pale green weeds wave in the River Nore's quiet stream, and trout ripple the waters as they rise after flies. Grey walls and red roofs ascend in cliffs above the river as in Mediterranean towns.

The Thomas of the market town's name was Thomas FitzAnthony Walsh, Seneschal – or Governor – of Leinster in the 13th century. He built a wall around the town with 14 towers, a religious house and a castle. Having done that, Walsh built another keep, Grenan Castle, along the river, where its ruins now stand, large and forlorn. Bits of the fortifications still survive in Thomastown.

The main street of the town is brightly coloured and pretty, with shops and pubs hung with flower baskets. In keeping with its agricultural clientele, the chemist's shop gives equal prominence to make-up, lotions and animal medicines. At the top of Thomastown is the Water Garden, a walk between herbaceous borders, water plants and tinkling fountains. George Berkeley (1685-1753), Protestant Bishop of Cloyne and philosopher, was born at nearby Dysart Castle. It is after him that California's Berkeley University takes its name.

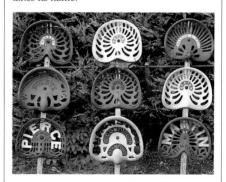

TRACTOR-SEAT TABLEAU *A display of tractor seats adorns Thomastown's Water Garden.*

175

# Where St Declan Landed

*Red-sandstone mountains glittering with corrie lakes rise from valleys threaded with rivers that meander to the sea. It was here that St Declan landed, one of the earliest missionaries to bring Christianity to Ireland. Now, people come to this region to walk the paths that crisscross the gorse-covered and boulder-strewn slopes, or fish the dimpled waters of the River Blackwater for its salmon and trout.*

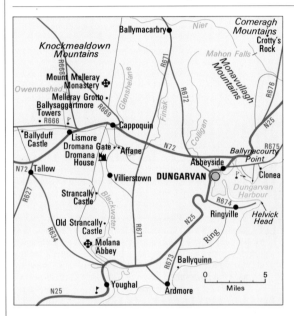

accommodate weavers brought from Ulster.

**EVENTS**

**Irish music** Ring (Gaeltacht), 6m from Dungarvan: Tigh an Cheoil, Thur nights, Sat, Sun; Mooney's Pub, most summer evenings; Marine Bar on N25, Mon, Thur, Sat and Sun nights.

**Lismore Community Festival** Aug.

**Tallow Horse Fair** Sept.

**SPORT**

**Angling** Coarse fishing: Dromana Lake and River Blackwater. Game fishing: Rivers Blackwater, Colligan, Finisk, Nier and Owennashad, and Nier lakes. Sea fishing: Ardmore, Clonea, Dungarvan Harbour, Helvick Head and Ringville.

**Bathing** Ardmore, Ballyquin, Dungarvan, Ringville.

**Golf** Dungarvan Golf Club, 9-hole course. Tel: (058) 41605.

Dungarvan Sports Centre (pitch and putt). Tel: (058) 41111.

Lismore Golf Club, 9-hole course. Tel: (058) 54026.

**Pony trekking** Ballymacarbry. Tel: (052) 36147.

**Sailing** Ardmore, Dungarvan.

**Tennis** Dungarvan.

**INFORMATION**

South-East Tourism. Tel: (051) 75823. Waterford Tourist Information Centre. Tel: (051) 75788.

## OTHER PLACES TO SEE

**Affane** Scene of 1565 battle between Earls of Ormonde and Desmond. A segment of wall marks burial spot of many who died.

**Ballyduff Castle** Fortified house, also called Clancy's Castle, built 1628 by Earl of Cork, above River Blackwater. Not open to public.

**Ballymacarbry** Pretty village set in beautiful woodland near bend in River Nier.

**Ballyquinn** 4m NE of Ardmore. Attractive isolated beach with long stretch of sand, rocky coastline and beautiful clifftop walk.

**Mahon Falls** Splendid waterfall dropping from 2300ft above sea level.

**Mount Melleray Monastery** Gothic-style Cistercian monastery at foot of Knockmealdown Mountains, founded 1822 by French Trappist monks. Open to visitors and to those wishing to go into retreat.

**Ring** Irish cultural centre in Irish-speaking area near Dungarvan. Summer courses, traditional Irish music and folklore.

**Villierstown** Charming 18th-century village planned by Villiers-Stuart family to

ANCIENT SCRIPT *An old pillar stone in Ardmore Cathedral is engraved with ogham script, the Irish alphabet from the 4th to the 7th centuries.*

## Ardmore/Aird Mhór

The seaside village of Ardmore stands on a promontory known mainly for its association with St Declan, the 5th-century missionary who brought Christianity to this part of Ireland.

St Declan is said to have been at sea when, in answer to prayer, a floating rock with his bell and vestments appeared near the boat. 'Wherever that lands,' vowed the saint, 'I will too, and there will my resurrection be.' St Declan's Stone can be seen where it supposedly came to rest, perched on rocks near the south end of the beach. To be able to crawl beneath the stone was believed to cure the rheumatism of all but sinners – but the act would also demand considerable athleticism. Past Cliff House Hotel, a path leads to St Declan's Well and a ruined church where the saint spent his final years. It includes a stone seat and a sunken bath where pilgrims bathed.

Above the village, a 12th-century Round Tower that tapers to almost 100ft is an unmistakable landmark. One of the best-preserved towers in Ireland, its unusual features are the regularity of the masonry, the projecting string courses at unequal intervals and the roll-moulding around the doorway, which is 13ft above ground level.

ST DECLAN'S WELL *Three medieval carvings of the Crucifixion adorn the stone above the well.*

The side of the tower and the stone walls of the adjacent 12th-century cathedral include a unique composition of arched panels containing low-relief sculptures, thought to have been taken from an older building and now set into the west gable. The subjects include the Weighing of Souls, the Fall of Man, the Judgment of Solomon and the Adoration of the Magi. Within the shell of the cathedral are several memorial stones and two ogham stones.

St Declan's oratory dates from the 9th century and is reputedly his burial place. Each year on July 24, pilgrims celebrate St Declan's feast day by making their rounds of the 'stations' beginning with St Declan's Well.

## Ballysaggartmore Towers

A signpost marks a circuitous woodland walk to the Towers, a marvellous monument to human envy dating from the 1820s. Arthur Kiely, whose brother owned Strancally Castle, lived in an ordinary house nearby. Urged by his wife to build a grander castle than his brother, Kiely built a long winding drive, a splendid Gothic gateway with battlemented symmetrical lodges in grey stone, and another, less imposing, inner gateway. But the venture proved too costly, and before work on the castle itself started he ran out of money. The Kielys were forced to spend their lives in their original modest home.

## Cappoquin/Ceapach Choinn

Small and unpretentious, the market town of Cappoquin stands in the woodlands at the foot of the Knockmealdown Mountains. Here the Rivers Blackwater and Glenshelane meet, making Cappoquin a famous centre for coarse-fishing enthusiasts and a popular point from which to explore the countryside. An imposing stone gateway in the main street leads up a winding drive to a large courtyard and Cappoquin House.

The original grand, two-storey, balustraded house, built in 1779, was destroyed by fire in 1923. Richard Caulfield-Orpen (1863-1938), brother of the celebrated painter Sir William Orpen (1878-1931), was engaged to rebuild it. He was faithful to every detail of the original, but reversed the front and back of the house so that the garden and the view beyond it across the Blackwater could be enjoyed by the occupants.

**Cappoquin House** *Apr to early July, 9am-1pm. Or visits by appointment. Tel: (058) 54004.*

GATEWAY TO NOWHERE *The Gothic gate to Ballysaggartmore Towers was all that was ever built.*

### AN IRISH ROBIN HOOD

Crotty's Rock, more than 2300ft high on the east side of the Comeragh Mountains, is a craggy landmark recalling the life of an 18th-century highwayman, William Crotty. A swashbuckling character, he robbed rich travellers on the road to Waterford, often to help the poor. His reputation was enhanced by his cavalier daring, frequently staging hold-ups in broad daylight. A cave at the foot of the crag was his hideout, and another one nearby was used for storage.

For years he eluded capture, often confusing his pursuers by reversing the shoes on his horse's hooves. He was finally caught by the treachery of his accomplice, David Norris, who was bribed to spike the highwayman's drink and then water his pistols. Crotty was trapped, arrested, tried and subsequently hanged at Waterford Jail on March 18, 1742.

In order to save himself, Norris compounded his treachery by accusing Crotty's wife of being her husband's accessory. She swore vengeance against Norris, and lived for several months as a fugitive in the mountains. She was finally trapped by the authorities near the peak, but rather than surrender she threw herself from the mountain to her death.

## Dromana House

What is left of Dromana House is dramatically sited on a rocky escarpment overlooking the Blackwater estuary. It was built in the 17th and 18th centuries as an addition to a 15th-century stronghold of the Fitzgeralds, badly damaged in the Civil War. Much of the house has been demolished, but the surviving parts include a particularly fine doorway. The huge curved area outside, overlooking the river, is the site of the former ballroom. The remains of the castle are on this side, too.

Sir Walter Raleigh was a guest there, and it was also the birthplace of Katherine Fitzgerald, the 'Old' Countess of Desmond, said by some to have lived to 120, by others to 160! In any event, she achieved celebrity because of her age and the manner of her death – she died in 1604 as the result of a fall from a cherry tree.

Dromana Gate – a mixture of Hindu-Gothic with ogee arches – was built in 1830 as a honeymoon gift for Henry Villiers-Stuart and his wife. It has recently been restored by the Irish Georgian Society.

## Dungarvan/Dún Garbhán

Unassuming and industrious, the market town and seaport of Dungarvan straddles the estuary where the River Colligan flows into the sea. It derives its name from St Garvan, who is thought to have founded a monastery here in the 7th century, but it was the Anglo-Normans, in the 1170s, who really settled Dungarvan and started the town's development. A motte and bailey at Gallowshill, which can still be seen, marks their original presence.

Legend has it that when Cromwell attacked the town in 1649 he would have completely destroyed it had not a Mrs Nagle drunk his health and offered refreshments to Cromwell and his men. Shipbuilding was important to Dungarvan and the town flourished in the early 19th century, but the effects of the Famine in the 1840s drastically reduced the population, and most of those able to emigrate left, never to return.

At the heart of the town, handsome 19th-century buildings cluster around Grattan Square, and busy, shop-filled streets radiate from each corner. Nearer the harbour, a network of narrow lanes and alleys thread their way between warehouses to lead to the quayside.

At the end of Parnell Street, off Grattan Square, is Old Market House, built in 1690

SAINTLY TRIO *Effigies of St Carthage, St Catherine and St Patrick decorate the 16th-century tomb of the McGrath family in Lismore's St Carthage Cathedral.*

GLORIOUS GLASS *This window in St Carthage's is by the Victorian artist Edward Burne-Jones.*

## VISIONS AT MELLERAY GROTTO

North of Cappoquin, a mile before reaching Mount Melleray Monastery, is a signpost to Melleray Grotto – a place of prayer where a statue of the Virgin Mary is set in the cliffside. On Friday, August 16, 1985, a family was about to leave after reciting the Rosary when one of them noticed the statue moving. Thinking she had imagined it, she looked away and then back again, to find that she was looking at a vision of 'Our Lady'.

Throughout the next nine days, other worshippers saw similar visions and received messages asking for prayers that there be 'peace and prayer and no more fighting in the world'. Crowds gathered and on one occasion many of those present claimed to have seen the statue move.

On August 24, 12-year-old Tom Cliffe, who had been seeing visions and receiving messages from the third day, asked: 'Are you the Mother of Jesus Christ?' The answer, 'I am', was the last he or others were to receive. The grotto has now become a shrine where the faithful hope to witness a repetition of that 'miraculous' week.

and now a museum, library and tourist office. A permanent exhibit records the tragic story of the *Moresby*, a full-rigged three-masted vessel which left Cardiff for South America with a cargo of coal in 1895. A severe storm forced the ship to anchor in the bay where it was ultimately driven onto the rocks and sank with a loss of 20 lives. In the cemetery of St Mary's Protestant church, a stone marks the mass grave.

Castle Street, to the left of Old Market House, leads to Dungarvan Castle, built by Prince John in 1185. The substantial remains include a keep, twin-towered gatehouse and sections of the original battlement walls. The castle was subsequently rebuilt several times.

A causeway and bridge link Dungarvan with Abbeyside, on the east bank of the Colligan estuary. A short walk leads to the Augustinian abbey, dramatically sited on a spit of land reaching out into Dungarvan Harbour with lovely views of Helvick Head and Ballynacourty Point.

The abbey was founded in 1290 by Augustinians who came from Clare Priory in Suffolk at the invitation of Thomas, Lord Offaly, Justiciary of Ireland. Much of it was destroyed by Cromwell's forces in 1649, but

the tower, nave and east window remain. They are incorporated with the 19th-century Catholic church, built on the site of the abbey living quarters.

### Lismore/Lios Mór

The massive square towers and battlements of Lismore Castle and the cathedral steeple rise above the surrounding woodland, announcing the approach to this market town. In AD 633, St Carthage founded a double monastic centre here – a monastery for monks and a convent for nuns. By the 12th century it was one of Munster's principal monasteries.

In 1185, Prince John, Lord of Ireland and Henry II's youngest son, chose the riverside as a site for a castle. The one that stands today was rebuilt in the 19th century by the 6th Duke of Devonshire with the help of Joseph Paxton (1801-68), and it is still occupied by his descendants. Most of the castle's 7 acre garden was laid out in 1850 with camellias, rhododendrons and magnolias as well as myrtles, roses and quinces.

Within the sight of the castle is 17th-century St Carthage's Cathedral with a tower and elegant spire. The bosses of the internal vaulting are emerald-green with carved roses picked out in blue and red.
**Lismore Castle Gardens** *May to mid-Sept, 2.45-4.45pm exc Sat.*

### Molana Abbey

On the west bank of the River Blackwater is the monastic retreat of the early 13th-century Molana Abbey. Wrought-iron gates open from the roadside onto a winding track through a valley fringed with reeds on one side of the river. A walk to the secluded ruins by the river's edge leads to one of the few remaining sprat weirs in Ireland. Sprat weirs were developed by monasteries to catch sprats in tidal rivers.
**Opening times** *Tues, Wed, Thur, 9am-4.30pm.*

### Strancally Castle

Overlooking the River Blackwater is the grandiose Gothic Revival mansion built by Richard Pain in the 1820s. The castellated building, with ornamental arches and arrow loops, has a keep beside it that is still inhabited. Three miles downstream on the same side is the original, medieval Strancally Castle, where a Fitzgerald is said to have cut his guests' throats and dropped their bodies into the river so as to acquire their land.

# Cut-glass Makers to the World

*Plunging cliffs, rocky inlets and unexpected bays with sandy beaches shape the south-east coast of Ireland, where friendly fishing villages and larger ports add a lively human bustle to the scene prepared by nature. The ancient city of Waterford, whose colourful terraced houses overlook the quayside, is a thriving port and producer of hand-cut crystal glass, a sparkling treasure exported the world over.*

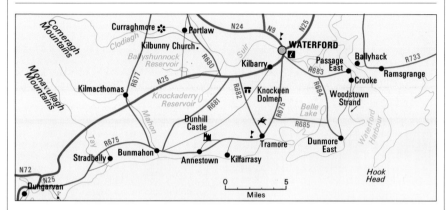

## OTHER PLACES TO SEE

**Bunmahon** 4m W of Annestown. Typical small fishing village with fine sandy beach. Exhilarating walk along clifftop gives stunning views. Disused copper mines inland.

**Dunmore East** Small fishing village and resort on west side of entrance to Waterford harbour. Major centre for offshore and deep-sea fishing, and yachting.

**Kilbunny Church** 2m SE of Portlaw. Recently restored stone walls of 12th-century church of St Munna (d.635), abbot of Taghmon monastery in Wexford. Fine 12th-century Irish Romanesque doorway.

**Kilmacthomas** Centre for climbers and tourists heading for Comeragh and Monavullagh Mountains. Birthplace of Tyrone Power (1797-1841), actor and comedian and great-grandfather of film star Tyrone Power.

**Knockeen Dolmen** 4½m SSW of Waterford. Fine Stone Age monument, 4000-4500 years old, across a field and hidden among trees (signposted from road).

**Portlaw** 19th-century model village built by Quaker industrialist David Malcolmson for his cotton workers.

**Stradbally** 18m SW of Waterford, near sea. Beautiful, unspoilt, horseshoe-shaped bay with sandy beach sheltered by tree-clad cliffs. Stream at rear, through glade of trees. Cliffside walk.

## EVENTS

**Tramore Open Surfing Championships** Late Mar, early Apr.

**Waterford International Light Opera Festival** Sept.

## SPORT

**Angling** Coarse fishing: Belle Lake. Game fishing: Ballyshunnock and Knockaderry reservoirs, Rivers Clodiagh, Mahon, Suir and Tay. Sea fishing: Annestown, Bunmahon, Dunmore East, Kilfarrasy, Passage East, Stradbally, Tramore and Woodstown Strand.

**Bathing** Bunmahon, Dunmore East, Tramore.

**Golf** Tramore Golf Club, 18-hole course. Tel: (051) 86170. Waterford Golf Club, 18-hole course. Tel: (051) 76748.

**Horse racing** Tramore.

## INFORMATION

South-East Tourism. Tel: (051) 75823. Waterford Tourist Information Centre. Tel: (051) 75788.

## Curraghmore House

A long driveway leads to a vast courtyard and the faded grandeur of Curraghmore House, seat of the Beresford family. Parts of the house date back to the medieval castle that belonged to the Le Poers, or Powers, which was rebuilt by James Power, Earl of Tyrone, in the 1700s. The design is said to have been inspired by Vanbrugh's Seaton Delaval in Northumberland, with rusticated arches, pilasters and pedimented niches with statues. The imposing tower above the main door, linking each wing of the house, is crowned by St Hubert's Stag, with a crucifix set between its antlers – the crest of the Le Poer family. The house is not open to the public, but visitors may walk around it.

The layout of Curraghmore's formal gardens evokes the scale and grandeur of Versailles – on which the plan is said to have been based. In the woods is Ireland's tallest tree, a 156ft Sitka spruce.

To the rear and right of the house stands a mid-18th-century curiosity, the Shell House, its interior decorated with thousands of shells by Lady Catherine Power, Countess of Tyrone. It contains a statue of her by John van Nost.

**Shell House and Gardens** *Thur pm and public holidays. Tel: (051) 87101.*

## Dunhill Castle

Looming above a little bridge that crosses a river stands an overgrown ruined hilltop fortress once owned by the Power family. It tells a vivid story. Towards the end of 1649, Cromwell, on his way to subjugate Dungarvan, called on the castle to surrender. The Baroness of Dunhill, in control during her husband's absence, resolutely refused. For three days Cromwell's men besieged the stronghold. But a skilful gunner on the castle's rooftop caused sufficient casualties for Cromwell to call off the attack.

When the gunner saw Cromwell leaving, he called for ale for his men. The baroness, known to be cautious, sent up jugs of buttermilk instead. Incensed, the gunner ran up the white flag. Cromwell promptly returned, entered the castle, took the baroness prisoner and hanged the treacherous gunner from a nearby tree.

## Kilbarry/Cill Barra

South-west of Waterford city is where the hand-cut Waterford crystal is made. Here, on a 40 acre site, 1500 people are employed in the largest industry of its kind in the world. There is a showroom with a permanent exhibition of glassware, where the crystal can be bought and a video presentation viewed.

AT THE WATER'S EDGE *Oystercatchers probe the beach of Stradbally cove, undisturbed by the wind-whipped white horses crashing upon the shore.*

### WATERFORD CRYSTAL – FROZEN LIGHT AND COLOUR

STEADY HANDS *A craftsman cuts the geometrical pattern on a crystal bowl.*

FINISHING TOUCH *Using a fine cutting tool, the bowl is inscribed with a legend.*

In 1783, George and William Penrose set up a business in Waterford aiming to make glass with the character and purity of crystal. For 68 years the business flourished, and its sparkling glass won several gold medals at the 1851 Great Exhibition in London. But by the end of that triumphal year the business had crashed, a victim of under-funding and crippling taxation.

Nearly a century later, in 1947, a small glassmaking factory was established once more in Waterford. Building on the tradition of its predecessor, the company has since grown to become the largest of its kind in the world, producing hand-crafted crystal coveted by connoisseurs and collectors alike. In 1990, sales worldwide amounted to Irf£86.986 million, with 69 per cent of the crystal going to North America.

The formula for the lead-crystal glass, which remains an industrial secret, means that objects of considerable thickness can be made. This thickness allows the characteristic deep cutting that gives the

glass its strong light-refracting properties and produces its diamond-like glitter.

The basic ingredients – silica sand, potash and lead oxide, among others – are mixed in powder form and placed in an oil-fired furnace for 36-40 hours, heated to 1200°C (2192°F). The craftsman or 'blower' takes a globule of molten crystal on the end of a hollow metal tube and, with an assistant's help, keeps the globule's symmetry by constantly twisting the tube. It is then lowered into a wooden mould, shaped roughly like the item to be made, where it is blown to fill the cavity. The mould is separated and, still spinning, the now hollow blob is refined with a combination of blowing and shaping with wooden tools. It is finally 'knocked off', cut or snapped from the tube, and set to cool.

After several days, the crystal goes to the 'cutters'. Each item is first marked with a grid pattern. It is then cut by the craftsmen on rotating stone wheels, with wedge or flat-shaped cutting edges, a skill that calls for a keen eye and a steady hand.

**Showroom** (*No children*). *Mon-Fri, 9am-5pm; May-Sept also Sat, 9am-12.30pm. Tours: 10.15am, 11am, 11.45am, 1.45pm, and 2pm. Tel: (051) 73311.*

### Passage East/An Pasáiste

It was at Passage East that Strongbow – Richard de Clare, Earl of Pembroke – landed in 1170, on his way to Waterford, and began the Anglo-Norman invasion of Ireland. Cromwell too made use of this small harbour village, which rests at the bottom of a steep descent, hugged by cliffs. Its colourful houses with their unpretentious exteriors, cluster around several small squares – a reminder that Passage East was once a garrison for Cromwell's men. Crooke, a village to the south, and the Hook Head peninsula, on the southernmost tip of the harbour, are said to be linked by Cromwell's vow – that he would take Waterford 'by Hook or by Crooke'.

The car ferry between Passage East and Ballyhack, a journey of four minutes, saves a 50 mile route by road.

**Ferry** *Apr-Sept: weekdays, 7.20am-10pm; Sun, 9.30am-10pm. Oct-Mar: weekdays, 7.20am-8pm; Sun, 9.30am-8pm. Tel: (051) 82488/82480.*

### Tramore/Trá Mhór

Set within a huge bay carved into the southern coastline, Tramore is renowned throughout Ireland as a seaside resort. Its long, sandy beach and more than 50 acres of leisure space include a permanent fairground, handsome promenade, miniature railway, boating lake, golf course and racecourse. There is also an established angling and wind-surfing centre.

### Waterford/Port Láirge

From the Kilkenny side of the River Suir, the striking features of Waterford are its mile-long quayside lined with blue, yellow, pink and white houses, and the cranes, barges and rows of warehouses that identify it as a busy seaport.

Behind the quayside activity and its backcloth of 18th and 19th-century buildings, a maze of narrow streets evoke the atmosphere of Waterford's medieval past. Scattered among a miscellany of crumbling structures and undistinguished developments are fragments of an ancient fortified wall recalling Waterford's 9th-century origins as a Viking settlement. The city's English name comes from the Norse *Vadrefjord*.

An outstanding landmark at the north-east corner of the city is Reginald's Tower, circular in plan and 73ft high, with walls 12ft thick at the base, tapering to 7ft thick at the top. A staircase rises within the walls, and the interior is divided into three floors: the ground-floor dungeon, and first and second-floor living quarters. Said to have been built in the 11th century by Reginald the Dane, the governor of Waterford, it was part of a fortified wall around the 19 acre settlement, protected to the north by the River Suir and to the south and west by swampland.

In 1170 the town was assaulted by Norman invaders. That same year Strongbow married Eva, daughter of Dermot Mac-Murrough, King of Leinster, and held the wedding reception there. The event is said to have lasted three weeks. Early in the next century, King John extended the city, adding 33 acres to the total enclosure.

Reginald's Tower has variously served as a royal residence, a mint, a military store and a jail. It now houses the Civic and Maritime Museum and contains many historical artefacts. Among them are the municipal sword

BOATS IN REPOSE *Fishing boats at rest rock gently in Dunmore East harbour.*

and mace, and ancient official documents including several royal charters.

In nearby Greyfriars' Street are the roofless but impressive remains of the tower and a fine east window of the French Church, one of Ireland's national monuments. Founded in 1240 as a Franciscan friary by Sir Hugh Purcell and also known as Greyfriars, it was enriched by Henry III. It survived the suppression of the monasteries to be used as a hospital for the aged. In 1695 it became a place of worship for Huguenot refugees – hence its common name.

Another intriguing ruin, with a surviving tower and arched windows, is Blackfriars' Abbey. Established in 1226, it is one of Ireland's earliest Dominican foundations, and thrived for 300 years until suppressed in 1541. Nearby is the west wall of St Olave's Church, all that remains of the original Viking foundation of AD 870.

Off Great George's Street, in Jenkin's Lane, is the 1750 St Patrick's Catholic church, the oldest Catholic church in County Waterford. During the time of the penal laws (instituted in 1695), it served as a corn store which the Jesuits secretly used as a place of worship. It has been delightfully restored, with terracotta paintwork offsetting the white pillars, gallery balustrades and ceiling.

Several important buildings and, unusually, both Catholic and Protestant churches were designed by Waterford's great builder, John Roberts (1749-94). They include the Chamber of Commerce, completed in 1795 as a town house for a shipping merchant. Its handsome blue façade, with window frames and fanlight picked out in white, is a testament to Georgian elegance. Inside there is a fine oval staircase with a spectacular upward view.

In Cathedral Square is Christ Church Cathedral, whose greystone spire towers above the city's skyline. In 1770, the authorities destroyed the existing Protestant church, which had stood there for 700 years, to make way for its replacement. The spacious interior has a massive colonnade of Corinthian columns, and the ceiling and its vaulted arches are decorated with fine stucco work.

In the south sanctuary is a renowned memorial to James Rice, a former mayor who died in 1490. A macabre piece, it represents Rice in a state of early decay on a massive sarcophagus, with worms emerging from between his ribs and a frog by his legs. It was carved in accordance with Rice's instructions,

GRACIOUS SIMPLICITY *The restored St Patrick's Cathedral has an air of unpretentious elegance.*

to serve as a warning to the faithless of the ephemeral nature of life on earth.

Holy Trinity, the Catholic cathedral in Barronstrand Street, was built in 1793-6 with a double-aisled nave. It too has Corinthian columns and a roof-lit stone canopy, or baldechino, over the altar. The baroque façade was added a century later. Also in

Cathedral Square is the former Bishop's Palace, a handsome three-storey building erected in 1741 and recently restored to house city offices. Although the design is sometimes attributed to Richard Cassel, it is probably Roberts' work.

In front of the other side of the palace – as seen from The Mall – are the

AFTER THE MASTER *The sumptuous nave of Christ Church reflects the style of Wren.*

recently excavated remains of St Martin's Gate, a twin-towered gateway built in the 11th century over the remains of the city's outer wall. The nearby City Hall, designed as Assembly Rooms in 1788, now houses the Victorian Theatre Royal.

Other interesting buildings in Waterford include the courthouse in Catherine Street, built in 1849. It overlooks the People's Park, covering 15 acres and laid out in 1857. Occupying a late 19th-century Methodist church, the Heritage Centre in Greyfriar's Street houses a permanent exhibition of the city's past with a model of the Viking settlement and a selection of artefacts recovered from archaeological excavations in 1987-8. These include a rare amber necklace, ring moulds, fragments of fabric and pottery, and board games.

**Civic and Maritime Museum** *Easter weekend to end Oct, Mon-Fri 9.30am-5.30pm, Sat 10am-2pm.*

**Heritage Centre** *Easter weekend to end Oct, Mon-Fri 9.30am-5.30pm, Sat 10am-2pm.*

# Troubled Land of Ancient Kings

*North-west Wexford is the land of the MacMurrough-Kavanaghs, the ancient kings of Leinster whose crumbling 13th-century castle at Ferns testifies to a bloody heritage. Its now peaceful valleys are crisscrossed, it is claimed, by more rivers and streams than any other county in Ireland. This flattish landscape is broken by Vinegar Hill and, to the north, Mount Leinster, with its hem of purple heather.*

## Bunclody/Bun Clóidí

The great 2610ft hump of Mount Leinster broods over this delightful town, with its tree-lined main street, The Mall, and a stream spanned by little stone bridges. The Barry-Maxwell family acquired the town and its lands in 1719, and it was Judith Barry-Maxwell and her son Bishop Henry Maxwell who then diverted water from the River Clody into a stream which provided the town with water. In the 1770s they also planted the trees that can still be seen.

In 1776, the Barry-Maxwells built the elegantly proportioned Protestant parish church, and Lady Lucy Maxwell developed the woods bordering the town. She had footpaths laid along the river banks, which gave access to a waterfall on the River Slaney, which joins the River Clody here, making this a delightful place to stroll. The family name was echoed in the English name of the town – Newtownbarry – until 1950, when it reverted to its Irish name, which means 'the mouth of the River Clody'.

Despite its peaceful environs, Bunclody has had its share of turmoil and bloodshed over the centuries. It was attacked during the 1798 Rebellion by Irish rebels, resulting in 300 dead and 40 houses burnt. Death came again in 1831 when a crowd protesting against their cattle being sold to meet tithes was fired upon by the local yeomanry, killing 14 and wounding 26 more. The event became known as the Battle of the Pound.

On a more domestic level, the ownership of the Bunclody estates involved one of the most lurid plots in family history. It began in 1727 when Richard Annesley (1694-1761) assumed the ownership of the Bunclody estates. He had the rightful earl – his 12-year-old nephew James (1715-60) – kidnapped and sold into slavery in America. James remained there until his period of slavery was over, and then joined one of the ships of Admiral Vernon's English fleet. He told his story to the officers, and Vernon brought him back to England in 1740. James began life-long legal proceedings that never recovered him his rightful titles, and he died a beaten man. Richard's granddaughter, Lucy, was the same Lady Lucy Maxwell who endowed Bunclody with its wooded walks.

At the top of Mount Leinster stand the Nine Stones – according to some accounts the meeting place for nine kings, while another tradition says that the stones were laid by nine shepherds to establish the right to graze sheep on the mountain.

## Enniscorthy/Inis Córthaidh

County Wexford's cathedral town bustles with shops that seem to shoulder each other out of the way as they cascade down the steep streets to Abbey Square beside the River Slaney. Above them rise the spires of the Catholic St Aidan's Cathedral and the Protestant St Mary's Church. Both were built in the 1840s, and the tower and slender spire of St Mary's – added in 1850 – is perhaps the more elegant of the two. St Aidan's was designed by that disciple of Gothic architecture Augustus Pugin (1812-52), and is a gloriously massive bulk of blue-tinted stone with an imposing west front and beautiful east window.

The town, whose name means 'the island of the Corthaige', a people who lived there in the 4th and 5th centuries, was first settled in the 6th century by St Senan, a follower of St Patrick. At the top of Castle Hill stands the turreted fortress founded by the Normans in 1205, but almost entirely rebuilt 400 years later. In the 16th century it was owned by the poet Edmund Spenser, given to him, it is said, by Elizabeth I for his poem *The Faerie Queen* (which flattered Her Majesty).

The castle is now the County Wexford Historical and Folk Museum. Its displays include two rooms dedicated to Ireland's uprisings of 1798 and 1916. Also to be seen is the sedan chair in which Lady Maxwell was

### THE BATTLE OF VINEGAR HILL

Almost every village in County Wexford has a commemorative plaque or statue to the 1798 Rebellion, when Irish insurgents virtually cleared the county of British troops and the hated yeomanries.

The spark that ignited their rage was lit when the villagers of Booleyvogue were making their way 4 miles north-west, to Ferns, to hand in their weapons. They were attacked by local yeomanry, and 20 houses and their church were burnt. Outraged, and led by their priest Father John Murphy, they rose up and attacked and defeated the yeomanry at The Harrow, 3 miles south-east of Ferns. In the succeeding weeks the whole of Wexford joined in, the insurgents took Enniscorthy and won battles all over the county.

On June 21, 18,000 insurgents — 'isolated, unorganised, un-officered' — took their stand on Vinegar Hill above Enniscorthy against 20,000 Crown forces including artillery and cavalry. Their command post was the stone windmill whose remains still stand there today. They suffered a crushing defeat with tremendous casualties and, although many were able to slip through a gap in the surrounding forces, the Battle of Vinegar Hill was the effective end of a 27-day revolt.

carried through her beloved landscape around Bunclody in the late 18th century.

The rocky Vinegar Hill stands on the east bank of the Slaney, and was the scene of a bloody battle during the 1798 Rebellion, when rebels used a ruined windmill as a makeshift fort and held out for nearly a month. From the site of the old windmill there are spectacular views of the river winding below, and far beyond to the blue-topped Blackstairs Mountains. It is said that on a

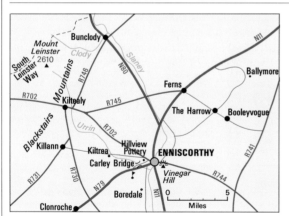

## OTHER PLACES TO SEE

**Boredale** 2m S of Enniscorthy. Once home of Admiral Earl Beatty of First World War fame. Lovely walks and river views.
**Hillview Pottery** Specialises in earthenware pots, as do nearby Carley Bridge and Kiltrea potteries.
**Killann** Shape of churchyard indicates ancient ecclesiastical centre. Blessed well. Home of John Kelly – 'the boy from Killann', hero of 1798 Rebellion.

## EVENTS

**Bunclody Summer Festival** July.
**Greyhound racing** Enniscorthy, Mon and Thur.
**St Patrick's Day Parade** Enniscorthy, Mar 17.
**Wexford Strawberry Fair** Enniscorthy, early July.

## SPORT

**Angling** Game fishing: River Slaney (no daily charge from Enniscorthy Bridge to Wexford harbour).
**Canoeing** Bunclody.
**Golf** Enniscorthy Golf Club, 18-hole course. Tel: (054) 33191.
**Hang-gliding** Bunclody, from Mount Leinster.
**Horse riding** Boro Hill House Equestrian Centre, Clonroche. Tel: (054) 44117.

## INFORMATION

Wexford Tourist Office. Tel: (053) 23111.

WALKING THE DOGS *Enniscorthy locals exercise greyhounds at the dog track before a race.*

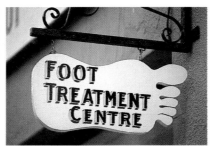

TRADEMARKS *Eye-catching signs advertise treatments and trades in Enniscorthy.*

MUSEUM PIECE *Lady Lucy Maxwell's sedan chair now rests in Wexford Museum.*

BATTLE-SCARRED TOWER *The old windmill on Vinegar Hill was a command post in 1798.*

GOTHIC RUINS *Still graceful, the sparse ruin of the 13th-century Ferns Cathedral thrusts up five elegant lancet windows of an arcade – which, along with the tower, is virtually all that remains.*

quiet summer evening you may hear the sounds of that battle of long ago.
**County Wexford Museum** *Feb-May, 2-5.30pm; June-Oct, 10am-6pm; Nov-Jan, 2-5pm.*

### Ferns/Fearna

History has burnt too fiercely for there to be much left of the town that was once the seat of the kings of Leinster. Burnt and looted time and time again, it was fought over in the 12th century by King Diarmuid MacMurchada, or MacMurrough, and the Irish who controlled the land north of the Blackstairs Mountains. What is left, however, is intriguing – especially the ruins of the cathedral with its tower and 13th-century roofless chancel, and the surviving round tower of the castle.

From the tower there are commanding views of the land that the castle once dominated, with mountains to the north and the sloping valleys to the south and west. The

MacMurroughs probably fortified themselves here in pre-Norman times, but today's castle – with its moat and 8ft thick walls, now ruined – was begun in the early 1200s by William Marshal, Earl of Pembroke, husband of Strongbow's daughter, Isabel de Clare.

The castle was burnt by the Irish in 1331 and rebuilt by the Bishop of Ferns. The MacMurrough-Kavanaghs held it from 1402 until 1550, and 100 years later it fell to the Cromwellians. In 1694 it passed to the

Donovan family of Ballymore, who still own it, although it is now under the guardianship of the state.

At the other end of the village stands the present Protestant cathedral, St Edan's, with part of its original Norman structure, 19th-century tower and chapter house. A few hundred yards east are the remains of tiny St Peter's. Its history of rebuilding is illustrated by an unusual window, Romanesque on the inside and Norman on the outside.

# The Wreckers' Coast

This part of Wexford's east coast is known as the Macamores, from the Irish 'An Maca Mor', or 'the Big Marl'. The name refers to a 5 mile long strip of marl, which is marine mud deposited inland by the Ice Age. The sandbanks 6 miles offshore have caught many unwary sea captains, but for tourists the coastline is a paradise with its picturesque villages, sandy beaches and wide, cliff-encircled bays.

VILLAGE PRIDE *A trim thatch and pebbled walls catch the eye in award-winning Blackwater.*

### Blackwater/An Abhainn Dubh

A profusion of colourful flower tubs, hanging flower baskets and floral gardens has more than once earned Blackwater the title of Wexford's 'tidiest village'. A shallow stream crossed by stepping stones runs through the village, and ducks sit on the bank by a miniature cottage, aptly named Duck House. Throughout the summer a local theatre company stages plays in the village, at the back of Etchingham's pub.

### Cahore/Chathóir

Cliffside paths lead through grasses and bracken alive with darting birds to Cahore

COURTOWN HARBOUR *The stone piers were built to provide work during the 1847 Famine.*

**OTHER PLACES TO SEE**
**Ballycanew** Craft centre in a restored creamery, with crafts ranging from pottery and glassware to knitwear and paintings.
**Curracloe** 3 mile sweep of clean, sandy beach with large sand dunes behind.
**Inch** Riverside village, once a border post of old Irish kingdoms. Irish legend over the post office door relates to the old kingdoms of the Cualu to the north and the Ui Chennselaig to the south.
**Kilmuckridge** Good beach, and interesting pub in village with traditional jazz on Sun.

**EVENTS**
**Ballycanew Flower Festival** May.
**Courtown Failte Festival** Aug and Oct.
**Courtown Harbour Golf Club Open Championships** May-Sept.
**Gorey Summer Fair** Aug.

**Gorey Summer Theatre** Tues, Thur, July and Aug.

**SPORT**
**Angling** Sea fishing: Blackwater, Cahore, Courtown Harbour, Morriscastle.
**Bathing** Ballyconnigar Strand, Ballymoney, Blackwater, Castletown, Clones, Courtown Harbour, Curracloe, Duffcarrick, Kilpatrick, Morriscastle, Tara Cove.
**Golf** Courtown Harbour Golf Club, 18-hole course. Tel: (055) 25166.
**Pony trekking** Gorey, Laraheen Farm. Tel: (055) 28289.
**Sailing** Cahore, Courtown Harbour. Tel: (055) 25207.
**Windsurfing** Courtown Harbour Board Sailing Club. Tel: (055) 25292/21397.

**INFORMATION**
Wexford Tourist Office. Tel: (053) 23111.

## THE WEXFORD WRECKERS

For some two centuries, the people who once lived on the coast between Kilmuckridge and Blackwater have been known as the 'kill-em-and-eat-ems'. The jibe does not refer to cannibalism among the local folk, though their crimes were little less dreadful: in times of poverty, local families engaged in 'wrecking'.

They would tie lights to donkeys on the sands so that ships might mistake them for a harbour and run aground. Then they would board the ships and loot them. Many ships fell for this nefarious activity, and on one occasion the wreckers boarded a ship that was crewless except for a parrot. The bird could only recite 'kill-em-and-eat-em', giving the boarding party a name that stuck.

Point and its now deserted pier. It was here, during the 19th century, that coal from Wales was unloaded from schooners lying offshore, before being carried inland by donkey or horsedrawn carts.

The beach has been largely washed away by the advancing sea, but there are pleasant walks along the cliffs with carpets of sea pinks sweeping down the cliffside. Seals and porpoises can often be seen just off the coast, and its waters are popular with anglers for the varieties and size of fish that can be caught here.

### Courtown Harbour/Cuan Bhaile na Cúirte

The River Owenavorragh reaches the sea at Courtown Harbour, crowded with colourfully painted fishing boats and dinghies bobbing in the protected waters. The piers were built by the Earl of Courtown in 1847. Beyond the harbour lies a curving 2 mile stretch of golden sand and grass-tufted dunes. This, and Courtown Harbour's claim to have the lowest annual rainfall in Ireland, make it one of the most popular resorts on the sunshine coast.

### Gorey/Guaire

Wide streets arranged in a grid pattern proclaim Gorey's 17th-century origins, when the town was built by the Ram family, one of whom was a bishop. The town was incor-

SPACIOUS SUNSPOT *With a generous 3 mile stretch of sand, Curracloe beach is rarely crowded.*

porated as 'The Borough and Town of New-borough', in 1620. The town's arms, granted in 1623, consist of a cross, lion, rose and swan, emblems that signify religion, forti-tude, unanimity and industry. They can be seen over the doorway of the Vocational School in The Avenue, and on the Market Hall in Main Street.

There are many examples of the impor-tance the town enjoyed in the two centuries until the corporation was abolished in 1825. They include St Michael's Catholic church, built by that prolific 19th-century church builder Augustus Pugin (1812-52). The mag-nificent building, with its massive square tower, was inspired by Dunbrody Abbey, near Waterford Harbour. St Michael's graveyard has links with the Irish travelling families, the 'tinkers', who erected elaborate memorials to their dead there. Pugin also built the nearby Loreto Convent.

The town's Protestant church, Christ Church, dates from 1861 and has some fine stained-glass windows. Installed in 1922, they are by Harry Clarke (1889-1931), acknowledged as one of Ireland's greatest stained-glass artists, and depict St Stephen, St Luke and St Martin of Tours. Clarke used a technique of etching the glass deeply with acid to give the windows a jewelled effect.

Gorey was in the forefront of the 1798 Rebellion, which is commemorated by a Celtic Cross to the west of the town. It stands close to the 418ft Gorey Hill, where the insurgents camped before moving on to Arklow in County Wicklow. Prisoners of both sides taken during the rebellion were held in Gorey's Market Hall.

In Market Square is the old cemetery. It contains the remains of Bishop Thomas Ram, who died in 1634, and the graves of the industrious Bates family, whose coachmaking business exported coaches all over the world in the 19th century.

To the north of the town rises the volcanic Tara Hill, a relic from the Ice Age, which presides over the Macamores like a huge dumpling. It is 833ft high and was once owned by the powerful and feared Gaelic poet, Dubhtach. The walk to its summit is worth the effort, for it gives superb views across to Courtown bay.

### Killincooly/Cill Leáin Chúile

This area of land is known only for its circular, stone-walled cemetery, and the blessed well that contains water reputed to be good for curing eye complaints. The cemetery holds the grave of John Mangan (1872-1916), an 18 stone heavyweight shot thrower and local champion, who set a new world record throwing the hammer a distance of 32ft 5in. He was also part of the village tug-of-war team (ten men who weighed over a ton) who won the all-Ireland championship at the turn of the century.

POIGNANT PIETÁ *Loving messages deck a tombstone in St Michael's, watched over by the Pietá. The cemetery at Gorey is the resting place of many tinkers, whose kin lavish mementos upon the graves.*

185

# A Norman Guiding Light

*A tongue of land, the Hook Head peninsula, guards Waterford Harbour and an inland area of 'lost' villages destroyed by tidal silt and floods. At the tip of the tongue a lighthouse built by the Normans still guides ships on their way to New Ross, 20 miles inland and Ireland's fifth largest port. Beyond New Ross rises the 1703ft Brandon Hill, pushing the Blackstairs Mountains into the background.*

## Ballyhack/Baile Hac

The five-storey sandstone castle that guards the head of Waterford Harbour at Ballyhack dates from the 16th century. Now roofless, the castle has a prison cell with no door, making it escape-proof. Prisoners were dropped into it through a hole in the ceiling. Directions to the holder of the key to the castle can be got from one of the residents of Ballyhack. It is a pretty village of terraced cottages with a small harbour from which a car ferry operates across the estuary.

About 2 miles south of Ballyhack is the 19th-century village of Arthurstown, set on the crescent-shaped King's Bay. The bay is so called because tradition has it that King James II boarded ship here on his way from the Battle of the Boyne in 1690. Like so many traditions, there is no supporting evidence for the claim, which it shares with Duncannon a few miles to the south.

## Duncannon/Dún Canann

Whether James II left Ireland from Duncannon or not, there is little evidence of a royal visit now. Today the village of fishermen's cottages with their colourful window boxes is a holiday resort, popular for its broad sandy beach which offers safe bathing and good shore angling.

The 16th-century fort, built to guard Waterford Harbour, resisted long sieges in the 1600s, and until recently was an army training centre. The area was of vital importance during the Napoleonic Wars, when the British built three Martello Towers to deter the French.

BALLYHACK *Colour-washed cottages contrast with the sombre castle overlooking the harbour.*

## Hook Head/Rinn Dúáin

The lighthouse at Hook Head is an astonishing building, if only for the fact that it was constructed some 600 years before the stone-built lighthouses pioneered in the 18th century by James Smeaton. It was a Norman, Raymond le Gros, who built it in 1172, giving it 13ft thick walls made of stone bonded with a mixture of mud and bullock's blood. Norman builders believed that bullock's blood gave strength.

The possibility that there is an earlier lighthouse on the point could help to endorse the legend that it was founded in the 5th century by a Welsh monk, Dubhand ('Hook').

The Norman structure consists of three bullet-shaped chambers mounted one above the other. Each has an arched cross of stone at the top to strengthen the vaulted ceiling and bear the weight of the chamber above. Together they rise to a height of 100ft, to support a light that has guided shipping for 1400 years. For most of that time the lighthouse was manned by monks, who carried timber and peat up 149 steps to the beacon fire, and who slept in rooms set in the walls. Now the light is run by electricity.

The lighthouse is well worth a visit for its views. On clear days it overlooks a bright blue sea pitted with grey, black and yellow limestone rocks. But in stormy weather the sea thunders through 'blow holes' that eject spectacular fountains of spray.

Permits to visit the lighthouse must be sought in advance through the Irish Lights Office, 16 Pembroke Street, Dublin 2.

## New Ross/Ros Mhic Thriúin

The town's arms proclaim New Ross as the 'Norman Gateway to the Barrow Valley', basing its claim on the town's foundation in the 13th century by Isabel, daughter of the Norman leader 'Strongbow' (Richard de Clare). She and her husband – William

of 5000 exotic trees and shrubs on 580 acres above the Kennedy ancestral home at Dunganstown. May-Aug 10am-8pm, Apr and Sept 10am-6.30pm, Oct-Mar 10am-5pm. Tel: (051) 88171.
**Tintern Abbey** 13th-century Cistercian monastery.
**Slade** Peaceful little fishing quay overlooked by castle.

**WALKS**
Carrickbyrne, 7m E of New Ross.

**EVENTS**
**New Ross Festival** Late June.
**Hook Angling Competition** Boat and shore. Early June.

**SPORT**
**Angling** Game fishing: River Owenduff. Sea fishing: Baginbun, Duncannon, Fethard, Hook Head, Slade.
**Bathing** Baginbun, Blackhall Bay, Booley Bay, Dollar Bay,

Duncannon, Grange.
**Golf** New Ross Golf Club, 9-hole course. Tel: (051) 21433.
**Horse riding and pony trekking** Horetown House Riding Centre, Foulkesmill. Tel: (051) 63786.
**Road bowling** Grange, 7pm every night, June-Aug.
**Sailing** Duncannon, Fethard, New Ross, Slade.
**Scuba-diving** Hook Head, Slade.
**Windsurfing** Shielbaggan Outdoor Education Centre, Ramsgrange. Tel: (051) 62213/62108.

**INFORMATION**
Hook Head Tourist Development Centre. Tel: (051) 97179/97129. Waterford Tourist Office. Tel: (051) 75788. Wexford Tourist Office. Tel: (052) 23111.

**OTHER PLACES TO SEE**
**John F. Kennedy Arboretum** 7m S of New Ross. Collection

---

### THE DEVIL AND MISS TOTTENHAM

Loftus Hall, a mock-Georgian mansion overlooking the sea on the Hook Head peninsula, was built in 1870 by the 4th Marquis of Ely for his bride-to-be, Victoria, the Princess Royal. It is a grand affair, with an Italian-made oak staircase, balconies and cornices carved with heads. But for all its grandeur it seems not to have enticed her, since the lady called off the engagement. Perhaps she had heard of the ghostly legend of Loftus Hall, which relates to an earlier house that stood on the site.

It is said that in 1750 the daughter of the house, Anne Tottenham, was playing cards with some guests and dropped a card to the floor. When she bent to retrieve it she saw the cloven hooves of one of the players. Her hysterical screams at the sight of this man, who was obviously the Devil, sent him disappearing through the roof in a puff of smoke.

It would appear that Miss Tottenham never recovered from this traumatic experience, even after death, for her ghost is said to haunt one of the bedrooms, her rustling skirt making her presence known. The house is now a hotel, but can be toured on request at the bar.

Marshal, Earl of Pembroke – built a bridge across the Barrow and developed the thriving port that New Ross still is. Its modern berths and warehouses handle a wide variety of cargo, including oil, gas, coal and timber. It has succeeded despite being 20 miles from the sea and despite the rivalry of nearby Waterford, largely because it was helped by a decree issued in 1215 by King John granting the right to collect shipping dues.

The town itself is attractively laid out on a grid pattern, with steep streets of terraced houses three and four storeys high and shops that have retained their character. Many are vividly painted in primary colours. In the town centre is the Norse-named Tholsel, or tollhouse, where payment was made for right of passage and now the seat of local government in the town. It was built in 1749, with a clock tower and cupola added later, and was designed by the architect William Kent.

Two of the town's treasures displayed in the Tholsel are its maces. The older one is the Mace of King Edward III, which was snatched from the Mayor of Waterford by the Sovereign of New Ross during an argument in 1374 over boundary rights. The other one is the Mace of King Charles II, presented to the

FAMILY TOMB *A skull and crossbones unites crests on a 17th-century tomb in St Mary's.*

town by the Marquis of Anglesea in 1699.

St Mary's Church, in Church Lane, is thought to have been founded by Isabel and her husband. The ruined Gothic chancel and transepts contain many tombstones, including one with the inscription *ISABEL LA FEM* which is possibly the tombstone of Strongbow's daughter. A poignant 13th-century tomb in the north wall of the chancel is known as the 'Bambino' stone. Its slab represents an infant wrapped in swaddling clothes flanked on either side by male and female figures, presumably the parents.

LIGHT OF DEVOTION *Monks first operated the lighthouse that guards wave-lashed Hook Head.*

NEW ROSS *Traditional shopfronts and colourful façades mingle happily on South Street.*

# A Viking Trading Post

*Wexford town's history began when St Ibar landed there in AD 420, a dozen years before St Patrick, and founded a monastery. Vikings plundered it in 819, and later set up a trading post which they called Weissfjord, or 'white fjord', from which the English name comes. But the county was first settled as far back as 9000 years ago, a past that is re-created in the Irish National Heritage Park, outside Wexford town.*

### Irish National Heritage Park

At Ferrycarrig there is a wonderland of history, where visitors can walk into the past, from faithfully re-created Stone Age and Bronze Age dwellings to a superbly reconstructed Norman castle. The River Slaney flows through the park, with a Viking longboat bobbing on its waters and huts made from mud, straw, wattle and animal skin on its banks.

Many aspects of daily life in ancient times are shown, including cooking equipment, hunting weapons, corn-drying kilns, a water mill and grindstones. There is an early Christian monastery, with its crude stone-built church, a stone circle and an ogham stone inscribed with the earliest form of Irish writing, which dates from the 3rd century.

The Norman castle is a set piece that would have gladdened the heart of Cecil B. de Mille. In gleaming white limewash, it has an imposing gateway towering above massive walls. But the centre as a whole presents far more than a romantic historical picture of life in the Emerald Isle. It shows vividly how men and women fought for survival against their environment, the elements, wild creatures and invaders.

**Opening times** *Mar-Oct, daily, 10am-7pm. Tel: (053) 41733/41911.*

### Johnstown Castle

Not a castle in the true sense, this magnificent building, with a 15th-century tower house at its core, is one of the finest examples of a 19th-century Gothic Revival mansion to be found anywhere. Towers, turrets, battlements and barbican – Johnstown Castle has them all. It stands in 50 acres of grounds which include some 200 kinds of trees and shrubs, three ornamental lakes, walled gardens and hothouses. The giant rhubarb *Gunnera manicata* almost rings one of the lakes.

The grounds also contain the Irish Agricultural Museum with its superb collection of farming implements, horse-drawn vehicles and country furniture, and its re-created blacksmith's forge, cooperage, and wheelwright's workshop.

**Gardens** *Daily except Christmas Day, 9am-5.30pm.*
**Museum** *Apr to mid-Nov, Mon-Fri, 9am-5pm, Sat and Sun, 2-5pm; mid-Nov to Mar, Mon-Fri, 9am-5pm. Tel: (053) 42888.*

### Kilmore Quay/Cé na Cille Móire

Thatched cottages with whitewashed walls, an increasingly rare sight in Ireland, decorate this picturesque village, tucked below Forlorn Point to the east of Ballyteige Bay.

The village's pride is its Maritime Museum, on board the retired lightship *Guillemot*. It displays ship models, maritime pictures and other antiques. The village pub is part of a ship that broke up in a storm and was brought ashore by the villagers.

**EVENTS**
**Kilmore Quay Seafood Festival** 2nd week July.
**Our Lady's Island Pilgrimage** 2nd week Aug.
**Tagoat Horticultural and Agricultural Show** Aug.
**Wexford Opera Festival** Late Oct to mid-Nov.
**Wexford Races** Feb-Oct.

**SPORT**
**Angling** Game fishing: River Sow, Wexford Reservoir. Sea fishing: Ballyteige Bay, Ballytrent, Carna, Kilmore Quay, Rosslare, Wexford.
**Bathing** Ballyhealy, Ballytrent, Carna, Cullenstown, Rosslare, St Helens.
**Golf** Rosslare Golf Club, 18-hole course. Tel: (053) 32113.
Wexford Golf Club, 18-hole course. Tel: (053) 42238.
**Sailing** Ballyteige Bay, Carna, Kilmore Quay, Rosslare, Wexford Harbour.

**INFORMATION**
Rosslare Terminal Tourist Office. Tel: (053) 33622.
Wexford Tourist Office. Tel: (053) 23111.

**OTHER PLACES TO SEE**
**Castlebridge** 3m N of Wexford. Relics of corn trade: granaries, lofts, water mill.
**Rathmacknee Castle** 6m S of Wexford, 15th-century castle, largely intact.
**Rosslare** Seaside resort with good sandy beach. To south is ferry port with services to and from Wales and France.

**The Slobs** Flat wetlands N and S of Wexford. North Slobs is wildfowl reserve with hides, lookout towers, etc. South Slobs is huge reserve for Greenland geese that overwinter there.
**Tacumshane** 10m S of Wexford. Windmill in working order, awaiting restoration.

COOPER'S CRAFT *Tubs and barrels await repair in the Agricultural Museum at Johnstown Castle.*

VIKING SETTLEMENT *Daily life in ancient Ireland is re-created at the Irish National Heritage Park.*

A short distance offshore are the Saltee Islands, where there are extensive colonies of gannets and other sea birds. The islands can be visited on day trips from Kilmore Quay. **Maritime Museum** *Daily, June-Sept, 2-8pm. Tel: (053) 29804.*

### Our Lady's Island/Cluain na mBan

This tiny island, surrounded by a salt lake and cut off from the sea by a sand bar, has been a place of pilgrimage since pre-Christian times. It was St Ibar who absorbed it into the Christian Church and dedicated it to the Virgin Mary. From the 12th century, Christians have made their way to do penance there, many crawling around its 12 acres on their knees, or walking with one foot in the water.

Today, outdoor seating is arranged beneath an altar set into the remains of a 15th-century castle, whose one remaining tower leans at an angle. Thousands of worshippers regularly attend a late summer service held on the island each year, between August 15 and September 8.

There is ample evidence of pre-Christian settlement around the island. Raths, or ring-forts, are thought to lie beneath clay mounds scattered throughout the locality, and at nearby Ballytrent and Carnsore Point are two important pagan shrines. Historians believe that the area was once quite densely populated and that Our Lady's Island – whose Irish name means 'meadow of the women' – was the home of druid priestesses. The present causeway is thought to have been built by pre-Norman monks.

The area's mystical past is still venerated at every funeral, when a wooden cross is placed in the hawthorn tree nearest the cemetery, a custom thought to be linked to druidical worship.

### Wexford/Loch Garman

Narrow streets only 12ft wide in places – a legacy of Viking times – are crammed along Wexford's waterfront, where the quays tell of the times when the town was a busy port. But the harbour silted up in the late 19th century and Wexford lost its trade to Waterford. The quaysides are wooden still, and are dominated by a statue of Commodore John Barry (1745-1803), a local man who became a founding father of the United States Navy and led naval operations in the American War of Independence in 1776.

Its narrow streets apart, there are relatively few reminders of Wexford's historic past, which includes the Norman invasion of 1170 and the sacking of the town in 1649 by Oliver Cromwell. Rising above the roofs of Abbey Street is the sandstone tower of the 12th-century Selskar Abbey, where Henry II spent six weeks of penance in Lent 1172, for his connivance in the murder of St Thomas Becket. In Cornmarket there is a section of

WEXFORD MORNING *The early sun casts a warm glow over Wexford Harbour and the town beyond.*

the town's 13th-century wall, and close by is the original Westgate. In the town centre is the 1760 Protestant St Iberius Church, a fine Georgian building on the site of the church founded by St Ibar, the oldest in Ireland.

Wexford also boasts an opera house, which was once a row of three cottages, but now hosts the international Wexford Opera Festival, at which celebrities such as Dame Janet Baker have performed.

# Glens of Refuge

*Craggy mountains and wooded glens define south-western County Wicklow, and have provided refuge over the centuries for rebels who fought British rule. It is a thinly populated landscape – left empty by a steady stream of emigration during the potato famines of 1844-7 – dotted with valley villages, dairy farms and great expanses of pastureland, and disfigured on the western fringe by quarries.*

FERTILE VALE *Croghan Valley's rich farmlands spread to the west of Croghan Mountain.*

### Aughrim/Eachroim

Cradled in a valley where the River Ow joins Derry Water to form the River Aughrim is this pretty market town. It is a major centre for livestock sales, held on Tuesday and Wednesday, when cattle and sheep are herded to the pens immediately south of the three-arched bridge over the Ow.

Running parallel to the River Aughrim is a narrow stream used by a fish farm, and on its banks is a river garden decorated with mill stones. Just north of the Aughrim bridge is the 100-year-old forge with its characteristic horseshoe-shaped stone portal. The forge is now empty but can be visited.

Half a mile east of the village centre is a huge flour mill, now abandoned – the relic of an industry overtaken by technological developments elsewhere. About 200yds to the east is the short-spanned Tinnakilly Bridge, from which fishermen cast their lines into the River Aughrim below.

Some of the higher, less-used mountain roads leading out of Aughrim are untarred and badly potholed along elevated stretches. But it is worth while braving them for the extraordinary panoramic views of the surrounding countryside from above.

### Baltinglass/Bealach Conglais

The approaches to this market town, which lies in a charming valley, are dominated by the verdant 1258ft mound of Baltinglass Hill. The main street of the town bustles with

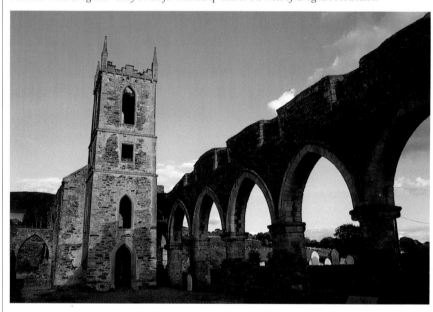

ABBEY AT BALTINGLASS *A 12th-century King of Leinster, Dermot MacMurrough, founded the abbey.*

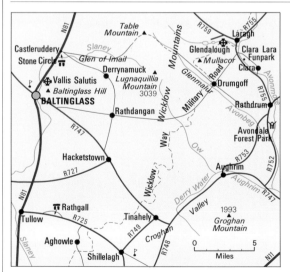

signposted ruins of ancient fort with three concentric stone walls, remnants of stronghold of kings of South Leinster and their burial place.

**WALKS**
**Wicklow Way** 82m walk from Dublin to Clonegall in County Carlow.

**EVENTS**
**Wicklow County Show** Tinahely, early Aug.

**SPORT**
**Angling** Game fishing: Rivers Aughrim, Avonbeg and Slaney.
**Golf** Baltinglass Golf Club, 9-hole course. Tel: (0508) 81530.
Coollattin Golf Club, 9-hole course. Tel: (055) 29125.

**INFORMATION**
Wicklow Tourist Office. Tel: (0404) 69117/8.

**OTHER PLACES TO SEE**
**Aghowle** Village with 12th-century church, once part of

6th-century monastery founded by St Finian.
**Rathgall** 6m W of Shillelagh;

lorries, since it is an industrial hub and centre for the manufacture of agricultural products. They make their way around the highlight of Main Street, a heroic statue of Sam MacAllister, dedicated to the memory of 18th-century rebels against British rule.

On the east bank of the River Slaney, half a mile north of the bridge in the town centre, are the remains of a Cistercian abbey, Vallis Salutis. It was founded in 1148 by Dermot MacMurrough, King of Leinster, in what was then called the Valley of Salvation. The surviving Irish Romanesque arches of the abbey are reminders of its lost magnificence.

The square tower was added later, in 1815. The abbey's remains are accessible through the grounds of the adjoining 19th-century parish church.

At the summit of Baltinglass Hill a Stone Age double ring of stones surrounds three passage-graves. Two of these tombs contain decorated stones. A much larger earthen ring was probably built a little later, in the Iron Age, and may have been a defensive structure.

### Clara/Clarach

It is said that the village of Clara is one of the smallest in Ireland: it has a church, a small schoolhouse and two houses. Near it, on the Rathdrum-Laragh road, is the Clara Lara Fun Park, once a trout farm and now a family recreation area. It has an adventure playground and a mock commando assault course, with provision for boating, fishing and barbecues.

**Fun Park** *Easter-Oct, 10.30am-6.30pm. Tel: (0404) 46161.*

### Glenmalur/Gleann Molúra

The Glenmalur valley is considered by many to be the most spectacular of County Wicklow's glens, by others to be sombre and forbidding. It carries the River Avonbeg and begins just south of Rathdrum, but becomes a long, narrow glacial amphitheatre, with steep sides, above Drumgoff. Where the Wicklow Mountains road crosses the valley, a ruined barracks dating from the turn of the 18th century stands guard.

The peaks of Lugnaquillia, at 3039ft the highest in the Wicklow Mountains, and Mullacor (2179ft) rise on either side of the road, which runs across humpbacked bridges and past cows grazing in the pastureland on the mountain slopes. Red deer and pine marten inhabit remote corners of the valley, and sheep forage on the heights between trickling waterfalls and fields of loose scree.

The road eventually becomes a rough track leading over Table Mountain (2302ft) to the Glen of Imail. There is fine walking in the valley and the hills above, but walkers should be properly equipped, carry maps, and stick to established paths.

### Glen of Imail/Gleann Ó Máil

The best way to approach the wild open Glen of Imail is from the top, along the road north from the crossroads village of Rathdangan, which runs across the brow of the glen. The road has splendid views of the region, across a patchwork of pastureland, both wild and cultivated, enclosed by woods and sprinkled with farmhouses. The River Slaney rises as a thin stream at the eastern end of the glen, on the high slopes of Lugnaquillia Mountain.

The valley's remote situation made it a stronghold of resistance to the British in the past. At Derrynamuck, above the glen, is the Dwyer-MacAllister Cottage, now a national monument, from which the rebel Michael Dwyer escaped from the British two centuries ago. It can be reached through Hoxey's Farm. The key to the cottage, which is 200yds from the road, may be obtained at the farmhouse.

On the way down westwards, to the main Blessington-Baltinglass road, the road passes through the townland of Castleruddery. On the rise to the east of the road, earthworks surround a stone circle of unknown antiquity.

### Shillelagh/Síol Éalaigh

Timber was once felled from the oak forests around this modest village to be used in the roofs of Dublin's St Patrick's Cathedral and of the Palace of Westminster in London. But the village is most famous for having given its name to the Irishman's proverbial cudgel. Shillelaghs were originally fashioned from oak grown in these forests, but later blackthorn was used as well.

The village sits snugly in the Croghan Valley, at the south-western edge of County Wicklow near the southern end of the Wicklow Way. Terraces of the traditional chimneyed cottages that line Shillelagh's main road are fronted by elaborately worked stone porches and decorative door frames.

HAPPY WANDERERS *Travellers and their bright caravans are still seen on Ireland's byways.*

# Valley of the Two Lakes

*Few villages and even fewer towns interrupt this rolling landscape of mountainous bogland, woods, vales, lakes and mountain streams. Many of the hamlets are little more than a road junction with a pub offering travellers rest and refreshment. But they lie on routes that have been followed for many centuries by pilgrims travelling to the monastic centre of Glendalough, founded by St Kevin 1400 years ago.*

### Blessington/Baile Coimín

The gateway to north-west Wicklow is a sleepy, one-street town. Its broad, tree-lined thoroughfare was laid out in the 1680s by Michael Boyle, Archbishop of Dublin, and Blessington was once a staging post for coaches between Carlow and the capital. Now it is a weekend haven for Dubliners.

A remnant of an illustrious past is the stately Georgian Downshire House on the main street. Once a residence of the Marquis of Downshire, it is now a hotel. The lion-fronted drinking fountain across the road from adjoining St Mary's Church (1683) was erected by the marquis at the turn of the 19th century to commemorate the coming of age of his son. The Georgian courthouse behind the fountain has been converted for use as offices.

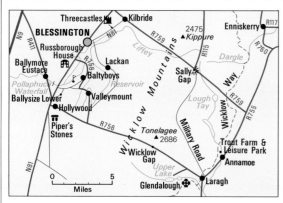

**OTHER PLACES TO SEE**
**Annamoe Trout Farm and Leisure Park** Swimming, canoeing and fish barbecues. Tel: (0404) 45145.
**Ballysize Lower** 1m N of Hollywood. Ancient granite cross.
**Baltyboys** Near Blessington, birthplace of Dame Ninette de Valois (1898-1988), creator of the Sadlers Wells Ballet.
**Kippure** 2475ft peak N of Sally Gap. Topped by television mast.
**Pollaphuca** 2m N of Hollywood. 150ft waterfall, once major attraction of

region now curbed by hydroelectric scheme. In pool at bottom, Puca, a malicious sprite, was said to cavort noisily.
**Sally Gap** High pass on military road in N Wicklow Mountains. Just to N are sources of Liffey and Dargle. Breathtaking views over Lough Tay to SE.
**Threecastles** 3m NE of Blessington, sturdy remains of 14th-century keep, from one of the three castles that once stood here.
**Valleymount** St Joseph's Church, 1803, Hispanic

façade designed by Mexican immigrants.
**Wicklow Gap** Second main pass over Wicklow Mountains, between Hollywood and Glendalough, overshadowed by Tonelagee (2686ft).

**WALKS**
**Wicklow Way** 82m hike from Dublin to Clonegall in County Carlow.

**EVENTS**
**Festival of Irish Music** Russborough House, June. Tel: (045) 65239.
**Rowing and sailing regattas** Blessington reservoir, summer. Tel: (045) 64209.

**SPORT**
**Angling** Game fishing: Blessington reservoir, Glendalough Upper and Lower Lakes, Russborough House.
**Golf** Tulfarris Golf Club, 9-hole course. Tel: (0405) 64574.
**Water-skiing** Blessington reservoir. Tel: (045) 64209.

**INFORMATION**
Wicklow Tourist Office. Tel: (0404) 69117/8.

ROMANTIC RETREAT *Precipitous mountains sweep down to enclose the wooded shores of Lough Tay.*

In a corner of the town cemetery, half a mile along the Baltinglass road, is the tall, austere 12th-century St Mark's Cross, with an unpierced ring. It was moved here when its original site was flooded in the 1930s to become part of the Blessington reservoir, which provides water – and electricity – for the city of Dublin.

The reservoir has delightful lakeside walks and drives, particularly along the eastern shore through the village of Lackan.

### Glendalough/Gleann dá Loch

The 'Valley of the Two Lakes' is one of Ireland's national monuments – for scenic, religious, historic and archaeological reasons. Approaching it from the east, or descending upon it through the Wicklow Gap from the west, is like entering an Irish Shangri-La, so shrouded is it in beauty, mystery and tranquillity. In the distance the rounded, towering purple peaks of the Wicklow Mountains fold gracefully into one another. The mountain forests of pine and spruce are reflected in the clear waters of the two lakes that give the valley its name.

Glendalough was a place of religious pilgrimage for centuries following its establishment as a monastic centre by St Kevin in the 6th century. By the 12th century it was an important diocese. But Viking raids from the 9th century onward did Glendalough much

RURAL CHARM *A bright window frame and a dozing cat grace Annamoe village.*

damage, and after a great fire in 1398 it declined as a religious centre. However, extensive restoration work was begun in the 19th century.

The remains of the main monastic complex are reached through the original stone portal, just beyond the Visitor Centre. The remarkably well-preserved St Kevin's Church is a simple one-roomed structure with a high-pitched stone roof and a 12th-century bell tower, which looked to local people like a chimney. The church therefore came to be known as St Kevin's Kitchen.

Nearby is an imposing 100ft high Round Tower, dating from between the 10th and 12th centuries. It served as a bell tower, a beacon to guide pilgrims from afar, and as a refuge in times of attack. The Priests' House, also originally of the 12th century, was a burial place for priests in the times when Catholicism was suppressed. It stands in the cemetery, to the east of which is the 11ft granite St Kevin's Cross, of about the same age. The Cathedral of St Peter and St Paul, built from about the 10th century in three phases, has an ornate east window.

Perhaps the only sites dating from St Kevin's time are higher up the valley, beside the Upper Lake, and can be reached only by boat: the reconstructed Teampull-na-Skellig (or 'Rock Church') and the cave known as St Kevin's Bed, in which the saint is said to have lived.

The Visitor Centre gives an audiovisual presentation and has a collection of antiquities. Guided tours are available.

**Glendalough Monastery** *Nov to mid-Mar, Tues-Sun 10am-4.30pm; mid-Mar to June, mid-Sept to end Oct, daily 10am-5pm; mid-June to mid-Sept, daily 10am-7pm. Tel: (0404) 45325.*

## Hollywood/Cillín Chaoimhín

The valley village of Hollywood slumbers astride an ancient pilgrims' road. Pious travellers from the west of Ireland began their ascent of the Wicklow Mountains here, before crossing the Wicklow Gap to reach the monastic community of Glendalough on the far side.

St Kevin is believed to have spent some time in Hollywood in the 6th century, before founding the Glendalough settlement. Both Hollywood's churches are dedicated to him, and a 1914 statue of the saint watches over the village from a mountain crag.

The Protestant church of St Kevin on the hill east of the village has a vaulted stone roof

dating back to the 17th century. Both Catholics and Protestants are buried in its partly overgrown graveyard. The central nave of the Catholic church of St Kevin, at the heart of the village, dates from 1789 with wings added in 1830.

Just south of Hollywood, on top of a hillock, is a Bronze Age stone circle, the Piper's Stones. Some of the stones are upright; others have fallen. One legend says they are a piper and ring of dancers turned to stone for

FINE ART *Exquisite plasterwork surrounds a harbour scene painted by Claude Vernet, at Russborough House.*

dancing on the Sabbath. Another suggests that they were named because fairies used to play the bagpipes among them at night.

## Russborough House

In 1741 Richard Cassel and Francis Bindon built a mansion to be the country seat of a Dublin brewer, Joseph Leeson. Its Baroque central structure is flanked by colonnades and the house overall exudes a feeling of wealth and power. The ceilings of the main rooms are 20ft high, many adorned with elaborate plaster flourishes. The house is furnished and decorated with priceless antique furniture, tapestries, carpets, porcelain, a collection of rare dolls, and other valuables.

It also contains the Beit Collection, one of the finest art collections in Ireland, gathered mostly by Sir Alfred Beit (1853-1906) who, with Cecil Rhodes, founded the de Beers diamond mining company in South Africa. The works include paintings by Goya, Murillo, Velazquez and Gainsborough. In 1974, 16 of the paintings were stolen to raise money for the IRA, but they were later recovered.

**Opening times** *Easter-Oct, every afternoon. Tel: (045) 65239.*

ALPINE VIEW *Mountain goats graze on the slopes above Glendalough's Upper Lake.*

# The Wicklow Mountains

*Wild and forbidding, despite their modest height, the Wicklow Mountains are also an integral part of Dublin's 'breathing space'. The 82 mile Wicklow Way, which starts just outside Dublin, enables the energetic to see the heart of this country by foot. And where the mountains slope down to the sea their beautiful wooded hills and the landscaped gardens at their feet provide a backdrop to seaside towns.*

### Bray/Bré

The sand and shingle beach and children's funfair draw locals and Dubliners alike to Bray. At the northern end of the beach esplanade a colourful terrace of houses extends upwards from the shore. No.1 Martello Terrace was James Joyce's family home from 1888 to 1891, and features in his novel *A Portrait of the Artist as a Young Man*. It is a private home and is not open to visitors.

At the bottom of Bray's Main Street sits the gabled old Town Hall which, in addition to the Tourist Information Centre, now houses a Heritage Museum. Among its exhibits are artefacts, records, maps and photographs of old Bray.

A footpath starting at the town's south end follows the shore past the sudden granite promontory of Bray Head (791ft), which dominates the coastline.
**Heritage Museum** *Wed, Sat, Sun 2.30-5pm; July, Aug, Tues-Sun 2.30-5pm. Tel: (01) 2862539.*

### Dargle Glen Gardens

Just off the busy Bray Road lies this verdant extravaganza of hillside trees and shrubs and eye-catching plants such as giant-leafed gunnera and fairy-wand astilbe. Many of the plants were imported from the Far East. A wisteria-covered bridge divides the private from the public sections of the gardens. The gardens are open all year round.

### Delgany/Deilgne

Christ Church, the 1790 Protestant parish church of Delgany, marks the site of a 7th-century church. It was founded by St Chuarog, a Welsh disciple of St Kevin, who founded the great monastery at Glendalough. In addition to superb stained-glass windows, it also contains a striking neoclassical monument to David La Touche (died 1785), a prominent 18th-century local figure. The Bellevue demesne, where La Touche lived, is now Delgany State Forest. Pubs on the main street also date back to the 18th century.

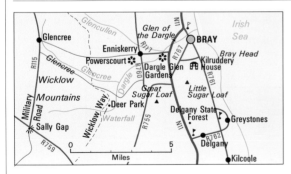

### OTHER PLACES TO SEE
**Glen of the Dargle** 2m W of Bray. Thickly wooded defile, through which the River Dargle runs. Scenic picnic spots.

### WALKS
**Bray Head** Magnificent cliff walk round foot of Bray Head starting from south end of Bray town.
**Wicklow Way** 82m path from Dublin to Clonegall.

### EVENTS
**Bray Seaside Festival** July.
**Kilcoole Horse Show** June.

### SPORT
**Angling** Game fishing: Rivers Dargle and Glencree. Sea fishing: Bray and Greystones.
**Golf** Bray Golf Club, 9-hole course. Tel: (01) 862484. Delgany Golf Club, 18-hole course. Tel: (0404) 874645/874833.
Greystones Golf Club, 18-hole course. Tel: (01) 876624.

### INFORMATION
Wicklow Tourist Office. Tel: (0404) 69117/8.

DAWN'S PALE FACE *Morning mist weaves a shroud in the valley below the Great Sugar Loaf.*

### Enniskerry/Áth an Sceire

The vast estate and gardens of Powerscourt House are Enniskerry's best-known attraction. They are approached through gates opposite the parish church, up the hill from the clock tower. A long avenue lined with towering beech trees leads past the house, which was built by Richard Cassel between 1731 and 1740 for Richard Wingfield, MP, who became the 1st Viscount Powerscourt. The central block of the mansion is now only a shell, having been gutted by fire in 1974, but it retains its dramatic façade.

The house overlooks flights of pebbled steps leading down to the duck-inhabited Triton pool with its 100ft fountain, flanked by grottoes and bronze statues of winged horses, emblems of the Wingfield coat of arms. To the left are Italian and American Gardens, and beneath them a Japanese Garden. The Bamberg Gates fronting the walled gardens, though of Viennese origin, are believed to have come from the German cathedral of Bamberg in Bavaria.

Three miles to the south of the gardens (or about 4 miles above a signposted path), in a wooded grove of Powerscourt deer park, is the highest waterfall in Ireland. The River Dargle tumbles 398ft over glistening granite into a pool at the bottom. The deer park is home to Japanese sika deer introduced in the late 19th century.

SOUND AND FURY *Bray's esplanade is no place to stand when a thunderous sea lashes it.*

GARDEN OF SERENITY *A splashing fountain evokes tranquillity in Powerscourt's gardens.*

The village itself centres around a 19th-century green-domed clock tower, with one of its faces missing. It is a picturesque place, which attracts many visitors drawn by the antique, fashion and craft shops that line its sloping three-sided 'square'.

**Powerscourt Gardens** *Mar-Oct, 9am-5.30pm. Tel: (01) 2867676.*
**Waterfall** *All year, 10.30am-7pm, or dusk in winter.*

### Glencree

The rugged valley of Glencree, with its small huddle of roadside cottages, sits at the foot of the military road that runs north-south through the Wicklow Mountains. The buildings off the road behind St Kevin's Church were originally military barracks for the troops patrolling the region against rebels of the 1798 insurrection. They have since been used as a centre for sectarian reconciliation and the headquarters of an Irish geological survey.

A path in front of the church leads down to a wooded walk along the bank of the stone-strewn River Glencree. Fifty yards down the road from the church is the entrance to a military cemetery established by the German government. The bodies of German navy men washed ashore during the two World Wars, and also airmen who crashed and died on Irish soil during World War II, are buried there.

### Greystones/Na Clocha Liatha

Like Bray, Greystones was a fashionable resort for the wealthy during the 19th and early 20th centuries. The imposing Victorian façade of the large seafront hotel near the harbour testifies to its former elegance. Even though the town is now within easy commuting distance of Dublin, it has remained a graceful place of calm, faded elegance. It has a fine seafront, a modest beach, and a small sheltered bay much used by the local sailing and motor yacht clubs. Its name comes from the grey rocks along the shore south of the town's harbour.

### Kilruddery House

On the coast road between Bray and Greystones is Kilruddery House, built in Tudor Revival style in 1820. The estate has been the family home of the Earls of Meath for more than 300 years, and the extensive Kilruddery Gardens have been cultivated even longer. Parts of the estate constitute the only such 17th-century complex still intact in Ireland.

Twin canals 500ft long, classical statuary, hedge-lined walks, terracing and angular gardens all testify to the strong continental influences at the various times when the sections of the grounds were designed and laid out. The Victorian house and the view of the Little Sugar Loaf mountain (1123ft) offset the austerity of this classical park.

**Kilruddery Gardens** *May, June and Sept, 1-5pm. Tel: (01) 2863405.*

# Where the Bright Waters Meet

*Between the harbours of Wicklow and Arklow runs a string of sandy beaches where families come to bathe in the summer and sea anglers cast their lines. Inland, the ground rises to the lower slopes of the Wicklow Mountains, and jade-green glens crossed by narrow roads and footpaths resound with birdsong. This is the sweet Vale of Avoca, which inspired Thomas Moore's poem, 'The Meeting of the Waters'.*

### Arklow/An tInbhear Mór

Legend has it that the Irish tribe inhabiting this region long ago called the early settlement at the mouth of the Avoca river Tulackinbhearmore. The Vikings who settled here were unable to pronounce the word and renamed it Arklow, allegedly after Aru-Kell, the Viking chieftain who settled there in the 9th century.

Today, Arklow is the main town of south-east County Wicklow. On weekends and holidays, people from the surrounding countryside join locals in the town's pubs, restaurants, cinema and bingo halls. They promenade beside the river, picnic on its banks and venture onto its waters in pedal boats.

There is music from the bandstand in the park off Main Street. The park was built over the burial ground of the parish church, demolished in 1908, and ancient, weathered headstones line the park walls. Sand and shingle beaches stretch to north and south of the town.

During the week, Arklow reverts to a more unruffled pace. The town was once an important shipbuilding and fishing centre, and both seamen and ships from the town were known in ports around the world. A small fleet of trawlers and fishing boats still operate from the harbour, and *Gypsy Moth IV* – in which Sir Francis Chichester sailed single-handed around the world in 1966-7 – was built here, by John, Tyrrell and Sons. The shipyard is still working.

Down St Mary's Road and past the stone-domed Church of St Mary and St Peter, 1840, is Arklow's Maritime Museum, sited in the District Library building. It contains varied memorabilia of the town's seafaring past, and includes model sailing ships, one of which is made of 10,700 matchsticks, ships' log books and other nautical documents. There is also a display showing Arklow fishing boats rescuing survivors of the *Lusitania*, sunk by a German submarine in 1915.

The new face of Arklow is presented by Arklow Pottery, run by a Japanese company, alongside the harbour. There are tours of the pottery operations every weekday in summer, and a shop sells the pottery's wares.

**Maritime Museum** *Mon-Sat 10am-1pm, 2-5pm. Tel: (0402) 328681.*
**Japanese Pottery** *Mon-Sat 10am-5pm. Guided tours 10am, 11am, 2.30pm. Tel: (0402) 32868.*

### Avoca/Abhóca

The Vale of Avoca begins 3 miles north of Avoca village, where the Rivers Avonmore and Avonbeg meet to form the Avoca, and is the setting for Thomas Moore's poem *The Meeting of the Waters*.

*There is not in this wide world a valley so sweet*
*As that in whose bosom the bright waters meet*

The tidy little village of Avoca straddles the river of the same name in its picturesque

SKILLED HANDS *A handweaver works deftly at the Avoca mill.*

vale. Near the old corn mill on the river is an internationally famous weaving enterprise, with daily public demonstrations of hand-weaving.

A mile farther north, towards Rathdrum, is a signposted turning to the Motte Stone, a large granite boulder on top of a hill covered in heather and gorse. On a clear day, the top of it commands a view as far as the mountains of Wales. Legend has it that the boulder belonged to the Irish hero Finn MacCool and was his hurling stone. Another legend tells that the large iron staples embedded in the stone were put there by a local landowner as rungs so that his bride could climb to the top and fully appreciate the size of his estate.

**Avoca Weavers** *June-Aug, Mon-Fri 9am-6pm; Sept-May, Mon-Fri 9.30am-5.30pm. Sat and Sun 10am-5.30pm. Tel: (0402) 35105.*

### Avondale Forest Park

Some 528 acres on the west bank of the River Avonmore make up this park, established in 1904 and the centre of reafforestation in Ireland. It contains one of Europe's finest collections of trees, brought from all over the world to assess which would succeed best locally. Special areas are reserved for species of elm, beech, oak, spruce, maple, Douglas fir, larch, ash and others. Most remain, or have regenerated, from the original plantings. Despite this botanical purpose, Avondale is

---

### OTHER PLACES TO SEE

**Brittas Bay** 2m long stretch of clean powdery sand, one of the most popular family beaches on Ireland's east coast. Sand dunes and clumps of tall shore grass give protection against coastal breezes.
**Devil's Glen** 3m NW of Ashford. Deep tree-shaded chasm where River Vartry tumbles 75ft over narrow precipice into Devil's Punchbowl rock basin. The Glen has well-marked walking paths and scenic picnic spots.

**Kilmacurragh Forest Park** Arboretum with oak, beech, eucalyptus, redwood and other trees interspersed with shaded clearings, wide meadows and miniature lake. Not signposted: turn W off N11 road 4m S of Wicklow, at Taps public house. Car park is at burnt-out shell of once fine 17th-century mansion.

### WALKS

**The Murrough** 3m long strip of land between the sea and River Vartry and Broad Lough.

### EVENTS

**Arklow Music Festival** Mar.
**August Maritime Festival** August Bank Holiday.
**County Wicklow Garden Festival** Mid-June.
**Round-Ireland Yacht Race** Starts Wicklow, June.

### SPORT

**Angling** Game fishing: Rivers Avonmore and Vartry, and Woodenbridge Trout Farm. Sea fishing: Arklow, Brittas Bay, Jack's Hole, The Murrough, Wicklow.
**Bathing** Brittas Bay.
**Golf** Arklow Golf Club, 18-hole course. Tel: (0402) 32492.
Blainroe Golf Club, 18-hole course. Tel: (0404) 68168.
Rathdrum Golf Club, 18-hole course. Tel: (0404) 46149.
Wicklow Golf Club, 9-hole course. Tel: (0404) 67379.
Woodenbridge Golf Club, 9-hole course. Tel: (0402) 35202.
**Mountaineering and canoeing courses** Tiglin Adventure Centre. Tel: (0404) 40169.
**Sailing** Brittas Bay.
**Windsurfing** Brittas Bay.

### INFORMATION

Wicklow Tourist Office. Tel: (0404) 69117/8.

Despite being the son of a country landowner – he was born at Avondale House, near Rathdrum – Charles Stewart Parnell (1846-91) became one of the greatest campaigners for Irish democracy and peasant rights. He first entered the Westminster Parliament in 1875 as the member for County Meath, after a campaign in favour of Home Rule for Ireland. Two years later, Parnell and Michael Davitt founded the Irish National Land League, and together campaigned strongly for agrarian reform, peasant land ownership and Home Rule.

But scandal struck when Parnell was cited in a divorce case in 1890. This caused a split in his party, most of whom voted to oust him as chairman. The following year, just five months after marrying Mrs O'Shea, the wife of a fellow MP in whose divorce case he had figured, Parnell died.

primarily a leisure park with river walks, duck pond, forest paths, picnic grounds and a coffee shop. It is also home to a range of wildlife, including badgers, rabbits, hares, hedgehogs and otters.

The park is the site of Avondale House (1779), birthplace of the Irish patriot and MP Charles Stewart Parnell. Part of the house is now a museum, with exhibits recounting Parnell's life and achievements, as well as his tragic end after an adulterous scandal.
**Forest Park** *All year, 8am to dusk.*
**Avondale House** *Apr-Nov, daily 11am-6pm. Tel: (0404) 46111.*

BARON'S BASTION *Black Castle, built to defend Wicklow against the O'Byrne chieftains, is now a ruin crumbling into the sea.*

## Mount Usher Gardens

What was once a single acre of green but derelict land with an old mill was turned in the late 19th century into the flourishing private gardens of Mount Usher. Edward Walpole, a Dublin businessman, acquired the land in 1868. His three sons inherited the site, bought more land around it and, over the years, gathered the plants that formed the basis for today's remarkable floral collection, among Ireland's finest, sprawling luxuriantly on the banks of the River Vartry.

The gardens now contain more than 4000 species of plants from many parts of the world, planted so as to make best use of the land's existing features. Camellias, magnolias and dogstooth violets flower in April; viburnum and handkerchief trees (*Davidia*) in May; and the Chilean fire bush (*Embothrium*) and mock orange (*Philadelphus*) in June. Some of the best views of Mount Usher can be enjoyed from the garden bridges, where you may spot the occasional heron and kingfisher.
**Opening times** *Mar-Oct, Mon-Fri 10.30am-6pm, Sun 11am-6pm. Tel: (0404) 40205.*

MOUNT USHER GARDENS *An old mangle finds a new use in these pretty gardens.*

## Wicklow/Cill Mhantáin

The name Wicklow is the modern version of Wykinglo – Viking's Meadow – the name of the 9th-century Viking settlement here. After the Vikings came the early Christians, whose traces remain in the fragments of a 13th-century Franciscan friary at the west end of Main Street.

Notable 18th-century buildings include the Town Hall, and behind it the remains of the Old Jail, built in 1702. This was the scene of executions until the end of the 19th century – including that of Billy Byrne, a leader of the 1798 Rebellion, commemorated by a monument in Market Square. The Old Jail ceased to be a prison in 1924, and is now a Heritage Centre and museum.

On a grassy knoll south of Wicklow's sheltered harbour are the remains of the Black Castle, successor to the castle built in 1169 by the Anglo-Norman Maurice Fitzgerald for protection against the O'Byrne chieftains who frequently raided the town.
**Heritage Centre** *9am-5pm daily. Tel: (0404) 67324.*

# CONNAUGHT COUNTIES

IN the remote west of Ireland the starkly beautiful mountains of Galway and Mayo drop down to a coastline of lace-like intricacy. Whitewashed cottages, their thatches lashed to their gables against the Atlantic storms, lie scattered along the shoreline, clinging to rare patches of fertile soil. The sweet and acrid smoke of turf fires hangs in the air. Mountains rise dramatically from the sea, and inland roads wind through woodland of beech, rowan, sycamore and wild rhododendron, before rising up to an open landscape of moorland – vast tracts of blanket bog where sheep pick their way over brightly coloured mosses and peat-darkened streams.

When the sun shines, the long, sandy beaches fill with families picnicking and bathing in the bracing sea, walkers take to the hills and golfers stroll out onto the many seaside links. On cloudy days, fishermen thank their luck and head for the lakes and rivers of some of Ireland's most prized fishing country in search of salmon, sea trout and brown trout. And

when the sea mists blanket the coast, the landscape reveals a new, mysterious nature, and the many prehistoric sites of this region take on an unworldly presence, surrounded by the muffled gloom. Bitter winter days apart, the temperatures are mild, warmed by the Gulf Stream. Palm trees grow in sheltered spots, and many roads are banked by hedges of fuchsia which, unrestrained by frost, grow in thick profusion.

Connaught is the old mid-western province of Ireland, bounded by the Shannon to the east and comprising counties Galway, Mayo and Roscommon, as well as Leitrim and Sligo farther north. It is divided from north to south by a chain of lakes – Loughs Conn, Mask and Corrib – running down from Killala to Galway and providing a natural border between the fertile lowlands to the east and the wild mountains to the west. The lowlands – covering parts of Mayo and Galway and all of Roscommon – have throughout history provided prosperity through cattle-raising and

TEAMPALL BHEANÁIN *The tiny roofless church on Inishmore is a remnant of a group of monasteries founded on the Aran Islands.*

SYMPHONY IN BLUE AND GOLD *The early sun gilds The Twelve Pins of Connemara, reflected in azure waters.*

agriculture. Here limestone plains form the beginnings of the rich pastures of the midlands, and open roads pass farms set in a green and wooded landscape, with tidy villages and bustling market towns.

But it was the remote and less accessible western side that provided refuge against invaders, and it is here that you will find the region's most beautiful scenery. The coast and mountains of Connaught were the last parts of Ireland to hold out against Tudor incursions and today people still speak Irish in some parts, notably in Iarconnaught, the Gaeltacht – or Irish-speaking area – that stretches along the north coast of Galway Bay, and in the Aran Islands.

Galway city developed as an unusual enclave, loyal to the English Crown and trading vigorously with Spain, France and Portugal from behind the walls built to keep out the hostile Irish clans which surrounded it. It is now a delightful and prospering university town.

Among the region's most celebrated beauty spots are Achill Island in County Mayo and the bleak Connemara mountains in County Galway. Straddling Galway Bay, the Aran Islands, with their gaily painted thatched cottages and pocket-handkerchief pastures, boast massive prehistoric fortresses, including Dun Aengus, with its back to the edge of a 250ft precipice. At every turn there are reminders of the early Christian and medieval monks who lived on the islands – beehive cells, tiny stone chapels and ancient graveyards among the sand dunes.

Throughout Connaught, the turbulence of the region is recalled by numerous fortifications, particularly the tower houses built by smaller landowners in the 15th and 16th centuries. Some, such as those of Aughnanure and Dunguaire castles in Galway, have survived in good condition; hundreds of others dot the landscape as crumbling ruins. The shells of countless monasteries, some gaunt and forlorn, others of touching beauty, also lie scattered over the country – Cong, Rosserk, Moyne, Kilmacduagh, Ross Errilly, Kilconnell, Boyle, to name but a few.

Later centuries produced the 'big house', and while many of these did not survive the Civil War of 1922-3, Strokestown Park House and Clonalis House in Roscommon, and Westport House in Mayo are

OBSERVING TRADITION *The Aran Islands are an outpost of the old way of life in Ireland. Here the traditional clothes are still worn, Irish is spoken, the islanders still spin, weave and knit using traditional patterns, and eke a living from the limestone soil and the wild sea.*

**INDEX OF TOURING AREAS**

notable exceptions, now open to the public. Two of the big houses have important places on the literary map of Ireland – Coole House in Galway and Moore Hall in Mayo. Coole House, which has been demolished, was home to Lady Gregory, a leading light of last century's Irish Literary Revival, whose mansion was a meeting place for a glittering array of literary figures. Many of them, such as George Bernard Shaw and W.B. Yeats, were encouraged to carve their initials on a tree in the grounds; it is the focus of literary pilgrimages to this day.

For those looking for an alternative to historical or literary sites, there are other, unique attractions. Galway is famous for its oysters, which are raised in oyster beds at the eastern end of Galway Bay. Galway city and nearby Clarinbridge both hold oyster festivals in September. For horse-lovers, Ballinasloe in Galway hosts a large horse fair in October, while Connemara has two shows for its famous ponies in August.

Like everywhere else in Ireland, the region has its own religious associations. In 1879, a vision of the Virgin Mary, St Joseph and St John the Evangelist was witnessed by a number of villagers at Knock in County Mayo. It has since become one of the most important Marian shrines in the world, with a huge, modern basilica. The adjacent international airport accommodates the thousands of pilgrims who come here each year in the hope of the vision appearing again.

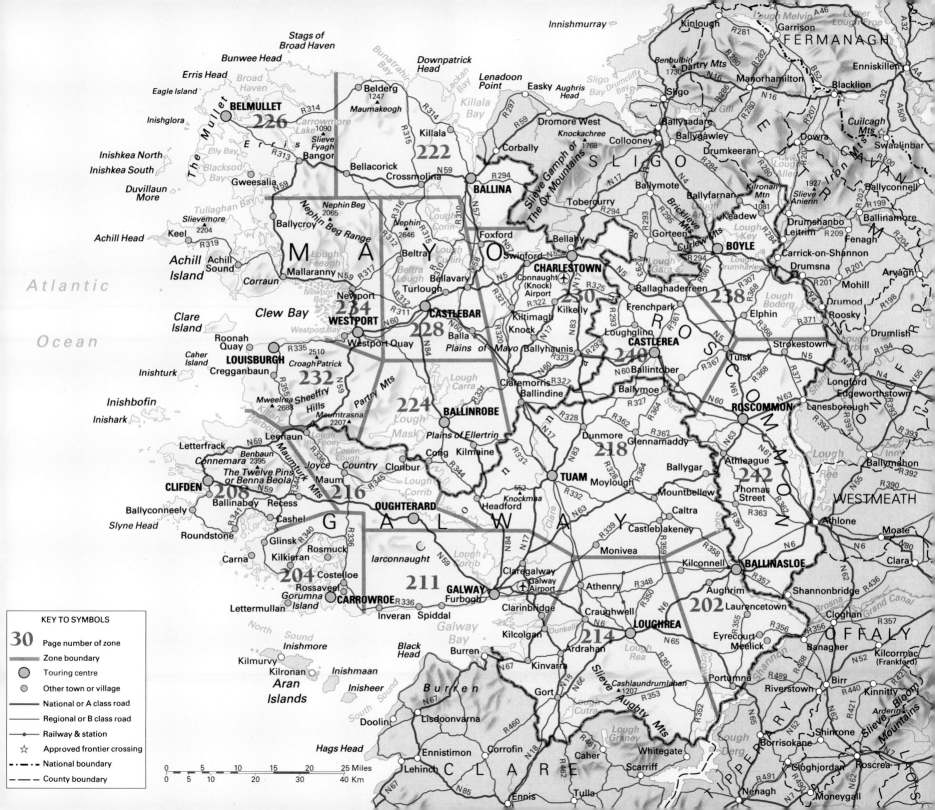

# Horse fairs and Navigators

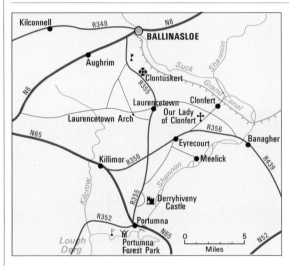

*Towards the great fertile plains of central Ireland the soil produces rich pasture for dairy cattle and, instead of the dry-stone walls so typical of the rest of the country, a living network of green hedges overlays the grazing land. The countryside is dotted with reminders of the past, from the ruined tower houses of the late-medieval gentry to the iron handpumps in the villages and the avenues to grand houses.*

HORSES FOR COURSES *At Ballinasloe horse fair, horses are raced as well as traded.*

## OTHER PLACES TO SEE

**Aughrim** Pretty agricultural village near battlefield where James II's Catholic army was defeated by Williamites in 1691. James's general, St Ruth, died in ring-fort close to road. Nearby is another ring-fort; both are about 100ft across.

**Derryhiveny Castle** 4m NE of Portumna, roofless, but well-preserved 1643 castle.

**Eyrecourt** 10m NE of Portumna, old-world agricultural village. Through graveyard of ruined church N of village is ivy-clad ruin of old Eyrecourt Castle, former seat of Earls of Clanrickarde.

**Kilconnell** Outside village are ruins of 1414 Franciscan friary; intricate vaulting and sculpture on ceiling of bell tower; nave contains beautifully carved tombs from late 15th or 16th century.

**Laurencetown** Typical 'landlord's village' with Georgian atmosphere. At crossroads 2m W of village is 'Laurencetown Arch', dilapidated but grandiose monument to Irish Volunteer movement of 1778-83.

**Meelick** 10m NE of Portumna, close to W bank of Shannon, Franciscan friary founded 1414. Fishing and boating.

**Our Lady of Clonfert** 1m SW of Clonfert, modern Catholic church with endearing 14th-century painted wooden statue of the Madonna and Child. Nearby,

on roadside, are remains of 16th-century tower house.

## TOURS

**Bog Tours** Mar-Oct, tours by narrow-gauge railway. Information from Bórd na Móna, Blackwater. Tel: (0905) 74114.

## EVENTS

**Ballinasloe Arts Week** June.
**Ballinasloe Gala Angling Week** May.
**Ballinasloe Great October Fair** (including horse fair), end Sept-early Oct.
**East Galway Gymkhana and Hunt** June.
**Galway County Fleadh Cheoil Finals** Ballinasloe, May.
**Lough Derg Rally** Early July.
**Portumna Summer Festival** Mid-July.

## SPORT

**Angling** Coarse fishing: Rivers Kilcrow, Shannon and Suck, and Lough Derg. Game fishing: Lough Derg and River Shannon.
**Golf** Ballinasloe Golf Club, 18-hole course. Tel: (0905) 42126.
Portumna Golf Club, 9-hole course, being extended to 18-hole course. Tel: (0509) 41059.
**Horse riding** Milcham Equestrian Centre. Tel: (0905) 76388. O'Sullivan Beare. Tel: (0905) 75205/75247.

## INFORMATION

Ireland West Tourism. Tel: (091) 63081.

## Ballinasloe/Béal Átha na Sluaighe

Businesslike streets set around a scooped-out green, a cattle grid spanning the gateway to the Catholic church and a harness-maker to be seen at work in the main street give Ballinasloe the air of a well-run stable yard. This was once the scene of one of the three greatest horse fairs in Europe. It has ancient origins, but really took off in the years after 1722, when the local landowners, the Trench family – Earls of Clancarty – were licensed to hold an annual livestock fair here. It became a hiring fair too, for labourers, but it was its horses that made it famous throughout Europe. By the end of the 18th century, agents from all the major European powers, especially France and Russia, were coming to Ballinasloe to buy cavalry horses, draught horses and ponies for the baggage trains of their armies. It is said that as many as 6000 horses would change hands in a single day. Local tradition also holds that Napoleon's horse Marengo was bought at Ballinasloe. Ballinasloe's Great October Fair attracts droves of visitors and 'interested parties' on the opening Sunday.

The Trench family provided a rare example of enlightened landlords, and are held in high esteem to this day. The many elegant grey limestone buildings in the town, including the Clancarty's town house (now a branch of the Bank of Ireland), were built when it prospered with the fair.

Ballinasloe's other charms include its pretty main streets and two churches of note. St Michael's Catholic church, built in the 1850s, has an impressive austerity to it, softened by some fine, modern stained glass, including work by Harry Clarke (1889-1931); the elegant tower of Protestant St John's, on high ground at the edge of the green, provides a backdrop to the fair.

## Clonfert/Cluain Fearta

A village in the vale of the River Suck, Clonfert became known for the monastery founded on this site by Brendan the Navigator in AD 563. Clonfert monastery was a famous centre of learning, but was destroyed five times between its foundation and the 12th century, by Vikings and by fire. However, much of the cathedral that was subsequently built here around 1200 has survived, largely because Clonfert is one of Ireland's few great medieval churches to remain in use for Protestant services.

Above the exceptionally beautiful round-arched west doorway is a triangular pediment filled with carved figures, animals and ornament. It is a lovely relic of Irish Romanesque decorative architecture.

## Clontuskert/Cluain Tuaiscirt

The well-preserved ruins of an Augustinian priory stand about a quarter of a mile's walk across fields at the edge of the vale of Suck. The original foundation on the site was by St Baetan in 805 and from 1140 it became a monastery of great wealth and influence. A disastrous fire destroyed it in the early 15th century and much of what is seen today was built in its place.

The carvings around the west door of the church date from 1471. In a neat row stand the angel-saint Michael holding a pair of scales on which the Christian soul will be weighed at the Gates of Heaven, while a demon crouches at his feet waiting greedily to

take care of the rejects. St Catherine of Alexandria is depicted with the wheel on which she was tortured (the catherine wheel). St John the Baptist and St Augustine of Hippo are also shown.

## Portumna/Port Omna

The River Shannon provided one of the historic barriers to the west, and Portumna was one of the few places where it could be crossed. The river was bridged here for the first time only in 1796. The latest of three bridges is an iron one built in 1910, with four sets of domed piers; it stretches for a quarter of a mile, with a swing section to let larger vessels through.

Portumna's broad streets of shops and houses retain hints of the town's Georgian past. The big family here was called Clanrickarde – a title blackened by the absurd miserliness of the last earl and marquis, who caused his tenants much anguish by persisting, against the general political climate, with high rents and evictions during the 1880s and right up until his death in 1916.

The Clanrickardes were among the descendants of the powerful Anglo-Norman de Burgo (or Burke) family. Richard Burke, the 4th earl, built Portumna Castle (1610-20), a fortified manor house that was then probably the most magnificent house in Ireland. It was gutted by fire in 1826, but its graceful proportions, rows of stone-mullioned windows and Dutch-style decorative gables are still visible, giving it an air of wealth, comfort and stability. Closer inspection justifies the name 'castle'. The gardens are defended by guard towers, slit windows in the corner towers give cover to the entrance, and the walls are as thick as a keep's.

In the grounds of Portumna Castle are the ruins of a Dominican priory surrounded by mature trees. It has a fine east window with its stone tracery intact, and a partially restored cloister. Patrick Sarsfield, hero of the siege of Limerick in 1690, married Honoria de Burgh, daughter of the Earl of Clanrickarde, in this church.

The 1400 acres of the Clanrickarde demesne on the shores of Lough Derg to the west of the town have been opened to the public as the Portumna Forest Park. This wildlife sanctuary is home to a large herd of deer and many other native mammals and birds. Forest walks are well signposted.

**Portumna Castle Grounds** *8am-4pm.*
**Portumna Forest Park** *9am-9pm, or dusk.*

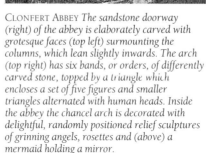

CLONFERT ABBEY *The sandstone doorway (right) of the abbey is elaborately carved with grotesque faces (top left) surmounting the columns, which lean slightly inwards. The arch (top right) has six bands, or orders, of differently carved stone, topped by a triangle which encloses a set of five figures and smaller triangles alternated with human heads. Inside the abbey the chancel arch is decorated with delightful, randomly positioned relief sculptures of grinning angels, rosettes and (above) a mermaid holding a mirror.*

# Where Old Ways Survive

*Boulder-strewn bog pitted with tiny loughs reaches right to the edge of a granite coastline shredded by erosion. The coast is skirted by a road known, simply enough, as Cois Fharraige, which means 'beside the sea'. A few miles offshore lie the Aran Islands, where Irish is the first language, the local traditions are still strong and a hard living has to be wrenched from perilous seas and recalcitrant soil.*

## Aran Islands

Postcards of the Aran Islands successfully capture the tranquillity of their whitewashed thatched cottages, their window frames and low wooden doors picked out in vivid colour, and the intricate network of dry-stone walls that bind together tiny green pastures. Yet much of the landscape is far more rugged. Vast pavements of grey limestone, fissured and crumbling, cover the interior. The dry-stone walls screen intermittent patches of vegetation, and in some of the fields there is no soil at all. In the past, islanders had to grow crops here by pounding at the limestone with sledgehammers, and salvaging soil from cracks in the rock which they fertilised with seaweed. Fishing from currachs, crop-growing and raising a few domestic animals

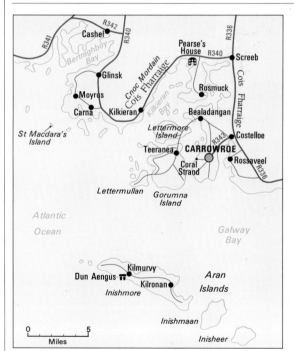

### OTHER PLACES TO SEE
**Costelloe** Pretty village at top of rocky bay; home of Irish-language radio station, Radió na Gaeltachta.

**Rosmuck** Hamlet on tip of peninsula jutting into Kilkieran Bay; coastal landscape with clusters of woodland, and fine views.

### St Macdara's Island
Uninhabited island famous for fine 12th-century chapel with sharply angled stone roof (fully restored) and antae; associated with St Mac Dara, patron saint of Connemara fishermen. Access in good weather by private arrangement with boat operators in Carna.

### EVENTS
**Féile Mhic Dara** Carna, mid-July. Traditional boat and angling festival centring on annual pilgrimage to St Macdara's Island.
**Féile na nOileán** Gorumna Island. Traditional boat festival. End July.

### SPORT
**Angling** Game-fishing: Aroolagh, Camus, Carna, Carrowroe, Gorumna Island, Inverbeg and Lettermucka loughs; Costelloe, Formoyle, Furnace, Invermore, Owengowla and Screeb systems; River Gowlabeg. Sea-fishing: Aran Islands, Carna, Rossaveel.

### INFORMATION
Ireland West Tourism.
Tel: (091) 63081.

IDYLLIC ISLANDS *A watchful cat (top) on the Aran Islands enjoys a Sunday morning, while islanders make their way to church, the older women in traditional black shawls (below).*

FENCED IN *Since timber is scarce on the islands, and stones are plentiful, farmers make their gates from piles of stones to fence in their cattle (below).*

in this unpromising terrain provided the islanders with a scant livelihood, and formed the basis of a distinctive pattern of traditions.

The resilience and warmth of the Aran islanders and the great beauty of the landscape have attracted writers, painters and film-makers for over a hundred years. The playwright J.M. Synge (1871-1909) was a frequent visitor to these islands, and was greatly moved and influenced by them. Robert Flaherty, the American film director, came here in the early 1930s and made *Man of Aran*. This remarkable evocation of one family's battle with the land and the sea was rendered in an innovative mixture of documentary and poetic storytelling that has made it a classic of the cinema.

There are three main islands in the group, which lie in a row in the mouth of Galway Bay: Inishmore ('the large island'), Inishmaan ('the middle island'), and Inisheer ('the eastern island').

**Inishmore**, with a population of about 900, is by far the biggest, 8 miles long and roughly cigar-shaped. There is just one road, which runs the length of the island and connects the main village and harbour, Kilronan, to the other villages. These are all on the north side, where the land is comparatively good, with pasture running down to the shore. To the south, by contrast, the land rises through an extremely rocky limestone landscape to a line of high cliffs. It is here, in the middle of Inishmore's southern coast, that the Aran Islands' most famous monument – Dun Aengus – is found, set precariously at the edge of a sheer drop of over 250ft to the sea.

Dun Aengus is a huge prehistoric cliff fort defended on the landward side by three semicircular rings of massive dry-stone battlements, and a broad band of vicious-looking *chevaux-de-frise*, sharp, upended rocks placed in the ground to impede any enemy. The innermost enclosure is some 50yds across.

There are three other such strongholds on the island, each as impressive in its own way. Dun Doocaher ('the black fort') is similarly positioned on the edge of cliffs, surrounded by acres of limestone pavement, whereas Dun Onaght and Dun Eochla are completely circular and set in the middle of the island, with fine views out over Galway Bay. No one quite knows who built these forts, or exactly when, but they are reckoned to be around 2000 years old.

INISHMORE *High cliffs and a rocky shore bound the largest of the Aran Islands.*

AN IRISH CLIFFHANGER *With its back to precipitous cliffs, its horseshoe-shaped walls holding off enemies from inland, Dun Aengus is the finest prehistoric cliff fort in Ireland.*

The Aran Islands, settled by early Christians in the 6th century, are dotted with early Christian remains. The great saint of the islands was St Enda, the teacher of many holy men such as St Jarlath of Tuam and St Kieran, who founded Clonmacnoise in County Offaly. Teampall Chiaráin, a church of about the year 1200 and bearing St Kieran's name, lies in pasture on Inishmore, not far from Kilronan. Each of these ruins has a haunting beauty, in their intimate scale, in the rigorous asceticism that they represent, and in their settings. Particularly beautiful are St Benan's Church (Teampall Mionnáir), a tiny 9th-12th-century oratory standing on the

BEAST OF BURDEN *The donkey is still favoured on the Aran Islands for carrying goods, particularly baskets of turf.*

KEEPING TRADITIONS ALIVE *A villager on Inishmaan prepares thatch before binding it to the roof of a cottage.*

crest of a hill overlooking Inishmaan; and Teaghlach Éinne, an 11th to 12th-century church associated with St Enda, which lies half-buried in sand dunes at the southern end of the island, surrounded by a graveyard said to contain the graves of 120 saints.

The early monks, pursuing the lives of hermits, used to live in tiny 'beehive cells', houses constructed entirely of dry-stone masonry which is staggered gently inwards to form a corbelled, dome-like roof. One of these, Clochán na Carraige, set in pasture on the northern coast near the village of Kilmurvy, has survived virtually intact.

**Inishmaan**, the least well served by ferries to the mainland, is the most unspoilt and traditional of the three islands: some of the older women still wear the old style of calf-length woollen skirt, with a colourful shawl and headscarf, and there are very few vehicles here. The landscape beckons to the walker, with paths across the rocky hillsides

to the south decked with wild flowers, or beautiful sandy beaches to the north.

Inishmaan has its share of interesting historical monuments, including the prehistoric Conor Fort, the most splendid of the circular (or oval) dry-stone forts of the islands, and the beautiful little chapel called Kilcanonagh at the eastern end of the island. The Teach Synge is a pretty thatched cottage where J.M. Synge used to stay; and there is a lovely little church of St Mary Immaculate, built in 1939, with radiant stained-glass windows from the studio of Harry Clarke.

**Inisheer** is the smallest of the islands, and has marginally richer terrain, sectioned off by countless stone walls. The main villages are in the northern part, where there are two sandy beaches. The north is dominated by the ruins of a 15th-century tower house called O'Brien's Castle, crowning a steep hill and surrounded by a large cashel. Among its early Christian ruins is the tiny 11th-12th-century

church associated with St Gobnat, who was said to have been the only woman allowed on the islands in the early Christian era. Teampall Chaomháin, called the Church of Kevin, has had to be excavated from a huge sand dune strewn with seashells. Chaomháin was said to be the brother of St Kevin of Glendalough, County Wicklow.

Inisheer also has a small folk museum where a variety of artefacts representative of traditional island life and photographs of the past are displayed. It is next to the Ceard Shiopa, one of several outlets for the Aran Islands' most famous product, the beautiful white hand-knitted sweaters, or Aran ganseys, with their distinctive patterning, still worn by islanders in cold weather. The sweaters are thought to have got the name gansey from Guernsey, to which every young fisherman was expected to sail to prove his manhood, and from which the patterns are thought to have come. Traditional costume is still worn by some islanders, especially on Inishmaan, and includes rawhide shoes suited to the islands' rocky terrain, and finger-braided girdles, or crois, of coloured wools.

**Ferry services** *From Rossaveel and Galway to Inishmore; from Doolin, County Clare, to Inishmore and Inisheer; from Spiddal in summer to all the islands.*

## Carna

The scattered coastal settlement is the largest on the western side of the peninsula. A scenic road leads west to the coast at Moyrus, with views of the offshore islands, and on to Glinsk overlooking deep Bertraghboy Bay, with The Twelve Pins, or Benna Beola, of Connemara beyond it.

The colours of the Connemara landscape are often compared to the natural dyes of the local tweed. In autumn the moor grass turns russet-brown and bracken dies back to a dry beige. There are mauves in the fading heather, glowing reds in the fuchsia hedges and vivid touches of yellow in the gorse.

## Carrowroe/An Cheathrú Rua

The village's Irish name means 'peninsula' and refers to the tongue of land on which Carrowroe sits, with its cottages tucked away among the dry-stone walls in the lee of the hillsides. There are some fine sandy beaches scattered along the mainly rocky coast, which can be reached by small roads and farm tracks. On several of the beaches, the tradi-

tional fishing boats known as currachs lie upturned on grass banks next to long lines of lobster pots.

The most celebrated beach is the so-called Coral Strand west of Carrowroe. What looks like yellow sand from a distance turns out to be, on closer inspection, millions of rounded fragments of limestone which form a crust around the branches of a seaweed called *Lithothamnion.*

## Gorumna Island/Garmna

The bay between Carrowroe and Kilkieran contains Gorumna Island, joined to the islands of Lettermullan, Lettermore and the mainland since the late 19th century by a series of bridges.

Despite great changes on the islands over the past 50 years, their inhabitants maintain a strong sense of their traditions. Currach racing is still a fiercely contested sport. Peat is stacked neatly on dry-stone plinths by cottage doors, and here and there crops are still grown on banks of raised soil called 'lazybeds'.

Aspects of traditional life, such as a poteen still and a pedal-operated loom, and historic photographs, are displayed in the small Island Heritage Centre at Teeranea on Gorumna Island.

CARROWROE CORAL *Fragments of coral bleached by the sun and smoothed by the sand litter the beach at Coral Strand.*

## A VERY VERSATILE CRAFT

Along much of the west coast, and particularly on the Aran Islands, the traditional rowing boats called 'currachs' are still used. For a coastal region where timber is scarce, these craft provide a practical and highly effective solution to boat-builders. They are made of a frame of wooden slats covered in canvas, which is then coated in several layers of black tar, although originally they were covered with hide.

The shape of the currach is distinctive, with a flat stern and a rising prow which rides high in the water. There are usually three seats, for traditionally currachs are rowed by teams of three oarsmen, each wielding a pair of narrow-bladed oars. The oars are held firm to the gunwale by a vertical spigot of wood which serves as a rowlock: the oar has a triangular piece of wood attached to it with a hole through it, and the spigot is inserted into this hole.

Currachs are versatile craft, extremely buoyant, and able to bear large loads. Although they are not particularly light, a crew of three can lift a currach over their heads and, looking like a long-legged beetle, carry it well up the beach for safe-keeping. They are traditionally stored upside-down, resting on stones or trestles, often with the oars and other gear sheltered beneath.

Nowadays, currachs are often fitted with small outboard motors, and wheeled in and out of the sea on dinghy trolleys, but nonetheless their basic design remains quite unchanged. Currach racing is a popular sport on the west coast, and this alone is likely to help to preserve the boat's use for many decades to come.

### Kilkieran/Cill Chiaráin

St Kieran, the 6th-century saint who founded the great abbey at Clonmacnoise in County Offaly, is believed to have stopped here on his way to see St Enda on the Aran Islands. Kilkieran is now a spacious village on a hillside above the long inlet of Kilkieran Bay. Near the pier lie heaps of seaweed waiting to be processed by the Arramara Teoranta Company, which turns seaweed into shrivelled chips that look like tea leaves by washing and then drying it in coal-fired ovens. The dried seaweed is transported via Northern Ireland to Scotland where extracts are made, mainly for use as thickeners in the food and cosmetics industries.

CURRACH RACING *Every year these boats are raced from Gorumna Island.*

DOWN TO THE SEA *As dawn breaks, a currach is carried across the flat sands to the water's edge, the start of a day's fishing.*

### Pearse's House/Teach an Phiarsaigh

Alone on a small hill overlooking a tiny lough is a traditional whitewashed and thatched cottage. It was built in 1910 by the writer and teacher Patrick Pearse (1879-1916), president of the provisional government of the Irish republic in 1916, who stayed here when holidaying to improve his Irish.

The simple interior is representative of the kind of home almost all rural and coastal families in Galway lived in until fairly recently. The front door opens onto the kitchen, with its stone floor and cast-iron range, which served as the main living room. The only other rooms are two bedrooms, one on either side of the kitchen.

The cottage is a national monument to the man who led the ill-fated Easter Rising in Dublin in 1916, and was shot for it. The key can be got from the house on the main road.
**Opening times** *All year, Mon-Sat 9.30am-5.30pm.*

# The Connemara Coast

*Wrapped around The Twelve Pins, or Benna Beola, and jutting out into the Atlantic is a landscape of wild, rocky bogland, of ragged coastline coloured with the autumnal shades of seaweed, and pine trees on tiny pincushion islands mirrored in the loughs. This is Connemara, a poor land where people have eked out meagre livelihoods by fishing, turf cutting and raising what they could from the stony soil.*

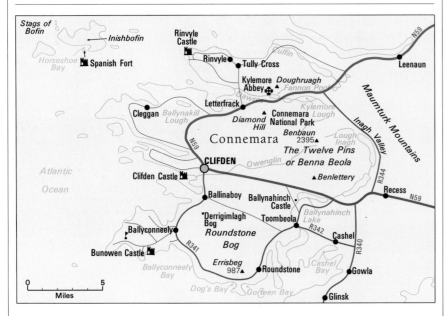

### OTHER PLACES TO SEE
**Ballyconneely** Scattered village at neck of a peninsula with fine sandy beaches; 2m SW is Bunowen Castle, impressive shell of early 19th-century neo-Gothic mansion never completed.
**Inagh Valley** Exceptionally lovely views of mountains, conifer forests and sea from road connecting Recess and Kylemore.
**Letterfrack** Quaker-founded village with good beach nearby for bathing; base for hill walking and mountain climbing.
**Rinvyle Castle** 3m NE of

Tully Cross, remains of 14th-century O'Flaherty tower house, overlooking sea at head of peninsula. Rinvyle peninsula has good sandy beaches.

### WALKS
**Clifden-Derrygimlagh** 10m walk takes in boat harbour, beaches, Lough Fadda, haunt of wild birds, and Marconi station.

### EVENTS
**Cashel Pony Show** Aug.
**Connemara Pony Show** Clifden, Aug.
**Roundstone Salmon and Lobster Festival** End June.

### SPORT
**Angling** Coarse fishing: Rivers Ballinaboy, Dawros and Owenglin; Ballyconneely, Ballynahinch, Ballynakill, Inagh, Kylemore and Roundstone loughs; Culfin and Gowla systems. Sea fishing: Ballyconneely, Cashel Bay, Cleggan, Clifden, Inishbofin, Rinvyle, Roundstone.
**Golf** Connemara Golf Club, 18-hole course. Tel: (095) 23502.

### INFORMATION
Ireland West Tourism. Tel: (091) 63081.

### Ballynahinch Lake/Loch Baile na hInse
This lake is the most westerly of a chain of loughs curling round the eastern flank of the group of mountains called The Twelve Pins. It is a pretty lake, open to the scree-coated flanks of Benlettery (1904ft) on its northern side, but wooded along the south.

On a tiny island near the western end of the lake the ivy-covered ruin of a castle recalls several highly colourful characters who lived here. It was one of the strongholds of Grace O'Malley, the 16th-century Pirate Queen from Clare Island, County Mayo. Later, it belonged to Galway city oligarch Richard Martin MP (1754-1834), who enlarged an inn near the south shore and named it Bally-nahinch Castle. It is now a hotel.

Martin, known as 'Hairtrigger Dick' from his fame as a duellist, introduced the bill that led to the founding of the Royal Society for the Prevention of Cruelty to Animals (RSPCA), and thus earned the new nickname 'Humanity Dick'. He apparently used the old castle on the lake to incarcerate anyone on his estate found mistreating animals.

Probably the best-loved owner of the house was the cricketing Maharaja, Prince Ranjitsinji, who spent part of every year at Ballynahinch from 1925 until his death in 1933. Visitors are welcome to the grounds.

### Clifden/An Clochán
The charm of the 'capital of Connemara', the largest town of the region, owes a lot to its site above an inlet of the Atlantic. The Twelve Pins provide a grand backdrop to the town against the eastern sky, and below the town the River Owenglin cascades into the bay.

Two spires give Clifden its distinctive skyline. The neo-Gothic Catholic church with great rose windows, built on the site of an ancient beehive-shaped stone hut, and the simpler Protestant church, enjoy equal billing in the building scheme. The town was founded in 1812 by local landowner John d'Arcy. The broad main streets are laid out in a T-plan, with painted shopfronts.

A scenic route called the Sky Road runs out along the peninsula to the west, with exhilarating coastal views. A mile along this road is a castellated gateway, the entrance to the old d'Arcy mansion called Clifden Castle, reached by a 10 minute walk down a muddy farm track. Now just a derelict shell, it was once a fanciful Gothic mansion with turrets, towers and crenellations.

MARKET DAY *Clifden's cattle market attracts farmers from the surrounding dairy country hoping to sell a cow or two.*

### Connemara National Park
The real gift of Connemara is its untamed natural beauty, 5000 acres of which make up the Connemara National Park, one of the region's top attractions. It consists of a sweep of mountainous land south of the Quaker village of Letterfrack, and contains the chisel-shaped peak of Diamond Hill and four of The Twelve Pins (including Benbaun, the tallest at

BEAUTY SPOTS *The towering Twelve Pins (left), mist-shrouded Kylemore Lough (above) and Ballyconneely Bay (below) are among Connemara's gems.*

2395ft). The park is involved in conservation projects, one of which has reintroduced the native Irish red deer to the park.

Two signposted nature trails start at the Visitor Centre. One traces a course through beautiful Ellis Wood; the other the Sruffaunboy trail, climbs rougher terrain and passes the paddock where the park's herd of Connemara ponies is kept. Beyond these trails, small paths lead out into the wilder more extensive landscape of The Twelve Pins. This is proper hill-walking country for experienced and seriously kitted-out hikers.

The park has a well-equipped Visitor Centre with car park.
**Opening times** *Apr-Oct. Tel: (095) 41054/ 41006.*

## Inishbofin/Inis Bó Finne

Although only 3 miles long, this little island off the coast of Galway has quite varied landscapes. Across the middle is a broad saddle of pasture, divided by stone walls and dotted with conical haystacks. The eastern side has beaches of fine white sand and a hazy blue view of the mountains across the bay. At the western end, by contrast, rich peat bog rises towards a line of blackened, craggy rocks. Offshore lies the spray-lashed cluster of rocks called the Stags of Bofin.

About 180 people live on Inishbofin, mainly on the southern coast around the large natural harbour. They are connected to the mainland by a regular boat service from Cleggan. The rhythm of life is tranquil now,

but the island has had a dramatic past. The harbour entrance lies under the eye of the Spanish Fort, a lonely ruined fortress on the eastern promontory, accessible only at low tide. It was occupied at one time in the 16th century by a Spanish pirate called Don Bosco, apparently after entering an alliance with the Pirate Queen, Grace O'Malley. Today its cluster of gables speak more of the castle's use as a fortified barracks during Cromwellian times, after 1653, when monks and priests were interned here.

To the east of the island is a little fishing village that lines the deep curve of Horseshoe Bay. Nearby, in a graveyard grazed by curly horned ewes, is the lichen-covered nave of a 13th-century church. It was built on the site of the 7th-century monastery established by St Colman, who arrived here with a group of dissenting monks, having refused to accept the Church's decision to abandon Celtic church practices in favour of Roman ones.

## Kylemore Abbey

An extravagant medieval fantasy in glistening white granite and grey limestone rises from the shores of Fannon Pool, one of a trio of lakes, backed by the thickly wooded escarpments of Doughruagh (1736ft). Kylemore Lough's Irish name, 'Loch na Coille Móire', means 'lake of the big wood'. The mansion was created in the 1860s after a Manchester magnate, Mitchell Henry, came here on honeymoon. He and his wife fell in love with the spot and determined to build a house on it.

Kylemore Abbey, a castellated neo-Gothic mansion of 70 rooms, is occupied today by an Irish Benedictine community of nuns who came to it from Ypres after the First World War. The grounds and part of the building are open to the public. The chapel in the grounds – a miniature replica of Norwich Cathedral, with good Victorian stained glass – is well worth a visit.
**Kylemore Abbey Grounds** *Feb-Nov, daily 10am-6pm. Tel: (095) 41146. Pottery and tea room. Tel: (095) 41113.*

## Roundstone Bog

An untamed, uninhabited, lake-spattered blanket bog, under the protection of Connemara National Park, stretches from the rocky protrusion of Errisbeg in the south to the foot of The Twelve Pins. Viewed from a height, its patches of water glisten like hundreds of tiny mirrors embroidered onto some exotic gown.

### ALCOCK AND BROWN

In May 1919, just 16 years after Orville Wright's plane hopped 120ft and proved that powered flight was possible, the *Daily Mail* offered a £10,000 prize for the first nonstop flight across the Atlantic. It was won on June 15 by Capt John Alcock, pilot, and Lt Arthur W. Brown, navigator, in a Vickers Vimy biplane bomber. They took 16 hours 12 minutes to fly the 1900 miles from St John's, Newfoundland to Ireland, averaging 120mph.

They sighted the Galway coast at 8.40am and tried to land near the Marconi telegraphy station at Clifden, where what they thought was firm ground turned out to be waterlogged peat. However, they survived, and the Marconi station radioed the news to London immediately. Alcock and Brown were both knighted, but Alcock died in a flying accident the same year; Brown died in 1948. Their plane is in the Science Museum, London.

The bog, which covers more than 10,000 acres, is a rare environment and one of the few strongholds of the otter left in Europe. One small road weaves its way across it, between the hamlets of Toombeola and Ballinaboy, with exceptional views of The Twelve Pins in fine weather.

In the north-western corner is Derrigimlagh Bog, where two major achievements of 20th-century technology occurred. Count Guglielmo Marconi set up the first transatlantic 'wireless telegraphy station' here in 1907, from which he sent the first radio signals across the Atlantic later that year. The installations were ruined in 1922, during the Irish Civil War, but the foundations of the generating room, the masts and domestic buildings can still be seen. To the south a monument commemorates the spot where Alcock and Brown crash-landed at the end of the first nonstop transatlantic flight in 1919.

### CONNEMARA PONIES

Most Connemara families had a workhorse in the past, a beast of burden that they took for granted. Only in the early 20th century were Connemara ponies recognised for their exceptional qualities. Hardy, companionable, resilient yet pliant, they are found exclusively in this harsh coastal terrain. If bred outside Connemara, the ponies begin to lose their distinctive qualities after two generations.

Their origin is uncertain. Probably they were a crossbreed of a native Celtic horse and Spanish-Arabs imported from Galicia in north-western Spain in the Middle Ages. Their qualities derive also from the particular combination of climate and terrain and the rigorous genetic selection that such an environment demands. Pasture in Connemara is scarce and the ponies eat very little of it. Instead they feed on the salt-tolerant grasses and seaweeds on the seashore.

In spite of their sturdy frame, the ponies are naturally elegant and have become popular everywhere for riding and showjumping.

# On the Shores of Lough Corrib

*The wide expanse of Lough Corrib divides this region into two distinct parts. In the east stretch limestone plains where sheep and cattle graze in rich pasture and the villages are compact and picturesque. To the west are hills covered with untameable bog, and a loose chain of villages which straggles along the northern shore of Galway Bay. This is Iarconnaught, an important centre for the Irish language.*

### Claregalway/Baile Chláir

The River Clare winds it way towards Lough Corrib just to the north of Claregalway, separating the village from the ruins of a Franciscan friary and the thickset keep of an old castle a field away. A tall bell tower with a crown of exaggerated crenellations gives the friary an unusually delicate silhouette, softened by the large sycamore trees that shade the domestic buildings. It was built in the 13th century and somehow survived the campaign of destruction waged against Irish churches, to remain in use until the 18th century. The gargoyles on the tower have grotesque puckered faces and fantastic animal heads, while a bearded face looks down from the octagonal boss in the centre of the vaulted ceiling beneath the tower. The chancel of the church must have been unusually light, with a fine east window and rows of six deeply recessed lancet windows on both sides.

The castle, by contrast, is now very much a ruin left to nature, squat and darkly grim. It was built in the 15th century by the Anglo-Norman de Burgo (or Burke) family to defend the river crossing, and the road still passes over a bridge at its foot. It follows the familiar pattern of the tower house, but with a slightly more complex interior afforded by its broader ground plan.

### Galway/Gaillimh

The fourth-largest urban area in the Republic is Galway city, for almost 1000 years a centre of economic importance, which it owes to the River Corrib that tumbles out of Lough Corrib into Galway Bay. Tucked away in a sheltered corner of Galway Bay, at the lowest crossing of the salmon-run Corrib river, the city is a natural trading post between the rich inland country east of the lough and the markets of Europe's Atlantic seaboard.

By 1240 the de Burgo family had built a castle here, around which the town grew up, prospering through trade with France and Spain. It was controlled by 14 families that Cromwell called the 'Tribes of Galway'.

Only traces of Galway's splendid medieval past survive here and there among the later buildings erected on the old street plan. The most complete is Lynch's Castle, on Shop Street, one of the finest medieval town houses remaining in Ireland. This was once the stronghold of the Lynch family, one of the 14 'tribes', and proclaims its noble past with a greystone façade, complete with gargoyle, carved coat of arms and stone-mullioned windows. It is now a branch of the Allied Irish Bank, and is the oldest Irish building used daily for commercial purposes.

Nearby is the Collegiate Church of St Nicholas of Myra, a saint held dear by seafarers. It was built in 1320 and enlarged

## EVENTS

**Clarinbridge Oyster Festival** Early Sept.
**Eyre Square Festival** Galway, early Aug.
**Galway Arts Festival** July.
**Galway Bay Sea Angling Festival** Salthill, May.
**Galway Race Week** July-Aug.
**International Oyster Festival** Galway, late Sept.
**Market Day** Sat, in Galway (by the Collegiate Church of St Nicholas).
**Salthill Harp Festival** June-July.

## SPORT

**Angling** Coarse fishing: Ross Lake. Game fishing: Rivers Corrib, Knock and Owenboliskey; Loughs Corrib and Kip. Sea fishing: Barna, Spiddal, Inveran.
**Golf** Galway Golf Club, 18-hole course. Tel: (091) 21827.
**Greyhound racing** Galway.
**Horse racing** Ballybrit, July-Oct.
**Horse riding** Claregalway.

## INFORMATION

Ireland West Tourism.
Tel: (091) 63081.

## OTHER PLACES TO SEE

**Annaghdown** Tiny ruined 15th-century cathedral on site of church founded by St Brendan; small 11th/12th-century church and largely 15th-century priory stand nearby.
**Clarinbridge** 8m from Galway, tiny village and focus of oyster festival. Also Clarinbridge crystal; showrooms open Mon-Fri 9am-6pm, Sat 10am-6pm. Sun 2-6pm. Tel: (091) 96178.

**Furbogh** Irish-speaking village and administrative centre for the Gaeltachtaí throughout Ireland.
**Inveran** Very pretty Gaeltacht settlement, the least spoilt on northern shore of Galway Bay.

## CRUISES

River and Lough Corrib guided tours by *Corrib Princess* of Aran Ferries, from Woodquay, Galway city. Tel: (091) 68903.

LOUGH CORRIB *Ireland's second largest lake, some 25 miles long and 7 miles across at its widest point, effectively cuts County Galway in two.*

211

and remodelled over the centuries. It has an unusually broad, open feel to it, and a sober calmness evoked by the grey pillars and stonework set against the cream-painted plaster. Tradition has it that Christopher Columbus visited Galway to find out more about St Brendan's voyages prior to sailing across the Atlantic to discover America in 1492, and came to this church to pray.

Bordering the churchyard is the remnant of a wall, Gothic doorway and a relief sculpture of a skull and crossbones. This is the Lynch Memorial, restored to this position in 1854, which marks the scene of a famous Galway story. In 1493 a young Spanish man was killed by the son of the mayor, James

### CLARINBRIDGE OYSTERS

The unique mix of fresh and salt water gives Clarinbridge, or 'Galway Bay', oysters their worldwide reputation for firm texture and full flavour. These are native wild oysters and breed in some 700 acres of beds spread across Dunbuleaun Bay where the Rivers Clarinbridge and Dunkellin converge. They are harvested when about four years old.

The name Clarinbridge is well known with oyster-lovers as the home of the annual oyster festival, of which Paddy Burke's pub is the focus. It is a pretty 17th-century building with a snug interior of panelled wood. The rich and famous had already joined his faithful regulars by the time Paddy launched the first festival in 1954. By the time he died in 1971, the festival had grown from an original attendance of 35 to registrations of over 1000. The Clarinbridge Oyster Festival that evolved around Paddy Burke's pub goes from strength to strength.

Nearby, at the weir on the River Dunkellin, Moran's Oyster Cottage is equally well known to enthusiasts. The festival takes place in early September.

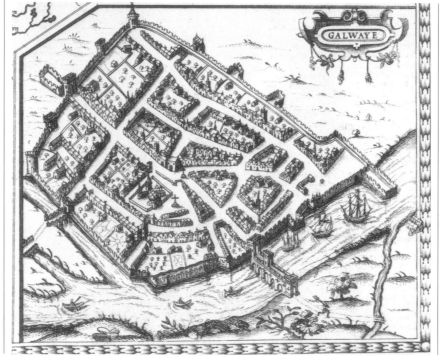

WATERFRONT REFLECTIONS *Galway harbour's Spanish Arch stands where ships from Spain once unloaded wines and brandy.*

A CITY WITHIN WALLS *The 1610 map of Galway drawn by the historian John Speed shows a small town with spacious gardens – it is now the Republic's fourth-largest city.*

Lynch Fitzpatrick. Nobody could be found to carry out the sentence of death, so the mayor hanged his own son before retiring into reclusion. Poignant though this tale may be, it has been widely denounced as fiction.

The city's trade with Spain was particularly strong, and the close association caused the 'Spanish Arch' to be built in 1584 beside the old docks. Next to the Spanish Arch is the small Galway City Museum, which houses a collection of historical artefacts from the old Claddagh settlement which lay just outside Galway's city walls, and which is now a suburb of the city.

The broad River Corrib washes the western side of the city, flowing under three bridges. Upstream a salmon weir stems its flow. In March and April huge numbers of salmon mass here in the clear water, preparing to jump the weir and run their way up to their spawning grounds.

Overlooking the salmon weir from the west bank is Galway's most prominent modern landmark: the Cathedral of Our Lady Assumed into Heaven and St Nicholas, completed in 1965. It is a Renaissance-style building with a copper-green dome and an impressive interior. Roughly hewn grey and grey-black limestone is offset by mosaics around the rim of the dome and modern stained glass. The apse at the north end contains a rose window, designed by George Campbell of Dublin, with six main panels: five represent the mysteries of the Rosary, and the sixth is a figure of Our Lady. A bronze statue beneath the window represents Our Lady holding the infant Jesus. The floor is surfaced with pale grey, green and red Connemara marble and the barrel-vaulted and coffered ceiling is lined with red cedar.

A little to the north are the original buildings of University College, founded as Queen's College in 1846 and imitating Oxbridge colleges in style. Nearby is the renovated, tiny, one-up one-down family home of Nora Barnacle, wife of the novelist James Joyce (1882-1941), in the Bowling Green.

**Galway City Museum** *Apr-Oct, Mon-Sat 10am-5.15pm.*

**Nora Barnacle's Cottage** *Apr-Sept, 10am-5pm.*

Nora Barnacle's Kitchen *The home of James Joyce's wife is open to the public.*

Man In The Street *A Galway citizen relaxes amid the bright signs on an Eyre Street restaurant.*

Storyteller *The celebrated Irish story writer Padraic O'Conaire is remembered by a statue in Eyre Square.*

## THE CLADDAGH RING

Over to the west of the Corrib river, just outside Galway's old city walls, lived a close-knit fishing community of some 3000 Irish-speaking people. But, like their rows of cottages, their once fierce independence was swept away, and since 1934, Claddagh, as it is called, has been a tidy suburb of Galway city. However, one tradition survives: the Claddagh ring, made of silver or gold, with the distinctive design of two hands presenting a crowned heart.

Claddagh rings were worn widely by women on the western coast and islands, often representing the sole major investment of a fishing family, handed down from mother to daughter. If it was worn by a girl on her right hand with the heart towards the nail it meant she was open to offers of marriage. Worn on the left hand, with the point away from the nail, it meant that she was engaged to be married.

The rings are still made in Galway city and are now popular all over the world.

### Spiddal/An Spidéal

A string of Irish-speaking villages lines the northern shore of Galway Bay, the most compact of which is Spiddal. It is set back from the sea on a rise, and has a large quay from which boats leave for the Aran Islands in the summer. Currach races are held here every summer.

On the main street stands Cill Einde, the Church of St Énda, a modern expression of Celtic Romanesque architecture designed by William A. Scott and completed in 1904. Every detail, inside and out, is faithful to the Celtic tradition, down to the extravagantly interlaced ironwork hinges on the main doors. The view up the aisle takes in abstract but richly coloured stained glass, a huge copper chandelier and a peach-red apse.

The Spiddal Craft Centre (Ceardlann), with its coffee shop, is one of the enterprises sponsored by the Irish-speaking organisation Udarás na Gaeltachta. Tel: (091) 83255.

# Meeting place of Poets

*Mile upon mile of dry-stone walls peppered with white lichen weave a net over undulating farmland right down to the frayed and rocky shoreline of Galway Bay. In the north, large areas of bog contrast with rough pasture where sheep and cattle pluck persistently at the tussocks. There are traces of numerous earthworks and ring-forts on these hills, left by ancient farmers who eked out a meagre existence here.*

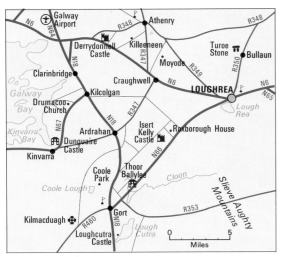

**OTHER PLACES TO SEE**

**Derrydonnell Castle** 3½m SW of Athenry, ruined tower house disintegrating under immense cloak of ivy.

**Drumacoo Church** 2m W of Kilcolgan, not signposted, ruined 10th-century church associated with nun, St Sorney; finely carved Gothic doorway c.1220, and ruined early 19th-century mausoleum of St George Tyrone family.

**Dunguaire Castle** Across Kinvarra Bay, 16th-century castle said to be on site of castle built by Guaire, 7th-century King of Connacht. Open Easter to Sept, daily 9.30am-5.30pm. Tea room and gift shop. Medieval banquets held there.

**Gort** Handsome 18th-century market town with large wedge-shaped marketplace complete with weighing house, huge scales and pump.

**Isert Kelly Castle** 4m E of Ardrahan, not signposted, ruined 16th-century tower house, rebuilt c.1617, with spiral staircase to second floor and elaborately inscribed chimneypiece dated 1604.

**Killeeneen** 'Graveyard of the Poets', set around ruined monastic church; burial place of local poets.

**Kinvarra** Colourful fishing village, where summer festival 'The Gathering of the Boats' is held; traditional sailing and fishing craft.

**Lough Cutra** Beautiful lake, dotted with wooded islands, forming natural parkland for Loughcutra Castle, 1810, not open to public; picnic area on E shore.

**Moyode** 4m SE of Athenry, walks in Moyode Wood.

**Turoe Stone** At Bullaun, rare and beautiful national monument, probably 1st century; 4ft tall, white granite, La Tène style decoration. Possibly featured in ancient fertility rites. Stands in field by farmhouse, fixed in concrete surrounded by circular cattle grid.

**EVENTS**

**Cruinniú na mBád** Traditional boat festival. Kinvarra, early Aug.

**International Festival of Traditional Irish Music** Gort, Oct.

**Market Days** Athenry: Fri, general market; Mon, Tues, Thur, livestock market. Gort: Fri. Loughrea: Thur.

**SPORT**

**Angling** Game fishing: Lough Rea, River Clarinbridge.

**Golf** Athenry Golf Club, 9-hole course. Tel: (091) 94466.
Gort Golf Club, 9-hole course. Tel: (091) 31336.
Loughrea Golf Club, 9-hole course. Tel: (091) 41049.

**Horse riding** Aille Cross Equestrian Centre. Tel: (091) 41216. Slieve Aughty Trail. Tel: (0509) 45246.

**INFORMATION**

Ireland West Tourism. Tel: (091) 63081.

## Athenry/Baile Atha an Rí

The town of the 'ford of the kings' is an old walled settlement that once lay at the intersection of three kingdoms – those of the O'Kellys, O'Flahertys and O'Heynes. The Anglo-Norman lord, Meiler de Bermingham, built a stout castle here in about 1240 and, as Baron of Athenry, made it his base in Galway. The castle still dominates the southern approach to the town – a mighty, austere keep barely penetrated by light and surrounded by a high-walled bawn or enclosure. Defence, not comfort, was clearly the priority of its builders.

Meiler de Bermingham founded the Dominican priory nearby at about the same time as the castle, and its ruined church, with its elegant stone tracery, can still be seen. It contains a number of interesting tombstones, including one dated 1682 which shows the tools of the blacksmith's trade. To get hold of the keys for the castle and priory, ask any of the local people, who will willingly give directions to the keyholder.

Part of a 15th-century market cross stands in the middle of the town, with a crucifixion on one side and the Virgin and Child on the other, badly weathered but an interesting piece of carving.

## Coole Park

At the end of the 19th century Coole House, the home of Lady Gregory, was a meeting place for a dazzling list of poets, playwrights, writers and artists, among them Yeats, Shaw, Synge, Masefield and Augustus John. The house was pulled down in 1941, but the surrounding parkland has since been salvaged and carefully rearranged. A tunnel-like arcade of huge holly trees leaning over the avenue provides a fittingly mysterious entrance to this former haunt of bards of the 'Celtic twilight'.

In the walled garden is the remarkable 'autograph tree', a copper beech on which famous guests carved their initials, still distinguishable, such as W.B.Y. and G.B.S. It is now protected by a large cylindrical grille to prevent lesser scribes from following their example.

About a mile south-west of the site of the house is the lovely Coole Lough, whose swans inspired Yeats' poem *The Wild Swans of Coole*. The lake is a 'turlough': its bed is porous limestone and its level of water varies greatly over the year depending on the height of the water table.

ROUND RETREAT *Kilmacduagh's tower was a haven for monks during attacks by marauders.*

## Kilmacduagh/Cill Mhic Duach

The massive 12th-century Round Tower – 111ft to the tip of its conical cap, with seven storeys inside, and leaning 2ft out of perpendicular – dominates this site on the eastern fringe of the Burren. Below it are the ruins of a small cathedral, which contains two finely carved crucifixions, and scattered remains of monastic buildings.

This was once a famous religious centre, founded about 610 by a local saint, Colman MacDuagh. An Augustinian monastery was established here in the 13th century by the O'Heynes, descendants of the saint's family. Its church contains some excellent carvings, on the capitals of the slender pillars of the chancel arches and in the pair of windows at the east end with their elegant, widely splayed recesses.

St Colman MacDuagh was a kinsman of King Guaire, the King of Connacht who built the original castle of Dunguaire at Kinvarra. It is said that King Guaire gave Colman land for a monastery in recompense for the grievous wrong that his father had done to Colman's mother, Rhinach. When King Guaire's father was king, he heard a prophesy that Rhinach would bear a child who would become greater than his own son. To prevent this happening, he persuaded some of his retainers to drown Rhinach. They tied a stone around her neck and threw her into a lake, but the stone miraculously

ILLUSTRIOUS CREATION *The Ascension window in St Brendan's Cathedral was executed in 1936 by Michael Healy, a follower of the Arts and Crafts style, and is among the great modern windows.*

In 1896 the poet W.B. Yeats went on a walking tour with a friend and met the wealthy widow, Lady Gregory (1852-1932). This meeting heralded the beginning of the Irish Literary Revival that rekindled interest in Irish myth, folklore and storytelling.

Born Isabella Augusta Persse, she grew up at Roxborough House, 8 miles from Coole. In 1880 she married Sir William Gregory, a man 35 years her senior who had returned after a distinguished career in India to his home at Coole House.

After Sir William's death in 1892, Lady Gregory devoted herself to literary pursuits, particularly Irish folklore. She taught herself Irish and, by visiting the homes of local people and talking to them, became a leading collector of tales and traditions. She wrote poems, short stories and more than 40 plays, and inspired the exploration of the distinctive Irish voice in literature that led to the creation of the Abbey Theatre in Dublin, a beacon of new Irish talent. She was a woman of immense energy and generosity, encouraging Yeats and helping him financially, and with him played an active role in the management of the Abbey Theatre. She died in 1932 and is buried in the New Cemetery in Galway.

She is remembered in Joyce's limerick:

*There was a kind Lady called Gregory,*
*Said 'Come to be poets in beggary'*
*But found her imprudence*
*When thousands of students*
*Cried 'All we are in that catégory'.*

floated, Rhinach survived and gave birth to Colman. Colman later became a hermit in the Burren, until he was discovered there by King Guaire.

The keys to the cathedral are with the caretaker, in the house opposite the car park.

## Loughrea/Baile Locha Riach

A market town that was formerly one of Connaught's administrative centres, Loughrea stands on the edge of the 'grey lake', as its Irish name translates. It grew up round a 13th-century stronghold of the de Burgo family, who installed Carmelite friars here in about 1300. The ruins of the priory church adjoin the later, 19th-century Carmelite house, where the keys may be obtained. The ground beneath the tower that rises over the chancel arch is one of several places where the French general St Ruth was supposed to have been buried after his death at the Battle of Aughrim in 1691.

The real glory of Loughrea is the interior of St Brendan's Cathedral, built 1897-1903. It is an example of the Arts and Crafts style in the Irish idiom.

THOOR BALLYLEE *The tower house was the home of W.B. Yeats for almost ten years.*

## Thoor Ballylee

In 1917, then in his fifties, the poet W.B. Yeats (1865-1939) bought and restored a ruined 16th-century tower house and cottage near Coole House, home of his friend Lady Gregory. It was a retreat for him, his young wife and two children, from the bitter political turmoil of the 1920s. The tower is sparsely furnished, as it was when Yeats lived there, and also contains a display of his work. It is a tranquil spot with the River Cloon passing the tower before winding through a wooded glade down to a mill. From the tower are views across rolling pastureland and coppices to the Slieve Aughty Mountains and the Burren.

Yeats wrote extensively there, often inspired by the mysteries and symbolism of his surroundings. In 1928 (his last year there), he published a collection of poems entitled *The Tower*, and another volume in 1933, called *The Winding Stair*, both titles suggested by the place.

Attached to the outside wall of the tower is this ditty:

*I, the poet William Yeats*
*With old millboards and sea-green slates*
*And smithy work from the Gort forge*
*Restored this tower for my wife George*
*And may these characters remain*
*When all is ruin once again.*

**Opening times** *May-Sept, daily. Tel: (091) 31436. Audiovisual programme, other recordings and readings. Tea room and bookshop.*

215

# Joyce Country

*In this border country the thrust of clans from the plains of north-east Galway and Mayo met the fierce resistance of the mountain people of Joyce Country and Connemara. In their wake they left clusters of ruined castles on and around the land bridge that separates Loughs Mask and Corrib – the 'Gap of Danger'. The area owes its name to a Welsh family who settled here in the 13th century and became a leading clan in the region.*

### Aughnanure Castle/Achadh na nIubhar

A six-storey tower house stands among trees on an outcrop of rock that over the centuries has been sculpted and pierced by the stream curling around it. The tower was built around 1500 by the O'Flahertys, the most powerful Irish clan of this region. It has since been beautifully restored, although its outer fortifications still lie in ruins. Views from the top reach north-west over the wooded western shores of Lough Corrib to the mountains of Joyce Country and south-west to the bleak moors that rise to Knocknalee Hill.

**Opening times** *Early June to mid-Sept, daily 9.30am-6.30pm. Tel: (091) 82214.*

### Castlekirk/Caisleán na Circe

One of Ireland's most romantic tumbledown ruins is the castle that sits on a lonely island in

SUMMER AT MAAM CROSS *A farmer (above) stacks bundles of dried grass for use in thatching. Nearby, Lough Shindilla's rippled surface is decked with water lilies (below).*

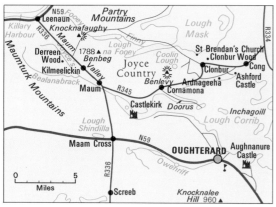

Brendan. Downstream at Maum, large 1820s pub built as HQ by Scottish engineer Alexander Nimmo (1783-1832). Forest walks at Derreen Wood.

**EVENTS**
**Oughterard Annual Agricultural Show** Aug.
**Sheep and Wool Festival** Leenaun.

**SPORT**
**Angling** Coarse fishing: Loughs Corrib and na Fooey, and River Finny. Game fishing: Loughs Corrib, na Fooey and Mask, and River Owenriff. Sea fishing: Leenaun.
**Bathing** Lough Corrib, at Ardnageeha; Lough na Fooey and Lough Mask.
**Golf** Oughterard Golf Club, 18-hole course. Tel: (091) 82131.
**Horse riding** Tel: (092) 46024.

**INFORMATION**
Ireland West Tourism.
Tel: (091) 63081.

Lough Corrib. This mighty rectangular fortress with bold square corner turrets was built in the early 13th century, by the King of Connacht. It was fought for by the leading clans of the region – the O'Connors, O'Flahertys and Joyces – and was eventually destroyed by the Cromwellians.

Its Irish name means 'castle of the hen', and refers to legends about an enchanted hen. But these have become entangled with the exploits of the 16th-century Pirate Queen, Grace O'Malley, who proved to be a doughty 'hen' to her people in rallying them to defend Castlekirk against the Joyces. Her husband Donal O'Flaherty earned the title of 'the cock' because of his courage in battle. The island can be reached by boat through private arrangement with a local fisherman.

### Clonbur/An Fhairche

The pretty village stands on the neck of land that separates Loughs Mask and Corrib, facing east to the plains and west to the mountains of Joyce Country. It is a good base

**OTHER PLACES TO SEE**
**Ashford Castle** 1m S of Cong, 1870 mass of 'medieval' towers and battlements with large Victorian windows, built for Lord Ardilaun of the Guinness family. Now a hotel.
**Benlevy** Easternmost mountain of Joyce Country, known locally as Mt Gable. Road leads to Coolin Lough, with picnic spot and walks up southern ridge to wide views.

**Doorus** Scenic peninsula in Lough Corrib, with views to east and west.
**Leenaun** Village near head of Killary Harbour and location of *The Field* (1990), a film about 1930s rural Ireland, starring Richard Harris and John Hurt.
**Maum Valley** Where Joyce's River and Bealanabrack River unite; at Kilmeelickin is church with Evie Hone stained glass depicting St

for forest walks. Just outside Clonbur is a geological curiosity: the stream that runs out of Lough Mask into Lough Corrib goes underground at three places on its 4 mile course. There are pleasant woodland walks to the north that offer wide views and lead to the shores of Lough Mask.

Near the lake a road signposted 'Cemetery' leads to St Brendan's Church, or Teampall Breandán, also known as Ross Hill Abbey. This ruin of a simple church stands on a large, oval-shaped plot of ground, surrounded by a dry-stone wall and framed by the conifer trees of Clonbur Wood. Its lintelled door and inclined jambs suggest early Christian origins, and it is believed to have been built on the site of an earlier church founded in the 6th century by St Brendan the Navigator. Some 60ft from the west door is a small, lichen-covered standing stone with crosses on both sides.

NEW FROM OLD *Superbly sited by Lough Corrib, Ashford Castle was built by the Norman de Burgo family in 1228, and was extensively enlarged in the 1870s.*

### Inchagoill/Inis an Ghaill

Uninhabited and tranquil, the 'island of the stranger' is one of the largest of the many wooded islets spattered across Lough Corrib. It has not only spectacular views of the Maumturk range, Joyce Country and the mountains of Connemara, but also two ancient, venerated sites, set close together in its woods.

St Patrick's Church, or Teampall Phádraig, with walls made from massive blocks of stone and with a flat-topped lintelled doorway at the western end, is in parts an earlier Christian building. Among the ancient gravestones surrounding it is one with Roman letters that read LIE LUGUAEDON MACCI

MENUEH ('the stone of Luguaedon, son of Menueh'). Menueh is believed to have been St Patrick's sister and her son his navigator. If the lettering is indeed from the 5th century, it is Ireland's oldest Christian inscription.

The tiny Church of the Saints, or Teampall na Naomh, a simple roofless nave and chancel church, glories in a beautiful sculpted Irish Romanesque west door of the 12th century. The jambs incline inwards with three orders of columns and arches, decorated with sculpted heads, floral patterns and grinning, grotesque faces. It is reached from Ashford Castle, from which a regular boat service runs, or by private arrangement with fishermen around Oughterard.

### Lough na Fooey/Loch na Fuaiche

Between the raw slopes of Benbeg (1788ft), in Joyce Country to the south, and the flank of the Partry Mountains to the north, is a lake of haunting beauty. In poor weather, when cloud and mist cloak the surrounding hills, Lough na Fooey is an eerie place, but when the weather breaks and the gold-fingered clouds drift high over the peaks, it is like a mirror raised to the sky.

A dramatic cascade at the western end tumbles down the tree-lined ravine of Ailldubh ('black cliff') to form the River Fooey which, after crossing rough pasture, feeds the lough. Just above it is a conical hill, Knocknafaughy (847ft), an easy climb which has beautiful views of the lake and the scooped-out hills around.

### Oughterard/Uachtar Ard

This charmingly old-world little town, the largest on the western side of Lough Corrib, lies a mile back from the shore. The approach from the west is particularly attractive, descending through a defiantly wild landscape of rocky bog, windswept loughs and conifer forests, before dropping down to Oughterard.

The little River Owenriff passes majestic beeches and serene Georgian houses with tidy gardens. In the main part of Oughterard (which means 'high ground' in Irish) a pretty row of painted façades lines the curving road. Some houses are still thatched.

The place is a well-known centre for fishermen, but obviously an agricultural one too, where your progress is likely to be slowed by cows being herded gently along the roads by farmers on their bicycles, aided by their wild-eyed dogs.

ALIVE, ALIVE, O! *A Leenaun fisherman unloads a fine catch of mussels.*

# A Legendary Queen's Tomb

*A broad green disc of farmland crossed by brooks and sluggish rivers spreads out from the town of Tuam, broken only by the bump of Knockmaa hill, burial place of legendary Queen Maeve. The relative richness of the area is expressed in the generous size of its farmhouses and their adjoining barns, and the black-and-white dairy cows that sway heavily along the country roads at milking time.*

### Abbeyknockmoy (Mainistir Choc Muaidhe)

The church of a ruined Cistercian abbey founded by Cathal O'Conor, King of Connaught, in 1190 stands surrounded by rough pasture. It has a bold, cathedral-like scale, but is austere and spare and makes the churches of other monasteries in the region seem warm and intimate by comparison.

The east end of the church has been tidily reroofed to protect one of the few surviving examples of medieval frescoes in Ireland. The paintings on the chancel wall date from the 15th century, but time and the weather have turned them into little more than pale outlines, and the conservation work now being carried out comes at the eleventh hour. Enough survives, however, to indicate how they must once have appeared – large-scale illustrations bearing severe messages. In the upper row three kings stand next to three skeletons wearing crowns; there was an inscription which apparently read: 'We have been as you are, you shall be as we are.' Below them, Christ, with a halo and his hand raised, stands next to a scene in which a couple of archers are grimly setting about the task of firing arrows into St Sebastian, who is lashed to a stylised tree.

### Glinsk Castle/Caisleán Ghlinsce

A ruined shell on a rise above a small, wooded river valley is all that remains of one of the many tower houses built in this area by the de Burgo family. It dates from the 1630s, by which time these defensive buildings began to evolve into more comfortable places to live in. It has large stone-mullioned windows on every floor, making the rooms lighter than before; a generous, rectangular ground plan and two fine sets of tall, square chimneys. Even so, the roof gables still hide behind the parapet and the main door is plain and small, presumably for better defence.

### Knockmaa/Cnoc Má

Five miles west of Tuam a prominent wooded hill rises 552ft from the plain, providing impressive panoramic views. The summit is crowded with prehistoric remains scattered among the hawthorns, bracken, heather and gorse, including a small cashel, or dry-stone fortress, of indeterminate age. It is only some 60ft across but has three sets of defensive walls 3ft thick, of successive heights. A short way to the east is a massive cairn.

These ancient remains are entwined in Irish mythology, for this is where Queen Maeve, the legendary Queen of Connaught, is said to be buried. It is also the hill granted by the pagan god Dagda to Finbarr, king of the 'people of the mounds', or the fairies. Delicate little stone steps built into the walls of a tiny cashel on the summit support this story.

### Monivea/Muine Mhéa

In the mid-18th century Robert Ffrench, a member of one of the 14 Tribes of Galway, set up an estate here, converting much of the bog to forests of oak, elm and beech. He developed a linen industry on the estate and built the village of Monivea to house the weavers and other workers and their families. By 1779 there were 276 houses here, with 96 looms and 370 spinning wheels, and a broad green for flax drying running through the village. However, the flax industry waned and linen is no longer produced here.

In a lonely patch of forest east of the village is a mausoleum, built from 1896 to 1900 for the last Ffrench, Robert Percy, by his only child, Kathleen. The monument, which cost perhaps a million pounds at present values, is a miniature castle. Inside it is a tiny funerary chapel, vaulted in white granite with a floor of white, grey and pink marble. Stained-glass windows, with elaborate floral designs around coats of arms, let in a soft, mystical light.

On a bed on the floor, his effigy swathed in blankets, hands clasped on his chest in prayer, lies the bearded figure of Robert Percy Ffrench, rendered in white Italian marble. It is said to be a perfect likeness. Kathleen died in 1938 when travelling in China, and was laid to rest next to her father. The key is available from the second house to the right of the entrance to the demesne.

KEEN AND PEACHY *Eye-catching façades in Ballygar have helped the village to win a number of 'Tidy Town' awards.*

---

of tower house, in corner of meadow backed by a wood; also known as Jenning's Castle. Originally built by de Burgo family in 16th century. **Kilbennan** Ruins of 15th-century Franciscan friary and part of 11th-century Round Tower on site of St Benan's monastery; he succeeded St Patrick as Bishop of Armagh. **Mountbellew** Small agricultural centre, home of the Franciscan Agricultural College. Forest walks and bird sanctuary in old Mountbellew demesne, with man-made lake.

### EVENTS
**Mountbellew Agricultural Show** (including Horse Show), Sept.

### SPORT
**Angling** Coarse fishing: River Suck. Game fishing: Rivers Clare, Dalgan and Sinking. **Golf** Mountbellew Golf Club, 9-hole course. Tel: (0905) 79259.
Tuam Golf Club, 18-hole course. Tel: (093) 24354.

### INFORMATION
Ireland West Tourism.
Tel: (091) 63081.

### OTHER PLACES TO SEE
**Ballinderry** 3½m S of Tuam, unsignposted; ivy-covered ruin of heavily fortified tower house, surrounded by pasture, with *sheela-na-gig* carved over doorway.
**Ballygar** Very pretty village; 1m N are woodland walks in Aughrane Forest.
**Cahermore** 3½m W of Monivea; site of huge cashel, or ring-fort, perhaps 1000 years old; ring of dry-stone wall visible, 2ft thick and 200yds across. Extensive views from top of hill.
**Dunmore** Little town on banks of River Sinking, with ruined church and tower of Augustinian priory, with decorated arch above west door; ½m W of Dunmore, 14th-century keep with mullioned windows.
**Feartagar Castle** Lonely ruin

BAR WITH A DUAL PURPOSE *Quinn's in Tuam, like many Irish pubs, combines a bar with a grocery.*

MARBLE MASTERPIECE *The superbly detailed effigy of Robert Percy Ffrench rests in the mausoleum built for him by his daughter, at Monivea.*

## Ross Errilly Abbey/Mainistir an Rois

Even though it lies in ruins, this Franciscan friary is unusually complete and gives an interesting insight into monastic life. Ross Errilly Abbey (or Ross Abbey) was founded in the middle of the 14th century by the de Burgo family, although most of what remains belongs to the 15th century. The castellated tower, built over the chancel arch, dates from 1498 and has an unusual gallery on the first floor with three squints that look down on the chancel. A doorway beneath the tower leads to the cloister, which was once surrounded by a covered ambulatory, or walkway. The collection of buildings beyond this include a kitchen, refectory and bakehouse. The kitchen has a well-like stone tank in one corner which was used for holding live fish, and in one exterior wall there is a channelled stone down which slops were poured. In the corner of the refectory is a stone seat next to the window, where a monk sat to read from the scriptures during mealtimes.

The overall impression is of a tightly knit, self-sufficient community, where domestic concerns were intimately connected with religious observances. However, the life of the abbey drew to a close when the English took it over in 1596, and the buildings were wrecked by Cromwellian forces in 1656.

## Tuam/Tuaim

Despite its 19th-century air, the large market town of Tuam (pronounced 'choom') has a long history. A monastery was founded here in the early 6th century, and in the 11th century the O'Conor kings of Connaught made it their base. Two of them, Turlough and Ruari, became High Kings and in their times Tuam was effectively Ireland's capital.

The chancel arch of the cathedral may have been built after a fire in 1184. It is now incorporated into the 1878 Protestant cathedral of St Mary. The arch is a splendid example of Irish Romanesque in richly carved red sandstone, 22½ft across and 16ft high. Its six orders of columns and arches are intricately decorated with chevrons and other geometric designs with interlacing and animal faces on the capitals.

The High Cross in Tuam's main square was created between 1126 and 1152, but the carvings on the head seem to have come from a different cross from the shaft, which is decorated with interlaced patterns.

On the eastern side of the town is the huge Cathedral of the Assumption, built

QUEEN MAEVE

*A panel on the outside of the Gundestrup cauldron, found in Denmark in 1891 and said to be from the 1st century BC, is thought to depict Queen Maeve.*

The legendary Queen of Connaught, Maeve (or, in Irish, Medb), plays the role of an anarchic goddess of war and fertility in Irish mythology. She features in numerous stories usually to do with the rivalry between Connaught and Ulster, involving the great Ulster warriors Cuchulainn, Conall and Laoire.

When Maeve was young she killed one of her sisters, Clothru, who was pregnant at the time. However, the child, Furbaide, was saved, and he eventually avenged his mother's death by killing Queen Maeve with a piece of cheese shot from his sling while she bathed in the waters of Lough Ree. She is said to have been buried on Knockmaa hill, near Tuam – although some also claim that her resting place is at Knocknarea in County Sligo. 'The Cattle Raid of Cooley' is the most famous story about Maeve.

1827-36, the second Catholic cathedral (after Newry) to be built in Ireland after Catholic emancipation.

Tuam's industrial past is re-created in the Mill Museum near the centre of the town, housed in a functioning corn mill. A steam train follows the scenic route laid out in the 1860s between Tuam and Athenry.

**Mill Museum** June-Oct, 10am-6pm. Tel: (093) 24463.

**Steam trains** July and Aug, Sat 1.45pm.

# THE LIVING TURF

*A precious resource for plants and wildlife, and treasures from the past*

If you have never seen a stretch of peatbog close up, or squelched across its spongy surface, it is easy to dismiss it as a flat, treeless piece of waterlogged land, of little use to man or beast. But walk across an Irish bog in early summer and you will see that it is a mosaic of hillocks and hollows, pools and lakes, its covering of mosses, grasses, lichens, heathers and sedges coloured silver-grey, pale pink, russet, purple, vermilion and golden-green.

High above, a hovering lark pours out its breathless song, while close to where you stand a snipe sits silently on her nest until you are almost on top of her and then explodes away in a series of frenzied zigzags. Crouch down and you may spot the telltale curve of flattened grasses where a hare has been resting, or catch a flash of metallic blue as a hungry damselfly darts among the vegetation.

THE DEVELOPMENT OF BOGS Peatlands, or bogs, originally covered one-seventh of Ireland, and although they have been largely destroyed this century, Ireland is one of the few countries where a wide range of peatlands still exist in their natural state.

Irish bogs began to develop more than 8000 years ago, after the last Ice Age. As the climate grew warmer, plants started to grow on top of shallow lakes and pools, and on poorly drained mountainsides. When the plants died, there was not enough oxygen in these waterlogged areas for them to rot down fully, so layers of compacted roots, stems, leaves, flowers, fruits and seeds accumulated.

Layers of what we now call peat built up to form two different kinds of bog – dome-shaped raised bogs, which develop on lake basins, and blanket bogs, spread over large areas of poorly drained soil. The peat in the raised bogs, found mainly in the midlands, can be as much as 40ft thick, whereas blanket bogs, in the wetter, western parts of Ireland, are rarely more than 20ft thick.

LIFE IN THE PEATLANDS Raised bogs are cushioned with clumps of different-coloured sphagnum mosses, while on blanket bogs tough grasses predominate. Flocks of the rare Greenland white-fronted goose feed on the roots of these grasses in winter, and in spring golden plovers and curlews nest in the drier hummocks.

Because the soil in bogs contains virtually no nutrients, the plants that live there depend on rainwater as their main source of minerals. But many plants have developed other ways of adding to their mineral supply. For example, there are 11 species of carnivorous plants that thrive in Irish bogs, such as sundews and butterworts, which trap and digest insects. And bog cotton and bog asphodel recycle the nutrients from their own dying tissues.

AN ARCHAEOLOGIST'S DREAM The lack of oxygen in bogs enables them to preserve almost anything they cover – from a pollen grain to fields, houses and tombs – which makes them a fascinating kind of history

STICKY DEATH *A dragonfly struggles in vain on the sticky leaves of the insectivorous sundew.*

book. Fields cultivated by Stone Age farmers have been discovered under bogs, evidence that the country's first settlers were doing their best to tame the landscape some 5000 years ago. They cleared the land of trees and grazed cattle in their walled-in fields, and when the soil became impoverished they moved on – and the bog moved in.

Hoards of tools, weapons, jewellery and other objects buried by Bronze Age man have been unearthed. Even early cooking pits called 'fulacht fiadh' (the cooking place of the deer), used by hunters, have been discovered.

Archaeologists believe that the hunters would light a fire, heat stones until they were white hot, and then drop them into a trough of water. A constant supply of hot stones would keep the water on the simmer while

THE BODY IN THE BOG *The body of an Iron Age man found in a Galway bog in 1821 still wore a cape and had hair and a stubbly beard, although these have since gone.*

CONNEMARA BOG *The islands of blanket bog that dot the many lakes of Connemara support rare heathers such as Mackay's heath.*

the meat was cooking. Archaeologists have also discovered great trackways made of oak logs, some stretching for more than a mile. These show that Late Bronze Age people and early Christians had trouble getting around the country because of the ever-expanding bog, which forced them to construct raised walkways.

Even human bodies have been found in the bogs, mostly from the 17th and 18th centuries. One from a Galway bog was complete with long black hair, leather tunic and shoes. And among the most common bog discoveries have been containers of butter. These caches were dug up so regularly that the people who found them used to sell them as axle grease.

FROM PEAT TO ENERGY Peat has been a source of fuel in Ireland for more than a thousand years. Each household would have a 'stripe' of bog and would set out at the first sign of dry weather, usually in April or May, to collect their peat. First they would slice off the top layer, or 'scraw', with a spade. Then, using a long-handled 'slèan', the cutters would slice down into the peat and with one stroke toss each sod up onto the bank where the rest of the family would spread them out to dry.

The family would return after a few days to pile up the sods, and finally they would draw the turf home – enough to last a year – in creels, or baskets, on their backs or strapped to a donkey. Some families still cut

PEATCUTTING PAST AND PRESENT *The traditional way of cutting peat was to cut out sods with a spade, spread them out to dry and pile them up. Today's methods of mechanised extraction have laid bare huge areas of bog and created a distinctive landscape.*

turf by hand, but increasingly they use a specialised tractor-mounted machine and then dry the turf in the traditional way.

The Irish Peat Board, Bord na Móna, set up in 1946, has excavated thousands of acres of bog to fuel power stations and provide electricity for the country, manufacture peat briquettes for domestic fires, and peat products for horticultural use. But the government has recently had to face up to the impact that such large-scale exploitation, along with afforestation and drainage, has had on this increasingly rare habitat.

Today, the Irish Wildlife Service and Bord na Móna are conserving expanses of bogland, and there is a strong lobby for peatland conservation. The race is now on to save the remaining bog, which naturalist David Bellamy has said should stand alongside Mount Everest, the Californian Redwoods and the Pyramids as a world heritage site.

JEWELS OF THE BOGS *The pale pink bog pimpernel, that forms mats on the bog surface, and the upright yellow tormentil, brighten the peatlands from May to September.*

BUTTERWORT *The sticky leaves of butterwort trap insects and dissolve them for food.*

BOGBEAN *Submerged roots support the bogbean in water-filled hollows.*

BELL HEATHER *A shrub that flourishes on dry hummocks of peat.*

BOG ASPHODEL *Another plant which grows on drier patches above the water.*

# Where French Invaders Landed

*This brownish-green landscape of bog is broken by conifer plantations, except where it slopes down to the coves and cliff faces of the coast. Towards the west the countryside softens into pasture, while the eastern part drains into the Moy valley. The River Moy, cherished haunt of game fishermen, runs towards the estuary at Killala Bay, landing point of General Humbert and his French troops in 1798.*

### Ballina/Béal an Átha

A population of about 7000 makes Ballina the second largest town in Connaught after Galway city. The main streets slope down to the broad River Moy, which is spanned by two bridges busy with anglers. The original settlement was at Ardnaree, on the east side of the river, which commanded a ford. The site is marked by the ivy-covered ruins of a 14th-century Augustinian friary, dwarfed by the stern Victorian greystone cathedral of St Muiredach.

In the 18th century Ballina developed on the west side of the river. The railway station is overlooked by the Dolmen of the Four Maols, three great hunks of rock capped by a massive flat boulder, dating from the Bronze Age. They earn their name from an incident in the early Christian era. Four foster-brothers named Maol murdered their master, a bishop, whose death was avenged by his own brother. The four were hanged and, supposedly, buried here.

At the end of the 18th century Franco-Irish forces under General Humbert captured the town, and the locals lit straw along a road to guide them in. The road is still known as Bothnar na Sop, the 'Road of Straw'.

### Bellacorick/Béal Átha Chomhraic

The great curving silhouette in the desolate expanses of bog in northern Mayo is the cooling tower of Bellacorick Power Station, one of Ireland's peat-burning power stations, built in 1962.

But a more beguiling aspect of the town is its musical bridge, built in 1820. The bridge might pass unnoticed, but for the sight of people running along its length pushing large pebbles along the top of the parapets. These are capped with a kind of stone which rings dully when struck, and each block gives out a different note. 'Played' together, they create a free-form tune – a happy accident of bridge building.

### Cèide Fields

One of the most exciting prehistoric discoveries of recent years in Ireland has been the Cèide (pronounced 'kay-jeh') Fields along the north Mayo coast. Buried and preserved beneath 6ft of blanket bog are the remains of a New Stone Age community, which lived here before 3000 BC.

Dry-stone livestock enclosures and dwellings with pottery and flint tools have been exposed by excavations. And tree stumps testify to ancient pine forests cleared by early settlers. There is also a dig near Belderg, 5 miles farther west, the site of a Bronze Age farm of around 1500 BC..

The discovery of the Cèide Fields reveals how well organised this Stone Age society must have been, for the extensive enclosed pastureland must have required a high level of social cooperation and cohesion.

It takes some imagination to visualise what the lines of unearthed stones represent but the site has been well organised for visitors and there are teams of archaeologists willing to help.

The French Revolution of 1789 reverberated through Europe, stirring to life other would-be republicans. It blew a fresh wind of rebellion across Ireland, and middle-class reformers, both Protestant and Catholic, formed the United Irishmen movement with the aim of overthrowing English rule. One of the chief organisers of the movement was the Dublin Protestant Wolfe Tone, who eventually went to Paris and persuaded the French to mount an invasion of Ireland.

In August 1798, three French men-of-war landed 1100 French troops, under the French General Humbert (above), at Kilcummin strand in Killala Bay. They moved quickly, taking first Killala, then Ballina. Marching over the mountains instead of taking the road running beside Lough Cullin, they surprised the English garrison at Castlebar and routed them. But organised local support for General Humbert's army never came to fruition, and those Irishmen who did join the French lacked experience and adequate weapons.

In September, Humbert realised his quest was hopeless and surrendered. The French were treated as prisoners of war, their Irish supporters hanged as traitors.

### Downpatrick Head/Ceann Dhún Pádraig

This great headland juts out into the sea like a huge splayed hand. Beneath the fingertips are cliffs that drop abruptly 130ft down to the sea, where they are pounded by a race of swelling foam.

Just off the forefinger is Doonbristy, a magnificent sea stack that has sheered off from the mainland. In places, the sea has gouged caverns into the rock, and as the waves heave in, plumes of spray shoot out of

---

**OTHER PLACES TO SEE**
**Belleek Castle** 1¼m N of Ballina; castellated 1831 mansion, now a hotel, with museum containing arms, armour, 16th-century furniture, etc. Open weekends only, 9am-6pm. Tel: (096) 22061.
**Breastagh Ogham Stone** 4½m NW of Killala, 8ft Bronze Age menhir, inscribed between AD 300 and 600 with ogham writing: MAQ CORRBRI MAQ AMLOITT, probably commemorating a dead person.
**Carrowkilleen** 3m W of Crossmolina, 120ft long, triple-chambered court tomb, largest in Mayo.
**Crossmolina** Little country town on River Deel, great centre for anglers.
**Deel Castle** 16th-century tower house with 18th-century extension.
**Glenree** Bronze Age farmstead preserved under bog for 4000 years.

**Kilcummin** Picturesque row of fishermen's cottages, tiny harbour and pier, famous as landing place of French soldiers under General Humbert.
**Rathfran Abbey** 4m NW of Killala, ruins of 13th-century Dominican friary on estuary, overlooked by shell of Summerhill House.

**WALKS**
Altnabracky woods.

**EVENTS**
**Killala Bay All Ireland Master Angler Boat Competition** Aug.

**SPORT**
**Angling** Coarse fishing: Loughs Brohly, Cartron and Carrowkerribly. Game fishing: Rivers Ballinglen, Brusna, Cloonaghmore, Deel, Glencullin and Moy, and Lough Conn. Sea fishing: Bunatrahir and Killala Bays.
**Bathing** Lackan Bay, Kilcummin, Ross beach.
**Boating** Lough Conn.
**Golf** Ballina Golf Club, 9-hole course. Tel: (096) 21050.

**INFORMATION**
Westport Tourist Information Office. Tel: (098) 25711/25908.

their blowholes. The most extraordinary of these 'caverns' is the tunnel that runs from the cliff face some 200yds under the turf-covered top of the headland. This can be seen by looking into a huge hole called Poulinashantinny in the middle of the headland, now for safety's sake surrounded by wire netting. In a large swell the sea surges into the tunnel, and bursts out of the hole in a cloud of spray. In 1798 a group of 75 people tried to use the tunnel as a refuge from the English after the rebellion, but they were drowned.

According to legend, Downpatrick Head was formed during a battle between St Patrick and the Devil. St Patrick struck the Devil so hard with his crozier that he fell, making the hole through the headland and breaking off land to leave the Doonbristy stack. The tiny ruined chapel on the headland commemorates this association with St Patrick.

### Killala/Cill Ala

Famous above all as the first place to be taken by General Humbert and his French troops after their landing here, the beautiful little coastal town of Killala has an air of history about it. The town rises above its small tidal harbour, with a skyline dominated by two pencil-thin monuments. One is a fine 12th-century Round Tower, about 80ft high and complete with stone cap. Its door is about 13ft off the ground. (The keys to the enclosure around the tower are with the caretaker next door.) The other is the spire of the Church of Ireland 'cathedral' of St Patrick, built in 1680 on the site of an ancient church believed to have been founded by St Patrick and handed over to his disciple, St Muiredach. Now a parish church, it is interesting for its complete set of box pews, where prominent local families could worship in semi-privacy.

### Moyne Abbey/Mainistir na Maighne

This large ruin of a friary shares much with its neighbour, Rosserk. Both compete for the title of largest and most impressive ecclesiastical ruins in Mayo. Moyne was founded as a Franciscan friary by the Burke family, built in late Irish Gothic style and consecrated in 1462.

The church has a nave and chancel separated from a south aisle by robust round pillars. The ruins are dominated by a tall bell tower built over the chancel arch, and a hole for a bell rope can still be seen in the ceiling. Incised in the plaster next to the west door is an unusual 16th-century picture of a ship.

BEACHHEAD OF REBELLION *Three French warships landed troops at Kilcummin strand in support of a rebellion against the English.*

There are enough domestic details left of the abbey to make it possible to imagine how the monks lived there. The abbey's life ended after 1590, when it was destroyed by Sir Richard Bingham, Elizabeth I's zealous governor of Connaught.

### Rosserk Friary/Mainistir Ros Eirc

Like Moyne Abbey, this is another splendid and comparatively complete ruin. Founded in 1460 for Franciscan friars by the Joyce family, it too was destroyed by Sir Richard Bingham in about 1590. It was built on the estuary of the River Moy, surrounded by green fields. The church is cruciform in plan, with a battlemented bell tower suspended over the chancel arch, a feat of architecture more noticeable now that the church is roofless.

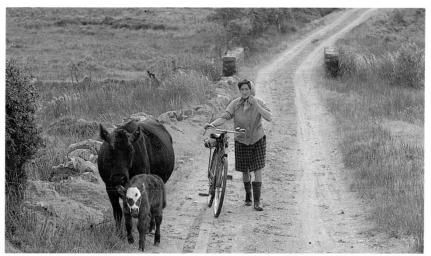

HERDING BY BIKE *A cow and her calf are shepherded gently along a Mayo country lane.*

COUNTRY CRAFT *A wheelwright plies his trade.*

223

# Anglers' Capital of the West

The very south of County Mayo is a landscape of rich
pastureland, with just a toe-hold on the northern tip of
Lough Corrib. Farther north is Lough Mask. To its west
are the bare escarpments of the Partry Mountains, crossed
by a single road. To its east is low-lying, undulating
countryside where prosperous farmland alternates with
untamed woodland and bog. Here prehistoric peoples built cairns and
ring-forts, and medieval monks prayed, fished and farmed.

WIDE WATERS *Ten miles long and four miles across, Lough Mask is almost an inland sea.*

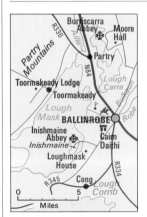

OTHER PLACES TO SEE
**Burriscarra Abbey** Ruins of
14th-century Carmelite abbey
(later Augustinian friary)
paired with 14th-century
parish church.
**Inishmaine Abbey** Ruins of
13th-century Augustinian
house, originally founded by
St Cormac in 6th century,
with fine carvings.

WALKS
**Ballinrobe-Inishmaine Trail**
From Tobercurry to
Rathowen hill-fort.
**Toormakeady Forest Trail.**

EVENTS
**Ballinrobe Agricultural
Show** Aug.
**Horse racing** Ballinrobe (five
meetings a year).

**Market Day** Ballinrobe, Wed.
**Queen of the Mask Festival**
Ballinrobe, midsummer.
**World Cup Angling
Competition** Ballinrobe,
Lough Mask.

SPORT
**Angling** Coarse fishing:
Loughs Carra, Corrib and
Mask, Rivers Aille, Bulkaun,
Finny, Owenbrin and Robe.
Game fishing: Lough Carra.
**Golf** Ballinrobe Golf Club,
9-hole course. Tel: (092)
41448.

INFORMATION
Westport Tourist Information
Office. Tel: (098) 25711/
25908.

## Ballinrobe/Baile an Róba

The 'Angling Capital of the West' is the largest
town in this part of southern Mayo. Its
Catholic church, St Mary's, has some
luminous stained glass by Harry Clarke
(1889-1931): two sets of lancet windows
depict the saints of Ireland, scenes from the
life of Christ, and of the Assumption and
Coronation of the Virgin Mary.

A road to the south-west towards Lough
Mask passes several prehistoric sites, the most
notable of which is the so-called Cairn Daithi.
This 22ft high pile of stones probably covers a
Stone Age passage-grave. It is associated with
the legend of the Battle of Moytura, in County
Sligo, in which the Fir Bolg inhabitants of
Ireland clashed with the invading Tuatha dé
Danann. In this battle King Eochaidh, the last
king of the Fir Bolgs, was killed.

A walk across four enclosed fields to the
north beyond the cairn leads to a small
ring-fort dating from about AD 500, with
good views of the surrounding countryside.

## Cong/Conga

The old-world feel of this village is to some
extent deliberate, for dearly Cong remembers
its role in *The Quiet Man*, partly filmed here in
1952 and starring John Wayne and Maureen
O'Hara. Cong Abbey, where the Cross of
Cong was kept, was founded for the Augustinian Canons Regular in about 1120 by Turlough O'Conor, High King of Ireland, on the
site of a 6th-century church associated with St
Feichin. Much of the surviving building dates
from the early 13th century. There are some
fine details in the carving, and a pretty cloister
overlooking a wooded river.

The properties of the limestone around
Cong were overlooked by engineers when, in
1845-50, they planned a canal to connect
Lough Mask to Lough Corrib. The canal was
built, but when the water was let in it
disappeared into the porous limestone bed.
The fine, stone-clad locks remain, marooned
in dry land.

## Lough Mask/Loch Measca

The waters of Lough Mask are wide enough to
produce choppy waves in rough weather, and
a seascape of racing clouds. The western side
is memorable for fuchsia hedges and stone
walls built from rugged boulders. The 'Lough
Mask Drive' runs along this side in the lee of
the Partry Mountains, from which lanes lead
down to picnic sites at the water's edge.
Towards the south, the road cuts inland

around the base of the mountains and heads
into untamed country along the side of a deep
inlet, and then over a low pass to remote
Lough na Fooey, just inside Galway.

The name Lough Mask will always be
associated with an incident in the Land War
of 1879-82. The National Land League
founded by Michael Davitt and Charles
Stewart Parnell waged a campaign for reduc-
tions in the rent paid by tenant farmers.
Captain Charles Boycott, who was the land
agent for Lord Erne and lived at Loughmask
House on the eastern shore of the lough, fell
foul of Parnell's campaign when he refused to
reduce rents by the demanded 25 per cent.
Local farmers duly put into practice the
policy advocated by Parnell of 'isolating him
from the rest of his kind as if he were a leper'.
In 1880, finding that no one locally would
harvest for him, he imported workers from
Ulster, which caused such resentment that he
had to be protected by the militia. Shortly
thereafter he left the country. From these
events the English language gained a new
word: 'boycott'.

## Moore Hall/Halle ui Mhórdha

On the east side of Lough Carra is the gutted
ruin of Moore Hall, the family home of the
writer George Moore (1852-1933), ranked by
many as the most important Irish novelist of
his day. He lived in Paris at the time of the
Impressionists and was a friend of Manet,
among other painters. He related his experiences of this time in *Reminiscences of the
Impressionist Painters* (1906). He also lived in
Dublin during the heady days of the Irish
literary renaissance, and played a role in
planning the Abbey Theatre. Between 1911
and 1914 he published *Hail and Farewell*, his
not always reliable memoirs of this period. He
died in London in 1933, but his ashes were
brought home and now lie under a cairn on
one of the islands of Lough Carra.

Moore Hall was also lived in by George's
grandfather John Moore, president of the
short-lived 'Republic of Connaught' in 1798,
and by G.H.Moore, MP for Mayo and leading
Home Ruler. It was burnt down in 1923.

The waters of Lough Carra have settled
into an anchor-shaped scoop amid gentle
pastureland, with the towering mountains
providing only a distantly menacing note.
This landscape is the subject of Moore's short,
poetic novel *The Lake* (1905). There are
woodland walks around the house and trails
beside the lake, which is safe for swimming.

MAN OF LETTERS *George Moore, the 19th-century writer, lived beside Lough Carra.*

## THE CROSS OF CONG

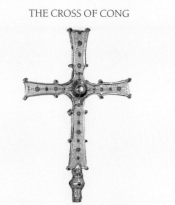

One of the great treasures of Ireland is the processional Cross of Cong, 30in tall and 19in wide, now in the National Museum, Dublin. It is said that it originally enshrined a piece of the True Cross, but this relic was lost in the course of the cross's precarious history.

Made in Roscommon in 1123, at the order of Turlough O'Conor, High King of Ireland, it has gilt-bronze plates over an oak base, which are richly ornamented with interlacing stylised mammals tussling with serpents – an interesting blend of Celtic and Scandinavian decoration.

The inscriptions read: *In this cross is preserved the cross on which suffered the Founder of the World, and Pray for Turlough O'Conor, King of Ireland, and Abbot O'Duffy, and for the artist Maol Iosa O'Echan.*

SUNSET SILHOUETTE *In the orange flow of the setting sun, the islands off the shore of Lough Mask seem to float on the water like desert mirages.*

WOOL ON THE HOOF *Suffolk sheep are a popular breed in Mayo's rich pastureland.*

### Toormakeady/*Tuar Mhic Éadaigh*

The only settlement of any size on the western side of Lough Mask is Toormakeady, a Gaeltacht, or designated Irish-speaking area, with a well-known Irish-speaking school on the shores of the lough. The Gaeltarra knitwear factory in the village produces hand-made and machine-made jerseys and cardigans in wool and linen – one of Udarás na Gaeltachta's many projects for boosting the local economy of Irish-speaking communities. In the village stand the roofless remains of a mid-19th-century Gothic church. The Church of Ireland Bishop of Tuam, Thomas Plunkett, is buried in the churchyard.

A small road signposted Toormakeady Lodge leads to a very beautiful riverside walk through woodland. At the end is a pretty waterfall where a stream tumbles down tall steps into a pool overhung by trees, ferns and heather-clad rocks.

# Rugged Cliffs and Jagged Rocks

*At every turn of Mayo's jagged peninsulas, islands and estuaries, fresh views lead the eye across more bays and headlands to the boldly pronounced mountains that hem this region to the south. In sunshine the sweeping horizons are speckled with highlights of delicate colour, but the moisture-laden Atlantic atmosphere can blot out the entire spectacle with days of mist, drizzle or blinding rain. That way, at least, no one takes the unsurpassed scenery for granted.*

## Belmullet/Béal an Mhuirthead

This seaside town was laid out in the 1820s in an extraordinary position at the narrowest part of the isthmus between Broad Haven and Blacksod Bay. The sea water withdraws from both sides at low tide to reveal expanses of mud dotted with seaweed and worm casts. A canal, usable only at high tide, has been cut just to the west of the town to connect the two bays and save boats the long journey around The Mullet.

Belmullet's colourful main streets have seen better days, but even now it is a busy town: as the largest town in Erris, it draws people from the scattered agricultural and fishing communities from miles around to buy their supplies. It also hosts an annual sea-angling festival, which coincides with the August fair, when Belmullet people from all over the world return to renew old acquaintances.

## Benwee Head/An Bhinn Bhuí

The cliffs on this startling coastline are dramatic, dropping from the highest point on Benwee Head 820ft down to the sea. The remote cliffs themselves are accessible by a rough road from the hamlet of Kilgalligan to a place where cars can be left. From here a walk of 20 minutes over damp, mossy sheep pasture leads to the headland.

The views are magnificent. They reach south-west to The Mullet peninsula and Achill Island beyond, and along the north coast of Mayo as far as the cliffs of Donegal. A mile and a half out to sea rear up the Stags of Broad Haven, an impressive cluster of jagged rocks.

Just to the south is the Irish-speaking village of Carrowteige (Ceathrú Thaidhg). There is a beautiful crescent-shaped beach beneath the scattered community of Portacloy, and farther east is the hamlet of Porturlin, a centre for lobster fishing beside a curving estuary.

## Erris/Iorras

The area around Belmullet and Bangor is known as Erris, one of the least inhabited, most desolate stretches of landscape in Ireland. Blanket bog stretches as far as the eye can see: across the peninsula, and from Bangor almost as far as Crossmolina, all the way up to the north coast and all the way south to Claggan Mountain. Here and there are small scattered communities and farmsteads, and occasionally a rare patch of bright green pasture where the land has been drained.

Peat is cut from the bog for fuel in the traditional way, and the piled ricks of turf can be seen drying through the summer months – small evidence of human activity in a vast and inaccessible landscape. In places these signs are more dramatic. To feed the voracious power station at Bellacorick, peat is scoured from the bog by bulldozers, which turn acres of landscape into flat, dark, velvety plains.

On a bleak overcast day this is a grim and threatening landscape, but in sunny weather this open unspoilt stretch of Ireland has great beauty, impressive in its immensity.

## Gweesalia/Gaoth Sáile

From Bangor the 'Coast Road' leads south-west through countryside laid waste by peat extraction towards a roughly square peninsula jutting into Blacksod Bay. The area is usually flat, and it is worth climbing the track up the last hill before the peninsula to the little modern chapel called Mount Jubilee Monument for a view of the snaking estuary of Tullaghan Bay, and huge Blacksod Bay.

The landscape south of Gweesalia (also known as Geesala) is enchanting. The road around the rim of the peninsula gives views of the Nephin Beg Range to the east, and of the towering Slievemore peak on Achill Island to the south.

Doohooma (Dumha Thuama), a settlement stretching along the southern flank of the peninsula, is said to have been the setting for J.M. Synge's play *The Playboy of the Western World*. This classic of Irish theatre caused a great stir on account of its blunt realism and earthy language when first performed at Dublin's Abbey Theatre in 1907, and 500 policemen were called in to control the outraged audience, itself numbering just less than 500.

WELL OF HOLY WATER *The bright shrine of St Dervila marks the site of a well whose water is said to be good for curing eye trouble.*

### Map

*Atlantic Ocean* — Stags of Broad Haven — Benwee Head — Portacloy — Porturlin — The Mullet — Kilgalligan — Carrowteige — Eagle Island — Broad Haven — Muingnabo — R314 — Ballyglass Lighthouse — Dooncarton — Doonamo Fort — Pollatomish — Corclogh — Knocknalina — Sruwaddacon — Cross Abbey — Pier — BELMULLET — Bellanaboy — Glenamoy — Inishglora — R313 — Barnatra — Lough Namackan — Slieve Fyagh 1090 — Carrowmore Lake — Glencullin — Inishkea North — Elly Bay — Bunnahowen — Mount Jubilee Monument — Bangor — Blacksod Bay — E r r i s — St Dervila's Church — Inishkea South — Gweesalia — Bellacorick — Fallmore — Blacksod Point — N59 — Duvillaun More — Doohooma — Tullaghan Bay — Owenmore — 0 5 Miles

## OTHER PLACES TO SEE

**Carrowmore Lake**
Signposted drive from Barnatra down western side to Bangor-Belmullet road – fine views E and SE to Slieve Fyagh (1090ft) and foothills of Nephin Beg Range.
**Duvillaun More** 1½m offshore (boats can be hired by arrangement from Blacksod Point); tiny, uninhabited island with early Christian remains.
**Inishglora** 1m offshore (boat by arrangement from Blacksod Point or Knocknalina); tiny uninhabited island with early Christian remains.
**Inishkea North and Inishkea South** 2½m offshore (boat by arrangement from Blacksod Point), pair of islands inhabited until 1930s. On them are early Christian remains associated with St Columba.
**Sruwaddacon Bay** Beautiful estuary of River Glenamoy with pine trees, rhododendrons, fuchsia hedges; coast road through Pollatomish village, past Dooncarton megalithic tomb (unsignposted), with views across Broad Haven to Ballyglass lighthouse on The Mullet.

## EVENTS
**Belmullet August Fair.**
**Belmullet Sea Angling Festival** Aug.

## SPORT
**Angling** Game fishing: Rivers Bellanaboy, Bunnahowen, Glenamoy, Glencullin, Muingnabo and Owenmore, Carrowmore Lake and Lough Namackan. Sea fishing: Belmullet, Blacksod Bay and Broad Haven.
**Bathing** Elly Bay, Portacloy.
**Golf** Belmullet Golf Club, 9-hole course. Tel: (097) 81093.

## INFORMATION
Westport Tourist Information Office. Tel: (098) 25711/ 25908.

THE MULLET *The long ragged tongue of land known as The Mullet projects into the Atlantic, its edges scalloped with shallow bays and sandy beaches.*

## The Mullet

The Mullet peninsula with its small farms comes as a refreshing surprise after the open expanses of Erris bog. This ragged piece of land is virtually an island, joined only at Belmullet. Sand dunes lie heaped along the western shore, and there are fine beaches, notably the shallow inlet at Elly Bay. At Blacksod Point near the south of the peninsula, one of the larger Spanish Armada ships, *La Rata Encoronada,* grounded and was burnt by her crew in 1588.

The 'Fallmore Drive' leads around the southern point to the little ruined 11th or 12th-century church of St Dervila in a churchyard above the sea, overgrown with grass, cow parsley and briar. The fact that the church is dedicated to a female saint suggests that there was once a convent here, but its history is not known. Some 300yds to the north of the church is St Dervila's Well, a spring said to be good for curing eye trouble.

West of the peninsula lie the uninhabited islands of Duvillaun More, Inishkea North, Inishkea South and Inishglora, once hermitages and probably places of pilgrimage. Farther up the west coast are the remains of 14th-century Cross Abbey, believed to have been associated originally with St Brendan. Only the foundations are left, but it has a fine position overlooking the Atlantic breakers as they roll in.

Yet farther north is Doonamo Fort, near Corclogh. This is a prehistoric promontory fort similar to those found on the Aran Islands. Little of it remains, but the line of the massive stone wall that sealed off this headland is still visible. It is in an exhilarating position with views along the coastline to the south, and directly overlooking a lighthouse built in 1835 on the bare rock of Eagle Island, a mile offshore.

BENWEE HEAD *An indigo sea laps the sheer cliffs and rocky inlets of this wild coast.*

227

# The Plain of the Saxons' Yews

*The county town of Castlebar looks out from the heart of Mayo onto rolling hills of rich pasture, where cattle, sheep and horses graze – though the pervasive bog is never far away. To the north, low olive-green hills preface the startling cone of Nephin, a punctuation mark at the end of the rambling Nephin Beg Range. At its feet are two woodland-fringed loughs, Conn and Cullin, separated by a thin land bridge.*

### Ballintober Abbey/Baile an Tobair

Unusually, this old and revered abbey is still in use, despite the Reformation and being vandalised by the Cromwellians in 1653. It is exceptional in that Mass has never ceased to be celebrated in it since it was built, over 750 years ago, except for five weeks during the Famine of the 1840s.

St Patrick is believed to have founded a church on this site in about 441, before Augustinian canons started their abbey in 1216, though the adjoining cloister (much ruined) is from the 15th century.

After Catholic emancipation in 1829, the restoration of the church and chapter house began. Today, the dominant note of the

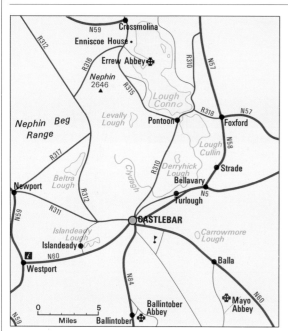

TRADITIONAL SOUNDS *In The Fishing Lodge on Lough Conn, local people celebrate St Patrick's Day with folk music and some good 'crack', or stories.*

restored interior is simplicity: unadorned, whitewashed walls and bold cruciform shape.

The de Burgo chapel, which doubles as a craft shop, was built to house the elaborate tomb of 'Pirate Queen' Grace O'Malley's son, Tioboid na Long (Theobald of the Ships), murdered near here in 1629.

The Tóchar Phádhraig, the pilgrimage road to the holy mount of Croagh Patrick, passes Ballintober. The pre-Christian flag-stones of the causeway can still be followed from either side of the abbey.

### Castlebar/Caisleán an Bharraigh

This is the county town of Mayo. The main street has the attraction of good-natured activity. By contrast, 'The Mall', on higher ground, is a picture of calm. This is a large green (unusual for Mayo towns) bordered by interesting buildings, including the old courthouse with cast-iron pillars built in the 1830s, and a pretty Methodist Hall with lancet windows and painted white and black. Its foundation stone was laid by John Wesley (1703-91), the Methodist evangelist, in 1785.

Nearby is the Imperial Hotel, where the National Land League was founded by Michael Davitt and Charles Parnell in 1879 to protect tenant farmers from eviction. The interior and particularly the wood-panelled dining room has retained an authentically Victorian air. The polygonal glass lamp over the front door is still lit by gas.

In 1798, Castlebar was the scene of a triumph of the Franco-Irish forces under General Humbert. So hasty was the flight of the British forces before inferior numbers that the engagement was gleefully labelled the 'Races of Castlebar'.

### Loughs Conn and Cullin/Loch Con and Loch Cuilinn

These two lakes are famous for their brown trout and salmon. Cullin is the smaller of the two, about one-fifth the size of Conn, and its rock-strewn, sandy shores are more accessible. Lough Conn by contrast is very coy, barely visible from any road that runs around it. With its wooded foreshores and the tower-ing backdrop of Nephin mountain, this is one of the region's beauty spots.

One way down to Lough Conn follows the road to Errew Abbey on the western side. This ruined 13th-century abbey on the tip of

with small folk museum and centre for N Mayo family-history research. Open to public by arrangement. Tel: (096) 31112.

**Islandeady** 3m W of Castlebar, magnificent scenery with mountains, lakes and crannogs.

**Turlough** Fine capped Round Tower, probably 11th century, next to ruin of 17th-century church.

### EVENTS

**Loughs Conn and Cullin Angling Festival** June.
**Castlebar International Four Days' Walks** June-July. Contact secretary. Tel: (094) 21339.
**Market Day** Castlebar, Sat.

### SPORT

**Angling** Coarse fishing: Loughs Carrowmore, Derryhick and Levally. Game fishing: Loughs Conn and Cullin, Beltra and Islandeady Loughs, and River Clydagh.
**Golf** Castlebar Golf Club, 18-hole course. Tel: (094) 21649.

### INFORMATION

Westport Tourist Information Office. Tel: (098) 25711/ 25908.

### OTHER PLACES TO SEE

**Balla** Brightly painted village on Castlebar-Claremorris road, with remains of probably 12th-century Round Tower.
**Beltra Lough** Pretty lough with small islands in SW corner; noted for salmon and sea trout; scenic route along eastern shore.
**Enniscoe House** 2m S of Crossmolina, overlooking Lough Conn – fine Georgian house built around 1790, now country-house hotel

MIRROR IMAGE *Lough Conn's reedy waters reflect the cloud-topped cone of Nephin mountain.*

a long promontory is reached by a short walk across meadows. The church is plain with no tombstones either inside or out. On one side of the cloister is a dark passage with four small lancet windows piercing the thick walls. About 100yds north are the remains of a nun's tiny chapel, which, despite its size, has massive walls 2ft thick.

## Mayo Abbey/Mainistir Mhuigheo

Lost in the countryside, and set in a gravel-strewn churchyard, is this ivy-covered ruin resonant with history. It was founded in the 7th century by English monks. They were dissidents from Lindisfarne, led by St Colman, who would not bow to the Synod of Whitby (664) and adopt Roman custom in place of the old Celtic tradition.

The monks settled first on Inishbofin off the Galway coast, but then 30 of them, with their Irish brethren, left to found their own community. The place they eventually settled at was called Mag nEo Sacsan, the 'Plain of the Saxons' Yews', later shortened to 'Mayo'.

The abbey's fame inspired Sir Henry Sidney, charged with dividing the old province of Connaught into counties, to name County Mayo after it.

STRADE STONEWORK *An exquisite tomb in the north wall of the chancel of Strade friary is faced with finely carved figures.*

## Strade/An tSráid

The ruined 13th-century Dominican friary of this small village contains some excellent 15th-century relief carvings. Beady-eyed saints and bishops line the remains of a tomb surmounted by fine stonework tracery. Adorning the stone altar is a primitive pietà in the same style, protected by two scaly angels.

Strade is, however, more famous as the birthplace, and burial place, of the reformer and founder of the National Land League,

Michael Davitt (1846-1906). There is a museum to his memory next to the abbey. It may be small, but it contains a wealth of information, including newspaper articles, police intelligence reports on his movements, mementos of his travels abroad, and harrowing photographs showing the eviction from their meagre cottages of agricultural labourers unable to pay their rent.

**Michael Davitt Museum** *Apr-Oct, Tues-Sat 10am-6pm, Sun 2-6pm. Tel: (094) 31022.*

The tireless reformer, writer and democrat, Michael Davitt, is one of Mayo's heroes. Born in the village of Strade in 1846, in the middle of the Famine years, he was four when his family were evicted and had to emigrate to Haslingden, a small industrial town in Lancashire. Michael left school at nine to work in a cotton mill, where, in 1857, he lost his right arm in an industrial accident. On recovering he went back to school, then worked in a small printing shop.

During this time he met Fenian activists and joined the Irish Republican Brotherhood. Arrested in 1870 on a charge of arms trafficking, he was sentenced to 15 years hard labour but was released on parole in 1877.

Ireland was then facing another famine, while tenant farmers were being squeezed by increased rents and the threat of eviction. In 1879 Davitt and the young Protestant MP for Meath, Charles Stewart Parnell, founded the National Land League to protect farmers. It led to mass action, which escalated into the 'Land War' of 1879-82 but won concessions from the British government. The weakening of the landlords' grip on the land was an important step towards Irish independence.

# Where Pilgrims Flock

*Low hills rise and fall, covered by green pasture patched with heather-coated bog. Divided and subdivided by hedgerows and dry-stone walls, the pastures reflect a long history of human occupation. There are few large houses, but the hills are dotted with one-storey cottages – some old, many modern. The market towns that serve these scattered rural communities are friendly, busy places with broad streets lined with cheerfully painted façades.*

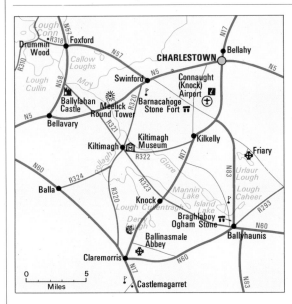

BOUNDARY PATTERNS *Dry-stone walls embroider the landscape around Barnacahoge.*

**OTHER PLACES TO SEE**

**Ballinasmale Abbey** 2m NE of Claremorris – ruins of late 13th-century Carmelite friary in rural setting.

**Ballylahan Castle** 4m S of Foxford – last ruined fragments of large castle (by the standards of the time), built in the 13th century by McJordan family.

**Braghlaboy Ogham Stone** ¾m W of Ballyhaunis, off the road leading N to Island Lake, standing stone, now at an angle, incised with ogham writing, on top of a small hill – fine views to E.

**Castlemagarrett** 2m S of Claremorris forest walks near the golf course, on old estate of Lord Oranmore and Browne.

**Claremorris** Cheerfully bustling market town and railway junction, with wide main street of shops and houses gaily painted in fashion characteristic of the region.

**Kiltimagh Museum** Small folk museum, well laid out in disused railway station, with restored railway carriages. Also birthplace of the poet 'Blind Raftery' lies close to Kiltimagh. Museum open daily 2-6pm. Tel: (094) 81132/81393.

**WALKS**

**Between Kilkelly and Charlestown.**

**Drummin Wood** Forest walks and picnic spots:

**EVENTS**

**Claremorris Ham Fair** Aug.

**Féile na Gabhair** Goat Fair, Foxford, May.

**Market Days** Ballyhaunis, Tues; Swinford, Wed; Claremorris, Fri.

**St Patrick's Week Festival** Kiltimagh, Mar.

**Swinford Agricultural Show** Aug.

**Western Rose Festival** Charlestown, Aug.

**SPORT**

**Angling** Coarse fishing: Loughs Caheer, Callow, Cullentragh, Derry, Eaton's, Mannin and Urlaur, Lakehill Pond, and Rivers Glore, Moy and Pollagh. Game fishing: Loughs Conn and Cullin.

**Bathing** Loughs Conn and Cullin.

**Golf** Ballyhaunis Golf Club, 9-hole course. Tel: (0907) 30014.
Claremorris Golf Club, 9-hole course. Tel: (094) 71527.
Swinford Golf Club, 9-hole course. Tel: (094) 51378.

**INFORMATION**

Westport Tourist Information Office. Tel: (098) 25711/25908.

## Ballyhaunis/Béal Átha hAmhnais

This agreeable market town was founded at a crossroads and has spread up the sides of a gently sloping valley. As in most of the towns of Mayo, the houses and shops are terraced, but each has its own individual style, and each its colour scheme, often vivid reds and blues. There is an atmosphere of quiet bustle here, as people from the agricultural surrounds visit the shops and go about their business. To the north of Ballyhaunis is a sprinkling of pretty little lakes set in rolling country, among which is Urlaur Lough, with its ruined 15th-century Dominican friary.

## Barnacahoge Stone Fort/Caiseal Cluain Meirg

Near the runway of Connaught (Knock) International Airport, on a grassy knoll within a bow-shaped ring of hills, stands Barnacahoge Stone Fort. It is a good example of the small fortified enclosures in use from the late Iron Age (c. AD 500) and may have been occupied as late as the 1700s. Encircling the flat summit are the remains of a wall some 5ft thick and about 50ft in diameter. Within the shelter of these massive walls would have been thatched dwellings of mud and wattle, and pens into which livestock could be herded when raiders threatened.

The practice of herding over the centuries has turned the landscape into a quilt of small pastures. Many of these robust dry-stone enclosures have no gates: when a farmer moves livestock, he simply takes down a bit of wall, replacing it when the animals have gone through.

## Charlestown/Baile Chathail

The origin of this trim little market town with its wide streets and neatly painted houses and shops is unusual. Until the 1840s, Bellahy, just over the border in Sligo, was the rural area's centre. It belonged to the Knox family, with whom the owner of this part of Mayo, Lord Dillon, was at odds.

Lord Dillon's agent, Charles Strickland, offended by Lord Knox, decided to build an alternative town, and offered 100 acres for the first fire lit in the hearth of a completed house on a site on the Mayo side. The prize was won in 1846.

Connaught International Airport, the crowning triumph of Monsignor James Horan who had it built to bring pilgrims to the holy site at Knock, lies to the south, nearer to Charlestown than to Knock itself.

### Foxford/Béal Easa

On the River Moy east of Loughs Conn and Cullin is this pleasant market town and centre for anglers. It is known for the Woollen Mills, established in 1892 by Mother Arsenius of the Irish Sisters of Charity to try to stem the tide of emigration from the town. The nuns helped to run the mill until the late 1980s. Now privately owned, it still produces high-quality blankets, tweeds, furnishing fabrics, and even blue serge for garda uniforms. The machines today are mainly modern, but the buildings are still redolent of the 19th century, with the original motto overlooking the factory floor: 'God's Providence is our Inheritance.'

**Foxford Woollen Mills** *Daily, 9am-5.15pm exc Fri, 9am-1pm. Guided tours, Mon-Fri 11am and 2.30pm. Closes for three weeks in July. Craft shop, May-Sept. Tel: (094) 56104.*

FROM FATHER TO SON *A boy learns the trade at a Claremorris cattle market.*

### THE APPARITION AT KNOCK

On the wet evening of August 21, 1879, in a year marked by the beginning of the bitter Land War, Mary McLoughlin walked past her parish church in the village of Knock and saw, at the gable end, what she thought was a group of religious statues. She hurried on to visit her friend, Mary Byrne.

Half an hour later, returning along this road, they both saw these figures, hovering about 2ft off the ground, quite stationary and silent. They recognised three life-size figures as the Virgin Mary, St Joseph and St John the Evangelist.

To one side was what looked like a simple altar, on which stood a lamb haloed by stars or angels, and a wooden cross. The whole scene, illuminated by an inexplicable globe of bright light, lasted some two hours, during which a total of 15 villagers came to witness it.

Six weeks later, the formidable Archbishop of Tuam, John MacHale, then aged 90, held a commission of enquiry. The witnesses were interviewed and cross-examined. The vision was declared genuine. Again, in 1936, three surviving witnesses were interviewed, and once again they convinced the commissioners of the truth of what they had seen.

Crowds of some 20,000 would gather there on feast days in the early years, but the shrine remained a comparatively modest pilgrimage centre until recently, when the number of pilgrims began to accelerate rapidly, making it now one of the world's major Marian shrines.

### Knock/An Cnoc

In 1879 the figures of St Mary, mother of Jesus, St Joseph and St John the Evangelist were reported to have appeared in a vision before 15 people from the village of Knock. Since then this village has been a centre of pilgrimage, drawing over a million pilgrims every year.

To accommodate such numbers, the huge Basilica of Our Lady Queen of Ireland was built in 1976 to hold 20,000 people. Its rather functional polygonal concrete structure is brought to life by the thronging crowds and processions. Knock is not a place of cure, as is Lourdes, but it is widely held that all devout believers will receive some kind of blessing from their visit. Despite the very serious purpose of the visitors, the atmosphere is infectiously joyous.

The original church (built 1828) remains. It has a very beautiful interior, with some fine stained-glass windows by Harry Clarke (1889-1931). The exterior gable, where the apparition was observed, is now protected by a glass-walled oratory.

Knock also has the best folk museum in Mayo, well laid out in a modern building near the Basilica. It contains artefacts and photographs relating to the apparition as well as items of rural Ireland at that time and a reconstructed interior of a traditional cottage.

Monsignor James Horan was the parish priest of Knock who fought tirelessly to promote the shrine. He raised over one million Irish pounds in donations and cajoled the government into funding an airport to serve the thousands visiting Knock each year. The airport was opened in 1986.

**Knock Folk Museum** *May-Oct, daily 10am-6pm, July and Aug 10am-7pm. Tel: (094) 88100.*

### Meelick Round Tower

This lonely finger of masonry rises to over 65ft in an open landscape of pasture and hedgerows. From the hillock on which it stands, some 3 miles south-west of Swinford, there are fine, open views across to Slieve Gamph, or 'The Ox Mountains', in the north and the Partry Mountains to the south-west. The tower's cap is missing but its doorway, 11ft off the ground, is still visible. The tower served as a refuge, presumably for monks from St Broccaidh's monastery, which is believed to have occupied the site.

### Swinford/Béal Átha na Muice

This 18th-century town is a busy rural centre stretching along the main Castlebar-Dublin road. Behind the small modern hospital is a poignant reminder of the devastation caused by the 'Black Years' Famines of 1845 and 1847. In Mayo some 250,000 people died of starvation in those years, 564 of them buried unceremoniously in a mass grave behind what was then the workhouse. A discreet modern memorial stone beside the orderly lawns and flowerbeds of the hospital grounds signals its tragic contents.

TOKENS OF REMEMBRANCE *Souvenirs at Knock Shrine cater for every pilgrim's taste.*

# St Patrick's Holy Mount

*The conical peak of Ireland's holy mountain, Croagh Patrick, steals the limelight in this corner of County Mayo. It is also the focus of one of Ireland's most important pilgrimages. To the west is a plain of moist farmland and tiny loughs, and a coastline of empty, curving beaches of white sand which look out to Caher Island and Inishturk. This coast is sparsely inhabited, but prehistoric and early Christian remains show it has been lived in for many centuries.*

### Bunlahinch Clapper Footbridge

Near the hamlets of Killeen and Killadoon, in pretty, remote coastal pasture, is a narrow footbridge a few centuries old. It is a low, curving construction, 130ft long, formed of 38 boulders spanned by slabs of stone, and takes walkers across a wide but shallow ford. The hills and plains nearby are scattered with prehistoric remains.

### Clare Island/Cliara

The only island in Mayo's waters reached by a regular ferry service is Clare Island. In fine weather it has exceptional views, south down the coast to Connemara, to the east across Clew Bay, and north to Achill Island. Some 140 people live there now, but the island's 4000 acres supported 1700 people before the 1840s Famine. Witness to this are ruins of

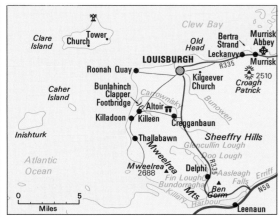

**OTHER PLACES TO SEE**
**Altoir** Megalithic wedge-tomb, about 2000 BC; so named because its great capstone was used as an altar for saying Mass in 'penal times' during 17th and 18th centuries.
**Caher Island** 4m offshore, boats by arrangement from Clare Island or Roonah Quay; remains of early Christian settlement associated with St Patrick.

**Inishturk** 7m offshore, boats will take visitors across by arrangement, from Clare Island, Roonah Quay, or Cleggan (County Galway). Small island with attractive hilly landscape, good beaches and lovely views.
**Kilgeever Church** 1½m E of Louisburgh, tiny ruined church associated with St Patrick; devotional 'stations' performed here by pilgrims to Croagh Patrick.

**Thallabawn** On beach W of village, cone of rubble, which is all that remains of church founded by St Colman, about AD 668.

**WALKS**
**Clare Island** Information from the Centre for Island Studies. Tel: (098) 25048/ 25412.

**EVENTS**
**International Sea Angling Competitions** Clew Bay, Apr-Oct.
**Open Boat Competition** Clare Island, June-Aug.

**SPORT**
**Angling** Game fishing: Carrownisky system, Rivers Bunowen and Erriff, and Doo, Fin and Glencullin loughs. Sea fishing: Clew Bay, Clare Island, Louisburgh, Roonah Quay.
**Bathing** Clew Bay, Leckanvy.
**Canoeing** Louisburgh.
**Surfing** Louisburgh.

**INFORMATION**
Westport Tourist Information Office. Tel: (098) 25711/ 25908.

cottages and extensive ribs of land where potatoes grew in soil banked up to shed rain.

A 15th-century tower overlooking the tiny harbour was once the stronghold of the O'Malley's, who used the island as a base for pestering trading ships with their manoeuvrable little craft. The tower is now a sad ruin, defaced after being converted into a coastguard's tower in the 19th century. The ruined Cistercian church (founded 1224), a mile and a half to the west, has rare trompe l'oeil vaulting and a spidery red dragon painted on the chancel ceiling. It also contains a simple tomb spanned by fine stone tracing, now green with damp. This is said to be Grace O'Malley's final resting place. Her family crest is displayed on a stone panel next to the tomb, with a motto that reads: *Terra Mariq[ue] Potens* (Mighty on Land and Sea).

Ireland's first open-sea salmon farm lies in the bay south-east from the lighthouse on the northern tip.
**Ferry Crossing** *From Roonah Quay, west of Louisburgh. Lasts 25 minutes. Tel: (098) 26307.*

HOLY MOUNTAIN *Pilgrims of all ages (above and right) climb the slopes of Croagh Patrick.*

### Croagh Patrick

The stark and soaring pinnacle of Croagh Patrick (2510ft) is a persistent landmark throughout central and southern Mayo. It was once sacred to the pagan god Crom, but St Patrick spent the 40 days of Lent here around AD 441 and won the mountain for Christianity. Furthermore, when he rang his bell at the edge of the mighty precipice on the south side, all the toads and snakes of Ireland leapt to their deaths, except the natterjack toad, thus ridding Ireland of all these reptiles but one, forever. Since that time Croagh Patrick has been the focus of pilgrimage.

Throughout the year people of all ages and all degrees of devotion trek up the rocky path to the summit, a stiff walk of two hours or more. The main pilgrimage, however, takes place on the Sunday before the Lughnasa feast on August 1. Some 60,000 pilgrims make the ascent, starting at a point just above

Murrisk Abbey. They climb the mountain throughout the day, beginning in the darkness of early morning, when they are guided by hand-held lights. Mass is celebrated in the tiny chapel on the summit. The broad path cut by the feet, and knees, of millions of pilgrims over the centuries is clearly visible for miles around.

ST PATRICK'S BELL

Inside this ornate shrine is a plain iron bell, shaped like a large cow bell, said to have belonged to St Patrick. There is another, similar bell associated with St Patrick, which is one of Ireland's most sacred relics and plays a significant part in a number of Ireland's most treasured legends. It was at the sound of this bell that snakes and toads, except for the natterjack toad, departed Ireland for good. It also broke the spell cast upon the children of the ocean god Lir by their jealous stepmother, to tread the waters of Lough Derravaragh for 300 years as swans.

The bell has a tarnished, blackened look, said to be from the fires of hell when St Patrick battled with the pagan gods on Croagh Patrick: it symbolises the coming of Christianity and victory over paganism.

Both bells and the shrine are now in the National Museum, Dublin. The richly ornamented case, made in about 1100 in Armagh, is decorated with silver and gold filigree, with exquisite gilt-silver openwork featuring interlaced birds and snakes, offset by studs of rock crystal and glass. The back is remarkable for the ingenious simplicity of its geometric design, an openwork panel of 32 interlocking crosses.

### Doo Lough/Loch Dúlocha

South of Louisburgh, in a steep bowl between the Sheeffrey Hills, Mweelrea Mountains and Ben Gorm, lies the rightly named 'black lake'. The southern tip of the lake leads into a wooded dell where Fin Lough (or Fionnloch) and the River Bundorragha lead to Killary Harbour. The 2nd Marquess of Sligo – Byron's travelling companion in Greece – was so reminded of home by the site of the oracle at Delphi that when he built a fishing lodge here in the 1830s he called it 'Delphi', still the name of a small settlement and an adventure centre.

### Killary Harbour/An Caoláire Rua

The deep furrow of Killary Harbour divides Mayo from Galway. Not a harbour in the usual sense, it is a long, narrow inlet that winds in from the Atlantic to meet the outflow of the River Erriff. It is Ireland's only true fiord, steeply banked by the 2688ft peak of Mweelrea on the Mayo side, and by the Maumturk Mountains in Galway. Killary Harbour, which offers capacious deep-water anchorage, has a muscular beauty, brooding and menacing in foul weather.

### Louisburgh/Cluain Cearbán

The Irish name of this tiny town means 'meadow of buttercups', but it was renamed in honour of an uncle of the Marquess of Sligo, who had played a part in the capture in 1758 of the French fortress of Louisbourg on Cape Breton Island, Nova Scotia. Its broad streets of terraced houses, each individually fashioned, have remained more or less intact since it was laid out in the 18th century. The Granuaile Interpretive Centre on the edge of the town is devoted to the story of the Pirate Queen Grace O'Malley and other aspects of local history.

**Granuaile Interpretive Centre** *Easter to end Oct, 10am-6pm. Sat 10am-4pm. Tel: (098) 66195.*

### Murrisk Abbey/Mainistir Muraisc

At the base of Croagh Patrick, lapped by the waters of Clew Bay, stands the greystone ruin of an Augustinian friary, the pilgrims' traditional starting point for their route up the mountain. Founded in 1456 by the O'Malley family, it was destroyed by the English in the late 16th century.

The fine stonework of the east window, with delicate bar tracery, indicates something of what was lost. Surrounded by a windswept cemetery and bent hawthorn trees, there is a sense of grim determination here, a note struck by an inscription commemorating the rudimentary restoration of the oratory: *'AD 1942, on the eleventh day of August after a lapse of nearly four centuries since the destruction by heretics of this Abbey of Murrisk, the holy sacrifice of Mass was again offered for the first time in this oratory.'*

MAYO MARSHES *The white heads of marsh plants dance over the dark waters of a peatland.*

# Haunt of a Pirate Queen

*Clew Bay, studded with hundreds of little green islands, in fact, 'drowned drumlins', is at the heart of Mayo's western seaboard. The jewel in this crown is Achill Island with ever-changing cloudscapes brushing its peaks, a place of wild beauty. Around Westport and Newport there is a mixture of rich pasture and bog. To the north are the vast rocky screes and uninhabited blanket bog of the Nephin Beg Range.*

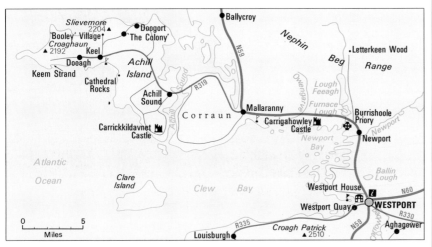

## OTHER PLACES TO SEE

**Ballycroy** Tiny village on Mallaranny-Bangor road; exceptional views of Nephin Beg Range and Achill Island.

**Burrishoole Priory** Hauntingly beautiful ruin at edge of tidal estuary, founded as Dominican priory in about 1469 by Richard Burke.

**Letterkeen Wood** Forest and riverside walks in Nephin Beg Range, above Loughs Feeagh and Furnace.

**Mallaranny** Also, Mulrany; scattered seaboard village with fine sandy beach in sheltered corner of Clew Bay, famous for fuchsia hedges and other plants prospering in its mild climate.

## WALKS

**Croaghaun mountain** On Achill Island, 7m walk round its base.

**Leenaun to Westport** 25m hike.

**Nephin Beg Range.**

## EVENTS

**Bangor Annual Trail Walk** June.

**Market Day** Westport, Thur.

**Newport Sea Angling Festival** Early Aug.

**Westport Arts Festival** Oct.

**Westport International Sea Angling Festival** June.

**Westport Street Festival** July.

## SPORT

**Angling** Game fishing: Ballin and Carrowbeg loughs, and small loughs and rivers on Achill Island and the Corraun peninsula. Rivers Carrowsallagh, Newport and Owengarve.
Sea fishing: Achill Island, Clew Bay.

**Golf** Achill Island Golf Club, 9-hole course. Tel: (098) 43202.
Mulrany Golf Club, 9-hole course. Tel: (098) 36185.
Westport Golf Club, 18-hole course. Tel: (098) 25113.

**Horse riding** Drummindoo Equitation Centre. Tel: (098) 25616.

**Rock climbing** Nephin Beg Range, Slievemore (Achill Island).

**Sailing** Glenans Sailing Centre. Contact tourist office.

## INFORMATION

Westport Tourist Information Office. Tel: (098) 25711/ 25908.

## Achill Island/Acaill

Ireland's largest island is also one of its most spectacular. Achill's great hills plunge down to the sea, truncated by some of the most impressive cliff faces in Europe. On the southern coast are the strangely architectural Cathedral Rocks, and at the western end, Croaghaun (2192ft) tumbles down a 2000ft precipice to the sea. Here and there the hills soften into sheltered bays with golden beaches. The Atlantic Drive takes in some of Achill's best scenery, the green and khaki of bog and poor pasture interspersed with heather and fuchsia hedges and the unwieldy, corrugated forms of wild rhubarb.

On the lower slopes of Slievemore (2204ft) is 'The Colony', once a Protestant mission established in 1834 to convert stubborn western Catholics. Offering education, food, clothing and shelter to children as the reward for becoming Protestant, the mission thrived while the rest of Ireland reeled under the famine. Not far off is a deserted 'booley' village, where herdsmen lived with their families during the summer pasturing.

Guarding the southern entrance to Achill Sound, which separates the island from the mainland, is Carrickkildavnet Castle, an elegant 15th-century tower house believed to have been one of the pirate Grace O'Malley's network of strongholds. And at Dooagh is a Folklife Centre, a late 19th-century cottage furnished in the style of the period.
**Folklife Centre** *June-Sept, 10am-6pm. Tel: (0506) 21627.*

## Aghagower/Achadh Ghodhair

This pretty little agricultural hamlet centres upon a ruined church and a thin Round Tower rising to over 50ft over it. The tower served as both bell tower and refuge, and probably dates from about AD 1000. The original door stands 7ft above the ground, and the tower itself was divided into four storeys. It has lost its cap (now preserved in the local Catholic church), and the upper part was apparently destroyed by lightning. The door at ground level is more recent, but affords a glimpse of the narrow interior and 3ft thick walls.

A church is said to have been founded here by St Patrick and then handed over to his disciple, St Seanach. However, these ruins are mainly 15th century. Aghagower is on the Tóchar Phádraig, the pilgrimage route to Croagh Patrick, and there are sites associated with St Patrick around the churchyard, such

THE SIMPLE LIFE *Patchwork fields provide a modest living on Corraun peninsula.*

as the dried-up well to the north and the gnarled old tree to the south-east, where special devotions are made during the pilgrimage in July.

## Carrigahowley Castle/Carraig an Chablaigh

'Castle' is too grandiose a term for this square-built stronghold, also known as Rockfleet. It is little more than a tower set on the rocky foreshore of an inlet of Newport Bay. It belonged to Richard Burke (or de Burgo) and later became the home of the Pirate Queen, Grace O'Malley. The story goes that in 1566 Grace entered into her second marriage, to Richard Burke, on the understanding that either of them could annul it after one year. Grace is said to have done just this. A year later, as Richard arrived back at the castle after a pillaging expedition, she locked the door and leaned over the parapet to shout 'I dismiss you!'

The castle is in good order and has been carefully restored to a rudimentary but sound condition. By means of a steep flight of wooden steps and a narrow spiral staircase, visitors can see what cramped conditions the great Pirate Queen was accustomed to. The thick walls are pierced only by narrow defensive slits. Only the upper storey, with its fireplace and larger window, provides some measure of comfort and space, and was possibly richly furnished with the trappings of a life spent in trading and piracy.

### Newport/Baile Uí Fhiacháin

Overlooking the River Newport where it flows into Clew Bay is this 17th-century town. It is mainly an angling centre, and its focus is Newport House, a vine-covered Georgian mansion on the edge of the village, and now a hotel.

Above the town is the monumental neo-Romanesque Catholic church of St Patrick, built in 1914. Inside, its pale sandstone, with massive pillars supporting a barrel-vaulted roof, makes a restrained setting for exuberant stained-glass windows. The windows of the north and south aisle depict the Garden of Gethsemane and the Adoration of the Magi. But the real focus of the church is the exhilarating Last Judgement over the altar, filled with rich blues, greens and reds, by Harry Clarke (1889–1931).

### Westport/Cathair na Mart

Westport was laid out as an adjunct to the Marquess of Sligo's Westport House in the late 18th century, and its legacy of town planning can be seen in the comfortably spacious streets. The town focuses on the canalised River Carrowbeg, which tumbles gently over low steps through the tree-lined avenue called The Mall. A column in the middle of the octagonal market square now supports a modern statue of St Patrick where one of George Glendenning, banker and benefactor, stood until 1922.

There are several buildings with fine Georgian features, recalling the days of Westport's prosperity, when it thrived on the cotton and linen trade. Among them is an exceptionally lovely Protestant church (built around 1880), which displays the sinuous organic qualities of Art Nouveau.

### Westport House

East of Westport Quay lies the home of the Browne family, Earls of Altamont and Marquesses of Sligo. It is the only stately home in Mayo open to the public. It was built 1730-80 on the site of an O'Malley castle, the dungeons of which are visible beneath the house. The interior has a fine hall designed by Richard Cassel and an elegant dining room by James Wyatt. The contents are hugely varied, with engravings, family portraits, a *Holy Family* by Rubens, and curios.

**Westport House and Gardens** *May, 2-5pm; June, 2-6pm; July and Aug, 10.30am-6pm, Sun 2-6pm; Sept, 2-5pm, house only. Tel: (098) 25430.*

TRANQUIL BAY *Evening clouds turn the waters of Clew Bay to polished pewter as a gentle tide washes the rocks and shingle on the foreshore.*

---

#### THE PIRATE QUEEN OF MAYO

The old province of Connaught long held the reputation of being the 'wild west' of Ireland. One of the most famous chieftains of these untamed shores was the Pirate Queen, Granuaile, or Grace O'Malley in her anglicised form.

She was born in about 1530, the only daughter of Owen O'Malley, chief of the O'Malley (or O'Maille) clan, which ruled the western coast from Achill Island to Inishbofin. At the age of 16 Grace was married to Donal O'Flaherty, son of the clan that ruled over territory to the south, around Connemara. These were days of continuous feuding, land-grabbing, cattle-raiding and piracy. Donal was murdered by the Joyces, but Grace rallied her clan and established her own power base on Clare Island, protected by a ring of forts around Clew Bay. From here, sailing with a small fleet of galleys powered by sails and oars, she could prey on the cargo vessels from Spain and Scotland that sailed along the Galway coast.

*The O'Malley crest on a plaque in Clare Abbey.*

In 1566 she married Richard Burke, from another powerful local family. In 1577 Grace was captured while plundering the lands of the Earl of Desmond. After 18 months of imprisonment in Limerick, she was released on condition that she abandoned her lawless ways.

When Sir Richard Bingham began to enforce English rule in Ireland by violent suppression, Grace decided to appeal directly to Queen Elizabeth I for protection and set off for London to seek an audience. This was granted, and in September 1593 an extraordinary meeting took place between the two queens. According to legend, Grace O'Malley was forthright to the point of insult. When offered the title of countess, she apparently retorted that Queen Elizabeth had no right to presume to offer such a title, for they were equals. Nonetheless, her attitude must have had some charms, for Elizabeth granted her the freedom to live in peace for the rest of her life. She died in about 1603.

# ISLAND OF SAINTS AND SCHOLARS

*Christianity in Ireland from its arrival to the present*

The coming of Christianity to Ireland in the early 5th century was unlike its arrival in any other country. Throughout much of the Roman Empire the religion was spread by sword and edict, imposed upon a conquered people by the occupying Roman administration. But in Ireland Christianity arrived not by the sword but by persuasive missionaries who brought the 'Good Word' to the pagan Gaels and established a vibrant Church.

THE ARRIVAL OF ST PATRICK Popular legend claims that St Patrick introduced Christianity to Ireland in the middle of the 5th century, but historians believe he was not the first Christian to reach these shores. More likely, lesser-known British missionaries paved the way for his successes. Indeed, there were apparently enough converts in Ireland before Patrick's arrival to encourage Pope Celestine in 431 to appoint Ireland's first bishop, Palladius, as overseer of 'the Irish believing in Christ'.

Two documents written by St Patrick late in his life roughly outline his career. The son of a Roman official living in western Britain, he was abducted by Irish raiders when he was 16 years old. He remained in Ireland for six years looking after his master's sheep before escaping. After training as a cleric, probably in Gaul, he returned to Britain, where he dreamed of the Irish people crying 'We ask thee, boy, come and once more walk among us'.

According to tradition St Patrick returned in 432, and for the next 30 years crisscrossed Ireland making converts and establishing churches. He chose Armagh as the ecclesiastical capital of Ireland, within 3 miles of Eamhain Macha, the great hill-fort once occupied by kings and queens of Ulster, and organised the Church along Roman lines.

AN INDEPENDENT CHURCH The Roman model of the Church, with bishops overseeing established dioceses, soon proved unworkable in a rural land that lacked the complex Roman structure of towns and villages. And with the collapse of the Roman Empire and Ireland's isolation from Europe, the Irish Church was cut off from Rome's direct influence. Not surprisingly, it soon developed its own character. For example, much to the Pope's displeasure the Irish insisted on adhering to the traditional dating of Easter instead of following the new method of dating it accepted by Rome in 1457. It was not until 716 that the Irish Church acceded to Rome's wishes.

Suspect Irish theologians also incurred Rome's wrath. In 418 Rome excommunicated Pelagius for denying the doctrine of original sin. Ireland's monks expressed their independence in their appearance, too. Instead of following the European practice of shaving the crown of the head, they shaved their hair at the front of their heads and let it grow long at the back.

In a further move towards independence, the growing number of converts who wanted to dedicate their lives to Christianity established monasteries, in large numbers. Some, driven by a desire to become 'pilgrims for Christ', sailed away from Ireland on 'holy exile' or left to bring the message of Christianity to foreign lands. Communities were established in Scotland, England, Europe and even in Iceland. One of the most famous of these missionaries was Columbanus, who left Ireland in 590 and founded monasteries in France, Germany and Italy.

THE GROWTH OF THE MONASTERIES Monasteries in Ireland were at first austere, simple groups of wood or wattle buildings that housed small communities of the faithful. During the 6th and 7th centuries monasticism spread rapidly throughout Ireland as men like St Columba, St Kevin and St Ciaran turned these monasteries into sophisticated centres of worship, learning and artistic enterprise. The gospels were recorded in lavishly illuminated manuscripts such as the *Book of Kells* and the *Book of Dimma*, now regarded as priceless works of art. Monasteries also fostered the art of metalwork, in reliquaries, book shrines, croziers and devotive plaques. Stone carving flourished there too, on High Crosses, as statuary and as decoration on architecture.

IRELAND'S PATRON SAINT *A carving of St Patrick portrays him standing above a snake. Legend has it that when he rang his bell on top of Croagh Patrick in County Mayo, all the snakes in Ireland fled.*

By the mid-6th century Christianity had largely displaced the ancient pagan rites. But it enhanced the native culture too. By introducing the Irish to Latin and the Roman alphabet, which quickly replaced the limited ogham script, Irish monks could preserve their country's oral traditions. A national written literature was born. The Church, in turn, was influenced by Celtic society. Christian legends were often embellished with details inspired by Celtic myths.

As their fame spread, monasteries such as Glendalough and Clonmacnoise – known as the 'University of the West' – lured students from England and Europe. The fervent faith and accomplishments of Ireland's monks and missionaries led it to become known as the 'Island of Saints and Scholars'. Spared the devastation that ravaged Europe during the barbarian invasions of the Dark Ages, the Irish Church reached a high level of intellectual and cultural achievement. Sadly, this Golden Age was not to last.

THE CHURCH UNDER ATTACK In 795 Viking longboats approaching the shore of Ireland marked the end of the island's long isolation. Over the next 200 years the Vikings plundered the land – especially its monasteries – and slaughtered many of the monks. Anglo-Norman invaders followed in the 12th century and Henry VIII's Protestant Reformation threatened the Irish Church in the 16th century. Some 100 years later Cromwell outlawed Irish priests, and the penal laws of the 1690s forbade Catholic worship.

The Irish Church survived these attacks only to be threatened in the 20th century by the declining interest that afflicts many Churches in the Western world. Today 95 per cent of the Republic of Ireland is Catholic (compared with 23 per cent of Northern Ireland) and the Church still has some influence on Ireland's society and culture. But the number at Mass is falling off and few are entering convents or the priesthood. However, people still make regular pilgrimages to shrines such as Lourdes, Fatima and – closer to home – Knock and Croagh Patrick. And rags and mementos are attached to trees around holy wells. So while Ireland may no longer lay claim to the title of 'Island of Saints and Scholars', the glories of its legendary founders are still remembered and their blessings invoked.

GLENDALOUGH *The Round Tower of the monastery at Glendalough (right) rises into the mists that shroud the Glen of the Two Lakes. The 6th-century monastery has been a focus for pilgrimage for centuries. In the early 19th century, 'patterns', or religious festivals, were held there, as recorded by the painter Joseph Peacock in 1817 (above).*

ILLUMINATED MASTERPIECES *The* Book of Armagh *(below), made in 807, used very little colour compared with the rich decoration of the* Book of Kells *(centre left) and the 'carpet' pages of the* Book of Durrow *(centre right). Many books, such as the* Book of Dimma *(far right), borrowed patterns from metalwork.*

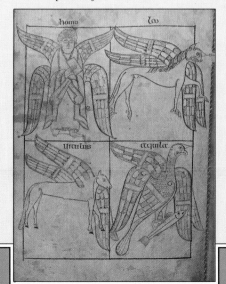

# Lake Islands and a Blind Harpist

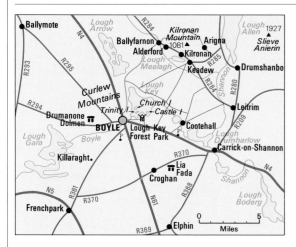

*The jewel among Roscommon's glittering lakes is Lough Key, lying amid the attractions of a forest park. But it is only part of a region rich in natural splendours where lakes teem with fish, wildlife abounds and rugged mountains and lush forests compete for attention. The bustling market town of Boyle nestles at the foot of the Curlew Mountains, its history imprinted on the shape of the ruins of Boyle Abbey and honoured in the restored grandeur of King House.*

### Arigna Scenic Drive

Cutting across the spectacular Kilronan Mountain is an uncut gem of a tourist attraction – the 25 mile Arigna Drive, from Cootehall to Boyle. It leads along narrow, winding and often bumpy roads that pass through tiny, immaculate villages like Keadew and some of the most magnificent scenery in Ireland. Red squirrels, stoats, fallow deer, badgers, rabbits and hares can be seen along the route, and among the birds to be spotted are goldcrests and pheasants.

### Boyle/Mainistir Na Búille

St Patrick is said to have passed through a tiny settlement in AD 435 and convinced St Attracta, the Abbess of Killaraght, that it needed better accommodation. Boyle town quickly grew round the hostel she founded. Later, legend says, St Patrick tumbled into the

LOUGH KEY *The golden tints of autumn highlight Castle Island with its 19th-century folly.*

**OTHER PLACES TO SEE**
**Drumanone Dolmen** 2m W of Boyle; one of the largest megalithic portal graves in Ireland, with 14ft by 10ft capstone.
**Keadew** Consistent winner of County Roscommon's Tidiest Village contest, and venue of O'Carolan International Harp Festival.

**Kilronan** 2½m SE of Ballyfarnon on shore of Lough Meelagh. Ruins of medieval church and burial place of Turlough O'Carolan. Holy Well of St Lasair on lough shore.
**Lia Fada** 9ft tall standing stone, said to have been hurled there by the Irish hero Finn MacCool.

**EVENTS**
**Boyle Arts Festival** July–Aug.
**Isle of Lough Key Festival** Boyle, July.
**O'Carolan International Harp Festival** Keadew, Aug.

**SPORT**
**Angling** Coarse fishing: Loughs Allen, Drumharlow, Key, Kilglass and Meelagh, and Rivers Boyle and Shannon. Game fishing: Kilglass Lough and River Boyle.
**Bathing** Doon Shore, NW banks of Lough Key and Lough Key Forest Park.
**Canoeing** Lough Key and River Boyle.
**Cruising** Lough Key and River Boyle.
**Gaelic Football** Abbey Park, opposite Boyle Abbey.
**Golf** Boyle Golf Club, 9-hole course. Tel: (079) 62594.
**Water-skiing and windsurfing** Lough Key Forest Park.

**INFORMATION**
Ireland West Tourism.
Tel: (091) 63081.

River Boyle and cursed the spot where he fell. Since then the fishing has been poor there.

The sport downstream, however, makes up for it. Boyle, and nearby Loughs Gara and Key, lure fishermen from all over the world for trout or coarse fishing, and host numerous international fishing contests. One local fisherman's tale concerns Constable O'Connor's Pike. On Good Friday, in 1900, Constable P.J. O'Connor landed a 53lb pike on Lough Key. He told *Fishing Gazette*, 'In spite of all we could do it brought us about where it liked through the lake'.

But Boyle is more than just a fisherman's paradise. On the northern edge of the town next to the river are the imposing ruins of a Cistercian abbey. It is Ireland's most impressive example of a 12th-century Cistercian church. Founded in 1161 and consecrated in 1218, the abbey was built during the period when Irish ecclesiastical architectural style was changing from the Romanesque to Gothic. On the north side of its long nave are pointed Gothic arches, while on the southern side they are rounded and Romanesque.

Wars, fires and plunderings damaged the building, yet it operated as a monastery until the end of the 16th century. From Elizabethan times to the end of the 18th century it served as a fort, and was known as Boyle Castle. Now it is administered by the Office of Public Works and there is a reconstruction of the original design in the abbey's renovated gatehouse. The lodge, cloister, kitchen cellars, sacristy and church remain.

Up the street from the abbey, dominating the town, is the stately mansion built for Sir Henry King, MP, in the early 1700s. It is one of the finest surviving town houses of the period, with a central block and two projecting wings. Boyle's Main Street was originally designed as an avenue leading up to it. The house became a barracks in the 1830s, but is now being restored to its original splendour.

The film actress Maureen O'Sullivan was born in Boyle. In 1988 she visited the town and unveiled a plaque on her birthplace, now a bicycle shop in Main Street.
**Boyle Abbey** *Mid-June to mid-Sept, daily 10am–6pm. Tel: (079) 62604.*

### Elphin/Ail Finn

This small market town between Boyle and Roscommon played an important role in the

STONES OF CONTENTION *Boyle Abbey was successively invaded by warring Irish chiefs.*

CURIOUS CARVINGS *Strange little men decorate a capital in Boyle Abbey's nave.*

spread of Christianity throughout Ireland, St Patrick established a bishopric here, on the site of a pre-Christian druidic house. Later, Elphin developed into an important Christian centre, with Augustinian and Franciscan friars establishing monastic houses here. But nothing now remains of the town's medieval churches and the bishopric today is in Sligo.

Many claim the writer Oliver Goldsmith (1728-74) was born in Elphin. In fact he was born near Ballymahon, County Longford, but was educated at Elphin's Diocesan School, as was Oscar Wilde's father, Sir William Wilde (1815-76), the antiquarian and oculist.

### *Lough Key Forest Park/Loch Cé*

The 3 mile wide lake, which is nearly circular, is the star attraction of the Lough Key Forest Park. Writers have chronicled the history of Lough Key for nearly 1000 years, starting with the year 1041 in the *Annals of Lough Key*.

The *Annals* were compiled on Castle Island, one of 33 islands in the lake, and are now preserved in Trinity College, Dublin, whereas the *Annals of Boyle* were compiled on nearby Trinity Island. Both tell of countless battles fought around the lake's shores and on its islands, as powerful local chieftains, such as the MacDermotts, fought off attackers.

The islands also became famous for the monasteries that were established on them. Trinity Abbey, on Trinity Island, is the only surviving Irish example of a monastery of White Canons, an order founded in France by St Norbert during the 12th century. On Church Island are a gable and church doorway of a 9th-century Celtic monastery.

The legend of the ill-fated lovers Una Bhan MacDermot and Thomas Láidir McCostello figures strongly in the lough's folklore. Although from rival families, the two fell

Turlough O'Carolan (1670-1738) may have lost his sight at 18 after an attack of smallpox, but he never let his handicap prevent him from becoming one of Ireland's most famous musicians. He gained great renown both as a harpist and composer, and his songs such as *O'Carolan's Cottage, The Lamentation of Owen O'Neill* and *Planxty MacGuire* still enchant listeners.

O'Carolan grew up in the Roscommon village of Alderford near Ballyfarnon, where he was apprenticed to a harpist after losing his sight. When he was 21, his patroness, Mrs Mary MacDermott Roe, provided a horse and servant so that he could travel throughout Ireland. He visited many great houses where he literally played and composed for his supper. In Dublin he met Dr Patrick Delaney, professor of oratory at Trinity College, and through him was introduced to the music of 18th-century composers such as Corelli and Vivaldi – music which was to become a strong influence on him.

The melody *Bridget Cruise* is said to have been inspired by a love affair when he was a young man. In later years, he was helping pilgrims onto a ferry on Lough Derg, and at the touch of a woman's hand recognised his love from the past.

Turlough's death in 1738 was an occasion of national sorrow. It is reported that on his deathbed at Alderford he called for his harp and played his *Farewell to Music*. He then asked for a cup of whiskey,

*A life-size bronze of O'Carolan stands in the town centre of Mohill, County Leitrim.*

but being too weak to drink it, kissed the cup explaining that old friends should not part without a kiss. Ten harpists played at his four-day wake, and he was buried at Kilronan Cemetery. Happily, more than 200 melodies of this last of the great Irish bards have survived.

deeply in love. Una's father was enraged and confined her to Castle Island where she became ill and died. Heartbroken, McCostello swam out to Trinity Island every night to visit her grave until, weakened by the cold waters, he fell ill with pneumonia. On his deathbed he pleaded with Una's father to be buried alongside his loved one. So they were reunited in death and, the story goes, two rose trees grew over their grave and became entwined in a lovers' knot. The bushes can still be seen. The poet W.B. Yeats (1865-1939) became so enchanted with the castle on Castle Island that he planned a place there 'where a mystical order would retire for a while for contemplation'. The idea came to nothing.

The 800 acre Forest Park, most of which was the Rockingham Estate, was owned by Sir John King and his successors until 1957, when it was sold to the Irish Land Commission. Rockingham House, designed by Nash in the early 1800s, was completely gutted by fire in 1957, though some of the outbuildings still stand, such as the ice house, or food store, and the shell of a former estate chapel. A modern structure, the Moylurg Tower, offers fine views of the estate and its islands.

The park also includes a large area of woodland, gardens, nature walks, archaeological remains such as the Carrowkeel court cairn, ring-forts and underground chambers, or souterrains, and the shell of a former estate chapel. A modern structure, the Moylurg Tower, offers fine views of the estate and the surrounding countryside from its top deck.

**Boat tours around Lough Key** *From Rockingham Harbour, or rowing boats can be hired.*

# Home of the Connaught Kings

*Some of the Irish nation's most celebrated ancestors once lived here, and in this century, the Republic's first president. Rathcroghan, graveyard of the ancient kings, is dotted with burial mounds and megalithic tombs that testify to the region's early occupation. Here also lived the later High Kings of Ireland and two of the country's most powerful old families – the O'Conors and the MacDermotts.*

## Ballintober Castle/Baile an Tobair

From the early 1300s, when the castle was built, until the 1600s this massive fort was the headquarters of the mighty O'Conors of Connaught. From here the family fought off attackers and maintained their grip on the surrounding countryside.

In 1652 Charles O'Conor lost the castle and all his possessions to Oliver Cromwell's forces, but they were restored to the O'Conors in 1677. After the Battle of the Boyne (1690), at which the O'Conors had backed the loser, James II, the castle was again confiscated. It began to fall into ruin around 1700.

Today the substantial remains of Ballintober Castle dominate the village of the same name. The polygonal twin-towered gatehouse, corner towers and much of the wall still stand. The 22ft high walls, almost 1000ft in length, were surrounded by a moat, and within the protection of the walls was an area of 1½ acres which is thought to have once contained several rows of houses, or cabins, although there are no remnants of these. Ballintober is an important structure because

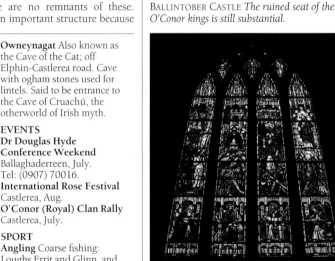

BALLINTOBER CASTLE *The ruined seat of the O'Conor kings is still substantial.*

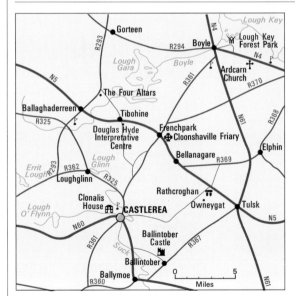

**Owneynagat** Also known as the Cave of the Cat; off Elphin-Castlerea road. Cave with ogham stones used for lintels. Said to be entrance to the Cave of Cruachú, the otherworld of Irish myth.

### EVENTS
**Dr Douglas Hyde Conference Weekend**
Ballaghaderreen, July.
Tel: (0907) 70016.
**International Rose Festival**
Castlerea, Aug.
**O'Conor (Royal) Clan Rally**
Castlerea, July.

### SPORT
**Angling** Coarse fishing: Loughs Errit and Glinn, and River Suck. Game fishing: Loughs Errit, Glinn and O'Flynn, and River Suck.
**Golf** Ballaghaderreen Golf Club, 9-hole course.
Tel: (0907) 60295.
Castlerea Golf Club, 9-hole course. Tel: (0907) 20068.

### INFORMATION
Ireland West Tourism.
Tel: (091) 63081.

**OTHER PLACES TO SEE**
**Ballaghaderreen** Small market town with Gothic Revival St Nathy's Cathedral.
**The Four Altars** Built during penal times, when Mass was said outdoors.
**Loughglinn** 7m NW of Castlerea, 18th-century mansion.

in the 12th century, and of Ireland's first president, Douglas Hyde (1860-1949). Oscar Wilde's father, Sir William Wilde (1815-76), was also born here.

Just to the west of Castlerea off the Castlebar road, behind a green veil of sycamore, ash and chestnut trees close to the bank of the River Suck, stands Clonalis House. This is the ancestral seat of the fabled O'Conors, a clan that included 11 High Kings of Ireland and 24 Kings of Connaught.

The present mansion of 45 rooms was built relatively recently, in 1878, replacing the 'old' Clonalis House, which was built in 1700. The 'new' house contains a priceless collection of archival material that documents Irish history and the history of the O'Conor clan as far back as the 5th century BC.

The joke goes that the senior surviving branch of the Conor clan spells the name with one 'n' rather than two because they never could make n's meet – a tale possibly borne out by the fact that Denis O'Conor was so impoverished that he walked barefoot to Dublin in 1720 in order to fight a law case to recover a small portion (800 acres of poor land) of his ancestral lands.

The family's place in history is first brought to the attention of visitors even before they pass through the Italianate entrance to the house. To the left of the door is the Coronation Stone of the Kings of Connaught, a squat lump of rock that dates from druidic times and was originally at Rathcroghan. The newly chosen king would place his foot on the stone during the ceremony.

Tours of the house begin in the handsome entrance hall with its Ionic columns of pink Mallow marble. Visitors are led through rooms furnished with antiques ranging in style from Louis Quinze to Georgian Regency and Victorian. Specially interesting are an exhibition of lace garments, Georgian, Regency and Victorian silver, a 17th-century chalice designed for easy concealment during the anti-Catholic penal times, and the harp of Turlough O'Carolan, the blind harpist who was a frequent visitor to Clonalis House.
**Clonalis House** *June-end Sept, Mon-Sat 11am-5pm, Sun 1-5pm. Tel: (0907) 20014.*

## Douglas Hyde Interpretative Centre

The burial place of Douglas Hyde, first President of Ireland and founder of the Gaelic League, is at Tibohine on the road to Ballaghaderreen, 5 miles west of Frenchpark. The

GLOWING GLASS *A.E. Child's stained-glass window decorates the Catholic church at Tulsk.*

it is thought to be the earliest example of an Irish stone castle. Traditionally the Irish built in timber.

## Castlerea/An Caisleán Riabhach

This small market town was the birthplace of the last High King of Ireland, Felim O'Conor,

## IRELAND'S FIRST PRESIDENT

As a child, Douglas Hyde became fascinated with the colourful folk tales and the rich Irish language he heard all around him in the counties of Roscommon and Sligo, where he spent his childhood. It was a fascination that led him to high office in the state and to acclaim as an authority on Irish.

He was born in 1860 at Castlerea, County Roscommon. His father, the Reverend Arthur Hyde, became rector of the Church of Ireland church at Tibohine. As a boy, Douglas was tutored at home and learned Irish from the local farmers. He never lost his love for the ancient tongue and devoted much of his life to reviving it. At Trinity College, Dublin, he was a versatile scholar, earning prizes in history, and gaining a law degree.

With the poet W.B. Yeats, he formed the Gaelic League in 1893, a society aimed at preserving the dying Irish tongue. The League became very influential in forming a national consciousness at the time, and many later revolutionaries were among its founders. However, he became disillusioned with the League's increasing politicisation and resigned to teach modern languages, first in Canada and then at University College, Dublin, where he became Professor of Modern Irish. In 1938 he became Ireland's first president, an office he held until his term expired in 1945. He returned to his home in Frenchpark where he died in 1949.

Dr Douglas Hyde, 78 when he became Ireland's first president, retired when he was 85.

former Protestant parish church where his father was rector now houses the centre, which contains photographs and mementos chronicling the life of the late president. Dr Hyde is buried in the church's cemetery.
**Opening times** *May-Sept, Tues-Fri 2-5pm, Sat and Sun 2-6pm. Tel: (0907) 70016.*

### Frenchpark/Dún Gar

This unpretentious village is named after the now demolished redbrick house designed by architect Richard Cassel in 1729. It was the home of Major General George Arthur French, first commissioner of the Canadian North-West Mounted Police, the 'Mounties'. In the grounds of the former house is a five-chambered underground refuge, or souterrain, and to the east are the remains of the 1385 Cloonshaville Dominican friary.

### Rathcroghan/Cruachan

Sadly, one of Ireland's – and Europe's – most important archaeological sites has not been fully excavated, preserved or signposted. This traditional coronation and burial place of the Kings of Ireland and Connaught covers several square miles and includes some 53 ancient sites, among them ring-barrows and ring-forts. Some of them are prehistoric and some of early historic dates. They are all pagan locations that were abandoned with the arrival of Christianity.

But since access is difficult – the land is still privately owned – and there is no visitor or interpretative centre, those seeking glimpses into Ireland's past will have to arrange their expeditions carefully and make sure they obtain permission from the farmers before crossing private land. A brochure with

MUSICAL MEMORIES *In the drawing room of Clonalis House stands the harp of Turlough O'Carolan, who was blind and often played at the house.*

ROYAL LINEAGE *The family tree of the O'Conors, in the library of Clonalis House, traces back the line of Kings of Connaught and of Ireland for 60 generations.*

a map of the ruins is available from the County Heritage Centre in Strokestown.

One of the most accessible sites is the earthwork known as Rathcroghan. This is named after Cruachú who was the handmaid of Etáin, mother of the legendary Queen Maeve. The small, steep-sided hill has been formed into a ring-barrow and was reputed to be Queen Maeve's residence. It is 3 miles to the west of Tulsk, just before the crossroads to Castlerea.

About 120yds north of the hill is a large stone, now on its side, formerly a 9ft standing stone. It is known as Maeve's Lump, but its purpose is unclear. Some believe it has magical associations.

Relig Na Ri, the burial ground of the kings, and Rath Na dTarbh, 'fort of the bulls', are nearby and deserve a visit. The Morrigan, a war and fertility goddess associated with Rathcroghan, is reputed to appear on occasion as a large, black crow.

### Tulsk/Tuilsce

'The hillock of the thorn tree' was the site of many battles between the O'Conor chieftains and the English. O'Conor Roe built here one of the strongest castles in Connaught, in 1406, and the foundations of its circular tower can still be seen. Across the road, in the cemetery, are the remains of the Dominican abbey founded in 1433 by Felim O'Conor. They include a double-arched doorway.

# A Hangwoman's Terrain

*Between the gently flowing River Shannon and the salmon-rich River Suck is an area of lush pastures, gently rolling countryside and island-bedecked lakes. This is prime cattle and sheep-farming country, where 'hardly a sod is turned', back roads are dotted with livestock farms, and towns, such as Roscommon, the county seat, regularly play host to bustling agricultural shows and noisy auctions of animals.*

### Donamon Castle

The castle is one of the oldest inhabited buildings in Ireland. There has been a fortress on the site from ancient times, but the earliest recorded reference is in the *Annals of the Four Masters* of 1632-6, which called it Dun Iomghuin ('fortress of Iomghuin'), and named it as the seat of the O'Finaghtys.

The O'Finaghtys, chiefs of the Conway clan, were dispossessed by the Normans in

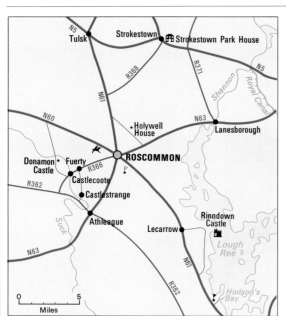

### OTHER PLACES TO SEE

**Castlestrange** 2m NW of Athleague, signposted stone across sheep meadow: oval granite boulder covered with intricate spiral patterns in Celtic La Tène style, dated to Iron Age (in Ireland 300 BC-AD 500); one of only four in Ireland and one of the best examples of decorated stones in Europe.

**Hodson's Bay** Recreational centre on shores of Lough Ree with boating, fishing, wind-surfing and camping facilities.
**Holywell House** 5m NE of Roscommon, remains of St Brigid's Church and St Brigid's Well. The Gunning Sisters, daughters of James Gunning of Castlecoote, whose beauty was toast of

London in 1750s, are said to have owed their envied complexions to the waters of the well.
**Rinndown Castle** 2½m E of Lecarrow, 13th-century ruins on peninsula jutting into Lough Ree. Permission to cross the fields must first be sought from the farmer.

### WALKS

**Roscommon Heritage Trail** Boyle to Carrick-on-Shannon, Strokestown, Roscommon, Ballintober, Tulsk and Elphin. Details available from Heritage Centre, Strokestown. Tel. (078) 33380.

### EVENTS

**Percy French Weekend** Roscommon, May.
**Horse racing** Roscommon, four meetings annually.

### SPORT

**Angling** Coarse fishing: Lough Ree, Rivers Shannon and Suck. Game fishing: River Suck.
**Golf** Hodson's Bay Golf Club, 18-hole course. Tel: (0902) 92073/92235. Roscommon Golf Club, 9-hole course. Tel: (0903) 6382.

### INFORMATION

Ireland West Tourism. Tel: (091) 63081.

## THEY ALL FELL FOR LADY BETTY

*Sally Dexter plays Lady Betty on stage.*

From 1780 to about 1810, the executioner at Roscommon Jail was a cold-blooded, brutal woman. She came from Kerry originally and lived in abject poverty on the west side of Roscommon with her young son. She was a silent, brooding person but was literate, an unusual accomplishment for those days, and taught her son to read and write. She also taught him that only money brought happiness, so when he came of age he emigrated to America to seek his fortune.

Several years later, one dark, stormy night, a tall, well-dressed stranger with a dark beard knocked on Betty's door asking for food and shelter. She took him in, but

while he slept she decided to kill him and take his money. Her dreadful deed done, she sifted through his papers and discovered, to her horror, that she had murdered her own son.

Hysterical, she ran out into the cold dawn, shrieking her guilt. She was arrested, tried and condemned to death. She and several other criminals were taken to Roscommon Jail for execution. On arrival, they were told that the executioner was ill, and the sheriff refused to execute them himself. Betty called out from the cart: 'Spare me, yer Honour, spare me and I'll hang them all.' The sheriff agreed. She performed the grisly task perfectly, and was appointed the jail's 'hangwoman', with a yearly salary and a room of her own.

Lady Betty, as she became known, acquired a fearsome reputation. Her method of hanging was to stand the victim on a wooden lapboard, a horizontal door hinged to the wall, outside her third-floor window. The noose around the neck was attached to an iron beam above her window. She would then pull the bolt that held up the lapboard, the hinged platform would drop and the victim was left to swing until dead. She also drew charcoal portraits of her victims on her walls and lived with this appalling record of destruction around her until she died, in the early 19th century.

**BATTLE-SCARRED BASTION** *Roscommon Castle defended the town until it was finally taken by Cromwell's troops in 1652.*

KING'S MEN *Effigies of mercenaries surround the O'Conor tomb in Roscommon friary.*

the 13th century. They returned, but it is said that in 1307 Nuala na Miodagh ('Nuala of the Dagger'), wife of the last O'Finaghty, murdered her husband, and married a Burke. In 1333, the Burkes took control of the castle and the Conway chieftainship and remained there until they were dispossessed in the Cromwellian Settlement of 1652.

The building, the oldest part of which dates from the 1400s and has been substantially updated over the years, is now occupied by the Divine Word Missionaries. It is not open to the public.

## Roscommon/Ros Comáin

About 1200 years ago Roscommon was a noted place of learning, with a monastery. It was founded in 746 by the town's namesake and first bishop, St Coman (the town's Irish name means 'Coman's Woods'). No trace of the monastery survives, but some local historians believe it stood on the site now occupied by the Anglican church of St Coman's in Church Street, built nearly 200 years ago.

Happily, other testaments to Roscommon's historic past have survived. On the southern edge of the town, in a fenced-off

enclosure by the side of a modern school, are the stately remains of the Dominican Friary of the Assumption. It was founded in 1253 by Felim O'Conor, King of Connaught, but destroyed by fire in 1308. It was rebuilt in the late 15th century and much of what remains dates from this period.

O'Conor's remains are said to rest in the late 15th-century tomb at the left of the long, narrow church. Although his effigy is defaced, some features can still be made out, such as the fleur-de-lis sceptre in his right hand and fragments of a crown around his head. A series of eight gallowglasses, or mercenaries, surround the tomb's base.

Roscommon was originally built on the southern slopes of a wide hill, near the top of which stand the remains of Roscommon Castle. It is found past a crowded cow pasture, down a lane at the northern edge of the town. A castle was first built there by the Normans in 1269, but was captured and razed by the Irish in 1272 and rebuilt in 1280. The large Tudor-style mullioned windows were added to the D-shaped corner towers and curtain around 1580.

In Roscommon's spacious square is the old jail, a castellated stone building that housed the county's criminals and was once the domain of Lady Betty, Roscommon's notorious 18th-century hangwoman.

## Strokestown/Béal na mBuillí

This modest village has what is reputedly the widest main street in Ireland outside Dublin, and it is a clue to Strokestown's heritage. A second clue is the imposing Georgian-Gothic triple arch at the end of the main street.

Behind this arch sits Strokestown Park House, the last major 18th-century manor house to survive in County Roscommon, around which the planned market town was developed. The house was built in the 1730s for Thomas Mahon, an Anglo-Irish MP, by the noted German-born architect Richard Cassel. It was the nucleus of Mahon's 30,000 acre estate, granted to his grandfather by Charles II for his allegiance to the House of Stuart during the Civil War.

Strokestown's wide main street is the result of a Mahon descendant's visit to Austria. He was so impressed by Vienna's Ringstrasse he decreed that Strokestown should have a similar main avenue.

Strokestown Park House stayed in the Mahon family until 1979, when it was bought by a local firm, restored and opened to the

public. Now it offers fascinating glimpses of Ireland's often stormy Anglo-Irish past.

Cassel's design for Park House incorporated a 17th-century tower house that stood on the spot. Only one room of the tower house remains, a still room in the cellar. Its restoration has revealed one of Ireland's most interesting early Georgian designs.

The house's design is basically that of a farmhouse expanded to the size of a stately home; it was copied by many of the landed Anglo-Irish gentry. The central block was the family's residence and wings either side housed the stables and kitchen areas.

The kitchen itself is noteworthy. A gallery runs its entire length, from which the lady of the house could oversee the kitchen staff without entering the kitchen itself, and from which, each Monday morning, she would drop a menu with instructions for the entire week's meals. The gallery is the last of its type in Ireland. Tunnels to conceal the comings and goings of staff and tradesmen link the house to kitchen, stable and bar.

The house's main reception rooms contain their original period furnishings which include an exquisite Chippendale bookcase and Regency wallpaper in the library. Antique toys fill the children's playroom, and the

bedrooms seem only recently vacated by their 19th-century occupants.

As well as the wealth of furnishings, the house has a collection of documents detailing the day-to-day lives of the Mahons and of the region over several centuries. Papers relating to the Great Famine of the 1840s which devastated Irish rural life and led to mass emigration are of special interest. The papers include details of the death of Major Denis Mahon, owner of the house during the famine, shot dead by tenants who accused him of chartering 'coffin ships' to send those evicted from his land to America. There are plans to set up a museum in the grounds devoted to those turbulent times.

At the other end of the town is the County Heritage and Genealogy Centre, which contains a display of ancient artefacts from the region and presents an audiovisual show on the history and heritage of County Roscommon. It also provides a research service into local genealogies, where more than 1000 people a year trace their ancestors.

**Strokestown Park House** *May-Sept, Tues-Sat 12-5pm. Tel: (078) 33013.*

**County Heritage and Genealogy Centre** *May-Sept, Tues-Fri 9.30am-5pm, Sat and Sun 2-6pm. Tel: (078) 33380.*

UPSTAIRS, DOWNSTAIRS *The gallery above the kitchen in Strokestown Park House overlooks an 18th-century scene where only the cooks and kitchen maids are missing.*

# THE NORTH-WEST

THE jutting borders of Northern Ireland almost cut the north-west region of the Republic in two. Donegal, still part of the province of Ulster, was given to the Republic in the partition of Ireland in 1921. It now stands alone like a wind-torn flag, attached to the Republic by the stick of land around Ballyshannon. The other two counties, Leitrim and Sligo, belong to the province of Connaught. The contrasts in this region are further stated in its geography – Donegal has wild mountains and a dramatic coastline, whereas Leitrim and Sligo have more quietly stated charms. The three counties are linked only by a quirk of history which threw them together in the Republic.

Donegal has always been held to have a character of its own, and the political divisions of the 20th century have only helped to isolate it further. The city to which it once gravitated, Londonderry (or Derry), is now in another country. Here is an empty landscape of grave, mountainous beauty, russet-hued like its famous tweed. Long valleys drop down from the mountains to a coast of rocky headlands, fishing villages and sweeping, sandy beaches. It is a landscape of grand gestures. Lough Swilly slices 20 miles inland from the north coast to Letterkenny. Glenveagh Castle, in the heart of the Donegal mountains, stands dramatically on a rocky outcrop overlooking Lough Beagh, embodying all the dreamy romanticism of the 19th-century medieval revival.

Here and there, as at Slieve League, the land ends in massive cliff faces, populated by guillemots, kittiwakes, puffins and razorbills. The sea rolls in from the north Atlantic, attracting surfers to Tory Sound and Donegal Bay. Malin Head, from whose weather station come weather forecasts for shipping, is the most northerly point of mainland Ireland. Tory Island, 9 miles off the coast, is a remote and peaceful corner, with its whitewashed cottages and grey slate roofs. Lobster fishing is the main source of income for the people of the island, although it is also noted for its school of Naive Art.

PUFFINS ON PATROL *Puffins watch the sea from the cliffs of Slieve League for signs of fish.*

FANAD HEAD *Sea loughs flank the low-lying peninsula that projects from Donegal into the Atlantic.*

This was the homeland of St Columba (also known as St Colmcille), raised in the Swilly valley in northern Donegal, who went on to found the monastery at Kells. Another saint, the powerful St Molaise, had his monastery on the island of Innishmurray in Donegal Bay, where the monks' beehive cells can still be seen. St Patrick is said to have fasted for 40 days on an island on Lough Derg, and in the summer months thousands of pilgrims visit the island for a gruelling three-day ritual of penitence, reminiscent of the self-denial of the early Christians. From Donegal came Red Hugh O'Donnell, who joined Hugh O'Neill, the Earl of Tyrone, in making an ill-fated stand against the English at the end of the 16th century. He was raised at Doe Castle, an impressive coastal fortress overlooking seaweed-strewn sands.

To the south is County Leitrim. It is split in two by Lough Allen, with the mountains to the north embracing deep valleys such as Glenade and Glencar, while to the south, the high plateaus of the Iron Mountains drop away through blanket bog to meet the rugged hillocks of the drumlin country around Mohill. This has always been fairly inaccessible terrain. The O'Rourkes ruled here until Tudor times, barely disturbed by the Anglo-Normans. Then came the plantation of Scottish and English settlers after the 17th century, who left their mark in towns with names like Jamestown and Manorhamilton. Leitrim soil favours forestry as much as mixed farming, which today is carried out in scattered smallholdings. This county is popular with fishermen, and the county town, Carrick-on-Shannon, is a noted centre for coarse fishing and river cruising.

To the west, farther round the coast, is County Sligo, where the road heads west from Sligo Bay, skirting the rocky, windswept flanks of the Slieve Gamph, or 'Ox Mountains', to reach Killala Bay and the popular resort of Inishcrone. Sligo is also 'Yeats country', a favourite haunt of Ireland's great poet. On Lough Gill is the island of Innisfree which Yeats celebrated in his poem *The Lake Isle of Innisfree*. The seaside resort of Rosses Point, now known for the championship links at The Sligo County Golf Club, is where Yeats and his brother Jack spent their childhood holidays. The poet lies buried in a graveyard below the stark table-top of Benbulbin, a mountain of haunting beauty.

Sligo appears to have been heavily populated in prehistoric times. There are numerous tombs, in particular the impressive concentrations of burial sites at Carrowkeel and Carrowmore, ring-forts and stone forts, and some 200 lake dwellings, or crannogs, in Lough Gara, inhabited over a period of some 2000 years. Later, Sligo became known for the 'Battle of the Books', said to have taken place at Cooldrumman, north of Sligo town. This was sparked when St Columba refused to give back a copy of a book of psalms to St Finian, the owner of the original. St Columba was banished to Scotland by St Molaise, and there founded his famous monastery on Iona.

Sligo boasts the only grand house of the region open to the public – the solid Lissadell. It was home to the poet Eva Gore-Booth, and her sister Constance Markiewicz, the first woman MP elected to the British Parliament, in 1918 – though she never took her seat.

TEELIN TRAWLERS *Fishing boats wait for better weather at Teelin, an Irish-speaking village whose name means 'house of the flowing tide'.*

LILIES OF THE LOUGH *Water lilies bejewel the wetlands of southern Donegal, north of Inver.*

Achill
Head

**KEY TO SYMBOLS**

**64** Page number of zone
〰〰 Zone boundary
⬤ Touring centre
◯ Other town or village
── National or A class road
── Regional or B class road
├─● Railway & station
☆ Approved frontier crossing
·—·—· National boundary
— — County boundary

Atlantic

Ocean

Malin Head
Glengad Head
Dunaff Head
Fanad Head
Malin
Culdaff
Inishowen Head
Carndonagh
Greencastle
Tory Island
Melmore Head
Fanad
Rosguill
Portsalon
*Inishowen*
Horn Head
Sheep Haven
R242
R238
R244
Dunfanaghy
R238
Bloody Foreland
N56
R245
Rathmullan
Millford
R247
Lough Swilly
BUNCRANA
**250**
2019 Slieve Snaght
Moville
Gola
Derrybeg
*Muckish Mtn* 2197
Loughsalt Mtn 1546
R246
Fahan
Muff
Limavady
Owey Island
Dunbeg
*Errigal Mtn* 2466
Kilmacrenan
R245
R255
R249
Bridge End
Lough Foyle
Londonderry
Airport
Eglinton
Aran Island
Gweedore
Dunlewy
Derryveagh Mountains
Lough Beagh
R255
R249
Carrigans
**258**
LONDONDERRY
Burtonport
The Rosses
R259
R258
**254**
Glendowan Mts
R254
RATHMELTON
N13
R237
A5
A6
Dungiven
DUNGLOW
R252
Glendowan Mts
LETTERKENNY
N56
R236
Raphoe
Claudy
B74
Dunnamanagh
Fintown
N56
**256**
Lifford
Castlefinn
N15
Strabane
B49
B48
Gweebarra Bay
R250
Aghla Mtn
R253
Stranorlar
Ballybofey
Sperrin Mountains
Plumbridge
B47
Dawros Head
R261
Glenties
Finn
**248**
Levagh More 2211
Blue Stack Mountains
N15
Castlederg
Derg
Newtownstewart
B46
Gortin
Loughros More Bay
Glen Head 1458
Slievetooey
ARDARA
R262
Lough Eske
**252**
B72
B50
Drumquin
B50
Omagh
A32
Carrickmore
1972
Slieve League
Carrick
Kilcar
Mountcharles
N56
DONEGAL
Ballintra
B4
Ederny
B84
TYRONE
Creggan
B4
Killybegs
Dunkineely
Dorrin Point
Lough Derg
R232
Pettigoe
A35
Dromore
Seskinore
A5
Ballygawley
St John's Point
Ballyshannon
N15
Lower Lough Erne
A47
Irvinestown
A32
Fintona
A5
Donegal Bay
Bundoran
Belleek
B52
A46
B46
B83
Tullaghan
R230
Enniskillen
Augher
B80
B107
Clogher
A28
Aughnacloy
N2
Innishmurray
Mullaghmore
Kinlough
Lough Melvin
Garrison
FERMANAGH
A4
B140
A4
Fivemiletown
Emyvale
Stags of Broad Haven
Benbulbin 1730
Truskmore 2120
Glenade
Kiltyclogher
Belcoo
B514
Brookeborough
Downpatrick Head
Dartry Mts
R280
R281
**264**
Glenfarne
Blacklion
Lisnaskea
Rosslea
R187
Monaghan
Belderg
Lenadoon Point
Easky
Rosses Point
Drumcliff
Glencar
Glencar
MANORHAMILTON
Cuilcagh Mts
Donagh
B36
Clones
R314
Maumakeogh 1247
Aughris Head
Sligo Bay
SLIGO
**268**
R280
R287
Dromahair
Killarga
R207
Cuilcagh 2188
Swanlinbar
A32
A509
Upper Lough Erne
MONAGHAN
Newbliss
R183
Belmullet
Slieve Fyagh 1090
Killala
Skreen
Strandhill
Ballysadare
Lough Gill
Drumkeeran
Dowra
Cuilcagh 2188
Ballyconnell
B200
Rockcorry
Broad Haven
R313
Killala Bay
Inishcrone
Dromore West
Ballygawley
Collooney
R284
Slieve Anierin 1927
Iron Mountains
R200
Belturbet
R205
R200
Coothill
Bellacorick
Crossmolina
Corbally
Knockachree 1768
**262**
Kilronan Mtn 1081
R209
Ballinamore
Cavan
R188
N59
Ballina
N17
SLIGO
Tobercurry
R294
Curlew Mts
Keadew
DRUMSHANBO
Fenagh
R204
Killashandra
Nephin 2646
R310
R294
**266**
Bricklieve Mts
Lough Arrow
Leitrim
Ballinamore
Carrigallen
R199
Foxford
Swinford
BALLYMOTE
R293
Boyle
CARRICK-ON-SHANNON
**260**
Crossdoney
Arvagh
Bellananagh
N3
Bailieborough
Beltra Lough
Gorteen
N4
Drumsna
Jamestown
Drumod
Annalee
R191
Newport
Bellavary
Charlestown
N5
Ballaghaderreen
N61
Mohill
R202
Roosky
Drumlish
Virginia
Castlebar
Connaught (Knock) Airport
Frenchpark
R368
Lough Gowna
R194
ROSCOMMON
LONGFORD
Granard

Scale: 0 5 10 15 20 25 30 35 40 45 50 Miles
0 5 10 20 30 40 50 60 70 80 Km

# The Home of Donegal Tweed

*The sounds of merrymaking are never far away in western Donegal, as the region seems to have a special affinity for good conversation, or 'the crack', and racing tunes played on fiddles which irresistibly set the feet tapping. This is also the home of the famed Donegal tweed and knitwear. But the region's traditions go back even farther in time – it is littered with the remains of prehistoric burial chambers, ruined churches and the forts of warlike chieftains.*

### Ardara/Ard an Rátha

Steep hills keep the worst of the westerly winds from the pretty village of Ardara (pronounced Ardrah). It is Ireland's capital of handwoven tweeds and handmade knitwear. No fewer than nine tweed and knitwear shops compete in the two main streets. Just out of the village are five factory-shops, where visitors can watch the wool being dyed and treated and woven into cloth, before browsing among the goods for sale. There is also an annual Weavers' Fair when weavers demonstrate their craft.

A century ago the Ardara weavers would display their wares on bales of straw laid down in the marketplace, and customers would come by horse and trap from all parts of Donegal to buy their cloth.

Traditionally a fungus called 'crotol' was scraped off the rocks, and the cloth was soaked in it to dye it brown. Today the tweeds are much more colourful.

Ardara is divided by the River Owentocker, which opens up into the unexpectedly wide Loughross More Bay. Its most prominent building is the 1904 Catholic Church of the Holy Family, painted black with white detailing, and notable for a circular stained-glass window created in 1954 by Evie Hone. In the porch is a map listing the sites of grave slabs and other religious antiquities in the area.

Ardara has many traditional pubs in which fiddle music is played. There are several fine sandy beaches nearby and scenic roads along the shoreline.

### Carrick/An Charraig

Set in the quiet valley of the River Glen, Carrick has a Gothic Revival church in dark sandstone, with a magnificently carved high altar designed by the 19th-century architect George Ashlin. The village is the starting point for a spectacular drive to the eastern end of Slieve League (1972ft), whose cliffs plunge 765ft before reaching the sea. A hairpin road with a sheer drop on the seaward side winds up from Teelin to Carrigan Head. Alternatively, just before reaching Teelin on the right there is a walk by way of One Man's Pass, past the ruins of Slieve League church, to the summit of Carrigan Head.

### Glencolumbkille/Gleann Cholm Cille

A patchwork valley of browns, greens and ochres runs into the hills from Glen Bay, where white waves break on the beach. The valley, and its village, are named after St Columba, or Colmcille, of Iona, who is said to have lived there with his followers for a time during the 6th century.

On St Columba's feast day (June 9) a penitential tour 3½ miles long takes place round the 15 holy sites in the neighbourhood. The pilgrims walk in bare feet, starting at midnight, uttering prayers for the saint's intercession at every stopping point, and have to finish the course by sunrise. These Stations include chapels, cairns and pillars, or grave slabs, decorated with geometric patterns and cross motifs.

Glencolumbkille owes its present prosperity largely to the work of another man of God, the late Father James McDyer, who was appointed parish priest in 1950 when the glen had no electricity, and emigration was rife. He set up a vegetable-processing factory and a machine-knitting enterprise, and in 1967 opened the Folk Village Museum, consisting of traditional-style cottages that give an idea of rural life at various periods from the 18th century on. The cottage of 1720, for example, is little more than a hovel, with an earth floor, an open fire without a chimney, and little furniture. Among the items sold in the museum's 'shebeen' is an unusual kind of wine made from fuchsias.

ARDARA FALLS *In the hills above Ardara, fast-flowing water tumbles over rocky ledges in spectacular cascades.*

### OTHER PLACES TO SEE
**Doon Fort** Ring-fort on small island in Doon Lough with 17ft walls and believed to be 2000 years old. Reached from banks of Doon Lough.
**Dunkineely** Village at landward end of St John's Point, good fishing centre.

**Mountcharles** Hillside village by Donegal Bay; The Hall, a three-storey 18th-century mansion, is one of Ireland's finest Georgian houses, but is not open to the public.

### WALKS
**Clooney Wood** Scenic walk.

### EVENTS
**Ardara Weavers' Fair** End June-early July.
**Glencolumbkille Seafood Festival** Mid-June.
**Glencolumbkille Traditional Music Festival** Early June.
**Glenties Fiddlers' Weekend** First weekend Oct.
**Glenties Harvest Fair** Mid-Sept.
**Kilcar Village Fleadh** Third week in July.
**Killybegs Sea-angling Festival** Three-day festival, Aug.

### SPORT
**Angling** Game fishing: Rivers Glen, Gweebarra, Oily and Owenea, and Eany Water. Sea fishing: Killybegs.
**Bathing** Ardara, Fintragh Bay, Kilcar, Narin.
**Golf** Narin and Portnoo Golf Club, 18-hole course. Tel: (075) 45107.

### INFORMATION
North-West Tourism. Tel: (074) 21160.

A few miles south-west of Glencolumbkille, near the small beach resort of Malin More, are Stone Age dolmens – standing stones with massive capstones.

**Folk Village Museum** *Easter-Apr, Mon-Fri 10am-6pm; early May-Aug, daily 10am-8pm. Sept, daily 10am-6pm. Tel: (073) 30017.*

## Glenties/Na Gleannta

At the point where two glens converge is this picturesque little town, whose Irish name means, simply, 'the glens'. It has a late Georgian courthouse (now a heritage centre), and a covered market building which dates from the 1840s. The Catholic church, built in 1975, is a dramatic building, with a roof that swoops down from its apex to a height of 7ft.

The highlight of the year in Glenties is the week-long Glenties Harvest Fair, which is at least 200 years old and is celebrated in September with band parades, sports and other events. The first weekend in October is a 'Fiddlers' Weekend', at which folk musicians from Ireland and farther afield get together to perform, listen, learn new techniques – and raise the roof of the pubs.

MAN OF STRAW *A Glencolumbkille thatcher weaves the straw that will eventually provide a roof as trim as its neighbour.*

PAINTED COAST *An indigo sea washes the foot of the Slieve League cliffs, while cloud shadows, red bracken and snow dapple the cliff tops.*

**Glenties Heritage Centre** *June-end Aug, daily 10am-5.30pm. Tel: (075) 51265.*

## Kilcar/Cill Charthaigh

Mountainous views, a craggy coastline, two of Ireland's 'Top Twenty' clean beaches, and teeming fishing rivers, make the village of Kilcar a popular tourist centre. Like Ardara, it is also a centre of the hand-woven tweed and woollen industry. Kilcar gets its name from the 7th-century St Cartha, whose grave is in the churchyard.

During the third week in July the village holds a 'fleadh' or music festival, with fiddle competitions, street entertainers, story-telling and folk-music sessions that last well into the night.

Up the glen to the north-east is Kilcar Forest, planted on the slopes above the Glenaddragh river.

## Killybegs/Na Cealla Beaga

Seagulls swirl round the trawlers entering the port of Killybegs, one of Ireland's major fishing harbours. It is a rough and dynamic place, where foreign ships tower over the quayside, and smells from its ten fish-processing factories fill the air.

Though the town looks typically Victorian, it was a borough as long ago as 1616, and the harbour was recorded a century earlier than that. St Catherine's Church was built in the 1840s and is unusually large, about 100ft long by 40ft wide. Attached to the wall is a 16th-century tomb slab, probably of one of the MacSweeney family. It depicts a gallowglass, or mercenary, showing that he was one of the Scottish soldiers of fortune employed by the Irish chieftains.

Killybegs used to have a carpet factory, whose handwoven products adorn Buckingham Palace, the White House and the Vatican. Drumanoo Head, 3 miles south, is a famous local viewpoint with plenty of opportunities for walks.

249

# Ireland's Most Northerly Point

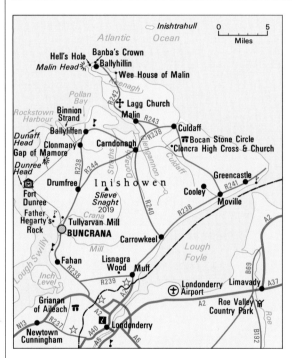

*Green valleys speckled with sheep and white cottages, and brown mountains that rise to the summit of Slieve Snacht, make up the inland areas of this region. To the north, like a crooked finger, the Inishowen (Inis Eoghain) peninsula points up into the Atlantic, and at its tip is Malin Head, Ireland's most northerly point. A 100 mile route called the Inis Eoghain 100 travels around the peninsula by way of Malin Head.*

## OTHER PLACES TO SEE

**Cooley** 2m NW of Moville, site of rectangular stone-roofed tomb called the 'Skull House', and 10ft stone cross with hole through its shaft, through which people would shake hands to seal a bargain.
**Fahan** 3m S of Buncrana; 7th-century monastic ruins and intricately carved St Mura's Cross, believed to mark grave of abbey's founder.

**Father Hegarty's Rock**
N along shoreline of Lough Swilly; where a Roman Catholic priest was martyred in 1632.
**Gap of Mamore** 7m N of Buncrana, 800ft above sea, spectacular view of Inishowen peninsula.
**Greencastle** Ivy-covered ruins of 1305 castle, built by Richard de Burgo, 'Red Earl' of Ulster, at entrance to Lough Foyle. It was destroyed

in 1555. Access through gate of Castle Inn.
**Lagg Church** 4m S of Malin Head, 1784 church set against 100ft high sand dunes; built on site where open-air Mass was formerly held.
**Moville** Village that was once a stopover for Atlantic liners, now a small tourist resort; it was developed in 1780s by Samuel Montgomery, ancestor of Field-Marshal Lord Montgomery.
**Tullyarvan Mill** Restored 19th-century mill, now a museum and visitor centre. Tel: (077) 62355.

### EVENTS
**Clonmany Sea Angling Festival** Mid-Aug.

### SPORT
**Angling** Game fishing: Rivers Clonmany, Crana, Culdaff, Donagh, Glengannon, Keenagh, Straths, and Inch Level lake.
**Bathing** Binnion Strand, Culdaff, Greencastle, Lisfannon and Pollan Bay.
**Golf** Ballyliffen Golf Club, 18-hole course. Tel: (077) 76119.
Greencastle Golf Club, 18-hole course. Tel: (077) 81013.
North-West Golf Club, 18-hole course. Tel: (077) 61027.

### INFORMATION
North-West Tourism.
Tel: (074) 21160.

## Buncrana/Bun Cranncha

The peninsula's largest town sprawls over the hillside on the eastern edge of Lough Swilly. Buncrana's Irish name means 'foot of the river of the trees', and one of its delights is the walk under beech, maple and lime trees beside the brown waters of the River Crana, which tumbles down from the high peatland over swirling waterfalls.

By the six-arched bridge across the Crana is the square keep of the 15th-century castle of the O'Dohertys. It was burnt by the English in 1602 when the local chieftain, Hugh Boy O'Doherty, was preparing to welcome an invading armada from Spain. Nearby, beside an ancient tower, is the 18th-century Buncrana Castle, where the Irish patriot Wolfe Tone (1763-98) was brought after his capture in 1798.

From more recent years Buncrana has a Vintage Car and Carriage Museum, which includes Victorian bicycles and model railway collections.
**Vintage Car and Carriage Museum** *June-Sept, daily, 10am-8pm. Off-season, every Sun; weekdays by appointment. Tel: (077) 61130.*

TRADITIONAL SOUNDS *The sweet trill of the tin whistle ripples through Buncrana in summer.*

## Carndonagh/Carn Domhnach

At the heart of Inishowen is this small market town dominated by a handsome Catholic church, built in 1945. On a nearby hill is the older Protestant church, on the site of a church reputedly founded by St Patrick.

Carndonagh's chief treasure is St Patrick's Cross, which stands by the roadside opposite the Protestant church. It has been dated to the 7th century and is said to be one of the oldest and finest carved stone crosses in Ireland. It is decorated with the Crucifixion, stylised birds and elaborate interlaced patterns, and reaches 11½ft high. The cross is set into a base with two smaller decorated stone pillars or stelae. Another pillar, in the churchyard, is known as the 'Marigold Stone', from a star pattern carved on it that has been wrongly interpreted as a marigold.

## Culdaff/Cúil Dabhcha

Bonnie Prince Charlie is said to have landed at Culdaff's little beach, fleeing across the 30 mile stretch of water from Scotland after the failure of the 1745 Rebellion. The village, on the Culdaff estuary a little way inland, is built round a triangular green. In the middle of the River Culdaff is a stone boulder known as 'St Buadan's Boat', on which, according to legend, the saint crossed from Scotland while fleeing from his enemies. The three holes in it are said to have been made by his fingers. Though it may have been mobile in the 7th century it has never moved since, even in the worst floods.

A mile south, in a field beside the road to Moville, is the Bocan Stone Circle, thought to date from 2000 BC. Sadly, the circle is far from complete, as many of the stones have been removed down the years.

Down a lane almost opposite the circle is the Clonca High Cross, 15ft high, carved with the miracle of the loaves and fishes. It marks the site of a monastery founded by St Buadan. Inside the ruined 17th-century church nearby is the 16th-century grave slab of a Gaelic warrior, possibly a Scotsman, decorated with a sword, a hurley stick and a ball, showing that he loved both fighting and sport. Hurley is an Irish game, played with a long curved stick and a ball.

## Fort Dunree/Dun Fhraoigh

The impressive fortifications that crown Dunree Head are a reminder of the strategic importance of Lough Swilly. In 1800, when Ireland was faced with the Napoleonic threat, heavy guns were mounted on the bluff of rock that commands the entrance to the lough. Martello towers were added to the fortifications in the next decade.

At the beginning of World War I the British Grand Fleet of 40 warships assembled

LAND'S END *In the north, Ireland ends in spectacular fashion, where the Inishowen peninsula stretches out between Lough Swilly and Lough Foyle to the rugged promontory of Malin Head.*

off Dunree Head. Throughout the war the Dunree guns protected the convoys that gathered there for the North Atlantic run, and by 1917 the United States had established a base there. The fort was handed over to Ireland by the British in 1938 and was last manned in 1952. In 1986 it was turned into a military museum tracing the development of coastal weaponry from 1800.

**Fort Dunree Military Museum** *June-Sept, Mon-Sat 10.30am-6pm, Sun 12-6pm. Tel: (074) 24613.*

## The Grianán of Aileach

The most spectacular man-made construction on Inishowen peninsula stands on the summit of a hill 7 miles south of Fahan, with spellbinding views in every direction. Known as the Grianán of Aileach, it consists of a terraced circular wall 17ft high and 13ft thick, forming an enclosure 77ft in diameter. It is thought to have been built in the last centuries BC for some long-forgotten ritual, perhaps connected with sun worship. The priests would have carried out their cere-

HEAVEN AND EARTH *From Grianán of Aileach there are spellbinding views across patchwork fields and Lough Swilly.*

GRIANÁN OF AILEACH *The stone fort crowns the 750ft Grianán mountain.*

monies at its centre, while hundreds of people watched from the terraces. The arrival of Christianity put an end to these rituals and the hill became for a time the royal residence of the O'Neills, kings of Ulster. Over the centuries it was damaged repeatedly by wars, but was finally restored in the 1870s.

## Malin/Málainn

The village of Malin, built round a neat triangular green, was 'planted' and settled after the great siege of Londonderry by James

II's army in 1689. Its ten-arched bridge, built in 1758, is the second longest stone bridge in Ireland. The stones were brought to the site on horsedrawn 'slipes' (sledges with iron runners). A variety of trees, including limes, sycamores, cherries and oaks, have been planted all round the green.

## Malin Head/Cionn Mhálanna

This spectacular headland, whose name is familiar from the BBC's weather forecasts, is Ireland's most northerly point. On clear days the promontory gives distant views of the Scottish islands of Islay and Jura, while during storms the sea boils ferociously at its feet. Its highest point, at 362ft, is known as 'Banba's Crown', after one of the pagan queens of pre-Christian Ireland. At its summit is a derelict Martello tower, which became a Lloyd's signal station for shipping in the early 19th century. The radio station that superseded it in 1910 is in the village of Ballyhillin, below.

Adventurous walkers can explore the rock formations of Hell's Hole, and the rock-cut cell known as the 'Wee House of Malin'. Monks used to assemble on the shoreline here each year on August 15, to bathe naked in the sea and wash away their sins – a practice long since discontinued.

# Fairy-tale Countryside

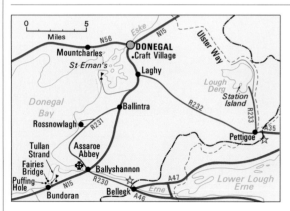

*The southern wedge of County Donegal is a land of gently rounded hills, its main towns standing on the green slopes beside Donegal Bay. It is perfect touring country, with good beaches and a hinterland dotted with lakes. The biggest of them, Lough Derg, contains Station Island, which is visited by thousands of pilgrims each year. In folklore south Donegal's secluded valleys are haunted by the fairies, and its legends have inspired generations of poets.*

### Ballyshannon/Béal Átha Seanaidh

This old British garrison town, once the frontier base of the O'Donnell clan, stands on the steep banks of the River Erne. Its name means 'mouth of Seanach's ford', after a 5th-century warrior killed by Conal Gulban, great-grandfather of St Columba.

Ballyshannon is a town of architectural contrasts, with groups of prettily painted Georgian shops set among more recent surroundings. The 18th-century barracks are worth looking at for their entrance arch.

In former times the bridge across the Erne had ten arches and the river was twice its present width. In the 1950s the river was embanked in the interests of a hydroelectric scheme, and made narrower. The old bridge was knocked down and the new one has only a single arch. Main Street and Castle Street meet at the river to form a steep-sided 'V'.

Half a mile out of the town on the Rossnowlagh road are the remains of Assaroe Abbey, built by the Cistercians in the 12th century. The Cistercians were experts in the use of water power, and local enthusiasts have recently renovated two water wheels originally installed by the monks. There is now an interpretative centre powered by the wheels, with a craft shop and display centre.

### Bundoran/Bun Dobhrain

The mile-long front at Bundoran attracts so many summer visitors that the town's population swells from 1700 to a peak of

HIGH TIME *Ballyshannon's imposing clock tower dates from 1878.*

some 20,000. The long sandy beach, Tullan Strand, is claimed to be the cleanest in Europe. At the southern end of the beach are fantastic rock formations, with fanciful names such as the Fairies Bridge and the Puffing Hole. Surfers can ride the rollers that sweep in from the Atlantic, and walkers can stride the cliff tops.

### Donegal/Dún na nGall

Donegal, whose name means the 'Fort of the Foreigners', is situated at the point where the River Eske flows into Donegal Bay. It has the finest centrepiece of any town in the country – the old market 'Diamond' (triangular rather than four-sided), which consists mainly of three and four-storey shops and hotels, with a sprinkling of dignified houses built of the local sandstone. The streets that radiate from it were laid out to the plans of Sir Basil Brooke, who was granted Donegal Castle in 1607, after the 'Flight of the Earls' when several of Ulster's leading families fled to the Continent. Until that time the castle in Donegal was the stronghold of the O'Donnell clan. When Brooke took over the four-storey tower house, he adapted it to include a bay window and a fireplace with his coat of arms above it, and added a Jacobean-style wing.

On the estuary just south of the town are the ruins of Donegal Abbey, founded in 1474 by the wife of Red Hugh O'Donnell. It was raided and occupied by the English in 1601, and was largely destroyed when a powder magazine exploded. But a few walls survive, along with some graceful Gothic windows and cloister arches. Donegal people have a deep affection for the abbey, as it was here that the Franciscans began the compilation of the *Annals of the Four Masters*, a monumental history of Ireland which goes back to the time of Noah's grandmother, 40 years before the Flood. The work was completed in 1632-6, at Ross Friary on Lough Melvin. A 25ft tall obelisk in the Diamond commemorates the four Franciscans who wrote the annals, among them Brother Michael O'Cleary, the chief annalist, who came from a prominent local family. They are also recalled by St Patrick's Memorial Church of the Four Masters, built in Irish Romanesque style in 1932.

Donegal's biggest store, Magee's, dates back to the middle of the last century. The Magees were fabric merchants who sold locally made handloom tweed, with its distinctive flecks of colour, buying it from the nearby town of Ardara. Today Magee's employs 40 outworkers, in addition to its factory workers, producing tweed in the traditional way. A good handloom weaver can produce 140yds of cloth a week. The shop has its own handloom which is operated during the summer, when visitors can watch a weaver at work.

A mile out of the town, on the Ballyshannon road, is the Donegal Craft Village – an industrial development centre which has among its craft workers a potter, a ceramics artist, a weaver and a batik painter.

**Donegal Craft Village** *Mon-Sat 9am-6pm; May-Sept also Sun, 12noon-6pm. Tel: (073) 22053.*

### Lough Derg/Loch Dearg

For 1500 years pilgrims have been beating a path to this remote stretch of water set in a barren landscape. In the middle of the lake is the small Station Island, which is covered with buildings and looks – from a distance at least – like a detail from a Canaletto painting. The four-storey hostels, clustered round an octagonal church, are the centre for the pilgrimage known as 'St Patrick's Purgatory', which takes place between the beginning of June and the middle of August.

It was on Station Island that St Patrick is said to have spent 40 days of prayer and fasting, to expel the last evil spirits from Ireland. Today's pilgrimage lasts three days,

---

**EVENTS**

**Allingham Arts Festival** Mid-Nov.

**Ballyshannon Folk and Traditional Music Festival** Early Aug.

**SPORT**

**Angling** Coarse fishing: Lough Derg and Pettigoe lakes. Game fishing: Rivers Drowes and Duff, Erne estuary, Eske system and Lough Derg. Deep-sea fishing: Contact Michael Conroy. Tel. (072) 41280.

**Golf** Bundoran Golf Club, 18-hole course. Tel: (072) 41302.

Donegal Golf Club, 18-hole course. Tel: (073) 34054.

**INFORMATION**

North-West Tourism. Tel: (074) 21160.

---

**OTHER PLACES TO SEE**

**Ballintra** Village on Ballyshannon-Donegal road where a popular horse race-meeting is held on first Mon in Aug.

**St Ernan's** 1m S of Donegal, small island, now in the grounds of hotel, surrounded by a Famine Wall, so called because a 19th-century landlord paid for locals to build it during the starvation years of the 1840s.

during which time the pilgrims walk barefoot round the 'Penitential Beds' (the remains of monastic cells), perform devotional exercises, and eat only one meal a day, of bread and black tea. They are not allowed to sleep on the first night, but can stay in the hostels on the second. As many as 15,000 pilgrims visit the island each year, with up to 400 people at any one time. From June to mid-August pilgrims only are allowed on the island.

## Rossnowlagh/Ros Neamhlach

The wide sandy beach at the little resort of Rossnowlagh, the 'forked headland', is over-looked by a Franciscan friary where the pious making the circuit of the Stations of the Cross can look down on windsurfers riding the rollers ashore. The friary houses the museum of the Donegal Historical Society, whose collection ranges from an Armada anchor to the fiddle and bagpipes of Turlough Mac-Suibhne, a leading local musician at the end of the 19th century.

**Donegal Historical Society Museum** *Daily, 10am-8pm. Talks and tours by arrangement. Tel: (072) 51267.*

### POET OF THE WEE FOLK

Ballyshannon's most famous son was poet William Allingham who wrote *The Fairies*, the best-known of his poems, which recalls the local belief in 'the wee folk'.

*Up the airy mountain*
*Down the rushy glen*
*We daren't go a-hunting*
*For fear of little men.*

Allingham was born in 1824, in the building that is now the Allied Irish Bank, and his bust is on display there, together with a pane of glass from his bedroom on which he etched the rhyming inscription:

*Allingham.*
*This name's duration shall surpass*
*The hand that wrote it in the glass.*

The prophesy was correct, as Ballyshannon's bridge across the Erne is now called Allingham Bridge. Allingham died in 1889, and is buried in St Anne's churchyard.

PILGRIMS' ISLAND *Station Island's basilica of 1929 (above) has windows by Harry Clarke depicting the Stations of the Cross (below).*

# 'The Headlands'

*This area is known as The Rosses, or 'Na Rosa' in Irish, meaning 'the headlands'. Villages are scattered along the rocky and barren coast and on the offshore islands of Aran and Tory, where aspects of traditional Irish life that have largely vanished elsewhere are preserved. Inland, the reddish peat bog is broken here and there by grey rocky outcrops and bubbling streams that feed numerous loughs. The region's wealth of lakes makes it perfect for walkers and anglers.*

## Aran Island/Árainn Mhór

In spite of its small size, 7sq miles, Aran has a surprisingly large population of 900 people. From the mainland jetty at Burtonport it is half-an-hour's chug across the straits on a ferry. The boat runs past a cluster of smaller islands, low-topped and surrounded by weather-worn boulders fringed with reddish seaweed.

Aran's only trees are by the landing point at Leabgarrow. Like the smaller islands, it is hemmed with giant boulders, while its hillsides are speckled with spick-and-span cottages, evidence of prosperity from fishing, construction work abroad, and a self-build venture backed by EC grants. From the slopes there are fine views across to the mainland mountains, and near Leabgarrow are two

**OTHER PLACES TO SEE**
**Ards Forest Park** On W side of Sheep Haven Bay, 10,000 acre woodland, with wildlife and nature trails.
**Burtonport** Leading fishing port for salmon, herring and mackerel, and starting point for boat to Aran Island.
**Church Hill** Village containing Colmcille Heritage Centre which traces the role of the saint, also called St Columba, in Church history. Opening times: Easter week, mid-May to Sept, Mon-Sat 10.30am-6.30pm, Sun 1-6.30pm. Tel: (074) 21160.
**Falcarragh** Irish-speaking village, good angling centre, and base for walks up Muckish Mountain; neo-

Gothic church of 1792.
**Gortahork** Resort in Irish-speaking district, base for walks up Muckish Mountain.

**EVENTS**
**Dunfanaghy Golf Club Open Week** End July-early Aug.
**Mary from Dunglow Festival** July-Aug.

**SPORT**
**Angling** Game fishing: Lough Shore, lakes on Aran Island, Dunfanaghy lakes, Loughs Beagh and Nacung, Rivers Gweedore and Ray, The Rosses Fishery. Sea fishing: Portnablahy.
**Bathing** Marble Hill, Portnablahy.
**Golf** Dunfanaghy Golf Club, 18-hole course. Tel: (074) 36335.
Gweedore Golf Club, 9-hole course. Tel: (075) 31140.
**Sailing** Marble Hill.
**Water-skiing** Marble Hill.
**Windsurfing** Marble Hill.

**INFORMATION**
North-West Tourism.
Tel: (074) 21160.

good beaches. A village of holiday cottages is being developed, and the island's first-ever secondary school opened in 1990.

## Dunfanaghy/Dún Fionnachaidh

Gently rolling hills above the waters of Sheep Haven shelter Dunfanaghy, a small resort which makes a good base for exploring the glories of this part of Donegal. To the north are Horn Head, where the sun can be watched going down over the Atlantic, and its neighbour, Duncap Isle, visited by legions of seabirds. To the south is Muckish Mountain, where fine walking and climbing are to be had. Nearby are a bird sanctuary and deserted sandhills. On the coast south-west of Horn Head is a blowhole known as McSwyne's Gun, which the tide rushes through with a loud explosion.

## Dunglow/An Clochan Liath

The capital (although a very small one) of the area known as The Rosses is Dunglow (also spelt Dungloe), whose inhabitants make their living from the sea and the land, as well as tourism. A fine house built for the Sweeney family around 1850 and now a hotel, Sweeney's, is full of family photographs from the turn of the century. It is still run by the family of that name. But the real attraction of this region is that it has no fewer than 130 lakes, all teeming with fish. Fishing is so cheap that an outlay of a few pounds buys sport of a quality which elsewhere can cost hundreds.

## Dunlewy/Dún Lúiche

The white marble village church, dating from the 1840s, stands roofless and forlorn beside a wind-ruffled lake but still has a compelling beauty of its own. It lies in the heart of the Derryveagh Mountains; to the north rises Errigal Mountain, at 2466ft Donegal's highest, and to the south is Slieve Snacht (2240ft). The church and walled graveyard with its solitary gravestone have long been abandoned to nature. A track past the church leads to The Poisoned Glen, which gets its name from the legend that God dropped poison there, since when no birdsong is ever heard. Nearby is the Dunlewey Lakeside Centre, a complex which includes a farmyard and re-created weaver's cottage and hires out boats for fishing or picnics.
**Dunlewey Lakeside Centre** *June-Sept, Mon-Sat 11.30am-6pm, Sun 12.30-7pm. Closed Tues. Tel: (075) 31699.*

## Glenveagh National Park

Wild mountain scenery contrasts with the formal gardens of Glenveagh Castle, which lie in the 10,000 acres of Glenveagh National Park. The castle was built in 1870 on the shores of long, narrow Lough Beagh and the gardens have been laid out in the intervening years. An orangery and formally designed Italian and French gardens blend with the surrounding countryside, and a herd of about 600 red deer roams through the park.

About 4 miles to the south of the park is The Glebe House, a Regency mansion beside

ISLAND ARTIST *Tory Island is home to a school of naive art.*

Gartan Lough, also known as Lough Beagh South. It was formerly the home of the painter and art collector Derek Hill, who gave it to the nation in 1980. The house contains an art gallery with paintings by Degas, Renoir and Picasso.

**Glenveagh National Park** *Apr-Oct, daily, 10.30am-6.30pm; June-Aug, also Sun 10.30am-7.30pm. Tel: (074) 37088.*

**The Glebe House and Gallery** *Mar-Apr for a week, and end May-end Sept, Mon-Sat 11am-6.30pm. Sun 1-6.30pm. Tel: (074) 37071.*

### Gweedore/Gaoth Dobhair

The region known as Gweedore, north of The Rosses, takes in the old port of Bunbeg, the neighbouring village of Derrybeg, and the magnificent rocky promontory of Bloody Foreland. It is traditionally an Irish-speaking area, though holiday bungalows, which are sprouting everywhere, and new restaurants, supermarkets and tweed shops, give it a modern seaside atmosphere.

Bunbeg's harbour, west of the main road, still has a small fishing fleet. It claims to be Europe's smallest harbour, and is reached from the sea along a zigzag channel only a few yards wide in places. Bunbeg is the starting point for trips to the uninhabited Gola Island just offshore, and to Tory Island 8 miles north of Bloody Foreland – which is so called not because of any tragedy that took place there, but because the evening sun turns the rocks to a glowing red.

### Tory Island/Toraigh

On a clear day, the 15 mile boat trip to Tory Island from Bunbeg harbour offers views of towering cliff faces and seascapes sweeping round to Malin Head. But if the weather turns bad, visitors may be marooned on the island for days, even in summer.

Tory Island is bleak and treeless, and its 150 inhabitants tend to be shy and withdrawn, the opposite of most Donegal folk. The name 'tory' comes from the Irish 'toraidhe', meaning 'outlaw'. It was adopted in England in 1679-80 to describe those who opposed James II's claim to the crown, and later became the name of a parliamentary party in Westminster.

According to legend, Tory Island was the home of Balor, the one-eyed Celtic god of darkness. It is also reputed to have been the lair of a ferocious tribe of African pirates and was the site of a monastery founded in the 6th century by St Columba.

HEAVENLY HAVEN *Beneath cloud-cloaked hills, Dunfanaghy embroiders the shore of Sheep Haven.*

CROHY HEAD *West of Dunglow the pounding Atlantic has sculpted fantastic rock forms.*

SNOW-CAPPED PEAK *Mount Errigal's white quartzite cone lies hidden under snow in winter.*

# Mountains of Rainbows

*Towns with lyrical names – Letterkenny, Stranorlar and Ballybofey – sit along the banks of the Rivers Finn and Swilly, separated by high farmland and mountainous terrain, where even conifers find it hard to gain a foothold in the thin topsoil. The slopes of the Croaghgorm or Blue Stack Mountains are speckled with foraging sheep, and to the north they fan out towards Lough Finn, which shimmers below a steep glen, often with a rainbow arching overhead.*

## Ballybofey/Bealach Féich

With its twin town Stranorlar (or Srath an Urláir), Ballybofey holds a key position in the heartland of Donegal as the magnet for an almost entirely rural population. The two towns are separated by the River Finn, 40yds wide at the bridge that links them. Ballybofey has the shops and commerce, the local soccer and Gaelic football teams, while Stranorlar has the churches and schools – hence the jest by Stranorlar folk that people from Ballybofey are uneducated pagans.

Stranorlar was laid out at the beginning of the 17th century by Peter Benson, a London entrepreneur who made a fortune from building the walls of Londonderry and was granted the manor of Stranorlar by James I. In the Protestant graveyard at the top of the town is the grave of Isaac Butt (1813-79), the founder of the Irish Home Rule Party.

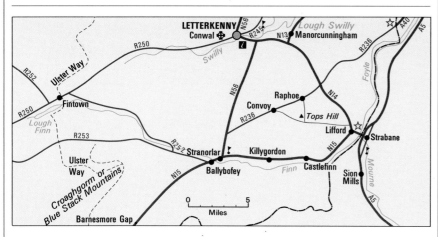

OTHER PLACES TO SEE
**Conwal** 2m W of Letterkenny, jumble of early Christian grave slabs, one with a cross carved into it, marks an ancient monastery. Nearby are two carved stone crosses and a holy well.

**WALKS**
**Ulster Way** 500 mile walk encircling the province of Ulster. The Donegal section, called Slí Uladh, is being set up by Donegal County Council. Tel: (074) 41066.

**EVENTS**
**Ballybofey and Stranorlar Twin Towns Festival** July.
**Donegal International Motor Rally** June.
**Gaelic Football** Ballybofey, Letterkenny, Sun.
**Letterkenny International Folk Festival** Aug.

**SPORT**
**Angling** Game fishing: Rivers Derg, Finn, Foyle and Swilly.
**Golf** Ballybofey and Stranorlar Golf Club, 18-hole course. Tel: (074) 31093. Letterkenny Golf Club, 18-hole course. Tel: (074) 21150.

**INFORMATION**
North-West Tourism.
Tel: (074) 21160.

There is an easy 1½ mile circular walk, which starts near Jackson's Hotel in Ballybofey, crosses a footbridge over the River Finn and then runs along its bank back to the main bridge. Hidden among the fir trees on the Stranorlar side of the river are the ruined walls of the Elizabethan Drumboe Castle, which was pulled down in 1944 after crumbling into decay.

## Blue Stack Mountains

The Blue Stack Mountains, also known as the Croaghgorm, or Na Cruacha, straddle the centre of Donegal, often lost in a cloudy haze. The only activity here is sheep-farming, and none of the towns or villages could be called the 'capital' of the mountains. Typical of them is Fintown, one of the larger villages, which straggles beside the 2½ mile long Lough Finn, but has no road signs to tell you that you have arrived there. Roads seem to peter out, leading to abandoned homesteads whose inhabitants gave up the unequal struggle with the terrain long ago.

Yet it is perfect away-from-it-all countryside. Brown trout and salmon can be caught in the loughs and rivers, there are boats for hire, campers and picnickers can settle down anywhere, walkers can pick up the Ulster Way long-distance footpath, and almost every weekend traditional music is played in the pubs. As compensation for the dampness of the climate, rainbows are almost always present.

The main road from Ballybofey to Donegal Town cuts through the Barnesmore Gap, which in the 18th century was notorious for bands of highwaymen. A garrison of redcoats was stationed there to safeguard travellers. The roadside pub, Biddy's of Barnes, is one of the longest-established pubs in Ireland. A much-loved former landlady, Rosie O'Callaghan, used to call 'Time!', make her customers kneel down to say the rosary, and then offer them another drink.

## Letterkenny/Leitir Ceanainn

The imposing 215ft spire of St Eunan's Catholic cathedral, one of the tallest in Ireland, towers majestically over Letterkenny, a small town on the River Swilly at the southern end of Lough Swilly. Its three-quarter-mile-long main street is one of the longest in the county. The cathedral, built at the end of the 19th century, is a huge building in late Gothic Revival style. Its oak furnishings, carved altar of Carrara marble

and colourful stained glass produce an overwhelmingly rich effect.

Across a small square is the 17th-century Protestant church, like every other building in the town, overshadowed by the cathedral. In its fascinating graveyard, which goes back to 1652, are the graves of a 17th-century outlaw, Count Redmond, his two sons, and Dr John Dinnear, a 19th-century champion of tenants' rights.

Up the hill is St Eunan's College, built in 1904 in a mixture of Romanesque and Celtic architecture, battlemented and with handsome conical turrets. The old workhouse, on the corner of the High Road and New Line Road, houses the recently restored County Museum, which contains displays on the history of Donegal.

According to legend, the Swilly gets its name from Suileach, a man-eating monster killed by St Columba. As the saint passed the pool where it lived, it rushed out at him, but he cut it in two with his sword, and though both halves then attacked him, he chopped them into small pieces. He then washed his sword in the Swilly, saying that henceforth its

PATRIOT'S ARREST

Letterkenny's Centre Spot restaurant has a historic link with the patriot Wolfe Tone. At the end of the 18th century, when Laird's Hotel stood on the site, Tone was arrested here in 1798, after having landed in Ireland with an invasion force from France. Dressed in a French uniform, he was assumed by his captors to be a French officer, but while eating breakfast at Laird's Hotel he was recognised by a former fellow student. He was clamped in irons and ridden to Derry surrounded by dragoons, and was eventually tried in Dublin.

LONESOME ROAD *Barren hills cradle the road that tortuously follows the course of the River Swilly through its valley, west of Letterkenny.*

water would wash away anger, as it had washed away Suileach's blood.

**Letterkenny County Museum** *Mon-Fri 11am-4.30pm, Sat 1-4.30pm.*

### Raphoe/Ráth Bhoth

This small cathedral town (whose name is pronounced 'Raffow') is built round the triangular 'Diamond' market square often found in 17th-century Irish Plantation towns, and has a good collection of Georgian houses at its centre. A 6th-century monastery here was raised to cathedral status in the 9th century.

HILLTOP RUIN *Raphoe's 17th-century Bishop's Palace was burnt down in 1838.*

The Gothic-style cathedral dates from the early 18th century; its tower, 24ft square, was built in 1738. Inside the porch is a 12th-century stone sculpture depicting the arrest of Jesus in the Garden of Gethsemane with St Peter standing nearby armed with a sword, and soldiers surrounding the group. The inner porch, now the baptistry, houses the delightful furnishings of the old consistory court, where wills were probated and marriage licences issued until well into the 19th century. The judge's bench is still furnished with quill pen and candle. At the eastern end of the cathedral is a memorial in Latin to William Archer Butler, who died of 'famine fever' in 1848. One of the finest Irish intellects ever, the post of Professor of Moral Philosophy at Trinity College, Dublin, was specially created for him.

Two miles south of Raphoe, on the summit of Tops Hill, is the Beltany Stone Circle, consisting of 64 standing stones said to predate Stonehenge, which was built around 1800 BC. The ring's name derives from the ancient Celtic festival of Beltane, held at the beginning of May to celebrate the rebirth of summer.

# Peninsulas and Sea Loughs

*Two dramatic knuckles of land, the Rosguill and Fanad peninsulas, pounded by crashing Atlantic waves, contrast with tranquil loughs inland. Lying between Lough Swilly on the east and Sheep Haven on the west, they are separated by the island-dotted sea lough of Mulroy Bay. It is a quiet region, where few visitors travel the road that runs round the bays, mountains, lakes and coves.*

## Doe Castle

Once a freebooters' stronghold, on a tongue of land that projects into Sheep Haven, Doe Castle dates from the early 15th century. Its name is an anglicised version of the Irish word 'tuath', meaning district or territory. In the 1440s it fell into the hands of the McSweeney (or MacSuibhne) clan, renowned for their constant changes of allegiance in the centuries-long tussle between the English and the Irish. Its remote position kept it safe for longer than most such strongholds, and it did not fall to the English until 1650, when the Cromwellians captured it in a surprise amphibious attack.

The rock-cut moat that leads into the castle was formerly guarded by a drawbridge and portcullis, but is now spanned by a bridge. The initials 'GVH' set into the north wall are those of General George Vaughan Harte, who altered the castle greatly in the early 19th century. He had served in India, and brought back with him an Indian manservant who is said to have slept fully armed on a mat outside his master's bedroom door.

In the nearby graveyard are several tombs of the McSweeneys and other clan chieftains.

DEFIANT STRONGHOLD *Doe Castle's massive keep stands more than 50ft high.*

## Fanad Head/Cionn Fhánada

A road leads along the west coast of Lough Swilly to Fanad Head, where on stormy days wild Atlantic seas beat against the cliffs. A short way to the south is the small resort of Portsalon, in a beautiful setting beside the broad sands of Ballymastocker Bay. Just west of the headland, at the former fishing village of Ballyhoorisky (sometimes spelled Ballywhoorisky), a local group of enthusiasts is restoring a cluster of stone-built cottages to their state before the Famine of the 1840s.

At Kindrum, 3 miles from Ballyhoorisky, on Mulroy Bay, is Daniel O'Callaghan's grocery store and pub, preserved since the early 1900s. Beautifully inlaid mirrors advertise brands of whiskey that no longer exist, two 36 gallon whiskey barrels stand in one corner, and pre-World War I posters recommend long-vanished brands of cigarettes and pipe tobacco. In the shop section, the numbered drawers once used for herbs and loose groceries such as rice still survive unaltered.

## Millford/Baile na nGallóglach

Two mountain ranges guarding this small village at the southern end of Mulroy Bay give protection from all but the occasional northerly winds. Loughsalt Mountain soars to 1546ft in the west, while the 1203ft Knockalla Mountain climbs to the east. Beyond is

friary which was suppressed in 1603.

**Kilmacrenan** Angling village on River Lurgy, where St Columba was fostered and later founded a monastery.

**EVENTS**
**Downings Angling Week** End Aug/early Sept.
**Downings Sea Angling Festival** End May.
**Leannon Festival** July.
**Rathmelton Market Day** Fri.
**Rathmullan Tope Fishing Festival** Early June.

**SPORT**
**Angling** Game fishing: Rivers Lackagh, Leannan and Swilly, Glen Lough and Lough Fern. Sea fishing: Downies.
**Bathing** Portsalon, Downies, Rathmullan.
**Golf** Otway Golf Club, 9-hole course. Tel: (074) 58319. Portsalon Golf Club, 18-hole course. Tel: (074) 59102. Rosapenna Golf Club, 18-hole course. Tel: (074) 55301.

**INFORMATION**
North-West Tourism. Tel: (074) 21160.

DOUBLE DEALING *O'Callaghan's pub in Kindrum also serves as a shop.*

**OTHER PLACES TO SEE**
**Doon Rock** 2m W of Kilmacrenan. Large isolated rock, where chieftains of O'Donnell clan were inaugurated from ancient times until 16th century.

Below it is Doon Well, holy well said to be responsible for miraculous cures.
**Killydonnell Friary** 2½m S of Rathmelton. Ruined church and domestic buildings of 1471 Franciscan

the blue of Mulroy Bay, zigzagging through a maze of promontories and islands to the Atlantic beyond. After a period of prosperity as a fair and market town, Millford is now mainly a tourist centre especially popular with anglers. Its Irish name means 'town of the gallowglasses'; these were Scottish mercenaries employed by Irish chieftains in their clan wars.

Nearby are some beautiful secluded glens, among them Bunlin Glen with its two waterfalls.

### Rathmelton/Ráth Mealtain

Sir William Stewart built this fine old plantation town, less formally spelt Ramelton, in the early 17th century for settlers from England and Scotland. It is curiously lopsided, with handsome Georgian buildings on only one side of the estuary of the River Leannan, which winds into Lough Swilly.

The Leannan was once navigable by ocean-going vessels, and Rathmelton's great days are recalled by the well-preserved 18th-century Fish House on the quayside. The town map on the Fish House wall lists almost 50 buildings worth seeing, from the 17th-century Presbyterian Meeting House, now called the Makemie Centre and being developed as a heritage centre and museum, to the two blue-painted cottages, built right over a bubbling brook, which were once the town's corn mill.

In more prosperous days, Rathmelton used to export grain, linen, butter, eels, salmon, and iodine extracted from seaweed, and was famous for its markets of pigs, cattle, turkeys and grain. A country-produce market is still held there every Friday morning.

A short way upstream from the town bridge is a salmon weir, which drops 12ft into a cauldron of foam. On the other side of town, the old, disused, ferry jetty juts 200yds into the water. In the past, passengers who wanted to attract the ferryman's attention could light a fire with wood kept stacked for the purpose.

**Rathmelton Heritage Centre and Museum** *Tel: (074) 51273.*

### Rathmullan/Rath Maoláin

An imposing battery fort shelters this small town on the shores of Lough Swilly. The fort, built in 1810 by the English as a defence against a possible Napoleonic attack, now houses the town's heritage centre, which tells the story, in documents and waxwork tab-

A WORLD AWAY *Whitewashed buildings with turf roofs stand amid dry-stone walls on the edge of Lough Swilly, relics of a simple way of life.*

leaux, of the 'Flight of the Earls', one of Ireland's most traumatic historic episodes, which put an end to the centuries-old rule of the Irish chieftains.

From Rathmullan pier, an attractive coastal walk leads between private gardens and the shore to woodlands of elm, hawthorn, snowberry, ash and sycamore.

**Flight of the Earls Heritage Centre** *End Mar-end Sept, 10am-6pm; Sun, 12.30-6pm. Tel: (074) 58131/58178.*

### Rosguill Peninsula

The 7 mile Atlantic Drive makes the circuit of this remote and unspoilt peninsula, which lies between Sheep Haven and Mulroy Bay. Every turn of the road brings a new view, either breathtaking or beguiling. Many of the inhabitants in the scattered settlements are Irish-speaking, and still live by traditional handicrafts.

Downies (also known as Downings) is the peninsula's main fishing village, where local boats land their catches of salmon, lobster, crab and turbot at the pier. Nearby is a Donegal tweed shop and factory, McNutts. All around are fine sandy beaches, two of them backing onto the fairways of the Rosapenna Golf Club, founded in 1893 by the 4th Earl of Leitrim.

Farther up the peninsula are the ruins of Meevagh church, with an early cross in its churchyard. St Columba is said to have built the original church at the point where his donkey lay down, too tired to go any farther. Crosses set in nearby walls mark the points at which it rested.

Tranarossan beach, a mile farther on, is strewn with pebbles and boulders in a wide spectrum of colours, indicating the variety of the local mineral deposits.

**McNutts Tweed Shop** *Mon-Sat 9am-6pm.*

# A Fisherman's Paradise

*South Leitrim is an area of loughs and rivers, the greatest of which, the mighty River Shannon, flows along the region's western boundary. It is a fisherman's paradise. But it is a rambler's heaven too. Rising above the waters is a series of small hills, or drumlins, and there is a large area of flatland peppered with historic ruins and grand houses.*

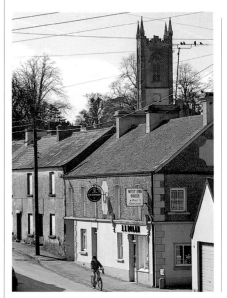

### Carrick-on-Shannon/Cora Droma Rúisc

The 'weir of the marshy ridge', with a population of 2000, is the smallest county town in Ireland, and its inhabitants are well outnumbered by the local cormorants and swans. For centuries it was merely a crossing point on the River Shannon, but in the early 17th century it was fortified and garrisoned to protect the new settlers.

Carrick's lock and waterworks date from the early 1800s, and it was a bustling centre in the early 19th century when water transport was vital and when recurring famines meant plenty of cheap labour. Today it is a popular centre for Shannon cruising. To go boating not more than a mile from the town is to explore an unspoilt and tranquil wilderness: the river glides past ghostly castles, ravaged stone crosses and deserted hamlets.

CARRIGALLEN *A lone cyclist rides through the deserted West End of Carrigallen village.*

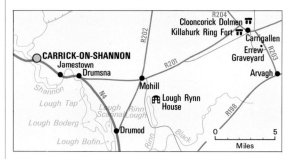

**OTHER PLACES TO SEE**
**Carrigallen** The three provinces of Ulster, Leinster and Connaught meet at a point in the corner of Carrigallen parish. Nearby are many fishing waters, well stocked with fish. Architectural remains in the district include Errew graveyard, Killahurk ring-fort and Clooncorick dolmen, a prehistoric tomb known locally as the King's Grave.

**EVENTS**
**Shannon Boat Rally** June and Oct.
**Shannon Regatta** July-Aug.

**SPORT**
**Angling** Coarse fishing: Rivers Rinn and Shannon. Game fishing: Loughs Boderg, Bofin, Scannal and Tap, and Rivers Black and Shannon.
**Boating** Carrick-on-Shannon. Contact Rowing Club. Tel: (078) 20063.
**Golf** Carrick-on-Shannon Golf Club, 9-hole course. Tel: (078) 67015.

**INFORMATION**
Sligo Tourist Office.
Tel: (071)) 61201.

FOUR MEN IN A BOAT *The placid Rinn Lough, whose waters flow into the River Shannon, provides a happy hunting ground for coarse fishing.*

At the junction of Bridge and Main Streets is Ireland's smallest church, the Costello Memorial Chapel, which measures only 16ft long, 12ft wide and 30ft high. The chapel was built in 1877 by Edward Costello, a wealthy merchant, as a memorial and burial vault for his wife Josephine. The interior is lined with yellow Bath stone. On both sides of the ornately tiled aisle is a sunken space, each of which holds a coffin lined with lead and covered with slabs of thick reinforced glass. The remains of both Edward and Josephine lie in them.

Carrick's courthouse was the scene of a mass execution in 1798, following the defeat by the British of the Irish rebels and a French army under General Humbert. The British commander, Lord Cornwallis, ordered that 17 captives were to be hanged. The prisoners were forced to draw pieces of paper from a

IN MEMORIAM *Carrick's Costello Chapel is Ireland's smallest church.*

hat, on 17 of which the word 'death' was written. Those unfortunate enough to draw these pieces of paper were promptly hanged outside the courthouse door.

Within a short distance of Carrick are many lakes stocked with fish, the focus of international fishing competitions.

## Drumsna/Droim ar Snámh

The often lazy, lordly Shannon hurries with suddenly unaccustomed vigour through Drumsna, as if anxious to reach the sea. Visitors should avoid making the same mistake, if only to take in reminders of the celebrities who lived in this village overlooked from the north by Slieve Anierin.

Novelist Anthony Trollope, then a senior civil servant, was sent here in 1843 to investigate the affairs of the postmaster who 'had come to some sorrow' over his money. While here he wrote his first novel *The McDermotts of Ballycloran*, published in 1847. A plaque marks the house where he stayed, now the village pub.

Adjoining the churchyard are the ruins of a preaching house founded by John Wesley. The brothers George and William Strawbridge were worshippers there and later were to travel to North America, in 1760, where they helped to establish Methodism, with a following today of 20 million.

LOUGH RYNN HOUSE *The 19th-century mansion was the home of the infamous 3rd Earl of Leitrim.*

### CARRICK'S JUNGLE EXPLORER

One of Leitrim's most famous sons was explorer Surgeon-Major Thomas Heazle Parke (1857-93). He was born near Carrick-on-Shannon, and in 1882 started his career as an army surgeon, serving in the Nile expedition and travelling with the desert columns sent to rescue General Gordon.

In 1887 Parke joined the Congo expedition led by Henry Morton Stanley, which involved the famous journey up the River Congo and the march through the Congo jungle. It was he who cured Stanley of his fever there.

Parke returned to England in 1890 to a warm reception, and was presented with gold medals from various associations, including the British Medical Association and the Royal Geographical Society. But his travels had taken their toll on his body and he lived in poor health until his death in 1893. His body was returned to Ireland and was buried at Drumsna, in Leitrim, in a tiny graveyard measuring 7yds by 18yds and said to be Ireland's smallest.

## Jamestown/Cill Srianáin

At Jamestown the River Shannon pauses in its 215 mile journey to the sea and sweeps back on itself to run north for 100yds or so. Sir Charles Coote founded the town in 1625 to safeguard the Shannon crossing and named it after James I. Despite his fortifications, the town was occupied by the O'Rourkes, a powerful local clan, in 1642. Only the lower part of one gateway survives as a memento of the 17th-century town wall, spanning the Dublin-Sligo road.

Today, Georgian houses line Jamestown's wooded river banks. Towards the river, from the Jamestown Arch, the last remains of the O'Rourke Castle can be seen.

## Mohill/Maothail

Streets that weave in and out of each other with a bar or quaint shops around almost every corner make Mohill an appealing place to wander around. Commanding the town centre is a life-size bronze bust of the blind harpist Turlough O'Carolan (1670-1738).

Nearby is Lough Rynn House, one of the homes of the Earls of Leitrim. The mansion, built in 1832, has been fully restored to its original glory and the grounds are being constantly upgraded and will soon become one of the major gardens of Europe. William Sydney Clements, 3rd Earl of Leitrim, was one of Leitrim's most notorious characters. He was eventually ambushed and assassinated in 1878, and after his death was accused in the House of Commons of exercising the *droit de seigneur* – the right to sleep with a bride on her wedding night before her husband did.

The estate covers more than 100 acres of woodland, ornamental gardens and open pasture. There are also 600 acres of lakes, and a lakeside turret house with memorable views of the countryside. The terraced walled garden, once a kitchen garden, dates from 1859 and covers 3 acres. The arboretum contains many exotic trees, including tulip trees, Californian redwoods and the oldest monkey puzzle (*Araucaria*) tree in Ireland.

Picnic sites with supervised play areas have been laid out near the old sawmill that once generated much of the estate's income. Nature trails are signposted and lead to various sites offering views across the lakes and countryside. One of the lakes has a 4000-year-old artificial island, or crannog. And on a hill within the grounds is a druidic altar on which human sacrifices were offered.

Mohill lies in the heart of Leitrim's lakeland at the head of Rinn Lough, surrounded by low-backed drumlin hills. The lakes abound with coarse fish, and a match stretch has been laid out on the lakes for international fishing competitions.

**Lough Rynn House and Gardens** *May-Sept, daily 10am-7pm. Tel: (078) 31427.*

# Peaceful Angling Towns

*The spectacular Lough Allen, the historic Shannon and a score of other waterways embroider this patchwork of land, cutting through mountains and across meadows where it is possible to wander for miles without encountering another person. It is ideal country for messing about in boats, biking up a mountain, walking in the glens or simply admiring the scenery.*

MUSIC-MAKERS *In August, Ballinamore hums to the sounds of its Irish music and dance festival.*

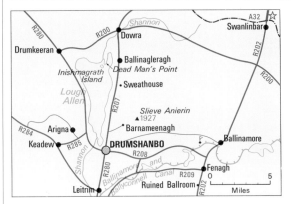

### EVENTS
**An Tostal** Week-long festival of traditional Irish music, song and dance. Drumshanbo, July.

**Ballinamore Festival of Irish music and dance** Aug.
**Drumshanbo Jamboree** Oct.
**Drumshanbo Open Coarse Fishing Competition** Lough Allen, July.
**Drumshanbo Teach Cheoil** (Music festival); Thur pm, June, July and Aug.

### SPORT
**Angling** Coarse fishing: Lough Allen and loughs around Drumshanbo, and River Shannon. Game fishing: Lough Allen and loughs around Drumshanbo, and River Shannon.
**Golf** Ballinamore Golf Club, 9-hole course. Tel: (078) 44346.
**Sailing** Lough Allen. Contact local yacht club. Tel: (078) 48044.

### INFORMATION
Sligo Tourist Office. Tel: (071) 61201.

## Ballinagleragh/Baile na gCléireach

In the north-east corner of Lough Allen is the peaceful angling town known as 'the town of the clergy' because it has been the birthplace of so many clerics. Among them was the local legend Father Charles 'Racey' Reynolds, who lived in Ballinagleragh in the late 18th century. A great sprinter, he is said to have been chased by pursuers for 7 miles before leaping right over a chasm called Poll an Chait. He said of his feat: 'Ah sure, I had a good run at it . . . seven miles or so.'

## Ballinamore/Béal an Átha Móir

Many loughs and several miles of river lie within easy reach of Ballinamore, making it an ideal touring centre. And the many low-backed ridges, called drumlins, that dot this landscape also attract ramblers. But the village has its own places of interest, including the Leitrim Heritage Centre which deals with enquiries from people who wish to trace ancestors that came from Leitrim. Ballinamore was the first town in Ireland to provide this service and now answers enquiries from all round the world, tracing relatives through registers dating from the early 1800s.

The Heritage Centre shares the same building as the town library and the museum. One of the most intriguing items in its collection is the shirt collar worn by the patriot Sean MacDiarmuid, when he was executed in 1916 for his part in the Easter Uprising. Other museum exhibits include old farming and kitchen implements, which tell a rich story of early life in Ireland.
**Leitrim Heritage Centre and Museum** *Mon-Fri 10am-5pm.*

---

### THE LOUGH ALLEN MONSTER

Anglers from far and wide can testify to the enormous catches yielded by Lough Allen . . . but locals reckon that the biggest of the lot has so far eluded them all.

A monster, many times larger than the 30lb pike for which the lake is famous, is reported to have made several appearances in recent years. It is described as 'massive' in length with several humps and an enormous head. A boatman who claims he was chased by the monster has vowed never to go on the lake again.

The monster would indeed be a prize catch. A £500 reward is on offer for anyone who can prove that it exists.

---

## Drumkeeran/Droim Caorthainn

The spectacular road to Drumkeeran, 'the ridge of the quicken tree', skirts the winding shores of Lough Allen. Boat trips are run to the 6 acre island of Inishmagrath, on which lie the ruins of an ancient church and disused graveyard. The island lies about 400yds from the lough shore and for centuries people of the district buried their dead there. In bad weather, when crossings were impossible, mourners would gather at Dead Man's Point on the mainland and keep watch over the dead until the weather had subsided.

FLUTE-PLAYER *A plaque in Drumshanbo remembers John McKenna, the flautist.*

## Drumshanbo/Droim Seanbhó

Drumshanbo, at the southern tip of Lough Allen, gives access to some of the best scenery in Ireland. Bordering the lough, to the north-west, are the Arigna mountains, and to the north-east Slieve Anierin (the Mountain of Iron), one of a range of heather-clad mountains pierced by steep-sided valleys that echo to the cries of grouse, pheasant, wild duck and a host of other wildlife. The Lough Allen Scenic Tour starts and finishes its 30 mile circuit of the lake, which is 8 miles long by 3 miles wide, in the town.

The name Drumshanbo means 'the ridge of old huts', a somewhat unromantic title for what has become a favourite hideaway for honeymooners. Trees, shrubs and flowers line the town's main street and it is a frequent winner of Leitrim's Tidy Town competition.

Outside the town, at Barnameenagh, is the stone of the legendary warrior-giant Finn MacCool, which he is reputed to have hurled at his enemies from the Arigna side of Lough Allen to near the top of Slieve Anierin. Indentations in the rock are said to have been made by MacCool when he gripped it. It is believed that people who place their fingers in the indentations will be rewarded with the gift of stamina – a useful tip to those walking or cycling in the area. MacCool's soldiers (called the Fianna) are said to lie sleeping in the mountains, awaiting his next call to battle.

Drumshanbo is one of the major coarse and fly-fishing centres of Europe, and sooner or later conversation there turns to angling. In addition to Lough Allen, there are several lakes and rivers a short distance from the town, all constantly re-stocked with trout.

On the road north from Drumshanbo is the Poor Clare Convent where nuns kneeling in pairs offer continuous prayers, or Adoration of the Blessed Sacrament, day and night. Pilgrims come here from all over the world to join in the worship.

### Fenagh/Fiodhnach

Two old churches lie in ruins on the site of a former monastery founded here by St Caillín in the 6th century. The church to the south has a 14th-century doorway and east window. The one to the north, built in the 15th century, has dressed stones from a pre-Norman building. Both have barrel-vaulted west ends. In the surrounding fields the paths that ran between the monks' cells can still be traced in the grass. *The Book of Fenagh*, completed at the monastery in 1516, contains a catalogue of lands and privileges of the monastery as well as a collection of 'wonders' alleged to have been performed by St Caillín. It is now kept at the Royal Irish Academy in Dublin.

Fenagh has two bars – Fianna Fail and Fine Gael, named after the republic's two main political parties. A telephone box which stood outside the Fine Gael pub was moved 30yds across the road to the Fianna Fail bar when the government of the republic changed.

Just out of Fenagh, on the Mohill road, is a 'Giant's Grave', a Stone Age two-court cairn. A mile on from Fenagh, towards Mohill, is a ballroom that once rocked to the big band sounds of the 1950s. Sadly the money made there was lost on two other ventures – a motorcycle wall of death and an unheated

ANGLERS' DELIGHT *At any time of the day during the coarse-fishing season, and in all weather, patient anglers are a familiar sight at Drumshanbo.*

## A CURE FOR ACHES AND PAINS

Once 'sweathouses', a sort of Irish sauna, were a common form of cure for sufferers from rheumatism, sciatica, and general aches and pains. One of these small stone buildings, of which there are 78 in County Leitrim alone, stands on the road between Drumshanbo and Ballinagleragh. It is 4ft high, 5ft wide and has an opening 2ft square onto a clay floor.

When the sweathouse was to be used, a fire would be lit inside it to heat the stones. Two people would then enter and have the entrance stopped with a stone behind them. They would stay for as long as the intense heat was bearable, before leaping into the nearby stream.

Sweathouses were largely abandoned after 1851 when the first dispensaries were established, although some are said to have been used up to the 1930s.

swimming pool – and the ballroom is now deserted and in ruins.

### Leitrim/Liatroim

This tiny village gave its name, meaning 'grey hill' to the county, a reflection of its past importance as the site of the stronghold of the O'Rourke chieftains. Their castle in Leitrim village was taken by the British in 1603 at the end of the Nine Years War, and today only a part of the castle wall can be seen.

With its old village pump still standing under a spreading chestnut tree, Leitrim seems to have been missed by the 19th century, except for the Ballinamore-Ballyconnell Canal, which joins the River Shannon here. The point at which the two meet can be clearly seen from the bridge. On the outskirts of Leitrim are riverside, canal and forest walks.

# The Abduction of Ireland's Helen

*Once, the glens of this land of battles echoed to the shouts of warriors, and it was here that the abduction of the 'Helen' of Ireland brought about the Anglo-Norman invasion that devastated the ancient kingdoms. Now the valleys are disturbed by little more than the sounds of wildlife and the rustle of trees, and the fiercest battles fought are between fishermen and salmon or pike.*

## Dromahair/Droim dhá Thiar

Around AD 440 St Patrick, patron saint of Ireland, settled in this valley, where the rushing sound of the River Bonet's rapids and waterfalls fills the air. During the following 17 years he founded a church, monastery and nunnery, but little is left of these ancient ruins – only a few stones of what is thought to have been the church.

Dromahair, which means 'the ridge of the air demons', then became the seat of the O'Rourkes, one of Ireland's most powerful families. In 1152, Dervorgilla, wife of the one-eyed Tiernan O'Rourke, Prince of Breifne, was abducted with all her cattle and possessions, while her husband was on a pilgrimage to St Patrick's Purgatory in Lough Derg. Her abductor was Dermot Mac-Murrough, King of Leinster. Thomas Moore's ballad *The Valley Lay Smiling Before Me* tells of Tiernan's homecoming and his dismay as he approached his castle and saw no light in his wife's window.

Fourteen years later Tiernan and his neighbouring chiefs dethroned Dermot and banished him from Leinster. Dermot appealed to Henry II of England to help him regain his kingdom, and enlisted the support of Strongbow – Richard de Clare, Earl of Pembroke. He was lured with the promise of marriage to Dermot's eldest daughter and the whole of Leinster on his death. Strongbow landed in Wexford in 1170, together with a group of Anglo-Norman barons who had been promised Wexford and neighbouring lands. So began the Anglo-Norman conquest of Ireland.

Dervorgilla was eventually returned to the O'Rourke castle but went straight to Mellifont monastery in County Louth, where she died aged 84. Despite the Anglo-Norman invasion, however, the lordship of the O'Rourkes lasted until the conquest by Elizabeth I. The O'Rourkes finally lost all power after the Battle of Kinsale, in 1601.

Sir William Villiers was granted 11,000 acres in the area in the 17th century and demolished the O'Rourke castle to provide the stone for a more grandiose fortified house, the Old Hall, completed in 1626. Today only the banqueting hall and walls remain.

Opposite this building, on the other side of the River Bonet, stand the remains of Creevelea Franciscan Friary. It was founded in 1508 by Margaret, wife of Owen O'Rourke, and was the last to be built before the suppression of the monasteries. A transept, east window and remarkably small cloister can still be seen, as can the kitchen and refectory, in the north wing. Among the stone carvings are St Francis preaching to the birds, and another showing the saint with the stigmata. In the grounds are the tombs of many of the O'Rourkes. The monastery was probably finally abandoned at the end of the 17th century. It is now a national monument.

The River Bonet is renowned for its salmon and trout, and the countryside around the town is ideal for hill climbing, cycling and pony trekking. In particular, a demanding climb to O'Rourke's Table, a flat-topped hill covered with ferns and mosses, rewards walkers with panoramic views of mountains and valleys.

## Kinlough/Cionn Locha

At the northern end of Lough Melvin is this little village and angling centre. It has an intriguing folk museum, part of which is the old McGurran's Bar. A half bottle of stout sits, still fermenting, on the bar and a poteen-still shaped like a diving bell stands by the wall.

VANISHED VOGUE *A mannequin advertises a hat in a Dromahair draper's window.*

[Map: showing Donegal Bay, Tullaghan, Bundoran, Belleek, Mullinaleck, Rossclogher Castle, Kinlough, Lough Melvin, Ulster Way, Ross Friar, Benbulbin ▲1730, Glencar Waterfall, Glenade Lough, Glenade, Killea, Kiltyclogher, Corracloona, Glencar, Corranmore, MANORHAMILTON, O'Rourke's Table, Sligo, Parke's Castle, Innisfree, Lough Gill, Dromahair, Bonet, Glenfarne, Killarga, 0–5 Miles]

**OTHER PLACES TO SEE**

**Corracloona** Prehistoric court tomb, 2500-2000 BC, known as Prince Connall's Grave.
**Glenade** Wild and rugged valley, with nearby Glenade Lough surrounded by high, cliff-like limestone hills.
**Glencar Waterfall** 50ft cascade through woodland. Signposted off road to Manorhamilton; road skirts Glencar Lough, and path leads to waterfall.
**Killarga** Traces of defunct Sligo, Leitrim and Northern Counties Railway – known as the Slow, Lazy and Never Come Regularly – can be seen from the village centre. Site of Holy Well of Killarga.
**Killea** Mountain resort which runs week-long camping and canoeing expeditions.
**Kiltyclogher** Village with memorial to Sean MacDiarmuid, a leader of the 1916 Uprising. Nearby, at Corranmore, is the cottage where he was born, now a national monument.

**Lough Gill** Lough praised by Yeats; boats sail from here to island of Innisfree.
**Parke's Castle** 4m N of Dromahair; 17th-century castle built by Thomas Parke, a planter. Square, three-storey building with large courtyard and two round towers.
**Rossclogher Castle** MacClancy stronghold, on crannog in Lough Melvin.

**EVENTS**
**Dromahair Agricultural show** July.
**Festival of Breifne History** Dromahair, June.
**Fleadh Cheoil** Manorhamilton, April.
**Manorhamilton Agricultural show** Aug.
**May Fair** Manorhamilton, May.
**Wild Rose Festival** Manorhamilton, Aug.

**SPORT**
**Angling** Coarse fishing: Loughs Gill and Melvin. Game fishing: Loughs Gill and Melvin; Rivers Bonet, Drowes and Duff.
**Boating** River Shannon.
**Pony trekking** Dromahair.

**INFORMATION**
Sligo Tourist Office.
Tel: (071) 61201.

---

### DOBHERCHÚ – THE MONSTER OTTER

Tread warily along the shores of Glenade Lough lest you encounter its monster, the dreaded Dobherchú. The name means otter, but this one is reputedly very big.

It is said that in September 1722, a local girl, Grace Connolly, failed to return home after going to wash clothes on the shores of the lake. Her husband went to look for her and found her mangled body with the beast sleeping over it.

The husband went back to his house, grabbed his spear, stole up to the Dobherchú and drove it into its body. But the man's troubles were not yet over. The brute's dying squeals awoke its companion from out of the placid waters – a monster more fierce than the one he had slain. Grace's husband ran home, chased by the monster, and he and his brother rode 20 furious miles on horseback to Castlegarden Hill, with the monster gaining on them.

At the hill they stood their ground and killed the beast. A tombstone over their grave in the local cemetery commemorates their feat and depicts the Dobherchú with a spear thrust through its heart. But it is believed that another Dobherchú lives in the lake still, which reappears occasionally.

Inside the museum, knick-knacks are crammed into every space, one of which is a newspaper cutting of Eamon de Valera on his way to the first sitting of the parliament (Dáil) of the Irish Free State in 1922. The key to the museum can be obtained from the grocery store across the road.

Near the museum is a 'Mass Rock' or 'Penal Altar', at which mass was celebrated during penal times by the people of the district. A holy water stoup, dated 1677, stands alongside.

The *Annals of the Four Masters*, one of the chief sources of Irish history from earliest times up to 1636, was completed at Ross Friar, on the southern shore of Lough Melvin. This massive task was undertaken by Brother Michael O'Cleary and three lay colleagues, known as the Four Masters.

Years of painstaking assembly and sifting of evidence from old manuscripts went into the production of the annals, which is now held at Trinity Library and the Royal Irish Academy in Dublin. A bronze monument commemorating their achievement stands on the bridge across the River Drowes, at Mullinaleck.

## Manorhamilton/*Cluainín*

Four mountain valleys sweep down to Manorhamilton which sits on a little plain, or 'little field' as its Irish name translates, at their junction. The surrounding peaks climb to 1500ft or so, and alpine plants such as saxifrage and mountain avens grow from a level of 800ft to the highest ground.

Manorhamilton was founded by Sir Frederick Hamilton, one of the many Hamiltons to bring settlers over from Scotland. In 1630, Charles I granted him 5000 acres of pastureland and 10,000 acres of woodland and bog. Sir Frederick's castle, once a good example of a 17th-century baronial mansion, is now roofless and covered with ivy.

The town is a base for bracing scenic walks and has easy access to the sea and five other counties. It is also the setting for the famous Wild Rose Festival each August, at which the Wild Rose Colleen is chosen. The festival commemorates the romance in the 1640s of Caitlin Ní Cuirnin, the Wild Rose of Lough Gill, and Edmond Tracy, foster son of Owen O'Rourke, chieftain of Dromahair. Candidates for the title are selected from eight places in Ireland as well as London and Madrid, places to which Caitlin is said to have travelled. The prize is a piece of Irish crystal.

GLENCAR LOUGH *Steep escarpments climb sheer from a rumpled landscape of fields and forest beside the lough's still waters.*

CREEVELEA FRIARY *Beside the tumbling River Bonet stands the ruined Franciscan abbey, abandoned by the monks towards the end of the 17th century.*

## Tullaghan/*An Tulachán*

The only village on the 2 mile stretch of Leitrim which borders the sea, Tullaghan is a fisherman's dream. It offers fishing in the Atlantic either by boat or from the shore, and excellent salmon fishing in the Rivers Duff and Drowes which flow to the sea on either side of the village. Tullaghan is also a picturesque base for exploring the neighbouring counties of Donegal and Sligo.

On a mound close to the village stands the Tullaghan Cross, an 11th or 12th-century relic that was recovered from the sea and placed in its setting by a local landowner called Dixon in 1770. It is thought to have come from a monastery that once stood near the shore of the River Drowes.

# A Land Carved by Ice

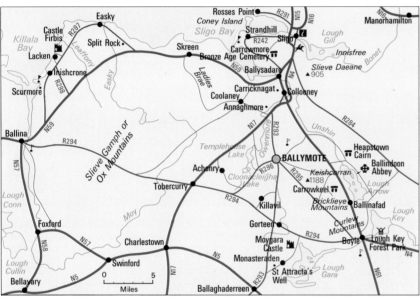

*About 200,000 years ago glaciers ground their way through southern Sligo on their way to the sea, carving the countryside through which they moved. When the ice receded 10,000 years ago, one of Connaught's most beautiful and unspoilt areas was revealed, sculpted with valleys and shimmering with lakes. It is also a region rich in tradition and home to some of Ireland's most famous musicians.*

## OTHER PLACES TO SEE

**Achonry** Remains of monastery founded by St Nath-Í.

**Annaghmore** Ancestral home of O'Haras. Visitors may walk around the grounds, which have many rare plants.

**Ballindoon Abbey** Impressive ruins of 16th-century Dominican priory overlooking Lough Arrow.

**Heapstown Cairn** Unexcavated 200ft wide Stone Age passage-tomb, traditionally known as burial place of Ailill, brother of Niall of the Nine Hostages.

**Keishcorran** Legendary mountain birthplace of Cormac MacAirt, High King of Ireland. A passage-tomb crowns the summit.

**Moygara Castle** 16th-century O'Hara stronghold with square curtain wall and one of six original towers.

**St Attracta's Well** 1m SW of Monasteraden, site where St Attracta took the veil from St Patrick.

## EVENTS

**Corran Festival** Ballymote, Aug.

**Midsummer's Fair Day and Busking Contest** Tobercurry.

**Old Fair Day Festival** Tobercurry, Aug.

**Western Drama Festival** Tobercurry, Mar.

## SPORT

**Angling** Coarse fishing: Templehouse and Cloonacleigha lakes, River Owenmore and Loughs Arrow and Gara. Game fishing: Rivers Easky, Moy and Unshin.

**Golf** Ballymote Golf Club, 9-hole course. Tel: (071) 3460.
Inishcrone Golf Club, 18-hole course. Tel: (096) 36297.

## INFORMATION

Sligo Tourist Office.
Tel: (071) 61201.

## Ballymote/Baile an Mhóta

The 'Red Earl' of Ulster, Richard Burke (de Burgo), built a castle here around 1300, which, with its 10ft walls and six towers, was once the strongest fortress in Connaught. The castle changed hands between the English and the Irish several times and was finally captured in the 17th century by the forces of Cromwell's chief officer in Ireland, General Henry Ireton.

The castle fell into disuse after 1690, and today is just a square shell surrounded by massive walls with a three-quarter tower at each corner. Two D-shaped towers defend the side walls, and the massive entrance gate is overshadowed by double towers.

Ballymote Castle is known for the *Book of Ballymote*, partially written there in 1391 for the McDonaghs, the keepers of the fortress. The 500 page book contains historical and genealogical tracts relating to County Sligo and provides a key to the ogham alphabet, an ancient Irish script. The manuscript is now in the Library of the Royal Irish Academy in Dublin. Part of the *Book of Ballymote* is also said to have been written at Ballymote Abbey, a Franciscan friary founded in 1450, whose ruins rest across the street from the castle. The keys to the castle's front gate can be obtained from the adjacent St John of God's Nursing Home.

Ballymote is also a centre for angling. A framed poem in Tighe's, one of the town's pubs, captures the essence of the area:

> *Oh it's grand to be out in the old grey boat*
> *With a friend and a rod and a fly*
> *And to feel the lift of the boat as we drift*
> *By the shoals where the brown trout lie.*

## Carrowkeel/An Cheathrú Chaol

Set high in the Bricklieve Mountains, projecting from the jagged edges of the hillside gorges, the Carrowkeel passage tombs have spectacular surroundings.

Most of the graves are round and built from limestone, and date from 2500 to 2000 BC. Cairn K, in the centre of the group, has a cross-shaped tomb with a sloping stone roof, and seems to have been designed as a kind of solar calendar, because it catches the rays of the rising sun on the longest day of the year.

To the east of the tomb site is a massive, flat limestone plateau dotted with the remains of 50 huts possibly from the Stone Age. They are believed to have been lived in by farmers who buried their dead in the tombs.

Carrowkeel should be approached only on the 1 mile drive in good weather, and should be left the same way and not down the eastern side of the mountains.

## Castle Firbis

This is the ruined stronghold of the McFirbis family, who were hereditary genealogists, or sennachies. The last of them died in 1671. The family supplied poets and historiographers to the O'Dowd clan, of Tireragh, from the 14th to the 17th century. Over this period, every head of the McFirbis family conducted a school of historical law at Lacken and played a leading role in the inauguration of each O'Dowd chief.

## Collooney/Cúil Mhuine

At the confluence of the Rivers Owenmore and Unshin, Collooney has long been the scene of battles fought and lives lost. The Collooney gap, a break between the eastern end of the Slieve Gamph, or 'Ox Mountains', and Slieve Daeane, was long protected by a castle built in 1225. The castle was much fought over, and little remains of it now.

Collooney's last battle was in July 1922, but it is an 18th-century battle that attracts today's visitors. The battle is commemorated by the Teeling Monument on the northern outskirts of Collooney. In 1798 an Irish-French force was heading for Ballinamuck, in County Longford (where it was subsequently defeated), but was pinned down at Carrick-nagat, near Collooney, by a British cannon, set on a hill. Captain Bartholomew Teeling, a 24-year-old Irishman serving in the French army, charged the hill, rode bravely through the enemy lines and shot the gunner dead on the spot where the monument now stands. The plaque that commemorates the battle reads: 'This brave and noble deed turned the tide and the English were routed.' Teeling and some 500 Irish soldiers were later executed for their part in the rebellion, although the captured French were accorded prisoner-of-war status.

## Inishcrone/Inis Crabhann

A 3 mile long sheltered beach, with spectacular views over the Atlantic horizon, draws holidaymakers to this town every year. But Inishcrone's real claim to fame is Kilcullen's Bath House, which offers its patrons seaweed baths, long popular as a treatment for the symptoms of disorders such as arthritis and rheumatism.

MORNING HARVEST *Seaweed is gathered each morning for use in Kilcullen's Bath House.*

ANCIENT TOMB *Carrowkeel's Cairn K has a long passage leading to a central chamber.*

Customers go to one of the bath house's seven immaculate rooms – families can opt for twin tubs instead of singles – which feature 7ft long porcelain tubs. A bucket of seaweed is then poured into the bath of piping hot sea water. The effect is instantly relaxing, though for novices, perhaps a bit surprising. There is little medical proof for the curative claim of the baths, although the seaweed's natural oil does give the skin a slightly slippery but luxuriant coating.

Near Inishcrone are the ruins of Roslee, a 15th-century castle and the third building to occupy this site. The 14th-century castle that preceded it was destroyed during battles between the MacDonells of Tireragh and the Burkes of Mayo in the 1500s. During this time Inishcrone was a strategic point on the road from Connaught to Ulster. The present castle was designed mainly as a residence during quieter times; even so the corner turrets were probably added as a safeguard against attackers.

**Kilcullen's Bath House** *Tel: (096) 36238.*

## Lough Gara/Loch Uí Ghadhra

During a drainage programme in 1952, the water level of this island-studded lake, 5 miles long by 4 miles wide, dropped about 4ft, and as the waters receded, workers were amazed to see a cluster of small islands appear. Archaeologists confirmed that they were man-made islands, or crannogs, which once served as easily defensible dwelling places. There are more than 200 in the lake.

Each crannog is circular, about 40ft in diameter, and built on oak pilings buttressed with stones in shallow parts of the lake. Floors of timber and brushwood were laid on these foundations and covered with wicker and reed shelters.

The settlement was probably inhabited for more than 1200 years, from about 200 BC to AD 1000. Finds include a bronze sword, dugout canoes, barbed arrow heads and exquisite pins and brooches. Many can be seen at the National Museum, in Dublin.

## Split Rock

During the last Ice Age, huge stones called 'glacial erratics' were deposited by glaciers on the coast north of the Ox Mountains. One of the most dramatic of these is Split Rock, which sits in a field about 1½ miles east of Easky on the south side of the coast road. It is known locally as 'Finn MacCool's Finger Stone'. According to legend, the great warrior and poet MacCool bet that he could throw the stone from the top of Ox Mountains across to the sea, but it fell a mile short of its target. The furious MacCool struck it and split it in two. It is said that the rock will close on anyone who dares to pass through the cleft three times.

## Scurmore

There is a mound here with seven pillar stones on top of it, the source of an ancient legend. An O'Dowd chief once came upon a beautiful mermaid by the sea. He snatched her cloak and hid it, thereby removing her powers. O'Dowd married her, and the couple had seven children. But one day, when he moved the cloak to a new hiding place, one of the children spotted him and told his mother where it was. She seized the cloak and fled back to the sea. Before departing, however, she took her revenge on her husband by turning the children into pillars of stone.

## Tobercurry/Tobar An Choire

Sheltering in the shadow of the Ox Mountains is a one-street market town that vibrates each July to some of Ireland's best traditional music, as its Summer School of Traditional Music and Dance gets under way. Along with the neighbouring village of Gorteen near the birthplace of the fiddler Michael Coleman, Tobercurry is the region's musical centre.

# 'Under Bare Ben Bulben's Head'

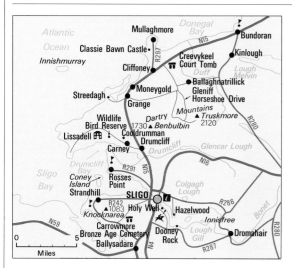

*From a coastline broken by bays and inlets the wooded countryside rolls inland around placid lakes, to be stopped abruptly by sheer limestone ridges such as Benbulbin, an outcrop that looms over Sligo like a beached ocean liner. This is a land whose images and mythology inspired Ireland's most famous poet, William Butler Yeats, for whom this was 'The Land of Heart's Desire'.*

**Sligo tour** Guided walks around town, departing from tourist office in Temple Street. July and Aug.

## EVENTS
**Feis Shligigh Festival** Sligo, Apr.
**Festival for Choirs** Sligo, Oct.
**Horse racing** Sligo, Apr-Sept.
**Mullaghmore Sea Angling Competition** Aug.
**Sligo Arts Festival** Sept/Oct.
**Strandhill Open Surfing Championships** Sligo, Aug.
**Summer College of Traditional Music Song and Dance** Sligo, Aug.
**Yeats International Summer School** Sligo, Aug.

## SPORT
**Angling** Coarse fishing: Loughs Colgagh and Gill, and River Garavogue. Game fishing: Colgagh and Glencar loughs, and Rivers Drumcliff and Garavogue. Sea fishing: Sligo Bay.
**Bathing** Mullaghmore, Rosses Point, Strandhill.
**Golf** Rosses Point Golf Club, 18-hole course. Tel: (071) 77186.
Strandhill Golf Club, 18-hole course. Tel: (071) 68188.
**Horse riding** Moneygold Riding Centre. Tel: (071) 63337.
**Sailing/Yachting** Sligo Yacht Club, Rosses Point. Tel: (071) 77168.

## INFORMATION
Sligo Tourist Office.
Tel: (071) 61201.

## OTHER PLACES TO SEE
**Cairn's Hill Forest Park** On top of Cairn's Hill is a tomb and a view across to a second tomb on the peak of Belvoir Hill.
**Creevykeel Court Tomb** Built between 3500 and 3000 BC. Entrance leads to oval open-air courtyard and two burial chambers.
**Gleniff Horseshoe Drive** Scenic route in Dartry Mountains north of Benbulbin.
**Mullaghmore** Fishing village and holiday centre with 2m beach: nearby is Classie Bawn Castle (private), former home of Lord Louis Mountbatten.
**Rosses Point** W.B. and Jack Yeats spent their summers here, now a resort with two beaches, golf club and yacht club.
**Strandhill** Seaside village and holiday resort with hard sand beaches.
**Streedagh Strand** Three ships of the Spanish Armada were wrecked here in 1588; wreckage is still visible occasionally. Good beaches and extensive sand dunes, and caves at southern end where fossils can be collected.
**Wildlife Bird Reserve** Near Lissadell House, on road to Carney; home to Ireland's largest colony of barnacle geese and other wildfowl.

## WALKS
**Knocknarea** Signposted walking route to Maeve's Mound.

## Carrowmore Bronze Age Cemetery/ Relig Meigiliotach an Cheathrú
This was the largest cemetery of megalithic tombs in Ireland, and the second biggest in Europe, after Carnac, in France. Yet in 1983 it was threatened by plans to turn it into a rubbish tip. Only after Supreme Court action was the cemetery saved.

About 60 tombs, a variety of dolmens, stone circles and passage-graves dot the site, spread over an area roughly half a mile wide and 1½ miles long, from north to south. Many consist of a stone burial chamber which contained cremated remains – cremation was common in prehistoric Ireland – topped by a roof cap and surrounded by a circle of large stones. Radiocarbon tests on samples from one tomb date it to around 4000 BC.

Archaeologists believe there were once as many as 150 tombs on this limestone plateau. But farming and sand and gravel quarrying over the years reduced the number, even before the rubbish-dump proposal nearly put an end to it.

## Cooldrumman
A rare and bloody battle over the copyright of a book took place at this spot in AD 561. The cause was St Columba's refusal to return to St Finian a copy of a psalter he had made from Finian's original, after a ruling in Finian's favour by High King Diarmuid, who declared 'To every cow its calf, and to every book its copy'. Columba took to arms to defend his copy, and in the Battle of the Books the rival monks clashed and more than 2000 died. Columba won the battle, but he was so consumed with guilt that he fled – or was banished – to Scotland to convert the heathen.

## Drumcliff/Droim Chliabh
At the foot of Benbulbin mountain is the village where poet and dramatist William Butler Yeats is buried, in the cemetery of the Protestant church. His grandfather had been rector of the church from 1811 to 1846 and Yeats asked to be buried here. Four months before he died in France in 1939, Yeats cited the spot in a poem:

*Under bare Ben Bulben's head*
*In Drumcliff churchyard Yeats is laid.*
*An ancestor was rector there*
*Long years ago, a church stands near,*
*By the road an ancient cross.*
*No marble, no conventional phrase;*
*On limestone quarried near the spot*
*By his command these words are cut;*
*Cast a cold eye*
*On life, on death,*
*Horseman, pass by!*

A simple tombstone engraved with the poem's last three lines marks the great poet's final resting place. Yeats was first buried at Roquebrune in the south of France, where he used to spend the winter, and where he died. But in accordance with his final wish his remains were brought to Drumcliff in 1948.

Around AD 575 a monastery was founded at Drumcliff, but it is now, unfortunately, bisected by the Sligo-Donegal road. But there remain the stump of a Round Tower, some walls and a 10th-century sculpted High Cross, the 'ancient cross' in Yeats's poem. The only High Cross in County Sligo, it has scenes from the Old Testament carved into its east face and images from the New Testament on its west face.

PIPES FOR ST PATRICK *A young piper joins the parade through Sligo to celebrate St Patrick's Day, on March 17.*

'BARE BEN BULBEN' *According to legend it was on the slopes of this limestone plateau that Diarmuid, who had eloped with the fiancée of the hero Finn MacCool, met his death.*

## A VOICE FOR CELTIC TRADITION

William Butler Yeats was born in Dublin in 1865, but spent much of his childhood in north Sligo, whose magical scenery and stirring legends he wove into his writing.

After a period at Dublin's Metropolitan School of Art (his father John and his brother Jack were noted artists), he concentrated on writing. His first poems were published when he was just 20. There followed a collection of Irish folk tales and his first book of poetry, *The Wanderings of Oisin and Other Poems*. Yeats soon became the leader of a group of writers who sought to preserve Ireland's ancient Celtic legends and myths. With Lady Gregory, a patron of fine arts, he founded the Irish National Theatre Society in 1902. His play *On Baile's Strand* opened the Abbey Theatre in Dublin.

For a time Yeats was drawn into nationalist politics, influenced by Maude Gonne, with whom he fell in love after meeting her in 1889. But she rejected his marriage proposal, and in 1917 he married Georgie Hyde-Lees. In 1922 he became a member of the Irish Senate.

Yeats's poetry earned him a central place on the world's literary stage, and in 1923 he was awarded the Nobel Prize for Literature. He died in France in 1939, and was reburied in County Sligo in 1948.

### Innishmurray/Inis Muirígh

About 4 miles off Sligo's untamed northern coast lies an uninhabited, windswept island that contains one of the best-preserved early Christian monasteries in Ireland. The monastery was founded by St Molaise in the 6th century and destroyed by the Vikings in 807. Three churches remain, enclosed within a 13ft high dry-stone wall, or cashel. The beehive hut was once the school.

The 200 acre island is also dotted with about 50 stone memorials, at which pilgrims performed the Stations of the Cross until 1948. Ironically, Innishmurray is also famous for its 'cursing stones' – used to cast ills upon enemies.

Boats to Innishmurray can be hired from Mullaghmore or Rosses Point.

ST MOLAISE *The wooden statue that once stood on Innishmurray is now in the National Museum, Dublin.*

### Knocknarea/Cnoc na Riabh

One of Sligo's most popular hikes is the path up the south-east flank of 1078ft Knocknarea, the 'Hill of the Kings'. At the summit is a 35ft high passage-grave and cairn, a 5000-year-old tomb which gives the mountain its characteristic cup-shaped peak. The tomb is estimated to consist of 40,000 stones and has a 200ft base, sloping to 100ft at its top.

Popular belief has it that this is the tomb of Queen Maeve, the legendary queen of Connaught, who features strongly in Celtic mythology. Archaeologists think it was more likely to have been built by Stone Age farmers around 3000 BC. However, the site has not yet been excavated, and no one is certain of its origin.

### Lissadell

On the northern shore of Drumcliff Bay is a Grecian Revival mansion, the only stately home in County Sligo open to visitors. It was built in 1832 for the Gore-Booth family and is still home to descendants of Sir Henry Gore-Booth (1843-1900), the Arctic explorer.

MONASTIC SECLUSION *A stone wall 13ft high surrounds St Molaise's monastery on the island of Innishmurray. The largest enclosure contains the ruined church, and behind it is a beehive hut which used to be the schoolhouse.*

The mansion is elegant but run down, with water-stained walls, peeling paint, and some of its glorious paintings and antiques in desperate need of restoration. But it is a treasure trove filled with the family's memorabilia and a window into Ireland's past.

The poet Eva Gore-Booth (1870-1926) and her sister Constance, later Countess Markievicz (1884-1927), grew up in Lissadell and were immortalised by Yeats in a poem:

*The light of evening, Lissadell,*
*Great windows open to the south,*
*Two girls in silk kimonos, both*
*Beautiful, one a gazelle.*

Constance became an Irish Republican activist and achieved fame as a leader of the 1916 Uprising. She was condemned to death for her part in it, but was later reprieved. She was the first woman to be elected to the British House of Commons, but took her seat in the Dáil (the Irish parliament) instead.
**Opening times** *June to mid-Sept, Mon-Sat 10am-4.15pm. Tel: (071) 63150.*

### Lough Gill/Loch Gile

The tiny island of Innisfree, known to many from Yeats's poem *The Lake Isle of Inisfree*, lies in the south-east corner of Lough Gill – a long lake surrounded by thickly wooded hills. There is little to see on the island itself, but the 24 mile Lough Gill Circuit gives glimpses of the lake and its islands, and includes the restored Georgian estate of Hazelwood, Half Moon Bay sculpture trail, a holy well and several tranquil picnic sites.

### Sligo/Sligeach

The River Garavogue cuts through the town on its way from Lough Gill to the sea. In the 9th century a settlement grew around the ford here, which was considered the gateway between Connaught and Ulster.

The Normans realised the importance of Sligo in their campaigns against the Irish, and the town grew rapidly after Maurice Fitzgerald, an Anglo-Norman lord, built a castle to guard the crossing in 1245. Numerous battles between the Irish and the Normans, and among the Irish chieftains themselves, took place during the following centuries, and the town fell to Cromwell's forces in 1645. Nothing remains of the castle, and the City Hall now stands on the site.

Modern Sligo is a marketing centre, and the largest town in the north-west of Ireland. Little, apart from Sligo Abbey, survives from

THE LIFFEY SWIM *One of Sligo's celebrated sons was the painter Jack Butler Yeats. He typically painted scenes from Irish life, such as this crowd of spectators watching a swimming race down the River Liffey in Dublin, and used a loose, expressionistic style.*

medieval days. The abbey was built by Fitzgerald for the Dominicans in 1252. It was burnt after a candle was overturned in 1414 and further damaged during the 1641 rebellion. Legend says that worshippers saved the abbey's silver bell, which now lies at the bottom of Lough Gill, where only those free from sin can hear it when it peals.

The nave, choir, arched tower and three sides of the cloister of the abbey church still stand. The choir, with its eight lancet windows, dates from the 13th century. Below is the high altar, the only example of a sculpted altar to survive in an Irish monastic church.

SLIGO SCENE *A colourful row of houses lines the River Garavogue that cuts through the town.*

Several of Sligo's 18th and 19th-century buildings were described by Yeats as having 'a kind of dignity in their utilitarianism'. These include the City Hall, the courthouse, St John's Church and the Catholic cathedral.

The Sligo Art Gallery includes a collection of watercolours, oils, and drawings by Yeats's father, John (1839-1922), and 27 works by his brother Jack, an artist of international renown. The gallery also contains paintings by modern Irish artists such as Paul Henry, Evie Hone and George Russell.

The most famous member of the talented Yeats family, William Butler, is commemorated in the Yeats Memorial Museum, a room in the Sligo County Museum and Art Gallery adjacent to the Library. It has a complete collection of Yeats's poems from 1889 to 1936, various editions of other writings and some unpublished letters. There is also the citation for his Nobel Prize for Literature. Tourism has to some extent overtaken Yeats, with key rings for sale featuring his profile, a sandwich bar that bears his name, Yeats pubs and even a W.B.'s Coffee Shop whose motto is 'Poetry in Food'.
**Sligo Art Gallery** *Mon-Fri 10am-5pm, Sat 10am-1pm. Tel: (071) 45847.*
**Sligo County Museum and Art Gallery** *June-Sept, Tues-Sat (Museum, Mon-Sat) 10.30am-4.30pm; Apr, May and Oct, Tues, Thur and Sat 10.30am-12.30pm. Nov-Mar by arrangement. Tel: (071) 42212.*

# POETS AND STORYTELLERS

### The literary fruits of this fertile land

'If you want to know Ireland, body and soul, you must read its poems and stories.' These words were written a century ago by William Butler Yeats, Ireland's towering poet and most famous man of letters. The advice is as good today as it was then, for Irish literature has long offered an unparalleled introduction to the island and its people.

FROM BARD TO PLAYWRIGHT The earliest Irish literature grew out of a thriving oral tradition where verses were composed by a hereditary class of professional poets, the aristocratic *filí*. It was not until the 5th century, when Christian missionaries introduced the Roman alphabet to Ireland, that these verses were written down. Most dealt with historical or religious topics.

In 'The Golden Age of Irish Literature', from 600 to 1200, the legends of ancient Ireland were recorded in great heroic sagas. In a colourful mix of narrative prose and verse, these tales – usually based on oral tradition – detailed the exploits of such heroes as Cuchulainn, Finn MacCool, Ossian, Deirdre and Queen Maeve, and told of war, death, love, famine and madness. Hundreds of these tales have survived, thanks to the medieval monks who laboriously recorded them in collections such as *The Book of the Dun Cow* and *The Book of Leinster*.

By the 1700s the English influence was paramount and was being reflected in Ireland's literature, by writers who were increasingly using English rather than Irish. One of the most important was Jonathan Swift, Dean of St Patrick's Cathedral in Dublin. His most famous work, *Gulliver's Travels*, is a biting satire on the vices of mankind. In another work he wrote that: 'All government without the consent of the governed is the very essence of slavery.'

After Swift, in the late 18th century, two Irish-born playwrights became known, among others, writing for the English stage: Oliver Goldsmith, who wrote the play *She Stoops to Conquer*, and Richard Brinsley Sheridan, whose plays include *The School for Scandal*. Both had moved to England and wrote primarily for English audiences, but both were deeply influenced by their Irish background.

THE IRISH RENAISSANCE During the early 19th century, Irish novelists and poets increasingly drew their inspiration from their countrymen and their roots. In *Castle Rackrent*, Maria Edgeworth portrayed the excesses of wasteful Irish landlords, while John and Michael Banim drew on the rich heritage of the Irish peasantry in *Tales of the O'Hara Family*. Musician and poet Thomas Moore became internationally famous as the national poet of Ireland with his patriotic and romantic poems set to traditional Irish folk songs.

Nationalism also played a major role in the late 19th-century literary phenomenon that has come to be known as the Irish Renaissance. Spearheaded by Yeats, this movement sought both to create a new national literature from purely Irish roots and to expand the political consciousness of the long-oppressed 'sons of Ireland'. Gathering other like-minded writers around him, Yeats proclaimed: 'Every Irish writer must either express Ireland or exploit her.' The movement was both a literary and political success. It gave birth to the Irish National Theatre Society whose Abbey Theatre produced plays by Yeats, Sean O'Casey, John Synge and others. It also played a part in inspiring the uprising against the British in 1916 that contributed to civil war and eventual independence from Britain. Ireland would never be the same. As Yeats wrote in a poem about the rebellion: 'A terrible beauty is born.'

Other writers chose to go farther afield to produce their work. Playwrights Oscar Wilde and George Bernard Shaw left their native Ireland to write for the British stage. Shaw once noted: 'As long as Ireland produces men with sense enough to leave her, she does not exist in vain.' Disenchanted with Ireland's strict religious and nationalistic attitudes, James Joyce moved to Europe. There he published *A Portrait of the Artist as a Young Man*, *Ulysses* and *Finnegans Wake*, which revolutionised the literary style and structure of the novel. Later, the novelist and dramatist

Samuel Beckett left Ireland and went to Paris where he joined Joyce as his personal secretary in 1938. In an effort to strip his works, such as *Waiting for Godot*, of any nationality or particular style, Beckett often wrote them first in French and then translated them into English. Like Shaw and Yeats before him, Beckett was awarded the Nobel Prize for Literature.

Among other modern Irish writers, Liam O'Flaherty, Frank O'Connor, Flann O'Brien and Sean O'Faoláin have based much of their writing on the activities of everyday Irish people. And some, such as Brendan Behan,

SAMUEL BECKETT (1906-89) *Among the self-exiled writer's plays is* Waiting for Godot.

BRENDAN BEHAN (1923-64) *A Republican activist, his experiences fill many of his works.*

MULTIPLYING WILDE *Max Beerbohm's caricature of Oscar Wilde (left) could have been inspired by Wilde's statement 'The only way to intensify personality is to multiply it', and depicts the many facets of the writer. Born in Dublin in 1856, Wilde adopted Englishness like no other Englishman, yet his eccentricities were considered at the time as 'peculiarly Irish'.*

W.B. YEATS AND THE IRISH THEATRE *Edward Dulac's ink, pencil and watercolour cartoon of Yeats (above) surrounds him with symbols of Ireland – a shamrock, a man and woman in 'traditional' Irish dress, and a harp. They refer to his Irish nationalism and his creation of a native Irish theatre, in the Abbey Theatre, Dublin, founded in 1904.*

were fiercely nationalistic, writing in Irish as well as English.

A powerful creative force, at least 2000 years old, has given Ireland a rich body of national literature quite out of proportion to its size. And it thrives still. The international renown of Ireland's writers today – from the poet Seamus Heaney to the playwrights Brian Friel and Frank McGuinness and the novelist Jennifer Johnston – serves to remind the world that the spark of Ireland's literary genius shows no sign of diminishing.

SEAMUS HEANEY *(b.1939) He is one of Ireland's leading contemporary poets.*

GEORGE BERNARD SHAW *(1856-1950) A playwright, he also wrote political essays.*

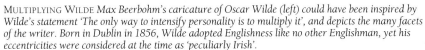

# NORTHERN IRELAND

NORTHERN Ireland has some of the most enchanting landscapes on the whole island – untouched by the strife that keeps the province in the news. From the rugged Atlantic-torn cliffs of Antrim in the north to the warm, wooded shores of Carlingford Lough in the south, this region offers all the variety of historical charm and fine scenery that can be found on the other side of the border.

In the ancient province of Ulster, Celtic kings and a queen ruled from Eamhain Macha, west of Armagh. Their palace, said to have been protected by the legendary Red Branch Knights, is now just a mound. Ulster is also where tradition has it that St Patrick first landed as a missionary, beside Strangford Lough, in about AD 432. He built his first church nearby, at Saul, and founded a monastery at Armagh, which became the ecclesiastical centre of Ireland. St Patrick is said to be buried at Downpatrick Cathedral.

After St Patrick, Christianity spread fast. Churches and monasteries sprang up throughout the north – only to become easy prey for generations of Vikings, who were hit-and-run raiders. The invaders who followed them, the Normans, came to stay. The Normans built castles like those at Carrickfergus and Dundrum to control the land they seized. But they never gained complete control, and for 400 years Norman barons and Irish chieftains ruled their fiefdoms – more or less under the English Crown.

Then Queen Elizabeth decided to impose more direct rule from England. In the ensuing war Ulster put up strong resistance to her armies, but lost. Rebel lands were confiscated and from 1603 onwards were heavily planted with Scottish and English settlers. The result is that today the majority of Northern Ireland's population is Protestant. Under the Anglo-Irish Treaty of 1921, Ulster was divided. Six counties – Antrim, Down, Armagh, Tyrone, Fermanagh and Londonderry – formed Northern Ireland, and three – Donegal, Cavan and Monaghan – were incorporated in what later became the Republic of Ireland.

MUSSENDEN TEMPLE *The neoclassical folly hugs the edge of the rugged Antrim cliffs.*

SOOTHING CONTOURS *The Mourne Mountains roll across Down, pinpricked with wild flowers and grazed by sheep.*

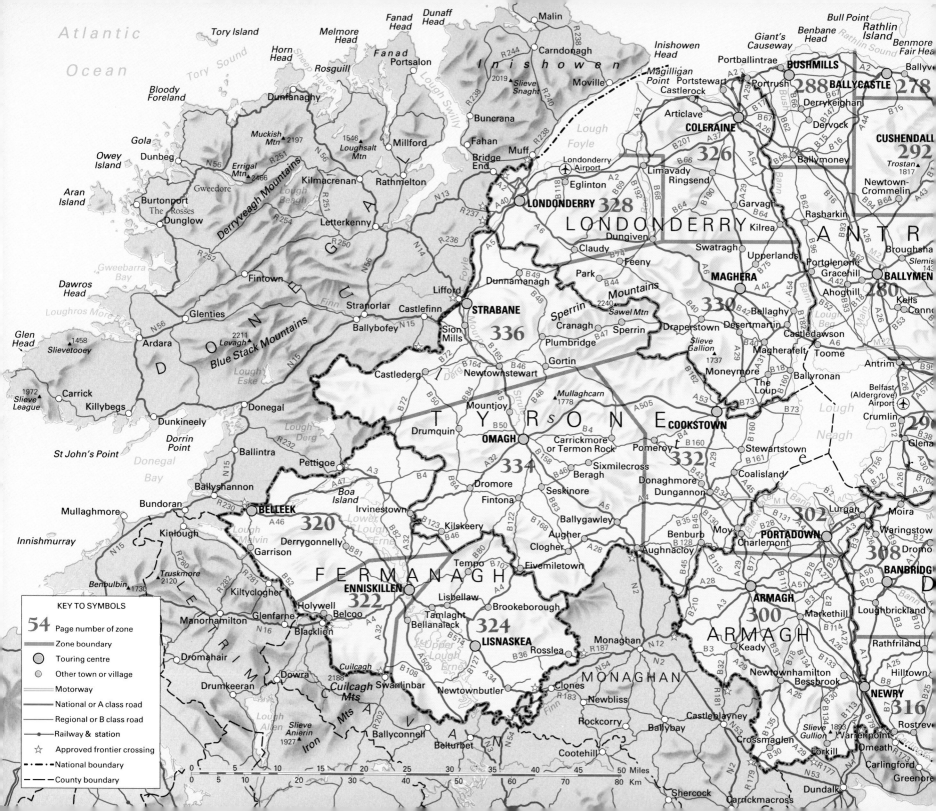

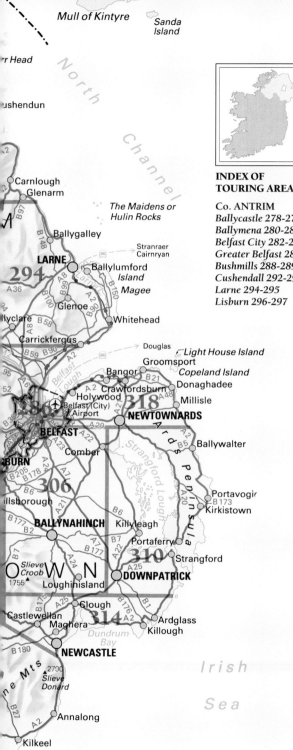

GLENARRIFF FALLS *The Glenarriff river tumbles between wooded banks, in one of the nine glens of Antrim.*

But Northern Ireland has its far more peaceful and beautiful side, like the Mourne Mountains, with their famous Silent Valley, and slopes rolling down to the pretty beaches and fishing villages of the Down coastline. To the north, the glens of County Antrim run down to a coastline of exceptional beauty. And near the northern tip is one of the great natural wonders of the world – The Giant's Causeway – where cooling lava has solidified into a series of stepped polygonal columns of such geometrical precision that people assumed they must have been placed there by a giant. Fermanagh, in the south-west, is Northern Ireland's lakeland, where the sprawling path of the River Erne swells into Lower and Upper Lough Erne. Several of the islands in the loughs contain early Christian relics, including the monastery and Round Tower of Devenish Island, and a set of mysterious weather-beaten statues on White Island.

North of the lake country are the sparsely populated moorlands and forests of County Tyrone, bordered to their north by the softly contoured Sperrin Mountains, and County Derry. Londonderry stands at the head of the broad estuary of the River Foyle. The city's great walls still carry the cannon that helped them withstand the siege of 1689.

Belfast, Northern Ireland's largest city with a population of just over 360,000, was built with 19th-century industrial money, giving it a marked Victorian character. It is beautifully set at the head of a sea lough ringed by hills. A few miles east of the city is Strangford Lough, a virtually landlocked arm of the sea and one of the richest maritime habitats in Europe; it is also the gathering place for thousands of migra-tory birds including the rare pale-bellied brent geese. Lough Neagh, west of the city, is the largest lake in the British Isles. Five of Northern Ireland's six counties – all but Fermanagh – meet around the lake.

Across the whole region the old Anglo-Irish 'big houses' have survived far better than in the Republic, where many were destroyed in the Civil War of 1922-3. A number are open to the public, including Castle Coole and Florence Court in County Fermanagh; and in County Down, Castle Ward near Portaferry, and Mount Stewart, near Newtownards. Mount Stewart also has one of the finest gardens in the British Isles, rivalled by nearby Rowallane. Indeed, the whole province is richly endowed with flourishing gardens that thrive in its mild climate.

# MacDonnell Castle Country

*The jagged coast of north Antrim is a wild vista of escarpments of layered rock sweeping majestically down to the shore, where they end abruptly in broad sandy beaches or reach out as rocky promontories. These outcrops are studded with the ruins of 16th and 17th-century castles, most of which were strongholds of the local MacDonnell clan. From these cliffs Irish chieftains lit bonfires to signal to their Scottish cousins 13 miles away that they were at war and needed help.*

## Ballycastle/Baile an Chaistil

Every year Ballycastle, the largest town in the Antrim glens, overflows with market stalls and herds of animals for the Ould Lammas Fair, Ireland's oldest and most popular fair. The fair has probably been held since the 1400s – and at first near the 15th-century Dunineny Castle, since the name means 'Fort of the Fair'. The castle ruins are scattered on the cliffs above the bay. The fair is now held on the last Monday and Tuesday of August in the town centre's Diamond, or square.

Sales of sheep and ponies are an important part of the fair, while the streets are filled

TRADITIONAL FARE *A Ballycastle lady sells the local delicacies of dried seaweed and yellow toffee at the annual Lammas Fair.*

with stalls overflowing with all kinds of goods. Traditionally sold at the Lammas Fair are 'dulse', an edible dried seaweed (also known as 'dillisk'), and 'yellow man' which is a bright yellow toffee, so hard that it often has to be broken with a hammer.

The fair has been immortalised in the song by local songwriter John Macauley (1873-1937):

*Did you treat your Mary Ann
To some dulse and Yellow Man
At the Ould Lammas Fair in Ballycastle – O?*

There is a plaque on the composer's house in Anne Street where he lived and worked as a bog-oak carver.

Ballycastle grew up around a castle built in 1625 by Sir Randal MacDonnell in the Diamond area of the town. In 1606 he obtained a charter enabling him to hold six fairs in the local area. The town was industrialised in the 18th century and a local landlord, Hugh Boyd, was responsible for much of its development. He built the imposing Protestant Holy Trinity Church in 1756, on the site of the old castle. The church is in the Doric style with a stone spire, and has a remarkable star-studded blue ceiling. It contains memorials to the Boyd family.

Boyd also leased the collieries, now disused, and constructed a harbour, now filled in for tennis courts. Glass, soap, salt and iron were all manufactured in the town during his time.

Ballycastle has a good sandy beach and a modern harbour where there is a memorial to Count Marconi and his assistant, George Kemp. From a cottage in Ballycastle they established radio contact with Rathlin Island in 1898, and with Lloyds Coastguard Station at Torr Head.

On the Ballycastle to Cushendall road is the state-owned Ballypatrick Forest where flat peat plains stretch for miles in a bleak landscape. A local lake, known as 'the vanishing lake' because of the sporadic and unexplained drop in its water level, is called Loughareema – 'the lake that ran away'.

Just outside Ballycastle, at Ballyvoy, is a sign for a scenic drive to Murlough Bay and Benmore, or Fair Head. This area, which is National Trust land, contains some of the most beautiful scenery in Antrim. Along the route is a stone cross memorial to the Irish patriot Sir Roger Casement (1864-1916), a Ballymena man executed for treason by the British Government after he attempted to

edifice overlooking Rathlin Sound. Long cliff walk leads to remains of gatehouse built by Sorley Boy MacDonnell's brother, Colla Dubh, with good views to Rathlin.
**Lough na Cranagh** Largest of three lakes with crannog in the middle.

**EVENTS**
**Ballycastle Apple Fair** End Oct.
**Ballycastle-Coleraine Yacht Club Regatta** Aug.
**Ballycastle Irish Folk Dancing Festival** Oct/Nov.
**Fleadh Agus Rince** Irish Music and Dance Festival, Ballycastle, mid-June.
**Ould Lammas Fair** Ballycastle, end Aug.

**SPORT**
**Angling** Game fishing: Rivers Carey, Glenshesk and Margy.
**Golf** Ballycastle Golf Club, 18-hole course. Tel: (02657) 62536.
**Pony trekking** Watertop Open Farm and Trekking Centre. Tel: (02657) 62576.

**INFORMATION**
Ballycastle Tourist Information Office.
Tel: (02657) 62024.

**OTHER PLACES TO SEE**
**Ballycastle Forest** Forest on NE slopes of Knocklayd Mountain, with nature trail.
**Benmore** Cliff 665ft high with glorious walk across heathery scrub; peregrine falcons and buzzards soar in the skies above.
**Carrickarade** Swinging bridge of wooden slats and wires, 80ft above the sea, connects mainland to tiny island 60ft away, where commercial salmon fishery has been established for two centuries. The bridge is taken down in Sept when salmon fishing season ends and is put back in Apr.
**Kinbane Castle** Outside Ballycastle; 16th-century

MUSIC IN THE SQUARE *Musicians hold a 'fleadh cheoil' in Ballycastle's Diamond.*

guide German ships into County Kerry in 1916, to stage an Irish rebellion. Access is by a steep path known as The Grey Man's Path.

Near Ballycastle, also, is Corrymeela ('Hill of Harmony') Peace and Reconciliation Centre. It was founded in 1965 as a neutral venue at which Catholics and Protestants could meet to heal sectarian divisions.

### Bonamargy Friary/Bun na Margy

At the meeting point of Glenshesk and Glentaisie lies the 15th-century friary, burial place of the MacDonnells. It is reached on foot down a pathway from the main road. The friary was built by the local ruler, Rory MacQuillan, who was defeated by the Mac-Donnells at the Battle of Orra in 1559. South of the altar is a vault which Randal Mac-Donnell built for the burial of his family. A 17th-century descendant of Rory, a prophetess known as Julia the Black Nun, requested that her remains be placed at the entrance so that people would walk over her and thereby help her to earn extra penance. The bones of one of the most famous MacDonnell chieftains, Sorley Boy, who died in 1590, are contained at Bonamargy.

### Rathlin Island/Reachlainn

A 45 minute boat trip away from Ballycastle harbour is Rathlin Island, said in legend to have been dropped into the sea by the mother of the legendary hero Finn MacCool, on her way to Scotland. The habitation of this 6 mile long, L-shaped island is ancient – flint implements and a porcellanite factory that may be 6000 years old have been discovered on the west side.

The Kebble Nature Reserve at Bull Point, on the west of the island, has tens of thousands of birds, up to 175 species nesting in the 350ft high cliffs and sea stacks. Puffins, kittiwakes, razorbills, guillemots and numerous other seabirds perch on the ledges near an 'upside-down' lighthouse, so called because it has its light at the bottom rather than the top.

To the east of the island, near another lighthouse, is the cave where the Scottish leader Robert Bruce hid after being defeated by the English at Perth in 1306. Watching a spider in the cave spinning its web taught him the virtue of patience, and he later returned to Scotland to become victorious at the Battle of Bannockburn.

Rathlin was allegedly the first place in Ireland to be raided by Vikings in the 8th

KINBANE CASTLE *Only the gatehouse remains of this 16th-century castle built by Colla Dubh MacDonnell, spectacularly sited on Rathlin Sound.*

DAUNTING PROSPECT *A rope bridge 80ft above the sea joins Carrickarade on the mainland to a salmon fishery on an island.*

century. Legend recalls that the King of Norway, Nabghoden, sent a delegation to Ireland to find him a wife. On Rathlin they found Taisie Taobhgheal, daughter of Donn, the King of the Island, who was already betrothed to Cobhghal. They tried to take her away by force as the wedding celebrations were underway, and in the ensuing battle the Norwegian king was killed. Land on the mainland was given to the newlyweds to build a palace in the area now known as Glentaisie.

In 1551, Sorley Boy MacDonnell captured Rathlin, but he was ousted from it by English forces in 1575, and they massacred the islanders. In 1642, the Campbells killed many of the next wave of islanders by brutally throwing them to their deaths over the cliffs.

A monastic site was established by St Comgall in the 6th century at Church Quarter, near the harbour, where two churches, one Catholic, one Anglican, now stand. An amenity centre was opened on the island in 1990, built with money donated by the millionaire businessman Richard Branson who landed in his balloon near the island and was saved by the island's rescue service.

# A Volcanic Landscape

*Threading through prosperous agricultural land interspersed with thick forest plantations, the glorious River Bann, Northern Ireland's longest river, teems with eels, trout and salmon. Slemish mountain, a small, extinct volcano, dominates the rainwashed skyline around Ballymena, once a busy linen-producing area. Historic sites abound and nature trails wind through the state-owned forests that stretch towards the shores of Lough Neagh.*

### Ballymena/Baile Meadhaonach

The geographic centre of County Antrim is Ballymena, on the River Braid. In the 13th century, Ballymena became part of the estate of the local clan, the O'Neills, but in 1626 it was handed over to William Adair, a Scottish planter, with a charter to hold regular fairs and markets. The Adairs developed it as a prosperous textile centre, and it is now a busy market town, surrounded by some of the richest pastureland in Ireland. Its market, held on Saturdays, is 350 years old.

Ballymena was dubbed the 'city of the seven towers' by Sir Alexander Adair (1811-86), afterwards Lord Waveney, who from a nearby hill picked out seven landmarks – four churches, the old town hall, the spinning mill and the castle. Only four of these structures remain, and the Seven Towers Leisure Centre stands on the site of the original Adair Castle.

The local grey basalt rock is used in many of the town's buildings including the Gothic Revival St Patrick's Church of Ireland, in Castle Street, built in the 1850s. In Church Entry is the oldest Protestant church in the town, Old Parish Church, which retains its 1721 tower and has a 19th-century graveyard. In marked contrast to the surrounding dark buildings is the 1924 Town Hall built in white Portland stone, with the borough's bright coat of arms, featuring seven towers, over its entrance. It also has an impressive copper dome. At the foot of Bridge Street is Braid Water Mill, once a centre of the linen industry.

Remains of Norman mottes, or earth mounds, can be seen around Ballymena, with a particularly fine one at Harryville, on the banks of the River Braid south of Ballymena. The rectangular bailey stands to the east of the motte.

### Gracehill/Baile Uí Chinneide

Drive into this village and you go back in time to the 18th century. Gracehill was founded as a Moravian settlement in 1746 by Reverend John Cennick and its streets are still lined with the original cottages and terraced houses of black basalt, with latticed and shuttered windows. Traditional street lamps and hanging flower baskets decorate the square village green, which is overlooked by an 18th-century school and a church with a square clock tower and fine stained-glass windows. The adjoining cemetery still follows the Moravian custom of separating the graves of men and women.

### Lough Neagh/Loch nEathach

Six rivers converge to form the largest inland lake in the British Isles. Lough Neagh covers

## OTHER PLACES TO SEE

**Bracknamuckley Forest** Walking trails and picnic areas.

**Connor** One of the oldest ecclesiastical dioceses in Ireland. Scene of Anglo-Norman battle in 1315, won by Scottish Edward Bruce, brother of Robert.

**Cullybackey** Ancestral home of Chester Alan Arthur, President of United States (1881-5); whitewashed, thatched farmhouse restored with authentic details. Craft demonstrations in summer. Open May-Sept, Mon-Sat 2-5pm. Tel: (0266) 44111.

**Kells** Ruins of an ancient abbey.

**Movanagher Fish Farm** Tours of hatchery and talk on life cycle of trout. Mon-Fri 10am-4.30pm, exc Bank Holidays. Tel: (0265) 40533.

## EVENTS

**Ahoghill Civic Week and Pipebands Championships** June.

**Autumn flower and produce show** Ballymena, Sept.

**Ballymena Arts Festival** During Oct.

**County Antrim Agricultural Show** Ballymena, June.

**Northern Ireland Game and Country Fair** Shane's Castle, July.

**Point-to-Point meeting** Galgorm, Mar.

**Spring flower and produce show** Ballymena, Apr.

**Steam Working Rally** Shane's Castle, May.

**Vintage and Classic Car Rally** Shane's Castle, mid-June.

## SPORT

**Angling** Coarse fishing: Rivers Bann, Braid, Clough and Main. Game fishing: Rivers Bann, Braid, Clough and Main, Kilgad Lake and Dungonnell Dam.

**Golf** Ballymena Golf Club, 18-hole course. Tel (0266) 861487/861207.

## INFORMATION

Ballymena Tourist Information. Tel: (0266) 44111/653663.

AUGUSTINE HENRY MEMORIAL GROVE *The grove in the forest outside Portglenone is dedicated to a 19th-century pioneer in forestry.*

153sq miles and reaches a depth of 45ft. According to legend, the lough is the water-filled hollow left after the hero Finn MacCool lifted a piece of land and hurled it into the sea, where it became the Isle of Man.

The waters are said by locals to have medicinal properties. However, the lough is most famous for its eels, the source of a thriving industry which yields 10 tons of eels a day. It is believed that eel fishing was carried out in the Iron Age by Celtic settlers, and traces of boats and implements have been found at nearby Newferry. A local delicacy is eels stewed with a white sauce.

## Portglenone/Port Chluain Eoghain

The River Bann divides this village in two, with part of the population living in County Londonderry and the rest in County Antrim. They are connected by a wide bridge.

Black basalt stone has been used in many of the buildings in the village, particularly the churches, such as the 18th-century Protestant church that dominates the scene. A plaque on Main Street marks the place where a local boy, Timothy Eaton, learned his trade as a draper in the mid-19th century. An industrious boy, he worked 16 hours a day and slept under the counter. He later emigrated to Canada and established a chain of retail stores bearing his name.

South of the village is a Cistercian monastery, founded in the 1950s in a Georgian mansion. The monks, in their flowing brown-and-white robes, can be seen working the land and in their gift shop, which sells organic flour, jams, souvenirs and linen. There is also a tea shop.

## Shane's Castle

Near Antrim is the 16th-century stronghold of Shane O'Neill, Shane's Castle, which is still inhabited by O'Neills. The name given to the castle is believed to have originated when James 1 of England granted it to Shane McBrian O'Neill. The O'Neills have one of the most traceable family histories in Europe, dating back to AD 360, and are descendants of the Royal family of Tara, who ruled in Ulster from the 5th century until the submission of Hugh O'Neill in 1603.

The castle was badly damaged by fire in 1816 but still retains a number of original features. The conservatory, designed by John Nash in 1812, houses a collection of camellias and has an underground passage. Some of the castle ruins are preserved in the lakeside

SLEMISH MOUNTAIN *Pilgrims climb this extinct volcano every year on St Patrick's Day.*

demesne which also has a deer park, bird sanctuary and nature trails.

In 1971 Shane's Castle Railway was opened, with a narrow-gauge locomotive that used to work in the 19th century. It runs for 1½ miles along the shores of Lough Neagh. **Railway and Nature Reserve** *End Mar-Aug, Sun and Bank Holidays; June, Wed also; July and Aug, Wed, Sat also. 12.30-6pm. Tel: 08494 63380.*

## Slemish mountain/Sliabh Mis

The small, extinct volcano, Slemish mountain (1433ft), visible from miles around, is best reached through Broughshane in the Braid valley. Broughshane village has a thatched inn and a 19th-century Protestant church, St Patrick's, painted bright red in contrast with its dark grey stone.

It was on the slopes of Slemish that St Patrick, patron saint of Ireland, who introduced Christianity to its inhabitants, is said to have tended sheep and pigs as a youth. He had been captured as a slave from Britain in the 5th century, and was put to work for the local chieftain, Miluic.

### EEL FISHING

Toomebridge, at the north-easterly mouth of Lough Neagh where it meets the River Bann, has the largest eel fishery in Europe. Local fishermen, using traditional 'long lines' baited with up to 100 hooks, fish by night for 'brown' or maturing eels. On a good night, up to 4000 eels can be caught by the 200 boats on the lough. The lines are lifted at dawn and the eels are collected each morning by lorry from the fishery, sorted, packed and sent for export to Holland and Germany, where they are smoked and sold as delicacies. In autumn, mature 'silver eels' make their way down the River Bann to their spawning ground in the Sargasso Sea near Bermuda. They only migrate on the darkest nights of the month. Nets are spread at Toome to catch them, during a fishing period which is limited to ten days a month between August and December.

Eel larvae drift slowly towards Europe on the Gulf Stream, until, at the age of 2½ years, when they are almost 3in long, they reach the European coast. They metamorphose into elvers (young eels) in the sea, and then in May or June swim upriver to lakes and ponds. They can take between 11 and 14 years to mature.

# A City of Industry and Elegance

*Hills and mountains rise to the north and west of Northern Ireland's capital city, which stands at the mouth of the River Lagan that flows through the city. Belfast's name – 'béal feirste' in Irish, meaning 'mouth of the sandspit' – first appeared in the 15th century. The settlement dates from 1177, when the Anglo-Norman John de Courcy invaded Ulster and built a castle nearby, establishing his rule over south-eastern Ulster, east of the River Bann. But Belfast's history really begins in 1603, when the castle and lands of Belfast came into the possession of Sir Arthur Chichester, Governor of Carrickfergus, who planted the land with settlers from Devon and Scotland. Ten years later Belfast was granted corporation status, with the right to send members to the Parliament at Westminster.*

*Belfast's linen industry thrived in the 17th century, helped by the influx of Huguenots who fled there seeking refuge from religious persecution in France. The Huguenots also encouraged the intellectual and cultural life of the city, so much so that it became known as Ireland's 'Athens of the North'. The Industrial Revolution brought new prosperity in the 19th century, with engineering and shipbuilding among the main industries. Many fine buildings from this time grace the city still, and are reminders of its prosperous past.*

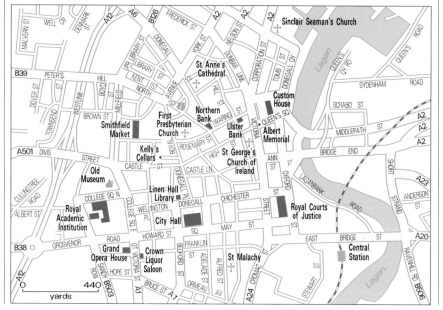

MISTY CITY *The Ormeau Bridge spans the steel-grey River Lagan that flows through Belfast.*

### The Albert Memorial

Belfast's answer to Big Ben in London is this huge clock tower, designed by William Barre in 1869. It flaunts Prince Albert in the flowing robes of the Order of the Garter, with four lions guarding the base. The tower leans slightly because its foundations are gradually sinking. It is not open to the public.

William Barre also designed Royal Avenue nearby, when in 1880 the city authorities decided to carve out a wide street in the centre, and lined it with buildings mainly in the Italianate palazzo style.

### St Anne's Cathedral

Once known as Belfast Cathedral, this Anglican cathedral was built between 1899 and 1927 on the site of the old parish church and still incorporates part of the original building. The cathedral is neo-Romanesque, 300ft long with a 120ft nave, and divided into six bays.

There are splendid mosaics above the West Door. The baptistry roof is made up of 150,000 pieces of glass representing The Creation and symbolising air, earth, fire and water, with the hand of God held in benediction above in a glorious sunburst of gold. The central dome is decorated with gold and silver mosaics with four seraphims holding a lamp, a chalice, a cross and a scroll.

Mosaics in the Chapel of the Holy Spirit celebrate the landing of St Patrick at Saul in AD 432, and the floor is laid with stones from every county in Ireland. The chapel's 85ft nave has a floor of maple and Irish marble and is lined with pillars whose capitals represent the 'occupations of mankind', among them Science, Industry, Healing and Womanhood.

### City Hall

Belfast became a city in 1888, and the city fathers commissioned the architect Brumwell

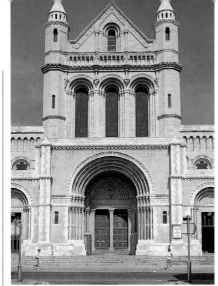

celebrates its traditional industries – spinning, weaving, shipbuilding and ropemaking.

The Council Chamber, Visitors' Gallery and Robing Room all have beautifully hand-carved oak panelling. The Great Hall is 120ft long and 57ft wide, with a lofty vaulted ceiling lit by stained-glass windows that depict sovereigns who have visited the city, and the shields of the Provinces of Ireland.

### The Crown Liquor Saloon

This 'gin palace' is undoubtedly one of the finest Victorian buildings in Belfast. Its exterior is decorated with colourful tiles. Inside it is a riot of stained and painted glass and tiles,

IMPOSING PORTALS *The superb west front of St Anne's Cathedral dominates Donegall Street.*

carved oak screens, gaslights, polished mahogany, glinting glass and gleaming brass pipes and taps. Heraldic lions and griffins crouch on top of the carved oak-panelled 'snugs', or booths.

The saloon was originally designed as a railway tavern, and has a glorious mosaic-tiled floor, and a ceiling with red-and-yellow arabesques in high relief. It was last restored in 1988, and is now owned by the National Trust, although it still functions as a public house. It is open daily during licensing hours. Tel: (0232) 325368.

### The Grand Opera House

With onion domes topping its façade, it is small wonder that Belfast's opera house in Great Victoria Street has earned the nickname

Thomas to build a city hall worthy of Belfast's new status. It was completed in 1906, on the site of the former White Linen Hall. Its 300ft long façade of Portland stone, with graceful columns and a splendid portico, dominate Donegall Square. Each of the four corners is surmounted by a tower, and a central copper dome rises dramatically to 173ft. The gardens around it include a Garden of Remembrance. The City Hall in Durban, South Africa, is an exact replica.

A grand stone entrance leads into a marble-lined octagonal vestibule with a memorial to Frederick Robert Chichester, Earl of Belfast (1827-53) and a floor richly decorated with black-and-white marble. An elegant staircase, of three different marbles, sweeps up to the principal landing. The domed ceiling has elaborate rococo plaster-work and below it seven stained-glass windows depict the history of Belfast Corporation. A mural by Belfast artist John Luke illustrates the founding of the city and

QUEEN OF BELFAST *A bronze figure symbolising Spinning sits at the foot of Queen Victoria's statue in front of City Hall.*

CITY HALL BAROQUE *The sumptuous domed ceiling of City Hall rises to a dizzying 173ft.*

JUNE IN BELFAST *Flower sellers outside City Hall enjoy the balmy air of a summer day.*

'the eastern palace'. It was lavishly designed in 1894 by Frank Matcham (1854-1920), the leading theatrical designer of the day, and the eastern theme is continued inside with an Asian motif in the ornate ceiling panels. Over the years the theatre deteriorated badly and finally closed in 1971, but a massive programme of restoration was begun in 1975, and in 1980 it reopened with a production of *Cinderella.*

Many famous performers have trodden the boards of this opera house in the past, including Pavlova, Orson Welles and Sarah Bernhardt. Today, international ballet, theatre and opera companies are restoring this *grande dame* to her former status.

THE CURTAIN RISES *The jester on the front of the Opera House (top) would have smiled when it reopened in 1980 with* Cinderella.

### Linen Hall Library

This building, at the north-west corner of Donegall Square, was originally a warehouse built by Charles Lanyon in 1864. It is the oldest library in the city and was begun in the White Linen Hall in 1788 as a public subscription organisation for the Belfast Society for Promoting Knowledge. The present building is of Scottish fire brick with Scrabo stone crossings, and the interior is of finely polished mahogany and oak. It houses what is probably the best collection of early Belfast-printed books in Ireland. Its 'Political Collection' is well known and contains more than 50,000 publications, which address every aspect of Northern Irish political life since 1966. And its genealogical records are available to people wishing to trace family trees.
**Opening times** *Mon, Tues, Wed, Fri 9.30am-6pm; Thur, 9.30am-8.30pm; Sat 9.30am-4pm. Tel: (0232) 321707.*

### First Presbyterian Church

Roger Mulholland, the local architect who designed Belfast's grid street plan and many of its fine buildings, created this elliptical Presbyterian church in Rosemary Street in 1783. Inside it has curved aisles and a radial plastered ceiling. A graceful staircase winds up to the pulpit, and the pews are made of mellow boxwood. The gallery is supported on wooden Corinthian columns. John Wesley, the evangelist and Methodist leader, preached here in 1789.

### Royal Academical Institution

A day school usually known as 'Inst', this was erected in 1810-14 for well-heeled medical and science students. It is based on the designs of Sir John Soane, the Neoclassicist architect. The poet-physician William Drennan (1754-1820) thought the school was a place 'where the youth of Ireland might sit together on these benches and learn to love and esteem one another'. Drennan helped to found the United Irishmen Society, and it was he who first coined the phrase 'emerald isle', to describe his beloved Ireland. The school can be visited, by appointment. Tel: (0232) 240461.

### St George's Church of Ireland

This was the first Protestant parish church to be built in Belfast, in 1819. Its handsome Corinthian façade came from Ballyscullion House in County Londonderry, one of three palaces built by the Earl-Bishop of Derry.

VICTORIAN GIN PALACE *The Crown Liquor Saloon (top and above), though now a museum piece, is still a working bar.*

JOHNSTON'S BROLLY *There's more than one way to advertise your wares on a street.*

STREET THEATRE *A juggler amuses passers-by.*

ST MALACHY'S CHURCH *The exuberant stucco ceiling resembles parasols twirling overhead.*

## OTHER PLACES TO SEE

**Custom House** Belfast's finest building, designed by Charles Lanyon in 1857. Mellow stone, with grand portico and sculpted pediment depicting Britannia flanked by a lion and unicorn, and supported by reclining Neptune and Mercury. Now VAT centre.

**Kelly's Cellars** Atmospheric 'singing' pub built about 1780, said to have been secret meeting place of the Society of United Irishmen, who also met in the roof of the First Presbyterian Church.

**Northern Bank** Mid-18th-century market house redesigned into Assembly Rooms in 1776, and later transformed into present palazzo-style building based on London's Reform Club.

**Old Museum** First purpose-built museum in Ireland, designed in 1831 in Greek Revival style. Now an arts centre and theatre.

**The Royal Courts of Justice** Famous for its 'Four Courts', in Chichester Street, built of Portland stone in 1933.

**Sinclair Seamen's Church** Presbyterian church designed by Charles Lanyon in 1853, furnished like a maritime museum, with port and starboard lights above the organ, ship's bell and compass rose, and model ships and lighthouse circling the ceiling. Services still held.

**Smithfield Market** For hunters of bric-a-brac and old books, behind Castle Court Shopping Centre.

**Ulster Bank** Designed by James Hamilton, Scottish architect, in 1860, dressed in yellow sandstone, and with the air of a Venetian palace.

### INFORMATION
Northern Ireland Tourist Board, 59 North Street, Belfast BT1 1ND. Belfast Tourist Information Centre. Tel: (0232) 246609.

285

# Greater Belfast

*During the 19th and early 20th centuries Belfast's industries boomed and people from the countryside flocked to the city seeking work in the shipyards, linen mills and factories. Terraces of two-up two-down houses were built to accommodate them. At the same time the city's flourishing cultural life was reflected in the building of such institutions as Queen's University and the Ulster Museum.*

### Belfast Castle

The Scottish Baronial pile that stands on the lower slopes of Cave Hill was begun in 1862 and completed in 1870, to replace Belfast's earlier castles that had burnt down in the 12th and 18th centuries. It was designed by W.H. Lynn for the 3rd Marquis of Donegall, and obviously with Scotland's Balmoral very much in mind.

A tower of six storeys dominates the building, and an elaborate staircase, added in 1894, winds upwards from attractive formal gardens. Inside the castle, the oak-panelled rooms, ornate fireplaces and a grand ballroom echo the lifestyle of the previous owners, including the 9th Lord Shaftesbury, who was Belfast's Lord Mayor in 1907. Lord Shaftesbury presented the castle

BELFAST CASTLE *The stately mansion stands on a hillside 400ft above the city.*

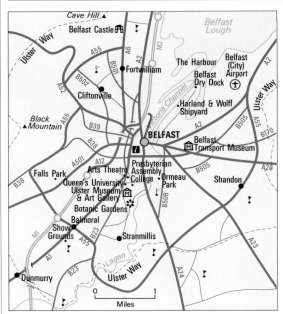

## EVENTS
**Belfast Marathon** May.
**Civic Festival** May.
**Lord Mayor's Show** Apr.
**Orangeman's Day** July 12.
**Royal Ulster Agricultural Show** Balmoral, May.
**Ulster Motorcycling Grand Prix World Championship** Aug.

## SPORT
**Angling** Coarse fishing: River Lagan.
**Boating** Belfast Lough.
**Golf** Balmoral Golf Club, 18-hole course. Tel: (0232) 381514.
Cliftonville Golf Club, 9-hole course. Tel: (0232) 744158.
Fortwilliam Golf Club, 18-hole course. Tel: (0232) 370770.
Ormeau Golf Club, 9-hole course. Tel: (0232) 641069.
Shandon Park Golf Club, 18-hole course. Tel: (0232) 401856.

## INFORMATION
Northern Ireland Tourist Board, 59 North Street, Belfast BT1 1ND.
Belfast Tourist Information Centre. Tel: (0232) 246609.

## OTHER PLACES TO SEE
**Arts Theatre** Botanic Avenue. Specialises in modern plays.
**Falls Park** At foot of Black Mountain; waterfalls, bridges, fishing and boating.
**Ormeau Park** Pretty walks on bank of River Lagan.
**Presbyterian Assembly College** Built 1853-5; housed the Northern Ireland Parliament in late 19th century.

and grounds to the city in 1934. It is now a restaurant. Tel: (0232) 776925.

### Belfast Transport Museum

The 1939 locomotive *Old Maeve*, the largest steam locomotive ever built in Ireland, is the museum's proudest possession. It stands amid an array of exhibits that includes early street trams and fire engines, vintage cars, motorbikes and 'penny-farthings'.
**Opening times** *Mon-Sat 10am-5pm. Tel: (0232) 451519.*

### Botanic Gardens

Set in more than 38 acres, the gardens are devoted to a glorious range of exotic and native plants. The Palm House is a superb structure of cast iron and curved glass panels. It was built between 1839 and 1852 by the Dublin iron founder Richard Turner, and is one of the earliest examples of its kind in Europe.

Opposite the Palm House a balcony overlooks the Tropical Ravine, a sunken, steamy glen of tropical plants.
**Opening times** *Gardens: dawn to dusk. Palm House and Tropical Ravine: Apr-Sept, Mon-Fri 10am-5pm; Oct-Mar, Mon-Fri 10am-4pm. Sat and Sun 2-5pm. Tel: (0232) 324902.*

LOFTY LIFTERS *Like giant goalposts Belfast's shipyard cranes dominate the city skyline.*

### The Harbour

The Port of Belfast lies nearly 12 miles from the sea, at the head of the deepwater Victoria Channel that runs from Belfast Lough. The quays stretch for 7 miles along the River Lagan, with the cross-channel ferry berths at Donegall Quay less than half a mile from the city centre.

In the 19th century, only Liverpool and London docks were larger. Today, ferries, colliers and container ships still make this one of the busiest ports in the United Kingdom. There are also four dry docks, including the 800ft Thompson Graving Dock, for the repair of tankers and liners.

Around the quays is a labyrinth of tiny streets, known as the Entries, lined with rows of two-up two-down houses and several colourful pubs.

### Harland and Wolff Shipyard

The United Kingdom's largest shipyard makes its presence known on the Belfast skyline with two giant cranes, affectionately known as Samson and Goliath. The yard was founded in 1862 by Edward Harland, a

CAP AND GOWN *Dons at Queen's University walk in procession on Graduation Day.*

Yorkshireman, in partnership with Gustav Wilhelm Wolff, a marine draughtsman from Hamburg. Together they built up the great shipyard that constructed some of the world's largest ships, including the ill-fated *Titanic*, the P & O cruise ship *Canberra* and the oil tanker *Myrina*, the largest vessel ever built in Europe when she was launched in 1967. Despite foreign competition, the shipyard still echoes to the sound of the riveter's hammer, and its busy repair dock can take vessels of up to 200,000 tons.

### Queen's University

Looking out over trim lawns, this Tudor-Gothic building with its red-brick façade, stone facings and stone-mullioned windows is all that a university building should be. Indeed, its central tower closely resembles the Founder's Tower of Magdalen College, Oxford. The architect was Sir Charles Lanyon, designer of several of Belfast's most distinguished buildings. When the university was founded in 1849, it was known as Queen's College, and it received its university charter in 1908. It has an international reputation and more than 8000 students.

### Ulster Museum

The building standing in the grounds of the Botanic Gardens was begun in 1923, and has a pleasing façade of Portland stone, with 25ft columns rising from the first floor. It was greatly extended in 1971 to house a wealth of exhibits ranging from Iron Age bronzework to oil paintings and watercolours.

Its displays also include a demonstration of spinning and weaving techniques since prehistoric times, and a reconstruction of the court cairn at Ballintaggart. One of the museum's major attractions is the gold and silver jewellery salvaged in 1967 from the wreck of the Spanish Armada galleon *Girona*, which sank off the Antrim coast in 1588.

The Art Gallery has works by many Irish painters, such as Sir John Lavery, William Conor and Jack Butler Yeats, and a fine international collection, including works by Stanley Spencer, Walter Sickert, Vanessa Bell and Camille Pissarro. Among the gallery's watercolours are works by George Petrie, Samuel Palmer and Paul Sandby. And there are two impressive Henry Moore sculptures – one entitled *Oval with Points* and the other a three-piece draped, reclining figure.
**Opening times** *Mon-Fri 10am-5pm, Sat 1-5pm, Sun 2-5pm. Tel: (0232) 381251.*

# The Mark of a Giant

*Epic struggles between warring Gaelic families caused many castles to be built in defensive positions along the north Antrim coast. But the ruggedness of their ruins is nothing compared with the coastal landscape, which is most spectacular at the Giant's Causeway, a marvel of volcanic activity with thousands of hexagonal columns rising up from the seashore, in the shadow of towering, multilayered cliffs.*

### Ballintoy/Baile an Tuaighe

A winding road leads down to Ballintoy's limestone harbour, set into cliffs where sea birds swirl and fishermen sit and mend nets near the bobbing boats and dinghies. Sheep Island, which has a huge cormorant colony, can be seen clearly across Boheeshane Bay. On the road to the harbour is a Protestant church built by a local landowning family, the Stewarts, some time before 1641, and

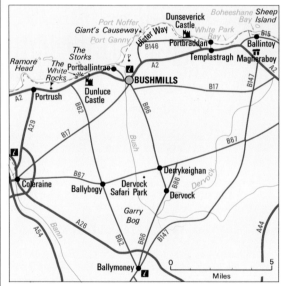

**North Antrim cliff path** Part of Ulster Way, which runs round whole province.
**White Park Bay** 1m trail along beach.

### EVENTS
**Ballymoney Agricultural Show** June.
**Ballymoney Irish Dancing Festival** Apr.
**Blackbush Amateur Golf Tournament** Causeway Coast, early June. Played over four courses.
**North Antrim Horticultural Show** Ballymoney, June.
**Portrush Country Music Festival** Sept.
**Portrush Historic Motor Vehicle Run** July.
**Portrush Irish Folk Dancing Festival** Mid-July.

### SPORT
**Angling** Game fishing: Rivers Bush, Dervock and tributaries of River Bush. Sea fishing: along coast.
**Golf** Bushfoot Golf Club, 9-hole course. Tel: (02657) 31317.
Royal Portrush Golf Club, two 18-hole courses and one 9-hole course. Tel: (0265) 822311.

### INFORMATION
Ballymoney Tourist Information. Tel: (02656) 62280.

### OTHER PLACES TO SEE
**Dervock Safari Park** 5m N of Ballymoney. A lion park with an amusement arcade for children. Tel: (02657) 41474.
**Magheraboy** 1m SW of Ballintoy. Chamber tomb in round cairn.
**Portballintrae** 5m E of Portrush. Quiet village with pebbledashed houses and old hand-pump.
**Portbraddan** 5m E of Bushmills. Village with pretty painted terraces and remains of what is one of the oldest churches on the north coast.
**Portrush** Seaside town famous for scenic golf course and wide sandy beaches. Has watersports and recreation centre, nature reserve and fossil-rich cliffs.

### WALKS
**Giant's Causeway to Portballintrae** Two-hour walk.

ROOMS WITH A VIEW *Terraces of three-storey guesthouses add to the charm of Portrush harbour.*

partially rebuilt in 1811. The tower, which tapers curiously inwards at the top, is part of the original edifice. The church spire blew off during a storm in 1894. It is said that during an Irish rebellion against the local Protestant landlords in 1641, Protestant women and children took refuge there and were kept from starving by a local Catholic priest, who was later killed by the rebels for his actions.

In the late 18th century Ballintoy's landlord was Dawson Downing, a relative of Sir George Downing, who founded Downing College in Cambridge, and after whom Downing Street in London is named. When Ballintoy Castle was demolished in 1795, its oak staircase and panelling were removed and installed in the Cambridge college.

### Ballymoney/Baile Monaidh

Lying in the heart of prime agricultural land on the edge of Garry Bog, the largest bog in Northern Ireland, is Ballymoney, a typically 'planted' town. It was settled by Scottish families who came over during the Plantation of Ulster in the 17th century and developed a thriving linen industry, as they did in neighbouring Ballymena. A wide main street leads to fine Georgian terraces in Charlotte Street. The Masonic Hall is a late 18th-century building with an attractive Italianate bell tower added in 1852. On the outskirts of the town is St Patrick's Church, a late 18th-century building of grey basalt.

### Bushmills/Muileann na Buaise

The world's oldest licensed distillery is in a village on the banks of the River Bush, known for its salmon fishing. The distillery, Old Bushmills, has been in operation since 1608, when James I of England granted a licence to the 'planter' landlord Sir Thomas Phillips.

Records of the 13th century mention that local soldiers were fortified with draughts of *aqua vitae*, 'the water of life', before going into battle. The Irish phrase *uisce beatha*, from which the word 'whiskey' comes, has the same meaning. The 'e' in 'whiskey' is used to distinguish it from Scottish whisky.

Locally grown barley and the surrounding peat that was used to fuel the kilns enabled the early producers to complete the process in one area. Now, peat is no longer used as fuel and the barley is imported. The water from the Bush tributary, St Columb's Rill, which flows through the distillery, is still used, and the copper pots in which the fermented mash is distilled three times, preserve the shape of the originals.
**Bushmills Distillery** *Mon-Thur 9am-12, 1.30-3.30pm; Fri 9am-11.45. Tours by arrangement. Tel: (02657) 31521.*

ROCKS OF AGES *Time and tides have carved the cliffs near Portrush into caves and arches.*

## Dunluce Castle

The rambling ruins of the castle with its towers and gables cling precariously to a black basalt crag, almost surrounded by the sea. Richard de Burgo (or Burke), the Red Earl of Ulster, built Dunluce in the early 1300s. The castle had an escape route through a cave which led from the cliff to the seashore (accessible only by boat), and the ruins include a 17th-century gatehouse in Scottish style, two 13th-century towers and the walls of the great hall.

In the 16th century, Sorley Boy Mac-Donnell (Sorley means 'yellow-haired') seized

DUNLUCE CASTLE *The castle was abandoned soon after a 1639 storm washed part of it into the sea.*

Dunluce from the MacQuillans. Shane O'Neill later managed to capture it by threatening to starve Sorley Boy to death, after taking him prisoner. After O'Neill's death and Sorley Boy's release in 1567, the castle became the MacDonnell stronghold, except for a short period in 1584 when the English, under Sir John Perrott, commanded it. Sorley Boy hatched an ingenious plan to regain it by getting one of his own men, who was employed in the castle, to haul some of the MacDonnells up the castle walls in a basket. They managed to overcome the garrison and take possession again. Sorley Boy repaired the damaged castle with money he received from the wreck of the Spanish Armada ship, *Girona*, which sank off the Causeway in 1588.

A car park, tea room and visitor centre lie at the entrance to the ruins, which are at the end of a hilly path.
**Opening times** *Apr-Sept, Mon-Sat 10am-7pm, Sun 2-7pm. Oct-Mar, Tues-Sat 10am-4pm, Sun 2-4pm.*

## Dunseverick Castle/Dun Soghairce

This was the capital of the ancient kingdom of Dal Riada, and is thought to have been one of the three great 'duns', or royal forts, visited by St Patrick in the 5th century. It lay at the end of an ancient route from Dundalk in County Louth, and there are extensive Celtic circular earth banks on the headland. Vikings captured Dunseverick in AD 871 and destroyed

it in 934. The ruined 16th-century tower is all that has survived from the period of struggle between the area's main warring families – the MacDonnells, O'Neills, O'Cahans and MacQuillans.

'The fate of the Children of Uisneach', the oldest of Ireland's love stories, claims that Dunseverick was the landing spot of Deirdre of the Sorrows. Deirdre, although betrothed to King Conor, eloped with his handsome bodyguard, Naoise, and his two brothers to Scotland. Eventually, persuaded by Fergus, Conor's deputy, that it was safe to return, they came back to Dunseverick. But the king took revenge. He slew the brothers and demanded Deirdre for his own. In her anguish, Deirdre killed herself and Fergus, outraged, destroyed the castle.

## Giant's Causeway

Perhaps the best-known tourist attraction in the whole of Northern Ireland is a coastline where tens of thousands of hexagonal basalt columns rise out of the water at the foot of 300ft cliffs. The Causeway stones can be found between Port Ganny and Port Noffer.

The Visitor Centre has an exhibition and audiovisual theatre, which outline the geological history of the Causeway.
**Visitor Centre** *Sept-June, Mon-Fri 10am-6pm, Sat and Sun 10am-6.30pm. July and Aug, daily 10am-7pm. National Trust tea room (Mar-Oct) and gift shop. Tel: (02657) 31855.*

# THE BLACK ...

*The story of Guinness and whiskey,*
*Ireland's best-known drinks*

Walk into any pub in Ireland and it won't take you long to realise that Guinness is the most popular drink. Rows of tall glasses filled with that rich velvet-black liquid, generously topped with a creamy-white head, testify to its unrivalled position. Though it is on sale in 120 other countries throughout the world, and is actually made in 31 of them, the right place to drink a Guinness, as far as most Irish imbibers are concerned, is Ireland. This could be due to the softness of the water, or because only Irish barmen have the art of pulling a good pint – slowly, and in stages, so that it can form a good thick head – or simply because their ancestors have been drinking Guinness for over 200 years.

ARTHUR GUINNESS *(above) His brewery once transported stout by barge from Dublin (right).*

THE BUILDING OF AN EMPIRE Arthur Guinness, who founded the brewery at St James's Gate in Dublin, bought a disused brewery in 1759 and started making traditional Irish ale. Shortly afterwards a new London-brewed drink, made from roasted barley, appeared in Dublin. Arthur had a go at making this 'porter', so called because of its popularity with the porters of Covent Garden and Billingsgate, and by 1799 had switched all his production to porter. The first export shipment, bound for Britain, left the brewery in 1769 and by the 1820s Guinness was being drunk across the world.

During the recession that followed the Napoleonic Wars, when other brewers were watering down their beers, the second Arthur Guinness produced a stronger 'extra stout' porter, shortened over the years to 'stout'. By the end of the century the St James's Gate brewery had become the largest in the world and its produce was reaching such remote areas as the Samoan Islands, to which Robert Louis Stevenson brought his own supplies, and the South Pole, where explorer Douglas Mawson left a few bottles at his base camp.

The brewery can produce some 2.5 million pints of Guinness per day, with the aid of modern technology. But it still uses the same strain of yeast pioneered by Arthur Guinness. And the basic brewing process – involving roasted Irish-grown barley, which

GUINNESS GALLERY *Guinness advertisements are renowned for their amusing images. Even the cartoonist Gilroy contributed to the gallery (centre left).*

A PINT OF PLAIN *Surrounded by Guinness memorabilia, a customer enjoys a Guinness in a bar in Carrick, County Donegal.*

gives it the characteristic dark colour, soft, pure water, hops and yeast – has not altered.

Since its creation, Guinness has promoted its wholesome image, which was summed up in the 'Guinness is good for you' campaign, launched in 1929. Its benefits were praised by one of Wellington's officers, wounded at Waterloo, who wrote in his diary that Guinness had 'contributed more than anything else to my recovery'. And by the mid-19th century, Guinness was being recommended to nursing mothers.

# ... AND THE GOLD

THE WATER OF LIFE Irish drinkers often 'chase' their pints of Guinness with a glass of the other national drink – Irish whiskey. Compared to Scotch whisky, an 'Irish' – as it is called in the pubs around the country – is claimed to have a milder, smoother, more delicate taste. Purists drink their whiskey neat or diluted with water, but there is always a demand for a 'hot Irish' too – lemon, cloves, brown sugar and boiling water are the added ingredients. Another variant is 'Irish' or 'Gaelic' coffee – black coffee, sugar and whiskey topped with a thick layer of cream.

Irish whiskey is made from a mixture of malted and unmalted barley, yeast and water. It is distilled three times in giant copper stills and then matured in oak casks for between five and eight years. The art of distillation, using an apparatus called an alembic, was probably brought to Ireland from Asia over 1000 years ago and experimented with in the monasteries. It did not take long before the ordinary people had developed their own stills which produced a spirit they called *uisce beatha* (water of life), anglicised first into 'fuisce' and then 'whiskey'.

Initially, distilling was carried out in homes around the country, and in impressive quantities among some of the gentry. Sir Walter Raleigh stocked up with a 32 gallon cask of the Earl of Cork's home brew before embarking on his epic voyages to America. But at the end of the 16th century the English government in Ireland, viewing spirit drinking as a cause of unrest, declared martial law in Munster against all makers of whiskey.

Later the government instituted a system of licensing for distillers, and the tax-dodging exploits of illicit distillers became a great source of entertainment for the people. At the beginning of the 19th century, customs warehouses were set up, where whiskey could be stored without payment of excise duty until it was needed for the market. This led to the practice of maturing whiskey in casks and in 1915 it became compulsory to store it in casks for at least three years.

The great Famine of the 1840s, followed by an anti-drink campaign by the Church, put many distilleries out of business. By 1900, just 30 of the original 1000 licensed distilleries were still in operation, along with

THE FOUNTS OF 'THE WATER OF LIFE' A *1920s photograph (top) shows casks of Irish whiskey being sent for export from John Jameson and Son's distillery in Bow Street, Dublin. In the past the Jameson's label bore three stars, denoting excellence (right). Another major distillery, Old Bushmills (above), in County Antrim, has produced whiskey since 1608, making it the world's oldest licensed distillery.*

## THE APOSTLE OF TEMPERANCE

In 1838 Father Theobald Mathew signed the pledge of total abstinence, with the words 'Here goes – in the name of the Lord'. His Temperance Movement soon gathered thousands of disciples, and by the end of 1842 about 5 million people – nearly half the adult population of Ireland – had taken the pledge of abstinence. The production of whiskey was halved, duties on Irish spirits fell and the rate of crime decreased. But a few years later, famine struck Ireland, the crusade was checked, and the production and consumption of liquor continued.

an unspecified number of illicit stills that made fiery poteen. In 1966 the three remaining major distilleries – John Jameson and Son, The Cork Distilleries Company and John Power and Son – merged to form the Irish Distillers Group. They were joined in 1974 by the oldest licensed distillery in the world, Old Bushmills.

The mellow, golden spirit favoured by Queen Elizabeth I and Czar Peter the Great is still the chosen drink of millions of connoisseurs around the world today. And many would agree with the 16th-century English chronicler, Holinshed:

> *It keepeth the reason from stifling,*
> *the stomach from wambling . . .*
> *the sinews from shrinking,*
> *the veines from crumpling . . .*

# The Glens of Antrim

*The high plateaus of this region are broken by steep glens and plunging coastal cliffs with dramatic sea views. From the winding coastal road, the patterned fields of mountain farms with sheep grazing the slopes can be seen. Apart from the many glens that give this area its name, there are expanses of peatland, conifer forests, tranquil loughs, tumbling waterfalls and ancient sites in abundance.*

### Carnlough/Carnlach

At the foot of Glencloy is the fishing village with its sandy beach, long seafront promenade and good harbour. The black-and-white Londonderry Arms Hotel that stands on the main street was built in 1848 as a coaching house by the Marchioness of Londonderry, Frances Anne Vane Tempest, who was a descendant of Randal MacDonnell, 1st Earl of Antrim. It later passed to her great-grandson, Sir Winston Churchill.

The Marchioness and her husband, Charles William Vane, played a major role in the development of Carnlough. In 1855 they started the limestone quarry, and built a harbour pier and the narrow-gauge railway which carried the limestone to the south pier to be exported to Scotland. Their home, Garron Tower, a blackstone mansion overlooking the North Channel, is now St McNissi's College, named after the founder of the monastic see of Connor.

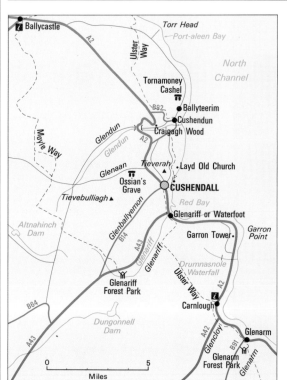

**OTHER PLACES TO SEE**
**Ballyteerim** Outside Cushendun, cairn of the chieftain Shane O'Neill. He died in 1567 in a brawl between his followers and the MacDonnells.
**Craigagh Wood** Contains Mass Rock of Inispollen, where Catholics celebrated Mass in secret in last century.
**Tiveragh** Outside Cushendall, an ancient mound also known as Fairy Hill, where the 'wee folk' are said to be seen.

**EVENTS**
**Feis na nGleann** The Irish Festival, Glenariff, July.

**SPORT**
**Angling** Game fishing: Rivers Glenariff and Glendun. Sea fishing: Carnlough.
**Bathing** Carnlough.
**Boating** Glenarm.
**Golf** Cushendall Golf Club, 9-hole course. Tel: (02667) 71318.

**INFORMATION**
Cushendall Tourist Information. Tel: (02667) 71180.

COLOUR CHANGE *A blanket of snow clads Red Bay, turning its red sands to glistening white.*

In the grounds of St McNissi's College are the mound and scattered stones of Dunmaul Fort, thought to be the remnants of an ancient inauguration site. Drumnasole waterfall lies just outside Carnlough.

### Cushendall/Bun Abhann Dalla

'The Capital of the Glens' sits below Glenballyemon, its streets sloping steeply up the sides of the glen. Its most prominent landmark is the red-sandstone tower known as the Curfew, or Garrison Tower, which stands at a crossroads in the village centre. Built in 1809 as a prison 'for riotous persons' by local landowner Francis Turnely, it has an opening at the lowest window on each of its four sides for pouring hot oil on would-be intruders. The tower is now a private home.

The ruins of 13th-century Layde Old Church lie in a copse a mile outside Cushendall. It is second in importance only to Bonamargy Friary as the burial place of the MacDonnell clan. A Celtic cross there is inscribed to the memory of Dr James MacDonnell, 18th-century patron of Irish harpists and one of the first doctors to use chloroform in surgical operations. The

MUSIC MAKERS *Musicians entertain in the streets during Cushendall's fleadh.*

ground was once the site of St Kieran's friary, and a well named after the saint survives nearby.

Off the road from Cushendall to Ballycastle is Ossian's Grave, a Stone Age court cairn, or burial mound. It is in the heart of Glenaan, 'the glen of the little streams', and is reached only after a steep walk up Tievebulliagh, climbing the path to about 600ft.

WILD GLEN *The Glendun river, spanned by a redstone viaduct, flows through Glendun, the 'brown glen', wildest of the 'Nine Glens of Antrim'.*

ROADSIDE SCENE *Long-haired sheep are a familiar sight on the road to Torr Head.*

The cairn, which now consists only of a ring of boulders, dates from 3000 BC, although Ossian, the legendary warrior-poet, lived in the 3rd century. From this windy spot there are fine views over the patchwork fields of the glen. The Ulster poet John Hewitt, who celebrated the glens in his works, which included *Time Enough* published in 1976, was buried beside the cairn in 1987. A plaque marks his grave.

## Cushendun/Bun Abhann Duinne

At the foot of Glendun is Cushendun, with its charming rows of whitewashed cottages and shuttered windows. The architect Clough Williams-Ellis, who designed the village of Portmeirion in Wales, was asked to build the village at the request of Lord Cushendun and his Cornish-born wife, Maud Bolitho, in 1812. Maud Cottages, facing the bay, are named after her. The village is now a conservation area, with a National Trust tea room and gift shop.

Behind the River Glendun are two hotels flanking the bay, which hide the Cushendun caves. Carved out by the action of the sea on the sandstone cliffs, the caves can be partially explored.

On the headland is a white house once owned by Moira O'Neill, 'the poetess of the glens', born in the late 19th century. Her daughter is Molly Keane, the Irish fiction writer.

A winding road leads to Torr Head, jutting out beyond Portaleen Bay. On the road are the ruins of an old coastguard station and in summer red-and-mauve fuchsia bushes blaze at the side together with wild yellow gorse and bright heathers. The Tornamony cashel on a hill to the left of the road is believed to date from AD 500 to 1000. It reaches 50ft across with walls 10ft high and 20ft thick.

## Glenariff/Gleann Aireamh

'Switzerland in miniature' is how the English writer William Thackeray described Glenariff in 1872. Of all the Antrim glens, this is the best known. It contains a state-owned forest park and the village of Waterfoot, also called Glenariff. The village is known for its traditional music and hosts a festival of Irish music every year, in July.

Between Waterfoot and Red Bay pier, on the way to Cushendall, is a series of caves with an interesting history. 'School Cave' was where the children of Red Bay had clandestine lessons in the 18th century, when the penal laws forbade Catholic education. The 40ft 'Nanny's Cave', the largest in the series,

was the home of Ann Murray. She was a 'shebeen queen', a distiller of poteen, who died in 1847 aged 100 years.

## Glenarm/Gleann Arma

Surrounded on three sides by wooded valleys, the narrow streets of Glenarm lie in the shadow of chalk cliffs that bear the scars of limestone mining in the last century when both limestone and chalk were exported. Now a conservation village, in the 17th century it was the seat of the MacDonnells, a warring clan, originally from Scotland, who dominated the north Antrim coast. The popular meaning of Gleann Arma is 'glen of the army'. Randal MacDonnell built his castle near the mouth of the river in 1636, and his descendants still live there. It is not open to the public.

A reminder of the village's belligerent past is seen in the barbican, visible from the bridge of Castle Street. It was built in 1636, with seven 'murder-holes', used to pour boiling liquid on would-be invaders.

Now, small fishing and pleasure boats bob peacefully in the harbour. St Patrick's Anglican church lies on the coast road at the northern end of the village, on the site of a former 15th-century Franciscan friary established by Robert Bissett. Fragments of his friary are preserved inside the 18th-century church, which also has an original 'Walker' organ.

Glenarm is the birthplace of Eoin Mac Neill (1867-1945), a noted Celtic scholar and founder of the Gaelic League, which promotes the Irish language and culture.

Glenarm Forest, part of the former Mac-Donnell demesne, has pleasant walks and picnic areas beside the river.

# A Gateway to Ulster

*With its busy port of Larne, from which ferries cross to Scotland, and separated from the Scottish coast by only a few miles of choppy sea, this area is a gateway to Ulster. Limestone and basalt cliffs form rugged headlands and spectacular coastal roads hug the high ground giving glimpses of white, sandy shores below. Inland, heathery moors and woodlands stretch north to the deep green of the Antrim glens.*

### Ballygalley/Baile Geithligh

A turreted castle in Scottish Baronial style dominates the village of Ballygalley. Built in 1625 from local stone by John Shaw, a Scottish landowner, it has 5ft thick walls, which withstood siege in 1641. The castle once had high walls, a steep roof, dormer windows and corner turrets, but it has been converted into a hotel and changed, although it retains much of its original character. Its coat of arms is inscribed over the main entrance door which led to the tower. A member of the Shaw family, a Madame Nixon, is reputed to haunt the castle, knocking on bedroom doors.

Above the tower loom the Sallagh Braes, where a walk on the summit provides some of the most delightful scenery in Ulster. To the north is the volcanic plug of Scawt Hill, which also gives breathtaking views. There is good fishing to be had around The Maidens, or Hulin Rocks, a cluster of rocks north of Ballygalley, while the ruins of O'Halloran's Castle, once owned by a recluse poet, crown Ballygalley Head.

### Carrickfergus/Carraig Fhearghais

In the 17th century, Carrickfergus was more important than Belfast, and was the only place in Northern Ireland where English was spoken instead of Irish. Its massive castle, built on a basalt promontory in 1180 by John de Courcy as a means of securing power along the coast, is the only covered Anglo-Norman tower remaining in Ireland. It consists of three wards and a four-storeyed 90ft keep with 8ft thick walls. Today the castle faces Marine Highway with its pleasant parks and shingle beaches.

Castle Green, in front of the castle, was a traditional meeting place, and it was here in 1690 that the townsfolk gathered to greet King William of Orange, whose forces garrisoned the castle after routing the French forces of the Catholic King James II. A bronze statue of 'King Billy' now stands on the green.

In the 18th century, the castle became a prison, and in 1928 it was bought by the Ministry of Defence who used the keep as an air-raid shelter in the Second World War. Although it has been renovated, the castle still has a Great Hall, dungeons and a 37ft well.

Carrickfergus town has a Williamite Trail, which starts at the seaward end of King William Pier and passes the landing stone where William of Orange stepped ashore in 1690. The trail leads to the town walls, built in 1608.

St Nicholas' Church, in North Road, was built in 1180, and is one of the few churches of this age in Ireland still with its roof and used for services. The Irish poet Louis MacNeice (1907-28) lived at the Rectory on North Road, and the 17th-century author of *Gulliver's Travels*, Jonathan Swift, preached at Kilroot, nearby.

A mile east of Carrickfergus is the Andrew Jackson Centre, an 18th-century thatched cottage which re-creates a domestic interior of the time and traces the president's family tree. Nearby, a plaque marks the site of the home of the parents of Andrew Jackson (the American president from 1829-37, and hero of the Battle of New Orleans).

**Carrickfergus Castle** *Apr-Sept, Mon-Sat 10am-6pm, Sun 2-6pm; Oct-Mar, Mon-Sat 10am-4pm, Sun 2-4pm. Tel: (09603) 51273.*

**Andrew Jackson Centre** *June-Sept, Mon-Fri 10am-6pm, Sat and Sun 2-6pm; Oct-May, Mon-Fri 10am-4pm, Sat and Sun 2-4pm.*

**Larne Folk Dancing Festival** Apr/May.
**Lughnasa Festival** Carrickfergus Castle, Aug.
**Mounthill Traditional Horse Fair** Larne, Oct.
**Nine Glens Festival of Irish Dancing** Carrickfergus, during Oct.

### SPORT

**Angling** Game fishing: Rivers Glenwhirry, Glynn and Larne, and Killylane Reservoir. Sea fishing: Ballygalley, Carrickfergus, Hulin Rocks, Larne, Portmuck, Whitehead.
**Bathing** Drains Bay, Island Magee, Larne Lough, Portmuck, Whitehead.
**Golf** Ballyclare Golf Club, 18-hole course. Tel: (09603) 22696/42352. Cairndhu Golf Club, 18-hole course. Tel: (0574) 83324. Carrickfergus Golf Club, 18-hole course. Tel: (09603) 63713/62203. Larne Golf Club, 9-hole course. Tel: (09603) 82228. Whitehead Golf Club, 18-hole course. Tel: (09603) 53631/53792.
**Sailing** Belfast and Larne Loughs.

### INFORMATION

Larne Tourist Information. Tel: (0574) 70517/72313.

### OTHER PLACES TO SEE

**Ballylumford** Village with dolmen in front of house; the single-chambered grave with four supporting stones and a capstone dates from around 2500-2000 BC.
**Carnfunnock Country Park** N of Larne, 375 acre park with forest trails, camping sites, a maze and excellent views over Larne Lough.
**Whitehead** Seaside town and centre of Railway Preservation Society of Ireland. Summer excursions on the Portrush Flyer, a famous steam train. Also has remains of Castle Chester built by Sir Moyses Hill in Elizabeth I's reign.

### EVENTS

**Carrickfergus and Larne Flower Show** Larne, Aug.
**Larne Drama Festival** Feb/Mar.

FAMILY TOMB *A monument to the Chichesters of Carrickfergus stands in St Nicholas' Church.*

CARRICKFERGUS CASTLE *The 90ft keep dominates the skyline of the harbour.*

### Glenoe

The whitewashed cottages of Glenoe cling precariously to the steep slope of the hill and all around is gloriously wooded countryside.

A signpost points the way to Glenoe's spectacular waterfall, now National Trust property. The waterfall tumbles over rocks through a tunnel of green trees, filtered by sunlight, to splashy pools below. It is a place of intense beauty where all that can be heard is the sound of crashing water, and the only company is that of an inquisitive trout or a bird in flight.

### Island Magee/Oileán Mhic Aodha

This 7 mile long peninsula juts out into the sea like an arm, protecting a near land-locked stretch of water in Larne Lough. Island Magee is renowned for the slaughter that took place here in 1642, when a number of local Catholics were thrown over the cliffs to their deaths, probably in retaliation for the previous year's killing of several Protestants. It also has a reputation for witchcraft, and in 1711 a local woman was pilloried in the last trial of its kind in Ireland.

The Bissett family held the tenancy of the peninsula in Elizabeth I's reign, their rent being 'an annual offering of goshawks'. These birds and many others breed on the rugged white chalk cliffs nearby.

### Larne/Latharna

In the 10th century the Vikings sailed up Larne Lough to the town of Latharna, bent on pillage and destruction. Now commercial shipping plies the channel, making Larne the second largest port in Ulster and its most important ferry terminal for freight and passenger services to Stranraer and Cairnryan in Scotland. It is also the gateway to the Glens of Antrim by way of the Antrim Coast Road.

At Curran Point, at the entrance to the harbour, is Olderfleet Castle, a crumbling 16th-century tower. The century before it was built, Edward Bruce, brother of Robert, landed in Olderfleet in 1315, anticipating his crowning as High King of Ireland. He was killed in battle three years later.

On Chaine Memorial Road, just past the ferry terminals, is a striking monument, Chaine Tower, a reproduction of a Round Tower 90ft high and built of granite. This was constructed in 1888 as a memorial to James Chaine, a local MP who developed the steamboat service between Larne and Scotland. The tower is now a lighthouse.

GLENOE FALLS *Overhanging trees and lacy ferns frame the cascading water, churned to silvery-white as it thunders over rocky ledges.*

Another memorial recalls the death in 1953 of 128 passengers on the *MV Princess Victoria*, which ran into a gale shortly after leaving Scotland and sank off the Irish coast.

In Victoria Road, the Larne and District Historical Centre has exhibitions of 18th-century domestic furniture, a replica of a country-house kitchen from the turn of the century, a milk house with plunge churn and butter maker, a smithy, agricultural implements and handicrafts. It also has histories of the families of the area.

St Cedmas' Church, originally an Augustinian friary, dates from probably around the 16th century. It has fine stained-glass windows including one known as The Leper Window, and outside is a carved head believed to represent the patron saint, St Cedmas. In Bridge Street stands the original First Larne Presbyterian Church, built in 1626 when the first Presbyterians arrived from Scotland.

**Larne and District Historical Centre** *Tues-Sat 2-5pm. Tel: (0574) 279482.*

### Larne Lough/Loch Latharna

A steep hill leads down to Brown's Bay which has good views over to Ballygalley Head. Around the other side of the peninsula is Portmuck beach, from which the fine chalk cliffs, known as The Gobbins, are visible.

The area around Larne Lough is noted for its birdlife, from the puffins on The Gobbins to the huge colony of roseate terns on Swan Island. Flocks of brent geese feed along the flats and shorelines oblivious of the boats that sail on the lough.

# Country of the Linen Weavers

*Undulating countryside is crisscrossed by sparkling rivers and lakes. On one of these – Lough Neagh – is the largest eel fishery in Europe. The small towns dotted around the area include Lisburn, famous for its linen industry in the 19th century, now a busy market town, and historic Antrim, which dates back to 5th-century Christian settlements and has a magnificent Round Tower.*

## Antrim/Aontroim

In the 5th century, Aodh, a disciple of St Patrick, founded a monastery here, on the banks of the Six Mile Water, which flows into Lough Neagh. The settlement grew into Antrim. All that remains today of Aodh's monastery is a Round Tower in Steeple Park, on the edge of the town. One of the finest in the country, it is 93ft high and 50ft in circumference with 4ft thick walls that taper towards the top. The door is 7ft off the ground, to deter attackers. The four windows at the top gave the monks a clear vantage point, so that with adequate warning they could take refuge in the tower and protect themselves and their treasures from marauding Vikings.

The town has seen many bloody battles, including a major naval engagement on Lough Neagh in 1643 between English forces and local captains. In an uprising led by General Monro in 1649, the town was destroyed by fire, and almost 50 years later, 3500 United Irishmen under Henry Joy MacCracken marched on the town but were routed and fled. Their commander, Lord John O'Neill, was killed.

A plantation castle which was built in 1662 by Sir John Clotworthy, later Lord Massereene, burnt down in 1922. A turreted gateway opposite the town's 1726 courthouse leads to beautiful gardens in the grounds of the former castle, now a public park, with the Six Mile Water meandering leisurely through. It has ornamental fish ponds, a Norman motte and a 19th-century coach house, Clotworthy House, now an arts centre with an open-air theatre.

Off Church Street is an 18th-century cottage called Pogue's Entry, the birthplace of the evangelist and writer Alexander Irvine (1863-1926), noted for his missionary work in the Bowery, in New York, and for the novel *My Lady of the Chimney Corner*, which features this cottage. The key to the cottage can be collected from the Antrim Forum. Irvine's remains are buried in the 16th-century Anglican church, All Saints, which also contains monuments to the Massereene family and some Renaissance stained glass.

## Crumlin/Cromghlinn

The name of this village means 'crooked glen', after its position in an awkwardly shaped

### OTHER PLACES TO SEE

**Belfast Zoo** 13 acres on slopes of Cave Hill, with animals in fenced enclosures. Good monkey house, aquarium, aviaries and reptile house. Specialises in breeding llamas, lions and wolves. Open Apr-Sept 10am-6pm, Oct-Mar 10am-4.30pm.
**Cave Hill** 1182ft high, and northernmost peak of hills that overlook Belfast city to the west. On top is MacArt's Fort, named after Brian MacArt O'Neill; in 1795 Wolfe Tone and members of United Irishmen's Society plotted Irish independence here.
**Collin Glen** On Glen Road, 5m SW of Belfast, wilderness with streams, woodland and wild-flower area, on slopes of Collin Mountain.
**Dixon Park** 18th-century estate covering 128 acres on outskirts of Belfast; has a walled garden, azalea walk, ornamental yew hedge and renowned displays of roses.
**Lower Ballinderry** 6m S of Crumlin. Village with Moravian church.
**Upper Ballinderry** Village with late 17th-century church with original interior.

### EVENTS
**International Rose Trials** Dixon Park, July-Sept.

### SPORT
**Angling** Coarse fishing: Loughs Beg and Neagh, River Lagan. Game fishing: River Ballinderry, lakes around Lisburn, Stoneyford Reservoir.
**Bowling** Musgrave Park.
**Golf** Ballyearl Golf Club, 9-hole course. Tel: (0232) 848287.
Dunmurry Golf Club, 18-hole course. Tel: (0232) 610834.
Lisburn Golf Club, 18-hole course. Tel: (0846) 677216.
Malone Golf Club, 9-hole and 18-hole courses. Tel: (0232) 612758.
Massereene Golf Club, 18-hole course. Tel: (08494) 28096.
**Tennis** Musgrave Park.

### INFORMATION
Belfast Tourist Information. Tel: (0232) 246609.

SPINNING THE TALE OF LINEN

*The Barbour Campbell factory at Hilden.*

The year 1685 saw great upheavals in France, for it was then that the Edict of Nantes was revoked, prohibiting Huguenots from practising their Protestant religion. They fled France and some, led by Louis Crommelin, King William of Orange's Overseer, came to south Antrim. Many of the refugees were weavers, and so linen weaving was brought to the area.

At first weaving was a cottage industry. Flax grown on farms was spun by women and children, and woven into fabric. It was then sold, unbleached, as brown linen at fairs, along with cattle and sheep. Brown Linen Halls were established by drapers to purchase cloth directly from the weavers.

A local man, William Coulson, became the first manufacturer in the north to produce damask in 1764. He subsequently became a supplier to the Russian, Swedish and British royal families.

In 1784 a Scottish settler, John Barbour, applied water power to twisting machines, and in 1823 he established a works at Hilden which introduced flax-spinning machinery and became the largest linen-thread works in the world. Linen and synthetic threads are still made at the Barbour Campbell factory for export.

valley where the River Crumlin flows gently into Lough Neagh near Gartree Point. The village is within easy reach of several good fishing spots – Glenavy and the Stoneyford Reservoir. A clock tower and weather vane in the village were erected in 1897 to Reverend Arthur Pakenham, whose family resided on the Pakenham estate, granted to them in the 17th century. The kitchen garden of the Pakenham demesne, now called Talnotry Cottage Bird Garden, has the largest variety

**COLD FEET** *Belfast Zoo flamingos try the snow.*

of species of quail, partridge and pheasant in the country.

In pre-plantation times Crumlin formed part of the lands owned by the O'Neills of Clandeboye. Part of the estate is now Crumlin Glen, a 15 acre site of mixed woodland beside the River Crumlin where nature trails wind past tumbling waterfalls, home to a variety of plants and birds.

**Talnotry Cottage Bird Garden** *Easter-Sept, Sun and Bank Holidays 2-6pm. Or by appointment. Tel: (08494) 22900.*

## Lisburn/Lios na gCearrbhach

This town, which slopes down to the River Lagan, was a highly important and prosperous linen centre in the 19th century, part of the famous 'linen triangle' that was formed by Belfast, Armagh and Dungannon. Half the linen output of the province of Ulster came from this area at that time.

Linen weaving was brought to Lisburn by Huguenots, who fled France after the revocation of the Edict of Nantes in 1685. The River Lagan was used to wash the fabric, and there were a number of 'bleaching greens' along its banks, the first established at nearby Lambeg in 1626. It took its name from the enormous goatskin Lambeg drums used by King William III's army, and traditionally sounded in Holland at weddings to drive away evil spirits. They are still used by Orange marching bands during the July 12 parades. Lisburn's Brown Linen Hall had the largest annual sale of brown linen in Ulster in 1816. It is now the post office.

In 1707 a fire destroyed most of the town. The 18th-century Assembly Rooms survived, and now house the town's museum, and arts and crafts exhibitions. The museum has an exhibition detailing the growth of the linen industry, with weaving looms dating from the 17th, 18th and 19th centuries. Flax continued to be produced during the Second World War when linen firms diversified – 2 million linen parachutes were made in Northern Ireland. The Huguenots' tombs can be seen in the churchyard of Christ Church Cathedral, not far from the museum.

In Bow Street, the heart of the shopping area, is a bronze monument to Brigadier General John Nicholson, born in Lisburn in 1822. He led the assault on Delhi during the Indian Mutiny in 1857.

**Lisburn Museum** *Apr-Sept, Tues-Sat 11am-4.45pm; Oct-Mar, Tues-Fri 11am-4.45pm. Tel: (0846) 672624.*

CITY VIEW *Cave Hill, to the north of Belfast, overlooks the sprawling city below.*

## Templepatrick/Teampall Phádraig

St Patrick is believed to have visited Templepatrick in AD 450, where he baptised converts at a holy well (now dry) and established a church. It is claimed that the 'old church' was taken over by the Knights of St John who settled here and built a castle. In 1619, the castle was granted to Captain Humfrey de Norton, who sold it 14 years later in order to disinherit his only daughter, who had run off with a soldier. It was sold to Captain Henry Upton, after whom the castle is named.

In 1770 the Scottish architect Robert Adam built the Stable Yard, an exact copy of the old Fish Market in Edinburgh, and the Mausoleum. Peacocks and deer wander in the gardens, and the stables house an art gallery.

The castle is said to be haunted. A portrait of an Upton, who was burnt to death by her husband for refusing to become Catholic, hangs in the house and is said to be surrounded by ice-cold air. The castle is not open to visitors.

**Castle Upton** *Art Gallery and Stables: daily 11am-6pm. Tel: (08494) 32466.*

CASTLE UPTON *Informal gardens offset the stark outlines of the castle's tower and battlements.*

# THE GIANT'S CAUSEWAY

## One of the natural wonders of the world

The towering cliffs of northern Antrim overlook an extraordinary promontory. Some 40,000 dark columns head out into the sea, each formed with such geometrical precision that it seems as though some supernatural hand has been at work. This is the Giant's Causeway. Altogether, it is an astounding sight, set against a 4 mile stretch of cliffs that soar some 400ft into the air.

The Causeway juts out from the base of the cliffs and has been eroded into three parts – known as the Grand, Middle and Little Causeway. About half of the columns are hexagonal; others have four, five, seven or eight sides. Many of them have horizontal cracks that divide them in lengths of 12-14in.

THE LEGEND Although the more prosaically minded will tell you the Causeway is the result of ancient volcanic activity, the legend is almost more convincing. It is said that the Causeway was built by the Ulster hero Finn MacCool as he hurried to Scotland, perhaps to fight a rival, or maybe to visit his lady love. Certainly, the flat tops of the columns form excellent stepping stones, and a similar rock formation re-emerges on the Scottish island of Staffa.

PIPES OF ROCK *Precipitous columns of basalt rise sheer from the sea to create the structure known as the Giant's Organ.*

THE GEOLOGISTS' VIEW According to geologists, the Causeway was formed some 60 million years ago as a result of repeated outpourings of volcanic basalt, during the Tertiary period of the earth's evolution. The columns were formed by the slow and even cooling and contraction of molten lava. The fine-grained basalt columns stand on a thick base of medium-grained basalt, in places over 300ft deep. Between these two dark layers is a striking strip of reddish soft rock, formed during a long break in volcanic activity when the climate was subtropical.

Elsewhere along the Causeway cliffs, the basalt has been thrown up into a number of bizarre structures which have been colourfully named by generations of local guides – the Wishing Chair, the Keystone, the Honeycomb and the Giant's Loom, the Giant's Organ, the King and his Nobles, the Horse Back, the Harp, and others. The Chim-ney Tops, separated by erosion from the surrounding cliffs, so confused sailors of the Spanish Armada that they reportedly mistook them for a castle and opened fire. One of their ships, the *Girona,* sank off the coast in 1588 with the reported loss of 1300 lives. The wreck was discovered in 1967 off Port-na-Spaniagh, or Spanish Point, and was found to contain treasure, some of which is displayed in the Ulster Museum in Belfast.

The scientific 'discovery' of the Causeway in the 17th century helped British and European scientists to understand the nature of volcanic rocks such as basalt. The Causeway also attracted thousands of travellers, including Dr Samuel Johnson, Sir Walter Scott and William Thackeray. Today, it is Northern Ireland's most popular tourist attraction and is protected by the National Trust. It was declared a World Heritage Site in April 1987, the only one in Ireland.

BIZARRE FORMS *The erosion of layers of lava on volcanic outflows, at different rates, has produced what is called 'onion-skin weathering'.*

A GIANT'S EYE *Partially weathered 'bubbles' of basalt, which formed around gas or liquids, have formed 'Giant's eyes' in the rock (above).*

STEPPING STONES TO SCOTLAND *The geometrical stepped columns of the Giant's Causeway (left) reappear on the Scottish island of Staffa.*

# Ulster's Camelot

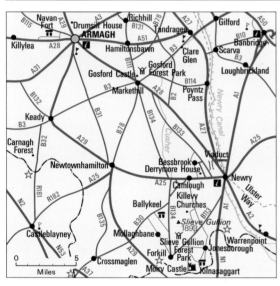

*From the wild hillsides of Slieve Gullion in the south to the peaty lowlands that bound Lough Neagh in the north the land is moulded by the gentle shapes of drumlins – little hills – and water lies everywhere. This is The Orchard of Ireland, but it is also the centre of mythical Ireland, at the hilltop fort of Eamhain Macha.*

### Armagh/Ard Mhacha

'Macha's Height' is named after Queen Macha, a legendary warrior queen with golden hair said to have reigned from 658 BC until her death seven years later. Her palace was a few miles to the west, at Navan Fort, also called Eamhain Macha.

In the 5th century, St Patrick built the first of his two churches here, at a place he called 'my sweet hill'. It grew to be the

**Mullaghbane** On W slope of Slieve Gullion, little thatched cottage Folk Museum furnished as traditional south Armagh farmhouse. Open by appointment. Tel: (0693) 888278.

**Slieve Gullion** Hill crowned with passage-graves; at south end is forest park with walks and viewpoints. Features in prose epic, *The Cattle Raid of Cooley.*

### WALKS

**Carnagh Forest** Natural woodland with lakes and anglers' inn.

**Clare Glen** 4m walk from pretty village of Tandragee to Clare old bridge and cornmill.

### EVENTS

**Armagh Agricultural Show** June.

**Irish Music Festival** Apr.

**Ulster Road Bowls Final** July/Aug.

### SPORT

**Angling** Game fishing: River Cusher.

**Golf** County Armagh Golf Club, 18-hole course. Tel: (0861) 522501.
Tandragee Golf Club, 18-hole course. Tel: (0762) 8740727.

### INFORMATION

Armagh Tourist Information. Tel: (0861) 524052/527808.

### OTHER PLACES TO SEE

**Ballykeel** Splendid dolmen by the roadside.

**Gosford Castle and Forest Park** Norman Revival castle, built 1819 with great round tower at one end and square keep. Castle not open to the public, but the park, with walled cherry garden and arboretum, is open 8am-10pm all year.

**Keady** Village with trout lakes and derelict watermills.

**Killevy Churches** 10th and 13th century churches.

Earlier church has massive lintelled door. Site of 5th-century nunnery founded by St Monenna. Her grave is said to be under a granite slab in the graveyard.

**Kilnasaggart** S of Jonesborough on S slopes of Slieve Gullion, elaborately carved upright stone with ten cross-inscribed circles on north face, one on east face and another on south. Bears inscription in Irish to Ternoc, died 716. Nearby are ruins of 1601 Moyry Castle.

Soaring Glory *St Patrick's Cathedral in Armagh is a triumph of the 19th-century neo-Gothic style.*

ecclesiastical capital of Ireland, a small elegant city glowing with the soft pinks, yellows and reds of the local limestone. Francis Johnston (1761-1829), the architect who made Dublin so beautiful, designed many of Armagh's most splendid buildings.

The Georgian Mall is perhaps his, and Armagh's, masterpiece. The green sward of The Mall was once the city's racecourse and cockpit. It is now a graceful and beautiful 'square', edged with the neoclassical courthouse, Georgian houses, the Royal Irish Fusiliers Museum and the County Museum.

The County Museum has a fine library and an art gallery with paintings by local artists such as George Russell (AE) (1867-1935), and James Sleator (1885-1949). Its local exhibits include military uniforms, 18th and 19th-century costumes, and lace.

Armagh's planetarium, with its computerised 'Theatre of the Stars', beside the Observatory, was established in 1967. Inside it are mock-ups of a Gemini spacecraft, the Space Shuttle, and Voyager. The Observatory, founded in 1790, was designed by Johnston.

Armagh's Church of Ireland cathedral, built on the site of St Patrick's second church, was restored by Francis Johnston in the 1770s. Much of his work has since been replaced, however. Carved heads staring into space form a frieze around its exterior. Brian Boru, first King of Ireland who drove the Norsemen out in 1014, is buried in the graveyard, his burial place marked by a slab in the north wall.

From the tower of the cathedral the medieval core of the town can be seen, with narrow streets radiating out to a ring that marks where the wall of the old fort, or rath, ran around the city. Across a valley to the north is the Catholic cathedral of St Patrick, started in 1840, with its exuberant colouring and almost Byzantine interior. The blue ceiling and walls are decorated with angels and Irish saints and its joyful carillon of 39 bells peals across the city.

A small neoclassical temple adjoins the Archbishop's Palace built for Archbishop Robinson by Thomas Cooley, and in the grounds are the ruins of a Franciscan friary. This was established by Archbishop Patrick O'Scannail in the 13th century and is Ireland's longest friary church at 163ft.

**Armagh County Museum** *Mon-Sat 10am-5pm. Tel: (0861) 523070.*

GOSFORD CASTLE *The first Norman Revival castle to be built in the British Isles stands in 580 acres of forest, with nature trails and an arboretum.*

**Royal Irish Fusiliers Museum** *Mon-Fri 10am-4pm. Tel: (0861) 522911.*

**The Planetarium** *Mon-Sat 2-4.45pm. Star shows, Sat 3pm, and Mon-Sat in July and Aug. Tel: (0861) 523689.*

### Bessbrook/An Sruthán

At the top of Slieve Gullion (1894ft), railway buffs gather once a year to watch the Slieve Gullion S-Class 4-4-0, pride of the Railway Preservation Society of Ireland, steam over the longest viaduct in Ireland, half a mile long. Built in 1851, the viaduct still carries the main Belfast to Dublin trains.

Bessbrook was founded by John Grubb Richardson in 1845 to house workers from his flax mill. It was the earliest of the Quaker model towns and was a model for Cadbury's Bournville. No pub, pawnshop or police station was deemed necessary, and the solid slate-roofed weavers' houses are grouped companionably around two squares, each with a green in the middle. The old water mill is a reminder of the village's industrial past

when Bessbrook Spinning Company linens were world famous.

In 1859, the Richardsons bought Derrymore House, with its thatched roof and bays that contain 80 window panes. It is one of the few surviving examples of the 'cottage orné', fantasies of what townspeople imagined rural cottages looked like. In the late 18th century such cottages were built as follies to create an architectural feature in the landscape. It is not open to the public.

### Navan Fort/Eamhain Macha

The ancient royal capital of Ulster, Eamhain Macha, now known as Navan Fort, was the centre of ancient Irish culture. It was founded by Queen Macha and is associated with Cuchulainn, the legendary Ulster warrior.

The fort is a huge, circular 16 acre hilltop enclosure with a large mound in the centre, and was probably a ritual site rather than a defensive one. It was part of a complex which included nearby Lough na Shade, in whose dark waters bones and skulls and four

bronze trumpets were found in the 19th century; the King's Stables; a Bronze Age ritual site to the north-west; Haughey's fort, to the west; and ancient tombs in the hills to the north. One of the houses in the enclosure obviously belonged to an important figure, since it contained the skeleton of a Barbary ape, presumably a gift from North Africa.

The fort is thought to have been in use from 4000 to 5000 years ago, and was occupied from about 700-100 BC, when the sagas of the hero Cuchulainn are connected with it. The fort was destroyed in AD 332.

Excavations show that in 94 BC it was a sophisticated, conical structure, 120ft in diameter, made of five concentric circles of about 275 posts, with a large central post, 36ft high, and a roof. Soon after the building was erected it was burnt to the ground, probably for religious reasons, and the whole circle was filled with cobbles to the height of a man's head. The stones were piled with brushwood and covered with earth to a depth of 10ft, creating the mound that can be seen today.

# The Peatlands of Lough Neagh

*The industrial towns of Lurgan and Portadown, once famous for their linen, lie near the rich peatlands of Lough Neagh's flat shores. This is excellent fishing country, threaded by the Rivers Bann and Blackwater, and is a birdwatcher's heaven, with the shores of Lough Neagh providing shelter for thousands of wildfowl. To the south is a countryside of distinguished country houses and tiny prosperous farms.*

### Ardress House/An tArdriasc

A gentleman farmer's house, Ardress was built in the 17th century, more in the English than Irish style – until Sarah Clarke, the daughter of the house, married George Ensor in 1760. The Ensors spent many years changing Ardress House. It is therefore puzzling why they should have arranged the house so that guests would have to brave the Armagh weather to pass from the drawing room to the dining room. Ensor's supporters say it was so that the magnificent plasterwork in the dining room would not be disturbed by building work around it. Other surprises include the fact that among the fine rows of windows to the front, five windows are fakes. But the house has a real warmth, and the plasterwork of Michael Stapleton, who decorated some of the finest Dublin houses, is magnificent. His stucco plaques depicting the seasons have a freedom about the curves that is rarely seen.

The house has a herb garden, farm buildings and rare breeds of fowl that pick for grain among the cobbles. There are also picnic sites in the woodland and nature trails. **Ardress House** *Apr-May, Sat, Sun and Bank Holidays; June-Aug, daily exc Tues; Sept, Sat and Sun 12-6pm. Tel: (0762) 851236.*

### The Argory/Ard Garraidhe

In 1824, Walter McGeough built his house, The Argory, on a rise overlooking a gently curving stretch of the River Blackwater that flows north into Lough Neagh. Its Irish name means the 'hill of the garden'. Its front entrance faces the river and is guarded by an affectionate-looking stone lion. Inside the gleaming entrance hall are more 'guardians' – a splendid bronze mastiff and greyhound. The walls are still covered in their original marbled and wood-grain finishes, and the light fittings, once lit by gas, are still there. Time stands still here: the cues still rest

SAILS IN THE SUNSET *Yachts on Lough Neagh, Britain's largest lake, return to shore at sunset.*

the Orange Order. Key obtained next door.

**SPORT**
**Angling** Coarse fishing: Rivers Bann, Blackwater and Callan. Game fishing: Rivers Bann and Blackwater.
**Golf** Craigavon Golf Centre, 18-hole course. Tel: (0762) 6606.
Lurgan Golf Club, 18-hole course. Tel: (0762) 322087.
Portadown Golf Club, 18-hole course. Tel: (0762) 355356.

**INFORMATION**
Armagh Tourist Information. Tel: (0861) 5240752/527808.
Portadown Tourist Information. Tel: (0762) 353260.

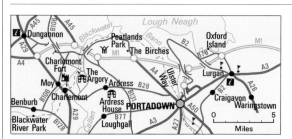

**OTHER PLACES TO SEE**
**Blackwater River Park** Extends for 3m, with ancient castle and priory. Famous for bream, canoeing over weirs, sub-aqua training and fossils.
**Charlemont Fort** 3m SW of The Argory, impressive outline of 1602 artillery fort with star-shaped bastions, built to defend area against O'Neills. Burnt down in 1921.
**Loughgall** Centre of apple growing area and village where the Orange Order was founded in 1795. Containing the Orange Museum, with sashes, flags and first signature of membership to

SILENT SENTRIES *Visitors entering The Argory's west hall are greeted by bronze statues of a mastiff and greyhound. The stove in the hall once provided a warmer welcome.*

on the billiard table, and the dining table is set for dinner.

**Opening times** *Apr-May, Sat, Sun and Bank Holidays; June-Aug, daily exc Tues; Sept, Sat and Sun. 12-6pm. Tea room and shop. Tel: (08687) 84753.*

## Lurgan/An Lorgain

Although the town has an unpretentious name, meaning 'a strip of land', it was once a prosperous strip, made so by the manufacture of linen-damask at adjacent Waringstown. The small courtyards and lanes that lead off the broad main street recall the weavers' pattern of life.

This is also peat country; there is a saying that a mournful person has 'a face as long as a Lurgan spade', a reference to the length of the blade necessary to get the best cut out of the local peatbogs.

Lurgan is known too as the home town of Master McGrath, a dog that won the Waterloo Cup for coursing greyhounds on three occasions between 1868 and 1871. The dog is celebrated in a ballad, in the town's coat of arms, in a stained-glass window in the parish church, and in a statue outside Brownlow House, once his master's home.

## Oxford Island/Oilean Ath an Daimh

The south shore of Lough Neagh is an important site for overwintering wildfowl, and these and other shoreline birds can be seen at the nature reserve at Oxford Island. There are 5 miles of walks with bird hides and picnic spots. Lucky visitors might even hear a corncrake at dusk.

The reserve has a commonsense system of observation posts at which there are co-ordinating notes about the birdlife. Visitors should bring binoculars and a good bird book, but be prepared for the Lough Neagh fly, a midge which, though not a biter, swarms in millions in the summer. Boat trips for birdwatchers can be arranged.

The peninsula was once an island farm, mainly for cattle, hence the name 'Ox-ford'. Boats can be hired to visit the island and there are nature trails.

**Oxford Island Information Centre** *Mon-Fri, 9am-5pm. Tel: (07622) 22205.*

## Peatlands Park

This delightful and informative nature reserve was started by the Irish Peat Development Company when it acquired the estate in 1901. Almost too late, Ireland has realised that the traditional process of peat cutting, which destroys bog environment irrevocably, must be slowed, and Peatlands Park is a nature reserve which tries to explain why. Displays and audiovisual presentations at the Visitor Centre put forward the case for preservation admirably.

The company put in 8 miles of narrow-gauge railway with trucks, which at first were pulled by men and later by donkeys. The rail was electrified in 1907, and diesel was introduced in the 1950s. Sections of the railway have been revived and wander through the reserve, while wooden pathways allow visitors to walk through restricted areas without causing any damage. It is a beautiful place in summer, when the white tufts of bog cotton nod in the breeze and butterflies, damselflies and dragonflies dance over the pools of water.

A few miles east is The Birches, ancestral home of Stonewall Jackson (1824-63), the Confederate general of the American Civil War. A blue plaque on the courtyard wall of the farm marks the association.

**Peatlands Park** *May-Sept, daily 9am-9pm; Oct-Apr, 9am-dusk. Visitor Centre: July-Aug, 2-7pm; Sept-June 1-4pm. Railway Easter-Sept, 2-6pm. Tel: (0762) 851102.*

### THE BALLAD OF MASTER McGRATH

*The champion greyhound Master McGrath stands in front of Bob at the Bowster.*

Lord Lurgan's great greyhound which won the Waterloo Cup in 1868, 1869 and again in 1871, is remembered in this traditional poem.

*1868 being the state of the year,*
*Those Waterloo sportsmen did grandly appear,*
*To gain the great prizes and bear them awa'*
*Never counting on Ireland and Master McGrath.*

*On the 12th of December, that day of renown,*
*McGrath and his trainer they left Lurgan town;*
*John Walsh was the trainer, and soon they got o'er,*
*For the very next day they touched England's great shore.*

*And when they arrived there in big London Town*
*Those great English sportsmen they all gathered roun'–*
*And one of these gentlemen gave a 'Ha! Ha!'*
*With: 'Is that the great dog you call Master McGrath?'*

*Then Lord Lurgan steps forward and says: 'Gentlemen,*
*If there's any amongst youse has money to spen'–*
*For youse nobles of England I don't give a straw–*
*Here's five thousand to one on my Master McGrath.'*

*And Rose stood uncovered, the great English pride,*
*Her master and keeper all close by her side;*
*They have let her away and the crowd cried 'Hurrah!'*
*For the pride of all England – and Master McGrath.*

*McGrath he looked up and he wagged his ould tail,*
*And he winked at his lordship to know he'd not fail;*
*Then he jumped on the hare's back and held up his paw–*
*Give three cheers for ould Ireland and Master McGrath.*

## Portadown/Port an Dúnáin

Once a linen town, Portadown now concentrates on manufacturing carpets and synthetic fibres, as well as canning fruit from nearby orchards. It has a wide main street, widening at each end into 'triangles'.

The River Bann, which flows through the town, has shoals of roach which attract thousands of fishermen who come here from all over Europe for competitions. The anglers repair to McConville's Pub on West Street, little changed since it was built in 1865.

# IRISH MYTHS AND LEGENDS

*The deeds and feats of heroes and heroines in the great Irish sagas*

The mythology of Ireland combines the homespun with the epic – one of the most famous legends is about a cattle raid – yet the tales of heroic feats and fierce battles have a grandeur to rival the sagas of the Greeks and Romans.

THE MYTHS' CREATORS Ireland's myths were fashioned hundreds of years ago, when formal storytelling, accompanied by lavish feasting and drinking, was the most widespread entertainment among the early Irish Celts. At the time, there was a distinct and very important class of professional learned men, the druids. Among their many duties they passed on history and religious readings by word of mouth, from generation to generation. They were divided into groups of men with different roles. One of these groups was the *filí*, the poets and storytellers.

A *file* had a long apprenticeship, learning to narrate 'the chief stories of Ireland's kings, lords and noblemen' – a fully trained 12th-century poet was expected to be able to recite at least 350 tales. Each poet had a patron – the *file* of the 6th-century Irish king, Mongán, was said to have entertained his master with a story every winter night from the first of November to the first of May.

The poets tended to group their tales according to theme, but when the stories were later classified by scholars they were put into four main groups: the Mythological Cycle, which deals mainly with the gods and goddesses of the Irish Celts; the Ulster Cycle, which relates the exploits of the warriors of Ulster, or the Ulaid, and their youthful hero Cuchulainn; the Kings' Cycle, which comprises tales from the reigns of various kings; and the Fenian Cycle, which centres on the hero Finn MacCool (or Fionn mac Cumhaill).

THE MYTHOLOGICAL CYCLE Irish monks working in the monasteries first wrote down their native myths in the 6th century. One of the earliest complete books, the 12th-century *Book of Invasions*, describes the arrival of people in pre-Celtic and Celtic Ireland, in successive waves. These tales are dealt with primarily in the Mythological Cycle. For

THE GUNDESTRUP CAULDRON *The silver cauldron unearthed in Denmark is thought to depict scenes from the Cattle Raid of Cooley. Here, Cuchulainn attacks his enemies with a broken chariot wheel.*

On a stamp showing a bronze statue:

éIRE 32

POBLACHT NA H EIREANN.
THE PROVISIONAL GOVERNMENT
of the
IRISH REPUBLIC
TO THE PEOPLE OF IRELAND.

1 Samhain 1916

1991

THE DYING CUCHULAINN *The hero, whose statue (above) stands in the Dublin Post Office, is commemorated on an Irish stamp.*

LAKE OF SORROW *Lough Derravaragh, in Westmeath (left), is where the Children of Lir were doomed to spend 300 years as swans.*

example, in the Battle of Moytura, the Tuatha dé Danann (the people of the goddess Danu), defeat the invading Fomorians. Later, when the Milesians arrive, the Tuatha dé Danann are banished to the magical world of the burial mounds.

Scholars now believe that the Túatha dé Danann were the gods of the Irish Celts and that the Christian scribes demoted them, though they still allowed them to be a powerful race, skilled in druidic magic. However, some of these deities retained their importance, in the form of Christian saints – St Brighid for example, was the Celtic goddess of poetry and learning.

The tales of this cycle tell of a time when people appeared to have little fear of death, for druidic teaching held that the soul did not die, but passed into another body. The Otherworld, known as Tír inna mBeo (the Land of the Living) and Tír na nÓg (the Land of Youth), is described as a blissful place, where flowers are always in bloom and women always beautiful. It was believed to be on an island off the west coast.

THE ULSTER AND FENIAN CYCLES One of the first Irish sagas to be written down, the *Táin*

*bó Cuailnge* (the Cattle Raid of Cooley), is contained in the Ulster Cycle. In it, Maeve, Queen of Connaught, invades Ulster to steal the mighty brown bull of Cooley and, because the Ulster warriors are struck down by a strange illness, it is left to the hero Cuchulainn to defend the province alone. He eventually defeats the men of Connaught, but is mortally wounded. He dies, standing up, strapped to a stone pillar.

The stories of the Fenian Cycle belong to a later period – some even describe Finn's son Ossian entertaining St Patrick in the 5th century. Finn was a giant and, like Cuchulainn, expert at fighting. Whereas many of the Ulster Cycle stories revolve around court life, Finn and his elite band of warriors, the Fianna, were constantly on the move, hunting, fighting and feasting throughout the provinces of Leinster and Munster. One of the most popular tales of this cycle is the love story of Diarmuid and Gráinne – said to have inspired the French romantic tale of Tristan and Iseult. It tells how King Cormac's beautiful daughter, Gráinne, given in marriage to the ageing Finn, puts a *geis* (spell) on the raven-haired Diarmuid to force him to elope with her. After many years on the run, Diarmuid is eventually killed in a fight with a great boar, on the slopes of Benbulbin in Sligo. As he slays the boar, it rips his stomach open, fulfilling a prophecy that he would die in this way. The lovers are remembered in the great number of dolmens scattered around Ireland, which are known as 'the Beds of Diarmuid and Gráinne'.

MYTHS IN THE MODERN WORLD The decline of the Irish nobility under English rule meant that by the 17th century there were no native patrons to employ the poets. It was left to others to revive these great myths – the 18th-century Scottish poet James Macpherson wrote a series of poems about Finn, and after him, others, including Lady Gregory and W.B. Yeats, gathered Celtic stories, and reproduced them in English.

The myths live on in the memory of the Irish people, and are fixed in the landscape, too. If you stop to chat to local people about a place, they will soon start telling you how Queen Maeve was buried in that mound, Finn slew a giant by this lake, that the Shannon is named after Sionna, granddaughter of the sea god Lir . . .

# Giants' Graves and Gardens

*When the ice sheets ground their way south during the last great Ice Age, they left in their wake little hills of boulder clay called drumlins. These undulations give the area a gentle feel in tune with the even temperature and the soft rain. It is a mysterious place with suggestions of cairns and dolmens, or 'giants' graves', in many fields, and rings of trees on the hilltops. The skyline is dominated by the large shape of Slieve Croob mountain.*

## Ballynahinch/Baile na hInse

The Earl of Moira, whose family seat was Montalto House, laid out Ballynahinch in the 1640s with impressive wide streets and a market square. The town was badly damaged in 1798 but there are still some attractive buildings. St Patrick's Catholic church (1843) has a beautiful classical interior, some good Victorian stained glass and a baptistry, and the pretty 1772 parish church nearby overlooks the Montalto woods and the river valley. The restrained blackstone Second Presbyterian Church catches the eye as does a shop with a fine tiled front at the corner of Dromore Street.

On the road out to Newcastle is a working water-powered corn mill and beside it an old flax mill, now used for drying grain. The town lies in a beautiful valley, and from a stump on Windmill Hill the whole of the wooded demesne of Montalto can be seen. Montalto House itself is not open to the public but there is an attractive trout lake where anglers may fish.

The valley is famous for the great, and last, battle of the United Irishmen's rebellion in 1798. The rebels had the opportunity to take Ballynahinch, and in doing so could have won themselves an important strategic position, but they eventually lost. There are some rousing local songs about 'brave General Monro' defeated in the battle and captured on Slieve Croob (1755ft). With the execution of Monro, and Henry Joy MacCracken at Lisburn, the death knell was rung for the United Irishmen.

Just outside the town is The Spa, a fashionable watering place in the mid-18th century. The formal gardens and maze no longer exist, but the old assembly rooms and chalybeate (iron-rich) water springs still remain, and the water is bottled for sale.

South-west of Ballynahinch is Slieve Croob, crowned by 12 cairns. Traditionally the locals would appease the old gods here, at the Feast of Lughnasa, held to celebrate the harvest on Blackberry Sunday, the first Sunday in August.

## Comber/An Comer

At the junction of the little River Comber and the River Enler is Comber town, just far enough off the main road to give it a quiet, contented look. Blackstone houses dot the main thoroughfare on the way out of town.

There are a few antique shops in the town, but it is best known for exceptionally early potatoes. It was once also known for its whiskey, but the distillery is now closed.

In the spacious square is a statue to the military hero Sir Robert Rollo Gillespie (1766-1814), who was born in a large house on the south side of the square, and died in action in Nepal.

## Giant's Ring

The gargantuan proportions of this earthwork have earned it its name – it is 600ft in diameter, almost 12ft high, and 60ft wide at the base – large enough for the local gentry to hold horse races inside it. Now it is a big, rough grassy saucer, with views over Belfast city to the north. Almost in the centre of the saucer is an impressive tomb with five upright stones and a large capstone over the chamber. Other stones lie about. The ring dates from about 3000 BC and may have been a ceremonial or assembly site in the late Stone Age.

## Legananny Dolmen/Lag an Eanaigh

On the south face of Cratlieve, 850ft above sea level, is a dolmen with a splendid view of the Mourne Mountains to the south. This is

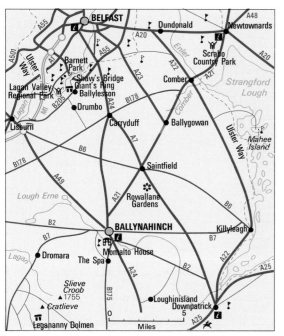

**OTHER PLACES TO SEE**
**Drumbo** Parish church, built 1788, has fine campanile with eight bells.
**WALKS**
**Minnowburn Beeches** 128 acres in Lagan river valley.
**Ulster Way** Along western shore of Strangford Lough.
**SPORT**
**Angling** Game fishing: Montalto lakes and others owned by the Department of Agriculture.
**Golf** Belvoir Park Golf Club, 18-hole course. Tel: (0232) 646113/491693.
Gilnahirk Golf Club, 9-hole course. Tel: (0232) 448477.
Knockbracken Golf and Country Club, 18-hole course. Tel: (0232) 792108.
The Spa Golf Club, 18-hole course. Tel: (0238) 562365.
**INFORMATION**
Belfast Tourist Information. Tel: (0232) 246609.

From an early age Robert Rollo Gillespie got what he wanted. At the age of ten, as was the custom of the day, his parents bought him a commission in the 45th Foot, and by 1783 he was a Cornet of the 3rd Horse garrison at Clogher, in County Tyrone. Gillespie then eloped with an heiress and married her. Later, at Athy, he was the second at a duel and argued with the opposing second, Mad Will Barrington, starting another duel. He shot his man dead, being saved himself when Barrington's bullet deflected off his jacket button.

Gillespie considered it wise to leave for the colonies, where he became involved in plans to destabilise the French colonies on Santo Domingo (now Haiti). He was captured by the French but saved himself with a masonic handshake. Back in Cork a punch-up in a theatre forced him to leave the country disguised as a nursing mother. He returned to the West Indies, where eight disgruntled settlers alleged that he had cheated them. Six he put to the sword.

His adventures continued. He forestalled his own kidnapping on a boat on the Bosporus, and cured a sheik, thus gaining a protector across the desert sands to Baghdad. He fought in India, Java and Nepal, where on October 31, 1814, impetuous as ever, he led an attack on a small hill-fort, ahead of the agreed assault time. His Royal Irish Dragoons followed him, the English troops hung back and he fell, sword in hand with a bullet through the heart, and the words 'One last shot for the honour of Down' on his lips.

SCARLET CARPET *In late spring the floor of Rowallane Gardens is covered with rhododendron petals.*

FLAX FIELDS AT SEAFORDE *Sheaths of cut flax are left to dry before being processed to make linen.*

WOODLAND WALK *Minnowburn Beeches offers quiet walks through woodland and fields.*

megalithic stonework at its most impressive. Whereas many dolmens are only semi-structured groups of fallen boulders, here the great capstone, 10ft by 4ft by 2ft, stands clear of the ground supported by three stones 7½ft high, looking like a huge tripod.

### Loughinisland/Loch an Oileáin

The three ruined churches of Loughinisland are seen at their best on a summer's evening when the only sound on the lough may be the swish of a casting line, the plop of water dropping off oars, or the throb of a distant tractor. A narrow causeway leads to the peaceful ruins in their wistful setting. The Middle Church probably dates to the 13th century. The larger North Church was built in the 15th century, probably to replace the earlier church. It was used until 1720. And the South Church, the smallest of the three, has the date 1636 carved over the door beside the initials 'PMC' – Phelim MacCartan.

### Rowallane Gardens

One of the great gardens of the British Isles, Rowallane was started by the Reverend John Moore in the last century, in the spirit of the great Victorian plant collectors. Its 56 acres include a pierrot's bandstand which was rescued from Newcastle Promenade and re-erected where John Moore preached.

In 1903, Hugh Armitage Moore, a distinguished plantsman, inherited the house and estate. He then redesigned this brilliant garden, where amazing showers of rhododendrons and azaleas burst into bloom in the spring, thriving on the light acid soil of the drumlins of County Down. The garden, 200ft above sea level and protected by an effective windbreak of beech, pine, holly and laurel, is the Ulster headquarters of the National Trust.

Driving to the gardens it is easy to miss the village of Saintfield, the 1990 winner of the Britain in Bloom award, with its lovely Georgian and Victorian houses and fine market house. In the graveyard are tombstones of men who were killed in the 1798 rebellion.

**Rowallane Gardens** *Daily, Jan-Mar, Oct-Dec, Mon-Fri 12-4.30pm; Mar-Apr, July-Sept, daily, 12-6pm. May and June, daily, 12-9pm. Tel: (0238) 510131.*

# Blackstone Villages

*The winding back roads of west Down are lined with big stone walls and the mature beech and chestnut coppices of great estates. Heavy stone gateposts mark the entrance to tree-lined avenues leading up to 17th and 18th-century yeomen's and planters' houses. Whinstone bridges mark each tributary of the rivers Bann and Lagan, along whose banks lie the occasional abandoned corn or linen mill and villages of blackstone houses brightened by flowers in window boxes.*

## Banbridge/Droichead na Banna

An important stop between Dublin and Belfast in earlier times, Banbridge is now the industrial centre of the area. In 1834 an underpass was cut into the hill over which the broad, steep main street runs, to enable the Royal Mail coaches to move more easily through the town. As a result, the coaching inn had to be moved from the Bunch of Grapes to what is now the Downshire Arms.

Banbridge is a pleasant town with riverside gardens and an extravagant suspension bridge built in 1845, which leads to an old mill. In Church Square there is a commanding statue of Captain Francis Crozier, discoverer in 1848 of the North-West Passage. He is flanked by four polar bears and panels depicting two ships locked in the Arctic ice – Crozier's ship and that of Sir John Franklin who also tried to find the passage. Crozier was descended from Huguenots who settled in the area in the 1680s and established a linen trade. A Blue Plaque on a Regency house across the street from the statue marks his birthplace in 1796.

On the Dromore road out of the town, another house bears a Blue Plaque, to the hymn writer Joseph Scriven (1819-86), whose best-known work is the hymn *What a friend we have in Jesus.*

## Dromore/Druim Mór

This small town is given some stature by its Norman motte and bailey, and its tiny Protestant cathedral of Christ the Redeemer (1808), the third known on the site since St Colman established an abbey here in the 6th century. The cathedral's rector will show visitors carved misericords depicting the history of the building, and a tomb and monument to the bishops Jeremy Taylor (1613-67) and Thomas Percy (1729-1811). Percy is remembered for his *Reliques*, a collection of old English ballads which influenced Wordsworth's *Lyrical Ballads*, written in 1798.

The town's important buildings were destroyed in 1641 and all that remains are a stone in the cathedral, called St Colman's Pillow, and a 9th-century High Cross set into the graveyard boundary. Outside the Town Hall are the original stocks, used in fun during the town's festivals.

## Hillsborough/Cromghlinn

The steep main street of this town is lined with attractive little houses, including several craft shops. At the bottom of the hill is one of Ireland's most elegant Gothic Revival churches, St Malachy's. At the top of the hill round the square are some fine Georgian houses and also the massive wrought-iron gates of Hillsborough Castle, formerly the residence of the Governor of Northern Ireland. The very fine ironwork in the gates and screen came from Richhill Castle in County Armagh and is dated 1745.

Off the central square, opposite the courthouse, stands Hillsborough Fort. It was built in 1650 by Colonel Arthur Hill, after whom the town is named, because it commanded the road from Dublin to Carrickfergus, along which warring Irish rebels might approach. The original gatehouse was remodelled in the mid-18th century for family feasts and parties, and a gazebo was erected in memory of Bishop Taylor, who lived here with the Hills in the 1660s. It is said that William III spent the night in the fort on his way to the Battle of the Boyne in 1690.

Behind the gatehouse lies the great star-shaped artillery fort with towers, walls and ramparts. Beyond this is a forest park with a lake, where fishing and canoeing are possible. The Shambles, nearby, was once a cattle market, but is now an art gallery.

**Hillsborough Fort** *Apr-Sept, Tues-Sat 10am-7pm, Sun 2-7pm; Oct-Mar, Tues-Sat 10am-4pm, Sun 2-4pm. Tel: (0846) 683285.*

SEEING FOREVER *On a clear day the view from Katesbridge stretches to the Mourne Mountains.*

HILLSBOROUGH FORT *The 1650 fort was built to defend the road to Carrickfergus.*

**OTHER PLACES TO SEE**
**Gilford Castle** Built around 1864 and the focus of antique auctions every year in Mar, June, Sept and Dec.
**Scarva** Pretty village and site of annual pageant re-enacting the Battle of the Boyne.

**EVENTS**
**Banbridge Civic Festival** June.
**Battle of the Boyne** Scarva Demesne, July.
**Dromore Horse Fair** Late Sept.

**SPORT**
**Angling** Coarse fishing: River Lagan. Game fishing: Corbet Lough, Hillsborough lake, Lough Brickland and River Bann.
**Golf** Banbridge Golf Club, 12-hole course. Tel: (08206) 62342.

**INFORMATION**
Banbridge Tourist Information. Tel: (08206) 62799.
Hillsborough Tourist Information. Tel: (0846) 682477.

## Loughbrickland/Loch Bricleann

Bricriu, the legendary poet after whom this lough and its tidy town were named, had such a reputation for slander that he became known as 'Bricriu of the bitter mouth'. The *Annals of the Four Masters*, a historical record set down by four monks between 1632 and 1636, documents a feast he gave at his palace at Dun Rudraige, for King Conor and his Ulster warriors. The feast ended in slaughter because Bricriu divided the portions in such a way that he inspired intense rivalry between his guests. The Feast of Bricriu is one of the major tales in the Ulster Cycle, one of the four groups of tales in Irish mythology.

Today the town has more peaceful associations – with trout fishing. It is a typical Down town with blackstone houses and hanging flower baskets.

## Moira/Maigh Rath

The broad hilly main street of this elegant town is planted with rowan trees and lined with 18th-century blackstone houses, each with curved carriage archways and fine fanlights over the front doors. The market house, built in 1810, marked the completion of the village. St John's parish church stands to the north at the end of a grassy avenue from where you can see the woods and ponds of the demesne of the former Earls of Moira.

FLORAL FANTASY *A donkey and cart made of pots of flowers decorates a street in Moira.*

William Butler Yeats, grandfather of the poet, was curate here in 1835, 110 years after the church was built.

Moira is near the site of a battle fought on June 24, 637, which gave rise to a host of the most celebrated Irish legends. During the battle Domnall II, King of Tara, defeated his foster son, Congall. The horrors of the battle caused the madness of Suibhne Gelt, Congall's right-hand man and son of the King of the Dalriada, a south Antrim tribe. The tale of Suibhne's torment later inspired the contemporary Irish poet Seamus Heaney to translate it, in *Sweeney Astray*.

## Waringstown/Baile an Bhairínigh

The original Flemish and Huguenot cottages of this spic-and-span village were rebuilt in

the 1930s. Towering over the town is the pink and flaking Waringstown House, built in 1667 by a pupil of Inigo Jones and with a deceptive façade that disguises the house's composition of stone and rubble.

When the 17th-century writer Jonathan Swift was Prebendary at Carrickfergus he proposed marriage to the town founder's niece, Jane Waring, whom he nicknamed Varina. She brushed aside his advances but later, cynics say, when his prospects had improved, she attempted to reopen the affair, to little avail.

The parish church, built in 1681, has a Jacobean interior furnished almost entirely of Irish oak from local woods. There is a beautiful choir screen and fine panelling.

# Where St Patrick First Landed

*Historic castles command a landscape formed from rocky outcrops that thrust into sea and lough. Even before the castles were built, St Patrick, Apostle of Ireland, landed at Saul, and was buried in Downpatrick. The mild climate of the east coast ensures that many rare plants flourish, seen at their finest in the magnificent Mount Stewart Gardens.*

## OTHER PLACES TO SEE

**Kilclief Castle** Said to have been built a little after 1413 by John Sely, Bishop of Down, who lived here until 1443 when sacked for adulterous liaison with Lettice Savage, a married lady who lived with him in the castle. Has four floors with twin towers on east side and entrance on inner wall of south-east tower.

**Kirkistown Castle** Near Portavogie; 1622 tower house with part of its curtain wall, and stumps of two turrets.

**Portavogie** Important fishing port famous for giant prawns named after it; these and other fresh fish sold each evening from the quay.

**Sketrick Castle** On causeway linking Sketrick Island to mainland are ruins of mid-15th-century castle. Large central room on ground floor, revealed by storm damage, was probably a secure boat bay.

**Strangford Castle** 16th-century castle built to control ships entering Strangford Lough. Just above castle door is a gaping hole which seems to be an old entrance. Open daily, exc Mon in July and Aug. Sat and Sun, Apr-June and Sept.

## WALKS

**St Patrick's Way** Paths centred around Saul retracing steps of St Patrick from his landing place at mouth of River Slaney.

**Ulster Way** Part of the 500 mile trail runs along western side of Strangford Lough, starting at Killyleagh and finishing in Newtownards.

## EVENTS

**Downpatrick Race Course** Horse racing throughout year. Tel: (0396) 612054.

**Sketrick Island to Hen Island Race** Oct.

**St Patrick's Day Celebrations** Mar 17.

**Strangford/Portaferry Festival** July.

**Ulster Harp National** Downpatrick, Feb.

## SPORT

**Angling** Coarse fishing: River Quoile and Tullynagee lakes. Game fishing: River Quoile and Loughs Cowey and Morey. Sea fishing: Portaferry, Portavogie, Strangford Lough.

**Golf** Downpatrick Golf Club, 18-hole course. Tel: (0396) 2152.
Mahee Island Golf Club, 9-hole course. Tel: (0238) 541234.

**Sailing** Portaferry Sailing Club. Tel: (02477) 28770.
Quoile Yacht Club. Tel: (0396) 612266.
Strangford Lough Yacht Club. Tel: (0238) 541202.
Strangford Sailing Club. Tel: (0396) 613711.

## INFORMATION

Downpatrick Tourist Information. Tel: (0396) 614331.

## Audley's Castle

On a rocky outcrop that thrusts into Strangford Lough is the strategically sited Audley's Castle, built by the Audleys in the 15th century. Visitors can enjoy panoramic views from the rooftop and scan the lough and surrounding countryside, much as the castle's inhabitants would have done centuries ago when trying to protect the castle from enemies.

About 1 mile west, off a lane running north from the road to the castle, is Audleystown Cairn, excavated in 1952. It is a long burial mound with eight chambers containing 34 Stone Age skeletons, buried with pottery and flint implements.

## Castle Espie

The Wildfowl and Wetlands Trust, whose creator was Sir Peter Scott, runs Castle Espie Wetland Centre just south of Comber. This is the trust's showpiece in Northern Ireland.

Water ripples and flows in the old clay pits of a now disused brickworks dating back to the 1870s. Around it, hides enable visitors to watch the overwintering ducks, geese and swans from the Arctic. There are waders everywhere, and in the lagoons exotic species from a private collection, with their wings partly clipped, mix with the commoner visitors, making up Ireland's largest collection of wildfowl.

The castle, in fact a 19th-century country house, has an art gallery and a collection of beautifully preserved stuffed birds – a reminder of the Victorian approach to birdwatching. It also has a tea house and souvenir shop.

**Castle Espie** *Mar-Oct, Wed-Sat 10.30am-5.30pm; July-Aug, also Sun 2-6pm; Nov-Feb, Sat only. Tel: (0247) 874146/872517.*

## Castleward House

The splendour of Castleward House is two faced. The front is in classical style with pillars and pediments, while the back is Gothic with pointed arched windows topped by battlements and finials. Inside, the classical columns and doorcases contrast with Gothic rooms, such as the boudoir with an extravagant fan-vaulted ceiling, modelled on Henry VII's chapel in Westminster Abbey. The curious division reflects the disagreement between the 1st Lord Bangor, Bernard Ward, and his wife, for whom the house was built in the 1760s. He favoured the classical style while she preferred the Gothic.

The house stands on high ground overlooking Strangford Lough near the centre of an 800 acre estate and surrounded by fine gardens and pleasure grounds. The working centre of the estate is down by the loughside. There the original Castle Ward, a tower house of 1610, stands in a farmyard along with a restored corn mill and saw mill. An information centre is sited in the old slaughterhouse.

**Castleward House** *Apr-Aug, daily exc Thur, 1-6pm; Sept and Oct, weekends and public holidays only. Shop and restaurant as for house, but open from 12 noon. Tel: (0396) 86204.*

**Estate and grounds** *All year, dawn to dusk.*

**Strangford Lough Barn** *May and June, weekends, public holidays, 2-6pm.*

## Downpatrick/Dún Pádraig

When St Patrick arrived here he may have found two great duns, or forts, on twin hilltops. They stood half a mile apart, above the waters of a tidal inlet of Strangford Lough. The water has now gone, but the hills remain.

Since the 7th century, Downpatrick has claimed to be the recognised burial place of St Patrick, the Apostle of Ireland. If so, he is more likely to be buried under the cathedral than beneath the massive granite boulder that bears his name, and which was placed in the graveyard in 1900.

The present cathedral dates mainly from the early 19th century, though it incorporates remains of earlier churches that were built, destroyed and rebuilt over 14 turbulent centuries of Irish history. A worn 10th-century High Cross outside the east end of the cathedral faces the Mall, which leads between the red-brick houses of the Southwell Charity of 1733, and the Down County Museum, built as the county jail in 1789-96. A section of the museum tells the story of St Patrick, while the main galleries recount the history of the people of Down over the centuries, with a collection of pictures, documents, costumes, tools and other artefacts. Two buildings, much the same in size, stand in the jail courtyard. One of these was the governor's residence, the other the cell block which housed 100 prisoners. The best-known prisoner was Thomas Russell, leader of the United Irishmen, whose rebellion was crushed in 1798. Russell was hanged in 1803 outside the gatehouse, from the sill over the entrance gate through which today's visitors pass. The holes made to support the gallows, now bricked up, can still be seen. In the churchyard of the Protestant parish church, a

HOW'S THAT! *The most English of games, enjoyed by two men, is played at Downpatrick.*

CASTLEWARD HOUSE *Freshly laundered linen hangs in the stone-flagged Victorian laundry.*

stone inscribed 'The grave of Russell' marks the rebel's burial place.

**Down County Museum** *Tues-Fri 11am-5pm, Sat 2-5pm; July and Aug, also Sun, 2-6pm. Tel: (0396) 615218.*

### Grey Abbey

Thanks to being retained for parish worship for much of the 17th and 18th centuries, more remains of Grey Abbey church than of many other Irish monasteries. Built on Strangford Lough, it is set in mature parkland and has an atmosphere of monastic calm. The abbey was founded in 1193 by Affreca, daughter of Godred, the Norse King of Man, and wife of John de Courcy, Norman conqueror of Ulster. It was probably built by the same Anglo-Norman masons who raised the great castles of Carrickfergus and Dundrum.

The abbey's masterpiece is the west door, an elaborate multi-arched confection of dog-tooth moulding supported by two clusters of carved pillars. A memorial on the nave wall recalls the fate in 1652 of Sir James (Montgomery) 'by pirates shot and thereof dead, by them i'th sea solemnly buried'.

### Inch Abbey

Within sight of Down Cathedral and the Mound of Down in Downpatrick stands 'Island Abbey' on a low mound beside the River Quoile. It was once surrounded by marsh on three sides, and the present approach road follows the line of the monks' causeway across the marsh. The abbey's site failed to protect it from the Vikings, who destroyed it in 1001 and again in 1149. The present remains date from its re-foundation in 1180 by John de Courcy. From the start the

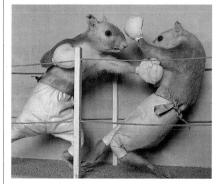

FURRY FIGHTERS *Stuffed boxing squirrels are in Castleward House morning room.*

abbey was meant to be a centre of Norman influence and an edict of 1380 debarred Irishmen from joining the community. The three striking lancet windows that remain, at the eastern end of the church, once lit the altar. It was here, separated from the nave by screens, that the monks congregated for worship. The abbey's manual workers, the lay brothers, were kept to the nave. Other buildings on the site include a chapter house and an infirmary as well as a bakehouse with an enclosed well.

### Killyleagh/Cill O'Laoch

From a small harbour, a long uphill climb leads to a two-towered, crenellated and romantically turreted castle. Here the young Hans Sloane was encouraged to educate himself in the library by the owner, the Earl of Clanbrassil. Sloane (1660-1753) went on to become physician to George II and founder of Kew Gardens and the British Museum, which he started with his own unusual and vast collection of books, manuscripts and curiosities. He is commemorated by a stone at the castle gatehouse.

Prince Andrew, Duke of York, was created Baron Killyleagh on his wedding day because his wife's forebears came from the area. The castle is not open to the public.

### Mount Stewart

A magnificent collection of fine trees and rare shrubs from all over the world flourishes in the gardens of Mount Stewart. They are spread throughout 17 separate enclosures, woods, drives and walks and include mimosa (*Acacia*) trees, eucalyptuses, palms, bamboos and tree heaths. The gardens were created by Edith, Lady Londonderry from 1921. Mount Stewart is now rated among the top gardens in the United Kingdom.

The huge airy windows of the creeper-clad south front of the house overlook a formal Italian garden. George Dance, surveyor to the City of London, and architect of Newgate Prison, designed the house, which is full of memorabilia of the best known of the Stewarts – Robert Viscount Castlereagh, War Minister and Foreign Secretary throughout much of the Napoleonic Wars. The 22 chairs he brought back from the Congress at Vienna in 1814 are now in the dining room, while the Castlereagh Room contains portraits of the statesman and many of his papers, including correspondence with Nelson and Wellington. There is also some fine furniture, porcelain

CLASSICAL ELEGANCE *Two classical nudes, carved in Rome in 1856, stand in the hall at Mount Stewart. The Carrara marble font is of the same period. The hall was designed in the late 1830s by the Irish architect William Vitruvius Morrison.*

## SHEARWATER NIGHTS

They come in by night, low over the waves, silhouetted against the orange glow of Belfast city, at the top of Belfast Lough. They fly with little short bursts of power from their narrow, angled wings, each burst followed by a short glide. Some come straight in from the open sea, others settle first, a raft of dark shapes crying on the black, shifting waters. These are the Manx shearwaters coming home to roost and breed on Light House Island, after their 5000 mile flight back from their winter quarters off the coasts of Brazil and Argentina. The shearwaters come at dusk each evening to avoid their larger would-be predators, the great black-backed gulls, and make their way to the old rabbit burrows they have occupied, to lay their solitary eggs.

The Vikings disliked these birds, which flew over them on the night sea, hearing in their odd, plaintive cry the spirit of evil. Today the birds are regarded more favourably. Their 1000 pair colony is the real interest of the Copeland Bird Observatory Club. The observatory was set up on the island in 1954 for the purpose of observing and ringing birds of passage. Since then its members have ringed more than 12,000 birds and their reports each year list a number of surprise visitors among the old familiars.

---

and paintings, including one by Stubbs of the racehorse Hambletonian.

**House** *Apr, May, Sept and Oct, 1-6pm, Sat, Sun and public holidays. June-Aug, daily except Tues. Tel: (024774) 387.*
**Gardens** *3-6pm, days as for house.*

### Nendrum

Two causeways and a narrow road that snakes the length of Reagh Island lead to the monastery of Nendrum on Mahee Island in Strangford Lough – where it lay forgotten for 400 years until the middle of the last century. The 6 acre site on a low hill was founded in the 5th century by St Mochaoi and is considered to be the finest pre-Norman monastic site in Northern Ireland. It consists of three concentric enclosures. The outer one may have contained gardens, orchards and fields. Excavated finds in the middle enclosure indicate that timber huts housing workshops once stood there. Iron styluses, used for writing on wax tablets, found within stone foundations close by, mark it as the site of the monastery school.

The inner enclosure houses the graveyard, remains of the church and a Round Tower, and an evocative reconstruction of the monks' sundial, its three main rays etched to mark the times of the three main services: terce, sext and nones.

### Portaferry/Port an Pheire

The broken grey tooth of Portaferry Castle sticks out above the neat white houses that line the town's waterfront to Strangford Lough. The south end of the waterfront serves fishermen and yachtsmen.

Beneath the ruin of the early 16th-century castle is the late 20th-century Northern Ireland Aquarium. In 20 or so huge tanks swim, or lurk, representatives of some of the 2000 species of marine creatures that live in the lough.

From the aquarium, Castle Street climbs up to the Square and some handsome Georgian buildings, including the Market House, now a community centre, and a smart stuccofaced house with a pillared portico.

East of the town, overlooking the Irish Sea, is the romantic pile of Quintin Castle, complete with massive battlemented keep, walls and turrets. Dating from the 15th century, it has been restored many times.

**Aquarium** *Sept-Mar, Tues-Sat 10.30am-5pm, Sun 1-5pm; Apr-Aug, Tues-Sat 10am-8pm, Sun 1-8pm. Tel: (02477) 28062.*

---

### Quoile Pondage

A tide control barrage, built in 1957 to stop the River Quoile from flooding the low-lying parts of Downpatrick, brought the town's long history as a port to an end and established one of the first National Nature Reserves in Northern Ireland. The pondage is a 450 acre holding area for flood water from the river which is released through the barrage on the ebbing tide. The banks are rich with wild flowers and the water with wildfowl. A 2½ mile walk along the east bank of the River Quoile starts at a car park and picnic site near the Quoile Bridge. The walk takes visitors past the old sailing ship quays, and the skeleton of a coal schooner, destroyed by fire in 1922. Farther on is Quoile Castle, the ruin of a 16th-century tower house. Beside it is a Visitor Centre with displays on the history and wildlife of the reserve.

**Visitor Centre** *Apr-Sept, 11am-6pm, exc Mon. Oct-Mar, Sat and Sun 1-5pm. Tel: (0396) 615520.*

### Saul/Sabhall

St Patrick is said to have established his first church in Ireland here, in the barn of a local chieftain ('Saul' comes from the Old Irish *sabhall,* meaning a 'barn'). The church and Round Tower that now occupy the site were built in 1932 to mark the 1500th anniversary of St Patrick's arrival. Nothing remains from his time, but there are some cross-carved stones dating from the 8th to 12th centuries, relics of a monastery that stood on the site until dissolved in the 16th century. Just a mile east of the church, on Slieve Patrick's summit, is a massive statue of the saint also placed there by the Roman Catholics in 1932.

### Struell Wells

Off a road past the Downshire Hospital in Downpatrick is a rough signposted track to Struell. Here lie four wells known as St Patrick's Wells, although there is no written record of them before the 14th century. The stone buildings, along the course of an underground stream, date from about 1600. Beside the shell of an old church is a drinking well, a small circular building with a domed roof. Next is the eye well, rectangular with a pyramidal stone roof. The large building is the men's bathhouse, which has a dressing room lined with stone seats and is connected to the bathing room. The roofless shell opposite is the women's bathing room. The wells were a place of pilgrimage until the 1800s.

# STRANGFORD LOUGH

*A sea inlet and wildlife reserve of great beauty and variety, one of Europe's richest maritime habitats*

The Irish Sea cuts deep into the rolling hills of north-eastern County Down, forming Strangford Lough, one of the largest sea inlets in the British Isles. Through a narrow, fiord-like entrance, known simply as 'the Narrows', the tidal waters surge into the main body of the lough at speeds of up to 8 knots (from which came the Norse name, *Strangfjord* – 'strong ford'). The lough washes some 150 miles of twisting coastline and the shores of about 120 islands.

Strangford Lough is a place of great natural beauty and variety. It has a dramatic rocky shoreline to the south, 160ft drumlins (rounded glacial boulder-clay hills) to the west and bird-trodden mud flats to the north, as well as islands, shallow reefs (known as pladdies, and which are eroded drumlins), bays, headlands and marshes.

THE WILDLIFE Vast quantities of microscopic plankton are swept into the lough every day by the currents, and the constant movement of water distributes them and an abundance of other nutrients to every part of the lough. The plankton provides a ready supply of food for an enormous range of creatures – Strangford has more than 2000 species of marine animals, making it one of the richest places for maritime life in the whole of Europe.

The 100ft deep bedrock of the turbulent 'Narrows' is carpeted with brilliantly coloured sponges and soft corals. In the shallow areas

of muddy sands to the north, plaice, dab and flounder feed on burrowing creatures, while out in the mid-water depths, huge shoals of herring fry and sand eels chase after plankton. Occasionally a massive basking shark, the world's second largest fish, is spotted cruising around the entrance of the lough, feasting on plankton. And giant skates glide through the depths, weighing up to 198lb. If anglers catch them they are expected to return them to the waters, after weighing them. The lough has the largest colony of common seals in Ireland – over 800 – and also attracts pilot whales and porpoises.

Strangford's marine life draws a huge number and variety of birds. In September flocks of pale-bellied brent geese arrive from Arctic Canada, heading for the swards of eel

*LIFE IN THE LOUGH Early summer in Strangford Lough sees colonies of seals on rocks and low reefs giving birth to pups (above). A grey heron (below) and oystercatchers (bottom) are among the birds that thrive on the rich supplies of food that are constantly replenished by the waters of the lough.*

grass on the northern mud flats. Wigeons, too, make the journey, from Iceland and the Soviet Union, while knots from Greenland join flocks of turnstones, lapwings and bar-tailed godwits in the salt marshes. As the winter winds bite, shelducks and whooper swans from Iceland also take shelter here.

With so many small islands offering a variety of good cover, plenty of food nearby, and little human disturbance, Strangford Lough is an ideal nesting site for up to 40 different species of birds. Among the noisiest and most successful of its spring and summer visitors are the terns – sandwich, common, arctic and the rarer roseate tern. Their teeming colonies may be made up of as many as 1500 nests squashed together at a single site.

The National Trust, which runs the Strangford Lough Wildlife Scheme, also protects the rich plant life of the area  the lichens, stonecrops and sea pinks encrusting the rocks along the shoreline; the gorse, sea campion and orchids on the islands; the grasses, sea aster and sea lavender of the salt marshes.

VISITING STRANGFORD The lough has attracted people to it for centuries, from prehistoric settlers who hunted wildfowl in its marshes and woods and collected shellfish along its shores, to the 18th-century owners of Castle Ward House and Mount Stewart who established magnificent parklands and gardens there. Strangford continues to draw large numbers of visitors. There are birdwatching tours, boats for hire, excellent viewpoints of the wildlife all around the lough, and bird hides at Castle Espie, Reagh Island and The Gasworks at Mount Stewart.

# Forest Parks and Beach Resorts

*The mild climate and glorious coastal scenery make this an attractive place to spend time. To add to its interest there are historic castles, ancient stone circles and Northern Ireland's National Arboretum, centred at Castlewellan Forest Park. This is fine walking country, especially in the Mourne Mountains which dominate the landscape with their spectacular and unparalleled beauty.*

### Ardglass/Ard Ghlais

The sprucely painted houses and cottages with colourful gardens that curve round the harbour road are the peaceful successors to a chain of six tower-house castles and fortified warehouses. They were built by local merchants to protect the harbour of Ardglass in the troubled times of the 14th to 16th centuries, when Ardglass was the busiest port in Ulster.

Jordan's Castle, which looks as forbidding as the day it was built, held out from 1598 to 1601 against the forces of the Earl of Tyrone in rebellion against Queen Elizabeth I. The castle owes its survival to restoration early this century by Francis Bigger, a Belfast antiquarian who also provided the antiques that furnish it.

A stroll round the town reveals three other castles in ruins, two incorporated in a modern building, and a row of fortified warehouses, now a golf clubhouse.
**Jordan's Castle** *June-Sept, Tues-Sat 10am-7pm; Sun 2-7pm. Tel: (0232) 230560 for group bookings.*

### Ballynoe Stone Circle

A five-minute walk, signposted off the Downpatrick to Rathmullan Lower road on the south side of Ballynoe, leads over a massive five-step stone stile through a hawthorn tunnel to a double circle of standing stones in a well-grazed field. An inner ring surrounds a mound in which two Stone Age graves were found. The outer ring, about 35yds across, consists of huge, close-set stones, many standing 6ft or more above the present ground level. Others have fallen, and a few more are scattered round the field. Whatever the circle's purpose – astronomical, ritual, or both – is not now known. But it has clearly been useful in recent times; many of the stones have been rubbed smooth by cattle seeking relief from itching hides.

### Castlewellan Forest Park

Northern Ireland's National Arboretum, one of the finest in the British Isles, is the centrepiece of Castlewellan Forest Park, which covers 1100 acres in the northern foothills of the Mourne Mountains. The core

NATIONAL ARBORETUM *The 15 acre walled garden contains rare shrubs from around the world.*

of the arboretum is a 15 acre walled garden containing exotic and indigenous plants. One of its gigantic Wellingtonias bears the planting date 1854 – just one year after the species was first brought to Europe. Other choice trees include cabbage palms, eucalyptuses and eucryphias, which flourish in the mild climate. Tender plants are displayed in greenhouses, one of which also shelters a flock of colourful, tropical birds.

Outside, in the park, the Scottish Baronial castle of Castlewellan (now a private conference centre) looks out over a mile-long lake stocked with trout. In the mature woodland surrounding the lake, lofty beeches and gnarled oaks mingle with other hardwoods. The outer reaches of the park are run as a commercial forestry of mixed hardwood and conifers. There are waymarked walks, which enable visitors to see the best of the park without getting lost.
**Castlewellan Forest Park** *Open all year. Tel: (03967) 78664.*

### Dundrum Castle

Even today, nothing can stir for miles around without being seen from the battlements of Dundrum Castle. The castle stands on a hill overlooking Dundrum Bay and its fine natural harbour, commanding the view far out to sea.

The oldest part of the castle, dating in part from the 12th century, crowns the top of the hill where a round keep towers within a lofty wall enclosing 2½ acres. Its stones sheltered defenders for more than 400 years, from a siege by King John in 1210 to a final battering by Cromwell in 1652. They now shelter mosses, ferns and wild flowers in their crevices. A lower walled enclosure, where venerable beeches and sycamores shade a well-kept lawn, once protected the castle's domestic and farm buildings. It contains the gabled shell of a 17th-century house.
**Opening times** *Apr-Sept, Tues-Sat 10am-7pm, Sun 2-7pm; Oct-Mar, Sat 10am-4pm, Sun 2-4pm.*

### Maghera/Machaire Rátha

Tucked away behind the neat, cement-rendered 19th-century parish church is the ruin of its predecessor, which dates from around the 13th century. Its gaunt gable stands on a slight rise amid a churchyard studded with ancient tombstones. A short way into a neighbouring field stands the 18ft stump of a Round Tower. The oval hole in which the door once stood, about 5ft above the ground, reveals the 3ft thickness of the lower wall. It marks the site of a monastery founded in the 6th century by St Donard, after whom Slieve Donard is named.

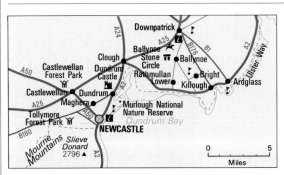

Newcastle, July.

**SPORT**
**Angling** Game fishing: Castlewellan Forest Park.
**Golf** Ardglass Golf Club, 18-hole course. Tel: (0396) 841219.
Bright Castle Golf Club, 18-hole course. Tel: (0396) 841319.
Royal County Down Golf Club, 18-hole course. Tel: (03967) 23314.

**INFORMATION**
Newcastle Tourist Information. Tel: (03967) 22222.

**OTHER PLACES TO SEE**
**Murlough National Nature Reserve** Coastal reserve with abundant birdlife.

**EVENTS**
**Ardglass Festival Week** Aug.
**Pipe Band Championships**

## PERCY FRENCH, IRISH TROUBADOUR

William Percy French (1854-1920), singer and writer of some of Ireland's most popular songs, was born in Roscommon, the son of a landlord. For a man with his musical talents he studied an unlikely subject – engineering. After graduating from Trinity College, Dublin, he became an inspector of drains in Cavan, living in Farnham Street, in the stone terraced house that stands next to what is now the Tourism Office.

During this seven-year period he wrote some of his best-known songs, including *Abdulla Bulbul Ameer* (1877) and organised a minstrel troupe known as the Kinniepottle Komics.

French then left Cavan for Dublin, where he worked for a time as editor and illustrator of a satirical magazine called *The Jarvey*. He made ends meet with solo performances in which he sang his own songs while drawing 'smoke pictures' with coloured chalk on brown paper; as the song finished he would turn the image upside down when, to his audience's glee, it would become another image entirely.

His most famous songs include *The Mountains of Mourne* and *Come Home Paddy Reilly to Ballyjamesduff*. He even wrote light operas, among them *The Knight of the Road*, which was staged several years ago as *Freeny!* He died in Formby, Lancashire, leaving a wealth of ditties that have become fixed in the Irish tradition of folk songs.

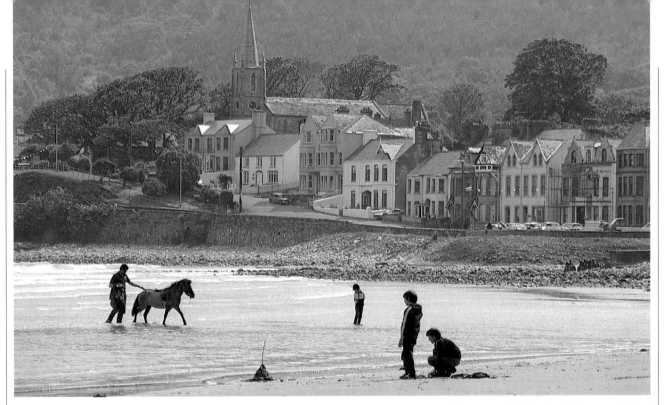

MISTY MOURNES *The Mourne Mountains provide a purple backdrop to the fields around Clough.*

NEWCASTLE *St John's chapel of ease overlooks the town's Victorian seafront.*

### Newcastle/An Caisleán Nua

Approaching the town from the south, the coast road rises to cross the toe of Slieve Donard, revealing one of the country's most popular resorts stretched out in a mile-long curve round the sandy shore of Dundrum Bay. The red-brick Slieve Donard Hotel marks the northern end of the town, while beyond the hotel is the Royal County Down Golf Club, one of the world's finest courses.

There are three notable memorials on the seafront. On the Central Promenade is a fountain commemorating the songwriter Percy French, composer of *The Mountains of Mourne*, the song that brought fame to this part of County Down.

Behind the Leisure Complex an inscription on a huge boulder records the aeroplane flight made along the beach at Newcastle in 1910 by Harry Ferguson, later famous for his tractors. A large ship's anchor near the swimming pool at the south end of the town bears a plaque linking it to I.K. Brunel's *Great Britain*, which was shipwrecked for the first time in Dundrum Bay in 1846. It was later salvaged, repaired and, after years of service, wrecked again in the Falkland Islands, before being towed to Bristol and restored.

### Tollymore Forest Park

Waymarked walks crisscrossing Northern Ireland's most popular forest park offer everything from a mile-long stroll to a 9 mile hike. Many of the walks in the 1200 acres pass through the pleasure grounds of what was the estate of the Earls of Roden, where fine specimen trees include giant redwoods, Douglas firs and Wellingtonias. The River Shimna, which flows through the park, carries fine runs of salmon between July and November, and these can often be seen in the pool below the Ivy Bridge. Quiet watchers may even spot an otter or kingfisher.
**Opening times** *10am to sunset.*

# 'The Mountains of Mourne'

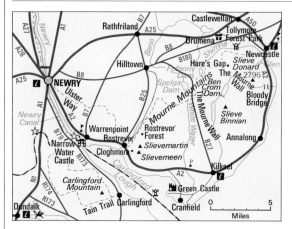

*The beautiful Mourne Mountains really do 'sweep down to the sea' as in the song that made them famous. Slieve Donard (2796ft), highest of the peaks, looks down on a rich patchwork of farmland and homesteads with many picturesque harbours, and boats bobbing on the sea.*
*Castles and ancient remains dot the landscape giving an historical flavour to this lovely place, while forests and riverside walks provide attractions for the active visitor.*

**WALKS**
**Hare's Gap** 4m walk to a high point of 1410ft.
**Glen River** 5½m strenuous walk up Slieve Donard.
**Slieve Binnian** 7m strenuous walk, to a peak of 2449ft.

**EVENTS**
**Carlingford Lough Regatta** Sept.
**Fiddlers Green Festival** Rostrevor, Aug.
**Kingdom of Mourne Festival** Annalong, July.
**Newry and Mourne Festival of the Arts** Oct.
**Newry Canal Festival and Agricultural Show** June.
**Newry Musical Feis** Apr.
**Warrenpoint Feis** Feb.
**Warrenpoint Gala Week** Aug.

**SPORT**
**Angling** Coarse fishing: Newry Canal. Game fishing: Rivers Newry and Shimna, Spelga and Fofanny dams. Sea fishing: Carlingford Lough, Kilkeel, White Water.
**Golf** Kilkeel Golf Club, 9-hole course. Tel: (06937) 62296.
Warrenpoint Golf Club, 18-hole course. Tel: (06937) 72219.
**Pony trekking** Rostrevor Forest. Tel: (06937) 38284.

**INFORMATION**
Newry Information Centre. Tel: (06937) 66232.
Kilkeel Tourist Information. Tel: (06937) 64666.

## OTHER PLACES TO SEE

**Annalong** Harbour village with barn museum containing old farming implements and domestic items, such as hand churns, and a simple wooden cradle. Open June-Aug, 2-6pm. Also 1800s water-powered corn mill, marine park and coastal path.
**Bloody Bridge** Through gate and squeeze-stile on Annalong-Newcastle road; bridge where a group of prisoners taken in 1641 Rebellion were massacred. Path to old bridge is start of Brandy Pad, old smuggling trail over Mournes.
**Drumena Cashel** Signposted off hilly lane; dry-stone wall about 6ft high and 10ft thick encircles area 132ft by 108ft. Near the centre a hole in the

ground leads to a T-shaped underground chamber. Remains of above-ground buildings in enclosure thought to have been farmstead in 6th-10th centuries.
**Rathfriland** Hilltop village with remains of castle built by the Magennises, chiefs of Iveagh. Wide views over surrounding plain.
**Silent Valley** Holds two dams that supply water to Belfast; Ben Crom most recent, built 1957, measuring 230yds across and 155ft high. Nearby is The Mourne Wall, 22 miles long, 8ft high, built 1904-22 to enclose 9000 acres of Mournes that feed reservoirs; connects summits of 15 mountains. Visitor Centre and walks.

## Green Castle/Caisleán na hOireanaí

Even with a whitewashed barn in front of the keep, a farmhouse running along its outer wall and cattle grazing below the moat, Green Castle looks formidable. Standing on a rocky knoll, 300yds from the shore, it commands the narrow entrance to Carlingford Lough. Henry III ordered its building in 1252, but it was soon captured and destroyed by the Irish. This was the start of a turbulent history. Rebuilt in 1261, it was taken by Robert Bruce's brother Edward in 1316, then by the Magennis clan in 1375 and again by the Irish later in the same century. By Queen Elizabeth I's time it again housed a royal garrison. It was finally vacated early in the 17th century after 350 years of active service. The ivy-covered ruins of a medieval church crouch in a field below the castle, and 240yds farther west a mound rises behind a row of six spruce, white Georgian cottages. The mound may have been a motte raised for a predecessor of the castle. The cottages were built to house the keepers of the lighthouse on a rock in Carlingford Lough.

## Kilkeel/Cill Chaoil

Green nets, orange buoys and lobster pots line the quayside. Red, white and blue hulls sway on the water with masts and spars thrusting out at all angles. Kilkeel claims the biggest fishing fleet in Ireland. The boats are packed together so tightly that it would be possible to walk along the harbour on their decks as easily as on the quay. When the time comes to sail, the boats have to squeeze out through a series of channels into the sea.

Appropriately, Kilkeel means 'church of the narrows', the church concerned being half a mile inland from the harbour, at the town centre. Now a ruin surrounded by old graves, it stands in an earthwork behind a high wall on Bridge Street. The pinnacled tower of its replacement, Christchurch, looms up behind it 100yds away in Newry Street.

## Newry/An tIúr

A town hall built on arches over the River Newry, and guarded by a cannon captured in the Crimean War, is accompanied by three notable firsts from Newry's long past. The Newry Canal, now disused, which runs beside the river through the middle of the town, was completed in 1741 – some 20 years before the Bridgewater Canal became the first canal to be built in England. In Hill Street, one street back from the canalside

### HILLS THAT SWEEP DOWN TO THE SEA

Red, purple, grey according to the sky – and often white in winter – the Mourne Mountains fill the south-eastern corner of County Down between Rostrevor and Newcastle, 80sq miles of granite rising to 2796ft at Slieve Donard and with ten other summits over 2000ft.

Only one road runs through the Mournes, climbing from Kilkeel on the coast to top 1200ft, where it overlooks the dark water of the Spelga Dam, before descending to Hilltown. A complete circuit of the Mournes – Newcastle – Rostrevor – Hilltown – Newcastle – extends to about 60 miles, and cuts through 'the Kingdom of Mourne', the name given to the strip of farmland that lies between the Mourne Mountains and the sea.

But the heart of the Mournes can be explored only on foot, on a web of old tracks, many with evocative names like the Brandy Pad (the old smugglers' route from the coast to Hilltown), the Black Stairs and the Trassey Track (used by the quarrymen who once hewed the mountain granite). The tracks lead into a world of heather and bilberries, moss and cotton grass, where ravens, red grouse and peregrine falcons fly and the silent visitor may spot a mountain hare or – at dusk – a badger.

Mall, is the Catholic cathedral of St Patrick and St Colman, the first to be built in Ireland since the Reformation. It was completed in 1829 and has many later additions. The interior is richly decorated in mosaic, marble and glowing stained glass. High above the cathedral and canal stands Ireland's first Protestant church, dedicated to St Patrick, which dates from 1578. A gate across the street facing the tower leads into Heather Park, once Gallows Hill – Newry's old-time place of execution.

## Rostrevor/Ros Treabhair

A 100ft obelisk alongside the coast road from Warrenpoint celebrates this quiet resort's most famous son – Major-General Robert Ross, who captured Washington and burnt the White House during the war of 1814. Even in General Ross's day the main occupation of most local people was the peaceable one of looking after holidaymakers who came to enjoy Rostrevor's mild climate and attractive surroundings.

Bridge Street, which runs down to the River Rostrevor from the town square, has some fine old Victorian shopfronts. By the tree-arched bridge over the river is a cluster of ivy-clad, early 19th-century houses with neat gardens.

On the far side of the bridge a public footpath runs upstream beside the river through the Fairy Glen. The peat-brown water of the river bubbles down over a series of small falls through a tunnel of giant oaks, sycamores and beeches, lined with wild flowers where the sun breaks through.

Rostrevor Forest, a National Nature Reserve, clings to the steep side of Slievemartin (1597ft) above Carlingford Lough, just south of the town. A path from the eastern side of the reserve zigzags up to the Cloghmore, or 'great stone', which sits about 900ft above sea level on a spur of Slievemartin. This is an enormous solitary boulder that was carried by an Ice Age glacier and eventually deposited on the mountain. Locally it is said that the legendary Ulster giant Finn MacCool threw the boulder from Carlingford Mountain, 4 miles away on the other side of the lough.

North of Rostrevor, along the River Kilbroney, are the remains of a church on the site of a 6th-century monastery.

## Warrenpoint/An Pointe

A tree-lined promenade, broad streets with handsome brightly painted Victorian villas, and busy shops that run into a huge square, tell of one side of the double life of Warrenpoint. This resort has been popular with holidaymakers for more than 150 years. But Warrenpoint was founded as a port – at the end of the 18th century – and in recent years has developed into one of the busiest ports in Northern Ireland. The old town dock, which runs up to the square, has one small berth offering entertainment to visitors when a ship is loading or unloading. But the bulk of Warrenpoint's commercial activity is hidden from them in large modern berths farther up the lough.

Beyond the port area, beside the Newry road, stands the aptly named Narrow Water Castle, strategically sited on a promontory commanding the entrance to the River Newry. A substantial stone tower surrounded by an outer wall, or bawn, it was built in the 1560s to house a royal garrison. It has since been well restored.

**Narrow Water Castle** *Tues-Sat 2-5pm.*

HEARTACHE HILLS *The Mourne Mountains are symbolic of an Irishman's homesickness.*

ROOFTOP VIEW *A grand house overlooks Narrow Water Castle on the banks of the River Newry.*

### AN IRISH FIRST

In 1742, the sailing ship *Cope* entered Dublin harbour with all flags flying and firing its guns in celebration. It was carrying the first load of coal from Coalisland in County Tyrone – and the remarkable achievement being celebrated was the fact that 18 miles of the voyage had been made by canal. All this happened some 20 years before James Brindley completed his first waterway, the 10½ mile long Bridgewater Canal on the outskirts of Manchester.

The Irish canal was 18 miles long and ran from Lough Neagh to Newry and the sea at Carlingford Lough. It had 14 locks – a device not used by Brindley until 1766, on the Trent and Mersey Canal. But, in common with those in England, the canal declined in the face of competition from the railways, and in the 1950s it closed.

317

# The Ards of Down

*The coastal road along the southern shore of Belfast Lough plays hide and seek with the sea, like the railway that runs alongside it, and darts in and out of the hills giving glimpses of sandy beaches, yacht clubs and busy harbours. Away from the coast are the beginnings of the rounded drumlin hills of the Ards Peninsula, unexpectedly rural so near to Belfast, and good walking country.*

### Bangor/Beannchar

Whichever way you come into this north Down town, your heart will lift as you drop over the brow of the 'peaked hill', the meaning of its Irish name, and see the sea catch the sunlight in the bay beyond the harbour.

Bangor has had two glorious pasts. Of the first, St Comgall's Abbey of the Regular Canons, founded in AD 558 and once the premier seat of Christian academic learning in all Europe, there is not a stone left. The only trace of it is a manuscript called the Bangor Antiphonary, the oldest-known Irish-written hymn sheet, which dates from the

MAGNIFICENT MAN *A full-scale model of the plane Harry Ferguson flew over his father's farmland in 1909 is in the Ulster Folk and Transport Museum. Ferguson was the first Irishman to fly a plane.*

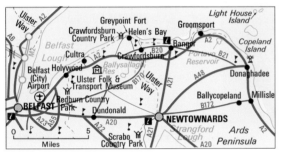

## OTHER PLACES TO SEE

**Ballycopeland** Village with late 18th-century windmill, still in working order. Open Apr-Sept, Tues-Sat 10am-7pm, Sun 2-7pm; Oct-Mar, Sat 10am-4pm, Sun 2-4pm.
**Copeland Island** Boat service from Bangor, Donaghadee and Groomsport to three tiny islands once inhabited by Irishmen, and grazed by cattle and sheep, now overrun by wild flowers. Light House Island has a bird observatory.
**Greypoint Fort** With sister fort across the bay at Kilroot, it guarded Ulster's eastern approaches during the two World Wars. Two powerful 6in breech-loading guns, engine house, stores and quarters. Open Easter-Oct 9am-5pm; Sun 2-5pm.

**Groomsport** Pretty harbour, where Marshal Schomberg landed with 10,000 men for the Williamite cause in 1689; tiny 18th-century cottages, one thatched.
**Scrabo Country Park** 130 acre park with 1857 Scrabo tower built in memory of 3rd Marquis of Londonderry; has 122 steps, and view at top across to Scotland. Visitor Centre explains natural history of area. Wildlife includes feral goats. Open Wed-Mon 12-5.30pm.

## WALKS
**Ulster Way** 18m stretch of this route, from Holywood to Portavo.

## EVENTS
**Game and Country Fair** Bangor, June.

## SPORT
**Angling** Game fishing: Ballysallagh, Holywood and Portavo reservoirs. Sea fishing: Belfast Lough, Donaghadee.
**Bathing** Bangor.
**Golf** Bangor Golf Club, 18-hole course. Tel: (0247) 270922.
Carnalea Golf Club, 18-hole course. Tel: (0247) 465004.
Clandeboye Golf Club, 18-hole course. Tel: (0247) 271767/473706.
Donaghadee Golf Club, 18-hole course. Tel: (0237) 888697.
Holywood Golf Club, 18-hole course. Tel: (02317) 2138.
Kirkistown Castle Golf Club, 18-hole course. Tel: (02477) 71233/71353.
The Knock Golf Club, 18-hole course. Tel: (0232) 2249.
Royal Belfast Golf Club, 18-hole course. Tel: (0232) 428165.
Scrabo Golf Club, 18-hole course. Tel: (0247) 812355.
**Sailing** Newtownards Sailing Club. Tel: (0247) 813426.

## INFORMATION
Newtownards Tourist Information. Tel: (0247) 812215.

BALLYCOPELAND WINDMILL *The mill's tower has walls 2ft thick and 33ft in diameter.*

680s, and is now in the Ambrosian Library in Milan, Italy. The abbey's wealth tempted the Vikings, the English who favoured the dissolution of the monasteries, and later the O'Neill earls. Even later, in the early 1600s, Scottish settlers were granted the lands and founded the little town.

Two centuries on, Bangor experienced its second era of glory with the arrival of the Belfast, Holywood and Bangor Railway Company, which gave free first-class ten-year season tickets to new householders. Bangor turned into a pleasant seaside resort with elegant stuccoed Victorian and Edwardian houses with slate roofs and sash windows. Today the town is fringed by golf courses, and offers a summer season of amateur theatre, band concerts on the sea front, four yacht clubs, sea fishing and trips around the bay.

### Crawfordsburn/Sruth Chráfard

This 'watering place by a stream', Crawford's Burn, is on the old route from Holywood to Bangor. The village's little cluster of white houses includes the part-thatched Old Inn, possibly the oldest inn in Ireland, dating from 1614, where bees hum in the garden in summer and silver service clinks in the panelled dining room. Round the village lies Crawfordsburn Country Park, originally an estate acquired by Scots Presbyterians. There are walks and glens, a Californian giant redwood, bursts of brilliant rhododendrons, trickling streams, campsites and a restaurant. The best walks are either through the glen, under the elegant railway viaduct and up to the waterfall, or from the sandy beach at Crawfordsburn to Helen's Bay at the eastern end of the park.

**Crawfordsburn Park** *Summer, 8.30am-8.30pm.*

## Donaghadee/Domhnach Daoi

From the 16th to the 19th centuries, the sheltered harbour of Donaghadee (the name means the 'Church of St Diack'), was the only safe refuge for the many boats negotiating the treacherous reefs along the coast. The Belfast road sweeps into the crescent bay past the golf links and small hotels along Shore Street, past The Parade, and down to the large harbour. There, a lighthouse dominates the scene. It was designed by the men who built the Eddystone Light off Plymouth – Sir John Rennie and David Logan.

Several famous people are associated with Donaghadee: Boswell stepped off the boat here in 1769, Keats came in 1818 on a visit to the Giant's Causeway and stayed in the old Grace Neill's Inn (1611) in the High Street; Franz Liszt arrived with a piano, marooned here for a few days due to bad weather, and Wordsworth also disembarked here. It is said that Peter the Great stayed in the inn between 1697-8 and learned about shipbuilding. The writer Brendan Behan also spent time in Donaghadee – and ended up painting the lighthouse.

The 140ft mound between Shore Street and Moat Street, with its 19th-century castle folly, was used as a gunpowder store during the construction of the harbour in the 1820s. At that time the harbour was greatly enlarged, in the expectation that the town would remain the main mail packet station for Scotland. Alas for the town, in 1849 the Stranraer-Larne service was chosen instead. Local fishermen tried to maintain a ferry service to Scotland and on calm days passengers could be rowed across for £5.

At low tide the dulse gatherers go out in boats, armed with small scythes to collect the edible seaweed with purple fronds known as dulse. The dulse (also known as dillisk) is then spread out in the sun to dry and sold, ready to eat, or to be cooked in soups and stews. It is a delicacy favoured by locals.

SCRABO TOWER *The tower is a memorial to the 3rd Marquis of Londonderry's charity.*

## Holywood/Ard Mhic Nasca

This dormitory town, whose name means 'Height of Nasca's Son', has a Norman motte and the remains of a Franciscan friary of the 15th century. In Church Street is a 70ft mast topped by a weather vane, the 'Maypole'. There has been a mast here ever since a Dutch ship went aground in 1700. The Bishop of Down's former palace, a splendid Gothic dwelling on the main road, is now the Culloden Hotel.

A walk along the shores of Belfast Lough to the east brings you to the magnificent Ulster Folk and Transport Museum. The old Cultra Manor estate, stretching over 136 acres of rolling countryside, has been transformed by a reconstruction of the province's recent past. Buildings were moved, stone by stone, from their original settings and rebuilt on the estate. There are tiny thatched cottages furnished in traditional style, a rectory dating from 1717, taken from Toome, and a village. The tiny houses of Tea Lane came from Belfast's Sandy Row and there is a church from Kilmore, a school and a courthouse. The collection also includes a flax mill from County Tyrone, a Fermanagh forge and a County Down bleach-green watchtower – a conical stone hut, which once housed a watchman with his musket who guarded linen laid out in the sun to bleach.

There are changing exhibitions in the gallery and picnic areas in the grounds. Across the road from the 'folk' area is the transport museum, displaying a range of vehicles from a 1980s De Lorean car to a monoplane from 1909, and a three-masted schooner.

**Ulster Folk and Transport Museum** *Apr-Sept, Mon-Sat 11am-6pm, Sun 2-6pm; Oct-Mar, Mon-Sat 11am-5pm, Sun 2-5pm. Tel: (0232) 428428.*

## Newtownards/Baile nua na hArda

The 'new town of the ards', the heights of the gentle drumlins of north Down, sits neatly at the head of Strangford Lough, 10 miles east of Belfast, among green, fertile market gardens and the plain sheds of light industry. Despite its name its history is long. The town dates from the 13th century, when Walter de Burgh founded a Dominican priory here. The ruins incorporate the nave of the original church together with a 17th-century square tower in Court Square. The Londonderrys, who succeeded the Montgomerys as landlords, have their family vault here.

At the east end of the High Street is the attractive old Market Cross, broken in 1653 and repaired, though not completely, in 1666. The tiny space inside it was used as an early 'lock-up'. The 1765 Market House, now the Town Hall, dominates the other end of the High Street and Conway Square.

On the Millisle road are the remains of the 13th-century church of the 6th-century Augustinian Abbey of Movilla. The church contains some Anglo-Norman grave slabs carved with foliate crosses, and a sword or a pair of shears, signifying whether a man or woman was being commemorated.

# The Lake of Stone Heads

*Lower Lough Erne, an island-flecked lake ringed by castles, covers much of northern Fermanagh, its western shores only 7 miles away from the Atlantic. In the west are two villages – Belleek and Pettigoe – bisected by the border with the Republic. It is a remote area with strange relics: on Boa Island is a two-faced statue, and White Island has some curious early Christian figures.*

### Belleek/Beal Leice

The Irish name means 'flagstone ford', and at one time the ford crossed the River Erne here at Belleek, the most westerly village in Northern Ireland. It is also the home of the renowned Belleek Pottery.

A museum in the Visitor Centre traces the history of the pottery, which has been owned for many years by a syndicate of four families. On show are fascinating examples of early sanitary ware, including some elegant hand basins, as well as elaborate figures and basketware.

The current range of Belleek pottery is displayed for viewing and for sale at the spacious showroom. There is a restaurant at the pottery.

**Pottery tours** *Mon-Thur 9.30am-4.15pm; Fri 9.30am-3.15pm.*
**Visitor Centre** *Mar-Sept, Mon-Fri 9am-6pm; Sat 10am-6pm, Sun 2-6pm. Oct-Feb, Mon-Fri 9am-5pm. Tel: (0365) 65501.*

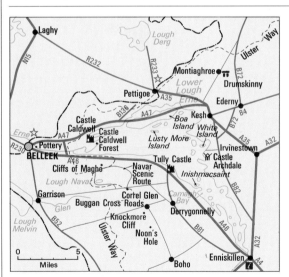

### OTHER PLACES TO SEE
**Lough Melvin Holiday Centre** Garrison. Activity holidays: canoeing, cycling, potholing, sailing, climbing. Tel: (0365) 658145.
**Lower Lough Erne** 20 mile long lough freckled with nearly 100 wooded islands. It is one of the least crowded waterways in Europe, and is very popular with trout anglers.
**White Island** In Lower Lough Erne; site of roofless church with arched Romanesque doorway. Inside is a grinning figure with crossed legs. Other figures include an abbot, a man with a short staff, one with birds and another armed with a sword and shield. Ferry for White Island leaves from Castle Archdale.

### WALKS
**Ulster Way** Part of the 500 mile footpath around Ulster, runs along top of Cliffs of Magho.

### EVENTS
**Cleenish Traditional Music Festival** May.
**Erne Boat Rally** May.
**Fiddle Stone Festival** Belleek, June.
**Lough Melvin Folk and Traditional Music Festival** July.
**Lough Melvin Open Trout Championships** Garrison, Aug.

### SPORT
**Angling** Coarse fishing: River Erne, Lough Melvin. Game fishing: River Erne, Lough Melvin, Lough Navar.

### INFORMATION
Lakeland Visitor Centre, Enniskillen. Tel: (0365) 323110.

A translucent, creamy lustre, delicate basketware, and elegant shapes and forms have made Belleek Pottery famous. The pottery was started in 1857 by John Caldwell Bloomfield, a farmer who was more interested in ceramics. When he noticed the sparkling white finish on the walls of his estate cottages, he surveyed the land and found the felspar and kaolin needed to make pottery.

He harnessed the river to provide a small millrace with sufficient flow to turn a millwheel and strong enough to grind components into 'slip', the potter's term for liquid clay. Soon a railway was built to Belleek, to bring in coal for the pottery's kilns and transport its products. The local inhabitants, trained by English potters, provided the work force and a team of skilled engravers was hired.

Soon the fame of Belleek's pottery spread, helped when Queen Victoria presented a Belleek tea service to the German royal family.

The pottery's appeal is based on the skills involved in creating each fragile piece. Basketwork is a delicate job, needing an apprenticeship of up to five years. Clay is first mixed with gum arabic to make it flexible before being extruded into fine strands which are woven into the bases. The potter's hands have to be greased with olive oil to prevent the strands sticking. The porcelain then undergoes three firings, during which the pieces shrink by about a third and acquire their lustrous appearance.

Motifs are then painted onto the pottery by hand, with fine brushes. These designs may include the traditional shamrocks and harps, or flowers and insects.

### Boa Island/Inis Badhbha

A glance into the overgrown graveyard on Boa Island, whose Irish name means 'island of cattle', will spot large eyes staring from a double-faced stone head roughly cemented onto a rock. The heart-shaped faces have crossed arms below them, traces of carved patterns decorate the sandstone sides, and on top of the 3ft high stone is a shallow depression filled with water. The purpose of this extraordinary Celtic idol is unknown.

Nearby is another, smaller idol, whose two faces have full lips and slightly plumper arms and may represent a woman. Despite its female attributes, the squat figure is known as 'Lusty Man', probably because it is believed to have been brought to Caldragh cemetery from nearby Lusty More Island.

The idols are thought to date from the prehistoric Iron Age. Heads were an important symbol to the Celts, who believed them to be the centre of the life force and therefore cut off their enemies' heads in battle. Two-faced and three-faced idols were thought to demonstrate an all-seeing, all-powerful god. The island is reached over a causeway.

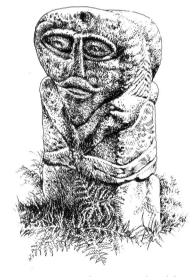

BOA ISLAND STATUE *The strange Celtic idol, with a face on both sides, cuts a curious figure in the Christian graveyard.*

## Castle Caldwell

Two arms of forested land stretch into Lower Lough Erne from the north shore to form Castle Caldwell Forest. Dating from 1913 it is one of Ireland's oldest state forests. It includes a nature reserve and a bird sanctuary. Blackcaps, chiffchaffs and willow warblers visit in spring, and in winter the alders provide food for siskins and redpolls. At the lake's edge is a hide for watching wildfowl, such as common scoters, a type of marine duck whose main breeding grounds are on the lough. By the forest shore, thick with rushes and wildflowers and bordered by spindly birches and alders, wildlife such as otters, mute swans and great crested grebes can also be seen. In the woods are the ivy-covered remains of the 1612 castle that gave the forest its name, and which was abandoned in the late 19th century.

Next to the gatepost at the main entrance to the forest is the Fiddler's Stone, a 5ft high fiddle-shaped memorial to Denis McCabe, a fiddler who went out on the lough on a barge to play music, drank too much and fell overboard and drowned. The last lines of the 1770 inscription read: 'On firm land only exercise your skill. There you may play and drink your fill.'

**Visitor Centre** *Tel: (0365) 631253. Or contact forest warden. Tel: (0365) 65328.*

## Garrison/An Garastún

The charm of Garrison lies at its centre, where a stone bridge crosses the rushing waters of the River Glen. The Glen plunges down the slopes of the west Fermanagh highlands in a series of waterfalls before flowing through the village and into Lough Melvin.

Garrison is best known as an angling resort for Lough Melvin, which claims to be the best-stocked wild fishery in Europe. As well as its brown trout, the lough is home to two unique species of fish. One is the sonaghan (*Salmo nigripinnis*), rather like a sea trout, which in August moves from deep water to the shallow bays before running up the rivers. The other is an evolutionary curiosity, the gillaroo (*Salmo stomachius*), which has a gizzard, and pink flesh from its diet of shrimps.

## Navar Scenic Route

The Lough Navar Scenic Drive takes in the entire lower part of Lower Lough Erne, and is a magnificent sight. The one-way route loops up through pine forests and heather-covered hills from Correl Glen east of Garrison. From

WELL-STOCKED WATERS *The mirror-like waters of lovely Lough Melvin teem with trout, wild salmon and the strange gillaroo.*

LOUGH MELVIN MARVEL. *The spotted gillaroo is said to be tastier than salmon.*

the top of the Cliffs of Magho, 1000ft above sea level, the dark blue waters of the Lower Lough spread below, pierced by the dark green forest of Castle Caldwell and the lighter green of the islands. From here it is also possible to see the Sperrin Mountains of Tyrone and the mountains of Donegal, Sligo and Leitrim.

Continuing to Derrygonnelly and then out to Buggan Cross Roads, the road skirts the sheer 600ft limestone face of Knockmore Cliff. Towards Boho, the hills to the west are pitted with swallow holes and caves. The deepest of these is Noon's Hole, at almost 300ft the deepest in Ireland.

## Tully Castle

A short, unhappy history lies behind the remains of Tully Castle, sited on a hill overlooking Lower Lough Erne where it bends to the west. The tall, fortified house, a cross between an Irish farmhouse and a Scottish castle, once had a thatched roof and a defensive yard with four flanking towers. It was built in 1613 for planter Sir John Hume, on land taken from the Maguire clan.

On Christmas Eve in 1641, Rory Maguire marched on the castle with a large band of followers to recapture the estate. The Humes were spared, but the other occupants of the castle, 15 men and 60 women and children, promised safe conduct, were murdered. The castle was burnt and was never lived in again. However, it is safe to explore, and from the windows of the first floor there are splendid views of the lake and islands. Beside the castle is a pretty parterre garden.

South-west of the castle, at Camagh Bay, a track leads to a footpath which crosses a pontoon to Inishmacsaint, the 'island of the plain of sorrel', on which lie the remains of a 6th-century monastery with a High Cross.

# Planters' Stately Homes

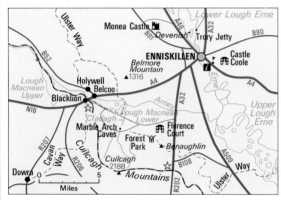

*Today, all the roads in Fermanagh radiate from Enniskillen, the hub of the county. But long ago, the great river system of the Erne was the highway, and the highlands that run parallel to it were a natural refuge for early people. There is scarcely a square mile without evidence of their presence – a chambered grave, or a crannog in a lake. Later, two of central Fermanagh's most successful planters established their mansions here – Florence Court and Castle Coole – on either side of Lough Erne.*

GEORGIAN GRANDEUR *Grey porphyry pilasters and an elegant frieze of swags echo the simple classical elegance found throughout Castle Coole.*

## WALKS

**Cuilcagh mountain** From Florence Court Forest Park, walk up north-east shoulder. Summit is 2188ft.

## EVENTS

**Annual Craft Fair** Florence Court House, Aug.
**Ardhowen Band Contest** Apr.
**Classic Fishing Festival** Lakes around Enniskillen, mid-May.
**Enniskillen Community Festival** Aug.
**Enniskillen County Agricultural Show** Aug.
**Lower Lough Erne Regattas** Apr, June, Sept.

## SPORT

**Angling** Coarse fishing: Loughs Macnean Upper and Lower, and River Arney. Game fishing: Loughs Macnean Upper and Lower, Lough Coole, River Arney.
**Golf** Ashwoods Golf Club, 9-hole course. Tel: (0365) 325321/322908. Castle Hume Golf Club, 18-hole course. Tel: (0365) 89205. Enniskillen Golf Club, 18-hole course. Tel: (0365) 25250.
**Yachting** Lough Erne Yacht Club. Tel: (0365) 81432.

## INFORMATION

Lakeland Visitor Centre, Enniskillen. Tel: (0365) 323110.

## OTHER PLACES TO SEE

**Belcoo** Sister village of Blacklion, in County Cavan; joining point of Ulster Way, which encircles province, and Cavan Way. Holy well once pilgrimage site for Lughnasa festival. Spring water behind fence at crossroads dedicated to St Patrick, said to cure 'nervous and paralytic' disorders.
**Benaughlin** 1221ft mountain near Florence Court Forest Park. Limestone outcrop known as the Speaking Horse, or the White Steed of Donn Binn, King of the Fairies. After galloping through countryside in May and June the 'horse' is said to address oracles to the fairies on the last Sun in July.
**Devenish island** In Lower Lough Erne, 1½m from

Enniskillen; site of St Molaise's House (12th-century church) and 81ft high Round Tower with Romanesque cornice with four human heads; also Teampull Mór (13th-century church), remains of St Mary's Augustinian priory (15th and 16th century), and museum, open Apr-Sept, Tues-Sun, 10am-7pm. Ferry from Trory Jetty.
**Monea Castle** Near Enniskillen. Best preserved of Fermanagh's Plantation castles, built for Malcolm Hamilton in 1618, with twin barrel towers. There is also a crannog nearby, in a partly drained lake to the south.

## CRUISES

**Lough Erne** From Enniskillen, on the MV *Kestrel*. Tel: (0365) 324368.

## Castle Coole

A long, oak-lined drive leads to the austere, silvery-white Castle Coole, with its great pedimented portico and colonnades linking the main block to pavilions at either end.

The castle was built between 1790 and 1793 for the 1st Earl of Belmore, and was intended to outshine Florence Court, the stately home of his brother-in-law, the Earl of Enniskillen, which stands 10 miles away. Castle Coole was constructed with Portland stone shipped from Dorset to Ballyshannon and taken from there by bullock cart to Lower Lough Erne and then by barge to Enniskillen.

The house has a lavish oval saloon with beautiful plasterwork on the ceiling, and mahogany doors, inlaid with satinwood, curved to follow the outline of the room. Upstairs is a lobby lit by three domed skylights and heated by iron stoves set in niches, their chimneys cunningly concealed in the hollow columns above.

Across the lawn from the house is Lough Coole, where greylag geese have nested for the last 300 years.
**Castle Coole** *Apr, May, Sept, weekends and public holidays, 2-6pm; June-Aug, daily exc Thur 2-6pm. Tel: (0238) 510721.*

## Enniskillen/Inis Ceithleann

'Ceithleann Island' was named after the wife of a chieftain, Balor of the Mighty Blows. It is set, like the waist of an egg timer, between the Upper and Lower Loughs of the great Erne system. Enniskillen later became the county town, and the twin-turreted 17th-century Watergate, which guards the approach to Enniskillen Castle from the Upper Lough, is a reminder of its military past.

St Macartin's Protestant cathedral stands out on the highest of the town's two hills, its 150ft tower and spire soaring above the main street. It was rebuilt in 1842, and part of the old 17th-century tower can be seen above the main door. The font dates from 1666.

Enniskillen is the only town in the British Isles to raise two regiments bearing its name, the Inniskilling Dragoons and the Royal Inniskilling Fusiliers, merged since 1968 as the Royal Irish Rangers. Inside the cathedral, regimental colours hang above the choir, and there is a regimental chapel where a Book of Remembrance records all ranks of the Fusiliers killed since the Battle of Waterloo.

Opposite the cathedral is St Michael's Roman Catholic church, whose south

PLASTER MASTERPIECE *Florence Court's lacy stucco is some of the finest plasterwork in Ireland.*

window commemorates St Molaise, the founder of the monastery on Devenish island in Lower Lough Erne.

The green copper dome and solid Victorian clock tower of the Town Hall on the second hill is another landmark. Figures of an Inniskilling Dragoon and an Inniskilling Fusilier stand above the main entrance and in the lobby a plaque commemorates Dragoon Captain Lawrence Oates who perished in the snow on Scott's ill-fated Antarctic expedition of 1912.

A great, fluted column bearing a statue of General Sir Galbraith Lowry Cole, one of

ENNISKILLEN GUARDS *The turrets of the Watergate still guard the approach up the River Erne.*

Wellington's generals in the Peninsular War and later Governor of Cape Colony, towers over the town's eastern end. Visitors can climb the 108 steps to the top for a fine view of the lakelands. Below the monument, in Fort Hill Park, is a cast-iron bandstand put up in 1895. It is a riot of decoration, with curving, iron dragons and lacy panels topped by a clock tower.

Enniskillen Castle is the old core of the settlement established in the 15th century by Hugh the Hospitable as a stronghold of the ruling Maguire family. With the arrival of the planters it became the nucleus of a town and an anti-Jacobite stronghold. The three-storey castle keep contains two museums, one showing Fermanagh's early history, with a collection of casts of the White Island figures and a video of the town's early days. The second museum is the Regimental Museum of the Royal Inniskilling Fusiliers.

Across the bridge from the castle, past the jetty where boats leave for island cruises, is the 18th-century Portora Royal School, a free school founded by James I in 1608. Portraits of Portora's most famous old boys include those of the playwrights Oscar Wilde (1854-1900), and Samuel Beckett (1906-1989) in cricket whites. It is still a school.

**Enniskillen Castle Museum** *May-Sept, Mon-Sat 10am-5pm; July and Aug, Sun afternoons as well. Oct-May, Mon-Fri 10am-5pm. Tel: (0365) 325000.*
**Regimental Museum** *Mon-Fri 9.30am-4.30pm, weekends by arrangement only. Tel: (0365) 323142.*

## Florence Court

The grandeur of the greystone early Georgian mansion is tempered by homely charm. The spacious rooms with their exuberant, rococo plasterwork also have much fine furniture

AN IRISHMAN IN PARIS

Samuel Barclay Beckett, born in Dublin in 1906, became an internationally famous playwright as author of *Waiting for Godot* (1952) and won the Nobel Prize for Literature in 1969. He studied at Trinity College, Dublin and in 1937 moved to France, where he became a close associate and friend of fellow Irish writer James Joyce.

Beckett frequently wrote first in French and later translated his works into English. They include *Murphy*, *Molloy*, *End Game* and *Krapp's Last Tape*. His plays, described as the 'theatre of the absurd', deal with meaningless and incoherent lives in which people cannot communicate successfully.

Beckett married Suzanne Descheveux-Dusmenil in 1961, and he died in Paris on December 22, 1989.

which looks comfortably solid and practical.

Sir John Cole of Enniskillen (1680-1726) first built a house on the site in the early 1700s for his Cornish wife Florence, and named it after her. The entrance hall is a dramatic introduction to the interior, with its decorated arch opening to the staircase and an elaborate plasterwork frieze. The staircase, made of pine, pear wood and yew wood, has beautifully stuccoed walls, probably by Dublin craftsman Robert West. His hallmarks of acanthus, flowers, baskets of fruit and flying birds appear throughout the mansion.

Below stairs, the kitchen has a parasol-like metal ceiling, added to protect the 3rd Earl of Enniskillen's fossil fish collection above from fire. Near the house is a 4 acre walled garden and a restored water-powered sawmill, built in the 1840s.

Florence Court Forest Park contains old oak forest, conifer plantations and moorland. And in a clearing towards the Cuilcagh mountain is the 220-year-old Irish yew (*Taxus baccata* 'Fastigiata'), said to be the parent of all Irish-type yews, characterised by the upward sweep of their branches.
**Florence Court** *June-Aug, daily exc Tues 12-6pm; Apr, May, Sept weekends only, 1-6pm. Tel: (0365) 82249.*
**Forest Park** *10am to an hour before sunset. Tel: (0365) 82497.*

## Marble Arch Caves

An eerie landscape, once open only to potholers and scientists, lies 160ft below the Cuilcagh mountains. Now there are guided tours of the most spectacular parts of this hidden world, its passages lit to reveal gigantic stalactites, translucent mineral veils and cascades of calcite that look like an overflow of petrified cream. One of the largest of these flowstones, the Porridge Pot, probably took 50,000 years to form from the drips from above. Boats take visitors across a silent, glassy, underground lake, a route first taken by Edouard Martel, the Frenchman who discovered the caves in 1895, making his way on foot and by collapsible canoe.

The Marble Arch that gave its name to the series of caves is in fact a natural limestone arch, formed by a collapsed cave, through which the River Cladagh rushes. It is at the southern boundary of Marble Arch Forest, a nature reserve situated along the wooded Cladagh gorge.
**Marble Arch Caves** *Daily, Apr-Oct, unless heavy rains cause closure. Tel: (0365) 828855.*

# A Reedy Maze of Islands

*Neat villages with well-kept churches and brown-and-cream half-timbered houses, conifer plantations, miles of moorland, and rivers, lakes and inlets distinguish this part of Fermanagh. Upper Lough Erne is a reedy maze of islands, with narrow roads winding their way down to lakeside farms. This part of Ireland was once important for textiles, particularly wool, and there are still clothing and cotton factories in the area's principal town, Lisnaskea.*

## Crom Castle

The 1350 acre Crom Castle estate is set on a peninsula surrounded by the glittering waters of Upper Lough Erne, and is one of the most important nature conservation sites owned by the National Trust. Its fine stands of oak support a variety of birds, the purple hairstreak butterfly and a colony of red squirrels, and its shorelines are bordered by sedges and ragged robin. In the grounds is a vast yew tree, which was planted in the 1600s and is one of the oldest in Northern Ireland.

Paths wind through the estate, skirting the castle, a huge, grey limestone building, built in 1834-40 for the Earls of Erne. The family still live there and the castle is private, as are the other buildings on the estate. These include a well-constructed stone house built in 1610, used for storing turf which was brought in by barge to fuel the fires in the mansion. There is also a restored, six-sided summerhouse, complete with a fireplace and chimney, and a fine, castellated boathouse on the lake below the sweeping lawns of the castle.

Cross a bridge to Inisherk island and from the slipway there is a view of Crichton Tower, a single tower standing on an islet at a point where five channels converge.

Another good view of the tower is from the ruins of the former Crom Castle, reached along a path from the boathouse. This Plantation building, built in 1611, was unsuccessfully besieged by Jacobites under Lord Galmoy in March 1689, and again in July that year under General MacCarthy. Despite their efforts the castle remained in the hands of the Crichton family until it was accidentally burnt down in 1764. The outer wall and two buttresses survive.

**Crom Castle grounds** *Easter-Sept, daily 2-6pm. Tel: (0365) 738174.*

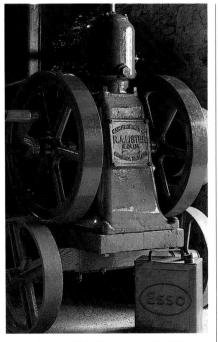

LISTER ENGINE *This 7hp engine in the Olde Barn Family Museum once powered a farm.*

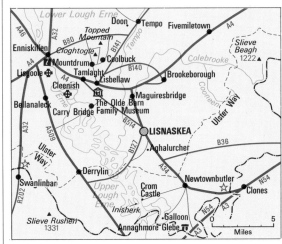

medieval church on site of 6th-century monastery and of dolmen on roadside.

**Tempo** 7m from Enniskillen; Jacobean style manor, built by Sir Charles Lanyon, 1862-7, on site of Maguire house, closed to the public.

**Topped Mountain** Round cairn on 910ft summit, and Bronze Age burial place, found with remains of male skeleton, traces of cremation, gold-mounted bronze dagger, and food vessel.

### EVENTS
**Cliff Smart Fishing Festival** Sept.
**Erne Open Coarse Fishing Festival** Sept.
**Erne Vintage Car Rally** Aug.
**King of the Colebrooke Fishing Competition** May.
**Romer Navigation Rally** Sept.
**Upper Lough Erne Water Festival** Lisnaskea, July.

### SPORT
**Angling** Coarse fishing: Upper Lough Erne.
**Boating** Upper Lough Erne.

### INFORMATION
Lakeland Visitor Centre, Enniskillen. Tel: (0365) 23110.

## OTHER PLACES TO SEE
**Aghalurcher** 1½m S of Lisnaskea, graveyard and burial place of Maguires, and site of 7th-century monastery founded by St Ronan. Medieval church guarded by old yew tree surrounded by superstition, because in 1484 a Maguire killed a kinsman on the altar.

**Annaghmore Glebe** 4m from Newtownbutler; Druid's Temple, circle of huge stones which surrounded a mound removed in 1712. It covered several Bronze Age burial chambers.

**Cloghtogle** Coolbuck church, with wedge-tomb; wedge-tomb also at Mountdrum.

**Doon** ½m SE of Tempo; two superimposed grey stones, 8½ft high. Lower boulder has some depressions; upper one is inscribed with two concentric circles.

**Tamlaght** N shore of Upper Lough Erne; remains of

CROM CASTLE *The castle and its 1350 acre estate are almost surrounded by Upper Lough Erne.*

### The Olde Barn Family Museum

A discreet sign on the road at Tamlaght points along a drive to a museum which gives a fascinating view of the history of Fermanagh through the eyes of several generations of the Carrothers family, who have farmed this land for more than 200 years.

The well-arranged display is housed in a converted barn and includes letters, photographs, historic documents, domestic and farm implements and antiquities carefully collected by the Carrothers.

A pikestaff, brought from lowland Scotland by the first Carrothers to settle at Farnaght in County Leitrim, and presumably for self-defence, hangs on the wall. An original deed of 1769 shows the granting of the land to Edward Carrothers and his two sons. A collection of letters from two Carrothers brothers who emigrated to Ontario, Canada, in the mid-1800s details an Irish emigrant's life and concerns at that time. And there is a touching series of letters written by John Carrothers, a young officer in the Royal Inniskilling Fusiliers, who was killed in the First World War aged 19.

Birds' eggs collected by Nathaniel Carrothers, a botanist, jostle with samples of patchwork sewn by the women of succeeding generations of the Carrothers family and domestic bills from the last century. Stone querns, used by early settlers for milling corn, are on view. One of them is 5000 years old.

The star exhibit in a display of restored agricultural machinery is a 1912 Lister, 7hp petrol engine, which was used for 60 years on the farm, to thresh and grind corn, saw firewood and pump water. The engine still works perfectly.

**Opening times** *Mon-Sat 11am-10pm. Tel: (0365) 87278.*

### Lisnaskea/Lios na Scéithe

East Fermanagh's chief town lies near Upper Lough Erne. It was first settled by the Fir Manach people, who came from the province of Leinster and gave the county its name. Later, the senior branch of the ruling Maguires lived here until the 1590s, but they were forced to move to Enniskillen to keep control over the western half of their territory.

Little remains of Lisnaskea's grand past, and most of the interesting buildings in the town date from the 19th century. In 1821 the town was bought for £82,500 by the 1st Earl of Erne. The market cross which stands in the marketplace off the main street was put up in

UPPER LOUGH ERNE *Like a jigsaw puzzle with a few pieces missing, the pattern of irregularly shaped fields is broken by the waters of Upper Lough Erne.*

1841 by the 2nd Earl of Erne to attract dealers and so build up the market. The cross was made and set on the massive, carved shaft of an earlier cross, dating probably from the 9th or 10th century. On the shaft is a Biblical scene representing a cheerfully prancing Adam and Eve. It is thought to come from an early church, perhaps from Galloon island to the south of Upper Lough Erne. The corn and potato market has an attractive brick and cobble square, and a surrounding colonnade of iron pillars supports a canopy.

The lake side of the town is dominated by Castle Balfour, reached through the churchyard of the Church of Ireland. This fortified house was built from 1618, in Scottish style, for the planter Sir James Balfour. The remains include corbelled turrets, high-pitched gables and tall chimneys. The castle was burnt down in 1803, but has been restored, and its upper floor still provides good views to the south-west.

### Upper Lough Erne

As it crosses the Cavan border on its way north to the Atlantic at Donegal Bay, the Erne creates the Upper Lough, a tree-fringed puzzle of islands, creeks and secret shores. Here a boat can cruise for hours in solitude, watched only by swans or a waiting heron. Dabchicks, moorhens, tufted ducks and mallards nest in the reed banks, and arctic terns fly over in search of food. Unusual flowers such as blue-eyed grass, water soldier and greater spearwort grow at the water's edge. Beneath the surface the lough teems with fish – the area round Carry Bridge is renowned for large pike.

Many of the lough's 60 islands are uninhabited, although some have the ruins of farms. At one time cattle would have been transported across the lough by 'cot', a big, flat-bottomed wooden craft with sloping ends, and the only practical way of carrying large loads through this watery region.

The water and its edges also provided early settlers with a safer place to live than the land, which was once covered by dense forest and treacherous bog. As a result the lake is dotted with crannogs, or artificial islands. These were built on mounds of stone and logs laid on the lake bottom, and were fortified with walls. They could be reached only by boat. The shore is speckled with earthwork rings, or raths, which protected homesteads and cattle from marauders.

Island monasteries were established at Cleenish, near Bellanaleck, and at Lisgoole. Galloon island, reached by a narrow bridge 3 miles south-west of Newtownbutler, has a sloping churchyard with the shafts of two 9th or 10th-century crosses and 18th-century gravestones with emblems of mortality, such as skull and crossbones, coffin, bell and sandtimer. The monastery was founded in the 6th century by St Tighernach, who also founded Clones monastery in Monaghan.

# Wide Strands and Towering Cliffs

*Some of Ireland's earliest inhabitants lived in this northernmost tip of the country – at Coleraine there is a settlement dating from around 7000 BC. It lies beside the River Bann, where it meets a dramatic coastline of towering cliffs. From these craggy heights can be seen the mountains of Donegal to the west and, to the east, Scotland and the islands of Jura and Islay.*

### Castlerock/Carraig Ceasail

Two jagged rocks on the shore, like the turrets of a castle, gave the name to this Victorian resort. At the crossroads above the village stands Hezlett House, a 17th-century thatched farmhouse now owned by the National Trust. Its construction, unusual in Ireland, consists of wooden ribs, called cruck trusses, arched at regular intervals between the load-bearing gable ends. A room in the house has had its ceiling stripped so that the method of construction and the materials can be seen. The house was extended in 1823, and this extension is now furnished in Victorian style, from the low, windowless servants' quarters in the loft to the fully equipped kitchen with its peat fire burning below a range of pots and pans. The wheat straw thatch was replaced in 1982, when it was discovered that in previous thatchings the old material had not been removed, and that the thatch had reached a thickness of some 6ft. It weighed almost 40 tons – a tribute to the house's sturdy construction.

**Hezlett House** *Last week Mar, daily; Apr-June, Sat, Sun and Bank Holidays; July, Aug, daily; Sept, Sat and Sun 2-6pm. Tel: (0265) 848567.*

BRIGHT INTERIORS *Inside Hezlett House, dark rooms, with their thick walls (right) and small windows, are brightened with colourful paintwork (below).*

[Map showing the Coleraine area, including Atlantic Ocean, Portrush, Portstewart, Portstewart Strand, The Barmouth, Castlerock, St Patrick's Well, Wilson Daffodil Garden, Downhill, Ulster Way, Bishop's Road, Hezlett House, Articlave, Lough Foyle, Binevenagh Forest, Binevenagh Wood, 1260, Grange Park, COLERAINE, Mountsandel, Springwell Forest, Limavady, Cam Forest, Ringsend, Aghadowey. Roads: B202, A2, A37, B201, A26, A54, A29, B186, B66. Scale 0–5 Miles.]

## OTHER PLACES TO SEE

**Aghadowey** Good centre for game and coarse fishing, and has old airfield now used for stock-car racing and parascending.

**Wilson Daffodil Garden** On university campus, large collection of Irish-bred daffodils. Garden is memorial to celebrated daffodil-breeder Guy Wilson. Free access to grounds.

### CRUISES

**Bann Cruise** *Maid of Antrim,* July. 10 mile trip from Lough Neagh to Coleraine. *The Cygnet,* 5-6 mile trip from Coleraine to river mouth.

**Riverbus cruises** Coleraine, June-Aug. Tel: (0265) 44744.

### EVENTS

**Coleraine 24-hour Yacht Race** Coleraine Marina, June.
**Coleraine Agricultural Show** June.
**Coleraine Irish Folk-Dancing Festival** Mar/Apr.
**Coleraine Music Festival** End Apr-beginning of May.
**North West 200 Motor Cycle Races** Portrush, May.
**Portstewart-Flowerfield Arts Festival** Oct.
**Portstewart Music Festival** Mid-May.
**Quadrathlon** Hutchinson's Quay, Portna, July.

## SPORT

**Angling** Coarse and game fishing: River Bann. Game fishing also in Binevenagh Lake. Sea fishing: Portstewart.
**Bathing** Portstewart.
**Canoeing** Coleraine Marina. Tel. (0265) 44768.
**Golf** Brown Trout Golf and Country Inn, 9-hole course. Tel: (0265) 868209. Castlerock Golf Club, 18-hole and 9-hole courses. Tel: (0265) 848314. Kilrea Golf Club, 9-hole course. Tel: (02665) 71397. Portstewart Golf Club, 18-hole and 9-hole courses. Tel: (026583) 2015.
**Pony trekking** Carrowclare Riding Centre, Limavady. Tel: (05047) 66869. Hill Farm Riding Centre, Aghadowey. Tel: (0265) 848629. Stradreagh Trekking Centre, Limavady. Tel: (05047) 64893. Timbertop Riding Centre, Aghadowey. Tel: (0265) 868788.
**Water-skiing** Coleraine Marina. Tel: (0265) 44768.
**Yachting** Coleraine Yacht Club. Tel: (0265) 44503.

### INFORMATION

Coleraine Tourist Information. Tel: (0265) 44723.

## Coleraine/Cóil Raithin

This sedate market town on the River Bann shows few signs of its antiquity. On the site of a 5th-century church, in the centre of town, is the 17th-century Church of Ireland church of St Patrick. Behind the church are the remains of the ramparts that surrounded Coleraine in the early 1600s. The University of Ulster, Coleraine campus, is modern, and its splendid town hall with its three-tiered clock tower is a typical example of the neoclassical style of the early 19th century.

Yet Coleraine stands close to the site of Ireland's oldest-known settlement – Mountsandel. A mile to the south of the town, it is a 200ft high grassy mound, hollowed at the centre. In the 12th century it became an Anglo-Norman fortification and was used until the 1600s, since it had such good views up and down the river. Close by, excavations have revealed the hearths of wooden houses that stood here 9000 years ago.

Another prehistoric mound, called Ballycairn, stands on the hill across the river from the university. It too was used as a fort by the Normans, and commands extensive views of the river.

On the outskirts of the town is a boating marina, and the River Bann is known for its salmon-rich waters.

## Downhill/Dún Bó

North-east of the craggy, 1260ft mountain of Binevenagh, which means 'terrifying promontory', stand the ruins of Downhill Castle. It was built in the 18th century for Frederick Hervey (1730-1803), 4th Earl of Bristol, who became Bishop of Derry in 1768. His two titles earned him the name of the Earl Bishop. Hervey appears to have enjoyed somewhat ungodly pastimes, indicated by a pair of his duelling pistols displayed in the chapter-house of Londonderry city's St Columb's Cathedral. His tastes seem to have been inherited, since he came from a family reputed for eccentricity; it was said that when God created the world he made men, women and Herveys.

The Earl Bishop's passions included travelling abroad – the many 'Hotel Bristols' throughout Europe are named after him – and building fine houses, one of which was Downhill Castle, constructed in about 1780. The house was burnt down in 1851 and is now a roofless shell, but two entrances to the estate survive, the neoclassical Lion Gate, and Bishop's Gate. The road past the Lion Gate

PORTSTEWART STRAND *The 3 mile beach has an uninterrupted view of fiery sunsets, one of which inspired the song* Red Sails in the Sunset.

leads to Portvantage Glen, also known as 'the Black Glen', with walks and picnic areas.

A short walk from the Lion Gate leads to the cliffs and to one of Hervey's creations – the splendid Mussenden Temple. This was built in 1785 as a summer library, and is a copy of the Temple of Vesta at Tivoli, which no doubt the Earl Bishop had seen during his travels. The pillared and domed rotunda bears a frieze with an inscription written by Lucretius, but translated by Dryden.

*Tis pleasant safely to behold from shore,*
*The rolling ship and hear the tempest roar.*

The Earl Bishop was also responsible for the construction of Bishop's Road, a scenic route from Limavady to Downhill, built to give access across the mountain.

Downhill Forest, with a walk planted with rare trees by the Earl Bishop for residents of the castle, is a beautiful spot, with waterfalls and a prehistoric mound, Dungannon Hill.

**Mussenden Temple** *Apr-Sept, daily 12-6pm.*

## Portstewart/Port Stiobhaird

The most notable feature of the bay of Portstewart is the 3 mile stretch of golden sand known as Portstewart Strand, owned by the National Trust. It makes a pleasant walk to The Barmouth, where the Bann flows into the sea, and is a spectacular sight in stormy weather when the white rollers break on the beach. Sunny evenings are remarkable for glorious sunsets, and it was one such scene that inspired the popular 1930s song *Red Sails*

*in the Sunset*, written by Jimmy Kennedy. The estuary at The Barmouth has large populations of nesting and wintering birds, and has a birdwatching hide. The key for the hide can be obtained from the warden. Tel: (0265) 848728.

The town is a quiet resort with a crescent-shaped promenade of shops and houses. It takes its name from the Royal Stewarts of Scotland, who built the first house here in 1790.

At the town end of Portstewart Strand is Tubber Patrick, or St Patrick's Well, probably a sacred well in pre-Christian times and a source of water for the prehistoric peoples who lived in the caves. Flint arrowheads, scrapers and other prehistoric tools have been found close by.

# The Maiden City

*The City of Londonderry is called The Maiden City because its walls have never been breached. It stands on the River Foyle, which flows to Lough Foyle and the Atlantic Ocean a few miles to the north. This was the course taken by the Vikings who plundered the old city in 812, and it was the outlet for hundreds of Irish families fleeing the famine of the 19th century to make a new life in North America.*

### Amelia Earhart Cottage

In Ballyarnet, north of Londonderry, is a specially constructed cottage, set in 150 acres of parkland. It commemorates Amelia Earhart, the first woman to fly across the Atlantic alone, and her landing here in 1932. The cottage contains an exhibition of the history of air transport.
**Opening times** *June-Sept, daily 2-5pm. Or by arrangement. Tel: (0504) 354040.*

### Dungiven/Dún Geimhin

The remains of the 12th-century Augustinian Dungiven Priory stand on a promontory above the River Roe. The priory is roofless except for the 13th-century chancel, which contains the tomb thought to be that of local chieftain Cooey-na-Gall O'Cahan, who died in 1385. It is considered the finest medieval tomb in Ulster.

The chief's effigy, wearing Irish armour, lies under a traceried canopy. Around the tomb are six kilted warriors – his Scottish mercenaries, known as gallowglasses. It was from these men that Cooey derived the suffix 'na-Gall', meaning 'of foreigners'.

Near the priory's entrance gate is a boulder with a hollow, known as a 'bullaun', which collects water and is said to cure warts. The overhanging thorn bush is covered with strips of rag left by people who claim to have benefited from the water's healing properties.

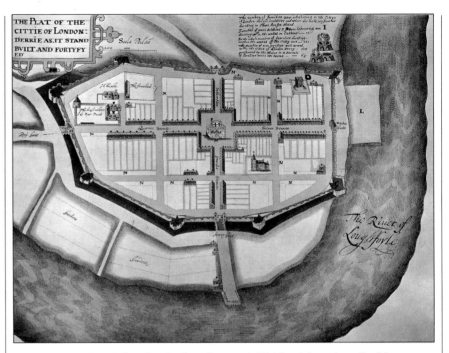

FROM TOWN TO CITY *A plan of Londonderry drawn in 1625 (above) shows the walls of the town clearly. They can still be seen today (below) even though the city has spread beyond its old walls.*

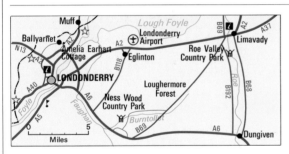

**OTHER PLACES TO SEE**
**Ness Wood Country Park**
8m SE of Londonderry, 46 acres of broadleaf woodland in Burntollet valley, with spectacular waterfall, Northern Ireland's highest, plunging 30ft into deep pool. Tel: (05047) 62074.

**WALKS**
**Loughermore Forest** 1m from Ness Wood, pretty walks amid wild mountain scenery.

**EVENTS**
**City of Londonderry Drama Festival** Feb.
**Dungiven Fleadh Cheoil** June.
**Feis Dhoire-Colmcille** Londonderry, Easter week.
**Foyle Head of the River Race** Londonderry, Feb/Mar.
**Limavady Agricultural Show** June.
**Londonderry Festival** Feb/Mar.
**North-West Arts Festival** Londonderry city, Nov.

**Relief of Derry Celebrations** Aug 12.
**Summer Foyle Festival** May/June.
**Ulster Orchestra Season** Sept/Oct.

**SPORT**
**Angling** Coarse and game fishing: Rivers Bann, Foyle. Game fishing also River Roe.
**Canoeing** Roe Valley Country Park.
**Golf** City of Derry Golf Club, 18-hole and 9-hole courses. Tel: (0504) 46369.
**Pony trekking** City of Derry Riding Centre. Tel: (0504) 351687.
Sinclair's Riding Stables. Tel: (0504) 44278.

**INFORMATION**
Limavady Tourist Information. Tel: (05047) 22226.
Londonderry Tourist Information. Tel: (0504) 267284.

### Limavady/Léim an Mhadaidh

This largely 18th-century town was the leading linen town of Londonderry. Cheap imports led to the decline of the industry, but today the town's buildings have been restored. They include several fine Georgian houses. One bears a plaque to Jane Ross (1810-79), who wrote down the music of the *Londonderry Air*, often rendered as *Danny Boy*, after hearing it played by a 19th-century travelling fiddler. The town's Irish name means 'leap of the dog'.

### Londonderry/Doire

To most Ulstermen, Ulster's second-largest city after Belfast is simply 'Derry', its original name when St Colmcille founded a monastery there in the 6th century. 'Derry' comes from the Irish 'doire', meaning an oak grove.

West of the River Foyle is the old city, built in the 1600s to replace an even earlier city destroyed by fire. The city was built by a consortium of City of London companies, which were granted land in return for developing the area and colonising it with English and Scottish settlers, a policy known as 'Plantation'. Thus in 1613 Derry received its prefix. The city's walls, a mile in circumference, date from this time. They are still intact, making Derry the only city in Ireland with a complete circuit of walls.

The city's defences were tested in 1689, during the Siege of Derry, when the Apprentice Boys locked the gates of the city against the forces of the Catholic King James II. The city was under siege for 105 days, a record in the British Isles.

Dominating the old city is St Columb's Protestant cathedral, dating from the early 17th century. Stained-glass windows commemorate the 'Shutting of the Gates' at the start of the siege. One window is dedicated to Mrs C.F. Alexander, wife of a former bishop of Derry and author of the Christmas carol *Once in Royal David's City*, and the hymns *There is a Green Hill Far Away*, and *All Things Bright and Beautiful*. Of a later date, 1851, is the sandstone Catholic St Eugene's Cathedral, with a spire that tops its rival by some 65ft. It has a granite cross 8ft high on top.

Outside the city walls, at Shipquay Gate, is the red-sandstone Guildhall of 1890, an impressive building in neo-Gothic style. Its clock tower has one of the largest four-faced clocks in the British Isles.

**The Guildhall** *Mon-Fri 9am-4pm. Tel: (0504) 365151.*

NEO-GOTHIC GUILDHALL *The red-sandstone Guildhall was built outside the city walls, a sign of the city's spread.*

### Foyle Valley Railway Centre

Londonderry's Foyle Road Station is a convincing replica of a station of the past. Its collection of majestic steam locomotives and early diesel railcars commemorates the railway history of the city that was once served by four companies. County Donegal Railways pioneered the use of diesel railcars and had two operating in the 1930s, making it the first company in the British Isles to give a regular timetable service by diesel. Visitors can take a trip on one of the diesel railcars built in 1934 along a mile-long stretch of the track by the River Foyle. There is also a Walt Disney-like train called *The Pup*, a railcar built in 1906 at a cost of £200, which was powered by a 10hp Ford engine and was run like a taxi, stopping on request along the line.

**Opening times** *Mon-Sat 10am-5pm. Tel: (0504) 265234.*

### Roe Valley Country Park

The woodland around the River Roe, which flows through cliffs and winding gorges, has been developed into a country park with a visitor centre that tells the story of the region, its people, wildlife and industry. Before the English arrived in the 17th century the area

THE CITY ON STAGE *Actors rehearse for the Londonderry Festival, with a backdrop of the city behind them.*

was ruled by the O'Cahan clan, and the remains of their castle can be seen deep in the woods. Their exploits are remembered in place names such as Dogleap Rock, where, when the castle was under siege, a faithful hound leapt across the raging river and brought allies to the rescue. O'Cahan's Rock celebrates the legend of an O'Cahan horseman who escaped from pursuers by

REQUEST STOP *'The Pup', a railcar which stopped on request along its route, now rests in the Foyle Valley Railway Centre.*

jumping his horse from the 80ft cliff to the other side of the Roe. A stone on the far bank is said to be marked by the horse's hoof.

There is also a power-house museum in the park, the site of Ulster's oldest hydro-electric station, built in 1896 and in operation until 1963.

**Visitor Centre** *June to mid-Sept 9am-9pm. Mid-Sept to May 9am-5pm. Tel: (05047) 62074.*

---

#### HEROINE OF THE AIR

In May 1932, the American aviator Amelia Earhart landed in a field at Ballyarnet, near Londonderry – the first woman to fly the Atlantic solo. Her true destination was Paris, but her emergency landing robbed France of the glory. Her flight took just less than 25 hours.

She was born in Kansas in 1898, and learned to fly in 1920-1, despite her family's protests. In 1928 she became the first woman passenger to fly the Atlantic. In 1937 she attempted a round-the-world flight from Miami, Florida, but radio contact was lost over the Pacific, and she disappeared without trace.

# The Country of Eel Fishers

*The Sperrin Mountains, in fact gentle hills not much higher than 2240ft, range for some 40 miles along Londonderry's southern border. Sheep roam these moorland heights, which are dotted with standing stones left behind by Stone Age people. In the south-east of the county there are trout and salmon rivers, such as the Moyola, and broad expanses of water such as Lough Fea; the county also borders the vast Lough Neagh.*

### Banagher Forest

The 4000 acre forest at Banagher, the largest in the county, takes its name from the Irish for 'the place of the pointed hills'. The hills referred to are the Sperrin Mountains, which rise to the south, although they are more rounded than pointed. There are some fine walks in the forest, especially around the Altnaheglish Reservoir.

Banagher Church stands on a small hill, a short walk from the road. Its well-preserved ruins date from the late 12th century, when it was founded by St Muiredach, though local tradition has it that it was founded by St Patrick in the 5th century. The Irish have a tendency to attribute all churches to their patron saint. The church was first mentioned in 1121 when 'the king of Clannacht was killed by his own kinsmen in the cemetery'.

Though roofless, the walls remain, and the 13th-century chancel has some elegantly carved windows. A large tomb in the graveyard is built in the shape of the church and has the carved figure of an abbot on the gable end. It is called a mortuary house, and is one of a number in Ulster. It is said to hold the remains of St Muiredach, whose family name was O'Heney.

Sand scraped from under the tomb is reputed to bring good luck – but only if your name is O'Heney. The best-known bearer of that name is the local poet Seamus Heaney, born in 1939 at Toome, County Antrim.

### Draperstown/Baile na Croise

In 1613, 12 City of London livery companies agreed to develop this part of Ulster, settling it with English families in return for land. Draperstown was built by the Drapers' Company. Today it is a market town, with broad streets of handsome houses around a triangular green. It is also an ideal base for a tour into the Sperrin Mountains. A straight road runs south-west through breathtaking scenery, to the area of the 'Six Towns'.

At Ballynascreen, one of the Six Towns, is a ruined church in the middle of a field, wrongly claimed to be the burial place of St Colmcille, or Columba. Locals also insist that St Patrick is buried there. The word *bally*, or *baile*, means 'town', and *screen* means 'box', referring to the reliquary in which the saint's body, or part of it, would have been held. The reliquary has long since disappeared.

### Maghera/Machaire Rátha

The streets of Maghera wind, unlike those of Plantation towns, which usually follow a grid pattern. This is because Maghera was developed before the Plantation of the early 17th century. Maghera Church dates from the 10th century and stands on the site of a 6th-century monastery founded by St Lurach. The church is in remarkable condition, and was used as the parish church until the early 19th century. It has a 17th-century tower and a 12th-century west door decorated with carved animal and floral designs, above which is a massive lintel carved with the Crucifixion. The key to the old church can be obtained from the recreational centre in the middle of the town.

Maghera was a linen-weaving town in the 19th century, and there was a bleaching green where the linen was laid out at nearby Upperlands. This village has a textile museum – Middle House Museum – which apart from textiles also contains linen finishing machinery from 1740. Upperlands was the birthplace of Charles Thompson (1729-1824), who helped to draw up the American Declaration of Independence.

North of Maghera there is a prehistoric monument, the Tirnony Dolmen, dating from about 4000 BC. It consists of two upright boulders with another boulder laid across the top, making a kind of sloping table, 8ft tall at its highest point.

**Middle House Museum** *Open by appointment. Tel: (0648) 42214/42737.*

### Moneymore/Muine Mór

The domed peak of Slieve Gallion rises 1737ft to the north-west of Moneymore, a town created by the Drapers' Company of London in 1613. Most of its buildings, however, date from Georgian times, including two market houses, two churches and fine houses along

GLENSHANE PASS *Sheep graze on frosted tufts of grass by the wayside high among the rounded shoulders of the Sperrin Mountains. The pass rises to 964ft above sea level.*

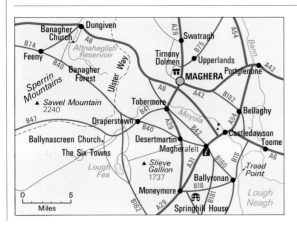

### SPORT
**Angling** Game fishing: Loughs Fea and Neagh, and River Moyola.
**Boating** Ballyronan.
**Golf** Moyola Park Golf Club, 18-hole course. Tel: (0648) 68468.
**Pony trekking** Marsh Kyse Riding School, Magherafelt. Tel: (0648) 33332.

### INFORMATION
Magherafelt Tourist Information. Tel: (0648) 32151.
Londonderry Tourist Information. Tel: (0504) 267284.

SPRINGHILL HOUSE *Built in the 17th century, the manor was the home of the Conyngham family for 300 years. It is said to be haunted by a relative whose husband shot himself in 1836.*

FISHERS OF EELS *Fishermen mend eel nets on the shores of Lough Neagh. This largest lake in Ireland is the centre for the largest eel fishery – not just in Ireland but in Europe.*

its broad main street. It was the first town in Ulster to have piped water, in 1615.

Just outside Moneymore is the elegant, whitewashed and grey-tiled Springhill House, a manor house built in the 17th century as part of a marriage contract between William Conyngham and Anne Upton. Later additions have made the house a truly superb dwelling. It is now owned by the National Trust, and is full of fine furniture and paintings. It is said to be haunted by the ghost of Olivia Lenox-Conyngham. Guided tours of the house are given.

The gardens include a herb garden, a large camomile lawn and several yew trees, one of which is said to be 1000 years old. The old laundry houses a costume collection dating from the 18th century to the present day, and includes a court dress made of brocaded Spitalfields silk in 1759-60.

**Springhill House** *Last week Mar, daily; Apr-June, and Sept, Sat, Sun and Bank Holidays; July-Aug, daily exc Thur 12-6pm. Shop and tea room. Tel: (06487) 48210.*

*The diatom* Stephanodiscus neoastrea *is one of the algae that live in Lough Neagh.*

### LIFE IN LOUGH NEAGH

Lough Neagh is the largest lake in Ireland, 20 miles long and 10 miles wide. At Traad Point, near the town of Magherafelt, is the University of Ulster's freshwater laboratory, which can be visited by the public. The laboratory studies every aspect of life in the lough and keeps a careful watch on algae which can endanger fish life. Fishing is an important resource of the lough – it has the largest eel fishery in the British Isles, and yields up to 4000 eels a day during the peak season.

By extracting cores of sediment from the lough the laboratory is able to gather information which helps to answer vital questions about the health of this and other freshwater lakes.

In 1986 the laboratory won an award for pollution abatement technology, with a device that uses bacteria to convert animal waste to an almost pure liquid.

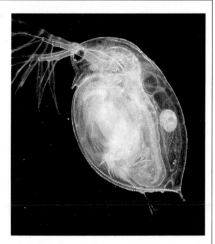

*The water flea* Daphnia *is a simple form of crustacean found in Lough Neagh.*

# A Water-bound Wilderness

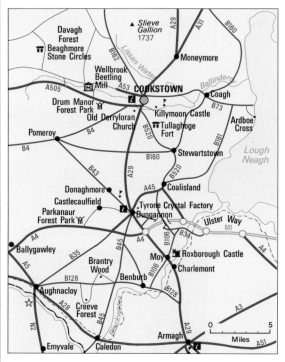

*Water surrounds east Tyrone on three sides – in the north, Lissan Water and the River Ballinderry, in the south the River Blackwater, and in the east the vast, 153sq miles of Lough Neagh, the largest lake in Ireland. The sandy shores of Lough Neagh bristle from May onwards when fishermen from all over the country set their mile-long lines, each bearing 1000 hooks, to catch the lough's eels.*

**OTHER PLACES TO SEE**

**Beaghmore Stone Circles**
Bronze Age group of circles with stone alignments indicating sunrise and moonrise at summer solstice.
**Caledon** 19th-century village with 18th-century church. Birthplace of Field Marshal Earl Alexander (1891-1969). On Caledon estate is 18th-century folly made from cattle's knuckle bones.
**Donaghmore** Graveyard contains 15ft 9th or 10th-century High Cross with Biblical scenes, probably made from two different crosses. Village has old Meeting House, where Irish Volunteers met in 1782 seeking parliamentary independence. Donaghmore Heritage Centre: Mon-Thur 9.30am-5pm, Fri 9.30am-3.30pm.
**Drum Manor Forest Park**
Contains copper beeches, cedars and oaks, special butterfly garden, walled garden and nature trails. Daily, 10am-dusk.
**Parkanaur Forest Park**
Home of herd of white fallow deer descended from pair given in 1597 by Queen Elizabeth to a god-daughter in County Cork; has two parasol beeches at least 150 years old. Daily, 10am-dusk.
**Tyrone Crystal Factory**
Conducted tours, and shop. Tel: (08687) 25335.
**Wellbrook Beetling Mill**
Apr-Sept, weekends only, 2-6pm. June-Aug, daily exc Tues 2-6pm. Tel: (06487) 51735.

**WALKS**

**Sperrin Mountains**
Permission to walk off public footpaths must be sought from landowners.

**SPORT**

**Angling** Coarse and game fishing: Rivers Ballinderry and Blackwater, and Lough Neagh.
**Canoeing** Benburb.
**Golf** Dungannon Golf Club, 18-hole course. Tel: (08687) 22098/27338.
Killymoon Golf Club, 18-hole course. Tel: (06487) 63762/62254.
**Horse riding** Erdergole Riding Centre. Tel: (06487) 62924.

**INFORMATION**
Cookstown Tourist Information Office. Tel: 06487) 62205.

MOLTEN MAGIC *Glassmakers attach a base to a vase at the Tyrone Crystal factory.*

## Ardboe Cross/Ard Both

The 6th-century monastic site of Ardboe is home to Ulster's finest carved cross, its impressive dignity enhanced by its lonely setting on a bleak, windswept stretch of Lough Neagh. The fenced-in cross stands 18ft high and has 22 carved panels of Biblical scenes. The carving is weathered and difficult to decipher, and parts of the sandstone top have crumbled. But the cross is still a credit to its 9th to 10th-century monastery craftsmen. At the bottom of the cross are Adam and Eve. On the east side, panels depict scenes from the Old Testament, and on the west, scenes from the New Testament.

Behind the cross, on a bluff overlooking the expanse of the lough, are the ruins of a 17th-century church and graveyard.

## Benburb/An Bhinn Bhorb

The estate village of Benburb has a long stone wall on one side of the street and gabled estate workers' cottages on the other. The 1888 redbrick mansion, built by the Scottish whiskey distiller James Bruce, director of Bushmills, is now a Servite priory, the hub of the village community. (The Servites follow the Order of Servants of Mary.) The chapel is in what was once the mansion's ballroom, which served as an operating theatre for the Allied Forces during the Second World War. The monks run an interdenominational conference centre and they are establishing a wildlife conservation area by the river.

The public can walk in the 147 acre grounds from which there are views over the valley and the ruins of 17th-century Benburb Castle. The castle stands on a cliff 200ft above the River Blackwater and has a small private house within its four massive stone walls.

WHITEWATER DAREDEVIL *With dextrous flicks of his paddle, an intrepid canoeist shoots the whitewater rapids on the River Blackwater near Benburb.*

Linen manufacture was once Ulster's most important industry, along with the cultivation of flax, and the province is scattered with abandoned mills where the fabric was produced. One of these is the National Trust's Wellbrook Beetling Mill, 4 miles from Cookstown, which was in commercial use for almost two centuries until 1961. 'Beetling' is a process in which the woven cloth is hammered in order to flatten the round flax fibres and produce a smooth sheen on the surface.

The water wheel at Wellbrook still revolves in a race off the River Ballinderry and powers the machinery in the long, whitewashed mill room. When the sluice gates are opened, the water turns the 16ft diameter wheel which powers a bank of seven beetling engines through shafts and gears. Each bank is a line of 32 beetles, square beechwood beams that hammer along the length of fabric, which moves slowly along on a roller below the beams.

At Wellbrook the beetled cloth was hung and dried on the upper floor where today an illustrated display tells the story of linen making, from 'pulling' the flax in the fields to 'retting', or wetting the bundles in cold water; 'scutching', which meant separating the core from the outside fibres; and 'combing'. The hanks were then sent for spinning and the linen was woven and bleached before being brought to the mill.

By the priory gates is the Church of Ireland Clonfeacle Church, built in 1618. A plaque by the altar commemorates James Hamilton, a Scottish lord who devised the Plantation scheme that resulted in Ireland being settled by the English and Scots. He was killed in 1646 at the Battle of Benburb when the Scots were defeated by the Irish confederate Owen Roe O'Neill.

## Cookstown/An Corr Chriochach

The distinctive main street of Cookstown is 130ft wide and points straight towards the silhouette of Slieve Gallion mountain (1737ft). The Stewarts of Killymoon, who were responsible for Cookstown's layout, wanted a main street to rival the avenues of Dublin. It is 1¼ miles long and changes its name eight times along the way, one of them being Main Street.

The west side of Main Street is dominated by the soaring spire of Holy Trinity Church, built in 1855 and designed by J.J. McCarthy. On the other side of the street is the pinnacled tower and spire of the neo-Gothic, greystone Derryloran parish church (1822). The tower is by John Nash, who was also responsible for the massive showpiece Norman-Revival Killymoon Castle beyond the golf club. This was Nash's first great Irish house. It was built in 1803 at a cost of £80,000 for Colonel William Stewart whose forebears had acquired the Cookstown estate in 1666 from its founder Dr Cooke, an ecclesiastical lawyer. The castle can be visited by arrangement. Tel: (06486) 64173.

In the 1880s Cookstown was a thriving linen centre with three factories along the River Ballinderry. The town is now the centre of a thriving agricultural area, with an important livestock market, and a lively street market on Saturdays. Its bacon factory is renowned for its sausages.

The ruins of the 17th-century Derryloran parish church are on a hillock by the River Ballinderry. There has been a church at this spot since AD 800. The name is from *doire Luran,* 'the oakwood of Luran'. Against the outside wall is the family vault of the Stewarts of Killymoon. The church was abandoned in 1822 when its successor was built in a more convenient place on Cookstown's central street.

## Dungannon/Dún Geannain

Textiles are now the main business of the busy town of Dungannon, built on a hill and with a sloping market square. A police station now stands on the site of the fort once occupied by druid's son Geannain who gave his name to the town.

Dungannon became one of the most important settlements in Ulster and was the seat of government for the ruling O'Neill chieftains who occupied the fort from the 13th century. In 1542 Con O'Neill submitted to the British and accepted the title Earl of

ERRIGAL KEEROGUE CROSS *The winter sun sets on this ridge-top graveyard and its unfinished cross.*

Tyrone from Henry VIII. The title was sold to Thomas Knox in 1692. His descendants, the Earls of Ranfurly, developed the town's markets and business.

Dungannon's greystone Royal School was founded by James I in 1608 and moved to its present site in Northland Row below the hill in 1789. On the lawn is a large, bronze statue of former pupil Brigadier General John Nicholson, killed during the Indian Mutiny of 1857. The statue was brought to Dungannon in 1960 from its former home at the Kashmir Gate in New Delhi.

## Moy/An Maigh

The immaculate village of Moy has a centre planted with shady trees and surrounded by 18th-century houses. In summer the neat flowerbeds on the manicured lawns are a blaze of colour. The village was designed by James Caulfield, Earl of Charlemont, who had been impressed by Marengo Square in Italy.

The austerely elegant St James Church (1819), has a bricked-up main door, the result, it is said, of a complaint about draughty pews by a lady from the manor house at Charlemont. The entrance is now at the side.

All that remains of the Charlemont family seat at nearby Roxborough Castle is a fine, curving black cast-iron screen and gates surmounted by red and gold dragons and unicorns.

## Tullaghoge Fort/Tulaigh Og

Now a hilltop circle of grass surrounded by a ring of trees, Tullaghoge Fort was once the dynastic centre and inauguration mound of the O'Neill chieftains. A short ascent from the car park leads to the earthwork, whose Irish name means 'little hill'.

The fort's saucer-shaped centre, 40yds across, is protected by a circular ditch and an outer bank, and has commanding views over the countryside, now partly obscured by trees planted by Victorians.

An early 17th-century map shows the fort with two gates, two thatched buildings and an inauguration chair on the Stewartstown side. This chair was broken up by Lord Deputy Mountjoy in 1602 when his forces were advancing against the O'Neills.

After Hugh O'Neill's defeat by Queen Elizabeth's armies in 1601, his tribesmen hid in Tullaghoge Forest. O'Neill is still a common name in these parts.

# The New World in Ulster

*West Tyrone is a surprising mixture of the bleak and fertile: thick pastures grazed by sleek cattle quickly give way to swathes of brownish bogland. In the south-east of the area, little whalebacked hills are separated by fertile valleys watered by clear trout streams that run through tidy villages with decorated gate posts. Here also is the Ulster-American Folk Park, a reconstruction of the life of emigrants to North America in the 18th and 19th centuries.*

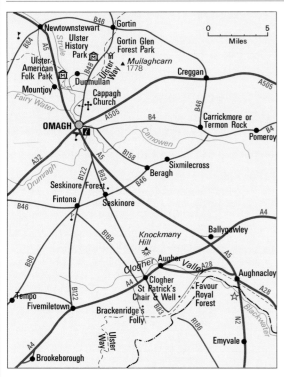

Mon, Tues, Fri 10am-6pm, Thur 2-8pm, Sat 10am-5pm. Closed public holidays. Tel: (03655) 21409.
**Gortin Glen Forest Park** 1000 acres of woodland, with paths up Mullaghcarn (1778ft).

### EVENTS
**Annual Arts Festival** Omagh, Oct.
**Aughnacloy Festival** July.
**Bilberry Sunday** Aughnacloy, last Sun in July.
**Carrickmore Drama Festival** Mar.
**Easter Bonnet Parade** Ulster-American Folk Park, Easter.
**Fourth of July celebrations** Ulster-American Folk Park.
**Hallowe'en Festival** Ulster-American Folk Park, Oct.
**Omagh Agricultural Show** July.
**Omagh-West Tyrone Feis** May.

### SPORT
**Angling** Game fishing: River Strule and Fairy Water.
**Golf** Fintona Golf Club, 9-hole course. Tel: (0662) 841480.
Omagh Golf Club, 18-hole course. Tel: (0662) 243160/241442.
**Pony trekking** Ballygowans Stables. Tel: (0662) 242903. Parkway Riding Centre. Tel: (0662) 245969.

### INFORMATION
Omagh Tourist Information. Tel: (0662) 247831/2.

### OTHER PLACES TO SEE
**Augher** Site of Spur Royal Castle; nearby is birthplace of William Carleton, novelist and author of *Traits and Stories of the Irish Peasantry.* At Augher Creamery, visitors can see the process of cheese making. Tours by arrangement. Tel: (06625) 48214.

**Aughnacloy** Royal Forest with St Patrick's Chair and Well, said never to dry out.
**Dunmullan** 4½m N of Omagh, ruins of medieval Cappagh Old Church.
**Fivemiletown Display Centre** Museum in village library, containing old photographs, kitchen utensils, craftsmen's tools.

## Clogher/Clochar

The handsome blue-grey stone cathedral of St Macartan's stands at the crest of Clogher's main street, which sweeps up the hill from the River Blackwater. The cathedral, rebuilt in 1744, claims to have been the centre of the oldest bishopric in Ireland, from the 5th century, until it was housed in the larger town of Enniskillen, in County Fermanagh. In the graveyard stand two High Crosses from the 9th or 10th century, decorated with geometrical motifs.

Beside the cathedral, lower down the hill, is the elegant former bishop's palace with a Georgian gate lodge, now a convent and home for the aged.

Next to the school, behind the cathedral, stands the Iron Age fort that was once the seat of the Kings of Oriel, a powerful local tribe. From it there is a clear view of Brackenridge's Folly, 2 miles to the south. The folly was built by the 19th-century squire George Brackenridge who, because he was not accepted into local society, built this conspicuous mausoleum so that people would at least take notice of him when he was dead.

## Knockmany Hill

The hill has a magnificent passage-grave with 12 massive upright slabs, three carved with spirals and whirls typical of Stone Age patterns and similar to those at Newgrange in County Meath. The grave is reached by a steep walk up the forested slopes of the hill.

The markings on the stones may depict an eye goddess worshipped in about 3000 BC. The stones are protected by a mound and have to be viewed through an iron gate, but the forest ranger will open it on request. From the top of the grassy knoll there is an excellent view of the 20 mile long Clogher Valley.

## Omagh/An Omaigh

Near the centre of Tyrone's county town the Rivers Camowen and Drumragh meet to form the wide River Strule. From this meeting point the main street sweeps uphill to the civic splendour of the 1814 neoclassical courthouse with its portico and four Doric columns. Behind it, on the crest of the hill, is a cluster of churches of four different denominations – Catholic, Church of Ireland, Presbyterian and Methodist – making it a difficult place to park on Sunday mornings. The unevenly sized double spires of the Catholic Sacred Heart church (1893-9) are the town's chief landmark.

Mirror Image *The uneven spires of Omagh's Sacred Heart church overlook the River Strule.*

Omagh has two particularly interesting bridges – the narrow, 17th-century King James Bridge over the River Drumragh, and the early 19th-century five-arched Bell's Bridge which spans the Strule just off the main street. Another, Strule Bridge, gives a fine view of the town, with the neo-Gothic Sacred Heart on one side, and the meeting of the rivers on the other.

From a green haven called Lovers' Retreat on the banks of the River Drumragh, salmon can be seen leaping and heron wading. There are picnic tables, benches and a riverside walk. 'Jimmy' Kennedy, who wrote the song *Teddy Bears' Picnic,* was born in Omagh in 1902.

A farm at Mountjoy, 4 miles from Omagh, is the home of the Tyrone Black, a handsome blue-black breed of cattle. The breed, developed over 20 years, is 62.5 per cent Aberdeen-Angus, and 12.5 per cent each of Charolais, Chianina and British Friesian.

## Seskinore Forest/Seisceann Odhar

The 500 acres of Seskinore Forest comprise one of Europe's largest game farms, and its birds stock the forest parks of most of Northern Ireland. In addition to pheasants and duck, Seskinore has a collection of rare birds, and indigenous birds include greenfinches and sparrowhawks. The wooded farm also has some rare sheep and an Irish dray mare and foal of the type once used to pull timber from the forest. Visitors can picnic in the grounds, but must telephone first. Tel: (0662) 841243.

## Ulster-American Folk Park

Ulster's contribution to the New World is set out at an open-air museum that re-creates the sights and sounds experienced by the flood of emigrants to North America in the 18th and 19th centuries.

The park's core is the thatched cottage in which Thomas Mellon was born, on February 3, 1813. Mellon left this whitewashed cottage at the age of five and sailed to America with his family, where he became a judge and banker, and founded a vast business empire. His son Andrew built up the steel town of Pittsburgh, and the Mellon family have contributed to the development of the Folk Park. In the kitchen of the Mellon cottage, smoke-wreathed from the fire in the hearth, traditional soda bread and oatmeal flatcakes are baked on iron griddles.

There are also authentic reconstructions of old Ulster buildings, a blacksmith's forge, a meeting house and a weaver's cottage. Local craftswomen card and spin wool at a wooden spinning wheel, and dye it in the traditional way, using birch bark to make a silvery-grey, onion skins for shades of orange and bilberries for soft pink.

The Ship and Dockside Gallery, depicting a quayside from which emigrants sailed from Ireland, has a full-scale replica of an early 19th-century two-masted sailing brig similar to the *Union* that carried members of the Mellon family across the Atlantic to Baltimore in 1816.

The New World part of the exhibition shows how early Irish emigrants lived in North America. The reconstructions include a log cabin and Pennsylvania log barn complete with two old breeds of pig, and a two-storey Pennsylvania log farmstead, a replica of the six-bedroomed Mellon home.

**Ulster-American Folk Park** *Easter-Sept, Mon-Sat 11am-6.30pm, Sun and public holidays 11.30am-7pm. Sept to pre-Easter, Mon-Fri 10.30am-5pm. Tel: (0662) 243292.*

## The Ulster History Park

An impression of life in Ulster several thousand years ago is given in the Ulster History Park, still in its first phase of construction. When it is completed the entire project will

ULSTER-AMERICAN FOLK PARK *A local woman spins wool in the reconstructed weaver's cottage (top), while candles are made in the kitchen of an Irish emigrant's Pennsylvania farmstead (above).*

LIFE IN AGES PAST *Historic dwellings are re-created in the Ulster History Park.*

include six sites, among them a Middle Stone Age home of 7000 BC, with its cosy, hazelwood, hide-covered dome, and a Later Stone Age house from 4000 BC to 2000 BC, its double-wattle walls filled with bracken for insulation. There will also be an interpretative exhibition centre with audiovisuals.

The 35 acre grounds already contain a crannog, or defensive island dwelling, made from stone and brushwood, set in a real lake. An early monastic settlement has also been re-created, with an outer wall 10ft high and 5ft thick, a Round Tower, an early church and a covered well. And there is a Norman motte with a bailey, from the 11th century.

Original building methods have been meticulously followed, and detailed plans and explanations of construction are displayed inside the entrance to the park.

**Ulster History Park** *Easter-end Sept, Mon-Fri 11am-6pm, Sat 11am-7pm, Sun 1-7pm. End Sept-Easter, Mon-Fri 11am-5pm. Bank Holidays 11am-7pm. Tel: (06626) 48188.*

### PICNIC TIME FOR TEDDY BEARS

A bored political officer who left the Colonial Service and became an internationally famous songwriter was born in Omagh. James 'Jimmy' Kennedy (1902-84), writer of the *Teddy Bears' Picnic*, was educated at Trinity College, Dublin, and joined the Colonial Service between the wars. He turned to songwriting in 1929 with *Hear the Ukelele* and the *Barmaid's Song*, both very popular in Blackpool. But it was in 1932 with *Teddy Bears' Picnic* that he sprang to international fame with record sales alone of 4 million. Others of his well-known hits were *Isle of Capri*, *Red Sails in the Sunset* and *Harbour Lights*, and together with Michael Carr he wrote the

old-time favourites *Siegfried Line*, the *Hokey Cokey* and *Chestnut Tree*.

Asked where he got his inspiration, Kennedy said: 'I don't think I've ever been inspired in my life.' After the Second World War he lived in Switzerland and later moved to Dublin; he was married three times. Kennedy won an Ivor Novello Award, became an Honorary Doctor of Literature at Ulster University and was awarded the Order of the British Empire (OBE). He was chairman of the British Songwriters Guild. His funeral oration at St Giles's Church in London, was given by Denis Thatcher, husband of the then British prime minister.

# Mountains of Gold

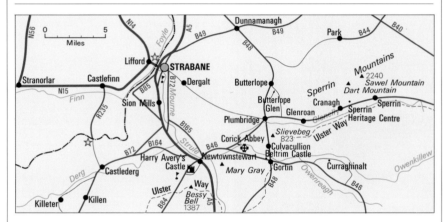

*There is an almost Tyrolean air here, with the Sperrin Mountains flanked by pinewoods, rough-coated sheep grazing rocky pastures, and the glistening ribbon of the River Glenelly winding below. Two other beautiful valleys are carved through the foothills by the Rivers Owenkillew and Owenreagh which, like the Glenelly, eventually find the sea at Lough Foyle, a large sea lough that reaches deep inland. These mountains have a rich secret which hides in the shining waters of their streams – they contain gold.*

## OTHER PLACES TO SEE

**Beltrim Castle** Remains of 17th-century castle, and site of Georgian house (built 1820). The house is not open to the public.

**Butterlope Glen** Remains of five stone circles.

**Culvacullion** On S slope of Slievebeg mountain (860ft), four stone circles and remains of chambered tomb.

**Drummond's Castle** Dunnamanagh; mid-17th-century castle never completed because Sir John Drummond's wife-to-be was drowned when the ship bringing her from France sank.

**Glenroan** N of St Patrick's Church; large stone with cup-shaped mark that local legend says is imprint of St Patrick's knee. In churchyard is stone with four cup marks. Nearby is Corickmore Abbey, 15th-century Franciscan friary church.

**Gortin** Village and gateway to Sperrin Mountains.

**Sperrin Heritage Centre** At Cranagh, display illustrating local gold exploration and facts on its history and the geological environment. Craft shop and café. Tel: (06626) 48142.

## WALKS

**Sperrin Mountains** 40 mile ridge straddling boundary between Tyrone and Londonderry. Rises to 2240ft. Walkers are advised not to stray from public footpaths, or must seek permission from landowners first.

## EVENTS

**Bessy Bell Classic** May 25, 26, June 1.

**Killeter Show** Aug.

**Sheep Dog Trials** Castlederg, June; Plumbridge, July; Killen, July and Aug.

**Strabane Golf Club Open Week** End June, early July.

**Strawberry Fair** Sion Mills, end June.

## SPORT

**Angling** Game fishing: Rivers Foyle, Mourne, Owenkillew and Owenreagh.

**Golf** Newtownstewart Golf Club, 18-hole course. Tel: (06626) 61466. Strabane Golf Club, 18-hole course. Tel: (0504) 382271.

## INFORMATION

Omagh Tourist Information. Tel: (0662) 247831/2.

## Newtownstewart/An Baile Nua

The quiet market town of Newtownstewart was once an important centre for the flax and woollen industries, founded in 1722 by planter William Stewart. Its main street, with its neat, mostly 19th-century buildings, runs downhill from St Eugene's (1724) Church of Ireland to the river. The road crosses a delightful 1727 arched stone bridge over the River Strule to the market buildings and livestock pens on the other side.

On the most prominent slope above the water, and situated rather incongruously behind a grocery store, are the three-pointed, crow-stepped end gable and chimney of the old Stewart castle, built during the Plantation on the spot where Tyrone chief Turlough O'Neill had a stronghold. During that time Newtownstewart was called Lislas. It was burnt by Felim O'Neill in 1641, and again in 1689 as the result of a bout of ill-temper by James II who stayed overnight in the vacant castle on his return from an unsuccessful assault on Londonderry. When he woke the next morning, he ordered the castle and town to be razed.

In the Northern Bank on the lower corner of Main Street is a gruesome reminder of a celebrated murder. A glass case contains part of the bloodstained counter where bank cashier William Glass was killed and robbed of £1600 in 1871. District Inspector of Police Thomas Montgomery, officer in charge of the investigation, turned out to be the culprit.

Two hills, Bessy Bell (1387ft) and Mary Gray (823ft) stand sentry over Newtownstewart on either side of the Omagh road. No one is certain who the ladies that they take their names from were, but the popular story is that the original Bessy and Mary were Scottish nurses who worked in the district at the time of the Famine.

On a high field below Bessy Bell, the massive remains of the twin towers of 14th-century Harry Avery's Castle stand against the skyline. Close inspection of the sturdy, thick stone walls reveals why they have survived for 500 years.

The castle is named after Henry Aimbreidh O'Neill. It is said that Avery had a sister with a head like a pig, and offered a large dowry as compensation to anyone who would marry her. But any suitor initially bold enough to carry out the bargain and who refused to marry the sister on seeing her would be hanged. Nineteen men decided to take that option.

PLANTERS' PRIDE *Newtownstewart, a Plantation town, is overlooked by the Sperrin Mountains.*

### GOLD IN THEM THAR HILLS

There have been periodic outbreaks of goldrush fever in the Gortin-Plumbridge area of the Sperrin Mountains for centuries, but as yet no one has made their fortune there. However, commercial prospecting revives the rumours from time to time and prospectors try their luck by panning in the boulder-strewn streams.

There is definitely gold in the area – it is thought that some prehistoric jewellery was made of Sperrin gold, and a mine has been opened at Curraghinalt, 6 miles east of Gortin. Tests have shown that some 80 sites in the Sperrins contain gold, making it the biggest commercial gold find in western Europe. But stories of lucky prospectors finding nuggets of gold in the streams are unlikely, as the ore has to be carefully sifted and chemically extracted – half an ounce of gold is yielded by every ton of ore mined. The lengthy process is carried out to produce objects for special occasions. A medallion made of Sperrin gold was presented to flyweight boxing champion Barry McGuigan in 1986. For those badly bitten by the gold bug, plastic dishes can be hired from the Sperrin Heritage Centre for panning in the stream outside.

## Sion Mills/Muileann an tSiáin

Black-and-white half-timbered buildings, neo-Gothic workers' cottages and streets lined with shady horse-chestnut and beech trees make Sion Mills still very much the mid-19th-century model linen village created by three Scottish brothers named Herdman.

On a bend of the River Mourne they converted an old flour mill into a flax-spinning mill and later built a handsome, yellow-brick factory behind it, a stately presence in what is now one of the most modern linen factories in Europe.

Most of the original houses in Sion Mills were by the English architect William Unsworth, designer of the Shakespeare Memorial Theatre at Stratford-upon-Avon, and James Herdman's son-in-law. His mock-Tudor theme is most apparent at the Gate-house at the top of Mill Lane.

Sion House, the Herdmans' former mansion, was remodelled with a red tiled roof and elaborate chimneys, and Unsworth also designed the attractive, red-brick stable block with a clock tower on the main road.

The same architect was responsible for the impressive Italianate Romanesque church of the Good Shepherd (1909), which is based on a Tuscan church and has arched windows, a tall campanile and marble steps and pulpits.

In contrast, the rectangular Catholic church of St Theresa is assertively modern, with a striking engraving of the Last Supper incised into slate, covering the entire front of the building. The engraving is by Oisin Kelly.

## Strabane/An Srath Bán

The town of Strabane is a busy gateway to the north-west, built along the banks of the River Mourne. The main street runs straight across

SUPPER ON SLATE *A large engraving incised on slate, depicting Christ breaking the bread at the Last Supper, decorates the front of the Church of St Theresa in Sion Mills.*

GRAY'S PRINTING PRESS *The 19th-century printing works (above) displays hand-printing presses.* RICH SECRET *The Sperrin Mountains (below), home to badgers and buzzards, also contain gold.*

the valley to Lifford in County Donegal. The linen trade was introduced in the 18th century and, although greatly decreased, it lingers on in shirt and collar making.

Tucked in among other buildings, near the main bridge from the south, is the curved Georgian façade of Gray's Printer's, the only surviving reminder of Strabane's importance in the 18th and 19th centuries as a printing centre. Once there were ten printing businesses in the town, and two newspapers.

John Dunlap, printer of the American Declaration of Independence and publisher of America's first daily newspaper, the *Pennsylvania Packet*, was born in Meeting House Street in 1746. He is reputed to have gained his first experience of the trade at Gray's.

To reach the print works, now preserved by the National Trust, visitors walk through a shop and across a yard to the upper floor of a slate-roofed, two-storey building. The most impressive of an array of well-maintained and decorative printing presses is a Columbian Press with a cast-iron American eagle on the cross-rod. Carved wooden letters, once used in poster printing, are stacked in wall racks. Type set in metal 'chases', or frames, lies on a bench. The shop also contains antique printing equipment such as a lead cutter.

James Wilson, grandfather of Woodrow Wilson, President of the United States from 1913 to 1921, is said to have served his apprenticeship at Gray's before emigrating to America in 1807. The Wilson family home, now a museum, stands on the slopes of the Sperrin Mountains in Dergalt, 2 miles southeast of Strabane on the Plumbridge road. It is a low, whitewashed farmhouse, with a flax thatching covering an under-thatch of sods supported by oak roof timbers. Inside, it is traditionally furnished. A dresser stands on the clay floor opposite the open hearth, where cooking pots and kettles still hang, and photographs of the Wilson family adorn the cottage. Over the fireplace hangs a painted portrait of Judge James Wilson, Woodrow's grandfather.

Members of the Wilson family still work the farm and live in the modern farmhouse nearby, where visitors should call for admission to the cottage.

**Gray's Printer's** *End Mar-Sept, exc Thur, Sun and Bank Holidays, 12-6pm. Shop open all year, 9am-5.30pm. Tel: (0504) 884094.*
**Wilson Farmhouse** *Apr-Sept, daily exc Sun, Thur and public holidays, 2-5.30pm, or by arrangement. Tel: (0504) 884094.*

# GLOSSARY

**Antae** Projections beyond the side walls of a building
**Arcade** Series of arches on columns
**Ard** A high place
**Ath** A ford
**Baile, or bally** A settlement
**Bailey** An enclosure for livestock, usually beside a castle or at the base of a motte
**Ballina** An entrance, or ford
**Barbican** A structure defending the gate of a castle
**Bawn** A fortified enclosure attached to a castle
**Bee-hive hut** A small hut built from stones laid in narrowing circles until they reach a point. Also called a clochán
**Beltane** Ancient Celtic festival on first day of May
**Boreen** Path, or lane, usually flanked by stone walls, originally for driving cows through
**Bullaun** Stone indented with smooth depression, often found in early monasteries. Probably used as a mortar
**Bun** End of a road; foot of a hill; mouth of a stream
**Caher** Dry-stone fort
**Cairn** A mound of stones, often indicating a tomb
**Capstone** A stone covering a dolmen
**Carrig, or Carrick** Rock
**Cashel** Stone enclosure, round a ring-fort, church or monastery
**Céilithe** (sing. ceilidh) Traditional dances
**Chancel** The east end of a church which houses the altar. Also called the choir
**Chevaux-de-Frise** Stones placed point upwards in the ground as a barrier, usually to a fort
**Clochán** A dry-stone hut, usually beehive-shaped
**Clogher** A stony place
**Cloister** A covered arcade, forming a square, usually around a garden, within a monastery

**Cluain** Meadow
**Colonnade** A series of columns placed at regular intervals
**Columbarium** A dovecote
**Corrie** A circular hollow at a valley head, often holding water
**Court-tomb** Stone Age tomb consisting of a long chamber divided into burial compartments with a courtyard in front of the tomb
**Crannog** Artificial island used as a lake dwelling, built from stone and wood. Its name is derived from *cran*, a tree, because of the large amount of wood used in the construction
**Cross-slab** A stone slab carved with one or more crosses; often an early gravestone
**Crypt** An underground vault or chamber, usually beneath a church and used as a burial place
**Cupola** A domed roof or ceiling
**Currach** A small fishing boat, formed of hides stretched over a lath framework, later of tarred canvas
**Dáil Éireann** The lower house, or House of Representatives, in the Irish Parliament
**Demesne** Enclosed park or garden surrounding a mansion; an estate
**Derg, or Dearg** Red
**Diamond** In Ulster, the central square or market-place of a Plantation town, often triangular in shape
**Dolmen** Stone Age tomb formed of three or more upright stones covered by a capstone, and once enclosed by an earth mound
**Dovecote** A roost for doves
**Drum, or Drom** A ridge or hillock
**Drumlin** A small hill, often oval in shape, formed by glacial action; much of Ulster

is divided from the rest of the island by a belt of such drumlins
**Dub, or Doo** (Irish *dubh*) Black, or dark
**Dun, or Doon** Fort
**Ennis, Inis, or Inch** An island
**Féis** Festival
**Fenian** Member of the Irish Republican Brotherhood, founded in 1858 to undermine British 'ascendancy' in Ireland
**Fianna Fáil** 'Sons of Destiny'; name of one of the two main political parties in the Republic
**Filí** (sing. file) Poets and storytellers
**Fine Gael** Meaning 'Race of the Irish'; name of one of the two main political parties in the Republic
**Fleadh** Music festival
**Fulacht Fiadh, or Fulacht fiann** Ancient cooking place. Cooking was achieved by heating stones and dropping them into a stone trough until the water came to the boil, then the raw meat would be dropped in
**Gable** The triangular end of the wall beneath a pitched roof
**Gaeltacht** Area in which Irish is the vernacular language
**Gallowglass** Mercenary soldier from Scotland, employed in Ireland from the 13th to the 15th centuries
**Glen, or Glan** A valley, or glen
**Gothic** A style of architecture prevalent from the late 12th century, using the pointed arch, rib vaulting and flying buttresses
**Henge** A ritual enclosure made of stone or wooden posts with a ditch inside the rampart
**High Cross** A tall ring-headed cross of stone, usually carved with figures, Biblical scenes and patterns
**Hill-fort** Fort encircling the summit of a selected hill. Sometimes it encloses as much as 20 acres within its

defences, which may be either stone-built ramparts or a steep bank and ditch
**Keep** A tower
**Kill, or Cill** Early monastic site, cell, or chapel
**Knock, or Cnoc** A hill; there are some 2000 townlands in Ireland with this prefix
**Lancet** A tall narrow window
**Lavabo** A building in which monks washed themselves, or a water bowl and water tank with a spout
**Lis** (Irish *lios*) Earthen fort, or enclosure
**Martello tower** Small round tower built as watch tower on many parts of the Irish coast to warn of invasion from Napoleon
**Mor** Big, great
**Motte** A man-made mound with a flattened top, used by the Normans as a fortification
**Nave** The central part of a church, flanked by aisles
**Og** Young
**Ogee** Double-curve, as in the letter *s*
**Ogham** The earliest known Irish script, formed of lines representing 20 letters of the Latin alphabet, used around the 5th century AD to notch memorial inscriptions on standing stones
**Oireachtas** Annual festival of Irish music, dancing, poetry, drama and painting. Also Irish national parliament, comprising the President, Dáil and Seanad. It means a 'gathering'
**Owen** A river
**Pale** The area, of varying borders but focused round Dublin, to which effective English control was confined from the 12th to 16th centuries
**Passage-grave** Stone Age grave in which a stone-lined passage leads to the tomb-chamber
**Pilaster** Part of a column, which projects from a wall
**Pillarstone** Standing stone
**Plantation** The settlement of Ulster with English and Scots settlers in the early 17th

century; also refers to architectural styles which introduced many features from Scotland during this time
**Portcullis** A sliding grille with points on the bottom, suspended above a gate, which could be lowered in time of danger
**Poteen** An illicitly distilled spirit usually made from potatoes
**Promontory fort** A stone-built defence placed across the neck of a promontory
**Rampart** A fortification surrounded by an embankment or wall, and often with a parapet
**Rath** Earthen fort or enclosure
**Ring-fort** A round or oval enclosure made from an earth or stone embankment, encircled by a ditch. In prehistoric times it was used as a form of community defence against marauders and wolves. Between 30,000 and 40,000 such forts have been found in the Irish countryside
**Romanesque** A style of architecture common from the 9th to the 12th centuries using rounded arches and thick walls
**Round Tower** Five-storeyed tower with conical roof, internal staircase and doorway several feet above ground. Built as part of a monastery, as a bell tower and as protection from raiding. The doorway was reached by ladder which would be pulled into the tower after the monks
**Sabhall** A barn
**Scellig, or Skellig** Lofty crag or rock
**Scoil** School
**Screen** A partition in a church, usually dividing the nave and chancel
**Seanchai** Traditional storyteller
**Sheela-na-gig** Sexually explicit or grotesque carving of a woman in religious or secular buildings, generally

thought to be connected with a fertility rite
**Sinn Fein** Meaning 'We Ourselves'; political party founded in 1905 for the furtherance of Home Rule, periodically illegal since independence
**Slieve** (Irish *sliabh*) Mountain
**Souterrain** Underground passage or artificially built chamber used as place of refuge and usually, though not always, connected to a fort
**Standing stone** A monument or prehistoric grave stone, sometimes inscribed in ogham with commemorative inscription
**Stone circles** Circles of free-standing upright stones, varying in number from five to 15. Sometimes a slab on its side, or a 'recumbent stone', lies in the centre. Used variously for burials, ancient rituals, as places of assembly and also as calendars, noting from the sun's shadows the coming and going of the seasons
**Stucco** Ornamental plaster work
**Sweathouse** Stone dome-shaped structure with a single opening used for sweat baths, heated by a fire. The procedure commonly ended with a cold plunge
**Taoiseach** Prime Minister
**Teampull, or Temple** A church
**Tholsel** Town hall, or toll-house
**Tobar, Tober, or Tubber** A well, often claimed to be holy
**Transept** The north and south wings of a church
**Transitional** Architectural style between Romanesque and Gothic and containing elements of both
**Turf** Word normally used where peat or peat-fuel would be used in Britain
**Vault** An arch forming a ceiling
**Wedge-tomb** Stone Age tomb wider at one end than at the other

# CHRONOLOGY

*An outline of the history of Ireland from the earliest settlements to the establishment of the Irish Free State*

## BC

**8000-7000** Evidence of first settlers in Ireland, in the midlands, and at Mountsandel, near Coleraine, Londonderry.

**3500** First evidence of neolithic settlements, and first megalithic tombs built.

**c.3000** Newgrange, one of the most impressive Stone Age tombs in Europe, built in the Boyne valley.

**c.1750-500** Bronze Age. Masterpieces of metalwork in bronze, copper and gold produced.

**c.500** Iron Age begins. La Tène style of decoration introduced around 3rd century BC. Eamhain Macha, legendary palace near Armagh, already in existence.

## AD

**c.300** Development of ogham alphabet, inscribed on stone.

**c.432** St Patrick arrives in Ireland.

**433** Easter fire lit by St Patrick on Hill of Slane symbolises arrival of Christianity.

**500-800** Monasteries established and monastic arts flourish.

**c.650** *Book of Durrow* created.

**c.700** Codification of Brehon Laws, setting out legal and judicial system.

**795** First Viking raid.

**800-1000** Periodic Viking invasions. *Book of Kells* created c.800. Vikings found Dublin c.840.

**c.850** First Viking-Irish alliance.

**1002** Brian Boru becomes High King of Ireland.

**1014** Danish command of east coast broken at Battle of Clontarf, led by Brian Boru. Boru is killed in the battle.

**1130-1200** Irish-Romanesque, or Hiberno-Romanesque, architectural style flourishes.

**1142** First Cistercian monastery built in Ireland, at Mellifont, Louth.

**1152** Dervorgilla, wife of Tiernan O'Rourke (Prince of Breifne) is abducted by Dermot MacMurrough (King of Leinster). Synod of Kells-Mellifont creates national Church under primacy of Armagh.

**1166** Dermot MacMurrough is driven out of Ireland and seeks help in England. Recruits Norman knights.

**1169** First Anglo-Normans arrive in Ireland, marking start of Norman invasion of Ireland. MacMurrough is given back kingship of Leinster.

**1170** The Anglo-Norman leader Richard FitzGilbert de Clare, also known as 'Strongbow', lands in Waterford. He marries MacMurrough's daughter, storms and captures Dublin, and invades Meath.

**1171** MacMurrough dies and Henry II of England arrives in Ireland.

**1172** Hugh de Lacy is granted lordship of Meath.

**1175** Treaty of Windsor signed, making Henry II of England Lord of Ireland.

**1176** Death of Strongbow.

**1177** Prince John of England made Lord of Ireland.

**1200-1300** Anglo-Normans establish themselves.

**1315** Edward, brother of Robert Bruce, allies with O'Neills, defeats English and becomes King of Ireland.

**1318** Edward Bruce is killed in battle at Faughart, near Dundalk.

**1366** Statutes of Kilkenny prohibit integration of Anglo-Normans and the Irish.

**1391** *Book of Ballymote* written. Provides key to the ancient ogham alphabet.

**c.1480** Existence of the Pale, an area of English jurisdiction centred on Dublin.

**1536** Reformation begins, followed by suppression of the monasteries.

**1541** Henry VIII is declared King of Ireland by parliament.

**1556** Laois and Offaly are planted with English settlers.

**1586** Start of plantation of province of Munster.

**1588** Ships from Spanish Armada wrecked off Irish coasts.

**1594** Rebellion in Ulster. Start of Nine Years' War when O'Neills try to oust English administration from Ulster.

**1599** Defeat of Earl of Essex by Owen O'Moore.

**1601** Battle of Kinsale, in which Hugh O'Neill (Earl of Tyrone) and his O'Donnell and Spanish supporters are defeated by Queen Elizabeth's army.

**1603** Treaty of Mellifont signed, and O'Neill surrenders.

**1606** Abolition of ancient Brehon Laws.

**1607** 'Flight of the Earls', in which Ulster's leading families flee to the Continent.

**1608-9** Plantation of Ulster with Protestant settlers initiated.

**1613** Derry City receives its prefix 'London' after James I grants the town to the citizens of London.

**1616**  Death of Hugh O'Neill in Rome.

**1619-21**  Plantations of Leitrim, Longford, Laois, Offaly and Westmeath.

**1632-6**  *Annals of the Four Masters*, a systematised account of Irish history.

**1641**  Insurrection spreads throughout Ireland. Rebels form the Confederate Catholics of Ireland, and set up their seat at Kilkenny.

**1642-52**  Civil war.

**1646**  Battle of Benburb in which confederate forces of Owen Roe O'Neill are victorious.

**1649**  Cromwell lands in Ireland; massacre of Drogheda and sack of Wexford.

**1653**  Cromwell's subjugation of Ireland complete. Irish landowners evicted and land handed over to Protestant settlers.

**1685**  Accession of Catholic James II to English throne.

**1688**  James II deposed and ousted by Protestant William of Orange. Siege of Londonderry by the Jacobites fails.

**1689**  James II lands at Kinsale, Cork.

**1690**  William III lands at Carrickfergus, Antrim. He and James II fight the Battle of the Boyne; William wins.

**1691**  Battle of Aughrim (July), and siege and surrender of Limerick. Catholic army defeated. Treaty of Limerick signed (Oct). Jacobites flee to Continent in thousands.

**1695-7**  Catholic clergy banished and penal laws instituted.

**1726**  *Gulliver's Travels* by Dean Jonathan Swift.

**1773**  *She Stoops to Conquer* by Oliver Goldsmith.

**1778**  Irish Volunteer Movement founded; Catholic Relief bill passed, giving Roman Catholics leasehold and inheritance rights.

**1782**  Irish Parliament formed with Henry Grattan as its leader.

**1791**  Society of United Irishmen founded.

**1793**  Catholics permitted to vote.

**1795**  Establishment of Orange Order, to counter popery.

**1796**  Unsuccessful French invasion of Bantry Bay; General Hoche's ships dispersed.

**1798**  Rebellion in Ulster and Leinster. Much fighting around the country, with the last battles of the United Irishmen fought at Ballynahinch, Down and in Co. Wexford marking the final defeat of the rebels. Franco-Irish forces under General Humbert and rallied by Wolfe Tone land at Killala Bay.

**1800**  End of Irish Parliament. Act of Union passed, joining Ireland with Great Britain. Publication of *Castle Rackrent*, novel tracing local family over several generations, written by Maria Edgeworth.

**1829**  Catholic Emancipation Act passed, allowing Catholics to sit in parliament.

**1842**  Young Ireland Movement formed. Growth of nationalist politics and arts.

**1845-8**  Failure of potato crop leads to famine, followed by mass emigration.

**1858**  Formation of Irish Republican Brotherhood, also called the Fenians.

**1866**  First transatlantic telegraph cable linked to Valencia Island, Kerry.

**1873**  Home Rule League founded.

**1879**  Irish National Land League formed by Michael Davitt and Charles Stewart Parnell, young Protestant MP for Meath.

**1879-82**  'Land War' in which the Irish National Land League protected tenant farmers from eviction and urged non-payment of rents and 'boycott' of landlords.

**1880**  Charles Parnell elected chairman of Irish Home Rule Party.

**1881**  Irish Land Act passed and Land League suppressed.

**1882**  Phoenix Park murders of chief secretary for Ireland, Lord Frederick Cavendish, and his under-secretary T.H. Burke by splinter group of Fenians.

**1884**  Gaelic Athletic Association (G.A.A.) formed.

**1885**  Gladstone's Home Rule Bill defeated in British Parliament.

**1888**  Belfast granted city status.

**1891**  Death of Parnell.

**1893**  Douglas Hyde and Eoin McNeill found Gaelic League. *The Celtic Twilight* is written by W.B. Yeats.

**1904**  Abbey Theatre founded in Dublin.

**1906**  Foundation of Sinn Fein by Arthur Griffith.

**1907**  Guglielmo Marconi sends first radio signals across Atlantic from County Galway; the play *The Playboy of the Western World* written by J.M. Synge.

**1913**  Formation of Irish Volunteers, Ulster Volunteer Force and Irish Citizen Army.

**1916**  Irish Republic proclaimed in Dublin, followed by Easter Rising, led by Irish Republican Brotherhood and Irish Citizen Army. Rebellion quashed and leaders executed.

**1919**  Dáil Eireann formed and Eamon de Valera becomes first president. Crash-landing of first nonstop transatlantic flight, flown by Alcock and Brown, near Clifden, Galway.

**1921**  Anglo-Irish Treaty signed, giving 'Southern Ireland' independence from Britain on certain conditions.

**1922**  Treaty ratified by Dáil, followed by war between supporters of the Free State and those against the treaty. Death of Michael Collins, guerrilla commander and leader of Sinn Fein, and important negotiator for 1921 Treaty. Inauguration of Irish Free State, excluding Northern Ireland. *Ulysses* by James Joyce.

**1923**  Ceasefire agreed and civil war ends.

## Adventure Centres

For those who want organised outdoor activities or an adventure holiday which could involve hill-walking, camping, cycling and canoeing, or sailing, surfing and scuba diving, Ireland has several outdoor pursuits centres.

The accommodation varies from hostels with bunks, to guesthouses and hotels. Many of the centres cater for children. Organisations that will provide further information on these centres are:

REPUBLIC OF IRELAND

Association for Adventure Sports, House of Sport, Longmile Rd, Dublin 12. Tel: (01) 509845/501633.

Outdoor Pursuits Centres Association, Little Killary Adventure Centre, Salruck, Rinvyle, Co Galway. Tel: (095) 43411.

Tiglin National Adventure Centre, Ashford, Co Wicklow. Tel: (0404) 40169.

NORTHERN IRELAND

Sports Council of Northern Ireland, House of Sport, Upper Malone Rd, Belfast BT9 5LA. Tel: (0232) 381222.

## Air Sports

Ireland's rounded mountain ranges lack the dangerous air currents found in higher, more jagged mountain ranges, and flying gliders and hang-gliders is possible all year round, although thermal activity is best from March to October. There are hundreds of flying sites around Ireland, from mountains to beach and dune sites.

Reliable instruction is available for air sports such as parachuting, hang-gliding and paragliding. The governing body for sport parachuting is the Parachute Association of Ireland. Its clubs offer weekend courses with expert instructors.

The Irish Hang-Gliding Association controls hang-gliding in the Irish Republic, and hang-gliding schools have to be registered and approved by them. Hang-gliding in Northern Ireland is controlled by the Ulster Hang-Gliding Club, which is affiliated to the British Hang-Gliding Association. Further information about these and other air sports, with addresses of clubs and tuition centres, can be obtained from the following:

REPUBLIC OF IRELAND

Dublin Ballooning Club, 5 Cill Cais, Old Bawn, Tallaght, Dublin 24. Tel: (01) 517184/682511.

Irish Aviation Council, 38 Pembroke Rd, Dublin 4. Tel: (01) 874474.

Irish Hang-Gliding Association, House of Sport, Longmile Rd, Dublin 12. Tel: (01) 509845/501633.

Irish Hang-Gliding and Paragliding Centre, 16 Mask Rd, Artane, Dublin 5. Tel: (01) 314051.

Irish Micro-Light Aircraft Association, 6 Wilfield Park, Ballsbridge, Dublin 4. Tel: (01) 696757.

Parachute Association of Ireland, 15 Henrietta St, Dublin 1. Tel: (01) 730093.

NORTHERN IRELAND

Ulster Hang-Gliding Club, 43 Rensevyn Park, Whitehead, Co Antrim BT38 9LY. Tel: (0232) 868141.

## Angling

All inland water in the Republic and Northern Ireland belongs to some person or organisation, and anglers must have permission from the owner of any water they intend to fish. A fee is usually payable, although fishing is free in some areas.

In the Republic and Northern Ireland all freshwater fishing is controlled by official bodies, and in addition to permission, anglers need an official licence from a state authority. In the Republic, anglers under 18 and over 66 do not need a rod licence for brown or rainbow trout or coarse fish. In Northern Ireland, anglers under 18 fishing exclusively for coarse fish do not need a licence, nor do anglers of any age fishing only for coarse fish in the Foyle area. No licence is required for sea fishing in the Republic or Northern Ireland, except on estuaries, where an official licence must be obtained to fish for sea trout. Licences are available from the appropriate authorities themselves, tackle shops, hotels and clubs in the area.

Size limits of fish that may be caught, and quantities, vary from one authority to the next. Any fish smaller than that stipulated must be put back.

A close season, during which fishing is banned in order to allow breeding, is fixed by the various authorities, but varies from area to area. Check with the appropriate body. There is no statutory close season for coarse or sea fishing in the Republic or Northern Ireland, or for rainbow trout in designated waters in the Conservancy Board area in Northern Ireland. The close season for salmon, sea trout and brown trout is roughly from the end of October to April or May. Addresses of authorities from which information and licences can be obtained:

REPUBLIC OF IRELAND

The Central Fisheries Board (and The Eastern Regional Fisheries Board), Balnagowan House, Mobhi Boreen, Glasnevin, Dublin 9. Tel: (01) 379206.

The Northern Regional Fisheries Board, Station Rd, Ballyshannon, Co Donegal. Tel: (072) 51435.

The North-Western Regional Fisheries Board, Ardnaree House, Abbey St, Ballina, Co Mayo. Tel: (096) 22623/22788.

The Shannon Regional Fisheries Board, Thomond Weir, Limerick, Co Limerick. Tel: (061) 55171.

The Southern Regional Fisheries Board, Anglesea St, Clonmel, Co Tipperary. Tel: (052) 23971/23624.

The South-Western Regional Fisheries Board, 1 Neville Terrace, Massey Town, Macroom, Co Cork. Tel: (026) 41221/2.

The Western Regional Fisheries Board, The Weir Lodge, Earl's Island, Galway. Tel: (091) 63118.

Irish Federation of Sea Anglers, 67 Windsor Drive, Monkstown, Co Dublin. Tel: (01) 806873/806901.

Irish Trout Fly Fishing Association, 26 St Margaret's Rd, Malahide, Co Dublin. Tel: (01) 450911.

National Coarse Fishing Federation of Ireland, 43 Shanliss Rd, Santry, Dublin 9. Tel: (01) 711020/423823.

There is also a computerised angling information service known as 'Hookline' which gives a weekly update on fisheries in Ireland. 'Hookline', 6 Lower Hatch St, Dublin 2. Tel: (01) 618172.

NORTHERN IRELAND

Department of Agriculture (Fisheries), Stormont, Belfast BT4 3PW. Tel: (0232) 763939.

Fisheries Conservancy Board for Northern Ireland, 1 Mahon Rd, Portadown, Co Armagh BT6Z 3EE. Tel: (0762) 334666.

The Foyle Fisheries Commission, 8 Victoria Rd, Londonderry BT47 2AB. Tel: (0504) 42100.

## Camping and Caravanning

Organised campsites with facilities for laundering and bathing are available throughout the Republic and Northern Ireland. Nearly all camping sites in the Republic and Northern Ireland are equipped with mains water and flush toilets.

Many campsites are open from Easter to September or October only, so it is advisable to check with individual sites before arrival. The AA publishes a list of sites in the Republic and Northern Ireland in its Members Handbook, and the Bord Fáilte lists sites in the Republic which it has inspected and which meet its requirements. Those sites approved by the Bord Fáilte display the 'Approved' symbol.

Further information on camping sites may be obtained from the following addresses:

REPUBLIC OF IRELAND

Irish Caravan Council, 2 Offington Court, Sutton, Dublin 13. Tel: (01) 323776.

NORTHERN IRELAND

The Forest Service, Room 34 Dundonald House, Belfast BT4 3SB, or Northern Ireland Tourist Board.

## Canals and Rivers

Ireland has about 600 miles of navigable rivers, canals and lakes, and about 300 square miles of cruising water on lakes. These are some of the cleanest waterways in Europe. They slow down the tempo of modern life; 15 miles a day is good going on a canal, for there are locks to negotiate and the speed limit is 4mph. Nature lovers will find wildlife plentiful, and the fishing on these waterways is excellent. Anglers will need permits and rod licences; see under Angling.

In the Republic it is advisable to hire cruisers only from members of the Irish Boat Rental Association, who are approved by the Bord Fáilte.

Experience in handling a boat is an advantage but not necessary, since handling a cruiser is easy. No licence is required, and half an hour's tuition by the operator is all that most novices need. There are charges for mooring boats, and fees at locks are payable either to the lock keeper or in advance to the waterways authority. Check with the local tourist office or the boat operator. Addresses to contact:

REPUBLIC OF IRELAND

Inland Waterways Association of Ireland, Stone Cottage, Claremont Rd, Killiney, Co Dublin. Tel: (01) 2852258.

Irish Boat Rental Association, 55 Braemor Rd, Churchtown, Dublin 14. Tel: (01) 987222.

Office of Public Works, Waterways Division, 51 St Stephen's Green, Dublin 2. Tel: (01) 613111.

NORTHERN IRELAND

Department of Agriculture, Dundonald House, Belfast. Tel: (0232) 650111.

## Canoeing

Hundreds of navigable rivers and lakes make Ireland one of Europe's most popular countries for canoeing. It offers all-year-round canoeing, canoe touring on rivers and waterways where larger craft cannot go, and for the experienced canoeist, white water canoeing, surfing and even marathon racing. The World Cup for canoeing was held in the Irish Republic in 1984 and 1987.

Beginners can learn how to handle a canoe by joining a club belonging to the Irish Canoe Union, which is affiliated with the International Canoe Federation, or at an adventure centre approved by the Association for Adventure Sports, or at a club approved by the Canoe Association of Northern Ireland. Organisations that will be of assistance:

REPUBLIC OF IRELAND

Irish Canoe Union, House of Sport, Longmile Rd, Dublin 12. Tel: (01) 501633. The headquarters of the Association for Adventure Sports is also at this address.

Tiglin National Adventure Centre, Ashford, Co Wicklow. Tel: (0404) 40169.

NORTHERN IRELAND

Canoe Association of Northern Ireland, House of Sport, Upper Malone Rd, Belfast BT9 5LA. Tel: (0232) 381222.

## Cycling

Ireland's empty roads make it ideal for cyclists, and cycling offers the chance to explore Ireland in great detail. For those planning a cycling holiday, suggested routes and accommodation are available from tourist offices in all main towns and cities. Bicycles can be rented in most towns. The bicycles range from tourers to tandems, mountain bikes and children's bikes. It is possible to rent a bicycle from one office and return it to another. A deposit is usually required. Bicycles hired in Northern Ireland cannot be taken into the Republic, and vice versa. Irish Rail offers a Rambler ticket for eight day and 15 day periods, which is a cheap way of travelling extensively by rail, and will take bikes by train, subject to space, for a small additional fee.

For those who would like the occasional bike ride, some adventure centres include cycling among their activities, and some hotels and guesthouses arrange bicycle hire and provide information on interesting local cycling routes. There are also guided cycle tours and Sunday cycle rides.

The Federation of Irish Cyclists controls cycling in Ireland and provides a calendar of races and touring events. For further information contact:

The Bike Store, 58 Lower Gardiner St, Dublin 1. Tel: (01) 725931.

Federation of Irish Cyclists, Halston St, Dublin 7. Tel: (01) 727524. (Also deals with Northern Ireland.)

Raleigh Rent-A-Bike Division, Raleigh Ireland Limited, Raleigh House, Kylemore Rd, Dublin 10. Tel: (012) 6261333. (Also has outlets in Northern Ireland.)

## Diving

Lying in the path of the Gulf Stream and with thousands of miles of varied coastline, Ireland has very good diving conditions, and a large range of sites, from sheltered harbours for beginners to steep cliff faces for experienced divers. Visibility underwater on the northwest, west and south-west coasts averages 40ft, and in summer, on good days, can reach up to 100ft, making the waters ideal for underwater photography.

There are sub-aqua clubs in almost every coastal county in the Republic, affiliated to the Irish Underwater Council. Most offer diving courses and have junior snorkelling sections.

By law, divers are prohibited from removing shellfish from the sea. They are also prohibited from diving on or interfering with wrecks of 100 years old or more, without a licence from the National Monuments Section of the Office of Public Works. Further information on clubs and courses may be obtained from this address:

REPUBLIC OF IRELAND

The Irish Underwater Council, National Maritime Museum, Haigh Terrace, Dun Laoghaire, Co Dublin. Tel: (01) 844601.

NORTHERN IRELAND

Sports Council for Northern Ireland, House of Sport, Malone Rd, Belfast BT9 5LA. Tel: (0232) 381222.

## Golf

Ireland is marvellous golfing country and has a large number of courses, in remote countryside, on rugged coasts and on the outskirts of towns and cities. They include championship courses such as Royal Portrush, on the north Antrim coast, and Portmarnock, outside Dublin. There are some 200 courses in the Republic and about 80 in Northern Ireland.

The large number of courses means that they are relatively uncrowded and there is little difficulty in getting a game, although to avoid possible disappointment it is always best to check with the club first.

Details of green fees, length of courses, and best days for playing can be obtained from tourist offices or the golf unions. Visitors can play at most courses without being a member, but have to pay green fees. Some clubs offer lower rates for young players, and many offer tuition for those new to golf. The best time of the year to play golf in Ireland is from April to September. Organisations that will provide further information are:

Golfing Union of Ireland, Glencar House, 81 Eglinton Rd, Donnybrook, Dublin 4. Tel: (01) 2694111. (Covers Northern Ireland as well as the Republic.)

Irish Ladies Golf Union, 1 Clonskeagh Square, Clonskeagh Rd, Dublin 14. Tel: (01) 2696244. Northern Ireland branch: 58a High St, Hollywood, Co Down. Tel: (02317) 3708.

## Nature Reserves and Sanctuaries

There are some 68 National Nature Reserves in the Republic and 44 in Northern Ireland, as well as more than 60 bird sanctuaries throughout. These are areas of importance for flora, fauna and features of geological interest, where taking animals by any means, or picking flowers, is prohibited. They include woodlands, wetlands, bogs, grasslands, dune systems and marine areas. Several organisations and trusts are responsible for these reserves and will give information on them and the best times to visit them:

REPUBLIC OF IRELAND

Irish Peatland Conservation Council, 3 Lower Mount St, Dublin 2. Tel: (01) 616645.

Irish Wildbird Conservancy, Ruttledge House, 8 Longford Place, Monkstown, Co Dublin. Tel: (01) 2804322.

Wildlife Service, Leeson Lane, Dublin 2. Tel: (01) 615666.

NORTHERN IRELAND

Department of the Environment for Northern Ireland, Countryside and Wildlife Branch, Calvert House, 23 Castle Place, Belfast BT1 1FY. Tel: (0232) 230560.

The National Trust, Rowallane House, Saintfield, Co. Down BT24 7LH. Tel: (0238) 510721.

Royal Society for the Protection of Birds (RSPB), Belvoir Park Forest, Belfast BT8 4QT. Tel: (0232) 491547.

## Riding

The horse holds a special place in Irish culture, and there are many stables throughout Ireland. Many have horses or ponies available for trekking or escorted trails, and many offer tuition. Some riding establishments offer riding holidays and arrange a variety of accommodation, from camping sites to hotels. Organisations to contact are:

REPUBLIC OF IRELAND

Association of Irish Riding Establishments (AIRE), Daffodil Lodge, Eadestown, Naas, Co Kildare. Tel: (01) 955990.

Equestrian Federation of Ireland, Ashton House, Castleknock, Dublin 15. Tel: (01) 387611.

NORTHERN IRELAND

British Horse Society, House of Sport, Upper Malone Rd, Belfast BT9 5LA. Tel: (0232) 381222.

## Sailing

Ireland's coastline and numerous lakes provide limitless opportunities for yachtsmen and boating enthusiasts. The oldest yacht club in the world is the Royal Cork Yacht Club, which was founded in 1720.

The national body that governs sailing in the Irish Republic is the Irish Yachting Association, which will provide information to visiting yachtsmen about chartering yachts, bringing yachts to Ireland, and conditions along the coast. It also provides information on registered centres for coastal or inland windsurfing. The Royal Yachting Association is the main body that deals with sailing in Northern Ireland. There are several sailing schools and centres around the Irish coast; reputable schools are affiliated to the Irish Association of Sail Training. Addresses of organisations that will provide information about sailing are:

REPUBLIC OF IRELAND

Irish Association of Sail Training, Confederation House, Kildare Street, Dublin 2. Tel: (01) 779801.

Irish Cruising Club, Cairngorm, Baily, Co Dublin. Tel: (01) 323421.

Irish Yachting Association, 3 Park Rd, Dun Laoghaire, Co Dublin. Tel: (01) 2800239.

NORTHERN IRELAND

Royal Yachting Association, Sports Council of Northern Ireland, House of Sport, Upper Malone Rd, Belfast BT9 5LA. Tel: (0232) 381222.

## Surfing

The Atlantic Ocean washes the west coast of Ireland with great swells that provide very good waves for surfing, particularly on the Donegal coast, where the European Surfing Championships were held in 1985.

Surfing clubs in the Republic are registered with the Irish Surfing Association, the governing body for the sport.

REPUBLIC OF IRELAND

Irish Surfing Association, Tigh-na-Mara, Rossnowlagh, Co Donegal. Tel: (072) 51261/ (073) 21053.

NORTHERN IRELAND

Sports Council for Northern Ireland, House of Sport, Malone Rd, Belfast BT9 5LA. Tel: (0232) 381222.

## Walking and Climbing

There are more than 1000 miles of completed waymarked trails throughout the Republic and Northern Ireland, and many more in the making. They include the 16 mile Cavan Way, the 82 mile Wicklow Way and the 500 mile Ulster Way. They take walkers along canal towpaths, through leafy woods and across the heathery slopes of granite hills. Accommodation, ranging from campsites and hostels to guesthouses, can be found in most areas, and lists are available from tourist offices or youth hostel associations. Maps of the Republic are available from the Government Publications Office in Molesworth Street, Dublin, and those for Northern Ireland can be obtained from HM Stationery Office in Belfast or from bookshops throughout. The Association for Adventure Sport organises mountaineering training courses and adventure holidays with walking and climbing. Contact addresses:

REPUBLIC OF IRELAND

An Óige (Irish Youth Hostel Association), 39 Mountjoy Square, Dublin 1. Tel: (01) 363111/364749.

Federation of Mountaineering Clubs of Ireland, 20 Leopardstown Gardens, Blackrock, Co Dublin. Tel: (01) 2881266.

Long Distance Walking Routes Committee, National Sports Council (Cospóir), Hawkins House, Hawkins St, Dublin 2. Tel: (01) 734700.

Mountaineering Council of Ireland, 17 Idrone Terrace, Blackrock, Co Dublin. Tel: (01) 509845.

Tiglin National Adventure Centre, Ashford, Co Wicklow. Tel: (0404) 40169.

NORTHERN IRELAND

Sports Council for Northern Ireland, House of Sport, Upper Malone Rd, Belfast BT9 5LA. Tel: (0232) 381222.

Ulster Federation of Rambling Clubs, (Sec.) 27 Slievegallion Drive, Belfast BT11 8JN. Tel: (0232) 624289.

Youth Hostel Association of Northern Ireland, 93 Dublin Rd, Belfast BT2 7HP. Tel: (0232) 324733.

## Sports for the Disabled

There are several associations which cover sports for the disabled and will provide information on clubs that have special facilities. For further information contact the following addresses:

Irish Blindsports, 23 The Strand, Donabate, Co Dublin. Tel: (01) 286833.

Irish Deaf Sports Association, 8 Dun Emer Drive, Dundrum, Dublin 16. Tel: (01) 956030 (after 4pm).

Irish Wheelchair Association, Aras Chuchuláin, Blackheath Drive, Clontarf, Dublin 3. Tel: (01) 338241/2/3; 333873; 333860.

## Automobile Association Centres

Information and advice on all aspects of motoring, from insurance to breakdown services, is available to Automobile Association members from the AA Centres throughout the Irish Republic and Northern Ireland, given below. Except in Dublin and Belfast, these offices close from 1300-1400 hours each day. For service during these hours telephone the after-hours number.

Members within the Irish Republic receive the same levels of cover they are entitled to when they are visiting Northern Ireland. The Relay service is not available to members visiting the Republic. Cars hired under Relay Plus in Northern Ireland may not be taken across the border.

**AA Members 24-hour Emergency Breakdown Service**: Republic of Ireland (Freefone) (1800) 667788. Northern Ireland (Freefone) (0800) 887766.

REPUBLIC OF IRELAND

**Athlone**: Shopping Centre, Dublin Rd, Athlone, Co Westmeath. Tel: (0902) 78875.

**Cork**: AA Ireland, 12 Emmet Place, Cork. Tel: (021) 276922.

**Dublin Central**: AA Ireland, 23 Suffolk St, Dublin 2. Tel: (01) 779481.

**Dublin Headquarters**: AA Ireland, 23 Rock Hill, Blackrock, Co Dublin. Tel: (01) 2833555.

**Dundalk**: Shopping Centre, Dublin Rd, Dundalk, Co Louth. Tel: (042) 32955.

**Galway**: Shopping Centre, Headford Rd, Galway. Tel: (091) 64438.

**Limerick**: Patrick St, Limerick. Tel: (061) 418241.

**Port Laoise**: Shopping Centre, James Fintan Lalor Ave, Port Laoise, Co Laois. Tel: (0502) 21692.

**Sligo**: Wine St Car Park, Sligo. Tel: (071) 62065.

**Waterford**: Meaghers Quay, Waterford. Tel: (051) 73765.

NORTHERN IRELAND

The Automobile Association, Fanum House, 108-110 Great Victoria St, Belfast BT2 7AT. Information line: (0345) 500600.

# ACKNOWLEDGMENTS

*Many people and organisations assisted in the preparation of this book. The publishers wish to thank all of them, particularly*

**Pia Henderson** (Researcher), **Valerie Kirkpatrick** (Designer), **Susan Mennell** (Picture Researcher), Jean Gay (Indexer), and individuals within Cork Kerry Tourism, Dublin Tourism, Ireland West Tourism, Midlands-East Tourism, Shannon Development, South-East Tourism, North-West Tourism, and the tourism departments within Northern Ireland's City and District Councils. Also, Boosey & Hawkes Music Publishers Ltd (Archives); Bord na Gaeilge; Bord na Móna; Dr Robert Brown; Central Fisheries Board, Dublin; County Libraries and Heritage Centres across the Republic; Deirdre Davitt; Gaelic Athletic Association (GAA); Giant's Causeway National Trust Visitor Centre; Guinness plc, Guinness Ireland Ltd; Irish Distillers; Irish National Stud; Dr John Jackson; Mary Angela Keane; National Sports Council; National Trust; Offices of Public Works; School of English, Trinity College, Dublin; Philip Watson.

*The publishers also wish to thank the following people and organisations for permission to reproduce photographs belonging to them (names with an asterisk denote an illustrator or photographer commissioned by Reader's Digest) – t = top, c = centre, b = bottom, l = left, r = right.*

*Ace Photo Agency* 15 b; *Aerofilms Limited* 41, 52 t, 61 l, 68-69, 97 tr, 165, 205 b, 221 tr, 253 t, 257, 270 r, 317 t, 325; *Allsport* 34 cl, 153 b; *An Post, Dublin* 305 r; *Heather Angel* 206 r, 220, 221 b, 313 c & b; *Simon Annand* 242 t; *Robert Ashby* 295, 302-3, 318 b; *Peter Barrett** (illustrator) 195; *Richard Bonson** (illustrator) 28, 39, 48, 49 c, 57, 61 r, 62, 67, 74, 85, 95, 105, 110, 121, 166, 167, 169, 170, 175, 193, 203, 213, 229, 257, 270, 312, 320, 321; *Bord Fáilte/Irish Tourist Board* 59 r, 88 r, 250; *British Academy of Songwriters, Composers & Authors* 335 b; *British Library* 212 bc ('Speed's Theatre' 1611), 171 t (MS. Harl.1319, Folio 9); *Richard Broomfield* 239 bl, 240 b; *Camera Press* 329 b; *Joe Cashman* 35 t; *Cork Examiner* 92 c; *Country Life/IPC Magazines* 153 t; *Cumann Luthchleas Gael (Gaelic Athletic Association), Dublin* 157 tr; *David H. Davison* 59 bl; *John Dodd* 258 b; *Bill Doyle* 2-3, 9, 118, 200, 206 l, 207, 211, 214, 216 t, 223 bl & br, 245, 259; *Guinness Ireland* 290 c far left & tr; *Guinness Museum, Dublin* 290 tl; *Christopher Hill* 111, 248, 249 t, 251 b, 274-5, 278 r, 279 b, 282, 283, 284 tl, bl & br, 285 tl & bl, 286, 287, 291 c, 293 tr, 294 r, 296, 297, 307, 308, 309, 311, 312, 315 br, 319, 322 b, 323 tl, 324 br, 326, 329 tc, 330, 331 tl, 332 br, 333 r, 337 tr; *Barry Hitchcox** 28 br, 29, 30, 31 tr, 32, 33 r, 37, 38, 40, 78, 81 t, c & b, 166, 170 tr, 190, 196, 197 tr; *Neil Holmes** 43 t & bl, 44, 45, 47 tr & br, 48-49, 50, 51 t & c, 54 r, 55, 57 tl, 65 t, 66, 67, 69, 73, 74, 75, 76, 77 l, 82, 83, 84, 85, 90 t, 91, 97 t, 100, 101, 102, 100, 104, 105 tr, 106, 107 b, 108, 109, 112, 113, 114, 115, 116, 117, 119, 120, 123, 124, 125, 126, 261 tl, 263 b; *Hugh Lane Municipal Gallery of Modern Art, Dublin/David Davison* 215 tr; *Hulton Picture Company* 36, 42 (portrait), 65 r, 171 b, 210 tr, 229 tr, 241 tl, 253 bl, 291 tr, 303, 306, 323; *Illustrated London News* 52 b; *Inpho Sports Photography, Dublin* 98, 99; *Irish Distillers, Dublin* 291 tl; *Jarrold Publishing* 20 br, 53, 59 tl, 95, 97 b, 193 br, 215 tl, 253 br, 323 br; *Tom Kelly* 8 cr, 12-13, 17 c, 19 tr, 23 t, 25 t, 27 tr, 39, 54 l, 58, 77 r, 79, 87, 93 t, 102-3, 128-9, 130, 159 t, 162-3, 167, 185 l, 208 t, 223 t, 229 tl, 231 br, 233 br, 246, 251 tr, 254, 262 tr, 264, 265 t, 270 tl, 305 l; *Courtney Kenny* 315 l; *Valerie Kirkpatrick* 19 bc; *Kos Photos/Kaoru Soemata* 107 t; *Landscape Only* 321; *Tony Lodge** (illustrator) 123; *Steve Lowry* 331 bl & br; *Susan Lund** 8 tr, 137, 152, 154 b, 155, 156, 157 tl & b, 158, 159 b, 172, 173 tl & b, 174, 175 b, 176, 178, 179, 180, 181, 183, 184, 185 r, 186, 187 t & br, 188 b; *Magnum Photos/Erich Lessing* 219 tr, 304; *John Man* 43 br; *Mansell Collection* 197 tl, 328 tr; *Mary Evans Picture Library* 42 (signature), 49 tr, 51 b, 96, 182, 184 br, 222, 225 tl, 256, 261 b, 273 tc; *Anthony Mason* 160 c, 203 b, 212 bl, 213 r, 235 b; *Eric Meacher* 60 b, 273 br; *National Gallery of Ireland* 22, 33 l, 271 b, 273 l; *National Library of Ireland* 20 tr, 127 r (J.T.Gilbert's National Mss of Ireland vol 4, no XXII); *National Museum of Ireland* 72, 154 t, 160 l & r, 161, 220 bl, 225 bl, 233 c, 236; *National Portrait Gallery, London* 273 tr; *National Trust Photographic Library* 275, 298, 299, 303, 313 t; *Network/Barry Lewis* 231 t; *Northern Ireland Tourist Board* 278 b, 280, 285 tr, c & bc, 288, 292 br, 294 l, 300, 314, 315 tr, 317 b, 318 t, 334, 335 tr, 337 br; *O'Donovan's Hotel, Clonakilty* 93 b; *Pearse Museum, Dublin* 27 br; *Peter Newark's Western Americana* 122, 170 tl; *Mrs Eva Reichmann/Ashmolean Museum, Oxford*, 272; *S & G Press Agency* 34 cr; *Slide File* 17 t, 18 t & br, 21, 24, 25 b, 26, 27 l, 31 tl, bl & br, 34 b, 57 tc, 61 c, 64, 81 r, 88 l, 92 b, 94, 105 tl & br, 142, 163, 177, 195 b, 199, 203 tl & tr, 204 c & b, 208-9, 216 b, 217 t, 220 br, 221 tc, 232-3, 233 bl, 239 tl, 251 l, 252, 255, 265 b, 269, 279 t, 281, 289, 292 t, 293 l, 301, 328 br; *Gill Tomblin** (illustrator) 142; *Topham Picture Source* 103 r; *The Board of Trinity College, Dublin* 47 l, 63 r, 237 b; *The Trustees of the Ulster Museum* 237 tl, 273 bc; *John Vigurs** 129, 132, 133, 134, 135, 136, 138, 139, 141, 144, 144-5, 146, 147, 148, 149, 150, 151; *Paul Wakefield* 56, 121, 140, 143, 198-9, 202, 205 t, 235 t; *John Watney Vintage Pictures* 333 l; *Timothy Woodcock* 8 l & br, 175 t; *Jon Wyand** Cover illustration, 4-5, 71 t, 217 b, 218, 219 tl & bl, 224, 225 tl & br, 226, 227, 228, 230, 231 bl, 238, 239 r, 240 t, 241 r & b, 242 b, 243, 260, 261 tr, 262 tl, 263 r, 267, 268 b, 284 tr, 320, 322, 324 tr, 327, 329 tl & tr, 331 tr, 332 tr, 335 tl & c, 336, 337 bl; *Anne Yeats and Michael B.Yeats/The Syndics of Cambridge University Library* 127; *Peter Zoeller* 1, 13, 15 t, 19 tl, bl & br, 20 tl, bl, bcl & bcr, 23 b, 34 t, 35 b, 63 l, 65 b, 71 b, 86-87, 94-95 t, 169, 173 tr, 187 l, 188-9, 189, 191, 192 b, 192-3, 193 l, 194, 195 t, 197 b, 204 t, 206 c, 209, 210, 212 t, 213 bl & br, 215, 234, 237 tr, 244-5, 249 b, 258 t, 271 t, 277, 290 cl, cr, c far right & b, 291 b.

CARTOGRAPHY Cosmographics, Watford; Thames Cartographic Services Limited, Maidenhead; Map Data Management Limited, Kendal; and Colourmap Scanning Limited, London.

*The publishers acknowledge their indebtedness to the following books which were used for reference:*

**Ancient Legends Of Ireland** by Lady Wilde (reprinted by O'Gorman Ltd, Galway); **Baedeker's Ireland** (Jarrold and Sons, Ltd); **Belfast** HMSO (The Universities Press (Belfast) Ltd); **A Biographical Dictionary Of Irish Writers** by Anne M. Brady & Brian Cleeve (Lilliput Press); **Blue Guide Ireland** by Ian Robertson (A&C Black, London, W W Norton, New York); **The Book Of The Irish Countryside** by Frank Mitchell & others (Blackstaff Press); **Castles of Ireland** by Brian de Breffny, photographs by George Mott (Thames and Hudson); **Celtic Mythology** by Proinsias MacCana (Hamlyn); **Claddagh Ring Story** by Cecily Joyce (Published by Cecily Joyce); **The Companion Guide To Ireland** by Brendan Lehane (Collins); **Constitution Of Ireland** Bunreacht Na hEireann (Government Publications Sale Office, Dublin); **Dictionary Of Saints** by John J. Delaney (Kaye & Ward Ltd); **Discovering Britain & Ireland** (The National Geographic Society); **Dublin Insight City Guides** (APA Publications); **Early Irish Myths And Sagas** (Penguin Classics); **Encyclopaedia Of Ireland** (Allen Figgis & Co Ltd, Dublin); **The Encyclopedia of Sports** (Marshall Cavendish); **Exploring Museums – Ireland** A Museums Association Guide by Sean Popplewell (HMSO); **Exploring Rural Ireland** by Andrew Sanger (Christopher Helm); **Fodor's 90 Ireland** (Fodor's Travel Publications, Inc, New York & London); **The Gardens Of Ireland** A Visitor's Guide by Jack Whaley (Poolbeg Press Ltd); **Gazetteer of Ireland** Prepared by The Placenames Branch of The Ordnance Survey (Brunswick Press); **A Guide To Irish Mythology** by Daragh Smyth (Irish Academic Press); **Granuaile** by Anne Chambers (Wolfhound Press); **The Great Cities – Dublin** by Brendan Lehane (Time-Life Books); **Guide to the National Monuments in the Republic of Ireland** by Peter Harbison (Gill & Macmillan); **Heritage – A Visitor's Guide** (The Office of Public Works); **The Heritage Of Clonmacnoise** (Environmental Sciences Unit, Trinity College in association with County Offaly Vocational Educational Committee); **Historic Monuments of Northern Ireland** (Department of the Environment for Northern Ireland); **History Of Ireland** by Desmond McGuire (Bison Books); **A History of the Irish Working Class** by P. Beresford-Ellis (Pluto); **Illustrated Ireland Guide** Bord Fáilte Eireann (Irish Tourist Board) (Dollard Printinghouse, Dublin); **In Search Of Ireland** by H.V. Morton (Methuen); **Ireland** by Micheál Mac Liammóir and Edwin Smith (Thames & Hudson); **Ireland: A Cultural Encyclopaedia** General Editor: Brian de Breffny (Facts on File – New York); **Ireland – A General and Regional Geography** by T.W. Freeman (Methuen); **Ireland Guide** (Irish Tourist Board); **Ireland – The Rough Guide** (Harrap-Columbus, London); **Ireland's Traditional Crafts** by David Shaw-Smith (Thames & Hudson); **Ireland Your Only Place** by Jan Morris & Paul Wakefield (Aurum Press); **Irish Art And Architecture** by Peter Harbison, Homan Potterton, and Jeanne Sheehy (Thames & Hudson); **The Irish Countryside** Edited by Desmond Gilmor (Wolfhound Press); **Irish Days** by Terry Wogan (Michael Joseph Ltd); **The Irish Heritage Series** (Jarrold and Sons Ltd, Norwich); **The Irish Language** by Maírtín O Murchu (Department of Foreign Affairs and Bord na Gaeilge); **The Land Of Ireland** by Brian de Breffny (Thames & Hudson); **Limerick The Rich Land** by Spellissy/O'Brien (Spellissy/O'Brien Publishers); **National Monuments Of Ireland** (Bord Fáilte Eireann); **Navan By The Boyne** A History of Navan and surrounding areas by Noel E. French; **The Noble Dwellings of Ireland** by John FitzMaurice Mills (Thames & Hudson); **Northern Ireland** by Ian Hill, Robert Blair & Bill Kirk (The Blackstaff Press); **The Oxford Dictionary Of Saints** by David Hugh Farmer (Clarendon Press, Oxford); **The Oxford Illustrated History of Ireland** Edited by R.F. Foster (Oxford University Press); **The Penguin Dictionary of Saints** by Donald Attwater (Penguin Books); **Pocket Dictionary of Irish Myth & Legend** Ronan Coghlan (Appletree Press); **Pocket Irish Phrase Book** by Paul Dorris (Appletree Press); **The Shell Guide To Ireland** Lord Killanin, M.A., M.R.I.A., and Michael V. Duignan, M.A. (2nd edition) (Ebury Press and George Rainbird); **The Shell Guide To Ireland** Revised and Updated by Peter Harbison (3rd edition) (Macmillan); **The Songs Of Percy French** Selected & Edited by James N. Healy (The Mercier Press, Dublin & Cork); **The Stone Circles of The British Isles** by Aubrey Burl (Yale University Press); **Treasures Of Ireland** (Royal Irish Academy, Dublin); **A Valley of Kings – The Boyne** by Henry Boylan (The O'Brien Press); **The Visitor's Guide To Northern Ireland** by Rosemary Evans (MPC Hunter Publishing Inc); **Where to Fish 1990-1991** Edited by D.A. Orton (Thomas Harmsworth Publishing Company); **The Wild Boglands, Bellamy's Ireland** by Dr David Bellamy (Country House).

SEPARATIONS Litho Studio Ltd, Dublin.
TYPESETTING Apex Computer Setting Ltd, London.
PAPER Cartaria Subalpina, Italy.
PRINTING AND BINDING Milanostampa s.p.a, Italy.

40-332-1

352